SIGNS & WONDERS

Marina Warner has an international reputation as a critic, historian and a novelist. Her many non-fiction works include *From the Beast to the Blonde*, *No Go the Bogeyman* and *Fantastic Metamorphoses*, while her most recent fiction includes the novel *The Leto Bundle*, and the short-story collection *Murderers I have Known*.

Marina Warner

SIGNS & WONDERS

ESSAYS ON LITERATURE & CULTURE

V

VINTAGE

Published by Vintage 2004

2 4 6 8 10 9 7 5 3 1

Copyright © Marina Warner 2003

Marina Warner has asserted her right under the
Copyright, Designs and Patents Act 1988 to be identified
as the author of this work

First published in Great Britain in 2003 by
Chatto & Windus

Vintage
Random House, 20 Vauxhall Bridge Road,
London SW1V 2SA

Random House Australia (Pty) Limited
20 Alfred Street, Milsons Point, Sydney,
New South Wales 2061, Australia

Random House New Zealand Limited
18 Poland Road, Glenfield,
Auckland 10, New Zealand

Random House South Africa (Pty) Limited
Endulini, 5A Jubilee Road, Parktown 2193, South Africa

Random House Group Limited Reg. No. 954009

www.randomhouse.co.uk/vintage

A CIP catalogue record for this book
is available from the British Library

ISBN 0 09 9437724

Papers used by Random House UK Ltd are natural, recyclable
products made from wood grown in sustainable forests. The
manufacturing processes conform to the environmental
regulations of the country of origin

Printed and bound in Great Britain by
Cox & Wyman Ltd, Reading, Berkshire

For G.

CONTENTS

4. FAITHS AND MARVELS

5. SHAKESPEAREAN TRANSFORMATIONS

6. CREOLE

What does it mean to say *I have survived*
until you take the mirrors and turn them outward
and read your own face in their outraged light?

That light of outrage is the light of history
springing upon us when we're least prepared,
thinking maybe a little glade of time
leaf-thick and with clear water
. . . is ours, is promised us, for all we've hacked
and tracked our way through: to this . . .

Adrienne Rich
from 'Through Corralitos under Rolls of Cloud',
An Atlas of the Difficult World, 1991.

ACKNOWLEDGMENTS

Writers used to have jobs: they were insurance brokers and bank clerks, spies and vicars, governesses, cooks and tutors; some writers do still do other things to get by, and many still emerge from other lines of work. In my case, I've tried to make time to write by writing, in a kind of paradoxical progress, somewhat like running up a down escalator. The essays collected here have been selected from over twenty-five years of this activity; they begin with some early journalism from the period I worked on the staff of one of the first colour supplements and they close with a version of the Amnesty lecture I gave in Oxford just over a year ago. They include articles, criticism, profiles, obituaries, tributes, memoirs, reportage, introductions, and longer reflections on certain topics, people, and issues; they were written for very different occasions and publications, for varied and distinct audiences and readers, and they communicate, I hope, my consistent interest in the cross-fertilisation of literature, belief and society, and in the interwovenness of cultural, aesthetic and political values. (My writings about the visual arts are appearing in another volume, next year.) This selection of essays on literature and culture has been edited by Jenny Uglow with incomparable attention and discernment as well as generosity: she culled and shaped and worried the heap I first presented her with, until we had drawn out a structure and a set of themes; working with her was an exhilarating experience. So my thanks go, above all, to her.

But I am also aware that I am lucky in my publisher as well as my editor: Alison Samuel at Chatto & Windus encouraged the idea of this collection from the start. My deepest thanks to her and to all those who have given me such support at both Chatto and Vintage; my gratitude, too, to Gill Coleridge and to her colleagues at Rogers, Coleridge and White.

Helena Ivins has compiled a fuller list of my work over the years, which can be viewed on my website www.marinawarner.com; many, many thanks to her for all the ways she has helped me and the detailed and patient sleuthing she has undertaken. Tom Fisher also tracked down lost items in the archives; so my thanks to him too. I also wish to acknowledge the many editors on magazines and newspapers who have asked me to review or write for them. Among them, I'd like to mention with especial gratitude Beatrix Miller on *Vogue* (my second and last full-time job, 1969–71), and Claire Tomalin, who started me reviewing books for her on the *New Statesman* and then on the *Sunday Times*. Since then, Mary-Kay Wilmers on *The London Review of Books*, Holly Eley and Lindsay Duguid and others on *The Times Literary Supplement*, have given me many opportunities, sending me books that I wanted to read but might never have come across or paid attention to in the way criticism demands. At *Raritan*, Richard Poirier and Jackson Lears have been the most open and inspiring of editors. I would also like to remember here the late Anna Rutherford, who spurred me to reflect on my background. My thanks also to the British Council for the readings and talks they have organised, and to the colleges, societies, museums and other places that have invited me over the years.

For permission to quote copyright material, I am grateful to Tom Disch, for 'On the Use of the Masculine-Preferred'; Faber & Faber Ltd for Ted Hughes, 'Tereus', *Tales From Ovid*; and Adrienne Rich and W. W. Norton and Company Inc, for 'Through Corralitos on Rolls of Cloud', from *An Atlas of the Difficult World*.

Marina Warner, Kentish Town, 2003

PROLOGUE: SEEKING THE SLANT

The writer Heinrich Böll, recalling his childhood in Nazi Germany, described a schoolteacher who taught *Mein Kampf*, as he was obliged to do, but had the idea of setting his pupils passages from the book to précis. To some extent, this wasn't a hard task, since so much of the writing was guff; but it was very difficult for the schoolchildren to produce a summary that was cogent, convincing, or in any way thoughtful, let alone appealing. In this way, the teacher helped Böll see the Fascist text for what it was – not by means of heroic resistance, but through covert enlightenment. As Emily Dickinson wrote,

> Tell all the Truth but tell it slant –
> Success in circuit lies.

In China, the Confucian emphasis on teaching by example inspired many sequences of stories that relate edifying acts: these include the famous 'Twenty-Four Acts of Filial Piety', in which heroes perform acts of self-sacrifice and self-abasement to bring happiness and dignity to their parents in their old age: Lao Lai-zi, for example, well into his own dotage, still capered and frolicked like a toddler to rejoice his venerable progenitors and make them laugh at his antics. (In illustrations, they're depicted gnarled as pickled walnuts but grinning widely as their ancient son gambols before them.)

The idea of the elevating anecdote in turn inspired the contrary notion of 'teaching by negative example': under Mao, some forbidden texts from the past or from the West could be analysed in class for their wickedness and corruption and deviation from the true way of Communism. By this means, which was admittedly highly circumscribed and remained perilous, some Chinese were able to smuggle knowledge past the censors and quietly absorb proscribed ideas, fiction and poetry. Scepticism can cut both ways, and the idea of error can refine the idea of truth beyond the control of demagogues or propagandists or simply lazy minds.

'Curiosity is the purest form of insubordination,' Nabokov once proposed. It's exhilarating to count on people's resistance to intellectual coercion; equally, it's dispiriting to lose faith in this human capacity, and so many contemporary horrors, dictatorships, national, tribal and religious conflicts, lead one inevitably to falter (the current, fearful craze for alien abduction stories may reflect this anxiety). But I have always thought that readers' – or viewers' – ability to disagree with a point of view or an argument and diverge from the prevailing tide of opinion is constantly being underestimated.

Historians and critics research and write under the sign of Doubting Thomas, probing the wounds of the past, but not content until the evidence has been uncovered, verified and analysed, and even then, still subject to challenge. I have always tried to question received ideas, customary arrangements, notions of natural order, as embodied in ideal and heroic figures like the Virgin Mary and Joan of Arc or, more recently in my work, the comical and despised old beldame storytellers like Mother Goose or the cannibal cradle-snatcher preying on babies as she – or he – roams the night.

Yet a convent schooling trains its pupils to believe more widely than in matters religious; nevertheless, it was through belief that I arrived, after many detours, at scepticism. In the convent where I boarded from the age of nine until A Levels, the New Testament wasn't the only book we were taught as gospel. Permitted reading included the pamphlets of the Catholic Truth Society on sale in the weekly 'Holy Shop' where we were allowed to spend our pocket money on rosaries from the Holy Land, holy water stoups, holy pictures – and booklets about figures in the Catholic pantheon. The heroes and heroines of the stories, like Confucian model children, conveyed thrilling lessons, but in lives of adventure, rebellion and violence. From the dull security of the begonia flowerbeds and murky rhododendron groves of suburban Ascot, the ingenious torments that afflicted martyrs far and wide opened vistas on unknown worlds: the remarkable heroism of Saint Francis, stripping in the public square of Assisi before his father, rather than be tainted by his family's material goods; the brilliant stand of Saint Catherine when she confounded the emperor and all his scholars in a public battle of wits in Alexandria; the dream oracle of the black dogs who appeared to Saint Dominic to call him to found the order that then inaugurated the Inquisition. All these stories filled the imaginations of us schoolgirls and drew irresistible images of possibility in the mind's eye.

Apart from the tales of heroism, there were the miracles, too: tales of blood that fell from the host in the hands of a priest who was racked by doubts about the Real Presence and so proved to him – and to all others – that the bread truly changed into the flesh of Jesus's body; the severed head of Saint Denis (and of other saints) that continued to sing praises to God when he picked it up and walked with it; the heavenly fragrance of roses that emanated from the wall where Teresa of Avila's body was interred; the flowers that appeared miraculously in the basket of Elizabeth of Hungary when she was discovered taking food to the poor by her wicked husband, who had forbidden her to do good works. We were wrapped in stories, in signs and wonders, in fantasies, myths and dreams.

The education stamped me with an abiding, irrepressible interest in the irrational, both as an expression of the mind in its most mysterious mode, and as a terrifying force in history. I still collect hagiographies, still visit remote churches to discover saints who once commanded international cults but are now forgotten: most recently, in East Portlemouth on the Salcombe estuary in Devon, the wonderfully named St. Winwalloe, who fled from Wales to Brittany from the Saxon invaders and founded a monastery, where he died in 520; his memory was brought back to the Devon and Cornish shore by monks of his order who reckoned him a saint. There wasn't much about Winwalloe to be discovered in his church, but the graveyard is full of pirates, smugglers, sailors and fisher folk who were wrecked and 'drowned', 'lost at sea', the epitaphs say. Stones, like oracular heads, sing out; stories cling to stories, grow one from another, lead on to new forks in the path.

In more secular vein, I was reading *The Blue, Green, Red, Rose Fairy Books*, which Andrew Lang edited, from a cornucopia of fairy tales gathered (as I learned later) by a team of lady writers and translators marshalled by Lang's wife, Leonora Alleyne. But the storybook that inspired me most indelibly was itself a parody of morality literature for children. *Struwwelpeter* was written for his own offspring by Dr Heinrich Hoffmann, a psychiatrist (then called an alienist), after he went out one Christmas to buy them a book, and, reportedly, could only find exhortatory tales and admonishments of interminable Victorian tedium. So he sat down and composed his gallows humour parody, peopled by Tall Agrippa who plunges bad boys in his giant inkwell and the Tailor Man with his long legs like a pair of shears who comes leaping in across the page to cut off the thumbs of the child who would go on sucking his. It was published in 1845 and was a huge, international success, translated into numerous languages and still selling.

My father was a bookseller, and he provided me and my younger sister Laura with a limitless supply of books from his shop. But *Struwwelpeter* was one I gave back to him, and asked him to burn it. He was having a bonfire in the garden, and he told me he'd thrown it in the flames. I had no need to fear the Scissor-man any longer. But a few weeks later, I found the book, hidden behind some others on a shelf. He hadn't burned it, because someone who loves and prizes books doesn't do that; besides, the bookshop he'd run in Cairo before moving to Belgium was torched in the Black Sunday riots of 1952.

Struwwelpeter was the first book I knew that I wished I didn't know, and its imagery entered my mind and lodged there, terrifying me. When I learned that its author intended it to be comic – its English subtitle is *Pretty Stories and Funny Pictures* – it seemed to me a perfect example of a document that can only be understood if its context is known: behind the story lies a history. Furthermore, it demonstrates how meanings proliferate beyond authors' characters, motives and the conditions of their times: around the particular historical instance lies a broader, denser thicket, the history of attitudes to children, to punishment, to curiosity, to sexuality, to amusement, to the difference between boys and girls. (There is only one naughty girl in *Struwwelpeter*, Harriet who played with fire.)

My father had a historical turn of mind: he would stride through a city – Paris, Ravenna, Brussels, Cambridge are among those I remember – telling stories about the streets where we found ourselves, the people who had made them, who had unmade them, who had remade them. He showed me the faded sign on the bricks of the Place de la Concorde, saying 'Place Louis XIV'. In Belgium, where he was manager of the W. H. Smith branch (and English tearooms, a feature of Brussels society in the 1950s), we lived near Waterloo.

Whenever visitors came from England, we drove off to the battlefield, explored the farms where the cannon balls' impact still gouged the walls, climbed the conical Wellington Monument with the lion on top and pored over the tiny figures of the Diorama, while my father talked of artillery deployment, pincer movements and flanking manoeuvres. The unfolding of the past was a matter of extreme urgency to him, and he liked its villains, as well as its heroes, not because he upheld what they had done or wanted to do, but because they raised the questions that need to be asked. I don't think we would have agreed very often about the answers (if we could have suggested some), but the excitement lay in the interplay of destiny, morality and psychology, as in the case of Napoleon, the arch-enemy so vividly commemorated in defeat on the tourist site of his final battle.

Hardly surprisingly, I no longer want to be a saint – or even to be like a saint, and I don't want to run away to fight the infidel any more – or at least, not in quite the same way as I was inspired to do at school. Nor am I frightened by 'The Dreadful Story about Harriet and the Matches'. I do find *Struwwelpeter* funny. But these childhood experiences of stories gave me a powerful sense of the presence of myth within diverse material.

My ethical and emotional upbringing was all mixed up with history and the way it was told – the Christian saints' lives and prodigies were presented as history, after all. Later, this sense led me to explore the shaping energy of myth on historical events themselves, as they occur and, above all, as they are reported, received and disseminated. I became interested in analysing the structures of dream and belief and desire that scaffold perception of events, of reality, of actuality: to find the slanted truth, to look at, if you like, the tension and the kinship between story and history, which in many languages are expressed by the same word – *la storia, l'histoire.*

1998

ONE

EARLY ENCOUNTERS

The Bitch Route 13

'You're not a real newsman till you've lost your first cameraman'
(attributed to an American news programme)

Each night in the restaurant of the Hotel Royal, Saigon, some of the 492 accredited journalists in Vietnam meet to discuss the war. As the empty cognac glasses multiply on the table and the witches' brew of Saigon's wildlife – rats, bats and cockroaches – come out to play in the curfewed town, the journalists tell stories. 'What did you do today?' they ask each other. 'Nothing much.' Went to Binh Dinh. Or went to Dat To. Or went to Can Tho. Or came back from Hué. For the last two weeks the exchanges have been frustrated and the newsmen listless: the North Vietnamese have dug themselves in, and the South Vietnamese don't fight. The stalemate was getting on everyone's nerves. 'The bad guys were really *hit* in Korea,' muttered one correspondent who has shorn his hair 'in order to move invisibly among the troops like a US adviser'. Most reporters agreed that Bangladesh had been far far more difficult to cover. One – usually nice – television man joked: 'Genocide must have been invented for the Bengalis.' Other wars, other campaigns and other years of the war in Vietnam stretch their shadows over this offensive. But this one, most journalists agreed, was a bitch.

The real 'bitch' is Route 13, the road from Saigon to An Loc. As the ARVN (South Vietnamese Army) edge their bitter pyrrhic way from their foxholes towards the flattened district capital, the last handful of North Vietnamese in the trees on either side of the road shower them with mortars, rockets and AK47 artillery fire. For the first weeks of the offensive, this was the focus of the world's interest because it was the journalists' own bullring, where they tested their mettle in the glare and the heat and the danger to get the story. To London. To New York. To

Washington. To Paris. To Stockholm. To Rome. 'It really must be a big story,' said one, 'even the Italians have come.'

For the last few weeks, Route 13 too had been a dead topic. Now however that An Loc, or rather what is left of An Loc, looks as if it is going to be relieved, 'Are you going up the Road?' has again become the question everyone asks each other over cognac in the restaurant of the Hotel Royal in Saigon.

Two Vietnamese army reporters have been killed and eight journalists wounded on Route 13 during this offensive. David De Voss of *Time* was abandoned riddled full of mortar in the trees by an ARVN platoon who reported, 'There is a round-eye lying over there. No rank. No weapon. Blah. We shan't go back.' Half an hour later, on American 'advice', he was rescued. His lungs were filled with blood. Yesterday Peter Arnett and another photojournalist (both with Associated Press; it was Arnett who reported the American major's classic remark 'we had to destroy the town in order to save it' in 1968) had half the radiator of their car destroyed by shrapnel and the windows shattered as they drove towards the besieged town. Yet a photographer, emerging unscathed, said in his urbane European drawl with his merry eyes alight, 'Vot I like eez boom boom. Oh yes.' Peter Gill of the *Daily Express* had anticipated this earlier. 'There is something fantastically exhilarating,' he said, 'about being terrified out of your wits.'

Each morning now journalists and photographers are again going up Route 13 to try to get into An Loc. Mountainous men girded with cameras and water bottles, strapped up in US army gear, swaddled in khaki flak jackets and surmounted with camouflage helmets, they swagger over to the old Pontiacs and Chevrolets outside the Continental Hotel in Saigon's main square and bargain with the Vietnamese drivers. The sixty miles up the road costs about £15 return. If you want to fly into An Loc you can: in this most mercenary of wars, you bribe the Vietnamese Air Force pilots to take you. That costs $200. To get out, you tell them you will wave a particular flag or make a particular signal, and then give them more money. Getting out is more difficult. Ru Rauch of *Time* managed it today after two days in the town but only because US General Hollingsworth picked him up in a fleet of helicopters.

There are hundreds of wounded Vietnamese soldiers in An Loc, soldiers who have been defending the town for two months and twelve days under an unrelenting rain of North Vietnamese fire and American bombing – sometimes 7,000 shells a day. The noise alone would burst the eardrums of the dead. Since helicopters have been able to fly into the town, they have been laid out by their mates on stretchers in the blistering heat, waiting to be evacuated. Only a few – about 400 – have so far caught this particular freedom bird. When Ru Rauch got out, he had to fight off those wounded soldiers who could still walk. This sort of thing happened at Kontum too. There, during the evacuation, journalists fought with Montagnard refugees.

When a journalist scoops a story – 'I was the first man into An Loc today . . .' – he is generous towards his colleagues. If he comes down the road from the fighting, those journalists who have not walked so brazenly to the front line cluster about him and pick his brains. He tells them what he's seen. In the hotel bars later, he tells some more. He looks hectic and excited. His audience looks crestfallen but gripped. Each one thinks to himself, mentally nail-biting, *I should have gone, I should have tried*. The needling is subtle and underhand, but each man feels it. And it often only takes one reckless/courageous newsman to set a whole gang-bang plunging forward. As one photographer remarked, 'Being out there is like having ten girls and ten orgasms all at once.'

The television men are the bravest. They have to go up front and stay there day after day and hour after hour to get the atrocities on film. The hunger of the editors at home pins them down in the blinding heat. A seasoned ITN war reporter said it was beginning to sicken him. 'Before they were satisfied with a corpse. Now they must have people dying in action. But when they really do get a film which shows what a mortar does to a man, really shows the flesh torn and the blood flowing, they get squeamish. They want it just so. They want TV to be cinema.'

Machismo, or masochismo, the goal of it all is the story. 'Did you get it?' is the cry. All the danger, the struggle, the *sauve-qui-peut* is to get the story running on the live wire home. Once it is written, the incident, however appalling, is shelved, except to be dusted and brought out again over the drinks at night, by which time it has become an exploit – turned and polished as a piece of literature.

Occasionally, a journalist will become involved. 'Goddam you. Leave me alone. Get the hell out,' shouted a *Newsweek* writer coming down Route 1 from the village of Trang Bang after the Vietnamese Air Force dropped napalm on their own side and burned two babies to death. He was waving his hands, shouting at the reporters clustered on the road who thirsted for his first-hand, eyewitness, report. But he was, for a moment, crazed, stomping down the road in fury and grief. Later, he came up to us, recovered. 'I'm really sorry. I didn't mean to cut up on you guys. It was just . . .' Everyone nodded and said, 'That's OK.' And then asked him to tell.

Peter Arnett, veteran newsman, says involvement is disastrous. The only way the press can stop anything happening is to stick to its job and write and photograph it. Doling out sympathy, rushing about trying to help does not work. As a result, someone like Peter Arnett is hardboiled as a Chinese thousand-year-old egg. But he is also one of many journalists who have valiantly altered and shaped the world's attitude to the Vietnam war.

Pity and compassion have nevertheless become the journalists' stock-in-trade. Emotions are really kept for the cables from home. YOUR SPLENDID AN LOC STORY MAKES DISTINGUISHED PAGE ONE LEAD MANY THANKS AND CONGRATULATIONS ON REALLY FINE WORK EDITOR is called a Herogram. YOUR SPLENDID AN LOC STORY UNFORTUNATELY SQUEEZED OUT IF IS ANY CONSOLATION TO YOU SPIFFING STORY OF MINE DIDN'T MAKE IT EITHER FOREIGN EDITOR is a matter for sullen resentment. 'I bloody nearly killed myself on that bloody road,' snarls the recipient.

Many journalists' careers have been built on, or at least strengthened by, a spell in Vietnam. They are – and they recognise it – living off the sufferings they describe. The byline under the headlines gives their ego a fillip as well. 'There is really nothing else,' they say. And so one comes to the central irony of the indisputably courageous and vital coverage of the Vietnam war. No matter how bitterly opposed to the war a journalist might be, it is really against his interests for the war to calm down. The bloodier the offensive, the more prominent the coverage. The more atrocities perpetrated, the more resounding his name and his dateline. However impassioned he is against the American presence in Vietnam – and many pressmen are – he does not really want the Americans to withdraw completely because it is their actions that make Vietnam a story of international concern. So the same criticism that many writers make against the Americans – that they care little or nothing for the interests of the Vietnamese people – can be levelled at the press.

Almost every night, between the anecdotes, solutions, or rather attempts at solutions, are thrashed out. There is never a consensus of opinion. The press corps in Vietnam is probably the most informed body of all about the war – though the politicians should be – and the deeper you get entangled in the war, the more intractable the riddle becomes.

This striving to understand is what makes covering Vietnam exciting. But there is the added element. War-reporting is the contemporary male's duel. When a newsman comes back from the road, from the challenge of enemy fire, he feels the pounding in his blood like any corny soldier, but without the contemporary taint of being a military man. As the photographer said, 'Boom boom. Oh yes.'

1972

The Crushed Butterflies of War

Bob Young, earnest and clean-cut, a young major in the US Army, asked his Vietnamese counterpart, Colonel Sinh, and Colonel Sinh's subordinate officers, to his quarters at the US Army base in Can Tho in the lush Mekong Delta. There was a floor show for the soldiers that night, and Major Young invited them to join him. At the door, they were turned away. Vietnamese were not allowed in the theatre, and strictly speaking, he was told, the whole base was off limits to them.

The major, who 'loves this country and loves its people' and has applied for a second term in Vietnam, is an unusual American officer. He was shaken and furious. But such contempt and prejudice for the ARVN and for the people of Vietnam ripple sourly through the most ordinary transactions and taint the Americans in Vietnam as occupiers rather than allies.

At dinner with Major Young and Colonel Sinh, which of course had to take place in the latter's rudimentary barracks, bare and humble except for complicated tape-recorder equipment that wailed sentimental medleys from old musicals ('I want to be in America/Everything's free in America'), Captain Muoi whispered his resentment to me as he ceremoniously tweezed another piece of spiced crab from his chopsticks into my bowl. Captain Muoi is an ardent Confucianist, who always acknowledges the presence of his mother's departed spirit at his table; he speaks excellent French: before he was mobilised he was a teacher.

Captain Muoi could vent his spleen freely, because Major Young (who is his friend – they go out dancing together) cannot understand French. Muoi's lustrous eyes glistened with emotion as he indicted the Americans. They had dislocated the traditional hierarchy of Vietnam, he said, lighting another cigarette and drawing on it excitedly, because he, a captain in the ARVN, got paid 600 piastres a day (60p) while a cycle driver, a coolie boy, made 1,000 a day. A GI is paid $300 (£120) a month; an ARVN private 3,000 piastres (£3). 'I can go into a bar,' said Captain Muoi, 'and I can have a drink. No one will bother me. The girls aren't interested. I haven't the money because my skin is yellow.' ('Je n'ai pas le fric parce que je suis jaune.')

Major Young had brought his girlfriend to dinner, a bargirl called Mai whom he proudly described to us as the daughter of a prominent Buddhist and, equally proudly, as having 'been all the way round the block'. She was painted and plump and seventeen years old. She spoke very little English, and that was rum. 'You don't know shit, soldier,' she would say, and Major Young would pat her knees and say to us, 'She doesn't know what she's saying.' He kept up an incessant flow of baby talk in her direction, and she would smile and say, 'Yeah, yeah', through her false eyelashes. She looked well into her twenties. As Vietnamese girls are slender, fragile-boned and youthful into middle age, it seemed that she had acquired, by mimesis, the physical tendencies of her host's country.

Captain Muoi cast a viperish look at her, and hissed at me: 'What the Vietnamese hate most about the Americans is that they have disrupted our culture and ruined our women – women like her.' Mai shifted nervously and Major Young patted her knees.

Mai had begged Major Young – or so he said – to give her a 'blue-eyed baby with blond hair and a cleft in its chin like mine' because 'all her friends have one'. He was terribly flattered and 'evaluating his response'. If he decided to, Mai's baby would join the estimated 15,000 to 50,000 métis children in South Vietnam – children of American soldiers, either half black or half white. Mai's prominent Buddhist father would probably ensure that she could afford to keep the baby, unlike other unmarried Vietnamese mothers who sign away their children at birth to one of Vietnam's squalid, teeming orphanages, or abandon them later, on the steps, when they realise that without means they cannot both work and rear their child.

Although American ground troops have generally withdrawn, the orphanages and hospitals report no corresponding decline in the number of métis births. A bargirl can of course only have one baby a year anyway, no matter how many nights she works. But another reason might be that more métis are being abandoned in ratio to the numbers born – hence the stable rate in institutions – because the principal flow of income has been staunched. Before, a girl would work the bars to keep her child. Now there are few soldiers and little work.

Above all, by order of President Thieu, all bars boasting piped music, massage parlours, steam baths, or other lupercalia were closed on 13 May when martial law was declared in Saigon, one of the select few towns in Vietnam which was not out of bounds to the US Army and therefore the fleshpot of the south.

Saigon tea, a weak iced brew, used to be the ticket to a girl's company in the bars. A few glasses, and she'd spend an hour with you; many glasses, and she'd spend the night. The bar chits were paid for by the client, and signed by the girl. The bar proprietor gave her a 50 per cent cut afterwards on her takings. No syndicates operated; the girls were self-employed and wandered at will from one gilt and velvet darkened dungeon to another. They also always reserved to themselves the prerogative to refuse, which gave them a bad name, both for iciness and for cheating. 'I bought you five goddam Saigon teas, you goddam bitch . . .'

Venereal disease was, and is, rife. The magazine *Soldiers* carries lurid warnings against the hazard, including pictures of women as death-heads wreathed in smiles. In the organised hangar-like bar-cum-brothel at the US base at Da Nang, posters proclaim 'Girls with tags are clean', 'Girls without tags are diseased'. There, at least, the girls were cared for, however degraded. As prostitution is illegal in this country, there are no VD clinics for women, but only for soldiers.

The bars are now, after one month, flickering back to life. The offending terms – 'Bar' and suchlike – are being summarily daubed out by a swift coat of paint in the right places, and the sign 'Restaurant' has been substituted. On the road out to the airport, one establishment that proudly proclaimed 'The Artistic Hand – Bar, Massage Parlour and Steam Bath' now reads: 'The Artistic Hand – Restaurant'.

But the bargirls have left Saigon and have returned to the families they probably supported all along, for, with the army pay so bad and full mobilisation, women have become all-important breadwinners. Only on the colonnaded terrace of the old and gracious Continental Hotel do the bargirls still sit, waiting for the journalists or for the handful of GIs who come into Saigon on Saturdays.

They sit together sipping iced tea or *citron pressé*. One wears a diamanté tiara and a long gown, another a silver plastic micro-skirt, another the traditional pencil-slim tunic called an *ao-dai* over black satin pantaloons. Some are ravishing, others clownishly painted. Some are men. In their handbags, the women carry albums of bright snapshots of their children and will show them to you when you buy them a drink. Sometimes they bring their children along: Vietnamese babies with blue eyes, in immaculate embroidered clothes. They charge (when they accept, and in these hard times that is frequent) about 5,000 piastres (£5) for a siesta, and 10,000 piastres for the day – a lot of money to them, little to their clients.

In the list of unused unaccompanied baggage which must be declared upon entry into South Vietnam are the following items: lipstick (5 items), face powder (5), hair spray (5), nail polish (5), eyebrow pencil (5), artificial eyelashes (5), and eye liner (5). The trade must have been brisk to warrant the Customs' close attention to such small quantities of make-up. Were GIs importing them for their girlfriends? Were the girls asking them to smuggle them in? Whatever it was, those girls on the terrace of the Continental, in all their cosmetic finery, belong to an expensive élite who can afford exorbitantly priced goods. They, out of many, have survived the closure of the bars and the crippling of their business.

Many women who lived in the wake of the American army, like birds settling in the furrow after the passing of the ploughshare, are scarcely surviving. Over the river, down a dust-filled street lined with shacks and booths, in two rooms that give out on to a stagnant backwater, live three women who worked in a desultory fashion as bargirls, leaving the job the minute they struck up a more enduring relationship. Between them they have eight children of assorted age, size, and blood. Some are their own, some belong to 'friends' who have left them there, and they all help each other, the eleven-year-olds feeding the babies, hoisting them out of the hammock where they sleep, mopping up their mess, and wringing the rags out in the yard outside.

Tra Kim Anh, thirty-five years old, with a bleak smile and white teeth, has a daughter, Thu, aged five, by a German, one of the many civilians who also traipsed after the riches of the American Army. Two months after he left Vietnam, Anh heard he had been killed in a brawl. Her son, Dung, aged four, lives with 'friends' for £9 a month. The household costs £30 a month to run; one of the three girls is sending money from Can Tho, where she has gone with her American captain boyfriend. 'She sends as much as she can,' says Anh. 'What will you do when that runs out?' I asked. 'I have saved some money.' 'How much?' About £40.

Anh now takes in sewing, but she is slow and unskilled and can only do repairs. So far, a month's work has earned her £4. The numerous children sleep on one high wooden Vietnamese bed; they eat rice and *nuoc mam*, a high-smelling sauce which the Vietnamese love, made from fish brewed and stewed and fermented in vats for month after month. It is fortunately highly nutritious.

A snapshot of Dung's father was produced and laid on the fly-blown table. Snub-nosed and fresh-faced in his crisp uniform, he grinned at us. This year, his payments towards his child's upbringing have dried up. He was unusual to bother at all; but now, as Anh writes no English, and has never written to him, she can't or won't communicate. When I asked her what she thought of Americans, she said it was hard for her to say. During the Tet offensive of 1968, she explained, she had been living with one GI when her mother had been killed by another. So it was hard to say. 'I was going to America,' she added, brightening, 'but the papers are very complicated.'

To emigrate from Vietnam is impossible for a single woman (unless, as always in Vietnam, you can touch those wheels within wheels); but GIs can and do – sometimes – take their wives home. There seem to be many degrees of wifeliness or wifehood in Vietnam. On every main street, signs are displayed: Marriage, Visas, Passport, All Documents and Papers Available. Inside some crooked agent sits, selling documents for crooked prices. (One agent asked £150 for an extension of a foreigner's permit to stay in Vietnam. On hearing the client was a journalist he amended his fee to £650. The extension costs nothing at the Foreign Ministry and is usually automatic, if slow.)

Marriage papers are granted by Vietnamese authorities through such agencies. An American walks in, swears an affidavit that no impediments exist to his marriage, pays a fee (swiftly assessed on his rank, means, etc.) and eventually endows his bride with a document which months and sometimes years afterwards she produces from her handbag along with the snapshots of her children. No wedding ceremony, civil or religious, is required in Vietnam, and, though the documents are legal and binding, they are meaningless. No bargirl has the means or the savoir-faire to sue a man in America for bigamy; an American wife, even if she hears of the affair, knows better than to bother about the whore he left behind. 'Cohabitation papers' are more common. In Vietnam, the classical module for corrupt Puritanism, living together is sinful, so to do it you have to have a permit. Unless a girl, walking with a foreigner at night, has such papers, the military police can pick her up as a prostitute, and sling her in gaol for the night

– but a few thousand piastres, slipped to the cop, can settle it. The man of course goes free anyway.

Louder, brawnier, bigger, American soldiers diminished the Vietnamese. They were fighting what was – in theory – their war for them, emasculating them, into Hanoi's phrase, like puppets; they seeped imperceptibly into the country's structure by altering that precarious balance between the sexes. For this reason, Captain Muoi lamented: 'For us there is nothing unless the Americans leave us. After that, there is still nothing. We have had it. Nous sommes fichus.'

1972

My Day

In Washington, where I live, deception is the order of the day. When I get up, white sunshine flows through the white curtains of our white bedroom; the winter sky is disarmingly blue; the tree-filled streets are lined by charming shuttered houses and the street lamps, now extinguished, remind one of pictures of Paris in the 1890s. Squirrels leap on our balcony and hurry away with huge nuts and pine cones pressed between their paws; a blue jay darts by. As we leave the house together, others are walking to work like us, hunched and muffled against the cold. William Shawcross, my husband, goes to the New Senate building, to the office of Senator Kennedy, to struggle with the Senator's Bill to establish a national health insurance – somewhat on the lines of the British system – in America, where nothing is free. I leave him one block before, and turn to the massive grey-green dome of the Library of Congress.

So monumental, so imposing, so gleaming, these governmental buildings. So pastoral, so tranquil, these residential streets of Georgetown or Capitol Hill. But, inside the vast edifices, the machinery of government turns upon itself in an ever-increasing inflationary spiral. Business begets more business. Papers, documents, suggestions, memos pile upon each other in an avalanche. More laws spawn more lawyers, more experts, scrutinising, sifting, matching and interpreting. The office of a minor Congressman employs fourteen full-time staff. Senator Kennedy alone employs seventy people.

Yet, just beyond the glorious neo-classical monoliths of Capitol Hill, the centre of Washington lies: the black ghetto. One derelict house after another, one corner shop boarded up after some incident that took place long ago – probably in the 1968 riots after Martin Luther King was murdered, one raggle-taggle of casual labourers waiting outside the local liquor shop for the pick-up truck which might come and give them work that day. When I first arrived, Washington reminded me of nowhere more than the degraded streets of South Vietnam; but what soon shocked harder was the strict demarcation between white and black, observed by invisible lines and an intuitive timetable. At midday, a restaurant is white, 'safe'; at night, it is closed, 'unsafe'. Two girls I know went to a black cinema; outside a young black reporter interviewed them about their motives. He was friendly, and curious. But their attendance was news. Only one area of Washington is integrated, and that is Capitol Hill, because the whites are moving back to the area they abandoned in the nineteenth century. So the prices go up, so the blacks are being pushed out. But the poverty of black Washington really bears no comparison to the poverty of anywhere else in the world, because it lies on the flanks of the most powerful government, a constant reminder, at best, of the impotence of the machine.

The Library of Congress, where I now go, mirrors the larger bureaucracy: armies of men and women marshal the slips made out by readers and hunt the shelves for the books in question; the catalogue alone fills three huge rooms; every book in the English-speaking world, and many in other languages, arrive there. Two hundred thousand books a year; more miles of shelf; more people to pore over the catalogue cards, to sort, to hunt, to record. The Library is metaphysical: in Jorge Luis Borges's imagination, libraries grow organically with an irresistible impetus, fill up with the works of men as yet unborn, with books that cannot be read, that will never again be seen.

I fill out dozens of request slips and take my place at a mahogany desk. Then I wait for the books I have asked for not to appear. I do what everyone does in libraries: moon at the ceiling, or stare at the other people who are mooning at the ceiling or staring at me. The golden dome of the Main Reading Room is emblazoned with edifying quotations. Some are mysterious: 'We taste the Spices of Arabia yet never feel the scorching sun which brings them forth.'

When my slips come back, saying Not on Shelf, I fill in some more slips requesting a Special Search. That takes a fortnight. So I then move to the Annexe. I walk down an underground tunnel for miles past library attendants struggling with books they have managed to unearth. They should have roller skates, I think, as they do in New York (or so I am told). By the middle of the tunnel I feel I could do with a pair.

The Annexe Reading Room is called after Thomas Jefferson, and the walls here are triumphantly painted with his words of liberation and equality for all. Even the irony is poor, nowadays.

So in the Thomas Jefferson Room staring at the people is better. There is the Eastern European contingent: refugees from the Cold War, in the Slavonic Studies Room, murmuring excitedly about the finer points of Bohemian fifteenth-century morphology. There is the historian of the Americas, a young man so devoted to his mounds of ruled copybooks covered with a close red Biro scrawl that he broke his leg and didn't have it set. I had watched him drag his useless leg up and down as he pulled one encyclopaedia off the shelf after another, and wondered what had happened to him. Then I heard him explaining to friends one day. Maybe he couldn't – in this country of private medicine – afford to have it set.

One book slip comes back. It refers me to the Rare Book Reading Room. Down a few floors in the lift. More tunnels. At the entrance to the carpeted luxurious study in which the Rare Books are kept, I swear not to use ink or Biro, break the books' spines or wear my coat when studying there. The book in question is reverently brought to me. The pages are uncut. I ask them if they could cut them so I can read. Oh no, they say. The book is an art object. For the vastness of the Library outruns its own usefulness – in this is it again a mirror of the governmental machine nearby? One librarian sighed: 'In Moscow they have double the readers and ten times less staff. We can't understand it.'

Back in the Main Reading Room I start reading Tertullian, a second-century Christian, on virgins. Or rather, on veiling virgins. (The book I am writing now is a study of the cult of the Virgin Mary and how it relates to what we still think is right and proper for women.) Tertullian is a delight. He rails against all the arts of women to deceive and ensnare men: nothing escapes him, the rouge of the cheek, the pretty slipper, the jewelled ear lobe, the casually falling tendrils of hair. On and on he goes, drinking every detail with that vengeful fire of observation – lust, indeed – that self-imposed chastity confers. The import is of course serious, for Tertullian is among the first Christians to identify sin with sex and sex with women in a closed syllogism that has bedevilled Western culture for centuries. I take copious notes on my index cards, and score them with exclamation marks and underlinings. Much later, talking to my sister, I am amazed to hear that we are descended from Tertullian: our mother's name was Terzulli.

By this time I am restless, hungry and exhausted. So I walk home, avoiding the underground cafeteria of the Library. At home I find the post, the greatest pleasure of the day for people living abroad. I ring up Willie to tell him he's got such and such a letter (if I recognise the handwriting) and often, a cable – the particular largesse of the journalist's world. He comes rushing over. We exclaim, read bits to each other and then swap. Then we poke at bits of cheese and tuna fish, and bread, though in America, as everyone always says, food might as well be polystyrene.

Back in the Library in the afternoon, the energy required for real concentration is drained, so I resort to horrid manuals of good conduct by parish priests this century. Everywhere the same message: submission, obedience, and sexual restraint are the qualities of a good Christian woman. And the model – the Virgin Mary. It disgusts me. But it gives point to my book at least. Millions of women are practising Catholics. More millions were, like me, indoctrinated in the Church's principles, and those principles have a way of sticking, when faith itself has long shaken loose.

Fed up with piety and strictures and the 'understanding' of celibate priests, I start back for home. It's now dark, and those 1890s lamps burn dimly. Scare stories from the staple conversation of Washington dinner parties – one girl has been raped, another guest mugged, and, just as I write, Senator Stennis was shot outside his house. I try and stifle the thoughts. Be fatalistic, walk tall, I say to myself, eyeing the rustling in the bushes, the shadows on the pavement. But fear resists the will, and I am always relieved when at last I reach our door.

This particular day, Willie is already back, shouting at me to hurry. 'The Chinese acrobats! The Chinese acrobats!' he calls down the stairs. The Shengyang troupe from Mukden in China have been touring Canada and the United States to ecstatic notices, and in Washington the enormous Kennedy Center has been sold out for months. But because it's the Kennedy Center, the Kennedy staff have been given a block of seats for the television performance – tonight.

And the acrobatics are fantastic. They defy all laws of gravity and nature. As the gongs and flutes and drums strike up the wild Chinese cacophony that I, for one, love, the troupe runs on to the stage in luminous pinks and lime greens. Thousands of plates twirl between their fingers on the ends of wands. Some acrobats turn somersaults, others stand on their heads, or on each other, all the while spinning these dozens of plates at the ends of their fingers. Later, a man positions a bamboo pole on his chest. It's twenty feet high. Another scales it nimbly, and then another. Together, at the top of the bamboo still perched on the man's chest, they perform dazzling feats: one holds on while the other stands on his head, one twists his leg round the pole and holds the other out to one side, horizontally, as if weightless. They show no signs of strain, and not a muscle quivers. The audience rubs its eyes, shrieks with tension and delight, applauds wildly.

Acts follow, each one astonishing, each one the same baraboum of virtuoso technique and straight circus fun. At the end, after all the colour, the cymbals, the prowess and gaiety, the troupe unfurls a huge red banner to a crescendo of percussion. 'LONG LIVE THE FRIENDSHIP OF THE UNITED STATES AND THE PEOPLE'S REPUBLIC OF CHINA.' 'Hooray!' shouts the crowd, rising to its feet. 'Hooray! hooray!'

That same day, the American bombardment of the People's Republic's allies in South Vietnam had been particularly thorough. Diplomacy proceeds from deception to deception, and, as I say, deception is the stuff of a Washington day.

1973

Jessica Mitford

Obituary

At around 4 am, Jessica Mitford would be up, tap-tap-tapping at her typewriter, which had the kind of typeface forensic experts match up to anonymous letters in spy movies: you could recognise a fax from Decca from any single wonky character. Also, from the abbreviations that peppered the page: her language was a kind of shorthand all of her own, her writing – sprinkled with dots and ellipses and ampersands and capitalised and truncated words, from her nickname, Dec or Decca (after one of her sisters' childhood lisping of her name) to her particular style for the place she had lived since her early twenties: 'Calif'. She liked to conduct exchanges in questions, exclamations, asides, and monosyllables:

'Go on, do tell!' 'Now, here's the thing!' 'Too good!' 'So long to know . . .'
When she gave a party, which she did, often, spontaneously, generously,
with no fuss, she drew up a guest list so that she could let you know exactly
who was coming (and why): she was businesslike as well as gregarious.
Even from such a list, her spirit jumped off the page, as if out of a bottle,
as if she were present talking to you with her merry eyes and her dry drawl:
no wonder some US archive was collecting every scrap of paper she'd ever
scribbled on. Even her shopping lists were idiosyncratic.

Struggling with smoking, she took to Nicorettes with a vengeance, and
was chewing twenty a day for the last few years of her life. She dreaded, she
said, that there would soon be announcements by the air hostess: 'There
will be no chewing on this flight'; the last time I saw her, at home in
Oakland, the doorbell rang and the delivery boy from the drugstore was
there, with a brown bag full of Nicorettes to tide her through the party.

Her style of talking and of writing was succinct, dry, and merciless: her
favourite method of demolishing an opponent was to make them listen to
themselves and crumble in embarrassment. She loved to quote exactly
word for word, showing up the hypocrisy/ pretension/folly of the
perpetrator. Among her favourite books were *Rotten Reviews Vol. 1* and
Rotten Reviews Vol. II, in which experts pronounce that *Wuthering
Heights* 'will never be generally read', or the *New Statesman* opines that
'there are no surprises' in *Brave New World*, and that *Buddenbrooks* is
'nothing but two thick tomes in which the author describes the worthless
story of worthless people in worthless chatter'.

Even if her aliveness to human folly was always too sharp to be
charitable, it would be a huge mistake to think of her as malicious or even
waspish: though her wit and turn of phrase belonged recognisably to the
grand cru vintage that produced her sister Nancy as well as Evelyn
Waugh, she was also affectionate, loyal, effervescent, generous: she once
handed my son $50, found him two friends to play with, and turned them
all loose to enjoy themselves in 'SF' (San Francisco) for the day. He was
overjoyed; I was dumbfounded: he was then eleven years old. She thought
my generation made far too much of a fuss about children and child-
rearing. She had opened her Running Away account at Drummonds at
the age of twelve, after all.

Life was an adventure, to be seized, to be lived to the hilt. It had proved
so for her, from eloping in 1937 at the age of nineteen with her first love
(later her husband), Esmond Romilly, to her blithe and irrepressible
political campaigns, first against the undertakers, then the obstetricians

(*The American Way of Death*, 1963, *The American Way of Birth*, 1992). She still subscribed to morticians' trade journals, and liked to read out the ads for the latest model coffins, chuckling over the trimmings. In revenge, one firm called a particularly modest version 'The Jessica Mitford'. 'All the right enemies' was a slogan she lived by.

This mixture of the satirist, the intrepid adventurer and the true-hearted, tonic friend comes through the list of her works, which could strike the reader as oddly inconsistent: *Poison Penmanship: The Gentle Art of Muckraking* (1979) mixed in with a biography of Grace Darling (1988); a personal tribute to Philip Toynbee alongside memories of the Communist Party, *A Fine Old Conflict* (1977). Her early masterpiece, *Hons and Rebels* (1960), combines both the personal and the political in this inimitable way: it begins with the hilarious (and now legendary) account of home life at the Mitfords, but becomes a memorably tender but utterly unsentimental story of her struggles as a young mother and widow. She wrote about Grace Darling because Darling was an intrepid heroine, the saviour of shipwrecks; and about Philip Toynbee because she loved him; he had been a friend of Esmond Romilly's, and she never abandoned her friends. She remained a tenacious protester and fighter, too. With Bob Treuhaft, the selfless civil rights lawyer whom she married in 1943, and who, equally caustic and droll, encouraged the mordant, pamphleteering side of her wicked talents, she struggled to establish justice on her home turf in Oakland – not in grand, headline-grabbing gestures (though she was no slouch at publicity) but in the boring, small-print detail of legal tangles and individual cases.

To read *A Fine Old Conflict*, her memoir of her life in America during the McCarthy period, is to realise how enterprising, dedicated, hard-working, serious and brave she and Bob were. This wasn't some kind of Mitford prank, as people all too easily think: she was committed, and she didn't take an easy path. Her class privileges may have given her a certain daredevil confidence, but she wasn't well off. Kay Graham, the owner of the *Washington Post*, who knew her in her first years in America, remembers how she used to bind her breasts and tummy so that her pregnancy would not show and she would not lose her job as a sales assistant in a clothes shop. The year that the Bay Bridge was damaged in the earthquake, I was staying with her and we were invited to a very grand party for the English-Speaking Union, given by Ann Getty in San Francisco across the Bay. Decca was rather frail that winter, but determined to go, so we took the ferry: she wore, with great panache, her best coat; it was A-line, short, and a little worse for wear; she had bought it from Dior under Nancy's supervision in Paris thirty years before with the money from *The American Way of Death*. She liked society, but was blissfully immune to the ruthlessness of style conventions. She also requested, as a fine last touch, that there should be no flowers at her funeral; donations were to go instead to 'Send a Piana to Havana'. Her son Benjy, a piano tuner, has been running the US blockade to Cuba with nothing more inflammatory than reconditioned pianos, so that the Cubans can enjoy music in tune once again.

She was hankering for England when I first met her, in the early Eighties: she wanted news of old friends and connections, gossip. She wanted to reconnect with the 'green unpleasant land'. She had not been 'home' for something like forty years, though it was hard to believe, from her English rose complexion and cornflower eye prettiness, that she had ever left the Cotswolds. Gradually, she picked up the dropped stitches, and began coming back, renting this house and that and writing articles and making films; most evenings would end with Decca singing. She knew French songs from her governess, and traditional parlour numbers from her mother, but her favourite was 'Maxwell's Silver Hammer', which had caught her attention when the Beatles first sang it. She'd learned every word: it had just the right mix of the deadpan and the grisly for her taste. 'Bang bang Maxwell's silver hammer came down on his head/Bang bang Maxwell's silver hammer made sure that he was dead,' she'd sing out. Her voice was slight, clear, wobbly and tuneful; it drew attention to the absolute peculiarity of the words.

To the end, Jessica Mitford had the quick-wittedness and hungry curiosity of a very young and very bright girl who has never pretended to know anything she does not know and is determined to find out more. Decca never missed a thing; she threw a different slant on all experiences, salting them, brightening them, bringing more vividly to life life itself, for those lucky enough to know her.

1996

Bob Treuhaft

Obituary

Robert Treuhaft was a civil rights activist, an indefatigable lawyer on behalf of hopeless causes, and a foot-slogging, door-stepping, envelope-stuffing campaigner. He must be one of the few successful lawyers who, as his wife Jessica Mitford blithely reported to her mother-in-law, left his job because the firm's fees were too high. Though his dedication was in earnest, Bob (or 'Bau-*awb*', as Decca called him) never failed to see the ironies and follies of life: his head cocked to one side, his slanted black eyes bright with indignant amusement, he would offer, in a soft drawl, the devastating facts and figures that exposed the corruption of his target, be it the segregationist actions of a housing association, the prison warders in the state gaols, or the fat cats in the funeral parlour business. Though he spent most of his life after 1943 in the Bay Area of California, he remained recognisably a New Yorker: he was born in the Bronx, the son of Jewish immigrants from Hungary or Czechoslovakia (depending on the shifting border). His mother Aranka was a milliner who eventually opened a hat shop on Park Avenue; she was then able to prod his father Albin, who was working as a waiter, into part-ownership of a restaurant on Wall Street, where Bob's gourmet tastes were formed.

'Bob and Decca' moved to Oakland in 1947, where they kept a famously bustling, open house for friends and fellow-workers and family for half a century; their hospitality was celebrated. Together they'd developed a way of talking that oddly anticipated text-messaging: a kind of staccato telegraph, based on plans and aims and jokes and nicknames long shared between them. Bob had something of Jack Lemmon and Walter Matthau combined: in this marriage, the dry wryness of the Bronx met the sparkle, malice and larkiness of the Mitfords and the result was a potent and brilliant chemical reaction.

His long life – he died on 11 November at the age of eighty-nine – encompassed at least four historic cycles of American politics; he found himself – or rather, he chose to put himself – in the thick of the most stirring and idealistic struggles of the last century. In 1930, he won a scholarship to Harvard Law School, and was the first student from his high school, New Utrecht in Brooklyn, to do so; he roomed with the architect Bertram Goldberg, as 'Harvard roomed Jews together in those days'. Through his mother, he began working on behalf of the

International Ladies' Garment Workers' Union, where his political opinions began to form. Suffering from epilepsy, he was not accepted by the Army when he volunteered in 1943, much to his disappointment; but it was at this time that he first met, in Washington DC, Jessica Mitford, who was a young widow with a small daughter, Constancia ('Dinky'): her husband, Esmond Romilly, had been shot down over Germany.

Decca moved to California in 1943, where Bob followed her. He opened an office with Bert Edises, to specialise in labour law – the firm was known affectionately as Gallstones, Gruesome, Sewer & Odious. When a teenage shoeshine boy, Jerry Newsom, was about to go to the chair for murder, Bob, who was not a criminal advocate, transformed himself and took up the case, for no fee, and successfully fought for Newsom's reprieve through no less than three retrials until the police testimony was in shreds. There were plans to film the case: until recently, Bob was still in touch with the client whose life he had, literally, saved.

The Communist Party in California, which Bob Treuhaft and Jessica Mitford joined in the Forties, was primarily occupied with establishing the rights of workers to fair conditions, and of blacks to basic American citizenship, which was to all intents and purposes still denied them. In 1953, he was summoned before the House Un-American Activities Committee in California and branded as one of the most dangerous and subversive lawyers in the country. It was an episode that did not rattle him, or Decca for that matter: there are advantages in having aristocratic aplomb as well as a Jewish sense of humour. They finally left the Party in 1958, but continued to sing the Internationale, together with 'Maxwell's Silver Hammer' and the Grace Darling song and other great ballads at any opportunity.

It was when Bob was representing the widows of longshoremen that he began to notice the profits undertakers were raking in (something that had also roused the indignation of the great campaigner in the East End of London, Maud Pember Reeves, in her 1917 classic, *Round About a Pound a Week*). Bob was the motive force behind Jessica Mitford's brilliantly merciless assault on the funeral trade, her first bestseller, *The American Way of Death* (1963), as she was the first to acknowledge. The subject perfectly united his fervour on behalf of the economically exploited with her macabre sense of humour: until his death, morticians' luxury catalogues were still arriving at the Oakland house and making him huff (and chuckle). The book helped shape legislation against profiteering, and Robert Kennedy was even influenced to choose a modest coffin for JFK.

The Sixties found Bob Treuhaft again at the centre of a new, different configuration of political protest, as one of the most engaged and selfless defenders of civil rights: from 1962 to 1978 he worked at his new law firm with Dobby Walker, campaigning on behalf of the East Bay Civil Rights Congress. Famously, he became the defence counsel for the demonstrators and sitters-in in the Berkeley protests, where he was himself arrested. He also structured many of Decca's star performances as a protester: as the sister of a duchess she could always win headlines in America. On one occasion, she successfully refused to be fingerprinted; on another, she travelled (with Bob) to Mississippi in the campaign against segregation and was arrested; his legal experiences inform the argument of her fierce critique of the prison system, *Kind and Usual Punishment*.

Well into his eighties, Bob continued the struggle; his interest, attentiveness, and old world courtesy helped many colleagues to succeed when they might have given up. One young black lawyer recalled, at the couple's fiftieth wedding anniversary, that Bob had pushed her and pushed her to persevere with law school. 'You were the wings under my wings,' she said. There was a spare room in the Oakland house, where I once sat down to write, and found myself suddenly at ease, inspired. I came down and told them; Bob told me it was the room where Maya Angelou had come to write too and where she had begun *I know Why the Caged Bird Sings*. They were both unfailingly encouraging to younger friends, directly and by example: Bob especially had a real feeling for writers and styles of writing and his later years were shadowed by the deaths of Jill Tweedie and of Sally Belfrage. But it gave him great pride and pleasure that J. K. Rowling called her daughter Jessica after Decca, her heroine.

2001

The Female Form Defined

Paris is a city of statues, most of them female. A building like the Opéra seems to be fashioned out of the limber and pneumatic bodies of Empire belles; they hold up the stairs, the ceiling, the balconies, the boxes, and all the lights. The outside swarms with numberless figures, vaulting, flying, supporting, embracing. Even the street lamps on the outer ring of the building are made in the shape of nymphs *en déshabille*.

On the Louvre, from the earliest pavilions on the Cour Carrée to the latest, Imperial additions, there are more allegories expressed in the female form than even a guide as exhaustive as Pevsner would list: every quality a ruler or politician ever wanted to possess finds expression in stone as sylph, caryatid, goddess, or nude. The historical statues with names and identities and stories are statesmen and Great Men of France. The female statues have no personae of this kind, being abstractions. The Emperor Napoleon III, for instance, the builder of so much of the Louvre as well as of Paris, appears once on his immense palace, surrounded by a female Peace and female Arts. This bitter breezy spring, he was gazing down on crowds gathering outside the marquees in the courtyard below for the trade fair of the rag trade, the *prêt-à-porter* collections.

Is there a connection between the spectacle of the collections and the French architectural tradition? An article recently published in the *New Yorker* by their fashion correspondent Kennedy Fraser led me to think that it might exist and might yield some fruitful reflections on the way we live and the way we think now, about ourselves, about women. Kennedy Fraser quoted the museum curator Susan Sidlauskas, who had written about the exhibition *Intimate Architecture: Contemporary Clothing Design* that she had organised at MIT: 'The recurring characteristics of this architectural vision are: a clarity of line, sharp edges, discrete shapes, and the impression that the garment possesses its own architectonic structure and could stand on its own without the necessity of a human wearer.' The allegorical figures of Justice and Peace who adorn the public buildings of Paris and cities all over the West are similarly impersonally vested: the person inside the ornamental dress – or undress – is not important as a person, but only as the vehicle of an idea, the repository of an inner fantasy. The women themselves are incidental to the form of which they are only a part, a prop. There is much discussion, by fashion observers today, about cut and structure, about how a designer like Montana 'builds' his look. Karl Lagerfeld, in his programme notes, opened with the heavily Barthesian line: 'Opposer dans un seul vêtement deux techniques (le Construit et le Déstructuré), c'est comme si on opposait la futilité à la sévérité et la frivolité à la rigueur.' ('To contrast in a single garment two techniques – constructing and deconstructing – is as if you contrasted futility with severity, and frivolity with rigour.') On the arch of the

Carrousel, just outside the Louvre, with its serious (severe) triumphalist claims for Napoleon III, and its light (frivolous) nymphs with garlands, one might make the same comment: heavy political boasts are lightened by the presence of the 'futile' girls at play upon the structure. The decorative girls on the fabric of the Louvre, and the decorative girls inside the tents, both make a claim on behalf of the originators: the palace proclaims the greatness of France, and all her qualities. The *prêt-à-porter* shows tell us a bit about the same, in a different way, but using the same metaphor, the abstracted impersonal figure.

The collections are now being held in the Louvre, and no longer in venues all over the city, because the Socialist government recognises the importance of fashion as a French industry. Expected puritan reactions to the frivolity and class snobbery of *la mode* weren't forthcoming. The reporter in *Libération*, the left-wing daily paper, gently reproved readers who might balk at the fantastic prices and lavish display of designers like Karl Lagerfeld for Chloé. Only a spirit of *chagrin*, a peevish killjoy, the reporter said, would miss the fun. Fun – and employment. Mitterrand's government has also just drafted a law, speedily nicknamed the *cache-sexe* or 'fig-leaf' law, threatening reprisals against sexist advertising or public images of women. Grace Jones as a caged panther with bloody chin was quoted as an example. Mitterrand's government is probably distinguished by its sense of seriousness rather than its sense of fun. But it is keen on manufacture and national businesses with a long tradition of specialised craft skills. Assembled in marquees in the Louvre, the *prêt-à-porter* shows became a specific prestige demonstration of French export drive, part of the *patrimoine* Mitterrand is keen to preserve and encourage.

But the collections aren't exactly the Motor Show at Earls Court. Money is not mentioned, does not change hands, does not . . . pollute the proceedings. The occasion has become too much of a sacred ritual, an initiate's exclusive ceremony. You can't buy a ticket to get in, not exactly. You have to be invited. The invitation cards mark out each show as an individual performance piece: Junko Koshimo's is a huge, red and black, bad-mannered flyposter, Castelbajac's was commissioned from Garouste, the current fashionable painter, the Girbauds' is a social-realist photograph of China in the Fifties. Designs of clothes do not figure. Not a few carry an image of the designer. But not all the invitation cards actually allow access. Some are like paper money after the fall of the old régime. You wave your card at the ushers, young, bank clerk types in red ties who stand at the crash barriers round the entrances, and they then cast an eye upon it and respond, obsequiously or bad temperedly, according to code marks thereon. The privileged few, with the marked cards, are wafted by: the foreign press, the buyers from Texas. Now and then, a suppliant at the crash barrier pleads, 'Is Chantal there? Or Christophe? Or Nadya?' Sometimes Chantal, or Christophe, or Nadya appears, at the tent flap. A wink, a gesture to the red-tie, a nod to the suppliant . . . access is gained, and the crowd closes up the gap against the barrier. At the last moment, the ordinary passes are finally permitted to enter; and if a corpse stood among them, it would be swept in on its feet by the tidal mass of the crowd. Inside, the event as sacred spectacle continues. Cleaners peep through the few neglected chinks in the tents, a thin photographer tries to snatch the invitation from my hand 'for a friend outside', then scavenges the floor to find one that might have been dropped. The movie cameras are banked up, their operators sometimes attached by walkie-talkie to their directors in the crowd; tic-tac signs pass between the photographers who huddle three-deep around the catwalk and their editors in the rows near the front. A single fire officer bravely deals with the persistent smokers.

Every single show begins late, half an hour, an hour. Waiting is part of the event, the whip of anticipation. The signal for the start is music: then the lights go down. The music is usually epic, spacy, Sibelius and Wagner rather than Haydn or Scarlatti. There is a distinct penchant for wild animals in the big beyond; Anne-Marie Beretta features a stampede of buffaloes, Castelbajac a horde of galloping horses, Montana adds the howling of wolves to yet more big sounds of the wild. The scale is set by music: we are not attending a chamber event, let alone watching the telly.

And the girls are huge, Titans, made on the scale of the gods. Raised up on what is no longer called a catwalk but a runway, they bear down with accelerating power, like radio-controlled missiles, flashing eyes over the packed audience, with cruel, disdainful stares and spurning mouths. Their glance is terrible. Their heads and necks remain motionless, their shoulders heave the air to one side and the other as they sweep down on us, often in a phalanx striding to a pace that's halfway between a frog-march and a swagger. The cruelty of their faceless faces, under the stiff brims and frequent dark glasses, is deliberate; without looking at the despised things (so small) that fasten their clothes, they snap open buckles and buttons with contempt. No model must admit that a coat or a glove needs to be looked at to be taken off; she shrugs herself free as if nothing ever could contain her strength. When the models do smile, as in Ungaro's show, or Sonia Rykiel's, they don't seem to have much affection for us in the audience. One usually takes the arm of another and they then share some private joke which we're too dumb to be told; or the smiles are through gritted teeth and sear us poor mortals without focusing, without acknowledgment. When they appear, these figures of intimidating and frigid potency, the photographers rise from their prayer mats by the runway and hold up their machines towards the apparition and then, having received the imprint of the sacred image, subside all together again in a heap. And the tent goes dark until the next sighting.

Only Saint Laurent showed his clothes quietly. His mannequins loped gently down the catwalk one by one to oddly loungey music, the repeating tapes of expensive but usually bad restaurants. He refused to deploy the models in squads or even connect the clothes to fantasy worlds other than the chic shopping street, the elegant drawing-room, the exclusive soirée. He used colour, lots of it, and in the most Fauve combinations. Given the blackness of hue and dire mood of almost all the other designers, he emerged as the most sweet-tempered, in a nostalgic, even dated sort of way.

The *défilé* – a word that is also used in French for military parades – has no story; it's a theatrical show with no incidents. In a sense we are shown possible variations of appearance over twenty-four hours, from day wear to evening wear. The changes are so swift, the numbers of outfits so great (two hundred is by no means unusual), and the accessorising so intense that it is impossible for anyone in the middle or back rows who is not gifted with needle-sharp eyes and years of expertise to see what exactly is happening. In a private salon show, as for instance at Azzedine Alaïa's (the new Tunisian-born number one seed of young fashion commentators), the ingenuity of cut, the perfection of detail, the beauty of stitch and seam could be seen and savoured. But in the tents, the couturiers become tribal chieftains, spending thousands to show how little they care about their investment of time and skill and materials, just as Native American potlatch parties smashed up all their fine ware and magnificent coppers to prove the tribe's disdain and superiority.

The designers no longer necessarily bring their shows to a climax with the bride. Gaultier ended his with a perverse brothel number, a transparent Mac over underwear. But the true culmination of the show is always the same: the appearance of the designer. And if he has created a bride, he takes her hand to be led out to the front of the runway and shown to the audience to receive the applause. He acts diffident, charmingly shy, and is usually dressed as if he had not expected to win such acclamation and had been caught over the draughtsman's table, in his scruffy, understated clothes. When he holds on to the bride and receives her kisses – and those of her attendants – it always looks as if we are attending the couturier's wedding. When the designer is a woman, her appearance is much more careful, and the bride then always seems daughter-like. Even if there is no bride, the memory print of her customary presence is still strong, so that when Castelbajac ended his show with a series of floating voile T-shirts, printed with images of famous men and women – Simone de Beauvoir and Sartre, the Kennedys – and brought the series to a climax with a picture of himself, I had the odd feeling that I was watching a different climactic union: the marriage of the couturier to his own best dream of himself. As an experienced observer of the Paris design world remarked to me, Castelbajac's Hall of Fame – which was received to rapturous laughter and applause – expressed the normative *pathétique* of the couturier who cannot bear to think that he is only that and not an artist, a philosopher, a worthy member of his own pantheon.

Castelbajac was the only designer whose show I saw who also posted a picture of himself at the end of the runway. He had posed, leaning reflectively on a book at a desk, wearing little professorial glasses, so that the girls literally issued from his head, as if surrounded by think bubbles. His didn't seem an especially self-satisfied face, in fact; rather, the two images of the designer truthfully revealed the relations between the clothes on show and their makers. The models in their magnificent array march forth from the designers' minds like so many daughters of fantasy. The women who are wearing the fierce clothes are blank; models and future customers are not interesting as people. They emerge in their plural combinations, in serried groups of sixes and sevens, with hidden eyes and swathed bodies, and do not express their own character at all, or any lived reality of women. (Giorgio Armani, in Italy, has obviously realised this, for he now shows his designs, in window-type displays, as still-lifes, with videos of the clothes being worn in the street, by women going about their accustomed tasks. He is re-siting his clothes in today's context, outside his personal dream.

The spectacles in Paris from the French designers conjured up the past: those huge shoulders, those narrow, bottom-hugging skirts, those great coats with their big belts that were everywhere, where have we seen them before? Jean-Paul Gaultier made the reference explicit: on the stars of Hollywood. He played his entire show to the wailing sax solo from *Judex* (remade in 1963, American style *film noir*,), and his girls, in their trench-coats, shining falls of blonde hair over one eye, were Lauren Bacall lookalikes. At Thierry Mugler, the clothes recalled Joan Crawford and Bette Davis, especially in their Hollywood incarnations as murderesses. He showed peignoirs and fluffy mules, the undress of Hollywood before nudity was allowed. His models toyed with little knives, even on the invitation card, and the theme colour of his climax was blood red. The French designers, showing to the sound of stampedes, produced some gaucho holsters, Mexican banderole belts, and even pistols. There was gunfire on the soundtrack of several shows; Montana ran a tape of a First World War dogfight, while aviatrices, in leather helmets, goggles, Biggles fur-and-leather greatcoats, brass aeroplanes for tie-pins, epaulettes, buckles, toggles, all the paraphernalia of the messroom, swaggered about like Amy Johnson clones. How old are most of these designers? Not old enough, surely, to have been alive when Amy Johnson flew to Australia in her Biggles gear, or to have seen the first run of Bette Davis in *Little Foxes*, or Lana Turner in *The Postman Always Rings Twice*. Lagerfeld, Mugler, Gaultier, Castelbajac, Montana are only in their thirties, or forties. These memories, so harshly evoked on the runways of the *prêt-à-porter*, recall their parents' youth: they are memories of mother. It is well known, for instance, that Karl Lagerfeld's mother wore couture clothes, and that her lavish taste formed his own love of what Hebe Dorsey of the *New York Herald Tribune* frankly calls the Big Bucks look. The look of the Forties, the fantasies of the Forties, exported worldwide from Hollywood, have received a new life from Paris designers, whose marriages for the most part will only ever be to the effigies summoned up from childhood, whom they send out on the runway to be stern and cruel and unloving towards the puny adorers clustered round their skirts.

The mass fantasy of the Bad Mother does not stop there. It manages to assimilate Big Bad Daddy too. Apart from the Hollywood Vamp, there were few evocations of women's traditional roles. We had a schoolgirl or two from Sonia Rykiel, a bride like a white lily from Anne-Marie Beretta, and some coy furry secretaries from Chantal Thomass. Sonia Rykiel showed the only dresses for pregnant women in Paris. (Though every coat could have accommodated quintuplets, the skirts worn under them couldn't accommodate most people's tummies after a cup of coffee.) But Action Man and toys for the boys were everywhere: not just gunmen and mobsters, pilots and trench soldiers, but admirals (Montana) complete with spaghetti frogging, naval cadets (Gaultier), bellboys, and parachutists in commando units. The colours were regimental as well: black, navy, grey. Kit, too, dominated: studs, cleats, belts (worn as necklaces), straps, buckles, and reached its apotheosis in Chloé's leitmotif, 'useless tools' (*outils inutils*), jewellery made of taps, spanners and gemmies, large as life, and sported, as the programme pointed out, 'humorously' by the models, whose Big Bucks look signifies that they never use them themselves, oh, my dear, no. Odd, really, to see these fantastic giants whose series of transformations deny the history of women's occupations and ape those of men's, proving that they are strong, domineering and relentless, and yet still stuck fast in the old axiomatic distinction between luxury and productiveness, between desirability and industriousness. If you are a Big Bucks Bitch, you mustn't wield a spanner effectively, just wear it with a diamond caught in its claws. All the same, luxury – as the French government's clever promotion of the collection reveals – has a lot to do with productivity: not a few busy and most probably female hands worked to make those taps into earrings, that diamond-crunching gemmy. Yet Karl Lagerfeld's wit at Chloé, with its old-fashioned equation of girls with luxury, is very much part of his huge commercial success, in a trade where the ability to renew yourself and replenish your imagination endlessly, productively, collection after collection, season after season, is very much at a premium.

It's perhaps easier to see why the designers, who are mostly male and often gay, should want Bad Mothers in black-uniformed plurality to issue forth down the runways. But why should women, who after all comprise some of the couturiers as well as most of the audience of editors and buyers and even photographers, let alone the potential customers, accept the projection at all? It was Sonia Rykiel herself who gave it its most extreme expression, ending her show with *fifty* girls, hip to hip like photographs of soldiers on parade, dressed in identical pencil tubes of black with minor variations in the diamanté legends they wore on their waists, informing us they were a 'special edition' or a 'work of art'. They came out very fast, as if punched out in a computerised series on ticker tape, and the effect was breathtaking, hilarious, but disturbing as the sight of uniformed individuals always is, even when the uniform serves no apparent master.

Masochism cannot be the whole answer. It cannot be that French women and the countless customers for French clothes in Great Britain and the United States have ingested a negative stereotype that denies them individuality and hangs a price tag where their face should be. An explanation can be sought elsewhere: in the tradition of using the female body as a *tabula rasa* for society's ideas about its own nature. This brings us back to the statues. The sculptured women on the Louvre are of a rather different shape from the current fashion, being bosomy and full-bellied and full-hipped, with great laps. But they are also huge. And, like the models of French *prêt-à-porter*, they look unbelievably strong. They are also arrayed, as allegories often are, with various weapons borrowed from men, breastplates and swords and helmets, enhancing and guaranteeing their impregnability. Such statues – and public images in many media – body forth a longed-for mightiness; the caryatids hold up the Louvre because it is the showpiece of French power, once royal, now republican. If the metaphor of physical strength, standing for moral authority and justice, can be properly applied to women, traditionally weak physically and fickle morally, then it can be applied to everyone. The allegorical figures embody a universal desire – and claim – to be unconquerable.

If you made a grid of the body and then marked the points that were emphasised by the French designers this spring, you would have found their attention focused first on the shoulders, the centre of the metaphor of supportive strength ('shoulder your burden', 'shoulder to cry on'), and secondly on the pelvis, which was wrapped and bound to stress its extreme narrowness. Through this small gauge tube, no child could pass. The fantasy women of the runway are daughters of the pill, childless and likely to remain so. The Bad Mother is also exclusive, and will have no more children. But even more interesting, this emphasis on the pelvis corresponds, like 'shoulder', to a basic linguistic turn of phrase that denotes strength: to gird one's loins. These fashions definitely showed loins well girt.

There was also another area on the body-map that had attention drawn to it, and that was the solar plexus, a traditional site of weakness that can be, and has to be, converted into strength by a muscleman or his surrogate, the Amazon. There were several high belts, and many corsets worn as outer clothes, like armour. The women's bodies were also presented as a single entity: very little cleavage, no erogenous attention to the crotch. No trousers, except at Saint Laurent, in spite of all the striding and masculine swaggering about. These women were made in one piece, extruded as if in a cylinder, with no bifurcation, nothing between their legs, no suggestion of the womanly part, or anything as humble or creaturely as that. Often the print or pattern on the evening dresses used the whole shape as one surface canvas – Chloé's much liked tableaux of gushing water and dramatic skyscrapers, for instance. Except from the back: there women were divided, by what the trade writers call 'the cupped *derrière*'. Gaultier showed dresses made from corsets laced tightly back and front. Fertility is not in fashion, homosexuality is.

Women accept, even enjoy, the projection of themselves as powerful. It's stirring to be titanic; aggression today is the best defence. It reflects growing economic reality to some extent, especially in businesses like fashion. It defends us against the crisis of identity that rapidly changing sex relations have provoked for so many men and women, by providing a clear, strong, defiant outline. But women also acquiesce in the image, even love it, because the female has always been traditionally invested with the virtues the society of her time most desires to possess. It's a variant on the old theme that 'men do, women are'. The current fantasy woman of high fashion appears like a giant, a bulwark, a citadel that cannot be stormed, because that's what the crisis-ridden West longs itself to be.

The extreme divergence between the Japanese and the French designers' ideas this spring was a commonplace of fashion comment: the Japanese, especially the newcomer, Rei Kawakubo of Comme des Garçons, created visions of beggarwomen, swathed in mournful indigo and bundled in rough-textured open-weave rags, with unkempt hair and peasant tie-on pattens. The voluminous layers and irregular folds, the formulaic but sensuous disguise of anatomy and sexual characteristics obviously derives from the beautiful structure of the traditional kimono. But the perversity of disguising oneself as a tatterdemalion in some of the most expensive swatches of fabric in the world can't be said to be just a part of the fun of it all, particularly since all the experts in Paris were quick to reproach the Japanese with a fatal lack of witty style – unlike the French, and Chloé *par excellence*. The French are in full *crise économique*; the Japanese, by contrast, are prospering. The French fashion designers project millionaire Amazons who never use spanners; the Japanese, secure in wealth and power, model their ready-to-wear on the vanishing peasants of their paddy fields, ragamuffins in home-dyed sackcloth with fastenings that predate the age of the machine: the knot, the swathe, the tuck. The French are more *soignées* than ever, their make-up classical, mask-like. The Japanese at Comme des Garçons wear blue lips, like strayed miners. The inversion seems almost too neat; the longing for symbols that turn the world upside down too clear. But the Japanese can afford to look like bag ladies, while the Westerners must vaunt their strength, cover all the areas of stress, and reinforce all points of weakness. At Issey Miyake, the models, who processed like tropical birds, fluttering with feathers and bright scraps of floating chiffon, were bound around the solar plexus with coils of rolled metal, recalling the quill-like armour of samurai warriors. It seemed as if the Parisian themes, of guarding against enemies, of warding off the crisis through the image of the undefeatable body, were receiving an Eastern echo. But then, as if by magic, to a chorus, rising in climax, the white bird (the bride) unclasped her metal girdle and held it aloft above her head like a trophy, and danced. Nothing could have been further in spirit from the hulking, gloomy, disciplining women in the visions of Gaultier or Montana. She took the risk of appearing weak and vulnerable, and then felt able to exult in it.

1983

Mrs Thatcher

An interview soon after she was elected leader of the Conservative Party, when she was receiving women's magazines.

The book Margaret Thatcher says has influenced her most profoundly is *A Time for Greatness* by Herbert Agar. She seemed impatient when I said I had not heard of it, and obligingly repeated the title twice and spelt the author's name. She is nothing if not thorough. She was nineteen or twenty years old when she read it, and she says now that, 'It is an interesting analysis of the problems of democracy at the beginning of the wartime period. It shows how vigilant you have to be to protect the freedoms you've got.'

A Time for Greatness was published in 1943. Agar was an American Anglophile and his book hymns the virtues of self-improvement and willpower and peppers the vice of 'softness' with energy and enthusiasm. It opens with a chapter on the Sickness of the West and closes with advice and a warning: 'We must also renew our traditions and serve them more faithfully. The liberals made democracy, and happiness and peace on earth sound too easy. As a result we relaxed. We lived like the heirs of an estate that could not be depleted, until we awoke one morning to find the bailiff at the door.'

Margaret Thatcher, like many other politicians and political thinkers at present, sees a grim parallel between our present depletion and the economic catastrophe that overtook Weimar during the Twenties and eventually led to the triumph of Hitler, and war. But unlike others, she adheres to the wartime philosophy contained in such books as Agar's. Her view is retrospective, and when she describes what she considers to be the traditional British character, she sounds old-fashioned because she is really describing a Churchillian world: 'We like to take the initiative and we dislike being pushed around. We have a healthy suspicion of government and bureaucracy, and we admire self-reliance and standing on one's own two feet. But we are also a people who believe it is one's duty to help others, and not because of legislation, but because we want to.' Self-reliance is the linchpin of her philosophy, and a word she often uses.

Mrs Thatcher's position as head of the Tory Party is revolutionary, but everything else about her is less surprising. Lord Blake, historian of the Tory Party, explained:

> When the Conservative Party finds itself in the doldrums it tries a new kind of person. Disraeli didn't fit into any of the usual categories of Conservative. Similarly with Bonar Law's election in 1911. The Party had lost three general elections running. Bonar Law didn't come from the social class you'd expect in the pre-war England Conservative Party. You could almost say Margaret Thatcher is in that sort of tradition though in her case it's the fact she's a woman rather than her social class. She is the first woman, just as Disraeli was the first leader of Jewish ancestry. Disraeli also embodied the traditional values of the Conservative Party – he wasn't specially progressive – Margaret Thatcher succeeding Ted Heath is very like Disraeli succeeding Sir Robert Peel. It is the same cry that has been raised, that the traditional values are not being upheld.

Mrs Thatcher's election was startling, and brutally revealed the thinness of the Tory front bench. The Department of Education is not the usual springboard to the leadership; but once Sir Keith Joseph had decided not to stand, there was no one else to challenge Heath's hegemony or his 'progressive' followers. 'There was,' she says simply, 'an opportunity which one took advantage of.' Once she was the clear runner, her qualities became obvious to many. Her friends and supporters extol her grasp, the incisiveness of her mind, her rapid command of the complexities of a brief. Patrick Cormack, the only MP who predicted the exact vote on the ballot for leadership, says:

> She is the least impulsive politician that I know. One would generally say women politicians were more impulsive than men, but she is the sort of person who would never do anything without thinking it through. She would not go out on a limb without testing the branch first. She does not do things 'lightly or wantonly' – to quote the Prayer Book. She has cold determination and analytic strength.

Her self-discipline is much praised. She rises early – around six o'clock – and goes to bed late, but no one has seen her look haggard. Norman St John Stevas, MP, her chosen Minister for Education in the Shadow Cabinet, calls her Blessed Mother Margaret and is said to have described her leadership success: 'It's not an election, it's an *Assumption*.'

St John Stevas also emphasises that she has the 'tremendous stamina' necessary for the job. She needs reserves of strength not only because of the enormous burden of work carried by the leader but also because she finds it difficult to delegate. Her close friend, the writer Patrick Cosgrave, declares perfectionism is her overriding characteristic. Consequently she bridles at leaving anything to others. 'She is *chronically able*,' he says. 'She is incapable of not doing things well. Perfectionism is her hallmark – in everything, cooking included.' He insists on her thoughtfulness, and describes how she stops outside the members' door of the House of Commons after late-night sessions to give lifts to colleagues, regardless of their political persuasion.

Conservatives are justifiably optimistic about the response she evokes on her walk-abouts. 'She can excite audiences,' says Cosgrave. 'She is a good speaker,' says Lord Blake, 'with an incisive tongue and an ability to put across a point of view with clarity and vigour.' Soon after her election to the leadership she was mobbed in Scotland by cheering women; later, at a Conservative rally, she was handed a broom to sweep the country clean of Socialism. 'Ted would never have taken the broom,' said one Conservative. 'Ted would never have been offered it,' retorted another.

Margaret Thatcher likes to pretend to an identity with housewives and plays up her popularity among working women. With extreme disingenuousness she said to me on the subject of unemployment: 'I feel strongly about it. I too only have a job.' Her followers are confident that she appeals to a wide sector and does not represent a narrow class interest. She has the courage of her views, and believes they represent the desires of many. Patrick Cormack says warmly:

> She is proud of what she believes in. She is not a guilt-ridden politician. The shoddy, wherever it exists, is a danger. The 'quality of life' is a phrase that really does have meaning for her. You are dealing with someone who has risen because of her own ability and determination. Quality for her is associated with an element of choice and competition. It must emerge through the competitive process.

But there are many, even within Conservative ranks, who view the prospect of Mrs Thatcher's prime-ministership with less enthusiasm. Partisans of Edward Heath are particularly bitter about her election and regard it as a disaster for the party. William Waldegrave, Heath's ex-private secretary, declared simply, 'She is the least experienced party leader ever elected since Ramsay MacDonald. She has no knowledge of economic management; and no foreign policy. She doesn't know how the party runs. It is all a closed book to her.' Her supporters claim that her post in Education equipped her to deal with questions of government spending. (She was the longest-serving Secretary of State for Education ever because Heath resisted all efforts to move her to a more prestigious post in the Treasury or to the chancellorship which she coveted.)

The most vicious criticism focuses on her ineptitude and insensitivity to privilege and its opposite. When she was at Education, *Panorama*'s Nicholas Harman was making a television profile of her and accompanied her to Highbury Comprehensive, where she visited a chemistry class. Mrs Thatcher has a degree in chemistry and she volunteered to demonstrate the experiment, which concerned the interaction of sulphur and silver. The class consisted of Cypriot, Irish and West Indian children for the most part. Holding up the blackened metal, Mrs Thatcher said in her best cheese-wire voice. 'And that is why, children, when you have a boiled egg for breakfast, your mother will never let you use the silver spoons.'

Margaret Thatcher's father was Alfred Roberts, who left school at the age of twelve. His father, grandfather and great-grandfather were all cobblers. He worked his way up until he owned two shops. One grocery cum-post office on the corner of North Parade in Grantham, Lincolnshire, was the home in which Margaret and her elder sister Muriel were raised. In 1927, two years after Margaret's birth, Alfred Roberts stood for the Council as an Independent. 'In those days,' explains Mrs Thatcher, 'Conservatives did not fight local elections.' There was always political harmony in the family. Roberts founded the local Rotary Club, became chairman of the board of governors of the local girls' grammar school which Margaret attended for seven years, and was Mayor of Grantham. The family was prosperous and successful, on a small, self-sufficient scale.

Margaret won a scholarship to Kesteven and Grantham Girls' at the age of ten, and then another, seven years later, to Somerville College, Oxford, where she read chemistry. She became president of the Oxford University Conservative Association and came down in 1947 with a second.

After university, Margaret Thatcher worked as a chemist for various industrial firms. She fought the solid Labour seat of Dartford in 1949. At the age of twenty-four, she was the youngest candidate in the election. She fought it again unsuccessfully in 1951 and on election day that year she announced her engagement to Denis Thatcher, who had inherited his father's local paint firm. In 1965, he sold out to Castrol, which was in turn bought by Burmah Oil, where he was a financial planning director until his retirement this June. He tactfully but firmly avoids the role of political 'wife' and rarely accompanies Mrs Thatcher on her public appearances, though he will escort her to dinners and other functions. Their twin children – Mark and Carol – were born in 1953 and sent to Harrow and St Paul's School for Girls respectively. Mark is now an accountant; Carol is doing her articles to become a solicitor, but she has moved out of London where it seems she found the publicity and attention intolerable. Their mother, who never wastes time, spent the first two years of her marriage studying law and was called to the Bar four months after the birth of her children. She specialised in tax and patent law, and sometimes produces the experience to prove her economic grasp and expertise and the clarity of her thinking. She has a scientist's attitude of mind, not a philosopher's or a writer's. Her speech is direct and plain, her metaphors mundane, her use of quotations almost non-existent.

She first achieved her ambition and began to demonstrate her political qualities when she was returned to Parliament as the member for Finchley and Friern Barnet in North London in the general election of October

1959, when she was thirty-five years old. Her meticulousness recommended her to Macmillan and he appointed her two years later to be joint parliamentary secretary at the Ministry of Pensions.

When the Conservatives were returned in 1970, she went to Education and Science and stayed four years. She was harshly dealt with by the press. 'Mrs Thatcher Milk Snatcher' – it was a cruel refrain. She is still very prickly with newspapermen. The slogan is not altogether deserved, as Labour have never rescinded her decision to stop free school milk. But the measure was seen to be symptomatic of Mrs Thatcher herself. She was headstrong and tough. At Education, she earned a reputation for riding roughshod over educationalists and teachers whose views differed from her own and she became unpopular with the National Union of Teachers when she fought hard to preserve selection in schools. She did, however, raise money to improve the primary school system and she passed more comprehensive schemes than she turned down.

The key to Margaret Thatcher's personality does not lie in her scientific or legal training or in her difficult initiation in ministerial experience. Alfred Roberts exercised a great influence over his clever daughter. He was a Methodist, a lay preacher in the local chapel, who did not allow newspapers on Sundays or drink in the house. Margaret Thatcher is not a teetotaller, but in more important aspects she has remained a low-church Christian. She was married in the Wesley Chapel in the City Road, London. Her religion is not a thin veneer: she became cross when I asked if she believed in God. 'What an extraordinary question,' she said, her blue eyes widening but nevertheless conveying grim annoyance. 'Of course, yes. I go to church, not every Sunday, but several times a year, and not just at Easter and Christmas.' The question touched a nerve. It is still important for the leader of the Tory Party to appear God-fearing, in the sober civic style of low-church Anglicanism. It is part of the Conservative image. But with Mrs Thatcher, the indignation runs deeper. If one stops to consider her values – the insistence on self-reliance, self-improvement, self-sufficiency, industriousness, thrift, neatness, organisation, efficiency, determination – these are specifically Protestant virtues. Margaret Thatcher is the embodiment of the Protestant ethic. Government helps those who help themselves.

In her own terms she has made a total success of her life, and in consequence she does not criticise the system through which she attained her eminence, but wishes to maintain it, and, where it has been eroded, to restore it. The daughter of a shopkeeper, she wants to protect the interests of the self-employed and the small businessman; the product of a grammar school, she pursued a vigorous policy of maintaining the grammar schools; her social mobility has led her to believe England allows social mobility; she has never felt it to be a disadvantage that she is a woman, so she pays lip service only to women's issues. She voted for the abortion law reform and against the relaxation of the divorce laws. When asked if being a woman had made any difference, she once quipped, 'Well, I've never been anything else.' Patrick Cosgrave says that at an early stage in the leadership struggle she felt that, as a woman, she could not win, but would rally behind Sir Keith Joseph. But when he decided against running, she felt she should take the chance. He concedes that 'she is uninterested in women's problems . . . she has no hostility to career women but she has shut off her mind to the dilemma of women's roles'.

She is a good-looking woman, much prettier than she appears in photographs. The etched sternness of her features in news shots is softened in reality by her blonde wavy hair and the excellence of her English peach complexion. She is lighter-boned too than she seems in the papers, with trim ankles and slender legs. She wears a lot of jewellery – real, but discreet. On the bright summer's day she granted me an interview, she was wearing a surprisingly frivolous dress: flower-printed on black chiffon, it was cut tight in the bodice, with long narrow sleeves and a high waist from which the skirt fell in knife pleats. She crinkles her eyes when she addresses you with a determined desire to please, but there is a granite edge to her graciousness and a chilliness at the core of her charm. She made me feel less like a frightened pupil than an anxious parent who has come with a complaint from her child, but, confronted with the imperturbable composure of the headmistress, cannot bring herself to broach the subject and leaves feeling foolish and ill at ease.

Margaret Thatcher runs so smoothly in the grain of her past in her ideals, her opinions, her prejudices and her manners that in a novel she would become too copybook to be anything but cardboard. This conformity with her origins is something she cherishes, and in interviews she recalls her childhood and adolescence and family milieu with clarity. There is no confusion in her mind about any part of it, it seems; no ambiguity or doubt. Ambiguity is as foreign to Mrs Thatcher as cooking in peanut oil and garlic was in Grantham when she was a girl.

She is not like a suburban woman, nor even a suburban man. She has the gift and the speed and the drive of the city dweller. She has no time for idleness. She does not play cards or any games of any kind; she has no passions on the side, unlike Heath with his music and his sailing; she enjoys opera, but she has not been for some time; she keeps up with 'the latest biographies and histories because otherwise one would lose touch completely with the cultural scene'. But politics are her passion and they leave little space for anything else.

Once or twice in speeches she has referred to Queen Elizabeth I. Patrick Cosgrave says that she once told him the Elizabethan age was 'the last time England was small and weak and great'. When I asked her about it, she pointed out: 'Curiously enough, inflation was a very great problem then.' But when I pressed her on a possible parallel between their personalities, she displayed embarrassment mingled with pleasure: 'Elizabeth had a marvellous grasp and grip and mental discipline. Mine comes from science and law. But no, the positions are different. She was a monarch. I'm just a politician.'

1975

Making It Big in the New World

The Staten Island ferry, at 25 cents a ride, rivals Kew Gardens for the best, cheapest entertainment in the world. You step on to the big-barrelled boat as if on to the travelator in an airport. The seamen – in long hair, headbands and jeans, like musicians from a Seventies rock album – hurl the ropes back on to the deck, and the ferry chugs out into New York harbour. It pulls away from the Manhattan skyline among tiny sailing boats like handkerchiefs waving you off, past sluggish container tankers, stacked with metal boxes so high they look as if a child has dared to see how far she can go before it sinks, past the tugs that nose in attendance like those birds that minister to hippopotamuses in the Nile, and gradually, as you lean on the rail gazing over the way, the view turns into a scenic whole, the most amazing urban panorama ever built. It sums up America, and it brings up all the conflicting pleasures and rebellion America produces in a visitor like me; with its daring, its giantism, its hubris, its flagrant immodesty, its nature-defying, God-challenging mass and height and density and artifice. It confronts you with the wealth and power of the Western world's capital, and you catch your breath, you want to say no, turn your back, but you can't.

The hyperbole is unmistakable. Bartholdi, the sculptor of the Statue of Liberty – which soon comes into view, a pygmy by comparison – wrote that he wanted to emulate the colossi of the ancient world, because they made the spectator feel big. Bigness, as everyone knows, is America's stock-in-trade. In the deli where I went for breakfast, my first morning in the city this time, I asked for an orange juice. 'Big or large?' asked the man behind the bubbling cooler. 'Which is which?' I asked.

I was taking the ferry to Staten Island to go to the kind of specialist library that institutions in America do better than anywhere else, I believe: the Center for Migration Studies. To the west from the ferry, the red-brick four-square turreted block of Ellis Island's Immigration Hall was visible, under a cross-hatching of scaffolding. It's being restored as a museum of immigration, with the proceeds of the Statue of Liberty's renovation campaign. Sixteen million people passed through between 1892 and 1934, and it's estimated that a hundred million Americans today are descended from them.

The centenary of the statue that became for so many their first sight of the New World, the symbol of their new life, the fixative of America's image in their eyes, has inspired a new curiosity, and a new *Roots*-style pride in the communities – German, Russian, Norwegian, Turkish, Armenian and Italian – who have previously been silent or unheard amid the clamour of other groups' history. The popularity and presence of Mario Cuomo, the governor of New York, and the razzle-dazzle cunning of Lee Iacocca, another Italo-American, have also contributed recently to the high profile of Italian immigrants in today's New York consciousness. Cuomo, for instance, tells the story of his arrival at Ellis Island as a child with his mother. He is genuinely affecting when he recalls it, for his mother had nothing to declare, no money, connections, skills. Except him. And declare him she did, he says. She promised he would turn out well. The inspectors were there to weed the healthy from the unhealthy, the hopeless from the promising, the indigent from the family of modest means, and to turn away undesirables. Single women were not allowed. They let Signora Cuomo pass.

Once the ferry docked, I waited for a bus to take me to the Center for Migration Studies. Staten Island is spread out and suburban, and its streets, with clapboard two-storey houses behind pretty trees, have an almost southern look. There were signs everywhere of the American mix: the Iron Den (a gym), an 'Egyptian Bazaar' at the corner of Baltic and Richmond Avenues, and, above all, O'Hunan's Chinese-Exotic Restaurant.

Many things in America are easier to work than they are in England: telephones, especially call boxes, last-minute meals (Korean groceries all over New York provide feasts of salads, smorgasbord-style, sold not by the item but by weight), coffee-makers, washing machines, and, as I have found in every library I've ever used there, from the Library of Congress itself to the Museum of Modern Art in New York, catalogues. The Center for Migration Studies was no exception. Here were the pamphlets issued in all languages by governments, benevolent institutions, doctors and priests, to help the new arrivals to settle down; here were the propaganda materials of campaigns against immigrants, here were photographs, memoirs, oral accounts, instructions, statistics. My own family, on my mother's side, emigrated from Puglia in South Italy in 1913; I was there to uncover, for a novel I'm writing, the circumstances of men like my grandfather and his brother, women like their sisters and their wives, my great-aunts and grandmother. I want to re-invent their lives, but I don't want to get the details, the atmosphere, the background wrong. Very quickly, using the admirably detailed, comprehensive and simple catalogue, I found that 1913 was a peak year, that in 1899, the US immigration authorities decided to distinguish arrivals no longer by country of origin, but by 'race' or 'people' instead, and that 'Southern Italian' became a distinct category because they were different by 'language, physique and character'.

From my grandfather's home province that year, 41,837 people emigrated. I was even able to determine, among this host, that he was one of seventy-nine professional men to leave (he was a lawyer), and that my great-uncle, who was a composer, was one of ninety-three musicians from Puglia that same year. My grandmother and her sisters and sister-in-law were entered under the much larger column, of 'housewives', 'semi-literate'. Usually it's important to turn people from statistics into individuals. But in this case, the knowledge that the characters whom I am trying to recreate in a novel were part of such an exodus gave me one of those shivers that I count as the most intense pleasures of the act of writing.

In the Public Library in New York, there's an exhibition about this wave of immigration: Lewis Hine, an unsparing, campaigning photographer, chronicled the pens at Ellis Island, the groups stepping off the boat with their bundles and cardboard suitcases and their prize possessions – a chair with a rush seat, in one instance. He posed southern Italian women as Madonnas, with kerchiefs over their heads and beautifully dressed babies, in lace caps and leather boots, on their laps. (The older children were barefoot, more like as not.) He noted that the main diet on Ellis Island was prune sandwiches.

Hine took his camera into the hovels of Hell's Kitchen and the Lower East Side and Little Italy, and photographed children doubled under heaps of piece-work for their mothers to finish, and families, from the parents to the last infants, assembling artificial flowers – just like Mimi in *La Bohème* – at their kitchen tables for 11 cents a bunch.

In California, later that week, I was listening to and questioning my Italian family. The first children who were born in America were gathered in Los Angeles for a family wedding. They and their children have become: a policeman (a cop in the LAPD specialising in Mexican homicide), a bank manager, a chiropodist, a real estate developer, a fireman, a stockbroker, an air hostess (at present grounded by the TWA lockout). They have traffic signals on their bar counters at home to give drinkers the go-ahead or otherwise; and swimming pools on their terraces far, far above Los Angeles and its spangled sprawl. They drive campers and convertibles and some of them travel hours on the freeways to get to work at 6am. In some cases they get up an hour earlier to put in some aerobics beforehand in the local gym. (This may seem unbelievable, but it's not only true, it's not even eccentric.)

'I owe, I owe, it's off to work I go,' runs one T-shirt slogan in America, and my Italian family have certainly got the hang of this American way. At the wedding there were sides of beef for the guests such as were never seen in Puglia, then or now. The ceremony took place by the side of a pool, where candle lotus blossoms were floating. The bride and groom came in to a Melissa Manchester ballad, and in the sermon, the pastor told them that when Adam saw Eve, he said, 'Right on, God!' The older members of the family remembered the past, but were anxious that I shouldn't dwell on it. They sighed when I asked them to recall their difficulties, their father's trials, their mother's work. 'The sacrifices they made, they made for us,' said one of my cousins, shaking his head at the thought of it. There were no more prune sandwiches and piece-work now. 'Why do you want to know about those days, darling?' said my eldest aunt, 'when everything is so beautiful now?' They have made it – big or large.

1986

Angela Carter

The Bloody Chamber wasn't the first book by Angela Carter that I read, but it was the one that turned the key for me as a writer. It opened on to a hidden room, the kind that exists in dreams, that had always somehow been there, but that I'd never entered because I'd been afraid. It is this room of her title that all her fictions inhabit: the centre of the labyrinth of desire, the eye of the stormy journey towards self-knowledge, the *ruelle* by the side of the bed where the deepest intimacies are exchanged, the cheval glass – called in French *une psyché* – of our inner selves. I say, our, but the way Angela Carter retells familiar fairy tales in *The Bloody Chamber* casts them as female stories, takes their heroines as the eyes and tongue and ears of the tales, and lifts the barriers that had come down to ring-fence them for the polite bourgeois nursery, that setting for the 'toilet training of the id' (one of Angela's many brilliant, dry reproofs of pedagogy).

I first met Angela Carter in the Sixties, in the offices of *Vogue*, a magazine she continued to write for rather surprisingly through to the Nineties, when she contributed a characteristically sharp-eyed piece about the new 'skirtless' fashion in leggings. Angela Carter was already known in the Sixties, and this early success did not help her later, when she appeared to belong to an earlier generation than writers who merely started later – Salman Rushdie is only six years her junior. She was already a prize-winning writer from the darker side of swinging London, who penetrated mysteries with a unique command of passion and its perversities, who was making, in one fiction after another, a new, fierce, interior map of women's curiosity and sexuality. The early novels – *The Magic Toyshop*, *Love*, *Heroes and Villains* – drew me as well as thousands of others into an expertise about the twists and knots of the psyche that was stunning, alarming, and thrilling. She had red hair then, and had just come back from Japan, where she'd fled with the proceeds of the Somerset Maugham prize, to escape her first marriage, she used to say. Her first collection of short stories, *Fireworks*, recounts some of her experiences there. Japan was tremendously important in the development of her writing, for it gave her, she said, a viewpoint outside England from which to look back at its familiar contours; she turned herself into a stranger in her own country, its traditions and its culture, and was able to explore it as an anthropologist might, and set out its oddnesses, its preconceptions, now to mock its hypocrisies, now to freshen its poetry. With these stranger's eyes, she was able to look again at stories everyone knows, that everyone is brought up on, and open them like quivering oysters. In many ways, *The Bloody Chamber* stands as the metafictional counterpart of the commentaries on style, music hall, books and films, that she was writing for *New Society*.

I had always loved fairy tales but I felt ashamed of liking them, of fantasising about enchanted forests of dog-roses and secret princesses arrayed in dresses the colour of time. The shame took two forms, really: at the time, it didn't seem grown-up enough to continue thrilling to 'The Maid without Hands' – when I was also reading *Vanity Fair* (Thackeray's), *Gone with the Wind*, *Rebecca*, *Silas Marner*. Babyish, and girly, too. Fairy tales were deemed lacking that signature of genius, that uniqueness of the true work of art – they were interchangeable, scanty, predictable, repetitive – and somehow, in spite of all their aristocratic preoccupations (or perhaps because of them), they were a literature of the poor and ignorant. Angela Carter, in her later Introduction to *The Virago Book of Fairy Tales*, points to just this aspect that attracted her to the genre: it has been made by those people 'whose labour made our world', she writes. But later, when I still loved fairy tales, with their fatal structure, their recurring enchanted motifs, I did not explore my feelings or write in response to them, but resisted and repressed them because in those days, the late Sixties, when I was first writing as an adult, 'Cinderella', 'Snow White', Perrault, the Grimms, et al. were coming under bitter attack from women who felt the fairy-tale heroine was a simple tool of male hegemonies who wanted a Stepford wife, or a blonde bimbo, or a Bobbsey twin, as in Anne Sexton's mordant variation on Cinderella. Princess Diana has since fulfilled the most doom-laden of these strictures.

But Angela specialised in provocation; she had a way of tilting her head, lifting the corner of her lips on one side and lowering her eyes as she delivered softly, in her near stammer, some delicious, poisoned barb at the pieties or thoughtless prejudices of her interlocutor. For this reason, she had an uneasy relationship to mainstream feminism in its Seventies shape: far too curious about perversity, masochism, collusion in women, far too enthralled by make-up and fashions and spectacle and performance for those days. 'Glamour' was a word she particularly liked, for example, and an appropriate liking for someone so in love with language, for 'glamour' derives from 'grammar', which used to confer status on its users.

The Sadeian Woman was a calculated affront to orthodox reformers and campaigners for female emancipation. I was frightened by it, and wasn't altogether sure I understood it. But *The Bloody Chamber* was another matter, for here were nursery standards rewritten in the light of her Sadeian woman, and they flung open that door in my head, on to the possibilities of women's reimagining the material that lies all about us, readily to hand. There was no need to tunnel into the depths and darkness of the past to recover a different story for women: we could improvise it from what we already knew and liked. 'This is how *I* make potato soup,' she wrote about the telling of old tales differently.

She didn't like my first novel, but she liked my last, which she read just before she died, and because she knew she was dying, it was overwhelming for me that she did so, that she rang me to tell me so. She had sent me a postcard a year or so before, from a Hindu scroll in the British Museum, the kind of narrative prop that the storytellers in the bazaar unroll as they spin out the episodes, pointing to the figures and the settings as they go. It showed a great white sea monster, who became, in *Indigo*, the cannibal fish Manjiku who terrorises the islanders. I had begun writing short stories, too, that attempted to give voice to the heroines of well-known stories: Ariadne, Susannah from the Old Testament, Martha from the New. 'The Belled Girl' forms part of this sequence; its immediate inspiration was a bronze sculpture called 'Ballerina' by the Spanish contemporary artist Juan Muñoz which shows a girl with staring eyes and bells for hands, but it echoes the theme of the maid-without-hands, a story much older than the Grimms' version. *La Manékine*, a medieval French poetic romance by Phillippe de Beaumanoir, already tells it: the heroine Joie slices off her hand to avoid marriage with her father. I wanted to express a contemporary twist on this sexual fear and place it in the context of today's emphasis on appearances and image: the culture that has produced beauty pageants for six-year-olds, and murdered child beauty queens like JonBenet Ramsey.

Angela Carter's effect on me, and on so many writers, goes beyond the way she unlocked the magic, light and dark, of everyday life, the way she showed up the unnecessary orientalism of fictions that go far and wide in search of new experience. The enchantments of the most familiar will meet all needs (*Wise Children* triumphantly conveys her baroque and extravagant celebration of the mundane). It even goes beyond the way she voiced female desire. She is a consummate writer of the English language; syntactically innovatory, verbally fertile, and with a thousand registers and tones and cadences, comic and heady and poignant; it is simply the most dazzling prose. I used to look up words all the time when reading her; but I also had to look up things she would mention, needing an illustrated encyclopaedia to understand the references to items and cuts of dress, to technical tools, to flora and fauna. I discovered what 'purple loosestrife' is from one of her books: it has always seemed apt that she should have known this unruly wild flower, a native to England, which self-seeds and flourishes in damp ground.

1998

TWO

WORDS AND SYMBOLS

Saint Paul: Let Women Keep Silent

My convent school was hard to find. There was one gate at the end of a private, unpaved road leading through the birch trees and azalea bushes of a dormitory suburb, and another entrance, turning abruptly off a side road, which opened on to the rhododendron-shrouded front drive. This approach was tarmacked and – at least in my memory – always reptilian-shiny from the rain. The school only emerged into view at the end of the deep drive, and seemed very imposing, the many tall red-brick buildings attached to the Gothic chapel like spokes to a hub. Also, after the dripping shrubberies on the way, it always looked preternaturally tidy. The begonias, which were installed in rows in the front flowerbed display, would drop their heads in the English damp: the only disorder in the sweep up to the small front door.

I went back once, in secret, just up the drive and then – quick turn around – out again, no harm done, the flypaper didn't catch me, and I experienced again the loneliness I used to feel at the beginning of term, when the school enclosed me back in its secluded world.

Saint Paul, by contrast, was a traveller, a man with contacts, on the move and firing off letters as he went. We followed his different journeys in different-coloured inks on maps of the Mediterranean; unlike the evangelists, who seemed separate from history, Paul could be grasped as a character in the past. Matthew and Mark were shadowy; Luke, the companion of Our Lady in old age and the painter of her portrait, had a bit of life in him, of a gentle, bedside-manner variety; John belonged in a vivid sequence of posed tableaux, ending in fierce old age sitting on his rock wrapped in visions. But there were adventure stories about Saint Paul that followed a familiar dramatic structure, of hubris and peripeteia, of shipwrecks and widows, riots and imprisonments, and, above all, the blinding moment on the road to Damascus.

Some years ago, in the Church of Santa Maria del Popolo in Rome, I came upon Caravaggio's painting of that conversion: the fallen saint, the stepping, bewildered horse, the penetrating radiance impacted together as if the edge of the picture had been cut down in order to tighten the drama. Paul, for all his movements, never lost contact with the centre of energy – or, rather, he carried it with him, like a magnet storing power. By contrast, enclosed at school, we were immobilised, and very far away from the heart of things. He enjoyed intimacy with the Lord, and all that meant in terms of power and love and light; we sat at our desks facing the blackboard in classrooms with high windows so that the view outside should not distract us, journeying with Paul on his many roads, by land and sea, along the lines of green and red ballpoint. In the fifth form (aged around fifteen) we could bicycle with permission to the local village beyond the shrubs and birch trees, but never farther afield. It was important to learn the love of Christ by sitting still and being good; Paul, dynamic, adventurous Paul to whom so much had happened, was the architect of this view of girls' proper conduct.

The result wasn't hatred of the saint, or even reproach. Saint Paul was beyond such familiarity. Besides, it was only much later that I ever heard of the idea that the New Testament might not be the revealed word of God but could be questioned, discussed, that individuals could take issue with it, that the Pastoral Letters, such as the First Epistle to Timothy, might not all originate from Paul but might have been composed pseudonymously by an interpreter who honoured him and wished to propagate his teachings.[1] No, Paul's heroism inspired in us love of those who had been fortunate to enjoy the company of this travelling hero, to participate in his adventures – like Timothy, characterised as young in the epistles (though commentators now reckon his age to be thirty or more), who had been adopted as Paul's beloved son.

At a boarding school, with parents visiting only three times a term, young women create – or at least try to create – clusters of affection around them which will replace the missing mothers, fathers, brothers, and sisters. Sometimes their absence is experienced as straightforward loss, and the substitutes simply become temporary surrogates. But sometimes, the family back home inspire turbulent emotions of anger and bitterness, for their disappearance can seem a kind of forsaking. In a convent, Christ's teaching that the true disciple leaves behind mother and father to follow him is fulfilled by the constant presence of nuns, who have renounced family even to the point of blotting out the name of their birth. Their choice complicates the issue of family love and loyalty, holding up the possibility that another family altogether could usurp the biological group of home and origin, that bonds could be forged willingly not by accident of birth but by election. Ah, the child who dreams, as Freud described, that she was switched in her cradle and given over mistakenly to these cruel and ordinary parents as their daughter, though she knows, if truth be told, that she is a princess, finds rich stimulus in the New Testament, where the constellations of relationships do not follow the usual social pattern, where Timothy can become the beloved son of Paul without the interference of a mother, shed all memory of earlier obligation or home, and fulfil his new father's orders like a hereditary prince.

Discipleship attracted us strongly, as a calling as well as a source of affection. We picked favourite nuns – and some among the community picked out favourite girls. When I was first sent to school, aged nine, Mother Barbara, the principal of the lower school, inspired deep attachments in many of the children. She was the lead voice in the choir, singing antiphons and masses composed by our Reverend Mother Cecilia, named for the patron saint of music. Mother Barbara had Italian blood and an Italian soprano's voice, surprisingly muscular for its pitch, and rather loud for the lullabies she chose after lights-out in the dormitory, where we lay in separate cubicles with our clothes folded on stools at the foot of the bed, beyond the flowered curtain.

> Sellellullellu bye bye
> If you want the stars to play with
> And the moon to run away with
> They'll come if you don't cry ...

We were – almost all of us – sure we preferred Mother Barbara to our own mothers; though I used to feel this was disloyal, especially as I already had one Italian mother.

The nuns themselves understood, however, that their care for us might not suffice, and they allowed the children in the lower school to be visited at bedtime by an older girl of their choice – not every night, but sometimes. The moment would come, as we were sitting up in bed, with our hairbrushes in our hands, when the prefects would enter the dormitory and disperse down the aisles, looking past the curtains for the little girl who had requested their goodnight kiss. There was sometimes competition for the same older girl – stars of the tennis court and the hockey pitch were in great demand. My first allegiance went to the head girl, known as P. J., who seemed to me then the most beautiful being in the world. But other people thought so too, and I had P. J. to myself only once. I think she found me rather intense; I think she also would have made my happiness then if she had said to me, as Paul did to Timothy, 'Go, my true and beloved child, take this message from me across the sea and defend it against all comers.'

Mother Barbara placed us all *in loco filiarum*, but she wasn't exactly a mentor; P. J. was my 'crack', as we called such passions, and I would have walked across a bridge of knives for her, as I say. I also longed to be tall and fair and cheerful and breezy like her, instead of stout and dark and anxious.

The relation of master-disciple, folded within the parent-child bond Paul and Timothy also claimed for themselves, did not really develop until later, when pupils reached the fifth and sixth forms, and then not among themselves but between teachers and girls, a certain nun and her student, though special friendships were terribly discouraged, of course. The imagined model tie was masculine, fraternal rather than filial, because the adventure of learning, the enterprise of travelling, even if only figuratively, was a male domain. When Sister Christina and I braved the lusts of pagan Rome in the company of Catullus, I saw myself as a wanderer in time, like Dante, or like Christian from *Pilgrim's Progress*. It was never me as I was then, in navy skirt and strap shoes and band holding my hair off my face.

At the time I didn't know the *Acts of Paul*, for we were sheltered from the New Testament *Apocrypha*. But when I came across the text later, and read there the story of Saint Thecla, I recognised something I had wanted to be. Thecla was forbidden to leave the house to hear Saint Paul preach, but she stood at the window of her parents' house in Iconium in Asia Minor to listen; accepting his message, she then rejected the rich marriage her parents had arranged for her, and proclaimed her new faith in virginity and Christ. Her rejected bridegroom had Paul driven out of town for leading young people astray. For her part, Thecla was condemned to death by burning alive. Miraculously, a rain cloud put out the bonfire, and she escaped. She then ran away to follow Paul. But Paul did not want her, because she was a girl. So Thecla cut her hair and put on boy's clothes and proved her devotion and courage until he at last agreed to allow her to preach as his disciple, like Timothy.[2]

When I lay in bed at night laying plans for my future, I saw myself intrepid, unstoppable, self-willed like Thecla – and in boy's clothes. When I read recently Karen Horney's critique of Freud's theories about femininity and the female castration complex, I was glad that someone within psychoanalysis had understood that young girls envy boys for social reasons, that Thecla did not cut her hair and put on the dress of a young man because she felt anguish at her lack of a penis but because Paul would not let her speak her mind in the shape of a girl.[3]

My school copy of the New Testament shows many places scored in the margin of the First Epistle to Timothy, for it is a letter in which Paul has a great deal to say about both women's behaviour and the correct Christian treatment of certain categories of women. He's above all concerned with women's tongues, as the author of the *Acts of Paul* was aware when he portrayed the apostle resisting Thecla's thirst to evangelise. It is in the First Epistle to Timothy that this verse appears: 'Let the woman learn in silence with all subjection' (2:11).

The nuns who taught us Scripture and church history as well as all the other subjects in our curriculum did not keep silence. At times, in their secluded quarters at one end of the convent buildings, they did not speak, and at times we kept vigil with them, during three-day retreats or in memory of the dead on certain feasts. But on the whole, their calling as teachers contradicted in its essence the injunction of Saint Paul. And indeed, Mary Ward, the foundress of the order to which they belonged – the Institute of the Blessed Virgin Mary – had been persecuted in her lifetime for her independent and resolute desire to establish an order of nuns who would teach girls in the same way as the Jesuits taught boys. (The order was suppressed by the Pope and was not restored until 1877.)[4]

Mary Ward did not believe in silence for women nor, perhaps, in their subjection. Her younger counterpart in New Spain, the poet and thinker Sor Juana de la Cruz (1648–95), also joined battle with the authorities when she listed many learned women of the past to whom she was beholden in her own studies and then continued with an attack on the male clergy's prerogatives: 'The interpretation of holy scripture should be forbidden not only to women, considered so very inept, but to men, who merely by virtue of being men consider themselves sages. . . . There are many who study in order to become ignorant, especially those of an arrogant, restless and overbearing turn of mind.'[5]

Saint Paul rather inclines to extravagant breast-beating, the attention-seeking gesture of a man who must always outstrip his peers, if only in abjection. In this First Epistle to Timothy, he writes of his turbulent past and calls himself, in the translation of Ronald Knox, which we used in the convent, 'a man of violence, author of outrage' (1:13).[6] (In the King James Version he calls himself 'injurious', in the Jerusalem Bible, 'a bully'. He reproaches himself for his sins: 'I was the worst of all' (1:15). But he never grows to consciousness – nor did we then, reading him – that violence remained with him, that he continued to show an arrogant, restless, and overbearing turn of mind when it came to discussing the expectations and potential of women.

'Let the woman learn in silence with all subjection' continues the ban at which Mary Ward and Sor Juana – and many others – chafed: 'But I suffer not a woman to teach, nor to usurp authority over the man, but to be in silence' (2:12). He then gives his reasons, moving in a characteristically Pauline way to an allegorical exegesis of the Fall: that Adam was made first, to symbolise his precedence over woman, and that since Eve, the type of all women to come, sinned through speech, by tempting Adam to eat, speech must be denied her daughters.

In the Vulgate, Jerome used *seducta* for Eve's transgression: the serpent led her astray, and she then 'seduced' Adam. The connotations of the verb are already sexual. Women's words are mixed up with women's wiles – beauty and expression go hand in hand, as Paul implies when he also lays down that women should dress modestly, without show of jewels or elaborate coiffures (2:9). Eve sinned by mouth: she bit into the apple of knowledge; she spoke to the serpent and to Adam; and she was in consequence cursed with desire, to kiss and be kissed ('Thy desire shall be to thy husband').

The seduction of women's talk reflected the seduction of their bodies; it was considered just as dangerous to Christian men, and condemned as improper. Paul, in the First Epistle to Timothy alone, proscribes at least five different kinds of speech which he attributes to women: the wives of deacons must not be 'slanderers' (3:11); Timothy must not listen to 'profane and old wives' fables' (4:7); young widows are 'not only idle, but tattlers also and busybodies, speaking things which they ought not' (5:13); he also fears gossip, and warns that young widows' behaviour will give rise to talk unless they remarry. By contrast, he exhorts his disciple to be 'an example of the believers, in word, in conversation' (4:12) and, at the end, to avoid 'profane and vain babblings' (6:20). The translators of the King James Version had no difficulty finding English words for these different types of condemned speech. In this matter, Catholics and Protestants were in agreement: garrulousness was a woman's vice, and silence – which was not even considered an appropriate virtue in the male – one of the chief ornaments a good woman should cultivate. It's a commonplace that what counts as articulateness in a man becomes stridency in a woman, that a man's conviction is a woman's shrillness, a man's fluency a woman's drivel. The speaking woman also refuses subjection and turns herself from a passive object of desire into a conspiring and conscious stimulation: the *mulier blandiens* or *mulier meretrix* of Ecclesiasticus 25:17–36 and Proverbs 6:24–6 comes in for much vituperation; the biblical text 'A man's spite is preferable to a woman's kindness' (Ecclesiasticus, 42:14) provoked much nodding of male heads.[7] Female curiosity had brought about the Fall and so must be quelled. The virtue of Prudence sometimes wears a padlock on her mouth, and sixteenth-century morality tales painted the portraits of the Wise Man and the Wise Woman, showing the latter with her lips firmly under lock and key:

> Everyone look at me because I am a wise woman . . .
> A golden padlock I wear on my mouth at all times
> so that no villainous words shall escape my mouth
> but I say nothing without deliberation
> and a wise woman should always act thus.[8]

The tongues of women were associated with curses and spells, the central activity of witches. There even exist, from the seventeenth century, scolds' bridles – contraptions like dog muzzles designed to gag women who had been charged and found guilty for something they had said; a law against cursing was passed in 1624.[9]

In cautionary children's literature of the late nineteenth century, a similar asymmetry between the value of men's and women's expressions governs the laws of good behaviour. The wife of Monsieur Croquemitaine the bogeyman comes for little girls who show too much curiosity and shuts them up in a trunk.[10] Father Flog, Croquemitaine's American counterpart, brandishes a knife with which he cuts the tongues of liars – in this case 'untruthful children' regardless of sex.[11] The other day, in a tobacconist's shop in Jalisco province in Mexico, I found two postcards, drawn in lurid caricature. In one, a bent old harridan hauls her shopping while two lounging men look on approvingly: she has a huge padlock through her lips. In the other, a sharp-featured woman's eyes are popping in terror as a hairy fist pulls out her tongue and prepares to cut it off with scissors.

We weren't discouraged from talking at school; the nuns carried on teaching us Paul's view of womankind in their articulate and independent way without alerting us to the contradiction. But it was odd and painful to read, in such places as Paul's First Epistle to Timothy, that there was another standard of conduct to which we should conform if we were to be proper disciples. No one could miss the apostle's tone when it came to women: in our own sex we were unworthy, in spite of being created equal and being saved equally and there being neither male nor female in Christ Jesus. And there was no means of redress, because the means – thought, learning, social reform – cut across the Scriptures' commands.

The First Epistle to Timothy tries to soften the blow against women by promising: 'Notwithstanding she shall be saved in childbearing' (2:15). We had a central notice board at school, in which notices of old girls' engagements were posted, and news of the babies born to them. Often the names were foreign – Spanish families, Italian families (preferably princely) were much in favour with the daughters of Catholics in England. The nuns would glow with approval, looking in their voluminous habits as if they were actually inflating gently. If the harsh self-immolation of Thecla eluded us, we could be saved by having a Catholic baby with a Spanish prince; it was a comfort. We believed it. I believed it, and in some ways still do, because I have found with age that although I see clearly the fallaciousness and the unkindness of fundamental principles I was taught, I bear the stamp of them ineluctably, and feel myself to be a renegade, a kind of voluntary outcast. For I sometimes feel a pinch of regret that I was not married in Saint James's, Spanish Place, wearing lilies and white lace, to the scion of an ancient Catholic line to whom I would bear an heir. For this was the secondary romance, after the high mission of Timothy and Thecla – though I was at odds with it, too, as well as called by it: I had read Shelley and became a votary of free love, scorning the designs for foaming lace wedding dresses which my classmates doodled in lessons.

Biblical scholars now argue that the mitigation of the apostle's usual stringent asceticism in the First and Second Epistles to Timothy and the Epistle to Titus points to a follower and imitator of Saint Paul who sought to 'domesticate' Pauline doctrine and adapt it to a traditional Jewish idea of the worth of marriage, the importance of hierarchy within the family, and tribal obligations to widows.[12] This explains, very satisfyingly, the contradiction on which we were impaled at school, between a heroic, otherworldly vocation on the one hand and the silent mission of motherhood and wifely obedience on the other.

Since leaving school, I have written about the Virgin Mary, and about Joan of Arc, and about many other Catholic heroines, imaginary and historical, who first captured my imagination when I was at the convent in the rhododendrons and I was taught to aspire higher and even higher. I was not schooled to silence; but I learned that a woman's silence is especially golden. Reading Saint Paul confirmed those longings I already felt to be other than what I was: I became a house divided against itself.

But I hope that the wind that blows in the cracks has a speaking voice.

1990

Christine de Pizan: *The Book of the City of Ladies*

In one of the most appealing and interesting anecdotes in this collection of women's lives, Christine de Pizan describes how Novella, the daughter of a law professor at the famed university of Bologna, taught in her father's place when he was busy, and in order to prevent her beauty from distracting her pupils, drew a curtain in front of her face. Beauty used to be one of the defining attributes of the female sex, virtually synonymous with feminine form; it was also presumed dangerous, and from Eve onwards, the naked female face (and form) were thought so potent they could unman the strongest of men. Novella's curtain did not just disguise her beauty, but her femaleness. Christine might well have written that Novella drew a curtain over her sex, just as in 1448, the editor of Christine's work of military ethics, *The Book of Feats of Arms and Chivalry*, decided to draw a veil over Christine's sex, and changed the text so that it appeared to have been written by a man. He was taking an elementary precaution against losing his readers. A work on the proper conduct of war, by a woman, would invite slurs of unreliability.

It was exactly this climate of prejudice that inspired Christine de Pizan's partisan works in defence of womankind. *The Book of the City of Ladies* is part of Christine's ardent campaign to rehabilitate her sex in her contemporaries' eyes.

Although *The Book of the City of Ladies* was written more than half a millennium ago, it is filled with potent observations for our times. The *querelle des femmes* – the woman question in late fourteenth- and fifteenth-century France – articulated its arguments in much the same way as today's debate about the equality of women. Here, in *The Book of the City of Ladies*, Christine intersperses her tales of formidable and exemplary heroines of the past with down-to-earth remarks about the wrongs done to women by society's attitudes and opinions. Her tone is not shrill, but forbearing; her comments trenchant; she never whines. She indicts men, Portia-like, from a position of superior benevolence, enacting the drama of women's greater moral qualities by refusing the line of violence or suppliant weakness. Christine de Pizan was born in a court and she was an adept of courtly ways; her strategy in her attack is courteous, and her courtesy, with its appearance of frankness, even artlessness, conceals a fair bit of cunning, and a deal of rage.

Recurring themes with resonance for today provoke in her a controlled indignation. She returns again and again, for instance, to the lack of access women have to education. She praises her own father generously for giving her an education against the conventional objections of her mother, and interjects defiantly that women's minds are 'freer and sharper' than men's. She laments the disappointment women of her day felt at the birth of daughters: she gives as its cause the need to provide young women with dowries. Yet today, when the economic reason has failed, the arrival of a girl baby is often greeted with less enthusiasm by grandparents, in-laws. Yet another barbarism that has not been modified in the long interval separating us from Christine appears in her pages; the accusation that women invite rape. Christine exonerates women from this suspicion with a fierce, felt regret, and ends by approving the supreme penalty for rapists. Elsewhere, touching what appears to be a personal note, she also pleads that women can be pretty and enjoy fine clothes without forfeiting their title to chastity. Her anger at the double standard, by which men, raping women, then blame women for exciting them to do so, still rings loud and clear today. She also paints a devastating and unchanged picture of violence in marriage, of drunken beatings and spendthrift husbands.

The Book of the City of Ladies uses a popular medieval convention, of an author's conversation with allegorical figures. In this book, Christine talks to the figures of Reason and Justice, familiar then from iconography as well as theology, but she also creates her own allegorical maiden, *Droiture*, Rectitude, 'Right-thinking', 'Right-doing'. Christine's introduction of this figure into the pageant of the regular female Virtues, Liberal Arts,

Heavenly Beatitudes, and other personifications found in the sculpture programmes of cathedrals, reveals her mental and emotional bent. In a book like *The City of Ladies*, Christine de Pizan is casting herself as a moral tutor rather than a poet; she is writing to instruct us, to shape our thinking and so incline us to right-thinking and right-doing. When she pleads for education for women, she gives as her reason education's close correlation with good conduct.

The contemporary reader might be unfamiliar with the medieval convention of allegory. Yet the appearance of Reason, Rectitude, and Justice as women reflects the entire purpose of Christine's *Book of the City of Ladies*: to bring back to memory the lives and deeds of virtuous women embodying those qualities, who have been neglected and forgotten by history. She is restoring speech to the silent portion of the past – one of the principal tasks of all historians. *The Book of the City of Ladies* resembles a visit to the shades of the dead, claiming their right to be remembered. Christine, drawing from her reading of classical and Renaissance sources, adds them to our store of knowledge and breaks the narrow moulds of female stereotypes. To achieve her vindication of women, she alters her source material in the most surprising ways, sometimes refreshing, sometimes bizarre.

Christine praises Medea for her herbal arts and her command of the elements – an interesting and justifiable example of reassessing witchcraft from a positive viewpoint. She thus frees a historical personality from the fears of ignorance and prejudice. But later, when Medea appears again among Christine's exempla of women's constancy in love, it is a trifle peculiar to find her story told without a mention of the demented dimension of her despair, with the murder of her children overlooked. Christine actually describes the great prototype of the wronged first wife turning merely 'despondent' after Jason leaves her. Similarly, Xanthippe, Socrates' proverbial shrew of a wife, emerges from Christine's pages as loyal and devoted and wise. Modesty also inspires Christine to change the famous story of 'Roman charity'. The dying old man who is suckled by a young woman is transformed into a female, the girl's mother moreover. Christine's redress of history's judgment can be enterprising and surprising (it had never occurred to me that Xanthippe might indeed have been maligned), but often the new, virtuous portrait strays towards a stereotype. Christine here is at her best as a storyteller when she writes from personal truth and emotion, and her rebukes rise from within the sting of lived experience.

Christine herself does not seem to distinguish between the levels of reality she seizes with her pen: her own life's lessons merge without interruption into the examples of heroines, legendary and historical. Reading *The Book of the City of Ladies* involves an odd trick of perception, for the circle enclosing Christine, Medusa, the goddess Ops, and Queen Blanche is one and the same without difference of degree, authenticity, or even time scale. Human experience is universal, Christine is telling us, and distance in time constitutes no effective barrier. But it is arresting – and charming – to find that Uranus was 'an extremely powerful man in Greece' married to a wife called Vesta, that Minerva figured in Christine's mind as the historical inventor of shorthand, arithmetic, weaving and spinning, the cultivation of the olive, and the forging of armour, and was not just the protagonist in a pagan myth of origin or a symbolic tutelary goddess of specific skills and arts. Christine was a devout Christian woman who saw Minerva as one of her predecessors in wisdom and industry; in the invocation with which she closes *The Book of Feats of Arms and Chivalry*, she asks Minerva to preside over her undertaking, as the goddess is a *'femme Italienne'* like herself. For Christine de Pizan, the centuries that had elapsed since Italy was part of Magna Graecia were but the winking of an eye; Minerva was her inspiration, her ally, and her compatriot.

The Book of the City of Ladies represents a determined and clear-headed woman's attempt to take apart the structure of her con-temporaries' prejudices; a reasoned but fierce counter-assault against baiting by the male. Christine was not a moderate; she believed deeply in sexual difference and she diagnosed, in this book and in other works, the nature and causes of sexual antagonism. She was always alive to injustice. Yet Christine, who herself resolved to remain a widow and sang of her decision in a famous *ballade, 'Seulete suy et seulete vueil estre'*, showed an admirably open mind when she counselled other women not to seek too much independence (even though her words sound like equivocation to our ears), for usually moralists command people to greatness they themselves cannot achieve. But she believed in the possibility of reconciliation: it was largely a matter of the right education leading to moral enlightenment. In this way, *The Book of the City of Ladies* is a work of optimism that is still by no means entirely justified by events. The task Christine de Pizan set herself has still to be done.

1982

Watch Your Tongues

Review of Howard Bloch, Medieval Misogyny and the Invention of
Western Romantic Love; *Margaret King,* Women of the Renaissance;
Brigitte Cazelles, The Lady as Saint: A Collection of French
Hagiographical Romances of the Thirteenth Century; *Fulvio Tomizza,*
Heavenly Supper: The Story of Maria Janis, *translated by Anne Jacobson
Shutte; Tina Krontiris,* Oppositional Voices: Women as Writers and
Translators of Literature in the English Renaissance

If Saints Jerome or Ambrose or Augustine or any of the grim Fathers had
been watching television in spring this year, they wouldn't have had much
trouble seeing Marlene Dietrich for what she was. Those lids, those lips,
that pillowy mink, those sidelong glances, those shimmering legs and –
above all – that voice, would have rendered her lightly accented modern
English as plain as the Latin of the Mass to the patriarchs and their friends
and forerunners in the penitential Thebaïd. The world, the flesh and the
devil embodied in a woman, and speaking in a woman's voice: the siren
incarnate against whom you have to plug your ears or else, like Adam, you
will feel the plunge as you fall. It is odd how wholeheartedly women have
given themselves to playing this part – to believing it, too. Or perhaps it's
not all that odd: the femme fatale offers more opportunities than several
of the other sacrificial parts in the repertoire. But it is remarkable how the
constituent elements of the contemporary fatal woman, the stories that
underpin her charms, as well as the ornaments she assumes, match the
fulminations of two thousand years ago against the counterfeit of
women's fascination and the seductions of their tongues.

As Howard Bloch points out in his short and combative study
Medieval Misogyny, the flesh was seen as feminine, set in opposition to
soul or mind, and the spirit wears the body like a concealing garment; to
adorn this fleshly raiment with yet more artifice and paint doubled the
distance that separated the incarnate and fallen world from the
disembodied condition of the angels. When Jean-Luc Godard, in his
update of the Nativity story, *Je vous salue Marie*, closed with his Mary
painting herself a bright red mouth as she looks in the wing mirror of her
car, he was offering an orthodox theological rebuttal of the ascetic
tradition, asserting the value of the material, of the sensual, the enfleshed
and female, in the person of Mary. But his Mary, a fleshly image
reproduced as illusion on screen, is also the vision of a seductress, Eve all

over again, whose body and speech could persuade a man to eat . . . anything. As Bloch says, the story misogyny tells is repeated again and again; it's a room with a hundred entrances and exits – different societies, different moments, different voices – but when you try each door in turn you find yourself back in the same room.

Does this mean that misogyny is an inevitable condition? Bloch writes at the start of his book: 'misogyny is a way of speaking about, as distinct from doing something to, women . . . It is a speech act.' But speech acts underlie as well as justify other acts, political, legal, economic. Fear of women's tongues connects to the historical restrictions on their public speech, misprision of women's minds as light and 'feminine' helps to explain the long reluctance to educate daughters as well as sons.

One of the first principles of misogyny sets up a huge stumbling-block in the path of any analyst or historian, for the misogynist thinks every women is All-Woman, that the varieties of the species don't make a bit of difference. The questor after the Eternal Feminine could find the face of the witch-hunter in his looking-glass; taking individual women out of their context, ignoring their class, place, work, family, to corral them in a realm of universal ascriptions constitutes the founding act of misogyny. All the books considered here wrestle with this problem, they reach for the particular moment, the detailed cluster of circumstances, the individual story, in order to avoid the prejudice of blanket categorisation. In this, they flow with the lively current of women's studies, which is bringing back the sound of different, personal voices and particular tales.

Margaret King's richly researched *Women of the Renaissance* explores the lives and works of foundlings and drudges, poets and princesses in a painstaking mesh of social, financial and legal detail. But it has to be said that the discourse of misogyny, divorcing women from history and reality, continues to seep through the growing evidence of women's defiance and achievement. That discourse was always something individuals had to reckon with and try to bend to their purposes; Margaret King describes how a determined and learned philosopher like Laura Cereta, of Brescia, spent a great amount of energy attacking women who conformed to more conventional notions of femininity than herself: 'I cannot bear the babbling and chattering women . . . Inflamed with hatred, they would noisily chew up others, [except that] mute, they are themselves chewed up within.' When Laura Cereta spoke up, she was trapped in the ancient conundrum, too: how to speak as a woman and not herself become a babbler or a shrew.

Finding a voice presented less of a challenge than getting a hearing; the Church offered a forum, on certain conditions – chastity, principally. *The Golden Legend*, compiled by the Dominican Jacopus de Voragine in the thirteenth century, has exercised an incalculable influence on Christian ideas about sanctity; its savage accounts of martyrdoms conjure images in the mind's eye more like the covers of slasher movies in video shops than anything pious, while its unabashed anti-Semitism prefigures modern demons of another kind. *The Golden Legend* was approved literature for well-born, literate women, when most other narrative works in the vernacular – romances, for example – were frowned on and banned. Margaret King, navigating the narrows the female sex had to ply, mentions copies of *The Golden Legend*, in English and French, being handed down from mother to daughter in the noblest families. The violent lives – and prolonged agonies in death – of the virgin martyrs were seen by these women as offering them lessons in life. Women are even known to have written such hagiography, but the two examples Brigitte Cazelles cites in the helpful Introduction to her collection of saints' lives unfortunately fall outside her chosen century. As does the most famous exponent of exemplary feminist biography, Christine de Pizan, who rebutted male poets' laments on female frailty with her own City of Ladies which gave room to heroines from Circe to Deborah.

Cazelles argues strongly that Christine did not insist on woman as victim in her section on the virgin martyrs; but she is stretching the evidence, I feel. After Sade the spectacle of cruelty can no longer be read as it was in the High Middle Ages – as innocently heroic. Cazelles has collected companion biographies to *The Golden Legend*, from the same century, and of similar ferocity. Bizarre, hyperbolic torments are visited on paragons like Saint Christina, who, after she has been beaten by her father, hanged, tied to a wheel, set fire to, thrown in the sea with a millstone round her neck, and had snakes fastened to her breasts, finally has her tongue cut out. Nothing daunted, she throws the severed portion at her tormentor: it pierces him through the eye. Her original fault lay in refusing to marry according to her father's wish, and insisting on proclaiming the true God. A woman could be a witness; she could, in certain circumstances, use her tongue to blind an oppressor.

Caroline Bynum, in her remarkable book about late medieval mystics, *Holy Feast and Holy Fast* (1987), put forward a startling theory of the female body's role in Christian tradition which none of the books discussed here attempts to confront, let alone integrate into their arguments (though most cite her reverently). She argued that the bodily practices of the women saints – severe fasting, stigmata, scourging, and other even more violent mortifications – were not a consequence of Christian contempt for the female. Rather the opposite: the incarnational doctrine led Christian men to honour the carnal condition and to want the experience of fleshliness in its consummate form, femaleness; that the bleeding, starving, broken, sacralised bodies of women mystics and martyrs were perceived to enact the *imitatio Christi* more perfectly and aptly than men's precisely because women were closer to the desired lowly condition of the carnal. For this reason, men found in women's bodies the instruments of their own quest for knowledge of God – the priest-poets who wrote the lives of martyrs like St. Christina spoke of their own salvation in the descriptions of her tortures, her torn-out tongue. In one sense, women's bodies became vehicles of men's speech; men defined themselves through the flesh they evoked, in the case of hagiographers, or beheld and consecrated, in the case of the confessors who accompanied most living saints and acted as witnesses and praise-singers.

Elizabeth of Hungary, a historical figure who was canonised four years after her death in 1231 by her friend Pope Gregory IX, was written up by the poet Rutebeuf among others: although she was married (the exception among exemplary women), she also turned her body into a spectacular theatre of divine manifestations, by giving up eating and drinking, having her servants beat her all night, until after death, 'in great haste, a crowd/ Came to cut out a piece of her;/ Parts of her hair and breast were cut.' Later still, her body in the tomb begins to exude myrrh: 'This oil oozed like so many drops of dew' – which brought about many cures. The saint's body becomes, like the Eucharist itself, a means to transcendence. But as the word 'martyr' implies, it also acts as a witness. Bynum's point is that women speak through their own bodies, their own 'suffering and generativity', rooted in biological metaphors like birthing and nursing, to which the female sex has a prior claim; female somatic presence abolishes the intermediary stage men occupy, which makes them need women to speak through, to think with.

As vessels of symbolic language and definition, however, they needed to be closely watched and controlled. Exchanges of symbolic meaning between bodies, food, language and law recur in the relations between fathers and daughters, emperors and subjects, husbands and wives in all the material surveyed by the books under review, in fact and fiction, and never more notably than in Renaut de Beaujeu's *Lai d'Ignauré*, recounted by Bloch. Ignauré, a knight, makes love to all twelve wives of the twelve peers of the realm, and is discovered. The husbands castrate him, kill him, and dish up his genitals and heart in a stew for their wives' table. When the women discover what they have done, they refuse ever to eat again, and die. This *lai* is a 'story prophane', as the writer Margaret Tyler would later call her translation of a Spanish romance, and it turns upside down the terms of the communion feast; but for all its impiety and even ribaldry, the poem doesn't alter the place of women as privileged participants in the great mysteries of love and transcendental union. Sacrilegiously, the adulteresses take the place of the Apostles at the Last Supper, but unlike them, they sacrifice themselves along with their beloved, paying the supreme price like the paschal victim himself: was Renaut de Beaujeu jesting against female piety's extremism as well as giving a new twist to tales of cuckoldry? Howard Bloch does not take his account this far, nor, for someone who professes interest in material circumstances, does he vouchsafe information about Renaut de Beaujeu's dates or context.

The case of Maria Janis, tried and condemned by the Inquisition in Venice in 1664, focused on food: as Fulvio Tomizza comments in *Heavenly Supper*, the verb 'to eat' is conjugated in every tense and mood in the trial transcripts he read in the Venetian state archives. His book has a strange publishing history, for it appeared as a *romanzo*, a novel, in 1981, under the title *La Finzione di Maria – The Pretence of Maria*, though 'make-believe' or even 'fiction' might catch the nuance of *finzione*. Tomizza's book belongs in the wave of micro-histories, which began with the voices of the accused of Montaillou, of Menocchio the miller, in Carlo Ginzburg's *The Cheese and the Worms*, and continued with Natalie Zemon Davis's *The Return of Martin Guerre*. Maria Janis, like these protagonists, makes herself heard from the pages of a trial, with a peculiar, powerful and, in her case, poignant story to tell: these are the particular lives which might topple the great monolith of misogynist discourse. Except that Maria Janis, in the tiny scale of her specialness, and the pathos of her ultimate defeat, only goes to prove the power of that monolith in the topography of the Counter-Reformation.

For Maria Janis wanted to be a saint, and she was a hundred or more years too late to be believed. Several sixteenth-century English women, Tina Krontiris points out in *Oppositional Voices*, chafed against the restrictions of their families, and consequently joined the old, forbidden religion: Catholicism at least offered the cloister as well as the hearth, whereas the Protestants only sanctioned the domestic and maternal role. But in Maria Janis's Italy, the old faith was stripping away the superstitious excesses of the past, the extreme fervour of the people and their cults, and through its Inquisitors assessing dubious claims to holiness. The advance of the Jesuit mission, for instance, tended to mark a corresponding retreat of popular faith: bleeding icons, visions in trees, apparitions in grottoes, all were examined and found to be hollow dreams. This was to be Maria Janis's fate too. She was the seamstress daughter of poor villagers from the mountains near Bergamo (the book badly needs a map) who joined up with a country priest, Don Pietro Morali. Don Pietro had won an enthusiastic local following as a preacher and miracle-worker, and she in turn gained his attention, and eventually, in her claims to sanctity, his allegiance and veneration.

Her God-granted 'privilege' was to live on communion alone. Like a thirteenth-century saint, she did not eat or drink anything except the Eucharist for five years. The priest administered it to her daily, and sometimes more than once, which was in itself heterodox, and he did so in the privacy of her room, as during their wanderings, he could not often enough obtain the correct permissions to say Mass in another priest's church. She kept the hosts in a pyx on a ribbon round her neck; as the first witnesses told the Inquisition, Don Pietro drew the little box out from between her breasts with his own hands. These witnesses were the couple's landlady's daughters, and they had been watching through a crack in the door.

Fulvio Tomizza considers his book a novel because he imagines the couple's thoughts and attributes motives to them; in other words, he flouts recent historiographical conventions about evidence. In his view, Maria Janis had a crush on the parish priest, and thanks to her *finzione* made it possible for herself to travel with him, cohabit with him and become as necessary to him as he was to her. He believed in her holiness, as did many others who gave them money and shelter and help, and testified on their behalf. But it was no good: Don Pietro was condemned, 'vehemently suspected of heresy', and she 'lightly' suspected of the same fault; his sentence was less severe, however – only four years' detention. Maria was enclosed at the pleasure of the Holy Office – that is, for ever – in a paupers' foundation. It is one of the many ironies of her story that she had originally wanted to enter a convent but did not have enough money for the dowry; she had managed instead to become a holy woman of temporary, local repute out in the world. She had also taught herself to read in the meantime, though not to write. Her signature on the trial confession was still only a cross.

Denied other routes, Maria Janis used prodigious self-denial to command attention, in the manner of the heroines of Christian folklore and history; though ecstatic mysticism still continued – with its somatic signs, like stigmata – the phenomenon dwindled as women gained access to literacy and other legitimate means of self-expression. Tina Krontiris's short, level-headed study of writers points out the notable, though overlooked, relationship between independence and literacy; the catch was that it was hard to achieve one without the other, especially within the traditional family. 'Placing out', the custom of sending girls away from home to work as servants in other households, turns out to have been the path that led to the library, where Margaret Tyler, for instance, taught herself Spanish so well that she published, in 1578, a translation of a romance – *The Mirour of Princely Deedes and Knighthood.*

Romance was a category much attacked by patriarchs and pedagogues: it could turn the minds of young women from their obligations. It could also, as Tyler's choice did, describe utopian codes of masculine conduct, in which men who offered violence were punished, love was esteemed and rewarded and adventures were sought by both sexes without censure. At a time when courtiers were composing odes comparing exemplary females to industrious silkworms, the romance stimulated dreams of possibility other than spinning cocoons. Isabella Whitney, too, though born into a literary family (her brother composed the famous emblem book), was placed out as a servant and there learned her letters, and became a poet. She solicited male patrons to recommend her enterprise and justify it too; an anonymous gentleman wrote in the foreword: 'She doth not write the brute or force in Armes.'

In fact, she did 'write the brute', for she protested, in 'A Copy of a Letter . . . to her unconstant Lover', against the betrayals of sworn suitors. But, as Krontiris comments, she was caught in the fine mesh of inherited metaphor, and when she warned against men's falsehood, she fell back on received imagery:

> Beware of fair and painted talk,
> beware of flattery tongues,
> The Mermaides do pretend no good
> for all their pleasant Songs.

The speaking woman, her tongue freed by the ability to write as well as read, found that the emblem books were still filled with the iconology of female wantonness and frailty and their contradictory companions, fatality and power. It was Whitney's art that she sang like a siren but made believe that she had another kind of tongue. That was the fiction that individual women felt required to offer to the old gods who had decreed:

> A woman's Tongue that is as swift as thought,
> Is ever bad, and she herself starke Nought.

The first wave of postwar feminist history and criticism, concerned with oppression, gave way to the celebration of heroic lives and the establishment of individual women's fame. The new feminist historiography tends to dissolve these simple oppositions, revealing how women often had to work with the grain of misogyny, and then found the timber broke their tools.

1992

Obscenity

Last year, Westminster City Council delayed the renewal of the Institute of Contemporary Arts' theatre licence, because they questioned the performance of Karen Finlay, a New York cabaret artist. In her solo impersonations of male pornographic fantasy, Finlay uses much foul language and explicit description of sexual practices; like another writer/entertainer, Kathy Acker, she shocks by passing far beyond the limits of conventional female speech.

At the private Council hearing, I appeared for the ICA and found that I needed to deny the obscenity of Karen Finlay's act in order to avoid falling into the Council's hands. To argue that something is not obscene because it is art makes nonsense of Finlay's mission of revolt, as it does of many plays, novels and other *causes célèbres* of the long campaign to withstand further censorship. Art *can* be obscene, and some of its essence is obscene.

Obscenity's relation to depravity and corruption is, however, very slippery indeed. Finlay, for instance, can be placed in a traditional nexus of lewdness, comedy and morality. Some of the most disturbing images of the High Renaissance – the drawings and engravings of Hans Baldung Grien and his followers, the Beham brothers – were inspired by the Reformers' strictures against sin. In a bitter, satiric fashion, Baldung's images of naked witches at their profane rituals warn against such transgressions. But they are so lascivious – and powerful – that they are only published now in order to illustrate the pathology of the witch-hunts, rather than the exemplary preaching of the Reformation. Admonition remains a constant in obscenity: the sexual assaults and other acts of violence in current movies are often heirs of this puritanism, characterising the desire aroused by women as sinful and worthy only of bloody annihilation. Similarly, the contemporary writer/entertainer like Acker or Finlay with women's issues on her mind uses filth pro-phylactically, like a Medusa's head to turn to stone all assailants, real and imagined. Sexual fears dominate, so sexual insults spew forth to tame those fears.

Obscenity reaches beyond limits, and in so doing helps to define them. The continuing endeavour of the arts to uncover ourselves to ourselves entails a portrayal of many things we find under heaven but hope not to find in heaven. But obscenity's complex functions do not only produce outrage and shock. Curiously, laughter often follows as well. Because so many of the satyr plays are lost, we have forgotten that the Greek tragedians' cycles were rounded off with bawdy, to send the audiences home stronger. In the story of Demeter and Persephone an old woman called Iambe meets the goddess as she wanders grieving for her lost daughter. Demeter has not smiled since Persephone's abduction, but Iambe plays the fool, tells her dirty stories and makes obscene gestures until at last she laughs. Iambe's very name associates her with verse and the curative powers of language. As *The Name of the Rose* points out, laughter issues a challenge against all comers, even God. When audiences laugh watching slasher films or the rape scene in *Blue Velvet*, they may be obeying the survival instinct Freud praised when he wrote, in the 1927 paper on humour, 'the ego refuses to be distressed by the provocations of reality, to let itself be compelled to suffer. It insists that it cannot be affected by the traumas of the external world; it shows, in fact, that such traumas are no more than occasions for it to gain pleasure.'

I do not offer these suggestions about the human nature of obscenity in order to make it all feel better; belittling the power of violent and pornographic representations does not help anyone, whether participants, creators or audiences. But the ordeal of obscenity to which so many people submit – with pleasure – raises a much wider question than the availability of hard-core magazines and home videos. Such materials enclose fantasies of power in order to face down fantasies of terror. They may exacerbate the intensity of the fantasies, but they reflect widespread and existing attitudes which will not disappear. Sexual self-loathing, women's otherness, the association between cruelty and power, between violence and authority, are not going to fall away at the snip of an official censor's scissors. The changes have to come before.

There are other laws besides censorship, to control acts, rather than the representation of acts. The camera's need for real subjects and live action has altered the conditions under which obscenity is produced, and it has become essential for the law to protect individuals – children especially. But the issue of consent here is far from clear-cut: the blitheness of a Cicciolina, the Italian porno star turned parliamentary deputy, cannot be considered representative of most models' feelings about the lens.

As someone who cannot call in Freud's self-protective super-ego and laugh at comparatively soft films like *Blue Velvet*, who flinches at those portraits of my kind in the magazines in the local newsagents', and fears the excitement they inspire and the consequences of that excitement, I find it hard to argue that obscenity is there for us to use, to define our own limits, and that in the practice of daily life we can make it work against fear, not on fear's account. Yet any reading of this century's history reveals what a great evil censorship is. Even in small ways, censorship distorts and destroys knowledge and judgment – as, for example, in the picketing of the recent exhibition of Surrealist photographs at the Hayward Gallery. Many of the images of women *were* profoundly disturbing, but if they had been taken out, Surrealism would have looked nice and sanitary, and its fundamental aims and philosophy would have been hopelessly mis-represented.

For women, the problem is, as ever, to take hold of language and put the matter from our point of view: Iambe needs a hearing, a showing (any imitation of male pornography, no matter how rancorous, remains in my view a kind of flattery). A novel like Toni Morrison's *Beloved*, which faces infanticide and slavery without euphemism and creates a language to convey these obscenities, can show the way.

1981

Fighting Talk

'Stunning maisonette' reads the estate agent's sign. 'What a knock-out!' stands in two-inch-high letters above the pin-up with the knockers. 'We was thinking of doing it just for the crack of it,' the gas-fitter tells me, of a plan he and his mates at the yard were cooking up to relieve the tedium. (He could have said 'for the hell of it', meaning fun, too.) A friend writes a postcard from Korčula, Yugoslavia. 'The scenery is ravishing,' he says. The playwright tells an interviewer, 'The tutors were dead for it, but not the students.'[1]

'Staggering', 'knock-out', 'stunning', 'smashing', 'stupendous', 'cracking', 'flabbergasting', 'helluva', 'dead' – they have been in current use as praise, in adjectival or adverbial form, since the late nineteenth century at least; they qualify – with enthusiasm – objects of admiration, desired states like success, moments and conditions of well-being. Some have an upper-class slant: 'ripping', 'cracking', and the Wodehouse words 'killing', as in 'a killing story' or 'killingly funny'. Some have a more working-class register: 'dead right that is'.

Probably before Catullus spoke of love in terms of excruciating agony, certainly since the medieval mystics borrowed Latin expressions of rapture, Zeus's abductions provided a model of ecstasy. Although the context never proposes that rape and religious ravishment are the same, the imagination seems to falter before the power of the experience and fails to find another way of describing it, beyond the sphere of erotic encounter and assault. At the same time as the statutes warned of the penalties for 'Felonious Rapes or Ravishements of Women Maydes Wieves and Damsells' (1576), Thomas Bowes was writing, 'This degree of love may be rightly called ravishing, in which the lover is so rapt out of himselfe, that he forgetteth himselfe' (1586).[2]

The vocabulary of pleasure depends on the imagery of pain. Terms of wonder, appreciation, and awe evoke the body dealt a blow, or otherwise assaulted. It becomes difficult, in one semantic zone, to comb out the tangle between feelings that feel nice and feelings that feel nasty. Can widespread masochism be the answer? Is Freud's diagnosis of the death instinct sufficient explanation or indeed, an explanation at all? In some places where language is born, the twofold drive towards annihilation and bliss may bring forth new images of hurt: some of the drug culture's slang conjures states of recognisable pleasure – 'rush', 'buzz', or 'high'. But much of its imagery sifts the lexicon of hard knocks: phrases like 'getting a kick' or 'a bang', 'it blew me away', 'it took the top of my head off'; words for the dose – the 'hit'; and street talk for the drugs themselves – 'smack', 'crack'. Though the gas-fitter's 'crack' is Irish for fun, for the wackiness, the dizziness, and comes down a different road from the new American drug, it arrives at a similar destination, at the image of splitting, breaking open, with the memory of a whip's passage somewhere behind it. 'Flabbergasting', if one pauses over it for a moment, turns into an ancient-looking word – laying flab to waste?[3] 'Thrilling', one of the oldest ways of describing the shivers and tingling of pleasure, derives from Middle English *thirlen*, to pierce, as in nostrils: nose-thrills or nose holes. With the verb 'to pierce', as well as associated images of penetration and delving, the metaphor of forced entry still remains live, inspiring sympathetic tremors, unlike so many current violent expressions for physical bliss, from which the colour and power have faded. Saint Teresa's angel makes himself felt, through the text, when he lifts 'a great golden spear . . . and plunged [it] into my heart several times so that it penetrated to my entrails'.[4]

Such imagery attempts to communicate the reality of the pleasure, its tone and pitch and volume, by locating it in sensations that familiarly bring the body to the forefront of consciousness. However, just as Elaine Scarry argues that pain is 'unspeakable', in that a sufferer cannot express suffering in terms that will convey its intensity and its fullness to another who does not experience the same torment, so language stumbles and falls over the complexity of pleasure, and seeks to make it feel real and strong by invoking experiences that by their very power introduce a dominant note, sweeping aside all other sensations. Scarry writes that the ascetics scourged and otherwise punished themselves not to deny the body but to feel its presence so acutely that they shut out all else: 'so emphasizing the body that the contents of the world are cancelled and the path is clear for the entry of an unworldly, contentless force. It is in part this world-ridding, path-clearing logic that explains the obsessive presence of pain in the rituals of large, widely shared religions as well as in the imagery of intensely private visions.'[5] The estate agent who declares the maisonette to be stunning wants a prospective buyer to think of nothing else, in the same way as if, were he to fetch his client a stunning blow, he would effectively focus his victim's attention.

Obviously, the effect of exclusion explains only one part of this peculiar language of delight. Another model of relations governs the metaphors: the model of contest. It is not a simple model, however, for it affords different points of entry, which alter the angle of vision and change the meanings produced. From one position, fighting talk identifies pleasure with winning: a person experiencing pleasure is cast in the role of a winner; proves his prowess; enjoys the pleasure of success. As in sports, the feeling is 'knock-out' (boxing), its 'smashing' (tennis, or boxing again), the actor in question is a 'smash hit'. 'To make a killing', meaning financial success not murder, passes into usage to describe a grand 'slam' in the game of bridge. From this aspect, the model of contest represents the pleasured person as active, an agent of experience, a maker and bringer of sensation, a knock-out opponent, a killer player. As Scarry says, 'the particular perceptual confusion sponsored by the language of agency is the conflation of pain with power'.[6]

The imagery of contest flies towards a simple goal, to narrow the field and bring the whole confusing business of feelings within range. The sports trope helps to do this, because typically it envisages two contestants, who may be champions of single combat, or at most two teams confronting each other; there must be a lone winner, a supremo. Technology searches out the ultimate victor, beyond human faculties' reach, with electronic split-second stopwatches, computerised cameras. As Primo Levi writes in *The Drowned and the Saved*, the crowd loves spectator sports because they divide the issue so simply. Grey areas, margins, mixed feelings, torn loyalties, the 'half-tints and complexities' are abolished – or at least banished. The Manichaean tendency 'is prone to reduce the river of human occurrences to conflicts, and the conflicts to duels – we and they'.[7]

The model of contest contains at least two participants, however, and can be looked at, and entered, from the point of view of the vanquished as well as the victor. Fighting talk, when applied to the pleasures of sex, frequently abolishes the difference between them, and presents sexual conquest as annihilating defeat (locating much pleasure therein). What is significant with respect to stunning pin-ups and flabbergasting blondes and staggering maisonettes and so forth is that a blow is imagined where there is no blow, where there is sometimes no action, no movement even.

In such a bout, the smash hit has happened in the imagination of only one of the participants. It circulates from its origin therein, travelling to the body that brought about the effect, and is then attributed to that entity, which becomes a smashing girl, a stunning flat. The knock-out lover can be a champion and a victim at once, can see himself, through this duplicity of language, as both knocking and knocked.

At this point, the observation of the lexicographer Jonathon Green becomes important: much adverbial usage of 'smashing' and 'staggering' and so forth might be euphemistic, especially as such words, many occurring first in the late Victorian period, are tinged with gentility. They may be substituting for stronger intensives expressing pleasure, while retaining the trace of the original thought: 'ripping' and 'corking' instead of 'fucking'. ('A fucking beautiful maisonette.')[8] With the help of this insight we may find that just as the internal switchback – the hypallage – in the epithet 'ravishing' transposes the impulse to ravish from the beholder to the beheld, so the girl who is a smash hit at a party may simply be fucking lovely ('a corker') to the men who behold her. The descriptions of affect, all those invocations of physical stupefaction and exhaustion, of thrust and its climax in victory, of diminished consciousness in order to communicate some state of bliss, of stunning and being stunned, of the conquering hero overcome, of corking and uncorking, amount to the obvious, really. Does it have to be spelled out?

Familiar expressions of pleasure, the vernacular of sought-after sensation, are grown in the experience of sex; and the experience is being regarded from within a male body, envisaged from a man's vantage point. We are outside the territory, passionately invoked by feminists in France like Hélène Cixous and Luce Irigaray, of 'writing the body' of woman.

The symbolised body from which many shared terms of pleasure issue forth is not necessarily the only possible male body, or the only body of male experience. But it is one that historically and culturally we have inherited, one we understand to be inhabited by people of the male sex. And the lexical constraints on the concept of maleness seem to be tightening: the circulating vocabulary of masculinity insists upon action, aggression, prowess and conquest ever more intensely, to the great distress of parents who have sons, and the confusion of those sons themselves, not to speak of the general dismay of women. It is not always easy to occupy a summit; there is a terrible oppression in being exhorted to be the master sex as well. (And in this case, sympathy isn't wasted, for we are all implicated, men and women alike, in the parcelling out of value to gender.)

Taking two mass markets, for instance, with clearly sexually defined targets – toiletries and toys – the buckles of gender roles make themselves felt, and painfully. Eaux de Cologne for men are called Polo, Denim, Aramis, and Brut (the last no doubt after champagne, but not ignoring other connotations). The cosmetic companies want to avoid sissy overtones, obviously, so they stress the robust, musketeering, sporty character of their fragrances. (Women's perfumes are brewed in some pretty wild alembics these days: the latest concoctions are named Anaïs, Opium, Poison, as the *odor di femmina* becomes ever more *fatale*.)

Toy manufacturers have an equivalent need to overdetermine the products' gender, in that they do not want small boys to think they are being soppy, playing with dolls. One series of 'action figures' – a bestselling line – contains the following cast of characters: Budo, a samurai; Muskrat, a swamp warrior; Spearhead, a pointman, and Max, his bobcat: Hit & Run, a light infantry man; Lightfoot, an explosives expert; Hardball Multishot, a grenadier; Blizzard, an Arctic attack soldier; Charbroil, a flame-thrower, Sneak Peek, advanced reconnaissance; Crazylegs, an assault trooper; Gung-ho, a marine; Tunnel Rat, a sapper; Chuckles, an undercover agent; Falcon, a green beret; Jinx, ninja intelligence; and Dodger, Blocker, Blaster, and Knockdown, who man vehicles and weapons with names like the Eliminator, the Dominator, the X-wing Chopper.[9] As with men's perfumes, the nomenclature of dolls for boys puts down its roots in warfare and sports; but it communicates action and power not only semantically, through the meanings of its images, but aurally too: the names of the warriors and the scents are short; plosives and gutturals appear far in excess of their usual distribution (there is an element of orientalism in this, of harking back to ancient gods whose names begin with or include lots of *z*s and *k*s and *x*s too). If a name runs longer than two syllables, it usually ends with a consonant to forestall any impression of yielding or weakness. Girl children, meanwhile, are sold toys with long, meandering names – My Little Pony, Lady Lovelylocks and the Pixie Tails.

Two or three years ago, the Chinese press reported that in Jiangyong county in the province of Hunan a women's language had been discovered.[10] It was very old indeed; so old the script resembled the earliest writing known to the world, the characters on the oracle bones of the Shang. The photograph showed two eighty-year-old women, heads tied in headclothes and inclined together over a paper they both held, where some of the six hundred surviving characters were no doubt inscribed. The *China Daily* reported the findings of the Chinese anthropologist who had uncovered this remnant: the women had kept the language alive among themselves while weaving, and songs and poems and fragments of autobiography survive, even though one of the last 'seven sisters' who knew the language burned documents in order to preserve its secrecy; the language had also been used in a local goddess's temple where women prayed for good husbands and fertility.

Since the report there has been no more word of the language's character, though a dictionary and an edition of the surviving songs and poems were promised. In their absence, the secrecy opens into a wide fair country of dreams: will this prove that place where the muffled voice of women will be raised? Where the opposition male/female will not generate strings of corresponding pairs, strong/weak, above/below, reason/instinct, active/passive, robust/fragile, Marauder Motorcycle Tank/My Little Pony, Brut/Anaïs, and so forth? It's of course much more likely that this is dream, that a language, however secret it's kept, cannot be produced pure, out of the woman's ground of being (whatever that is) without reflection of her social and historical conditions. There exist languages in which women speak differently from men in obvious ways, conferring their gender on their utterances, as in Romance languages' agreement of subject and participle, or in Iroquois, where a phrase like *my house* becomes a word of feminine gender on the lips of a woman, masculine on a man's. But such grammatical conventions yield scanty insights into tradition, history, or psychology.[11]

In English, no rules of grammar follow from the speaker's sex, and the language itself is politely neutral, conferring neither gender nor animation on objects that in French, for instance, are always feminine, like *la bête*, the beast or insect, and *la victime*, the victim. The poet Tom Disch has urged,

> It is a lovely language,
> English. One senses, instinctively, listening
> To it, that it was created, like chromosomes,
> In strict parity by women and by men:
> By Mother Goose and Father Time
> With their long memories, by the quick
> Co-equal wits of Mirabell and Millamant.[12]

But Mother Goose and Father Time have different memories, and English is gendered beyond the rules of grammar, as psychologists and sociologists are discovering. There's a wondrously rich and old vocabulary to describe precisely the different and varied character of female speech (which can be practised by men, but at their peril). To prattle, chatter (chit-chat), tattle (tittle-tattle), tongue-wag, gush, are not manly things; 'my gossip' used to mean 'my friend', spoken by a woman, of a woman; scolds, nags, tongue-lashers, wheedlers, complainers, screechers, railers are, notoriously, women; as many writers before me have pointed out, one man's oratory is a woman's stridency; one man's fluency is a woman's garrulity. Of course English isn't the only language to categorise women's talk so richly. In a carnival mood, the Dutch produced an anti-saint, Alwaere ('All-true'), patroness of raucousness and rowdiness, of strife and quarrelling, who wears a screeching magpie on her head and rides a braying ass.[13]

The very abundance of words denigrating women's speech tells us not that women kept quiet – hardly – but that they were guilty because they failed, in Emily Dickinson's word, to be 'still'.[14]

So, if women's disobligingness in the matter of silence rings down the centuries in the insults against their wagging tongues, can the particular language of female affect be found? And if it can, where? Women might buy a stunning maisonette, and like to look ravishing, and respond with excitement to the smashing prices at the supermarket, and so forth. But without being essentialist about women's bodies and universalising all female sensation, the historical witness of women's writings and other testimony, like the records of trials, reveals an inclination to a different set of blissful blazons, a different way of invoking pleasure, which imagines a woman's body as the site of well-being.

Besides the eye and the genitals, the other organs of sense pass on to women special information of pleasure. In Caroline Walker Bynum's eloquent study of female mystical practice and rhetoric in the High Middle Ages, imagery of nurturance (of mother's milk and the blood of generation, of flesh as food) dominates the visions of Catherine of Siena and her later compatriot, Catherine of Genoa, offering to the reader or hearer's senses – one could say dishing out – a personal eroticism.[15] While unsavoury to contemporary taste, this keyed-up language of appetite succeeds in transmitting undreamed-of states of pleasure, felt by women. The divine bridegroom here does not stun the visionary, or even pierce her, so much as offer himself in draughts of milk and blood, often presenting his incarnate body in the image of the visionary's renounced maternity:

'My beloved,' [Christ] said to her [Catherine of Siena], 'you have now gone through many struggles for my sake . . . I today shall give you a drink that transcends in perfection any that human nature can provide . . .' With that, he tenderly placed his right hand on her neck, and drew her toward the wound in his side. 'Drink, daughter, from my side,' he said, 'and by that draught your soul shall become enraptured with such delight that your very body, which for my sake you have denied, shall be inundated with its overflowing goodness.'[16]

Fancying a man today, young women still return to the metaphors of the mouth: 'Dishy,' they say, or 'very tasty'; they might find a caress 'delicious', a glimpse of tight jeans 'juicy'. This is not to claim that a man will not speak of a woman in these terms too, but just that in the current vocabulary of pleasure, women incline to metaphors of nourishment, not always of spectacle or violent action. Often, they are not themselves the imagined consumer, but offer themselves for consumption.

In the Sixties and Seventies, some polemicists were angered by endearments – and curses – turning women into food (sweetiepie, honeybunch) and their sexual parts into fruits (cherry, melons). But it has to be said that women, exploring union from a female somatic viewpoint, have themselves deeply enriched the trope. When the motif of ravishment appears, imagery of engulfment follows in the train of the threat to integrity, and the encounter comes accompanied by images of immersion and incorporation – analogous to the eucharistic union with Christ in the mystics' thought, the oneness with the saviour achieved by eating him. To take one example, from the nineteenth century: Emily Dickinson's famous poem, beginning 'I started Early', tells of her encounter with the tide, vividly personified in the poem as a pursuer:

> But no Man moved Me – till the Tide
> Went past my simple Shoe –
> And past my Apron – and my Belt
> And past my Bodice – too –
>
> And made as He would eat me up –
> As Wholly as a Dew
> Upon a Dandelion's Sleeve –
> And then – I started – too –
>
> And He – He followed – close behind –
> I felt His Silver Heel
> Upon my Ankle – Then my Shoes
> Would overflow with Pearl – [17]

The water's movement, imagined from the I's viewpoint with startling intimacy, begins by immersing her ('past my bodice – too'), then swallowing her (like dew drenching a flower), to spilling out of her shoes, in a sequence of metaphors that attribute to her pursuer, coming after her like a man giving chase in a dream, certain engulfing, oceanic, flooding, and devouring characteristics traditionally ascribed to the female body in the act of love. Describing her own state – and the poem conveys vivid, reverberating pleasure – Emily Dickinson pictures the assailing tide in the image of female sexuality, accomplishing a reversal comparable to that of the mystics, who taking Christ's body into their own in the form of the host feel themselves to be incorporated. The highly wrought erotic picture of the shoes, overflowing with pearl, first comes up before the eyes as Aphrodite foam, but does not stay there, as specular pleasure. It expands to excite the senses of taste and touch: to place before us cups and chalices brimming.

'Writing is precisely the very possibility of change,' writes Hélène Cixous in her rhapsodic manifesto 'The Laugh of the Medusa', where she rails at the silencing of women, their difficulty of speech because the dominant language belongs to the law-makers, the fathers.[18] Though not tongue-tied myself, though able, by privilege of education and profession, to express myself in language, and make myself heard (I think, sometimes), I recognise what Cixous is saying, because I find my voice falters in the site of pleasure, that I have no words for it, that there, I am gagged. The words that circulate don't suit ('That was smashing'? 'You're a knock-out'?). And far beyond the personal sphere of well-being and of sensual gratification, in ever widening rings, the language of appreciation is intertwined with metaphors of violence; consider the critics' stock of terms: *impact, force, explosive, searing*. Women don't avoid the imagery either. A fellow-novelist, writing about Louise Erdrich, says '*The Beet Queen* imparts its freshness of vision like an electric shock.'[19]

Catherine Clément, Cixous's collaborator on *La jeune née* (*The Newly Born Woman*), talks of the nervous cough Dora developed because she could not speak her story, and of Rosalie, a singer, who could no longer sing after she had witnessed her uncle's abuses; their pages are filled with so many Procnes and Philomels, the stifled voices of the exemplary heroic hysterics of the past, whom they idealise in the interest of their own impassioned rallying cry.[20]

Sometimes, this kind of desire to hymn women's oppression leads to exaggeration of their enforced silence, and a paradoxical diminishment of women's place in history and in culture; but it seems to me that in this matter, the expression of pleasure, the character of our metaphors shapes the character of those feelings. Is saying something violently saying it well? Is feeling something violently feeling it in the only possible way? Perhaps, if we were to set aside the language of pain, we might find our shoes, too, filling with pearl.

1990

Saint Cunera's Scarf

Talk given at the Writers' Conference, Dublin

In a world where violent nationalisms threaten, where refugees from despotism, famine and other ills grow in numbers daily, and America's solitary superpower status looms over all, the idea of Europe presents a safe house. But Europe is like the king in the story who leaves his daughter three caskets – the folktale Shakespeare uses in *The Merchant of Venice*: we are not the beneficiaries of a single bequest. We have to choose between many legacies – many more than the gold, silver and lead of the story.

To arrive at my idea of the European legacy I borrowed a tool used by historians of thought to trace shifting attitudes to male and female differences: discrimination by polarity. Man is the opposite of woman; perhaps, but both men and women are the opposites of – say – crocodiles, or teapots. Europe is the opposite of . . . America? Yes. And no. There are writers born in the United States here at this conference, like Edmund White, and many others who live there, like Joseph Brodsky, who dissolve any stand-off between the continents: we only have to think – to throw out a few names – of Cotton Mather's puritanism, Jefferson and Franklin's radical ideas of citizenship, or of Kate Chopin, Edith Wharton and John Ashbery, to see that the legacy of Europe can't be disentangled from US culture and history, can't be defined in opposition to America.

If we think of Europe as the Old World, then perhaps we can arrive at a pole on which definitions of Europe turn: Europe is old, Europe is the opposite of . . . Australia, say, or rather of Australia after it was settled by Europeans.

This casket has been buried deep and bulges to overflowing with a mass of stuff going far far back, to Euripides and Gottfried von Strassburg and Mme de La Fayette and Colette. Yet who can say Europe is the exclusive key-holder to this casket? Derek Walcott's great poem *Omeros* reveals how a single poet can swallow a whale – rather than the other way around – dream several months and days and nights with the whale of Western history in his belly and then tell a tale of the meeting of Old World and New in the Caribbean as a modern Odyssey. His vantage point can't be trapped within a definition of 'European', though the material, the references, the versification knowingly echo European masters.

In *Omeros*, Walcott writes: 'Time is the metre; memory the only plot.' The legacy of Europe lies in deep time, and the act of memory can order its higgledy-piggledy abundance into a story – a story which constantly changes, depending on who is telling it.

But when I say that Europe is old, I don't want to set up her bejewelled, encrusted body against the rest of the world in some superior relation: if we start that game, the Iraqis, with Sumer and Mesopotamia and Babylon, will win it, no contest, which is why Saddam Hussein thought he could redeem his Westernised military dictatorship by rebuilding the Hanging Gardens of Babylon. The appeal to the past as a legitimising move stinks of demagoguery: Le Pen spuriously lays claim to Joan of Arc and Chartres Cathedral as pure French. The notion of a pure tradition should be met with derision wherever it is raised: tradition must be impure, or it cannot thrive. As Primo Levi writes in *The Periodic Table*, 'in praise of impurity':

> [it] gives rise to changes, in other words, to life . . . In order for the wheel to turn, for life to be lived, impurities are needed, and the impurities of impurities in the soil, too, as is known if it is to be fertile. Dissension, diversity, the grain of salt and mustard are needed.

When I choose an old casket I do not want it made of stable gold, but of something changeable, like copper, turning different colours with time, or – if it were possible to make something tangible at all from this metal – of mercury. The most European country of all, it seems to me, from the geophysical perspective, is Holland: made out of the sea, constantly changing shape, moving dykes and channels to grow bigger here, smaller there, and yet unmistakably itself.

And Europe is also new – it is being made over new in all the countries of the Eastern bloc. It is being reorganised economically – and we realise how inexorably economics lead political change today. The UK's Thatcherite remnant, as you all know, still wishes to counter this new, political unity of Western Europe with its own Tom Thumb isolationist heroics. Here one European country becomes the opponent of others: the legacy divides its heirs and starts them quarrelling, as legacies do. There will be many practical problems for writers in this new Europe.

The Aristotelian list of related opposites includes:

oneness and plurality
right and left
straight and curved
stasis and movement
light and darkness
good and evil
black and white
odd and even

And of course male and female. Europe from the Eurocentric vantage point would belong to the male side; not female, not barbarian: enlightened, rational, democratic, light as opposed to dark. Europe's feminine origin, in the story of her rape by Zeus, has been forgotten. Europe has become the place where the handshake was invented as a sign of fellowship and trust, and the handshake has spread through the world as a tell-tale sign of the European spirit. (But it is of course a pledge that has been honoured in the breach as well as the observance.)

However, the casket I choose does not radiate the light of equality and reason in quite this sense, this philosophical, eighteenth-century sense.

To me, the legacy of Europe is above all an old story, a body of myths held in common, not a geographical entity or a political tradition or a collection of élite names – princes, poets, warriors. Though it is all those things. It is an old story which gives pleasure but does not quite convince; however, it unites those who hear it because it enmeshes common beliefs and imagery and a language of thought: the legacy of Europe is a certain cast of the imagination.

The most striking parallel with today's circumstances seems to me to be Hellenism; the condition of Graeco-Roman culture in the early Christian world. Dozens of different peoples, nations, races, creeds jostled in this world from the second century to the rise of Islam. In a recent book, *Hellenism in Late Antiquity*, G. W. Bowersock writes:

> Hellenism, which is a genuine Greek word for Greek culture (*Hellenismos*), represented language, thought, mythology, and images that constituted an extraordinarily flexible medium of both cultural and religious expression. It was a medium not necessarily antithetical to local or indigenous traditions. On the contrary, it provided a new and more eloquent way of giving voice to them.

This is what we are seeing – to view the matter in the most optimistic light – in Europe today: the mediation of English as an expressive language, used for personal as well as literary communication, corresponds to the currency of Latin in the Hellenistic world. That time was also polytheistic, in spite of the rulers' conversion: pagan oracles, divinities and rites continued to flourish, much to the anger of Christian Fathers. In several areas, at different times, heathens escaped persecution. Plurality of beliefs was considered a mark of civilisation. Belief is a complex concept – it can be allegiance, rather than creed, and this plurality too can be part of the legacy we accept, when Catholic fundamentalism as well as Islamic is on the march and the language of intolerance, to which the Christian Church is also prone, makes itself heard again.

The plural unity of the Hellenised world was woven of stories above all. Not only of religious myths, but of secular mythology too. This is the casket of the European inheritance which I would choose: Hellenism produced the great romances, tragicomic wonder-tales; sometimes called *erotia pathemata* – 'tales of erotic suffering'; Apollonias of Rhodes' *Voyage of Argo*; Lucian's *True History*; Ovid's *Metamorphoses* and the related book, Apuleius' *The Golden Ass*. This metaphysical adventure story, with its frank sexuality and its hero's angst, is a recognisable precursor of the modern novel, and more particularly of the contemporary hybrid novel, magical realist, sad and jolly all at once. Romance, a genre that was thoroughly despised until recently, is returning: obviously in popular literature, but also in cunningly wrought, profoundly thought out comedies: Angela Carter's new novel, *Wise Children*, exuberantly mines all the conventions of the genre in a tremendous act of homage to the Shakespeare of comic mischief and enchanted reconciliations: the Shakespeare of *A Midsummer Night's Dream*, not *Henry V*, of *The Comedy of Errors*, not *Hamlet*.

From this barnacled Hellenistic casket, I'm going to pick one bright object and show it to you, to illustrate what I mean, and to pay homage to our gathering here in Ireland.

I was recently in Utrecht, in the Netherlands, and in the Catharijneconvent Museum I came across a glass case in which lay a murder weapon from an old, medieval crime: it was a stole woven of fine cream silk with silver thread – Byzantine work, sixth century. It had been used, said the label, to strangle Saint Cunera, by a wicked queen who was jealous of the young woman's goodness and her beauty when she came to live at court.

The story will already have rung certain bells with those of you raised on fairy tales – this Saint Cunera is a predecessor of Snow White, her story belongs to the famous Constance cycle of folklore and turns up in different forms, in classical, medieval and modern stories all over the European, or – if I may – neo-Hellenistic world. Now, Cunera was the only survivor of the massacre at Cologne, in the seventh century, of Saint Ursula and her eleven thousand virgins: by a miracle, she was spared that fate at the hands of the Huns, only to fall victim later to a cruel woman.

Ursula and her maidens were from the westernmost part of the continent of Europe – Christians from Britain or Brittany – and they had travelled to Cologne, then an easternmost frontier of Christendom in fantasy. They had done so (according to one variation of the legend) in order to join Saint Maurice and the Theban Legion. Maurice is the black African soldier saint who, in the third century, refused to carry out an imperial order to murder innocent Christians, and was himself butchered in revenge, along with 6,666 men of his legion.

We may laugh. But these stories inspired not only the faithful, of course, but poets and musicians like Hildegard of Bingen in the twelfth century, Renaissance painters like Memling and Carpaccio, and pioneer educators like Angela Merici, who in the sixteenth century founded the Ursuline order to teach poor girls – maybe they saw, as we may see also, past the preposterousness of the plot to the metaphors it encloses: about persecution and suffering, about love and sympathy between people of like minds that transcend issues of nation, language, and race and geography.

There was a time when I would have attacked such a legend as a compendium of Judaeo-Christian bigotry, savage and sadistically misogynist. I've tried elsewhere in my work to criticise this aspect of the European legacy, and now I am more interested in reinterpreting it to yield up new meanings helpfully. When you have a rocky path ahead, it is best to make shoes with what you have, rather than go barefoot.

In those long ago times we are wrong to call dark, stories seem to have travelled fast, acquiring resonance and depth, imagining the world in the shape of need and desires – almost as fast and far as satellites transmit tales today: the scarf that strangled Ursula's last virgin was woven in Syria thirteen hundred years ago, lies in Holland today, and belongs in a story every child knows. This is a bit of the European legacy – and one of the places where I read about it was in Butler's *Lives of the Saints*, the gigantic work by Alban Butler, published in this city, Dublin, in twelve volumes, in 1779–80.

Taking this casket, the tinsel casket of folklore, fancy, and myth – even of superstition – doesn't mean consenting to its contents or affirming them – the salt, the mustard which make the material live are irony and humour, as Italo Calvino, Danilo Kiš, Dubravka Ugrešic, Salman Rushdie have shown us; scepticism and pleasure are not incompatible, as anyone who has loved knows – but I believe it is in this casket that we can find the vitality of local particularity and identity, thriving in tolerant coexistence.

1991

Language, Power, Fear

Talk given in Oxford on European Languages Studies Day, a fortnight after the attack on the World Trade Center

At the end of *Manon Lescaut*, one of the most powerful and elegant of eighteenth-century romances, the heroine is found guilty of immorality and sentenced to deportation from France, her native country: the novel was published in Paris in 1713 and so when the Abbé Prévost, its author, was setting the scene of Manon's exile, he chose a French colony. Manon is embarked for exile to La Nouvelle Orléans in *la Louisiane*, New Orleans in Louisiana, called after the great royal city and King Louis XIII, in the now southern states of America. Manon's piteously ruined state so inflames her fated lover, the Chevalier des Grieux, that he jumps on board the prison ship to be with her. In Puccini's impassioned opera *Manon Lescaut*, first performed in 1893, she expires in the last act in the empty, shelterless heat and dust of the American wilderness, while the Chevalier tries to find water for her. There she sings a long lament, a classic aria of a woman *sola, perduta, abbandonata* – alone, lost, abandoned.

In the eighteenth century, much of North America was French and francophone: in the north, Quebec had been settled by a pioneering Ursuline nun who brought with her the very efficacious relics of Saint Anne, mother of the Virgin Mary, which had been responsible for the conception of the Sun King himself; in the south, the Mississippi delta and many islands of the Caribbean bore the imprint of their owners' culture (Guadeloupe and Martinique are still *départements* of metropolitan France, and belong inside the zone of the Euro). The poet Aimé Césaire (born 1913), great voice of *négritude* in the Thirties, was Mayor of Martinique's capital, Fort-de-France, for many decades as well as the longest-serving *député* to the Chamber in Paris.

This French Creole culture threads rich nutrient-bearing capillaries through French and American writing: Baudelaire for one had it in mind in his famous 'Invitation au voyage', the poem which has given phrases that have become proverbial also in English:

> Là, tout n'est qu'ordre et beauté,
> Luxe, calme et volupté!

> (There, all is order and beauty,
> Luxury, calm and voluptuousness!)

Edgar Allan Poe, whom Baudelaire admired inordinately, and whom he translated, produced his novel atmosphere of the horrid and the uncanny from local ingredients: his southern Gothic is macabre, bizarre, grotesque and baroque – all words of French origin, not coincidentally.

In 1803, a generation before Poe was writing and a generation after the War of Independence from its colonial rulers the British, the new American republic bought Louisiana from the French – for $15,000,000. The historian Niall Ferguson recently edited a book of virtual history, full of 'counterfactuals' as he called them – imaginary turnings the flow of events could have taken. For example, what if Hitler had been killed in 1939? I don't recall if anyone asked what would have happened if the Louisiana Purchase had not been made. But if Americans spoke French, things would have been different. For the world, and certainly for all of us who speak English as well. It would have shifted the distribution of power

– I can't develop this theme here, even if I knew what it would have
entailed exactly – but I think you can appreciate the force of this
counterfactual. A language carries codes of identity, creates bonds and
allegiances across frontiers, communicates the stories of the past and local
principles of ethics and justice. It strengthens common bonds and is
formed by the circumstances of its use as it develops. Above all, a language
embodies power, reproduces positions of authority, and subordination.
To impose a language, or to forbid a language, represents a tyrant's first
move.

The threat which has cast its shadow on us since September 11 has
made me think hard about those conditions of freedom by which I live
now by right, casually, even instinctively. Among many things we are
suffering, we are certainly suffering mutual incomprehension, a
reciprocal incomprehension; monolithic enmities and crude dialectics
inevitably find linguistic expression.

The domination of English as the global language of markets, share
deals, air traffic control, credit cards, law, travel agents, film, satellite
television news, disturbingly mirrors the networks of power that have been
so fatally occupied and perverted by the terrorists. This hegemony has also
been growing fast: especially since the ending of the Cold War. It
reproduces some of the heedlessness which Western democracy has shown
– towards it own conduct as well as towards its neighbours and, above all,
towards human resources elsewhere. It's not just that assuming other
people will learn your language assumes the rights of a feudal lord when
the time for feudalism is up. My argument is less cynical, more humanistic
in its drift: knowing other languages opens up curiosity about other people
and their feelings and beliefs, it lifts ignorance and makes possible
plurality, complexity, subtlety – it sharpens intelligence, both as
information and as a quality of mind. Amin Maalouf, in his recent book
Les Identités meurtrières, writes, 'no one should be forced to become a
mental expatriate . . .' (translated as *On Identity* by Barbara Bray, the book
recently won the Scott-Moncrieff Prize). Monoglot globalism does not
equip us to adapt: in its limitations and myopia it strikes me as an
evolutionary trait about as enabling as the horns on a stag beetle that have
grown so big and heavy that the insect can't right itself when knocked over.

'We must love one another or die,' writes Auden in 'September 1939', his
tremendous poem, every line of which still calls to us now. But we can *think*
as well as love . . . or die, and languages are the tools of thought; without
them, memory, connection, mutuality and all that flows from them – law,

justice, legitimacy – weaken. And it is only by living by the internationally shared principles of democracy that we can make our stand.

Early in the same poem, Auden writes:

> All the conventions conspire
> To make this fort assume
> The furniture of home;
> Lest we should see where we are,
> Lost in a haunted wood,
> Children afraid of the night
> Who have never been happy or good.

By accidents of fortune, I was a child in other parts of the world: I first learned about fear in Egypt, when my father's English and French language bookshop was burned down in 1952, during the first significant insurgency of Arab nationalism and the last complacent period of the British empire. Black Sunday, as this riot was called, now seems a presage of what has happened. But I was also growing up, as it happened, in the polyglot, mixed, motley, international Mediterranean which had existed continuously since Hellenistic Greece and even before, since Phoenician times. French was the lingua franca (exactly so) of the cosmopolitan community in the southern and eastern Mediterranean; from Morocco to Lebanon, and it included Jews, Greeks, Arabs. It has been almost completely broken up. I also knew Arabic, but neither the later circumstances of my life nor my education fostered any development of *that* knowledge, unfortunately – and revealingly. Furthermore, my mother comes from Puglia, in southern Italy or Magna Graecia, where some of the most beautiful ruins of ancient Greece still stand. She had a brother called Pericles, and her nickname, because she liked to dance the Charleston, was Terpsichore, the muse of Dance.

After Cairo, where I went to French nuns, we moved to Brussels, and more nuns, Belgian this time: filing into class, we sang patriotic songs about Joan of Arc and against the Duke of Marlborough, and the school stood on the rue Edith Cavell, heroine of the French Resistance (I thought she was French). This is a very complex history, and I'm aware that the French imposed their language on their territories – in Algeria with terrible consequences – so that *francophonie* can't be held up as an unmixed ideal. The Belgian Congo, for example, featured prominently in national propaganda about the might and dazzle of the Belgian empire; we were taught to pray for the souls of black babies. But because my

French was learned outside France, as this lingua franca reaching far beyond ethnic and political boundaries, it helped to alert me to contingency, international tensions, and the relation of language to power. Later, as a student, I discovered another side to French culture, more Parisian, more to do with cafés, Juliette Gréco, Simone de Beauvoir and Jean-Luc Godard, and of course I still haven't begun to touch more than the surface of its great deposits.

The legacy of *francophonie* still includes a flourishing Caribbean literature. Derek Walcott has acknowledged the influence of his aunt Sidonie and her Creole stories in his Nobel Prize address and his poetry is richly inflected by Creole patois from the island where he was born, St Lucia, as well as from Trinidad where he worked for a long time in the theatre. In 'world music' the pattern can probably be felt most vibrantly of all: it can be heard on Radio Three's exuberant programme *Late Junction* and the programmes of the ethnomusicographer Lucy Duran.

When I was first invited to give this talk, before September 11, I suggested that I would talk about lullabies and children's songs: because they are the most common, easiest and best way into a new language.

When the French Symbolist poet Stéphane Mallarmé was working as a teacher of English in Paris, he became fascinated with English nonsense rhymes, ditties and catches; and he translated them into French for his pupils, expounding the rules of the language through such verses as:

> For this little cock-sparrow would make a nice stew
> And his giblets would make a nice little pie, too.

> 'Oh! No,' says cock-sparrow, 'I won't make a stew.'
> And he fluttered his wings, and away he flew.

A schools inspector chanced to come in just as Mallarmé was teaching the following rhyme to the children at the Lycée Fontanes in 1880, and translating it word for word:

> Liar liar lick spit
> Your tongue shall be slit
> And all the dogs in the town
> Shall have a little bit.

The report was withering: 'M. Mallarmé, as he is to remain a teacher of English . . . should learn English . . . he should not dictate . . . foolish rubbish like "Liar liar lick spit".' He then gave in full Mallarmé's polished version of the rhyme, and concluded, blustering, 'One is tempted to ask oneself if one is not in the presence of a sick man.'[1] However, it is likely that Mallarmé's pupils learned English rapidly and with relish.

The two themes – children's nonsense and international language circulation – are not as disconnected as they might seem. As utterances of children afraid of the night who have never been happy or good, they are linked both in theme and origin: the need to allay terror surges in many lullabies. These earliest songs express the dread of forces both unknown and in some cases known, and reveal how deeply we have all at one time experienced vulnerability and helplessness. And they are also above all part of the language of women and children, though many male composers and poets and singers – as well as fathers and grandfathers – have of course involved themselves in developing and transmitting them.

Such rhymes and songs are often anonymous and of uncertain date and origin all over the world; they have always been there, perhaps not in that precise form or tune, but in existence. On a practical point: learning such songs is one of the most efficient ways to pick up a language's phonetics – to shape its characteristic sounds. Linguisticians argue that human beings sing lullabies and nursery rhymes to their babies the world over in order to impart language: like birds, we acquire our species songs easily when young. This is not to say of course that it can't be done later – it can, but there will almost inevitably remain a trace of the first native song in the second language's lilt, tonality and shapes.

These songs also reveal language's first shoots rising in conditions not of power but of powerlessness. Or rather, to sharpen the focus more closely, they frequently express intimations of conflict and violence, of damage and harm. They are uttered by people without power, those who are first to suffer from war.

One of the first French nursery rhymes I learned as a child told the story of a little boy who goes to sea and sails the Mediterranean: the tune was jaunty, the words sounded gay and bright:

> Il était un petit navire (*bis*)
> Qui n'avait ja- ja- jamais navigué (*bis*)
> Ohé matelot!
> Matelot, navigue sur les flots!

(There was once a little boat
Which had never never gone to sea . . .
Hoho sailor!
Sailor, sail the sea!)

After being at sea five or six weeks, the little boat runs out of victuals and the crew begin to starve. So the men draw lots, and it's the youngest who draws the short straw. So it will be he who will be eaten, the song tells us, merrily:

Le sort tomba sur le plus jeune (*bis*)
C'est lui qui sera mangé (*bis*)
Ohé matelot etc.

Finally, in the same blithe spirit, the song describes how the sailors deliberate what sauce to cook him in and whether he should be fried or fricasséed.

Such nursery songs are by no means all so cheery in tone. A most terrifying ogre, *le grand Lustucru* (whose name means 'the Great-would-you-believe it?'), has stalked francophone children's imaginations since the seventeenth century at least. In this spookiest and most melancholy of lullabies, the bogeyman comes at night, clanking his chain, carrying the knapsack in which he bundles bad children who won't go to sleep.

Who do we want to identify with? Who are we? Whose side are we on? How do we stop Lustucru? How do we know if we are being Lustucru? How do we learn to think better? To feel more scrupulously? To guard what we value?

The conditions of vulnerability and correspondingly the threat of power are woven into the very tissue of language from the earliest stages of acquisition. Death by violence, famine, rapine and conflict is one of the most vivid personae inhabiting the nursery ballad or ditty. Ogres haunt children. The gaiety of the tune acts so as to defy the fear, as an apotropaic spell to ward off danger. The ironising and comic mode of the story toughens up the child listener. Or, again, to be more careful with meaning and implication, children are trained up to watch out for ogres: or, even more carefully, the menace that ogres brandish is both deployed and used to warn against ogreish behaviour.

Mallarmé was aware of this. He glosses accordingly one of the nursery rhymes which he taught – and which he translated into French. He takes, 'There was an old woman/ Tossed up in a blanket,/ Seventeen times as high as the moon' and with humour and irony tempered with genuine concern, he writes, 'Witch or not, those clowns should have first considered that they were dealing with an elderly woman.'

What does this tell us? That the task of dealing with our fears begins – perhaps haltingly – in the first dramatic scenes that language brings into being.

Italo Calvino in *Invisible Cities* describes Marco Polo telling the Great Khan all about the world, its variety, its fantastic places and peoples. But the Great Khan rebels against these fanciful accounts.

He protests, 'Why do you amuse yourself with consolatory fables?'

To which Polo answers, 'This is also the aim of my explorations: examining the traces of happiness still to be glimpsed, I gauge its short supply. If you want to know how much darkness there is around you, you must sharpen your eyes, peering at the faint lights in the distance.'

It helps to have more ways of reading the pinpricks of light in the distance; there are more of them, too, if they're intelligible, if the signals they flash speak.

2001

The Sign of the Dollar

Lecture given at the Palazzo Steri, Palermo

Like thousands, indeed millions of visitors to New York, I have a snapshot of myself on the Staten Island ferry, against a background of the Twin Towers. I didn't admire the towers, not especially, but they marked, as monuments do, the place: they unmistakably identified where I was. They would come to define, as I could not have known, a certain limited period of time when I could have been there, the quarter of a century between 1976 and 2001.

The harbour waters of Lower Manhattan of course enclose an older symbolic colossus, the Statue of Liberty, who has welcomed immigrants from her island to America since the nineteenth century. In *The Lost Father*, Davide Pittagora, the eponymous hero, is emigrating from southern Italy with thousands of others who left in the period around the turn of the nineteenth century. He beholds the statue as he arrives with his wife, having lost their first baby on the passage over, and for him Liberty announces a new life, a gateway to freedom, opportunity, wealth. My novel *The Lost Father* tracks the story of these hopes, how they become embroiled in the prejudice and hostility of Americans towards Italians, and how the family fails and returns to Ninfania, the name of the province in my novel. When that photograph of me was taken against the Twin Towers, I was researching the experiences of Italians in New York at the beginning of the twentieth century, and in the archives of the research center for the history of immigration on Staten Island I found that my grandfather's story, on which I based *The Lost Father*, followed the characteristic rise and fall of southern Italian migration in those years, and that 1921, the year that Luigi Terzulli gave up his American venture, saw the increasing crisis around the Sacco and Vanzetti case, the growing intolerance shown Italians on account of their association with labour agitation and syndico-anarchism, and the corresponding return, in huge numbers, of many Italians to the land of their birth. This political turbulence forms the setting of *The Lost Father*.

The destruction of the Twin Towers has closed a historical period of American politics, with direct bearing on attitudes to outsiders, to foreign-born, to migrants. We have entered a new phase of the Closed Door, which echoes what occurred in the Twenties when the Open Door of American mass immigration was also shut.

In this talk I am going to look at the complex multilayerings of the symbol of the doorway to America, and unpack the history behind the worldwide ciphers of its allure, its wealth, the dollar. The two signs – the dollar and the gateway of opportunity – are indissolubly linked.

You write '£' without thinking, and sometimes, even now, you might say '£.s.d.', meaning money, dough, cash, bread, dosh, moolah, though £ doesn't stand for any of those, except, possibly, for lolly. Any child over the age of ten can read the $ sign. At a guess, anyone anywhere in the world can now read the $ sign. It's entirely accepted, it's one of those invisible conventional signs that few question. Like many such invisible presences, put it under a lens and it turns out to be packed with stuff: like the first drop of water under the microscope, it's teeming with living phenomena, and some of them, with regard to the $ and the present global crisis, are full of meaning. It is, to pick up a phrase of Paul Ricoeur, a symbol that indeed gives rise to thought.

The story behind the £ sign is simple: it's the first letter of *libra*, meaning pound (as in Italian *lira*), and the two strokes through the upright stem signify, in standard scrivener's shorthand, an abbreviated word. Likewise, s. stands for *soldo*, and d. for *denaro* (all Italian words because the first Family, the Medici, pioneered banking). But $ doesn't look anything like a D for dollar.

Visit the Web and you will find there many theories, none of them worth the RAM they occupy. For example: that the two downward strokes on the $ sign lost their joining bit at the bottom and really stand for U – the U of United States.

Another theory came to my mind soon after 9/11 last year, and it tugged at my memory: according to an art-historical theory well known in Spain (for reasons that will become clear) but not much rehearsed elsewhere, the original dollar showed the Pillars of Hercules, and somehow, in some way I hadn't yet discovered, these pillars had turned into the $ sign. With help from the British Museum's Coins and Medals Department, I pieced the story together.

Rather surprisingly, I feel, it takes us back to no less a figure than Dante.

Rising through the stars, on the very edge of Cloud Nine, the fastest revolving, crystalline sphere of the heavens, Dante looks back earthwards, and sees, beyond the western edge of continental Europe, the passage of Ulysses into the Atlantic: 'On the one hand I saw, beyond Cadiz, the mad track of Ulysses, and on the other almost to the shore where Europa made herself a sweet burden.'[1]

The 'mad track of Ulysses' took him through and beyond the straits of Gibraltar to his death, according to Dante, and in this essay my own journey will follow in his wake, through the Pillars of Hercules, which stood at the limen where the Mediterranean opened on to the Atlantic Ocean; I will explore that gateway as a symbol of limits, and the columns as the 'renowned witnesses' to the '*suprema orbis meta*' – as Erasmus wrote, quoting Pindar – in other words, the uttermost ends of the earth beyond which lay 'nether darkness' (*zophos*). The extreme language of these classical metaphors may ring oddly, when so much traffic passed through the straits of Gibraltar in ancient and medieval times, but from Pindar to Dante, the tradition holds that the pillars set up by the hero marked some kind of voyage into the beyond. Summoning up the ghostly presence of both adventuring heroes – Ulysses and Hercules – I'll then look at the reappearance of those landmarks on the first coins minted in the Mundo Otro, as the Spanish conquistadors called the New World of the Americas, where their original ominous symbolism is transfigured. Eventually they coalesced into the familiar contours of the dollar sign, encoding its global ambitions. An important article of 1971 by Earl Rosenthal ('"*Plus Ultra, Non Plus Ultra*", and the Columnar Device of Emperor Charles V') suggested that the pillars do not only underlie the visual form of the sign, but, more resonantly, articulate a story of limits and excesses, of human striving and overreaching, of getting and spending. A minor incident of heroic myth will throw light, I hope, on the building of the Twin Towers, their destruction and the ensuing contemporary political crisis.

Dante in Paradise looks back at the Mediterranean, and his backward glance at Ulysses' 'mad track' returns the reader to the magnificent – and justly famous – Canto XXVI of the *Inferno*, in which Virgil speaks with the double-tongued flame enclosing Diomedes and Ulysses, and asks Ulysses to tell of his ultimate fate. At Virgil's ardent pleading, the epic hero relates how he was consumed with 'longing for experience of the world,/ Of human vices and virtue'.[2]

He gives the story of his last voyage, describing how he sailed through the Pillars of Hercules and on, till after five months he saw a dim mountain and was then violently struck by a storm and wrecked:

> ... I sailed out
> On the deep open seas, accompanied
>
> By that small company that still had not
> Deserted me, in a single ship ...
>
> ... My men were old and slow when we passed
>
> The narrow outlet where Hercules let stand
> His markers beyond which men were not to sail.
> On my left hand I had left Ceuta behind,
>
> And on the other sailed beyond Seville.
> 'O brothers who have reached the west,' I began,
> 'Through a hundred thousand perils, surviving all:

So little is the vigil we see remain
Still for our sense, that you should not choose
To deny it the experience – behind the sun

Leading us onward – of the world which has
No people in it. Consider well your seed:
You were not born to live as a mere brute does,

But for the pursuit of knowledge and good'.[3]

So Ulysses repeats the rallying speech he made to his crew, urging them to sail with him into the unknown, into the world at the back of the sun, that nether region invoked by Pindar, dark, unpeopled.

Primo Levi recalls, in the chapter called 'The Canto of Ulysses' in his classic memoir, *If This Is a Man*, how at Auschwitz he recited Ulysses' speech to his workmate Jean, known as Pikolo, after Jean, an Alsatian who spoke both French and German, expressed a desire to learn some Italian. On the walk to fetch the rations for their work-group, Primo Levi remembers how he was thinking:

Of this I am certain, I am sure, I can explain it to Pikolo, I can point out why 'mi mise' (I set forth) is not 'je me mis', it is much stronger and more audacious, it is a chain which has been broken, it is throwing oneself on the other side of a barrier, we know the impulse well. The open sea . . .

And the journey as well, the foolhardy journey beyond the Pillars of Hercules . . .

Here, listen, Pikolo, open your ears and your mind, you have to understand, for my sake.

And he quotes the line: 'Fatti non foste a vivre come bruti' ('You were not born to live as a mere brute does').

Then Levi writes, 'As if I also was hearing it for the first time: like the blast of a trumpet, like the voice of God. For a moment I forget who I am and where I am.'[4]

This impassioned chapter of a passionate book follows the stumbling of Primo Levi as he pieces the lines together from memory, but cannot quite reach for every verse. He slows Jean down, he has to impart to him, as urgently as one of the shades of the dead in the *Inferno* has to speak to

Dante, until he reaches the conclusion of the canto, when Ulysses and his men are swallowed up:

> for from the newfound land a storm had grown,
> Rising to strike the forepart of the ship.
> It whirled the vessel round, and round again
>
> With all the waters three times, lifting up
> The stern the fourth – as pleased an Other – to press
> The prow beneath the surface, and did not stop
>
> Until the sea had closed up over us.

Levi, remembering, writes:

> I keep Pikolo back, it is vitally necessary and urgent that he listen, that he understand this 'com'altrui piacque' ('as pleased an Other') before it is too late; tomorrow he or I might be dead, or we might never see each other again, I must tell him, I must explain to him about the Middle Ages, about the so human and so necessary and yet unexpected anachronism, but still more, something gigantic that I myself have only just seen, in a flash of intuition, perhaps the reason for our fate, for our being here today.

The chapter itself ends with the closing line of the canto when the ship is wrecked and goes down: 'Until the sea had closed up over us'.[5]

For Primo Levi, the concentration camp was a living Inferno, recreated in the here and now, and the drowning meted out to Ulysses by divine will the extinction desired for its prisoners by the camp's brutal creators.

The passage conveys powerfully how sharing the poetry gave Primo Levi strength, revived his hopes in his desperate struggle for survival in the camp, and how these lines in particular recalled both himself and Jean to a glimmering of their human status in spite of the degradation inflicted on them. But Ulysses' enterprise was also doomed, and later, the image of the drowned venture resonated with profound sadness in the metaphor that orders Primo Levi's lifelong meditation on the Nazi ideology and its prolonged, continuing costs to humanity.

Primo Levi became increasingly and profoundly fatalistic about the experience of the camps: the best were drowned, he wrote, the worst were saved. Dante's Ulysses prefigures in Levi's thought the best whom the Shoah obliterated, the questors, the venturesome, the strivers – the idealists. He grieved, in several later pieces of writing, including the book entitled *The Drowned and the Saved*, on the survivors' morality, on the petty, self-serving cunning and violence that allowed them to survive. He was continually troubled by this, for he too of course had not been drowned.

There also trembles, I think, beneath the bravery, defiance and heroic individualism of Primo Levi's claim on Ulysses, another, very different message, about oblivion and annihilation as a consequence of setting forth into the unknown. The contemporary ecologist Robin Grove-White, warning of the risks that have to be assessed today, speaks of 'unknown unknowns' – in a political sense, Nazism was an unknown unknown when it began: it was unimaginable before it revealed itself, horribly. Ulysses, and his journey beyond the Pillars of Hercules, into the unknown unknown as it then was, embody thoughts for us today that Primo Levi glimpsed so prophetically.

Recently, Adrienne Rich, lecturing in Cambridge, meditated with quiet and urgent eloquence on the role of poetry in opposing brutality and falsehood, in fostering relatedness and developing thought. She called us, her audience, to listen to 'old poets' oracular voices' – to find in their own stumblings and fumblings a passage through to a deeper understanding and a greater harmony. Dante's Ulysses, while harshly condemned to burn in the circle of those who abuse language, storytelling and intelligence – the false counsellors – radiantly contradicts his official sinfulness by his testimony to human striving and the pursuit of knowledge.

In the spirit of the imagined fate of Ulysses, and of Levi's tormented meditations on his story, it is possible, I think, to develop the eerie contemporary relevance of the Pillars of Hercules and relate them to the present times of war and atrocity.

The voyage Ulysses proposes to his men, which he successfully persuades them to undertake, in spite of their common agedness and exhaustion, involves following the sun westwards, and it takes them, as Ulysses describes, past the points beyond which men were not to sail.

Once past the columns demarcating the limits of the known world, after five months sailing, Ulysses and his men see in the distance a great mountain – a 'nova terra'. One of the editors of Dante, John D. Sinclair, connects this new land in the ocean with the Mount of Purgatory, and others have identified it with the Fortunate Islands, or Isles of the Blest (now the Canaries), but it could also represent the dreamed continent of Atlantis – which indeed gives the ocean its name. In two dialogues of Plato, the *Timaeus*, and then in the *Critias*, the legendary island of Atlantis rises beyond the Mediterranean where the ocean stream, the waters that engirdle the world, begins to flow. Atlantis is elaborately delineated there, and from the point of view of Dante's Ulysses and his voyage, it is worth noting above all that Atlantis falls under the divine jurisdiction of Poseidon, who encircles the island with ramparts and walls of water – so it may be the sea god's pleasure that decrees the wrecking of Ulysses' ship, rather than Dante's god, it seems to me, or a benighted demiurge in Primo Levi's enlightened historical perspective. Poseidon is Odysseus' implacable enemy, after his son Polyphemus' blinding – a story Aeneas also tells in Virgil's epic.

Mountainous, sea-girt Atlantis was rich in ores and vegetation, and was given over by Poseidon to his eldest son, Atlas, to rule. Atlas is also a name deeply associated with the adventures of Hercules, for the hero enlists the giant Atlas's help in stealing the apples of the Hesperides, the nymphs of the setting sun. Their Garden lies so far to the west that Hercules sends Atlas in his stead, because even he fears to make such a journey, and while the giant performs this task on his behalf, Hercules shoulders the burden of the world for a time. (It is Herodotus who first names the North African mountain range Atlas after the legendary giant, and his subsequent legends are very tangled. However, the overlap with Poseidon's eldest, the mountain king of Atlantis, who is also, in some legends, the father of the Hesperides, seems an easy confusion to make.)

Atlas takes Hercules' place: they are interchangeable heroic achievers in narrative terms; Hercules also makes several appearances within the cycle of Ulysses' myths, as his precursor and exemplar. Of all the classical heroes, Hercules sets the pace for exploits, more than Jason, more even than Theseus. In Dante, he prefigures Ulysses' endeavour in passing through the straits of Gibraltar, but Ulysses, being mortal, fails in the attempt, and is drowned. Ulysses as a man cannot do what Hercules as a hero can, for Hercules is a demi-god, destined for Olympian rank. Dante's Ulysses, by contrast, survives by deception and trickery and then trespasses against Providence's arrangements for humanity, and the Pillars of Hercules mark the boundary that he crosses in error.

The pillars demarcate a geographical limit that is more coherently a moral boundary, standing for human grandeur as well as littleness: the fabled map of the Mediterranean, teeming with exemplary and cautionary stories of the gods' adventures and humanity's fate, figures a psychological and ethical map as well, where everything is far less delineated and stable. The poet's sympathies fly out towards the grand, tall flame in which Ulysses burns in hell in epic dignity and he invites identification with him, as a doomed Everyman. And this hubristic Everyman reappears, in Canto XXVI of *Paradiso*, when Adam recalls the Fall, and also figures the sin of pride explicitly through the metaphor of passing beyond a permitted boundary or landmark: 'For it wasn't tasting of the tree, my son, that caused such a long exile, but only passing beyond the mark.'[6]

In the typological manner of medieval manuals, Dante's scheme foreshadows, in Ulysses' last voyage, Adam's eating of the fruit of knowledge: the two stories fall in the same position in their respective cantos. In the *Inferno*, the sunwise track of Ulysses also reverberates with two other classical myths of hubris: Icarus who flew too close to the sun on the wings his father Daedalus crafted for him, and Phaeton, who borrowed his father the sun god's chariot but could not control the horses. Dante chooses to allude to both tragic youths when he vividly conjures up his descent with Virgil into the abyss of Malebolge on the croup of the monster Geryon (Canto XVII). Geryon wheels down, planing like a modern hang-glider, making wide circles round the pit as Virgil urges him to do – one of Dante's utterly dramatic, imagined sequences:

> Onward he swam with motion more and more slow
> As he wheeled round descending . . .[7]

To describe the beast (*fera*) as he goes circling slowly on down, Dante likens Geryon to a falcon in a widening gyre who lands, exhausted: Geryon deposits his cargo at the bottom of the pit and vanishes, bringing Canto XVII to a mysterious, open-ended close. The passage foreshadows the fate of Ulysses' ship, which whirls around three times under the lash of the storm, before, on the fourth round, it plunges down into the abyss, and also closes this canto with its disappearance.

The monster Geryon belongs in the manifold myths about Hercules: he features in one of the Twelve Labours set by King Eurystheus; Hesiod specifies that Geryon pastured his fierce flocks on Erythea, a land beyond the sunset. The identification with Gades or Cadiz was made later. In some stories, it's when Hercules is on his way to kill Geryon and steal his flocks that he cleaves open the straits by separating the mountains of Calpe (the present-day Rock of Gibraltar) and Abyla (now Ximeira, or Ape Mountain, in Morocco), and thus opens the passage out of the Mediterranean.[8] It is Dante who, as Primo Levi perceived, follows the countervailing message of the story, and insists that Hercules' pillars issue a warning against voyaging on. A gateway, which can signal an entrance or an exit, a start or a terminus: this contradiction remains intrinsic to the 'riguardi' – the lookouts – of Hercules.

Geryon pastured huge flocks of animals, described as cannibal monsters in some sources, and they were guarded by a two-headed dog and the herdsman Eurython, who were both killed in Hercules' raid on his precious cattle. Geryon himself, in Hesiod's *Theogony* and as depicted on Greek vases, had three bodies, joined at the waist. Virgil alludes to this, but Dante doesn't follow this classical convention, and instead seems rather to take his imaginative cue from other classical monsters, such as Lamia, who haunted the North African shore. Geryon also recalls other antagonists – the terrifying hybrids Hercules dispatches in the course of other Labours, such as the ferocious Hydra and the stinking Stymphalian Birds. Dante's Gerione is a diabolical 'fiero animale', a 'bestia malvagia', a 'fera' with a scorpion's sting in his tail, and a serpent's skin scintillating with knots and weals. With his spotted hide and fair face concealing a wicked and savage nature – his 'faccia di menzogna', Dante's monster bears an affinity with sinners like Ulysses who have abused their powers of articulacy and communication: as Dante rises so powerfully to enflesh the damned soul of double-tongued Ulysses, the liar and deceiver, so the poet, sensitive to the affinities with his own powers of rhetoric and of literature, lingers feelingly on the falsehood of Geryon. With his wealed, iridescent pelt, Gerione thus looks forward to Keats's Lamia; he's one of Dante's most imposing infernal composites, as he lies on the edge of the pit like some lethal sphinx. (His handsome, false countenance inspired Botticelli to one of his most intense sequences of drawings, as he renders Dante and Virgil's whirling plunge on the monster's back.)

Today, Hercules has significantly receded from view as a model of manhood; especially compared to Odysseus/Ulysses who still commands moral and imaginative attention. But it was Hercules who, in the century after Dante, emerged in Florentine humanism as the pre-eminent exemplar of human striving and achievement, and though many aspects of his complex myth contributed to his salience in political and ethical philosophy, his persistent voyaging into the unknown figured above all his virtue and his knowledge.

The scholar Coluccio Salutati, Chancellor of Florence from 1375–1406, expanded on Hercules' moral choices: he maintained that Hercules had opened the passage out of the Mediterranean when he set up the Pillars. Cristoforo Landino, in the *De Vera nobilitate* (1487–90), interpreted Hercules' Labours in terms of Neoplatonist values, expanding on the moral topos of the heroic choice between Virtue and Vice, or Pleasure. These thinkers' impact might have remained perhaps a matter of recondite learning in intellectual Florentine circles, but, as can sometimes happen, their influence spread, and reached Milan, where another humanist, the physician Luigi Marliano, had become attached to the young king and future emperor Charles V and his court in 1516.[9]

Marliano was a fellow-Lombard and friend of Pietro Martire d'Angheria, the urbane, learned courtier who had been tutor to Charles's Spanish mother the Infanta when she was young; Peter Martyr, as he is known in English, wrote the highly influential history of the Americas, *De Orbe Novo* ('Of the New World') (1516), which circulated widely through his networks of diplomatic and scholarly connections. As the French historian Marcel Bataillon shows in an article written in 1960, it was Marliano who introduced the emblem of the Pillars of Hercules into the panoply of royal symbols, and combined them with the motto 'Plus Ultra' – literally 'More Beyond' – in other words, Ever Onwards – Ever Farther.[10] This phrase, which sounds so classical, actually embodies a mistake, as the proper form would be 'Ulterius'. But 'Plus Ultra' offers a recognisable twist on Dante's famous passage; it's a Latinised calque on the phrase Dante uses of the Pillars of Hercules set up to show: 'acciò che l'uom *più oltre* non si metta' (so that mankind should not venture farther).

Marliano introduced the device in his oration at the first gathering of the Order of the Golden Fleece presided over by Charles, then sixteen years old. There Marliano urged his student to become a new Hercules, a new Atlas, and take up the great burden of his global possessions; the following year, 1517, when the new king left his native Low Countries to occupy his throne in Spain, the sails of his flagship were painted with an image of the crucifixion between the Pillars of Hercules and the motto 'Plus Ultra'. During his subsequent reign, Charles happily prolonged the identification: in 1556, to commemorate fifty years on the throne, the humanist sculptor Leone Leoni created a beautifully modelled medal for him, showing Hercules in his lion skin and armed with his club, subduing the Hydra, a terrible monster with bat wings and six heads who sinks her talons viciously into her assailant's flesh.

Marliano returned to Italy as personal doctor to the ambitious new monarch, on his decisive and devastating expedition in Italy in 1527 to subdue his new subjects. The image of the Pillars of Hercules, another episode of the founding hero's life, was first struck on coins at the mint in Milan under Spanish control: the two pillars appeared side by side, under the Spanish crown, and interlaced with a baroque banderole spiralling round each column in a decorative manner (this flourish will take on another, profound significance). As Charles V travelled down through Italy after his conquest of Rome he fortified towns like Lecce and Otranto, raising over their gates the symbols of Spanish power, including the Pillars of Hercules. They signified the ends of the earth. They stood at the straits of Gibraltar, one in Europe, one in Africa, in modern-day Gibraltar and Ceuta, and the emperor stamped them on the coinage and armorial bearings of his new possessions to proclaim that he had voyaged beyond the limits of the known world, and made the unknown his own.

For soon after its first appearance in Charles's symbolism the classical device began to be charged with a specific energy; the geography of the unknown had been remapped, and the sea to the west no longer opened on to infinity but had become a road to conquests, fame and fortune – to American gold, and American silver. The Spanish used their mines there to mint their new imperial coinage; it was emblazoned with the Pillars of Hercules.

Writing to a rival contemporary monarch, Francis I of France, in 1523, the great scholar Erasmus issued an ironic warning about the belligerent ambitions of rulers:

> all the time there is an immense supply everywhere of those who rouse the spirit of princes to make war . . . One . . . murmurs, 'If you can add such-and-such a province to your dominions, you will easily add that other whenever you please.' Misguided guide! Why suggest how far they can advance the limits of their dominions . . .? Of the extending of dominions there is no end . . . Alexander the Great, having reached the ocean, deplored the absence of another world. Yet even Hercules could not pass beyond Cadiz. To our modern ambitions Cadiz is nowhere, the ocean does not exist.[11]

But the Herculean aspirations of the emperor grew, unabated, and the hero's exploits dominated Spanish imperial self-portraiture. *Reales* struck in Lima, Mexico City, and Bogota show the Pillars (*columnario* in Spanish), and with the inevitable motto 'Plus Ultra'. Charles V's son, Philip II, introduced some new, crucial features: the pillars stand on either side of crowned, superimposed hemispheres of the world, the American continent, North and South in front, the Old World behind. On the columns, 'Plus' and 'Ultra' appear on the two banderoles now twisted individually around each column, their feet standing in the turbulent ocean. This ocean view gestures openly towards the boundlessness of Spanish imperial ambitions.

These coins circulated as currency throughout the American continent and even as far afield as China in the eighteenth century. They were known as 'Mexican dollars' and their iconography strongly influenced the first big, silver, US dollars struck after 1776.[12] The largest were worth eight *reales*: these are the famous pieces of eight of pirate lore (remember the parrot in *Treasure Island* squawking 'Pieces of eight, pieces of eight'?).

Even more crucially, the emblem of the pillars shaped the *cipher* of the dollar sign itself. The S with the double or single downward stroke

Piece of Eight,
Lima, 1737

through its curves derives from the Pillars of Hercules in their baroque guise, or, more specifically, from the right-hand one on the eight *reales* coin of the Spanish New World. If you look at the right-hand column, you will see the dollar sign figured there: $, in the position on earlier *pesos* where appeared the numerical value of the coin, the figure 8 or the figure 4 or 1.

The 'columnar' device epitomised sixteenth-century humanist aspirations for virtue, for knowledge: Francis Bacon emblazoned the Pillars of Hercules on the title page of the *Instauratio Magna* 'The Great Instauration' of 1620, with the inscription appearing beneath a westbound galleon, 'Multi pertransibunt & augebitur scientia' ('Many will pass through and knowledge will be increased'). Seven years later, Bacon echoed the mythic theme of the world beyond the pillars with the title of his great manifesto, his dream of new human possibilities, *The New Atlantis*. On Bacon's Atlantis, the pursuit of Light occupies all its dwellers: the Merchants of Light, as he terms them, are thinkers, who aim to discover 'the knowledge of causes and the secret motion of things; and the enlarging of the bounds of the human empire, to the effecting of all things possible'. But the effects of conquest split imperial ambition from intellectual dream of voyaging ever onward.

When the ship Bacon imagined sailed on through the straits, the trade winds would blow her south – but, if she were able to fly as the crow flies, she would reach the east coast of the United States, and, almost at the same latitude as the straits of Gibraltar – only around six degrees north – the island of Manhattan, where, in 1976, the tallest buildings in the world had risen as twin pillars.

The architect of the Twin Towers, Minoru Yamasaki, died the year after they were completed, around twenty years after the complex was first mooted by the magnate David Rockefeller, the apostle of 'catalytic bigness'. The aesthetics of the buildings have not been of much consequence recently. Yamasaki was a much travelled, eclectic architect, a second-generation Japanese-American brought up in Seattle, who built very widely in the United States and elsewhere, including the Arabian Gulf; he was committed to the monumental, and declared his passion for skyscrapers and their symbolism: 'the sense of upwardness . . . this perhaps replaces to a degree the feeling of aspiration that the man [on the street] had in medieval days when he walked into a cathedral'. Yamasaki specialised in educational sites and in airports, saying of the Terminal he built at St Louis, 'Being the gateway to a large city . . . I had felt from the beginning that somehow this building should symbolize this sense of being a gateway . . . I . . . went to Grand Central Station and realized that . . . this great high room somehow gave you the sense of arrival to an important city.'[13]

Yamasaki's Twin Towers also set up a gateway, a pair of pillars that, from a certain vantage point, framed the Statue of Liberty; the buildings were even fluted, with ogival features at the base, references to the Gothic cathedrals so many New York skyscrapers also recall. They also reproduced an imaginary gateway, or, to use computer imagery, a virtual portal.

The Pillars of Hercules marked a limit, but that limit, once passed, became a portal: this is the ambiguity that the myth contains, when it features Hercules splitting the mountains to forge a passage out of the middle sea, but also setting up landmarks to warn of the dangers of passing through. It's the challenge that called to Ulysses and, after him, to others, to Francis Bacon and to Primo Levi.

When those towers were destroyed last year, the attackers adhered to an extreme development of the Islamic faith, in its present contemporary character, and, as we all sadly know, they were acting under instruction from the Al Qaeda sectarian leaders, who were at that time living under the protection of the Taliban regime in Afghanistan. The Taliban instituted a régime so deeply inimical to representation of any kind – visual and even aural – so suspicious and condemning of all Western-style image-making – that on the one hand it blew up the Bamiyan Buddhas, and on the other, pulled the tapes out of cassette-players and festooned the streets of Kabul with the ribbons, like trophies of war.

The Twin Towers iconically condensed the significance of Manhattan, New York City, as the financial capital of America. But it is worth bearing in mind that the complex of liberties and economics that the World Trade Center embodied was not exclusively national but international in character, and many of the thousands dead were not US citizens. The Twin Towers stood so high as the symbol of Western wealth, of the money-generating engine of Downtown, of the world stockmarket, of the global economy; and the currency, worldwide, which dominates the trade, is the dollar.

The Twin Towers were built in the flush of American hegemony, and were already criticised at the time of construction for anachronistic and inappropriate glorying in that power: they were then the tallest buildings to reach upwards, to embody the farthest, deepest reach of influence. They eerily embodied the conclusion of the 1957 global capitalist manifesto, a novel significantly entitled *Atlas Shrugged*, by the arch-conservative Ayn Rand, in which the protagonist looks up at the sky and a huge dollar sign appears emblazoned in it. The Ayn Rand Foundation today, if you visit its website, displays a skyscraper as its emblem and declares its credo: Reason is its absolute, rational self-interest, its guiding light 'not by permission of others, but by inalienable right ... [Rand] was adamantly opposed to altruism ... In her view, America was the tallest, brightest and most beautiful skyscraper built for man.' As President George W. Bush recently put it, 'Make the pie higher.'

Andy Warhol, an artist with a preternatural sensitivity to the potency of icons, painted a series of symbols of contemporary America, embodied in consumer and other cult objects, connected by a common morbidity: the Remington revolver, the electric chair, the car crash, Marilyn Monroe – and the dollar sign. Warhol was brought up in Pittsburgh as a member of a small Uniate community that belongs to the Catholic Church in Rome but observes a Greek rite, with all the Orthodox focus on venerating of sacred images. His work could be said to represent, iconically, as the objects of worship, a complete range of sacred symbols in contemporary culture. These were symbols by which America lived and died, so its leading deadpan pop artist recorded.

But as the dollar is not, needless to say, US currency only, and commands circulation across boundaries worldwide, I don't really need to add that it's consequently extraordinarily fitting that the Twin Towers, the tallest buildings in the world when they were built, soaring with the confidence of the world markets in the climate of free-for-all venture capitalism, may themselves echo the original model for the dollar symbol, the Pillars of Hercules as adopted and adapted by the most ambitious commercial and political – and ruthless – empire of the Renaissance. And that in the legendary history accumulating around the Pillars of Hercules, they were allegedly destroyed by the Moors in 1054 during an earlier conflict between Christendom and Islam in Europe. (No less an authority than Averroës, in his commentary on Aristotle – whom Dante read – relates this story.)[14]

The issues that open up if, like Ulysses, you wish to sail on, in search of the more beyond, touch on the present terrible conflicts. Without trifling with the human cost in lives on September 11 and in its aftermath, it is worth thinking about that act in a historical and symbolic context, and to place the psychology of the attackers in this perspective, rather than that of contemporary terrorism alone and the grievous attack on an American city. The destruction of the towers constituted an act of pure iconoclasm, a symbolic gesture of absolute extremism as well as a massacre of civilians. The crashing of the planes into the skin of the buildings literally defaced an image of the ideological values of the First World, in the same way as iconoclast attackers of an icon (Our Lady of Czestochowa in Warsaw, Michelangelo's *Pietà* and, indeed, the Bamiyan Buddhas, the two colossi destroyed six months before September 11) slash at or hammer or blow up a hated object of worship. The towers stood in Manhattan, but as vehicles brimful of significance, they belonged not within specific topographical borders, but in the realm of a collective belief system; this may not have been as apparent while they stood as it has become since they fell, for their iconic status has been enhanced, crystallised and consecrated in the aftermath. Never before were the two skyscrapers so cherished, so treasured.

But I think it is crucial to look at this symbolism from a less local angle. From the point of view of a woman like myself, with an Italian mother, a childhood partly spent in North Africa, and an English father, the range of associations stirred by the Pillars of Hercules and their history can hardly permit smugness: Fortress Europe, with its refugee camps and other manoeuvres to keep out asylum seekers and economic migrants, many of whom are fleeing conditions of poverty and civil strife in which our trade and foreign policies are deeply implicated, can hardly claim clean hands. Ceuta, the site of the southernmost, African column, one of the landmarks Dante's Ulysses notes as he sails past, is still a Spanish possession along with some islets – Perejil and Leila – in the straits of Gibraltar, and these last scattered uninhabited rocks actually became the objects of armed disputes between Morocco and Spain last July (2002). The conflict erupted over control of Europe's southern border, not only against the traffic in immigrants, but also that in drugs and other smuggled goods. The international traffic in narcotics supplies terrorists with a principal resource, and its reach is, needless to say, global. Ceuta, a Spanish territory in Africa, politically belongs to Europe and the European Union, and has consequently become the destination of thousands of desperate men and women who want to gain access to the First World and are excluded for ethnic and financial reasons. Jeremy Harding, in his fine study, *The Uninvited: Refugees at the Rich Man's Gate*, describes his visit to the Ceuta citadel, with its high triple fence of razor-wire to prevent the supplicants from entering. The Rock of Gibraltar, a British outpost in southern Europe, continues to be a source of bitter wrangling, again for control of the strategic position over the straits. And drownings take place daily in the Mediterranean, in the waters between Spain, Italy, North Africa and the Balkans.[15]

So the limits that Hercules marked, which Ulysses breached, still stand as a frontier, of the Eurocentric mindset, not only of its southern perimeter, and that border reverberates with associations of global trade and the privileges of plenty, as do – as did – the Twin Towers near Wall Street. The World Trade Center's architecture was compacted of signs denoting value and power, carried by a certain, historically evolved body of stories and a highly political set of beliefs; the dollar sign, international denoter of wealth, grew in the very ground of this ideology. Dante was absolutely prophetic – more prophetic than he could ever have dreamed – when he imagined the fatal dilemma at the core of Ulysses' voyaging beyond the Pillars of Hercules.

2003

THREE

BODIES AND MINDS

Harmoniously Arranged Livers

Review of Caroline Walker Bynum, The Resurrection of the Body in Western Christianity 200–1336

When a djinn appears in one of A. S. Byatt's fairy tales and grants the fiftyish academic heroine any wish her heart desires, she asks for her body 'as it was the last time she really *liked* it'. And lo, she finds herself once more housed in the 'serviceable and agreeable' form she possessed some fifteen years earlier, bearing some marks of experience (an appendix scar), but otherwise compact, neat, strong. She feels wonderful. 'I can go in the streets, she said to herself, and still be recognisably who I am — only I shall *feel* better, I shall like myself more.' She proceeds to great adventures of an earthly variety with the djinn himself.

This heroine knows her mind on such matters as her ideal physical identity rather more clearly than the medieval schoolmen who laboured to define what heavenly bodies will be like: what age would babies be when they were resurrected? Would bald men have their hair restored? Would the maimed warrior rise whole again? Would there be genitals in heaven? What of colons, what of teeth? (Tertullian decided that 'we will not chew in heaven, but we will have teeth, because we would look funny without them'.) And if a man has been devoured alive and has left behind no body in a grave, only macerated meat in a tiger's belly – what then? The questions grew more and more macabre and bizarre, the kind which gave Catholics their bad reputation of casuistry and for magical, even pagan, primitivism. What if a cannibal had eaten a pregnant woman? In what form would the embryo be found in the afterlife after the Day of Judgment?

Caroline Walker Bynum has made abhorrent corners of Catholic metaphysics her speciality. After remarkable work on the mortifying practices of female mystics in the Middle Ages (*Holy Feast and Holy Fast*), she has turned her attention to another aspect of early and medieval Christian cult in which the body is the crucial issue: the doctrine that we will all be reunited with our individual appearance after the last day. From the earliest days of Christianity, the resurrection of the body was a central plank of the faith: a tenet of the Nicaean creed, a testing-ground for heresy. At the last trump, the graves would yield up their dead and all – saints and sinners – would be reunited with their flesh. Saint Paul's prophecy drew the scene in the First Letter to the Corinthians, using the metaphor of a seed, planted in the ground, which grows into a wheat-ear: 'It is sown a natural body, it shall rise a spiritual body.' This natural image of transformation did not, however, meet believers' anxiety that individuals be recognisable in heaven (or hell), and other metaphors gained in popularity. Shattered pots or broken statues put back together offered a guarantee that the new body would be identical to the original: the smelting of ore to release gold dramatically envisioned God recovering cadavers from decomposition; Jonah vomited unharmed by the whale prefigured the escape of every human being intact from the jaws of death. Apocalyptic visions, as in the eleventh-century mosaic of Torcello, showed tombs gaping while angels and devils gathered up separated bones, and fish and animals spewed up any cadavers or parts thereof they had devoured. The chain of consumption threatened obliteration, but divine power would put it into reverse, and every swallowed and digested corpse would be regurgitated.

The wicked, however, would be returned to the relentless process of annihilation through devouring. Hell has a famous mouth; the maw of Leviathan, the triple jaws of Dante's Satan chew on sinners without respite; and devils as monster chefs with cooking implements – those pitchforks – turn sinners on spits and feed them into the ovens of hell. As Bynum says, flux, change, natural cycles of transformation profoundly disturbed early medieval thinkers and Fathers of the Church. Metempsychosis, the theory of the migration of souls on which Pythagoras built his moral system and his scale of rewards and penalties, afforded the early followers of Christ no satisfactory rationale and certainly no comfort; nor did the natural metamorphoses which Ovid, following Pythagorean metaphysics, invoked to make sense of nature and creation. By contrast to the world of flux and vanity, paradise would be a place of rest, of blissful stasis, in which degeneration, ageing, the organic cycles of fertility and decay come to a halt. Interestingly, these contrasting eschatological visions

– hell's mouth v. metamorphosis – are both embodied in that popular contemporary fantasy, *The Silence of the Lambs*, in the figures of the two serial killers – Hannibal Lecter whose mouth must be muzzled in an iron cage or else he will eat people raw, and 'Buffalo Bill' who dreams of turning his victims into fantasy frocks, as caterpillars turn into moths.

The Catholic emphasis on the body as food relates of course to the Eucharist, at the heart of Christian ritual, and led to charges of cannibalism against early worshippers; the body and blood of Christ, consumed by the faithful, united them in a food chain that reflects, in a paradisical mirror image, death's swallowing up of individuals. By eating the transubstantiated bread in communion the faithful Christian becomes one with Christ and, by extension, with other Christians.

Bynum has long studied, with brilliant tough-mindedness, these obsessional clusters of motifs in Christian belief, and this new book contains the chapter and verse of nearly a decade's reading and musing. She attempts in it to trace the development of the doctrine of the resurrection of the body, and the changes in approach to the problems the doctrine set in train, from early days to the fourteenth century. She is able to delineate one strong curve in the history of ideas: that the concept of material continuity between the corpse and transfigured eschatological flesh came under challenge, in the thirteenth century, from some of the most subtle thinkers of the Middle Ages – Aquinas and Bonaventure – but more particularly from lesser known philosophers, such as Durand de Saint Pourçain. The urgent need in earlier versions of the doctrine for angels to pick up and reassemble all the bits from the selfsame body that had lived and died was modified in the light of an Aristotelian concept of form. Each person has a body which is the material manifestation of their unique form; the body in the afterlife will rise again in this shape, bequeathing an identity of appearance, but not necessarily identical matter.

However, this position came dangerously near denying the literal resurrection of a person's body, which lay after all at the core of orthodoxy. Acquinas elsewhere contradicts his insight, while the work of others who contributed to the refinement of the concept was neglected or in certain instances condemned. Dante's metaphysics reflect his grasp of the formal identity between body and soul, but this solution did not really catch on: as Bynum readily agrees, the cult of relics, and hundreds of popular stories surrounding martyrs and their shrines, insisted that the blood in the gold and crystal ostensory was the glorious blood of the martyr who was now bodiless in heaven, and would be reinfused into his real flesh at the resurrection. Ditto with the splinters of bone and skulls on display in charnel-houses. The bones of Saint Ursula, and the eleven thousand virgins who were martyred with her, are still displayed on the walls of the Golden Chamber in her church in Cologne, as if in a floral arrangement, commissioned by pious ladies of the city: the long bones arranged to read as glorifying legends, the shoulder-blades in rosettes, the skulls in columns wearing embroidered visors in purple and gold (now rather dusty). All these will be gathered, sorted and reclothed in flesh.

Jacopus de Voragine imagines the martyr James the Dismembered sweetly apostrophising his body as he is tortured: 'Go, third toe, to thy companions, and as the grain of wheat bears much fruit, so shalt thou rest with thy fellows unto the last day . . . Be comforted, little toe, because great and small shall have the same resurrection.' Sophisticated mystical revisionism did not dent the faithful's need for direct, bodily contact and the conviction that loved ones will see one another again, face to face, whole and entire, as they were when they knew one another on earth.

The Resurrection of the Body is a work of unusual painstakingness: very few scholars today will commit themselves to reading so much scholastic logic-chopping with this degree of concentration. But in an essay on the same theme, which appeared in her remarkable collection of 1991, *Fragmentation and Redemption*, Bynum had already identified and summarised the issues at stake. There, in thirty sparkling pages, she argued that the absurdities of medieval ruminations about devoured embryos and maimed corpses shouldn't be mocked. The questions the medieval mind worried at underlie many lingering problems, and can usefully illuminate a roster of contemporary moral dilemmas, like surrogate motherhood, organ transplants, in vitro fertilisation from donor sperm and the preservation of human remains in museums. Should bog men, should mummies be given quieter resting places? Should a cow with a calf in the womb be sawn in half for display as sculpture? Should microbes preserved in amber from millions of years ago be reactivated and let loose in laboratories, as has just happened in San Luis Obispo in California? A story like *Frankenstein* continues to exercise its hold because it touches historically rooted notions of personhood and the body. But Caroline Bynum has not developed any of these insights any further in this much longer and more inspissated study; she piles on the schoolmen's texts with learning and diligence, until one understands the temper the divines of the Reformation (those forebears of Ian Paisley) showed when they made bonfires of Papist abominations.

There is a more fundamental problem than the unholy mix of logical hair-splitting and prurient gore. For another intellectual curve glimmers through the book: the resurrection of the body from the start put paid to the Platonic sense of the soul-body split, but as the doctrine was more and more elaborated, the body became more and more crucial to the idea of a person, so that, paradoxically for a faith which believes in the uniqueness of each created soul, the soul increasingly came to be seen as embodied in order to possess that particularity. As Bynum puts it, 'what self is (including what body is) will be packed into soul; body will be the expression of that soul in matter'. This principle departs radically from early Christian dualist lamentations (tinged with Gnosticism as well as classical disgust for the flesh) over that mortal part in which the shining, insubstantial, immortal soul was trapped, over the world of appearances as a cesspit into which spirit has fallen etc., etc. This affirmation of the incorporated soul, Bynum realises, accords with the religion's body worship, in the mystery of the God-made-flesh, in the cult of blood and bones and of immaculately incorrupt bodies of saints, in the penitential ecstasies of mystics – the marks of Christ's wounds on their hands and feet. So far so good; but as a consequence Bynum then dismisses the view that Christianity has been a religion which denies the goodness of the flesh. Goodness of the flesh is not at all the same thing as the presence of the body: while Catholicism's accent on the carnal has definitely enhanced its commitment to sensual excitements, in liturgy and image and holy rapture, it has – and Saint Jerome to James Joyce stand at a rather crowded bar here as witnesses – hardly promoted the beauty or value of the flesh. That radiant body in heaven, Aquinas wrote, will be possessed of the 'dowries' – *claritas*, *subtilitas*, *agilitas* and *impassibilitas* (difficult to define, but broadly speaking, brightness/beauty, penetrability/translucence, movement-without-effort, imperviousness/freedom from sensation) – i.e. it will be a body etherealised, absolved of almost all fleshly qualities as they are understood on this earth. (Augustine even implies that since nothing will be hidden or shameful, celestial bodies will be transparent, and we will even enjoy 'the sight of each other's harmoniously arranged livers and intestines in paradise'.) Although some schoolmen were certain that men and women would continue to have sexual organs in the afterlife, no one ever argued they would use them. The djinn from a

Turkish nightingale's eyes, was much more indulgent about bliss than
Thomas Aquinas, in Augustine's wake, could ever be.

Bynum writes in the sphere of Peter Brown's influence, and is one of the
historians who is revising attitudes to Christianity, not from an avowed
parti pris (she wasn't a cradle Catholic and has not converted), but from
a desire for intellectual provocation and a brisk contempt for *idées reçues*
(like Catholic sexual guilt). But this book, which shows such microscopic
discrimination in the differences of body and soul in a Giles of Rome,
does not squarely confront the deeper rift between concepts of carnality
and embodiment, or scan the hierarchical placement of flesh and spirit. In
Holy Feast and Holy Fast, she unfolded the fascinating strategy of mystics
who used the Church's aghast obsession with flesh, with its emissions and
transformations, to win themselves a voice of influence in matters of
Church and state in fourteenth- and fifteenth-century France, Italy, the
Netherlands, Germany, by making visible and active their prodigious
bodies (bearing stigmata, living on consecrated hosts alone). In *The
Resurrection of the Body*, she relates funerary customs – the laying out of
bodies with due care, the need for marked and hallowed burial grounds –
to Christian respect for the body, excited from the beginning by the
persecutions of the martyrs and the scattering of their remains. She also
makes a brief – all too brief – excursion into the rise of torture in Europe's
ecclesiastical courts and its connection to the historical picture of the
body's importance in personal identity, and alludes, again rather in
passing, to the beginnings of medical autopsy and experiments with
cadavers in the great schools of Italian medicine.

In the Museum of Human Anatomy in Bologna and the even spookier
Museo della Specola in Florence, wax models of organs and bodies in
various states of écorché and dissection were worked from the corpses
themselves, the veins injected with wax to take an impression as in the *cire
perdue* method, their limbs cast. It was done without compunction, and
under the Pope's patronage, and suggests, contrary to Bynum's argument,
that belief in the immortal soul's continued existence apart from the body
allowed investigative use and display of inanimate flesh in ways that strike
agnostic or atheist observers today as shocking desecrations. But on issues
such as these, raised by medical and political developments, Bynum refers
us to Marie-Christine Pouchelle and to R. I. Moore. Her book is not a
work of social history, and it suffers for it. For above all, Bynum does not
seize on the clear link between ideas of the soul's embodiment and the

Church's teaching today on contraception and abortion, which values bodies to the point where persons themselves don't matter, an interpretation of the importance of the flesh which is so partial – and intrinsically so negative – that it causes people to be punished for allowing the claims of the flesh at all. Bynum believes that too much energy has been spent on exploring issues of sexuality, eclipsing the overall picture of organic, psychosomatic unity in Christian theories of the body. But her keenness to tip the balance back has blunted her ability to empathise with what it means and what it felt like for many people to have a Catholic body.

1995

Magic Zones

Review of Richard Sennett, Flesh and Stone: The Body and the City in Western Civilisation

When Pasolini, disgusted with the fatted values of post-war capitalism in Italy, was dreaming up an alternative in his late trilogy, he found the imagery he needed in old collections of stories, and made *The Canterbury Tales*, *The Decameron* and *The Arabian Nights*. By turning from the uncanny, contemporary metaphysics of a film like *Theorem*, he was making common cause with the vulgar imagination and placing his hope in its vigour, in what he perceived to be its unabashed appetites and its laughter. *The Arabian Nights*, which sadly seems to have survived in this country only in a mutilated and dubbed print, is a period piece of Seventies hedonism. It opens with a jostling crowd in a souk in the Yemen and the auction of a slave girl; there follows much nudity, much touching and grinning in various combinations of partners, and under the aching desert moon, much passionate flesh. Some of the film is set in the jalousied interiors of Moorish bedrooms, or in desert cities such as Sana'a, with its towers of baked mud decorated with white scrolls and borders like piped icing. But on the whole, the freedoms of the flesh Pasolini dreams up take place in the open air, free of clothes or inhibitions – free of stone.

It's significant that Pasolini turned to the Orient to conjure his rather forced vision of primitive sanity, and that he expressed his resistance to

Western embourgeoisement through a honeyed, lyrical and comic picture of nomad culture and its pursuit of joyous, uncomplicated, promiscuous contact. His perception of sin (once a Catholic . . .) and his yearning for something other than Western hypocrisy led him to imagine a different geography of desire, rootless, unanchored, pastoral, with encounters taking place in an orange grove or in a tent pitched at will.

In Richard Sennett's study of bodies and cities in Western culture, flesh and stone are similarly inimical to one another, as the hint of a wound in the title suggests; stones build enclosures, which imprison the flesh as well as give it shelter. But since these are the Nineties not the Seventies, Sennett is less concerned with the flow of sexual desire than with the stemmed flow of fellow-feeling.

At the start of the book he recalls going to see a film with a friend whose hand had been shattered in Vietnam and replaced with a prosthesis. He describes how the audience, who had been watching the filmed carnage quite happily, shied from his friend's mutilation when they were leaving the cinema. Dulled by a diet of screen violence, they hurried away from an image of actual pain, dropping their eyes. Later, in his chapter on the Middle Ages, Sennett cites the fascinating theory put forward by the fourteenth-century Parisian surgeon Henri de Mondeville: he noticed that when a body is undergoing an operation, the other organs will compensate for the excised or wounded part as if in sympathy. Mondeville called the phenomenon 'syncope', and Sennett sees it as a metaphor for the working of the medieval Christian city, in which monks opened foundling hospitals and nuns succoured the sick and the mad in hospices attached to shrines; Knights Hospitallers on battlefields, and the confraternities burying plague victims, provided other kinds of care. Ideally, such a relation between people and places could be regenerated today in the modern cities of the West, though Sennett does not hold out much hope: the best we can manage, he thinks, is live and let live, as in his own neighbourhood of Greenwich Village.

Healing pilgrimages to places like Lourdes continue to give pride of place and dignity to bodies in pain; they do not hide away disfigurements or disease as if they were shameful, and in this they represent continuity with the ideals of Christian pastoral care. But the scene in the cinema with which Sennett opens could be interpreted in the opposite way: the audience may have flinched from the sight of a mechanical hand because they were still able to feel for someone who had suffered such a loss, despite the 'gory war epic' they had just sat through. Realistic film imagery of victims sometimes corresponds, in function, to Catholic iconography: the representation of the Madonna with the dead Christ is known as a Pietà because it is intended to evoke pity. That key work of compassionate representation, the Grünewald Altarpiece in Colmar, was painted for a hospital and features a Christ scored with the weals of Saint Elmo's fire, an illness which was ravaging the patients at the time the polyptych was commissioned. The screams and squeals that the most violent scenes in contemporary slasher and horror films excite from young spectators express their 'gut reactions' – the response of the flesh, their continuing capacity to wince. I'm not taking the argument so far as to say that *Full Metal Jacket* sensitises the body to empathy with others' destruction, but that the question whether it numbs and dulls remains open. Not averting one's eyes from a mutilation might express less sensitivity to its meaning for the sufferer, it seems to me, than looking away. Embarrassment does indeed prevent touching, but there are other ways, other senses with which we exchange awareness of one another.

Cities are places of exile from the lost paradise, Richard Sennett argues: Eden was a garden in which there were no buildings at all. The first town mentioned in the Bible was built by Cain, who gave it the name of his son Enoch; Genesis says nothing more about its history. The next edifice to be built (after the Ark) was the Tower of Babel; made of bricks to reach to the topmost heaven, it was blasted to punish the overweening pride of its architects; the result is the diversity of nations and tongues, still the most vivid prophecy of the great polyglot capitals to come, New York, London. Babel offers a variant on the original Fall: in both stories the human thirst for knowledge and power provokes jealous Yahweh's divine vengeance. As the distances between people grow, so do the places which mark their differences; Babel grew from the rubble. Setting aside altogether the countervailing traditon of an architecture of bliss – the Heavenly Jerusalem, the Eternal City – Sennett advocates an existential acceptance of permanent exile from radiance, to a realm of fragmentation, mistakes, doubts. All his cities are cities of the plain.

Flesh and Stone sweeps through Western civilisation from ancient Athens and the architecture of early democracy to New York today and the scoria of democracy's recent, dystopic manifestations (the homeless person's bender, the crack joint). In this attempt to map the urban world through time, Sennett proceeds by selecting an emblematic place or cluster of places in order to draw out the dominant significance of the relationship between men (women, sometimes) and their manmade environment. In Athens, he evokes the gymnasia where young boys wrestled naked and slippery, the forum with its open-air walks, the raked seats of the theatre which acted as a sounding board for the actor's voice (while he might be small and far away, his words resounded as if he stood much nearer), and the Pnyx hillside where the Ekklesiae or citizens' assemblies gathered for public discussions. These confident expressions of male participation are contrasted to women's seclusion in their rituals – the Thesmophoria, in which they re-enacted Persephone's abduction and return to earth, and the Adonai, in which they planted lettuce seedlings in memory of the youth whom Aphrodite had loved, and then left on their rooftops to droop and wither in the hot July sun. Greek practices like these have inspired some of the richest mythological analysis of recent years: there's an intriguing, speculative account of the Thesmophoria, for example, by Barbara Smith in the current issue of *Baetyl*. (This new journal coincidentally takes its name from the black stone into which the goddess Cybele metamorphosed in order to escape Zeus on one of his rampages – more flesh and stone in opposition.)

Sennett follows the approach of Marcel Detienne in his brilliant *The Gardens of Adonis* and interprets these rituals as creative expressions of the social and symbolic roles women fulfilled, as keepers of the codes of family and society. He regrets that 'ritual was not a tool people can use to investigate or reason about the unknown', but is very attracted to its discretion, its enigma. 'The spaces of rituals created magic zones of mutual affirmation,' he writes. It's not so certain, however, that their character inheres in stone, in the type of temple or dwellings where they took place. These were sometimes hearth ceremonies, but not always.

In Hadrian's Rome, by contrast, women enjoyed greater equality – they ate at the same table as their husbands, and could inherit and dispose of their own wealth – but its geography of power coerced its citizens and its slaves into submission; forced them into the ceremonies of imperial authority. The Romans erased the distinction between performance and reality: a gladiator playing Orpheus torn to pieces was literally mauled in full sight of all. 'Whatever fame sings of,' Martial wrote, 'the arena makes real for you.' In the same way, they founded cities in the image of Rome wherever they went, digging a central *mundus* for a capitol, and imposing spectacle, hierarchy and linearity in an unholy alliance.

In the section on medieval Paris, Sennett reveals most clearly his new-found sympathy 'with the Judaeo-Christian belief in the spiritual knowledge to be gained in the body'. Vulnerability, suffering, humbleness, victimhood: the upside-down value system Christ inaugurated developed an ideal urban economy of compassion. But while Sennett holds up the medieval monastery and the church as examples, he is finally too honest not to confront Christianity's devastating failure in this sphere.

The book's cover reproduces Piero della Francesca's famous painting of Christ's flagellation, which is set at the back of a serenely architectural loggia, with a mysterious group of two men and a youth standing in the foreground. Many bytes have been used up interpreting this image, and Sennett chooses Marilyn Lavin's explanation: she has identified the men as fathers of sons who died young through illness – the two groups are thus pendants, Christ's sufferings continuous with the men's human loss. But the composure of Piero's style is something less elegiac but rather more tranquil and austere than this theory suggests – which is, besides, only one among many. Nevertheless, the argument about Piero's vision of an eternal Catholic present, realised in a single unified space, makes real sense, for he also elaborated, in the famous frescos at Arezzo, the Triumph of the Cross over outsiders – over Jews and pagans, Romans and Saracens. The embrace of the Church, in all its saving forgiveness and healing, and vaunted egalitarianism and freedom from prejudice ('There shall be neither Jew nor Greek, bond nor free' etc.), could not tolerate those who refused conversion, who did not want to yield to its warm hold, as Sennett shows in the most brilliant section of his book, the chapter on the segregation of the Venetian Jews in the Ghetto. 'Send all of them to live in the Ghetto Nuovo which is like a castle,' the Venetian Zacaria Dolfin proposed, 'and [to] make drawbridges and close it with a wall; they should have only one gate, which would enclose them there and they would stay there, and two boats of the Council of Ten . . . would go and stay there, at night, at their expense.'

In 1516, the Ghetto Nuovo was built; a hundred years later, the Jews, many of whom had fled to Venice from persecution elsewhere, had effectively become strangers to most of their fellow-citizens, and were the subject of monstrous fantasies (that the men menstruated, and ate babies); in 1629–31, the ravages of plague were exacerbated when the Jews were not allowed to leave their dense, airless warren; in 1636, the Ghetto was attacked, torched and its inhabitants killed in one of the worst pogroms yet seen in Europe. Syncope had run out of energy. For Sennett, Shakespeare's portrait of the Christian merchants' 'lightness' of character, compared to the depths and consequence of Shylock's tragedy in *The Merchant of Venice*, marks the moment of entry into the modern world.

Meanwhile, torturers believed the Inquisitors when assured that it was only the devils who were screaming at the pain, not the human bodies whom they held at their mercy.

Sennett tells us that his book was begun fifteen years ago in collaboration with Michel Foucault. Foucault's influence is apparent in its interest in power, in its quest for understanding impulses towards abjection and dominance, in its intermittently personal tone, but above all in its preference for almost any state of being or feeling over indifference and passivity. 'Freedom which seeks to overcome resistance . . . dulls the body,' Sennett writes. 'It is an anaesthetic. Freedom which arouses the body does so by accepting impurity, difficulty and obstruction as part of the experience of liberty.' This commitment to stimulus can lead to some surprising judgments: describing the guillotine, Sennett deplores Revolutionary gravitas and the lack of drama between crowd and executioner, which had once been customary; discussing the death of Louis XVI, he objects to the phalanx of soldiers and to the speed and reticence of the deed, which prevented crowd participation in the King's pain. A hundred years on, and roads and railways increased the deadly isolation of city dwellers from one another and continued to lull and passify (*sic*) their flesh.

The author of *Flesh and Stone* can turn rather priestly at times: 'the moral divide between flesh and stone is one of the marks of the secularisation of society,' Sennett writes. But with the increase in ethnic conflict and the growing numbers of the homeless (nearly one person in two hundred in the summer in New York, 'placing the city above Calcutta but below Cairo in this index of misery'), practical measures seem to be needed much more than mystical symbols: the stones of an ordinary roof, of an ordinary hearth, not of temples or altars; a workaday saucepan, not a chalice. It may sound like stating the obvious, but as Christopher Jencks points out in *The Homeless*, the solution of homelessness is simply housing, and housing can be provided by an enlightened and effective housing policy.

The Australian playwright and historian Paul Carter has written eloquently on the settlement of the Yarra River and early colonial building in what became Melbourne; it would have been interesting to explore this. The opening up of Paris during the Revolution and the Second Empire, which Sennett discusses, throws light on the establishment of imperial authority elsewhere; in South Africa, there is new thinking on how to redraw the symbolic spaces of authority. Similarly, after looking so absorbingly at the different ways Athenian men and women inhabited their cities, *Flesh and Stone* could have followed up the continuing differences in contemporary life: women's gossipings in the neighbourhood, men's networkings on the business circuit. Few people who use London Transport, or attend football matches, concerts or demonstrations, would agree that modern cities have reduced resistance and difficulty or even stimulus – though the Criminal Justice Act has now outlawed some of these forms of association. Moshing, or churning with the crowd at the front near the band, and stage diving, surfing over the crowd's head, passed bodily from hand to hand, have become two of the new pleasures of our day, not quite the happy-go-lucky jostling of Pasolini's dream of lost pleasure, but, in keeping with the times, a more desperate bid for bodily contact.

1994

The Virtue of Incest

Review of Marc Shell, Elizabeth's Glass

The Romance of Apollonius of Tyre opens with the classic fairy-tale couple: the king and his daughter. Antiochus is powerful, she is beautiful, and of marriageable age – there is no mother. The difference is that, in this variation, she will not leave home to marry a prince, for her father Antiochus 'began to love her in a way unsuitable for a father . . . Since he could not endure the wound in his breast, one day . . . he rushed into his daughter's room and ordered the servants to withdraw . . . Spurred on by the frenzy of his lust, he took his daughter's virginity by force, in spite of her lengthy resistance.'

After the rape, the girl (who remains nameless) wants to kill herself, but her nurse (in romance and fairy tale, nurses almost always advance the immoralist argument for survival) persuades her to live and tolerate her father's passion. The King announces that he will give his daughter to the suitor who can answer a riddle – and candidates who fail will die. Enter Apollonius, who guesses correctly that Antiochus is living incestuously with his daughter: 'Nor did you lie,' he tells the King, 'when you said, "I eat my mother's flesh": look at your daughter.' Apollonius' discovery places him in great danger, and he flees – his adventures will disclose the proper pattern of paternal and filial love, as he first loses, then regains both true wife and true daughter. His multiple quest will involve him in redefining himself and others, in recognising concealed identities and in solving riddles, before the happy ending and the reconciliation are achieved.

The romance was one of the best known and most loved in the medieval world, and exists in numerous manuscripts and versions from the tenth and eleventh centuries onwards. Shakespeare follows its plot in *Pericles*, and it intertwines with many fairy tales: for example, Giambattista Basile's 'The She-Bear' (1636) and 'Donkeyskin', written down by Charles Perrault in 1694, though in both these stories the daughter escapes from her father by disguising herself in an animal skin.

Incest has now become one of the dominant focuses of moral panic, flourishing virulently in fantasy as well as occurring, often tragically, in practice, while these old stories, which deal with it, and which offer the consolation of an image reflected back, of a wrong unmasked, of authority shaken and realigned, lie overlooked on the river-bed of contemporary consciousness, as a turbulent current of terror, suspicions and despair rushes by. Through its own form of riddling, a romance like that of Apollonius encrypted emotional and social realities which helped its receivers at least to understand their situation a bit better.

In this remarkable study, Marc Shell has widened the range of genres dealing with the personal cost of the dysfunctional family to include a startling and unlikely candidate: a translation of a mystical meditation into English from French made by Princess Elizabeth, the future Queen. *The Glass of the Sinful Soul*, as she called it, was not an original work, but a good pupil's exercise, undertaken in 1544 at the age of eleven as part of her lessons. A long prayer by Marguerite de Valois, Queen of Navarre, it was written out and enclosed between embroidered covers, as a New Year's present for Catherine Parr, Elizabeth's fourth stepmother, and her last. This text has never been edited or analysed before, in spite of its fascination as a holograph manuscript by the future Gloriana, Astraea, Una, the Faerie Queene. Marc Shell expresses surprise at this, as well he might, for as he points out, the manuscript conjoins three of the most brilliant lively-minded queens of the era: Marguerite de Navarre was the compiler of *The Heptameron*, a collection of secular tales, as well as a Reformist sympathiser, friend of Calvin and patron of independent scholars; Catherine Parr also composed religious meditations, including the *Lamentacion of a Synner*. She was 'the first woman to publish in English', Shell says, 'with the intention of influencing the public'. All three once and future queens were united by their active interest in Protestantism: Marguerite gave protection to the Huguenots in France, and her own work was denounced as heretical by the Sorbonne.

Over Elizabeth and Catherine fell the shadow of another woman of gifts and intelligence, who was a queen herself for a spell: Anne Boleyn, Elizabeth's mother. In an age when Thomas More showed his radical mettle by according his daughters the same education as his sons, Anne had been allowed to cultivate her mind to an unusual degree; she had also corresponded with Marguerite, with whom she shared an interest in Reform theology and piety. The French Queen probably sent the English Queen *Le Miroir de l'âme pécheresse*. So when Anne's brilliant daughter Elizabeth began Englishing it and copying out her translation in her shapely, confident italic hand, she was also remembering the mother who had had her head cut off when she was three; the book is a kind of concealed memorial to Anne Boleyn. Elizabeth, who could probably not remember her, still wanted to picture her lost mother in her glass, like Miranda in *The Tempest*. *The Glass of the Sinful Soul* is her veiled girlhood tribute.

It does not make for easy reading now, unless the reader has a special taste for a brand of women's mysticism that began earlier, in Germany and the Lowlands, with the *devotio moderna*. Cries and ejaculations fly thick and fast, the soul seems to labour unavailingly, and sinks into a mire of bloated, yearning commonplaces. Marc Shell, however, has been able to read the braille of another tale beneath the rhetorical surplus, and to discover there the brightness of an individual imagination communicating strongly within given restrictions. His guidance is indispensable. Even Lacan was alert to the female mystics' intellectual adventurousness, though he did not expand on the way they seize on symbolic language for their own purposes. Peter Dronke has shown with great warmth and sensitivity how visionaries like Hildegard of Bingen in the twelfth century, and Marguerite Porete at the beginning of the fourteenth, developed an original, feminist subjectivity in their ecstatic writings. Marguerite de Navarre's intense personal ardour reveals the influence of Porete's *Mirror of Simple Souls*. This was a piety which dispensed with intermediaries: Porete's 'free soul' anticipated the Reformers' emphasis on individual conscience and their rage at Catholic priestly authority. For bypassing the clergy and speaking directly to God,

Marguerite Porete was burned in the Place de Grève in Paris in 1310 – perhaps the first female literary martyr.

The text the Princess Elizabeth translated, this long outpouring of divine prayers and praise, by turns rapturous and desperate, expansive and pent-up, chaste and erotic, thus affirmed a Protestant view of the relation of the individual and God, and looks forward, Shell argues, to the identification, in Protestant, Elizabethan Britain, of the monarch (anointed but not ordained) with the head of the Church, and to the convergence of patriotism and the Reformed faith in the soul of an Englishman/woman.

The political significance of the work as it circulated among royal women did not remain a private matter. In 1548, four years after the princess finished the translation, it was published by the Reformer John Bale, one of Elizabeth's mentors, under the purposively improved title, *A Godly Meditation of the Christian Soul*. Bale had his reasons, as Shell shows, and he encoded them (nothing was then written entirely *en clair*, it seems) in the learned Epistle Dedicatory and the shorter Conclusion which framed the work. He was the suitor who would grasp the contents of her riddle, claim her, and proclaim her true relation to the world.

John Bale's rhetoric has not attracted an editor's attention before, and in many ways he's an even more brilliant *trouvaille* than Elizabeth's *Glass* itself. A kind of Casaubon *avant la lettre*, polymathic, earnest, deploying references and invoking names in fistfuls, he also rants with splendid vigour: 'The monks in public schools . . . have advanced their idle monkery above the office of a bishop, and the friars with their scald craving beggary above the degrees of them both, as is largely seen in the brawling works of Richard Maydeston.' He thus contributes to the oratory of Protestant dissent which Ted Hughes and Tom Paulin have both evoked as a lost – or at least neglected – strand of the national tradition.

Bale blazoned his desiderata as much as he reviled the objects of his contempt. The Princess Elizabeth embodied all he hoped for. In his Conclusion, she represents the sum of a British tradition of queens, great ladies, brilliant female minds. His is a gripping, legendary, crazily partial account of the national history: 'Though none in this land have yet done as did among the Greeks Plutarch and among the Latins Boccaccio . . . that is to say, left behind them catalogues or nomenclatures of famous and honorable women, yet hath it not at any time been barren of them. No, not in the days of most popish darkness as appeareth by Eleanor Cobham, the wife of good Duke Humphrey.' For sheer entertainment, Bale far surpasses the religious turmoil of Marguerite/Elizabeth. In Bale, erudition becomes rapture, gynephilia euphoria.

Bale was a priest who married a nun, more, Shell thinks, to prove his Protestant credentials than to express his affections. The marriage of Luther to the Cistercian Catherine von Bora had been denounced as incest, because all monks and nuns were brothers and sisters in Christ. Incest therefore occupied a special place in the new faith: it was a badge of virtue, or at any rate, its value had to be recast in order to free it from its ancient taint. On Elizabeth's accession, Bale returned to England from Germany, where he had had *The Glass* published, but he died soon after, doubtless poised for influence, but robbed of the rewards of his enterprising fidelity – Shell does not expand.

The Glass was thus used, in conditions of acute political turbulence, to support the arguments for a queen in general, for Elizabeth in particular, and for a female defender of the Protestant faith, both before and after the fact, as three further editions between 1568 and 1582 suggest. But *The Glass* does not belong only in this frame of realpolitik. Shell pushes deep into what it suggests as to the nexus of psychic relations in the young Princess's life, and how they are enmeshed with questions of the legitimacy of her rule.

This motherless child, who, by 1544, had already seen so many 'mothers' come and go (Jane Seymour in childbirth seven years earlier, Catherine Howard beheaded five years after that), and who would see – and bring about – more women's deaths in her time, had also been made fatherless, when by Act of Parliament in 1536 Henry VIII proclaimed her a bastard. Like a figure in a riddle, Elizabeth's identity was wrapped in enigma, her status unstable, her name challenged: who was she, to what was she heir, to what was she entitled? The extraordinary act of decipherment which Shell performs reveals that Elizabeth speaks of herself and her predicament in the accents of the sinful soul whose implorings and rapture replicate her own quandary.

The soul addresses God in the allegorical language of the Song of Songs: the beloved is at once sister and spouse, little child and *magna mater*, wife and faithless adulteress. Like the Virgin Mary, she is both mother to the godhead, his daughter from the beginning, and his betrothed. Shell audaciously takes the mystical collapse of distinctions between lover, mother, bride and daughter, matches it with the situation in the Tudor court, and uses this religious vision as a template for the remodelled relation between monarch and subjects, reconstituting it as a passionate, aberrant, elective, spiritually incestuous family.

In this light, *The Glass* becomes 'a kinship riddle' in which the true princess was wrapped around by powers contending for control of the throne's significance. When Elizabeth expressed the symbolic incest of the soul, the child of God, with her father, the Creator and King of all, and then claimed equality with that 'sinful soul' as his spouse, she was laying the foundation of the modern state, in which the ruler, secular and religious (monarch and Pope), would be both brother and sister, mother and father, bride and bridegroom of the family of his/her subjects: she was casting herself, Shell writes, as a 'Mother Superior in a national siblinghood'. The origins of the Virgin Queen, hierogamously joined to her country, lie here. As she said in her accession speech: 'I have long since made choice of a husband, the kingdom of England . . . I beseech you, gentlemen, charge me not with the want of children, forasmuch as every one of you, and every Englishman besides, are my children and relations.'

The spectre of incest held the Tudor court in a permanent state of alarm, as surely as the Sphinx, that omen of aberration, had terrorised Thebes: Henry VIII divorced Catherine of Aragon because she had been married to his brother, he charged Anne Boleyn with committing incest with her brother George, and he himself had slept with her sister, Mary. Even more sharply, Thomas Seymour, Elizabeth's former step-uncle (as brother to Jane) as well as stepfather (he married the widowed Catherine Parr after Henry VIII's death), molested and later tried to marry her. Incest was widely defined in those days: according to Catholic laws of affinity, marriage between the godparents of the same child was forbidden, as was any union of children who shared a godparent. The notion of 'carnal contagion', a kind of theological Aids, decreed that anyone who slept with someone was joined to them, so that a third party might be committing incest too: 'when a man hath meddled with a woman, or a woman with a man, neither may be wedded to [the] other's kin, into the fifth degree . . . for if they do, it is incest'. The most extreme view condemned all sex as incestuous, because all are one in the family of Adam.

As a free-thinking Protestant, Bale was arguing against this mechanistic view of morality when he issued his impassioned justification of Anne Boleyn's daughter: 'true nobility' springs, he writes in the Epistle Dedicatory, from 'a famous renown obtained by long exercised virtue'. That Elizabeth was acutely aware that she was not only illegitimate, but possibly tainted by the incestuous union of her mother, was reflected in the translation exercises she chose to do as part of her education in virtue. From Beothius' *Consolation of Philosophy*, she rendered the lines:

> If your first spring and author
> God you view,
> No man bastard be . . .

The Catholic order, based on an outworn formulaic arrangement of kin, was to be replaced by the 'extraordinary kinship' of the Christian community. No one would be a bastard any more, if true to God, king (queen) and country. Everyone, like Luther, like John Bale himself, would be brother and sister, bride and groom. Spiritual incest was to lead to the first stirrings of democratic levelling between ruler and ruled in a new polity.

Does Shell overinterpret the evidence, as happens increasingly often with the more brilliant decoders working in America and influenced by French methods of inquiry? His essay is so fresh and so compelling that it seems grudging to offer objections. There are, however, several rucks in his ingeniously woven carpet: Elizabeth's sibling relation to her Faerie Kingdom and its folk needs development before it can become truly convincing, as her cult and her virginity elevated her far above the levelling voice of the 'sinful soul'. Did the model of the monarch as divine autocrat really change at this point, as Shell argues? Did its decline even begin here? Again, the taboo on incest survives, uninfluenced by Protestant revision, in Shakespeare's treatment of the Apollonius story in *Pericles* (1608) and in later variations. Indeed, in *Much Ado*, Beatrice quips that she may not marry: 'As Adam's sons are my brethren and truly I hold it a sin to match in my kindred.' It's one of her jokes, but it shows that old ideas about consanguinity and the incest taboo were still spooking believers. Moreover, Shakespeare had certainly not taken in his Queen's revolutionary ideas about bastardy.

There is a third, more fundamental objection to be made, however. The idea that mythic structures interact with social and political structures as in a mirror – but without inversion – runs contrary to much thinking about the sacred, its function and its means of expression. The mythic can only be conveyed through language which turns common laws, distinctions and relations upside down and inside out: hence celibate priests and cross-dressed shamans, virgin births, androgynous gods, and the 'Virgin mother, daughter to thy son' whom Dante invoked. By offering an image of difference, the sacred helps to set the rules, to define the norm. Shell argues that Bale and Elizabeth's joint work converts the transgressive, even tragic reality of incest into a utopian philosophy – that it brings the vision of the sacred family down to earth. The inversion makes the divine exception human. Perhaps the paradoxical cancellation of the incest taboo represents another of Protestantism's revolutionary freedoms; the new polity transgressed against the old order's distinction between sacred and profane, incorporating the mythic into the material order and the arrangement of power – as can be seen in Shakespeare's treatment of kingship. Shell's material could, however, be read exactly the other way round: to argue that Elizabeth was hallowed by the double anomaly of her unchaste kinship and her own chaste state: that they remained exceptional, and that therein lay the strong magic of the Virgin Queen.

This is a book of outstanding interest and subtlety, produced with model notes and glossary; it may overreach the evidence in boldness, but it unfailingly asks – and answers – acute questions, about the nation's identity, the permeable boundary between sex and politics, and the fascination of incest.

1993

The Marquise Unmasked: *Les Liaisons dangereuses*

Thirty years ago, various representatives of the French literary world tried to prevent Roger Vadim's 1959 film version of the novel *Les Liaisons dangereuses* by Choderlos de Laclos from being shown, claiming it would bring the nation's *patrimoine* into disrepute. Today, Christopher Hampton's version of the book, a huge draw on the London stage, has been adapted by him for the screen and become an even greater popular and critical sensation. Meanwhile Milos Forman has made another film version, called simply *Valmont*. Laclos's Don Juan has become a hero of our time, and his courtship – of the public at least – continues unopposed.

The Vicomte de Valmont, Laclos's male seducer, is six years older than Mozart's Don Giovanni (the novel appeared in 1782).[1] Both meet the description of the legendary Don Juan as Camus saw him: an embodied principle of desire which in itself provokes desire.[2] He is irresistible, and his dangerous reputation does nothing to thwart his conquests: the objects of his attention are all aware of it, seek to escape from the danger, but cannot. Elvira knows, pursues, succumbs again – almost. As for Mme de Merteuil, it is Valmont's fame as a seducer that spurs her original longing for him (one of the planks of the legend is that all women secretly want to appear in Don Juan's catalogue of conquests). Like Don Giovanni, he is aristocratic, too, while his partner in crime Mme de Merteuil shares a title with Laclos's real-life contemporary and *vicieux*, the Marquis de Sade. The focus of all feminine susceptibilities, Valmont is himself impervious; always aroused, securely virile, he is never touched. At least, not until he meets his nemesis, in the form of the Marquise's implacable revenge after his surrender to a rival, the Présidente de Tourvel.

Valmont's discovery of love with Mme de Tourvel represents a significant difference between Don Giovanni, as created by Mozart's librettist Lorenzo da Ponte for his opera and Laclos's seducer, and it makes Valmont a precursor of the hero of José Zorilla's popular romantic play, *Don Juan Tenorio*, written in 1844 and still performed annually in Spain today. In this romance, Don Juan is saved by the love of the pure virgin Doña Inés. But there are deeper points of contact and difference between Don Giovanni in the opera and Valmont in *Les Liaisons dangereuses*, as well as changed nuances of emphasis between the Laclos novel and the film version by Christopher Hampton. They reflect sharply current unease about sex and the state of play – of battle – in the bedroom; they pull the covers off the modern politics of seduction.

In *Don Giovanni*, as in earlier, Spanish versions of the Don Juan story, women are the immediate objects of the hero's desire but the ultimate targets of his exploits are men, the men who hold the women in their keeping; fathers, husbands, fiancés. In the first scene of the opera, Don Giovanni kills Donna Anna's father the Commendatore, who has been roused by her screams and rushes to help her. Later, on the eve of her wedding, Zerlina presents a specially piquant challenge, and Masetto, her rustic bridegroom, an amusing prey. Donna Elvira, however, unhusbanded, unmanned, stalking her seducer on her own, puts him to flight; in her case, there is no male protector, no masculine ownership to defy and outdo. According to the code of *omertà* that obtained in southern Europe throughout the era of chivalry and into the modern period, a man's honour was kept by the women of his house, by the daughters, the wives, the sisters, and, not least, the mothers. They could plunge a family into bloodshed for centuries by their folly, ruin a brother, husband, or father by their lapses, or redeem him, as Doña Inés does in Zorilla's play, by their goodness. A man's standing in society, as well as his immortal soul, was in hostage to his womenfolk. But their accumulation of virtue was highly vulnerable to attack: it constituted a store which could be raided like any other goods, and its guardians were not all like Doña Inés. Rather, like Eve, they were easily seduced, and the seducer, by robbing a man of his women's virtue, grew himself in reputation and stature as surely as if he had seized valuables of a material order. Don Giovanni allows us to glimpse, past the dazzle and high spirits of Mozart's *dramma giocoso*, this remorseless aristocratic economy, in which women are prizes at stake in a struggle for power between men.

Duelling is the inevitable consequence of such tension at the heart of Latin society: the violence by which Don Giovanni lives meets the violence with which first the Commendatore, then Don Ottavio, must defend Donna Anna. For every rapist, a knight errant; for every Don Juan, a Don Quixote. In fact, chivalrous males can do without women much more easily than without each other.

In *Les Liaisons dangereuses*, on the other hand, Valmont's manifest ambition focuses less clearly on the men behind the women; he is a thoroughgoing libertine, bent on pleasure and the sweets of power over women, especially resistant young maidens like Cécile Volanges, or honest wives, like Mme de Tourvel. But the Marquise de Merteuil performs with supreme art as a broker in men's honour: in her key letter (no. 81) when she analyses her methods to Valmont, she explains that she always extracts a secret from her lovers with which she can blackmail them, so that they can never unmask her and damage her honour. Her motive for debauching Cécile Volanges is revenge on the young woman's future husband; throughout the novel Laclos shows Merteuil gradually ensnaring and immobilising Valmont himself as poisonously as the famed black widow spider. Her own male protectors dead, a widow without parents or children, she plays with women too, as does Don Juan, in order to humiliate and disempower men; she has taken up occupation of a masculine place in the code of chivalry, and her scheming and pursuits seem in the novel all the more diabolical for this trespass across the boundaries of gender.

But what appeared unwomanly and anomalous, even fiendish, in the eighteenth century does not strike the present-day reader in the same light. The economics of chivalry have changed, and with them the objectives of seduction. Don Giovanni, with his Faustian heroics against fathers, law-givers, husbands, does not speak to our times as clearly as Valmont and Mme de Merteuil's partnership. With their different erotic objectives, the protagonists of *Les Liaisons dangereuses* reflect the business of sex today with more hardheadedness. For the Marquise, men are the paramount antagonists, including the Vicomte she cherishes so deeply for his villainy. When he offers her an ultimatum, demanding that she keep her word and reward him with a night in her bed, she hurls the curt message at him, 'Eh bien, la guerre' ('Well then, it's war'.) In the cinema, we expect from her half-smile that she will surrender to Valmont's eager charms, and her duellist's challenge (again, a masculine impulse) makes an effective *coup de théâtre*.

In this twentieth-century movie of the Don Juan myth, the woman on her own is no longer the piteous raving Elvira, driven to love and to save, to denounce the beloved seducer and then yield to him all over again, but a malignant and frozen sensualist who has learned never to confuse sex and love, the pleasures of love and the lover himself. Christopher Hampton had already translated Molière's *Don Juan*, in 1974. He once commented on the Molière: 'the harsh moral of his rigorous fable rings as true today as it ever has: if you let yourself be fucked, you will be'. His consciousness of the timeliness of such studies in cold-hearted eroticism may well have led him on to consider Laclos's novel, and in his skilful synthesis of a long book, Hampton pauses to dramatise the important moment of self-revelation on the Marquise's part, when she describes how she steeled herself to survive:

> I practised detachment. I learned how to look cheerful, while
> under the table I stuck a fork into the back of my hand. I became a
> virtuoso of deceit. It wasn't pleasure I was after, it was knowledge.
> I consulted the strictest moralists to learn how to appear,
> philosophers to find out what to think and novelists to see what I
> could get away with. And, in the end, I distilled everything down to
> one wonderfully simple principle: win or die.[3]

There is an apparent feminist edge to the Marquise's declaration, which the film script seizes, and on which the actress, Glenn Close, builds. In Laclos, the Marquise characterises herself as a Delilah, avenging her sex for the boredom and imprisonment inflicted on it by men ('Née pour venger mon sexe et maîtriser le vôtre', she writes: 'Born to avenge my sex and dominate yours.') In the film, the Marquise repudiates men as thoroughly as in the book, freezing out Valmont for his 'marital tone' when he tries to order her about. But she never adduces chivalry towards her own sex as a motive. In the 1980s, survival in the battle seems reason enough for her conduct.

A woman on her own, if determined not to capitulate to the seductions or the commandments of the male, has to find a *raison d'être*, or have one found for her by her creators. Mozart's opera proposes passion for vengeance in Elvira; Laclos presents Merteuil as unnatural, a monstrous usurper of a male sexuality. But Hampton, viewing the Marquise from the vantage point of today, finds something natural in her reaction to her female predicament. The film's choice of a Versailles-like *galerie des glaces*, a hall of mirrors, for the Marquise's apartments, points up her poker game of feints and illusion, the narcissism in the seducer's exercise of power, but it also stirs other associations. As long ago as 1929, the psychoanalyst Joan Rivière offered a depressing, influential insight into the changing character of sexual engagement since emancipation. Womanliness itself, she proposes, has become a masquerade.[4] Joan Rivière, inspired by her clinical studies, was writing about the 'new career woman', and noted, 'Not long ago intellectual pursuits for women were associated almost exclusively with an overtly masculine type of woman who, in pronounced cases, made no secret of her wish or claim to be a man. This has now changed.' Rivière went on to discuss one case history and described a performance of femininity, a 'masquerade' of compulsive twittering and coquetting. Glenn Close, playing the Marquise de Merteuil, is surrounded by mirrors, in which her perfected toilette and elaborate ornaments are continually refracted; schooling herself not to register her feelings on her face, practising detachment as fervently as a stylite, she is engaged in a lifelong masquerade too, because she has not been able to live openly the independent way she wanted, nor achieve her ends except by pretending to be a different kind of creature, a conventional woman, without appetite or intelligence, uninterested in sexual satisfaction or other power.

However, the film's sympathies with its evil genius only go so far: it would be reading against the text to invite compassion when the Marquise is publicly shamed at the Opéra. In the stage version, Hampton chose not to punish her so publicly and dramatically at the end, diverging from Laclos, who banishes her from society, and then disfigures her with smallpox. The playwright may have avoided the book's morality-tale ending in the stage version because it seemed too pat. If Mme de Merteuil's individual and extreme wickedness is wholly to blame, then the contemporary reverberations he had set in motion about her situation would go for nothing.

Some of the other changes to the novel in its journey from play to film tend to play down the glimmerings of sympathy for women's erotic life that *Les Liaisons dangereuses* can at times inspire. In *Dangerous Liaisons*, the director Stephen Frears follows Valmont's point of view more often than Merteuil's: Merteuil is more often beheld rather than the eyes through which we are watching and understanding the action. Within her masquerade, she remains to a great extent concealed from us too. It is Valmont, played by John Malkovich, who becomes the presiding consciousness of the film.

Valmont differs from his peer, Don Giovanni, in obvious ways: for one thing, he scores success after success, unlike Mozart's hero, who is comically checked at every turn. Also Valmont sometimes undertakes his seductions because he is told to by the Marquise; his pursuit of her, and his frustrated desire to renew their lost liaison effectively, provide a motive for most of the mischief in the plot. Like the legendary Don Juan, however, he is not to blame for the passions women excite in him: a Don Juan, as Ovid made clear in *The Art of Loving*, is God's gift to women, only giving them what they want:

> A man who kisses a girl and goes no further deserves to forfeit even the pleasure of kissing her. Obviously one wants to do a great deal more than that, and if one does not, one is being, not civilized, but silly.
>
> 'Oh, but I should hate to use brute force,' you say. Why, that is exactly what girls like: they often prefer to enjoy themselves under duress. The victim of a sexual assault is generally delighted, for she takes your audacity as a compliment; whereas the girl who could have been raped but was not is bound to feel disappointed . . .[5]

It is a principle of the myth of the eternal seducer that the raped are ravished by untold pleasure; the male fantasy in *Les Liaisons dangereuses* develops it further and shows the needs of women generously met not only by Valmont's prowess in bed (Cécile, raped, becomes an apt and lusty pupil) but by his submission to the Marquise's machinations, and prolonged obedience to the imperative of his frustrated desire for her. The necessary simplification of the novel for the cinema also points up a central, contemporary twist in the interpretation of the two protagonists' relationship, which twitches aside another mask from the Marquise, to reveal how she is beheld by the chief man in her life:

Merteuil: We loved each other once, didn't we? I think it was love. And you made me very happy.

Valmont: And I could again. We just untied the knot, it was never broken.

Merteuil: Illusions, of course, are by their nature sweet.

Valmont: I have no illusions. I lost them on my travels. Now I want to come home.[6]

The rake wants to come home.

Is this a meeting of husband and wife after a separation? Surely Merteuil's enmity towards marriage, surpassing even the traditional aversion of the professional seducer, must rule out an understanding that the pair are nostalgic for connubial bliss. No, in the late 1980s, when the rake asks to come home, he is not talking to a beloved mistress or a forsaken wife, but rather to another woman in his life – his mother.

Don Juan has no mother. Don Giovanni has no mother either, only a father figure; Elvira, Doña Inés and other women who have loved, forgiven and redeemed the rake fulfil a kind of maternal function in the legend, as intercessors for his salvation, like the Virgin Mary in early versions of the Don Juan legend, miracle stories about the deathbed repentance of daredevils and rascals. But Laclos shadows forth another kind of mothering in the famous seducer's life when he creates his monstrous Marquise, and Hampton caught his drift and rendered visible the invisible mother of Don Juan in the form of Mme de Merteuil: a perverted Phaedra, a cold-blooded Clytemnestra, Hamlet's mother Gertrude and Snow White's wicked Queen looking at themselves in mirrors.

To see Merteuil as Valmont's mother does not entail reading the novel itself, and its current avatars, as essentially Oedipal; nor agreeing with some interpreters who have analysed the whole Don Juan complex in those terms. (The Errol Flynn vehicle, written by a woman – Bess Meredyth – in 1926, provides the only instance I've come across of Don Juan's mother appearing in the story: she's caught *in flagrante* and harshly repudiated by little Juan's father, who then sternly warns the boy against all women, setting him on a lifelong quest for true love.) But listening to that odd filial note, 'Now I want to come home', does deepen the realisation that the misogynist aspects in the Freudian analysis of male sexuality inform the understanding and representation of female sexuality today. The mother shows her Medusa face and scares the little boy into manliness, dispatching him into the world outside the home, enabling him to turn his desire towards other women besides herself, and so further the existence of human society: in other words, his desire lies in her gift, at her command, arising from fear of the castration she inspires. (So orthodoxy would have it.) It seems to me that this is a model of sexual struggle that is becoming more widely and unquestioningly acknow ledged, as women express themselves strongly about their needs and wants, and men fail to develop a correspondingly articulate rebellion against the traditional perception of male desire as rampant, unfocused, violent, threatening and threatened. Somewhere, in the midst of the initial struggle going on about the character of maleness and of femaleness, a huge new population of fantasy females – hard women, sadistic specialists, phallic mothers – has grown, most obviously in the pornography industry, but also, pervasively, in other branches of entertainment and culture. The bridle that women were supposed to extend to their mates, according to Victorian models of sexuality, in order to tame and harness them, has become a goad, and a pretext for a renewed, but different, masculine claim that responsibility for male sexuality lies with the female.

This shift of the sexual burden, from men to women, can be seen through a comparison of *Don Giovanni* with Stephen Frears's film *Dangerous Liaisons*. In the opera, the entirely masculine figure of the Commendatore, father of Anna, embodies the law the libertine flouts. He has even been identified with Mozart's own father, who died while Mozart was composing the opera. A military commander transformed into a stone statue, he incorporates the values of solidity and rectitude and constancy and strength that the Don has rejected on his heedless whirl of changing partners and broken promises. The archetypal Don Juan, apostate and blasphemer, defies God the Father and his commandments and all his earthly representatives; *Le Festin de pierre*, an early dramatic version of the legend in France (1652/9), was actually subtitled 'Le Fils criminel'. Don Giovanni kills the Commendatore, defies his ghost, refuses to repent when he appears at the final banquet and is instead hurled down into hell. In a reversal of 'Là ci darem la mano', when he was wooing Zerlina with false promises, he takes the Commendatore's hand in good faith – and, for the first time, he himself tastes betrayal.

Mozart's Don Giovanni quickly became a hero of Romanticism precisely because he is so headstrong, seizing what is forbidden – sex – at the risk to his own life and soul. He dares be a man when the divine law denies him his instincts, and embraces his death. To the Romantics, his rebellion was magnificent, the divine authority of the patriarch could prevail over his body, but not his spirit: the opera ends with Don Giovanni's heroism exalted and purified by his damnation. He's the Faust who does not regret the pact with the Devil because he exults in his knowledge, he's Adam and Eve refusing to despair after the Fall, for they prefer mortality to Eden, human experience to perfect bliss.

Valmont also meets his death, at the hands of the Chevalier Danceny. He repents too, but betrays the Marquise with his last breath, one of his rare excursions into truthful utterance. He seals her fate, as assuredly as killing her. Just as the law is embodied by the Commendatore, so Valmont's law is laid down by the Marquise: though they claim to be equal allies, he is the tool of her intrigues and when he departs from her wishes, as in the case of Mme de Tourvel, becomes the target of her vengeance. Valmont is driven by her in a more straightforward manner than Don Giovanni is ruled by the Commendatore, and the shift from a prevailing male dynamic to a female one is a significant aspect of the contemporary revival of interest in Laclos's novel.

Don Juan is usually portrayed as needlessly self-willed; his drive to defy the patriarch does not provide an open reason for his conduct. In fact, he rarely offers a motive at all. As embodied desire, he merely acts, follows his nose, literally flaring at the *odor di femmina* on the air, a god liberated from the rules that govern mortal relations, as free to ravish as Jove himself. His 'mad pursuit', as Keats described the rape on the Grecian urn, only leads on to more, madder pursuits; Don Giovanni exults, during the 'champagne aria', his only extended solo in the opera, on the increase in his score, like a speculator contemplating a killing in the market. The music and the words imitate his stock-taking by their redoubled repeats:

> con questa e quella vo amoreggiar
> vo amoreggiar amoreggiar
> ah, la mia lista, doman mattina

d'una decina devi aumentar.
(I'll make love to one and then to another . . .
Oh! You'll have to add ten to my list tomorrow morning.')

Molière's Don Juan also acts on his own, wilfully flouting the received code of conduct and airing his views so thoroughly in the course of the play that he has little time left over – on stage – for flirtations; agnostic defiance, rationalism, anticlericalism, and a characteristic Molièrian repugnance for humbug animate his declared lust. Here, the century before Mozart and da Ponte, the chief mortal sin in the eyes of the Church – concupiscence – becomes the chief weapon of dissent. Molière's Don Juan speaks for the seventeenth-century Enlightenment, and succeeded too well in his challenge: the play was banned.

The rebel character of the hero made him a pattern of Romanticism: a loner, a kind of suicide, a saint of love and the personal quest for knowledge, whose final incarnation perhaps was Genet, seen through the eyes of Sartre. Although Valmont also finds love and damnation and death in the course of Laclos's novel, he could not become, alongside Don Giovanni, a fully fledged Romantic hero during the nineteenth century, because Laclos's pious intentions deny Valmont full responsibility for his actions. Don Giovanni is magnificent in his autonomy, his loneliness: he resembles the solitary watcher on the promontory or the wanderer in the forest of Caspar David Friedrich's paintings from the decades following the opera; he sins, and takes the consequences. In *Les Liaisons dangereuses*, it is Mme de Merteuil who takes the rap. Although her malice is hypnotising to the reader as well as to Valmont, her culpability ultimately diminishes the novel. The workings of desire in *Don Giovanni* magnify a struggle about carnality we all intuit within ourselves (regardless of gender), even if we are spared it in experience. But Mme de Merteuil is a special case, and Laclos's notion of blame a cowardly one. When Valmont parrots to Mme de Tourvel the farewell letter the Marquise has produced, he uses the Gallic shrug to devastating effect: 'Adieu, mon ange, je t'ai prise avec plaisir; je te quitte sans regret: je te reviendra peut-être. Ainsi va le monde.' ('Farewell, my angel, I took you with pleasure; I leave you without regret: perhaps I'll come back to you. It's the way of the world.') Then he repeats once more the refrain with which he has closed each line of this death sentence: 'Ce n'est pas ma faute.'

Cynicism about human nature and about society inspires him, he tells her. The original sin which drives Don Giovanni has become, in the world of *Les Liaisons*, a form of social mores. Though Mme de Merteuil and Valmont are both using languid pessimism as a weapon against the Présidente de Tourvel's pathetic struggle to be good, the novel still makes it clear that Mme de Merteuil, like the Tempter in the original miracle stories, not only whispers Valmont's misdeeds and then spurs him on, but, just like Satan, is fully cognisant of her own wickedness, and content. She has taken the place of Mephistopheles in the prototype of Faust, the tale of Theophilus who sold his soul to the Devil for a bishopric, but was saved by the Virgin Mary.

Between the page and the screen, something has changed this notoriously pitiless missive of Valmont to Mme de Tourvel. Hampton has translated Valmont's refrain 'Ce n'est pas ma faute' (simply, 'It's not my fault') as 'It's beyond my control.'

The scene when he renounces the Présidente is still horrifying, and Malkovich manages to convey how his words clash with his inner feelings more sensitively than fidelity to the book would call for. But this throws even more responsibility on to Merteuil, as does the phrase 'beyond my control'. 'Fault' is a general concept, roughly referring to the weakness of all men; 'ce n'est pas ma faute' is a coward's excuse, but it emanates from the same universe where Don Giovanni stands and defends the human against the divine judge, where men are possessed by lust and cannot do otherwise. (It has little to do, however, with Molière's hero's world, in which he alone elects, through reason, to follow the path he has chosen.) Mme de Merteuil, by contrast, filtered through Hampton's script and acted by Glenn Close, a star famous for performances in rawly violent films about sex (*Jagged Edge, Fatal Attraction*), is a contemporary creation for these times of sexual drive and purpose and independence; yet her relation to the principal man in her life is best characterised as incestuous. She goads him to perform, she delights in his success (but not so that he notices and slackens off), she defends her right to entertain a young lover in the face of his disapproval and jealousy, but her possessiveness leads her to cut him off when he falls in love, because she will accept no rival in his attachments. The power she has over him is convincing to modern eyes, both in the novel and in the cinema because it matches a recognisable and widespread power of women, one that is not forbidden to them: maternal authority. Her responsibility for his sexual exploits becomes acceptable too, for the same reason. Glenn Close herself hardly looks depraved, cruel, or sexually unscrupulous, whereas John Malkovich has sensually vulpine and sardonic features, perfectly expressive of Valmont's acid eroticism.

But it is a tenet of the new, mythologised female sexuality that even the coolest, blandest, and most cerebral of women can be possessed of insatiable desires which will impel them to stop at nothing in their hunger for gratification. Hence the casting of Glenn Close in the 1980s; in the late 1950s, the choice fell on the convincingly night-prowling Jeanne Moreau.

The post-Freudian dispensation draws us into pinning blame on women (and on Mother, above all) in a different way from before, and *Dangerous Liaisons* illustrates how: no one would now claim, with Ovid, that Valmont's victims were begging for it really, but many accept thoughtlessly that a man can remain under a woman's control like a small boy, and in the name of the 'phallic mother', locate the springs of masculine action in female authority. This particular form of the Don Juan myth holds sway now partly because it still seduces women themselves as well as men: motherhood is a site of female power and a legitimate social role which allows needs and desires to be expressed aloud. It is today's masquerade, the permitted face of woman, like the flirtatiousness of the Twenties, to which Rivière referred. The tyranny Mme de Merteuil exercises over Valmont can be thrilling to women, as much as Don Giovanni's boldness. (At the age of sixteen or seventeen, when I first read the novel, I too wanted that power, in kind and degree.) But one has to take care with this type of lure: a fantasy of control will always seduce the disenfranchised. (Unemployed teenagers wear combat fatigues and gigantic boots: prostitutes solicit business by boasting of their dominatrix methods.) This is perhaps the final twist in the seductions of Don Juan, that the victims are flattered into believing themselves in charge.

Don Giovanni hurls his challenge to women, principle, convention, sincerity and death itself, and finds that his life spins out of his control. As he plunges into the flames at the end of Mozart's opera, the three women sing like accomplices in his undoing, like the Moirae themselves: they have survived. Yet the closing triumphal sextet of the *dramma giocoso* hardly leaves us with a morbid image of the power of women or their responsibility for what has occurred. *Les Liaisons dangereuses*, on the other hand, reveals a preying-mantis universe in which men and women engage to the death, committed alike to destruction and self-destruction. At the end of the novel, the saintly Mme de Tourvel is dead, Cécile Volanges shut in a convent, and the Marquise imprisoned behind her ruined beauty; all varieties of closure that also strip disguises from the three women, and effectively put an end to pretences and dissimulation – and to seduction and sex.

The book's moral, which the film grippingly expands in a contemporary mode, offers a clammy warning in an age of material extravagance, conspicuous hedonism, sexual emancipation, AIDS, and deep anxiety about the place of sex in love. The compensations of such pessimism are obvious, and in some way similar to the surface satisfactions offered by Don Giovanni's come-uppance ('that's what you get'). But the fatal female libertine commanding the debauches of the male has returned as a compelling figure today because she embodies a contemporary fantasy about women's sexual domination and responsibility for men's desire. When Valmont looks at himself in the glass, he always sees the Marquise at his ear, urging him to do better. Every age gets the Don Juan it deserves; Valmont is the face of Don Giovanni for our time.

1990

'Wild at Heart': *Manon Lescaut*

The l'Abbé Prévost's novel and Puccini's opera

Manon is the only female character in the novel that bears her name, apart from one or two insignificant walk-on parts. In the opera she is not the only female voice we hear singing, but the only one who develops a personality; she is a peerless protagonist, as the parade of disgraced girls heading for deportation to the New World makes ruthlessly clear; throughout she becomes the cynosure of several sets of eyes, and the focus of the desires of many if not almost all the other characters.

Manon Lescaut, by the Abbé Prévost, is however told in the first person of the Chevalier des Grieux; it is only through his witness that Manon makes herself felt as a speaking subject of the story of which she is the centre, the dynamic, the meaning; the Chevalier's piteous confessions of his ruinous and violent love for her are made to two other men, and form a part – volume VII – of another, much longer masculine first-person novel *Mémoires d'un homme de qualité*. After its publication in 1731 the interpolated romance of *Manon Lescaut* won such intense favour with the reading public that it was immediately seized by the ever vigilant censors of the despotic state; this section of Prévost's long novel was subsequently reprinted separately to reach a growing audience; in 1753 Prévost made some amendments, and it has been in print without interruption ever since, and remained one of the most popular classics ever published, both in French and in translation. The book has been the principal source of the powerful, mythic figure of the femme fatale, the beautiful whore, who embroils men in her charms (fools for love) and then expires from passion.[1] Its position in Prévost's larger fictional enterprise even foreshadows Proust's *Un Amour de Swann*, another story of intense, destructive love similarly introduced into a long autobiographical work, which has taken on a life of its own, and evokes, through the eyes of the male lover, the delicious and tormenting caprices of a fascinating – and immoral – woman.

The Abbé Prévost (1697–1763) abandoned a Benedictine vocation, in the same way as his hero the Chevalier breaks off his clerical career when he falls in love with Manon; Prévost dubbed himself the *Abbé d'exiles* because he was expelled from France so many times for one delinquency or another; in this respect his adventures also echo the Chevalier's, and there have been many readings of *Manon Lescaut* which assume its autobiographical veracity. But the figure of Manon has not been identified with a real woman, unlike Alexander Dumas's variation on the femme fatale in his 1842 novel, *La Dame aux camélias*, and his stage version of four years later. His character, Marguerite Gautier, was modelled on the celebrated courtesan Marie Duplessis, who had been Dumas's mistress before she died at the age of twenty-three: the book appeared two years later. In real life, Marie Duplessis wore great bouquets of camellias; and she in turn inspired several golden-hearted whores of Romanticism who are also associated with flowers' full bloom and evanescence: Marguerite in the novel, Violetta in Verdi's *La traviata*, Mimì in Puccini's *La Bohème* ('i fior ch'io faccio non han odor'), which Puccini composed three years after *Manon Lescaut*. *Manon Lescaut* was his third opera, and helped launch his career as Verdi's heir.

But Prévost's classic, the ultimate source for this exploration of passionate love, male destruction and female immolation, is above all a young man's story: it was originally subtitled *L'Histoire du Chevalier des Grieux*, and it is very much its hero's tale; its intrigue, woven underneath the dominant plot of the lovers' struggle and failure to be together, concerns young men's rivalries – and alliances. *Manon Lescaut* is about dangerous liaisons, too: between men. It predates that novel by Choderlos de Laclos by half a century and was undoubtedly read by Laclos. Both these polished vehicles of Enlightenment sensibility, these subtle and perverse explorations of eroticism and social hypocrisy, brilliantly seduce the reader into believing that what is being described actually happened. The Abbé Prévost creates, in the Chevalier, a natural storyteller: from the moment the Man of Quality first meets him near Le Havre at the village of Pacy before embarkation to America, and then bumps into him again in Calais and hears his tragic story, to the end of the book when he breaks off almost abruptly because Manon is dead, Des Grieux gives the impression that he is talking to us on the page from his experience, and it becomes as fresh and painful to us as it is to him. As Jean Sgard, the leading scholar of Prévost and translator of the novel into English comments, 'The unstable relation between the relived past and an anxious, traumatised memory makes the Chevalier's narrative astonishingly mobile and alive.'[2]

When I first read, as a young woman, the romances of this period of French literature, Diderot's *La Religieuse*, Laclos's *Les Liaisons dangereuses* and Prévost's *Manon Lescaut*, I was completely taken in by the authors' tricks of framing the stories: 'I came across this bundle of letters,' one would say; 'I am publishing this terrible document because the world should know of these abuses,' another would write; 'I am just telling you what I heard the other day, as I was travelling to X, on the coach,' said Prévost.

The tragedy of *Manon Lescaut* catches us up in its authenticity of erotic gaiety, ecstasy and suffering; it has come to seem, through its many operatic descendants, from *La Traviata* to *La Bohème*, a story about the impossibility of love, for men and for women; but it is the women who die of it. The passionate heroines meet their ends – is it their deserts? The men survive to grieve – and repent. In Prévost's novel, poverty chiefly leads the lovers astray, and Puccini's several librettists reflect this theme in the last act, when Manon, unaccustomed to the hardships of a life of frontier settlements in the colony of Louisiana, fades away in Des Grieux's arms, cheated by fate from the marriage that would have granted her respectable social status as well as happiness. In the eighteenth century, individual destinies were psychologised within a web spun of power and money; they were not medicalised. Violetta and Mimì, by contrast, though assailed as well by economic problems and struggles for social status, are wasted by their creators in their very bodies: tuberculosis becomes the material embodiment – and the penalty – of sexual passion.

The financial theme of Prévost's *Manon Lescaut* acquires dramatic salience in the tumultuous scene when Manon tries to pack her jewels before eloping with the returned Chevalier from the house of her protector, Geronte di Ravoir. She scatters her acquisitions in her haste, a palpable correlative of the economic imprudence of her flight: the love of Manon and Des Grieux dissipates such resources as they have. He is, the narrator reports: 'a young man who obstinately refuses to be happy and deliberately plunges into the most dire misfortunes'. In the novel, her extravagance, love of luxury, of pleasure, of society, of riding in a good carriage and keeping an hospitable house, of wearing pretty and fashionable clothes and frequenting the capital, undo the natural virtue and industriousness of the Chevalier: in the book his conduct becomes criminal to a degree that the opera's librettists never dare approach. Incited and tutored by Lescaut, Manon's unscrupulous brother, Des Grieux learns to provide for Manon by card-sharping in an aristocratic gamblers' syndicate; he lies to the kindly superior of the establishment where he is confined by his father to reform him; when he makes his escape, he kills a servant. The experiences harden him: when Lescaut gets knifed in the street for a bad debt our hero wastes no tears on him, except to regret that the murder will attract attention and make the lovers' survival even more hazardous.

The friendships and enmities between men, family members and social contacts govern the development of Des Grieux and Manon's spiralling outlaw careers: Des Grieux, being very young (seventeen when he meets Manon, around nineteen at her death two and a half years later), deceives his father about his intentions when he touches him for funds. He tricks more money from his faithful confidant, Tiberge, whom he also entangles in his intrigues and lies; but above all, he engages in a form of ritual mating duel with his rivals for Manon's company (he has her love): the rich Messieurs de G. M., father and son.

In the opera by Puccini, Manon's wealthy patron is a single individual. In the much less evasive novel, she becomes first the father's mistress, then the son's: another instance of male rivalry in action, and in this secondary plot, directly Oedipal.

Prévost's hero Des Grieux also wants urgently to supplant men who enjoy more social power and prestige than he does, and he chooses to do so by demonstrating his superiority in matters erotic and personal: Manon's desire is the principle by which he can assert himself. But the stratagem eventually brings about the lovers' final excess of folly: when he agrees to Manon's proposal that they go to bed together in the younger

Monsieur de G.M.'s house and they give themselves up 'to the raptures of love', only to be discovered *in flagrante*. In Puccini, they are merely found together on the point of eloping. But Prévost's original is much more deeply perverse: the lovers want to humiliate the rich man with the one thing he cannot have: loving bliss at his table and 'between his sheets'. The holiness of the heart's affections is forged, in the eighteenth-century romance, in conditions of brutal worldliness. (Interestingly, in our own cynical times, the theme recurs, in the Pulp hit song 'Spy', in which Jarvis Cocker sings about adultery to the man whose bed he occupies, whose aftershave he uses in the bathroom when he is at home there making love to his wife.)

Puccini himself seems to throw out a similar challenge, a cockerel taking on the rooster, when he deliberately chooses the same subject for his opera as Jules Massenet's great success of a decade earlier; and again, when he competes with Leoncavallo at the very same time in adapting Murger's novel as *La Bohème*. His *Manon* has not eclipsed Massenet's; but his *Bohème* certainly succeeded in making Puccini cock of the walk.

A vivid scene in the novel, omitted from the opera, foreshadows the lovers' attempted humiliation of her patron; it is interesting because it casts Manon herself in a much more active and spirited part than she plays on the High Romantic operatic stage. When she and the Chevalier are living together in sweet and tender passion, she attracts the attentions of an Italian prince in the park where she takes the air in the afternoon; she invites him back, but she has a secret plan and asks the Chevalier to trust her: ' "Darling mine, I adore you," she said in her most bewitching tones. "I ask you for a moment's indulgence. One moment, only one moment and then I shall love you a thousand times more, and be grateful all my life." '

Des Grieux relates how he has a wonderful head of hair, which Manon likes playing with, dressing, grooming: when the Italian prince appears, bearing promises of riches and status for Manon if she will leave to live with him, she pulls Des Grieux from the bedroom where she had been amusing herself adorning him:

> she grasped my floating hair in one hand, seized her mirror in the other, and exerting all her strength hauled me in that state across the room, pushed the door open with her knee, and presented the stranger . . . with a sight that must have caused him no little astonishment . . .

Manon gave him no time to open his mouth, but thrusting her mirror in his face said: 'Look Sir. Have a good look at yourself and give me a fair answer. You ask for my love. Here is the man I love and whom I have vowed to love all my life. Compare for yourself . . . I declare that in the eyes of your humble servant all the princes in Italy are not worth one of the hairs I am holding in my hand.'

The Italian prince withdraws his offer. But not before commenting, quite reasonably in the circumstances, that ' "I have certainly had my eyes opened, and I see you are far less of a novice than I had supposed." '

This heroic – and ruthless – female champion of love, who can protest against the commodification of passion and against the market in women's favours, and who can at the same time buy a prostitute for Des Grieux to make up for one of her infidelities, loses flavour and force in the Puccini, to become instead much more vulnerable, a little more virtuous, and at the same time far more passive. Her fatality – to herself and to others – depends on her looking beautiful and enthralling men, rather than on her being intrinsically wild at heart; the troop of librettists Puccini employed seem one and all to have fought shy of Prévost's instinctive outlaw who wants certain social privileges without paying the price that they require. Manon in Prévost's novel is herself a libertine: a she-rake. She shares in the character of certain heroines created by female writers of the generation older than Prévost: the protagonists of such ironic and savage fairy tales as 'The Subtle Princess' by Marie-Jeanne L'Héritier, 'The Ram' by Marie-Catherine d'Aulnoy, and 'Bearskin' and 'The Palace of Vengeance' by Henriette-Julie de Murat.[3] In these tales of reluctant brides, the beast is the husband, and the happy endings entail his defeat, not his transformation. Several of these women were urbane and witty *salonnières* and their tongues – and their fictions – landed them in trouble with the censors, for they attacked, under the guise of the fantastic, the abuses of arranged marriages and other aspects of the erotic economy of the *ancien régime*. They themselves had suffered from some of the conventions that Prévost depicts in his novel: Marie-Catherine d'Aulnoy, for example, was abducted from a convent where she was being educated, by her husband, the Baron d'Aulnoy, a stranger many years her elder and a notorious debauchee, after he had struck some kind of bargain with her father.[4]

Many of these outspoken women writers of the *ancien régime* such as the group known as the *précieuses*, declared that they wished women to enjoy the same freedom as men to control their own money and marital choices; and if not, they wanted to be free to take lovers within marriage as did men. Prévost is not making a similar protest on behalf of Manon; but he does dramatise the frustrated, indeed lethal, quest to live by the truth of passion in a world where sexual pleasure was a luxury rich men bought exclusively for their own use. Manon, in her moments of spirited dissent from this code, also anticipates a character like Timberlake Wertenbaker's adventuress in her 1986 play *The Grace of Mary Traverse*, who wants the freedom of movement and choice and opportunity that social convention and male hegemony refused to women, and especially to unmarried and penniless young women like Manon. The opening of the story, when Manon is about to be put in the convent because there is no dowry to marry her off, sets out the theme in all its stark reality.

The more scandalous episodes in the youth of two inexperienced rakes on the make do not kill our sympathy with the hero – because the Chevalier is telling them himself: he is very skilled at charming us, at playing his cards quite beyond the value of the hand he holds. But Puccini's librettists baulked as well at the extent of his duplicities, of his twists and turns. Besides, the romantic tradition casts the emphasis on the fatality of the woman's beauty, and on the tragedy of love's victims, not on the rebellious transgressiveness of the young of both sexes.

Puccini's Manon embodies pathos *in extremis*: she woos us through her pitiful cries in the opera, and the Chevalier responds, in ever mounting tragic excitation. These erotic duets gather height and intensity, doing vocally the work that the novel naturally sets about achieving by other means. Interestingly, though Manon so ruthlessly brings her Italian prince face to face with the spectacle of his shortcomings, Prévost does not use fiction's great resources of picture-making, and lead us to visualise Manon's charms. In his novel, her captivating tenderness grows from her youth (she is even younger than the seventeen-year-old Chevalier, and her name ends in a diminutive associated with children, as in Cendrillon, Cinderella, or *mignon*, cute); but it also arises strongly from her sexuality: he recalls 'the most affectionate caresses', her tears, her kisses, the 'passionate abandon' of her love-making[5] (not in so many words – this is a work of most elegant euphemisms; certainly not one of the many explicitly pornographic romances of *l'Enfer*, the legendary locked bookcases of the Bibliothèque Nationale).[6] As a student of French literature, I was taught that one of the chief differences between the eighteenth-century novel and its nineteenth-century successors could be summed up in the simple surprising fact that we never learn the colour of Manon's eyes.

Physiognomy does not matter; she binds the Chevalier (and the reader) with a spell made from her touch and her gestures and the physical effect she has on him, the quivering and tears and ecstasy she provokes in him and in her other lovers by her demonstrativeness.

Prévost later translated Samuel Richardson's novels into French as *Pamela, Clarissa Harlowe and Grandisson*, and he adopts, in *Manon Lescaut*, a similar eighteenth-century concept of the passionate body, all sensation and emotion, convulsed by tears, swooning, in paroxysms of lamentations, shuddering, thrilling and vibrating, blushing and weeping and trembling and throbbing. These sensory signs of overpowering inward passion have become the clichés of pulp romance, a development which has unfortunately distorted their powerful and once innovatory means of conveying deep feeling.

Puccini's music for *Manon Lescaut* translates Prévost's lovers' bodies into sound with untrammelled lyricism: as a result, it does not quite seem right to say that the deaths of heroines like Manon result from a moral desire to punish them for their lived-out sexuality, as has been argued in essays about romantic opera.[7] The librettists do evince a certain need to pay lip service to the observance of sexual restraint, and so they give Des Grieux and Manon lots of breast-beating lyrics to sing. But the climactic duets of Violetta and Alfredo, of Mimì and Rodolfo, of Manon and Des Grieux mimic sexual passion – as we listeners know, consciously or not, from the first time we hear them; it may be a form of male self flattery that the female is extinguished by the *petite mort*, as the French call orgasm, and the male inflicts it on her again and again, but the metaphorical character of the music overrides the mechanics of the plot: we weep for the heroines' deaths, and if there is a moral lesson lurking there about women's predatory desires, about the folly of their prey's reciprocal passion, the frenzy of the music carries such warnings off and swirls them into a vortex of meaninglessness. This kind of opera only masquerades as moral: it only pretends to shake its head at the folly of love.

The contradiction lies at the heart of the opera: when Manon is deported, in the parade of other 'fallen women', our sympathies are aroused on their behalf; while society at large pushes passion's votaries and priestesses out beyond the pale, they are being included within the pale of the operatic stage, which is a special place where the female voice is not muffled, let alone silenced, and through it, love and passion assert their rights to be heard.[8] Manon's very name in Italian speaks defiance: 'Ma non!' – 'But no!' – so that as it resounds over and over again in the course of the opera, it literally issues a protest against compliance, compromise and convention. With an air of effortless storytelling from life, the Abbé Prévost explored this central and eternal conflict, between 'overmastering passion' and the social and rational ideals that should regulate the conduct of *l'homme moyen sensuel*; its later translation into song has not let this central human dilemma die along with its heroine, but rather made her the vehicle for the urgent and irrepressible claims of desire.

1997

In the Mirror of Madness: Elaine Showalter

Review of The Female Malady: Women, Madness and English Culture, 1830–1980

In the opening sequence of Robert Wiene and Carl Mayer's 1920s film drama, *The Cabinet of Dr Caligari*, a young woman appears, somnambulist, beautiful, with huge mysterious eyes. She is called Jane ('Crazy Jane') and dressed in white raiment down to the ground, like other stock figures of madness – Wilkie Collins's Woman in White, Miss Havisham. Her condition – moonstruck, lunatic – is familiar, even inevitable; she is suffering from the 'female malady': the derangement of the senses to which women are specially prone. Indeed since the Greeks diagnosed hysteria as rising in the wandering womb, women and madness have been seen to bear a natural affinity; it seems easily accepted that madness lay inside women, waiting to be let out. In general, the Victorians feared this ascribed susceptibility; the Surrealists, coming after, and longing for *le dérèglement de tous les sens*, admired it; both expectations had the effect of helping to drive women mad.

In this judicious book, which ranges lucidly and sanely over many bitter matters, Elaine Showalter describes the approaches of official medicine towards the problems of female madness. It is a most illuminating and readable narrative. Like other feminist literary critics, Showalter in her earlier work took up the question of the woman's body in the fictional text and showed just how closely metaphor and actuality are intertwined. In this new book, she works with the body of patients in history, and discovers in their ordeals a new set of diagnostic images for female difference.

Still maintaining a reasonable, level tone, she describes the harrowing cures, which proceeded by sympathetic magic, like shamans' exorcisms. Women crazed by lives of enforced idleness were confined for six weeks of stuffing food and bed-rest; young girls with sexual fantasies and anxieties had leeches applied to their genitals, or had their vulvae packed with ice. Control of the mad screens the wider issue of social subordination itself, and the study of its history provides a two-way mirror through which we can observe the psychiatrist and his idea of normality with as much clinical expertise and power as he showed when he applied his own assumptions of insanity. This mirror is of course angled for infinite recession: we are as bound by our own ideas about madness and female nature as Showalter's subjects.

Of all the Dr Caligaris whom she analyses, John Conolly, the presiding genius of the phase she names 'psychiatric Victorianism' (1820–70), emerges as the most benign and likeable. Conolly became the apostle of 'moral management' of the insane: discarding the impedimenta of the past, the gags and leg-irons and other restraints formerly used on lunatics. He advocated routine, quiet, privacy and gentleness; the asylums which opened during his period of influence, like the huge Colney Hatch (surviving as Friern Barnet) for over a thousand patients, were exemplary Victorian institutions, showcases of benevolent paternalism, humanistic reforms and belief in human perfectibility. Dances were held, and spectators attended, not to gawp at the frenzy of the inmates, as at Bedlam in the past, but to observe the seemliness. Dickens wrote of the Christmas Ball at St Luke's Hospital in 1851:

> There was the brisk, pippin-faced little old lady, in a fantastic cap – proud of her foot and ankle; there was the old-young woman, with the dishevelled long light hair, spare figure, and weird gentility; there was the vacantly laughing girl, requiring now and then a warning finger to admonish her . . .

This was surely an improvement on the horrors of past brutalisation? Yet, Showalter argues, the decorum of the mould into which the female subject was poured – that 'weird gentility' – was in effect a Victorian counterpart of the scold's bridle. She reproduces some of the photographs Hugh Diamond took of Conolly's charges – so many 'Ophelias' and 'Crazy Janes', posed and mute. Their words were not recorded, and their healers left no legacy of story about them.

In the same way as country midwives were ousted by male professionals, the matrons and other unqualified staff – often wives of the doctors – who had been so important to the mad were, with the growing respectability of public asylums, gradually forbidden to help. It wasn't until 1927 that the London County Council approved women doctors in asylums. The domination of the male doctor, as confessor, wizard, medicine-man, shaped the attitudes of Showalter's second generation, 'psychiatric Darwinists'. The leading exponent, Charles Maudsley, was Conolly's son-in-law. He could not, however, conceal his contempt for his tender-hearted predecessor. Even in his obituary, he reproved Conolly for his 'feminine' type of mind, which 'might even express itself in tears', and opined, 'a character most graceful and beautiful in a woman is no gift of fortune to a man having to meet the adverse circumstances . . . of a tumultuous life'.

Maudsley was dismissive, angry and Hobbesian in temper, seeing a hereditary taint in madness; he hoped to find a physical cause, such as syphilis, for all derangement, and maintained that women's reproductive cycle and organs inclined them to lunacy. He also noted however that the weary, stale, flat and unprofitable lives so many were required to lead contributed to the neurasthenia from which they began to suffer in increasing numbers among the middle classes. He did not, however, advocate any remedy, believing rather that education damaged girls' minds. The profession concurred; the American neurologist George Miller Beard blamed periodicals, steam-power, the telegraph, the sciences and 'especially the increased mental activity of women' for the 'sapping of American nervous strength'. Even a pioneer doctor, Margaret Cleaves, would acquiesce that at times work gave her a 'sprained brain'.

Showalter necessarily extends her focus on English practice to include Breuer and Freud, and their discovery, in the case of Anna O. (the remarkable and gifted Bertha Pappenheim), that a woman could be made better by talking. For the first time the 'alienists' were listening to the patient, and the woman's own experience of the female malady was breaking the surface of their consciousness. Showalter offers the fascinating perception that the *globus hystericus*, the choking sensation most hysterics experienced, actually reproduced physically the gag society placed upon their inner desires and thoughts. And in defiance of feminist critiques of Freud, she pays generous tribute to him for loosing it.

But she does also hint at the vexing insight that the female patient collaborates in psychoanalysis with the desires of her doctor, that even a brilliant and articulate subject like Anna O finds herself cast on the template of his expectations and wishes. For this reason, perhaps, so many women analysts past and present do not challenge the Freudian theory of women's inherent sense of deficiency, and the totemic and immovable place of the symbolic phallus. Showalter comes to grips with the problem of collusion between patient and doctor, and their united reinforcement of the prevailing symbolic order in her fascinating pages about Siegfried Sassoon's 'therapy' with W. H. R. Rivers in Scotland. Rivers restored Sassoon's belief in the war and in soldiering, in combat on the front line, as befitted an officer and a gentleman. But while Sassoon fortified himself against his homosexuality and rejected the unmanliness of his flight from the war, Rivers began to doubt the ethic he was inculcating. In this drama between men, Showalter counts the cost of sexual typecasting with implications beyond the madhouse. Shell-shocked soldiers were not permitted to break down. As Ford Madox Ford's character put it in *Parade's End*, 'Why isn't one a beastly girl and privileged to shriek?'

Showalter does not perhaps look closely enough at the strategic opportunities madness could present to women, especially young women. Being privileged to shriek may have had its moments. The relation between inspiration, religious experience and madness, between expressions of faith, female articulacy and early feminism – the milieu of *Adam Bede*, *The Bostonians* and *Jude the Obscure* – might have been worth more attention. The inspired, the vatic and the spiritual provided one outlet; could there be a sense in which women could rise 'armed with madness'? Under the sign of Folly, as at carnival time, there reigned a form of liberty; the drag queen in France, *la folle*, breaks the rules – and gets away with it.

Showalter's third phase, 1920–80, 'psychiatric modernism', concentrates on the personality of R. D. Laing. Her writing communicates the excitement she felt at his analysis of the oppression within the family and the damaging effects on daughters, but she has to indict him finally for his own deafness to the sexual conflicts in the doctor-madwoman relation. In this, Laing was, in his own words, 'a symptom of the Sixties'.

The Female Malady depends on the testimony of literate and creative women of genius – like Florence Nightingale and Sylvia Plath and Janet Frame. Can they really speak for the thousands of chronic patients who were never heard and still cannot make themselves heard? There is here an enormous emptiness. More information about background, incomes, work, age, could have been given (if available), and more awareness of unpleasant factors like cost-efficiency (ECT being rather cheaper than psychoanalysis; lobotomy being *final*, as it were). But these are cavils. Elaine Showalter has found that the asylum not the attic is the madwoman's place, and she has walked the long stone corridors to hear her, with unsparing but never sentimental humanity.

1987

Fasting Girls

Review of Joan Jacobs Brumberg, Fasting Girls: The Emergence of Anorexia Nervosa as a Modern Disease

A Californian supermarket has no precedent in reality; only in the folklore of hungry people should such heaps and stores of glittering food appear. Even the *Arabian Nights'* hoards are modest compared to the shelves and freezers of a normal US Safeway, stocked with edible stuffs that have passed far beyond identity as nutrition and entered another plane. Joan Jacobs Brumberg identifies the conflict between discipline and hedonism as characteristic of the present time in the West, and places at the centre of it the anorexic girl, who may deny her hunger altogether, or raid odd food in secret, or binge spasmodically and then starve for days or even weeks.

With *Fasting Girls*, Brumberg takes her place among the growing number of historians who describe society by analysing its illnesses, and find in the body of one patient the portrait of another. As in Peter Brown's *The Body and Society*, the significance of bodies is never confined to their physical symptoms, but belongs in the overarching order of the symbolic. The baffling and distressing disease of anorexia becomes emblematic of our times, a specific psychic dysfunction of plenty, not an organic or neurological or purely psychological illness, as some have claimed, for it is not found among the daughters of the poor in rich countries, or in poor countrics at all. It is a female malady: women's connections with the provision of food fit them for ailing this way (Brumberg dismisses the few male cases as different in origin and character).

The austerities of the saints, from the early Middle Ages to later ecstatics such as Margaret Mary Alacoque, included spectacular starvation and repugnant repasts (the blood and pus of the sick) and have led some writers to define anorexia as a latter-day secular mysticism. Brumberg will have none of this, nor of the feminist argument that anorexics are like hunger strikers, and champions of resistance. She notes keenly, however, how important the medieval examples were in the nineteenth century, when 'Fasting Girls' became media heroines, and their miraculous survival was used as proof of the sovereignty of mind over matter, of the divine spirit of mankind over the reductive pragmatism of the new men of science. A young girl called Sarah Jacob, 'the Welsh wonder', began starving herself at the age of twelve, in 1867, and soon her prodigious existence was drawing pilgrims to her village, and incidentally bringing in some money to her family. She lay in bed, adorned by her mother as a Pre-Raphaelite Ophelia, with coloured ribbons trailing on her pillow and a wreath of flowers in her hair; although her family were Chapel, a crucifix lay on her bed. Doctors from London became impatient with popular credulousness; the family agreed to a twenty-four-hour medical watch around Sarah's bed. Towards the end of the first week, when the girl was failing, the family still refused to allow food or drink. By the tenth day, medical science was proved right: Sarah Jacob was dead.

Later, a bottle-shaped depression was found under her arm, and her younger sister admitted she had fed Sarah morsels in kisses, like a bird. Soon after, in 1873, one of the Queen's physicians, Sir William Gull, first isolated anorexia nervosa as a discrete illness. 'The transformation of fasting behaviour,' writes Brumberg, 'from piety to disease captures the parallel process of secularization and medicalization.' Gull explicitly distinguished this kind of slow female suicide from hysteria. But in France, his contemporary Charles Lasègue rooted the problem in psychological distress, sometimes – very French, this – attributing it to disappointed love. The physician Charcot found a rose-coloured ribbon wound tight round the waist of an anorexic, and thereby diagnosed for the first time such patients' obsession with appearance, weight, materiality. Some of these Victorian sages were stern, and castigated the sufferers' 'morbid desire for notoriety'. Freud did not discuss the illness, but made a passing comment that was later taken up devoutly, inspiring Woody Allenish diagnoses of paternal fellation fantasies and phantom pregnancies.

The wrangles of the doctors are not as interesting, however, as Brumberg's own inspired account of the politics of the bourgeois family in the late nineteenth century, and the macabre mockery of paragon behaviour the anorexic performed, as she turned prescribed purity, demureness and delicacy into a living death. Parents, especially mothers, who were in charge of the table and the conduct of daughters, suffered profoundly, and revenge against maternal control may have been a partial motive. 'Parentectomy' was recommended as the most effective cure, and worked in some cases.

The twentieth-century sufferer does not, however, respond to leaving home in the same way. Anorexia is flourishing on American campuses among young women who hardly ever sat down to a family meal, but have 'grazed' and 'snacked' at will. They are destined for careers, have been encouraged in self-expression, and possess a physical freedom their ladylike predecessors never knew. The doctors are still at work defining new varieties of anorexia, but not one has lopped the *nervosa* label and suggested that it may be a virus, according to present fashion. Brumberg herself is distressed, and less able to give a coherent rationale for this epidemic, but she reproaches the American way of eating and the diet industry, worth an astonishing $5 billion a year. 'Sadly,' she concludes, 'the cult of diet and exercise is the closest thing our secular society offers women in terms of a coherent philosophy of the self.' She could have recorded more of the sufferers' own words, and tried to analyse more deeply the changing ethical attitudes towards envy, anger and lust and their sister, greed: as the other appetites lose their sinfulness, gluttony has risen in the scale of the deadly sins. (In California, courses in 'anger management' are offered, because 'your anger can be good'.) But *Fasting Girls* is a concise and penetrating book, and Joan Jacobs Brumberg shows compassion without sentimentality on behalf of these daughters of affluence, who want literally, it seems, to pass through the eye of a needle.

1989

Bloated

The skyscraper, the Cadillac fin, the flag, the cowboy boot under the jutting cuff of jeans, the steel-mill chimney all share a geometry, a sharp clarity of outline; they demonstrate power and energy rising, they take off. When I first started coming to America, the country would rise in my mind's eye, delineated with this cut and thrust. But if such symbols haven't become by now simply dated emblems of another time, they're actively denounced and repressed. The visual lexicon of American identity has changed emphasis; bigness still defines it, but a bigness grown pillowy and flaccid and fluffy and fat like baby flesh – the aesthetic of the animated cartoon writ large over aspects of the culture far beyond the world of entertainment where it began. The new aesthetic seems to me part of a generalised cult of childishness, fake infantilism. Its meanings run much deeper than the old cult of pioneer innocence or liberal hedonism; its roots lie in something far more important than the perennial anxiety about obesity. American gigantism was assertive; now it has turned escapist.

It used to be the case, family portraits show, that children were outfitted like their parents; now adipose, amorphous adults' bodies grow larger and more shapeless, swaddled in cushiony sweatsuits and bright baby colours, with squishy air-filled sneakers on their feet and travel mugs in hand so that they can suck every now and then and the dread day of weaning can be postponed for ever. Even the strongest of strong men are changing shape, so that Schwarzenegger has swollen pecs like female breasts and bulges in places John Wayne never would have dreamed of. Disney squishiness has filled out the streamlining of the automobile: no more sharp edges, no skinny-rib corners, no crests or spikes or tails. Even computer mice have turned bulbous.

Design that reveals an inner spine or underlying grid doesn't exorcise the appeal of the blob. Armature, as inner structure or exoskeleton, has come to define evil: the Terminator is a giant cockroach. Meanwhile the kind of shop that recurs every block has its window heaped with Care Bears, with bionic dinosaurs like Barney and pneumatic Beanie Babies, so popular the stores announce 'Maximum of six per customer'.

Today one symbol emerges above all others to characterise late Nineties infantilism: the large gas-filled balloon. The balloon is hard but rounded, firmer than a breast but without internal structure or scaffolding or skeleton. Buoyant, blithe and irresponsible, it manages to be full to bursting and light as air – the dieter's ultimate dream.

At first this focus on bigness and puffiness seems to carry a great cargo of guilt: on the immediate level of body size, fat people are cast as failures, socially and personally dysfunctional; diets fill the airwaves and the newspapers; fat-free foods guarantee eventual return to membership of the human race. The personal trainer has emerged as the indispensable companion of the heroes and heroines of the times: the one who can transform the exactions of excess and appetite into close-packed tissue, who can shed those pounds for you. . . . Madonna herself playing with balloons?

This nexus of ideas that have buried phallic hardness under an aesthetic of polymorphous billowing flesh could be considered an effect of the welcome change in women's position: that the tough guy and the myth of the frontier have been dethroned. But this would be glib – and wishful thinking. For it's not, in the end, the big breast that rules the emergent symbols of the blob and the balloon, but the big baby.

1997

Body Politic

Review of Madonna, Sex

Madonna's fans believe that she has pioneered a new concept of women's relation to pleasure, that she is in control of her image, as well as her business empire, and that she gives expression to female desire on her own terms. Her detractors find that she breaks no mould, but plays to conventional perceptions of women and hardens them, that she confirms the traditional split Virgin/Whore which her own baptismal name so aptly symbolises.

Steven Meisel's photographs for *Sex* imitate, in modish pasticheur style, many founding fathers of the medium: Man Ray, Brassai and Richard Avedon. The erotica in the text also parody well-thumbed predecessors: Lolita, Sade and the Italian *foto-romanza*. The problem with quotation can be staleness, and the brutal theatricality of the Fascist, biker, punk uniforms and torture-chamber props, followed by sentimental scenes of baby dolls and pubescent androgyny, reveal fancy dress charades to be a poor substitute for erotic fantasy.

Madonna has taken on a new persona for the book, Dita. *Dita* is Italian for a business or a firm, so the name's probably a killingly funny joke. *Dita* also means 'fingers'. This can hardly be a coincidence, since masturbation dominates the sex the book advocates and represents. There are no photographs of full coitus: they provide a kind of teasing primer for safe sex.

The scenes adapt many fringe practices for Madonna's purposes; they naturalise the taste for sadomasochistic tableaux, fist-fucking, masquerade orgies, kiddie porn, and obligation-free cruising. The only sexual orientation that excites criticism is exclusive male heterosexuality, but *Sex* is anxious not to exclude anyone, and elsewhere, in a confessional fantasy about how much she loves topless bars, Madonna makes it up to the he-men: 'I like all the guys in the front row in the baseball caps. They're usually truckers. . . .'

Madonna has anticipated objections on the new grounds that pornography's great for girls as well as for guys: 'Generally I don't think pornography degrades women,' she writes. 'The women who are doing it want to do it.' Later, she continues, 'I think that for the most part if women are in an abusive relationship and they know it and stay in it they must be digging it.'

Some of this would sound breathlessly naive, if it weren't in such bad faith: the photographs plug into risk to pack their charge (hitch-hiking naked: surrendering, bound and gagged, to the executioner), so the message that it's all good, safe, joky fun and games collapses on itself. She can dig her own abusive relationships, perhaps, and then swan out of them, but a brief visit to the red-light districts of most cities, to the prostitutes' haunts behind railway stations where women hitch rides to perform blow jobs for derisory sums with truckers in baseball caps, might give her pause. The economic realities of a photographic sex model's life should wipe the grin off her face.

Her idea of pleasure lies principally in play-acting, and you can tell that she is; she doesn't have the great actor or model's ability to look altogether lost in that moment. She's always rubber-necking, for the camera, for the fan-club, for the mirror. In the scenes in the gay nightclub, in which, gloved and glittering, she lounges among a group of naked or dinner-jacketed young bloods, her smile looks as regally fixed as Nancy Reagan's and her attention to the proceedings as incongruously absent-while-present as the Queen at a war dance of Papuan Mud Men.

Madonna's view of sex offers a syllogism that goes: 'I'm not a victim,

I'm in control. I'm a woman. Ergo, women aren't victims, women are in control.' If wishing were having, this might be true. But I think this idea that anyone can be, in any sexual situation, as completely in control as she presents herself expresses the deeper fantasy – the deeper fallacy – beneath all the sadistic make-believe and lesbian carry-on: that sex can be risk-free, safe at a psychological level just as much as at a physical-medical level. That it needn't matter, that it doesn't lead to attachment or to loneliness, to turmoil or to bliss in any deep or lasting sense; that it need bear no relation to the social fabric, to affection, to reciprocity, and that it is entirely distinct from love.

Her portrayal of sexuality unpicks the strong but delicate web that weaves together and tries to suspend in balance pleasure and altruism, cherishing and freedom, attention to individual others and gratification. The last words contain some agony-aunt counselling: 'A lot of people are afraid to say what they want. That's why they don't get what they want.' This presumes that people know, that they don't have to find out as they go along, in relation to one another.

Part of the revolution in sensibility which finds a figurehead in Madonna wants women to thrive on a radical break between sex and love: it recasts ideas about women and their erotic drives to make them more like truckers in topless bars or specialist gays in S&M groups. Ironically, it could be argued that while she herself hasn't been abused in these pages, her partners, paid to service her, are treated as less than human.

It would be ridiculous to prosecute the book, as has been feared; every newsagent carries more explicitly genital and more violent material as a matter of course. It would also be a serious error to imagine that Madonna's *Sex* represents the only view of eros held by the sceptics or opponents of Republican family values. Madonna here merely gives her endorsement to many of the fantasies which have hitherto been considered men's fantasies about boys, as well as about women – and not all men's at that; and the fantasy that the female erotic appetite is so devouring that they gotta have it has long provided a time-honoured pretext to let them have it in all kinds of other ways.

1992

Sites of Desire

Review of Peter Brooks, Body Work: Objects of Desire in Modern Narrative

In *King Kong*, the classic film of 1933, two scenes were censored by the Hays Office: the monster casually chomping on several 'native' victims, whose legs wriggle vividly between his teeth, and the first intimate meeting of Kong and Fay Wray. Both were restored recently, and audiences can now see how the giant ape, having carried Fay Wray up to a topmost crag, begins to investigate what exactly his new prize might be. He removes her dress in pieces, looks at the flimsy torn cloth and samples its texture, scatters it, and then smells his fingers. The nostrils of the animated model animal twitch appreciatively at this point. Kong may not have any language besides roaring and grunting, but he knows things through his other senses, especially his nose. This is what the censors could not accept.

The scene would serve to illustrate Peter Brooks's concern in *Body Work*, a densely argued study of desire as the motor of fiction and other narratives, of carnal knowledge in text and image. The first half of the book worries at the trope of Naked Truth, taking as its epitome a quotation from the eighteenth-century belle-lettrist and novelist, Charles Pinot Duclos, who wrote:

> I don't know why men have accused women of falsity, and have made Vérité female . . . They also say that she is naked, and that could well be. It is no doubt from a secret love for Truth that we pursue women with such ardour; we seek to strip them of everything that we think hides Truth; and when we have satisfied our curiosity on one, we lose our illusions and run after another . . .

In terms of Brooks's concerns, King Kong may stand as an exemplary man, because he is seeking to know the blonde he holds in his hand by stripping her, by scanning her, by possessing her with his eyes. 'My subject,' writes Brooks, 'is the nexus of desire, the body, the drive to know, and narrative: those stories we tell about the body in the effort to know and to have it, which results in making the body a site of signification . . . and itself a signifier, a prime agent in narrative plot and meaning.'

Story and body, semiotic and somatic, are intertwined. But Kong, by sniffing his fingers, also brings into play an alternative epistemological stratagem besides the gaze, and one which in its novelty and raw creatureliness dismayed the official watchdogs. In the second half of this book, Brooks shows a lively and at times persuasive interest in such possibilities, in finding challenges to the conventional procedures of desire, which have followed the track of the body and read its traces by different, dissenting means.

The territory Brooks traverses has been churned by contending armies and mapped by subtle surveyors using many different languages of measurement, as well as varying codes of conduct. His book places him in the thick of the most active controversies of the day (and the conference circuit), and touches on issues of justice, law, and politics (he ventures an excursus into abortion reform), as well as the changing and complex philosophy of identity. 'Discourse of the sexual body,' he judges, rightly, 'has perhaps replaced theological discourses of the arcane and the sacred for a desacralised era.' *Body Work* is, in consequence, a highly ambitious book, full of deep hard thinking and breadth of knowledge. The opposition between veiled masculinity and exposed femininity suggests that Brooks is engaging in sexual polemic, but he explicitly refuses dead white male breast-beating or other finger-wagging. This is not a product of the Kung Fu school of criticism recently popularised by American critics; non-violence remains its author's code.

Body Work does, however, give the reader a pretty rough work-out. It plays a medley of fast-paced, head-busting tapes, and tells us to keep flexing those muscles, to the beat of Lacan, of Derrida, of younger interpreters and glossers. But how fit are we expected to be? The book is sometimes inspissated with contemporary approaches to sexual difference, synthesised for the comparatively unexercised. In this guise, Brooks depends on the arguments of others and repeats them (with due acknowledgment). But his study does also aim at those who are long past foundation courses in intellectual aerobics, and it offers many genuinely invigorating, original and refreshing exercises in reading visually (and even olfactorily) a rich variety of texts and images.

Investigating the connection between narrative energy and the desire to see (stories as striptease), Brooks himself adduces two fables, which, while wearing an almost quaintly patriarchal air, still obtain powerfully in our contemporary culture: the story of Pygmalion and Galatea, and the biblical episode of the drunkenness of Noah. Galatea, sculpted from ivory by a man who is dissatisfied with all the women he has ever seen, comes to life under the pressure of his 'thumbs' and thus quickened, meets all his needs. Here is the object of desire sprung from the desiring subject without interruption: a dream which, in Brooks's account, also governs the making of stories by Balzac ('La Duchesse de Langeais', among others) and Flaubert (*Madame Bovary*) and Zola (*Nana*), but which finds itself collapsing from the inside as the body of the beloved still resists total intelligibility and can only be possessed in fragments or in death.

Like the painting of the female nude, which before the nineteenth century took place in private (male models were employed by the academics), the novel, Brooks avers, begins in intimacy, in Fanny Hill's dark closet, with whispered 'secrets de l'alcôve'. *Le Diable boîteux*, in which the devil lifts off the roofs of houses to peep inside, and *Les Liaisons dangereuses*, which by means of the false sincerity of letters enters the private passions of its libertines, are seen as evidence of the eighteenth-century equation of plot dynamics and the seducer's advance into the bedroom. It might have been interesting here to connect personal tale-telling with the earlier, very odd custom of the *précieuses*: great ladies received their guests in their *ruelle*, the gap by their bed, where they themselves would lie to listen to the latest gossip. The body's secrets can be prised from its recesses, too: in Diderot's famous *Les Bijoux indiscrets*, women's 'privates' speak, and Rousseau's avowals in the *Confessions* place his own body – for the first time (*pace* Augustine) – and its memory traces of pleasure and pain at the centre of his imaginative faculty. Rousseau produces in later *rêveries* potent fictions of bliss from the bruises of a schoolmistress's spanking.

'When one moves from Rousseau to the French Revolution,' writes Brooks, 'the process of assigning meanings to the individual's body leaves the domain of the individual to become a pressing concern for the state.' The public man was represented with his hand on his heart, as was the allegory of La République herself; he could have no inner secrets and must accept responsibility for all his actions. The rhetoric commemorating public figures flourished their corporeality: the heads of the guilty were displayed on pikes and the effigies of heroes placed in the Panthéon.

Brooks underplays here the Jacobins' imitation of Christian rituals. He marvels, for instance, at the digging up of the royal remains from Saint Denis and their dumping in a pit of quicklime – as happened to Catholic relics in the Reformation. He also has trouble finding convincing aesthetic examples for his account of the Revolution's reorientation of desire from the boudoir to the rostrum – he could have mentioned the pertinent, new and popular attraction of waxworks, made from the death masks of heroes (Marat) and villains (the King and Queen) – Galateas every one, except that no thumb would press life back into them.

Illustrating the argument from literary rather than political sources, Brooks anatomises a play that sounds like a precursor of *Ubu*, except that it was performed in deadly earnest – Sylvain Maréchal's *Le Jugement dernier des rois* (1793), in which all tyrants end up on a desert island and are done away with by a volcano. Virtue or terror, said Saint-Just, and the Terror in this play takes the form of incineration.

In the pursuit of another's body, the pursuer needs assurances that he does not proceed in error, that he is making headway, and that he has identified his goal correctly – the right king, the right girl; concomitantly, narrative itself needs to knot its threads to produce the figure in the carpet. Sometimes the two desiderata converge, in literal marks on the body, signs which bring about happy recognition (birthmarks, wounds), or trophies seized to register victory (scalps, maidenheads). Brooks has deciphered a remarkable collection, from Odysseus' scar to the shivery moment in Balzac's *Splendeurs et misères des courtisanes* when the police chief strikes Collin (Vautrin) to see if the letters TF – *Travaux forcés* – will appear in his flesh. But Collin has changed his own body: he has gouged out the brand of the deported convict and only seventeen holes materialise where he was struck.

Nineteenth-century innovations in policing by records of bodily data – through fingerprinting, mug shots, passports and *cartes d'identité* – swelled the descriptive files of realist fiction, though the subject, like Vautrin, like Macavity, continued to elude its stratagems. The rising number of women selling themselves as prostitutes in the increasingly populated and prosperous cities also inspired pursuit, desirous and other, as well as much ambiguous scrutiny. *Body Work* quotes Dorinda Outram's epigrammatic comment, 'The same arena which created public man made woman into *fille publique*.' Brooks offers a witty and devastating comparison of Zola's *Nana* with the slick nudes of fashionable salon soft porn, showing that although Zola the art critic recognised Courbet's achievement and satirised the 'sugared bonbons who melt under the gaze' of Bouguereau and Cabanel, he too fell on the air-brush when it came to seizing the body of Nana on the page. Yet, as an image of another consuming engine of Second Empire, wealth, Nana's sexuality functions like the locomotive, the coal mine, the stockmarket and the department store dramatised in his other novels: she offers another example of the personal and female body as a country where everyone may take up occupation except herself.

From Zola's failure to find a language to depict 'the mystic rose' of Nana's sex, Brooks then passes on to the phantasmagoric sadism of Barbey d'Aurevilly's story 'A un dîner d'athées', in *Les Diaboliques* (1874), in which the faithless woman is branded by her lover with the very seal she used on a treacherous love letter – and in the place where she committed her infidelity. This is another instance when Brooks acts as a social chronicler rather than a literary evaluator and needs (semi-apologetic) recourse to preposterous kitsch to make his case.

In the second, key fable of *Body Work*, 'the central scandal of our culture', Noah lies in a stupor and his nakedness is covered by his sons, who even walk backwards to approach him with the respectful veil. The patriarch, in the episode as filtered through Barthes's reading, represents the father who must not be unveiled, unlike Truth, unlike Galatea, unlike Fay Wray screaming in the monster's paw, unlike Nana, or the poor branded Rosalba in the D'Aurevilly horror story. The paternal principle – the phallus – lies so centrally at the foundation of culture and language and social relations that it cannot be handled or looked at, questioned and known, except as a cipher of power in someone's arsenal. Brooks points out that the Noah prohibition still governs public imagery, and that Robert Mapplethorpe's photographs were removed from view because, even in an America where constitutional rights to freedom of expression hold like Catholic dogma, they showed the penis.

To uncover – to listen to and sniff out – dissenting stories and ways of storytelling, to disturb the prohibitions governing narrative, Brooks turns to George Eliot and Henry James, and then produces two dense, inspiring chapters, on Gauguin's Tahitian paintings and Mary Shelley's *Frankenstein*. He parts company with feminist critiques of Gauguin and makes a vivid case for the artist's attempt to break out of the moral and psychological conventions of the nude. Brooks is not concerned with how badly Gauguin behaved, but with the utopian drive of his species of Orientalism; he was remaking paradise, not finding it, for Tahiti had been colonised for over a century when he arrived in 1891, and its culture was in ruins. His fictive refashioning of the lost Eden took two forms Brooks vigorously advocates: he managed to show the female body self-possessed and unabashed, and he blurs sexual polarities. Reading *Noa Noa*, the autobiography Gauguin wrote, with its title meaning 'Perfumed', Brooks quotes a wonderful passage, when Gauguin is following a youth through the forest and 'he seems to know the invisible paths by smell'. For a moment, Gauguin becomes confused by his androgyny and desires him; later, he feels 'all my old stock of the civilized' to be 'well-destroyed' and that he has come back 'another man, a Maori'. In this ambidextrous fantasy, Gauguin had grasped that the polarised body of 'civilized' society – the woman of stays and garters, unveiled in alcoves and closets, coveted by the eye alone – had to be destroyed in order to represent a lost, prelapsarian, sensory plenitude.

By contrast, Brooks's chapter on *Frankenstein* contains many dense pages of psychoanalytical insiders' terms, and it is a pity that it does not relate Mary Shelley to her book by including the kind of historical and biographical insights Brooks has no compunction about using – and using effectively – in his treatment of Gauguin. Nevertheless, when he writes that the Monster may well conceal within himself a woman who seeks to flee from the identity which others confer on her by their looking, he touches a real, revelatory nerve; when he analyses the Monster's attempt to make himself a person through his eloquent speech, by telling his own story, and then recalls how Frankenstein, the creator who loathes his creation, then 'compassionates' the Monster, Brooks makes us see Mary Shelley trying to move desire – and love – from the realm of the eye to the faculty of understanding. That consummation on these terms is not possible for the Monster provides the novel with the *perpetuum mobile* it needs, and at the same time involves all readers, regardless of sex and orientation, with the most fundamental carnal knowledge of all, desire endlessly denied.

1993

Love's Work: Gillian Rose

This small book contains multitudes. It fits to the hand like one of those knobbed hoops which do concise duty for the rosary, each knob giving the mind pause to open up onto new vistas and meditate on mysteries and passions; in the compass of a scant 136 pages it provokes, inspires and illuminates more profoundly than many a bulky work, and confronts the great subjects – death, illness, reason and unreason, family strife and family bonds, friendship and betrayal, today's political abdication and philosophical cowardice, the limits of feminism, of happiness – and it delivers what its title promises, a new allegory about love. 'Love's work' here stands in all defiance for the life's work, and the notion of living as an art turned into that harder thing, work, because this book has the best and most radiant qualities of an *askesis*, a discipline of spiritual exercises leading to understanding. As a testament and a memoir in fragments, its relative in the past would be Dante's *Vita Nuova*, with its rigour of self examination, and in more recent times, Roland Barthes's *A Lover's Discourse*, which does not flinch either at the constant companionship of pain. In one of its moments of diamond-sharp focus on human vulnerability, the author whispers to her friend Jim dying in a hospital bed, 'You are surrounded by friends who love you.' To which Jim pulls the sheet over his face. 'He was beyond language,' writes Gillian Rose, 'but not beyond the discomforts of love.'

Gillian Rose turns her back, again and again, on the invitations to ease and gladness which the well-meaning offer in various forms, consolations, placebos that she will not permit. Her epigraph, from the Cabbalist Staretz Silouan, 'Keep your mind in hell, and despair not', blazes an oxymoron over her text, a flaming sword at the gate of Eden. 'Existence is robbed of its weight, its gravity, when it is deprived of its agon.' By the end she has persuaded us to come with her into this hell, where despair can be bearable, even contained.

Love's Work begins with a friend in New York who was diagnosed with cancer at the age of sixteen, over seventy years ago. She has a prosthesis for her face, like a Groucho mask from a joke shop, but Gillian Rose comes to prefer seeing her with the smooth hole where her nose has wasted away. The first of many figures in the book who have been struck with disease, Edna fittingly opens it because inside her body, under her face, she is undiminished, her brilliance and generosity and vitality undimmed. Without ever labouring the point, Gillian Rose offers here a new map of body's relation to soul; she banishes all those equations between corruption, material and spiritual, that have flowed so cruelly and thoughtlessly into the prevalent use of illness as metaphor. For she too is desperately ill, and some of the book is about that.

But her revolt against all slackness of feeling and thinking means that before she takes up the question of her cancer, before she challenges the contemporary obsession with medicalisation as identity, with bodily history as the self's best narrative, she tells us about some other things.

Following her mind as it flashes on one turn and then another has the enchanting, surprise quality of being with a child, who knows nothing of conversation, or of ghastly meetings with planned presentations, but makes a sequence of sudden, wonderful confidences, which gradually crystallise into a pattern if only the listener lies in wait. In *A Lover's Discourse* Barthes has described this way of writing – though he disclaims aforethought more than Rose: 'Throughout any love life, figures occur to the lover without any order . . . Confronting each of these incidents (what "befalls" him), the amorous subject draws on the thesaurus of figures . . . Each figure explodes, vibrates in and out of itself . . . Amorous *discursus* is not dialectical; it turns like a perpetual calendar, an encyclopaedia of affective culture.'

In Rose's book, another of the early figures we meet is Yvette, a promiscuous, passionate, irrepressible friend, mother of five, teacher of Hebrew, who believes in having several lovers at once, and sometimes manages it. For that is one form of love's work, an energy of desire carrying the subject far beyond the pleasure principle with no shrinking back. These two older women, Edna the survivor of disease and Yvette the survivor of unrequitedness, counterbalance the older men who then enter Gillian Rose's confession: her two fathers. Both Jewish, one English and Protestant-style, the other (her stepfather, Irving) an 'Irish clown' figure, a hapless but much beloved gambler, they set up the poles which then exert tension over the life and the loves and the faith of the eldest daughter. The natural father is a guilt-inducing patriarch whose dues, exacted on Saturday afternoons, caused his eldest daughter to vomit weekly in apprehension; because of the bouts of accusation in his car, she has never dared learn to drive. On one of these occasions, he attacks her – for making her stepmother miscarry a son. Such a vengeful relation, grounded in a pitiless belief in accountability for error and catastrophe, inaugurates the challenge that Gillian Rose, grown up into a philosopher and a metaphysician, then mounts against the remorseless and punitive determinism of Protestantism. She expands later, in a fine outburst: 'If you lead a normally unhappy life, you are predestined to eternal damnation, you will not live . . . [but] to grow in love-ability is to accept the boundaries of oneself and others, while remaining vulnerable, woundable, around the bounds. Acknowledgment of conditionality is the only unconditionality of human love.'

At Seder with her mother's family, she and her sisters try to suppress their giggles as the lackadaisical stepfather intones, liberally sprinkling the sacred texts with four-letter words; later, the same child who stole *Hymns Ancient and Modern* from school will ask, as the eldest, for a copy of the Torah; later still, when her grandfather reverts on his deathbed to old High German, his mother tongue, she wonders whether her chosen path away from family into German philosophy, into Hegel and Kant and Adorno, has not in the end led her back home. But this home is intrinsic to the work of love she has undertaken; it is made in the mind and the heart, remade, doubled and redoubled: it is found in many places, but this does not scatter it, but lays one stratum upon another to a great depth.

Mothers, especially real, biological ones, hardly cast a shadow; and though the author remembers her sisters' ingenuity in love (Jacqueline Rose, Alison Rose), women of the family remain veiled. The Lover waits and watches, and men are feminised by this wooing, writes Barthes, but Gillian Rose strikes the reader here as a daughter to many fathers, and she strips herself chastely like Perpetua in the arena when she dreamed she was being rubbed with oil like a wrestler in the games.

Between the return journeys from Judaism and Protestantism and back again, she moors for a while with a father of a kind, a lover who is a Jesuit priest, a pagan who spreads his table with oysters and champagne for her, answers her Rilke with Dante; but when she becomes ill, he covers his face and says he feels old and tired. Perhaps lack of previous acquaintance with the mercilessness of the male Catholic conscience led her to expect too much. Yet no one has put better the purpose of priestly celibacy: as she walks and shops in his parish at his side, she realises that 'our emanation of eros afforded collective release, whereas the knowledge that we were lovers would have provoked a lynching. Not for the vow betrayed, but for the withdrawing of his gift of sex . . . from all to one.'

She remembers her love for this man in the accents of a mystic – Rilke, in echoes, but also Kafka with Felice, and even, Hadewijk and her Beloved, who is white and ruddy, the one whom the soul longs for from the Song of Songs. Yet in the midst of this rapture (always tautly expressed, never mushy), the observing intelligence never fails: 'Love-making is never simply pleasure. Sex manuals or feminist tracts which imply the infinite plasticity of position and pleasure, which counsel assertiveness, whether in bed or out, are dangerously destructive of imagination, of erotic and of spiritual ingenuity. The sexual exchange will be as complicated as the relationship in general – even more so.'

When the newspapers carry their daily stories of widespread or rare disease, when they show a child afflicted, they cheaply count on emotion leaping from the wellsprings of human fellow-feeling; Harold Brodkey's manifesto ('I have AIDS') seemed so finger-pointing and so nudging, he just assumed we would mind about him, when he did not attempt love's work, even as a beginner novelist understands it, to convey the character of the person who suffers, the individual who is threatened by the named plague. But after inhabiting Gillian Rose's thought under her guidance for half her book, the reader knows her presence, and cares for her, for her brilliance, her fierceness, the contrast between the authority of her mind and the modesty (it seems) of her claims on others, and so her particular stations of pain and her nearness to death come across in agony when she begins to tell that part of her story. No self-pity, no histrionics; even her reproaches are laconic, and the more effective for it. 'Medicine and I have dismissed each other,' she writes after the gruelling chronicle of surgery, chemotherapy, varied diagnosis of her stubbornly spreading cancer, doctors' disputes at her bedside. She decides to pioneer an account of colostomy: 'I want to talk about shit – the hourly transfiguration of our lovely eating of the sun', and it reveals her stout-heartedness that she frames her unblinking and perfectly scrupulous description of living without a colon with the reflection that the lack of sanitation arrangements at the camps brought about many *unplanned* deaths, but that historians who attempt to discuss this cannot get heard, because it makes people more uncomfortable than murder by gassing. This evasion, too, Gillian Rose contests with the honesty gained, she might say, from her passion for philosophy.

For in the book's closing chapter, in its knottiest and most compressed passages, she traces the course of this love and this work. Here she brings to mind Simone Weil, a true precursor in her radiant intransigence, and her engagement with the multiple home territories of Judaism and Christian metaphysics. Gillian Rose gives no quarter to those who have given up on philosophy's scepticism about its own purposes just because so little in the world is better than it was. She identifies this defeatism with Protestantism's refusal of hope, and advocates reason as the tool which distinguishes fantasy from reality and makes a theory of justice and political change at least possible. She yields nothing to the postmodernist philosophers who withdraw from applying reason to problems; in one of her compressed and inspired sentences, she wonderfully demolishes those who argue that rationality produced the unholy absolutes of totali-tarianism, the ruthless efficiency of Nazism, that reason goes hand in glove with tyranny: 'Relativism of authority does not establish the authority of relativism; it opens reason to new claimants.'

If I have quoted so often from *Love's Work*, it is because it conveys better than any paraphrase or criticism could how language can set courage against despair, and look hell in the eyes without covering one's own. She calls, like the true love of the *Vita Nuova*, to the high ground of a daily examined consciousness, and for many this is a hard place and a strait gate. But she's also on the side of whisky and revels and risk, and against the puritans and their recipes for soul sadness on the one hand, and seaweed brews and other New Age potions for health on the other. 'Earthly human sadness is the divine comedy,' she writes, and at times this is a funny book, too: 'It is love to laugh bitterly, purgatively, purgatorially, and then to be quiet.' But this is not a quiet book; its author knows how to cry out, and how to sing.

1995

Is There Another Place from which the Dickhead's Self Can Speak?

Review of Alan Hyde, Bodies of Law

Anatomical cabinets, displaying bodies bottled whole or in segments, are gripping artists' and writers' imaginations: the Enlightenment's relish for physical data banks excites awe, fascination and horror in inverse relation to the disembodiment and intangibility of knowledge in the contemporary computerised classroom. A pigmy woman who died in childbirth in London, where she had been brought to be exhibited, is preserved, in a complete half-section, in the Hunterian Museum. She inspired one of the last, unfinished works of the artist Helen Chadwick, who wanted to restore the unnamed pigmy to history, memory and human status as a person – to personhood, in short. University museums and hospital teaching departments are richly stocked with such specimens: a whole black man in a glass box in Chicago; quintuplet foetuses floating upwards, open-mouthed, like Donatello choristers, on a shelf in the Hunterian. Zarina Bhimji, another artist who, like Chadwick, expresses through photography her challenge to common, unexamined responses, has made a highly enigmatic, disturbing image of a black woman's breast, disfigured by a hideous slash. This exhibit comes from the forensic archive of a London hospital, where it is used to illustrate the effects of stabbing for the benefit of medical students: but the injury is itself framed by the jagged partition where the breast was severed from the anonymous victim – the scalpel repeating the pincers that appear, for example, in paintings of Saint Agatha's martyrdom.

A male cadaver known as 'Adam' can be inspected on a website; the images consist of wafer-thin slices (1,871 of them) through the frozen body and thus provide a microscopically detailed surgical map of his insides.* 'Adam' was a convicted murderer – Joseph Paul Jernigan, executed (by barbiturate poisoning) in Texas in 1993 – who donated his body to science. His bizarre, semi-eternal preservation represents the apotheosis of the displayed, reified, specular body of exploratory, scientific epistemology (the website is the pièce de résistance of the 'Visible Human Project'). But 'Adam' differs in two crucially late millennial respects from his antecedents in formaldehyde: first, he is science's current Everyman (and, until he's joined by a promised 'Eve', this is taken at all-embracing, generic force), whereas the eighteenth-century cabinets sought to define the norm through aberration, disease, deformity, monsters; secondly, he has been dematerialised and rendered imponderable, spectral, beamed digitally through the air. The diaphanous inventory of the website, or of the CD-ROM, allows global didactic display of what, if it were present for real (actual slices of flesh), would only be permitted to the public gaze under close certification as Art (cf. Damien Hirst).

Visual artists aren't the only ones to probe these distempered lesions in contemporary approaches to bodies and persons. Gaby Wood's essay 'The Sicilian Fairy' (1998), explored the voyeurism and plottings of freak aficionados and body-snatchers in Victorian London, while Hilary Mantel's fine, imaginative new novel, *The Giant, O'Brien*, dramatises the experiments and predations of the surgeon John Hunter, founder of the Hunterian, as he sniffs out his raw material – including one of the 'Irish giants' who showed themselves to the crowd for a fee in eighteenth-century London.

The new, modern sensitivity to these abuses grows out of the corpse of Cartesian dualism – which placed the individualising mind/spirit/soul inside a body as distinctly as vintage wine in a decanter – developing

---

* National Library of Medicine, Maryland

alongside a holistic understanding of consciousness as itself enfleshed. It's one of modernity's many contradictions that the materialist, atheist view of individuality has intensified the sacred character of the body, its rights and value and consequent claims to attention and respect. The High Renaissance popes who founded anatomical museums in Italy didn't worry about desecrating the living (or the dead) in the same way, because the soul had quit the body (Hamlet's 'shuffling off' hints at snakes, or even insects: crickets, for example).

These complex shifts have been accompanied – and deepened – by a myriad interpretative moves. The originality of Alan Hyde's *Bodies of Law* is that he is trying to apply psychoanalytic, structuralist, post-structuralist and feminist theories of the embodied individual to the analysis of American law. His approach depends on the Foucauldian tenet that while bodies exist in the world, they can take up that existence only through language: who speaks of them and how they speak of them, in medical, ethical, judicial discourse; who fashions them and animates them. Hyde joins forces here with radicals and utopians who want to change language to change thought to change bodies to change persons to change human nature, though nature, of course, only has being in language. He draws richly from such literary critics as Roland Barthes and Peter Brooks, but he is a member of that rare emerging species, the male feminist, and above all, he invokes Monique Wittig and Julia Kristeva, and heats the whole by the halogen sparkle of the supernovae of the American cultural empyrean – Judith Butler, Eve Kosofsky Sedgwick, Patricia J. Williams, Catherine MacKinnon. 'Can we conceptualise people as people in relations?' he asks. 'Can we create a bodily discourse of pleasure, or sexuality? Can we develop a constitutional jurisprudence of how we want to live with each other, so that rights could be secured for subjects by imagining them as other than isolated?' These are important questions, and Hyde, in his idealistic yearning to widen the range and impact of academic philosophy, thinks hard as he reaches for answers.

Bodies of Law lays out a historical taxonomy which attaches different laws to blood, spit, spleen, rectum, vagina, hands and other parcelled body elements. Hyde's examples almost all come from US case law, from lower-court decisions followed by Supreme Court decrees, and they exhibit a grim, callous, at times hilarious casuistry as the judges twist and turn between principles of liberty and privacy, anti-crime measures and constitutional rights. The body as the property of a person dominates much of this thinking. A woman who lived by selling her blood (she belonged to a rare group) was allowed to classify her body and its maintenance as a business expense, and deduct her food and vitamins against tax. A mother was upheld when she refused to allow her children's bone marrow to be donated to their half-sibling. A suspected robber, who was shot in the shoulder by the shop-owner, was also upheld when he refused to have the bullet extracted, as this intervention was deemed to constitute an intolerable invasion of his body. Much discussion of abortion ethics invokes women's ownership of their wombs. By contrast, a man who discovered that his spleen, which had been removed, had been used in experiments that led to a medical breakthrough was not allowed to claim ownership of the organ and a share of the profits. In the famous *Baby M* case, it was established that a woman can only assign her womb to another woman: she cannot sell it.

The metaphors that produce movie fantasies about possession and alien abduction, about medical experiments and body switching (as in the brilliant film *Coma*, the recent *Face-Off*, and many episodes of *The X-Files*), arise from this legal emphasis on the body as a kind of super gilt-edged bond in which the person is heavily – if not wholly – invested, and whose loss unseats that self that is Me. Fears about genetic engineering and cloning focus on the physical transmission of character traits along with body parts. If I'm a dead-ringer for someone else, where have I gone? Where is the self? How can I have a mind of my own in another's body? This wasn't something that very much bothered Mary Shelley at the end of the eighteenth century. *Frankenstein* doesn't suggest that the Creature inherits any of his miscellaneous forebears' characteristics through the genes of his stitched-together parts.

Only a few years ago, the sale of kidneys for transplants was condemned and surgeons who'd abetted it were prosecuted. But the illegal trade, as dramatised in *Coma*, continues, by all reports: the destitute, in Turkey or India, present themselves for the operation. Similarly, organised sex workers' argue that prostitution expresses their right to do what they want with their bodies. However, as the limits on commercial surrogacy reveal, and resistance to a market in organs, as well as to a market in sex, confirms, the commodity body is accompanied by its spirit shadow, what Hyde calls 'the sacred body', the habitat of persons, the ring-fenced zone of personhood, that must not be trafficked in (as in slavery), violated, alienated, reduced. 'A discourse in which the body was *always* unproblematically property,' he writes, 'would be incapable of creating human subjects, without whom neither market, nor any other, society could function. The body that cannot be property (. . . the *sacred* body) thus marks the boundaries of an aesthetic realm that defines the boundaries of, and supplements, market society.'

At the other pole from this sacrosanct vessel of personal identity stands the allegorical body, the impersonal bearer of multiple symbolic meanings, of nation and virtue, of history and the future, of health and vitality: individuals, in their bodies, get caught up in this language, and the law circumscribes their emissions, display and conduct according to specific cultural dreams of purity and danger (Hyde's arguments here depend on the social anthropologist Mary Douglas): at high-level meetings in Mao's China, the grandest officials' armchairs were flanked by imposing brass spittoons as if by armorial bearers; Edith Piaf, squatting on the stage to piss, was making a point about women's restrictions in the land of the public *pissoir*; Anthea Turner goes 'the full monty' on the cover of a glossy this month but the massive phallic snake and her gym-flexed limbs are still artfully arranged to conceal her nipples. Women fare unequally in this semiotic drama, required by law to look nice in public and all that entails: a motel receptionist in Alabama was fired for not wearing make-up to cover her spots, but the courts did not censure the employer for requiring this. Warrants have been issued for the search of the appellant's 'apartment and vagina'. Licit bodies have to be made visible: the law acts as a microscope, or a medical lens, tracing the passage of pollution in the larger body politic. Males are also subject to penetrative investigation: prisoners, especially young black detainees, are routinely subjected to body searches, while blood tests are required of US border guards and Customs officers to monitor drugs. Suspected of sex abuse, a policeman was offered a 'penile plethysmograph' to register his responses to erotic stimuli. He refused, and was dismissed. US law unveils the phallus with unprecedented eagerness, and unlike Adam, the 'owner' of the penis cannot choose to cover his nakedness. This process demystifies – up to a point. The veiling of the phallus, which used to enhance its power, has been replaced by a ritual unveiling that concentrates public fascination, so that we are all to become Noah's sons, looking at their drunken father in the vineyard. It must be disappointing to Alan Hyde that his book was finished before Monica Lewinsky continued Paula Jones's work of rendering public the President's privates. If fellatio is not a sexual relationship for the fellatee, then one reason for this is the penis's imagined distance from the person to whom it is physically attached: eyes meeting, lips touching – now, that would have been sex, surely, just like in the movies?

Hyde does not discuss proposals to control sex offenders by means of castration or drugs, but his analysis of the separation of organs under the law reveals that it could come to this, once unthinkable, measure. Judicial decisions in rape cases often appear to grant the penis autonomy, as if it were acting independently of the person's mind and control ('I couldn't help myself'; 'She made me do it'). 'If law were to construct . . . bodies that acted without minds, without "our leave", bodies that had their own civil and criminal responsibility,' Hyde writes, 'I am confident that the penis would become that body part par excellence to which independent agency would be attributed.' This interpretation would give a new slant to the American term 'dickhead', with its rueful, affectionate offspring, animated cartoon willies like Norbert. So, is there another place from which a dickhead's self can speak? Can Clinton plead that his libido acts distinctly from the self that does other things, like send in the missiles?

The metaphors which the laws apply for the body as tool, an object of exchange, a kit of disparate organs and limbs, fail to communicate the changing 'custom, piety, intuition and opinion' (in Terry Eagleton's phrase) which society observes. Legal judgments, in Hyde's view, continually attempt to 'model a system of rules and principles divorced from human empathy and identification', severed from those values and mores that render the hire of wombs repugnant and the philandering of Presidents somehow beside the point. But at this stage of its argument, *Bodies of Law* turns cloudy and by himself Hyde is unable to generate a new language of the self in the dock. He concludes that the 'law desperately needs new ways of "imagining", becoming one person with, our brothers and sisters, imaginings that do not depend on the visualised body', and proposes that persons qua persons should enter legal discourse, that the stories of victims be told, that 'narrated bodies' replace anatomies in the statute books. His appeal for empathy draws on new philosophies of feeling and subjectivity. It is clearly noble and idealistic, but it also conjures the spectre of an Oprah Winfrey-style legal rhetoric by which pleas persuade according to the intensity of their staging, and 'I feel your pain' becomes a moral principle and a criterion of judgment.

1998

FOUR

FAITH AND MARVELS

Wrestling with the Oldest Rules:
The First Commandment

The surprise is, there is no talk of love.

Casting back to Mother Bridget's catechism classes, I thought I remembered that God asks his people to love him, and no one else but him. There was a hint of charm about this, a lover's request, its claims mitigated by the swirling flow of emotion between the deity and his creatures. But what Yahweh says to Moses on the mountain is more stark, narrow and uncompromising, and carries not a hint of seduction: 'You shall have no other gods before me.'

What I had remembered was the first answer in the catechism, from the New Testament: that I should love the Lord my God with my whole heart and my whole soul. Over time, the Catholic Church had tilted the relation between humans and the supreme deity towards a reciprocal erotic fantasy, couched in the imagery of the Song of Songs, a far cry from the apocalyptic blasts of Yahweh.

What does this jealous God mean when he says, 'no other gods before me'? The people of the Book were notorious backsliders, straying into cults of the Babylonian Queen of Heaven and other pagan horrors, falling down in worship before the golden calf, easily distracted from the angry parent who keeps threatening to take care of them, or else. The phrase 'no other gods before me' could be Yahweh promising, with monotheism, a pact so intimate, so tight, that his protégés will not need intermediate divinities to make contact. There will be no pagan profusion, as in Egypt, the country Moses and company have left behind: no younger godlings like Horus, no goddesses like Nut or Isis, no divine messengers like jackal-headed Anubis, ferryman of the dead. But the phrasing still reveals an intrinsic problem: the God of monotheism is talking of other gods as if they exist, and exist as a threat to him.

I was taught that evolved societies worship one god alone, and that only primitive folk entertain a pantheon of gods and goddesses. But the Greeks' distribution of passions and functions and tasks among the Olympians reflects the complexity of human nature and culture. Zeus, who comes closest to Yahweh in his pre-eminence and thundering habits (though not in his sexual adventures), had to allow room for his siblings to rule by his side – and in that there's some kind of lesson in give-and-take, even though they do bicker and fight and deceive one another. The Hindu pantheon similarly embodies the polymorphous character of human aspirations and fears in its stories about Parvati, Krishna, Lakshmi, Shiva, Durga, Vishnu, Ganesa and . . . I could go on – so many female as well as male facets of wonder, passion and joy, of divine justice and wrath.

Now that I have returned to the Decalogue for the first time since childhood, the voice of the deity strikes my ear as that of a petulant and charmless tyrant who is covering up his own ineffectual promises with bluster, the kind of humourless boss who is given to loud renditions of 'My Way' at the annual office party.

1997

Signs of the Times: Touching Tears

Jules: Do you know what a miracle is?
Vincent: An act of God.
Jules: What's an act of God?
Vincent: I guess it's when God makes the impossible happen. And I'm sorry, Jules, but I don't think what happened this morning qualifies.
Jules: Don't you see, Vince, that shit don't matter. You're judging this thing the wrong way. It's not about what. It could be God stopped the bullets, he changed the Coke into Pepsi, he found my fuckin' car keys. You don't judge shit like this based on merit. Whether or not what we experienced was an according-to-Hoyle miracle is insignificant. What is significant is I felt God's touch. God got involved.

Quentin Tarantino, *Pulp Fiction* (1995)

On 2 February 1995, a state-employed electrician, Fabio Gregori, decided to leave the Church of Sant'Agostino in Pantano, near Civitavecchia, when his two-year-old son became restless, to give him and his sister Jessica, then aged five, their *merenda* – their tea – before returning to their mother Anna Maria and the service. It was the Feast of the Purification of the Virgin (the *Candelora*) and after the customary recitation of the rosary, Don Pablo Martin, the parish priest, was going to distribute candles to his parishioners to take home and keep alight all night in honour of Our Lady. Gregori was putting Davide back into the car when Jessica called to out him, 'Papa, la Madonnina piange!' ('Daddy, the Little Madonna is crying'). At first her father did not respond, so the child cried out again, 'Corri, corri, viene giù tutto sangue' ('Come quickly, come quickly, there's blood all coming down'). Fabio Gregori first checked her fingers, thinking she'd pricked herself on a rose bush; Jessica then specified: the blood came from the Madonnina. When Fabio saw the bright red tears streaking the statue's face, he touched them and felt 'a great blast of fire from head to toe, as if I'd fallen into a brazier'. He drove back to the church, 'at 140 kilometres an hour', he says, but had to wait till the service was over before telling the priest.

Don Pablo told Fabio to keep quiet, and Fabio continued as normal, going to work the next day, and leaving the statue in the niche in the garden. But within forty-eight hours, by word of mouth and with help from Radio Maria (broadcasting from near Como 'a Christian voice in your home'), the news was spreading, and relatives and strangers were gathering in the Gregori garden – only eleven people on 3 February but five times as many the following day. The Madonnina wept again, several times, or so around fifty witnesses declared – the tally varies. Fabio Gregori describes how he also dipped a handkerchief in the blood and the stain appeared, then faded immediately. Among the people who say they saw the Madonna's bloody tears fall repeatedly during those bitterly cold February days were some unexpected voices: a Jehovah's Witness who had been trying to convert Fabio (he has since been baptised and joined the family's prayer group), a photographer from the town, two policemen, a commander of the Vigili Urbani.

The parish priest decided it was time for him to call in his bishop and longtime associate, Don Girolamo Grillo. In response, the bishop denounced the whole district of Pantano as a hotbed of black magic and Satanist jokes; he had himself received hate mail, and even curses (tiny coffins filled with bones), from that parish. But he then announced a

Theological Commission to investigate the phenomenon and invited the veteran French Mariologist, l'abbé René Laurentin, aged seventy-seven, to serve on it. The contested statue was now attracting such crowds that Fabio Gregori hid it for safe keeping – in one of his relatives' homes – and began building a wall around his property; but on 10 February he agreed to hand it over to the bishop. Grillo, first taking the precaution of performing an exorcism, took it to a laboratory in the Catholic Hospital in Rome, where two experts submitted it to state-of-the-art analysis, including a CAT scan.

These attempts to understand the exudation (to use the technical term in theology) were helped – and hindered – by the descent on Civitavecchia of the contemporary media charivari, a garish, exuberant, noisy gang of pundits and scoffers, diviners and miracle-workers, gossip-mongers, television stars, and even a famous exorcist – Bishop Milingo, formerly of Zambia. The Mayor of Civitavecchia, Pietro Tidei, seized the commercial possibilities without a backward glance: he made provision for benches, water fountains, parking lots, portable lavatories, he issued licences to food carts, sandwich stalls, postcard sellers. An architect created a model, free of charge, showing the future sanctuary as a huge upturned azure waterlily, opening to the sky. At a press conference, Tidei spoke of hiring ferryboats to accommodate pilgrims, as if to fulfil the fantasy of the great dialect poet Tonino Guerra, who had once tried to convince the Mayor of Ravenna to build floating cathedrals out to sea. Cynics scoffed at the new mayor's opportunism: Tidei belongs to the PDS (Partito della Democrazia Socialista – the reconfigured Communist Party), and is the son and grandson of Communists. But he is nonetheless a believer, Italian-style, who has retained the crucifix hanging behind the Mayor's desk. The millennium would see a Holy Year to cap all Holy Years: millions of Catholics would be making the pilgrimage to Rome. As a local journalist commented, 'Rome is just down the road; if only a fraction of those pilgrims can be attracted here, just think how many bowls of fish soup that would mean.'

But after a month of high hopes and low motives, La Madonnina's fate changed: the law (the Procura) suddenly stepped in, sequestered the statue, and placed her under official seals. The faithful marched in protest, hundreds strong, into the town, to demand the Madonnina's liberty and her presence at the Easter ceremonies. She was becoming the prize in a religious version of a tug-of-love custody suit; a small outbreak of religious fervour threatened to start a major conflict between Church and state.

Nearly two acrimonious months were to pass before La Madonnina was let out, and although she was ceremoniously installed in the Church of Sant'Agostino on 17 June, her trials are by no means over. With no witnesses to see her in seclusion, she had not wept again in the sealed cupboard; to the disappointment of many, she has not done so since.

The statue is around 42 centimetres high (17 inches), her face the size of a large peach stone, disproportionately small in relation to her high-waisted, long-legged swathed body – very hard to see from any distance. The most fervent believers in the miracle of La Madonnina di Pantano count fourteen *lacrimazioni* in all from 2 February to 15 March; the Italian noun carries an active, performative charge, as if the Madonna actively engaged in a practical process, analogous to words like *torrefazione* (nougat) or 'manufacture', which lyrical English phrases like 'the shedding of tears' or 'tearfall' cannot catch; the nearest to the sense of purpose, though its jauntiness sounds a wrong note, would be the Woosterish slang about the sort of things girls do: 'turning on the waterworks'. But of course, in this case, the Mother of God did not cry tears of water, but of blood.

Catholic shrine souvenirs can have a fairy-light, gimcrack, sugar-candy charm that Jeff Koons has raised without irony into the canon of fine art: Our Lady in pink and blue with roses between her toes. But this Madonnina is slickly glazed all over in bathroom-tile white, and her maker pushed her without ceremony out of a mould with no craft, no detailing, no smoothing or rubbing; you can see the seam of the two halves of the mould, her hands look as if she's wearing gloves to do dishes, and her head under her veil is so lumpy she might have left in a curler or two under a headscarf.

The statue was bought in the market around the shrine of Medjugorje, the small town in the Catholic Croatian part of Bosnia-Herzegovina, in the diocese of Mostar, where several children began receiving regular visions of the Madonna in 1981. The visionaries are now grown up, and some have drifted away from the village, while others are still hearing and interpreting messages from the White Lady who appears to them as they recite the rosary at a certain time every day; she exhorts them to pray for the sins of the world in order to avert worse calamities than have already befallen. The Madonnina of Pantano near Civitavecchia has the word 'Medjugorje' inscribed on her pedestal – she was brought back by Don Pablo Martin in September 1994 and given to his parishioner and disciple, Fabio Gregori, to protect him. He felt that Fabio was straying, since he comes from a typical rural *mangiapreti* (priest-eating) anticlerical family, and used to work as a local councillor of the PDS (though it's perfectly possible that he combined Catholicism and Communism, like the Mayor).

The Gregori household is on the same road to the sea as Don Pablo's church, a bleak industrial stretch alongside the gigantic, roaring, coastal installation of the region's electricity generating plant, where Fabio Gregori and many of his neighbours work. He is reputed to be accident-prone: in 1982, he crashed his Fiat 500 and remained in a coma for a few days. He has also been severely electrocuted. The phalanx of pylons carrying energy march out of the Centrale like skeletal Pacmen; gradually they open out across the reclaimed marshes of the coast as they begin their advance southwards and northwards; three of the pylons – two very tall, one more squat – stand right behind the Gregori house. It's difficult not to imagine, when Fabio describes the shooting bolts of heat and radiance he received when he touched the weeping statue, that the electrical charge he himself must carry would set a lump of concrete crackling fire.

The God of the Old Testament displays his power through 'signs and wonders' (*semeia kai terata*): the phrase evokes the plagues of Egypt, the fire and frogs and rain of blood of Exodus and Moses' leadership. 'Wonders' imply the natural law suspended, the strike of the impossible, to which the only response is to marvel, as in Latin *mirari*, and so can sometimes be translated as 'miracles'; one of the prophets beseeches Yahweh, 'Send new portents, do fresh wonders, win glory for your hand and your right arm' (Ecclesiasticus 36:5). In the aberrational plagues that nature can produce, the God of the Old Testament demonstrates his might. In the New Testament, Jesus's signs take the form of kindlier miracles which overturn the laws of the physical universe: water into wine, cures of sickness, lameness, blindness – boon not bane. Jesus appears to scorn petitioners' hunger for prodigies, for whom 'seeing is believing'; but he does lift the fever from the dying son of the official from Capernaum, after reproaching his father – 'so you will not believe unless you see signs and portents' (John 4:48). The Gospel of Matthew warns that such wonders are dangerous, ambiguous, difficult to interpret: false prophets, in the service of the devil, can use them 'enough to deceive even the chosen, if that were possible' (Matthew 24:24). This is the crux: how can you tell if the bloody tears of the Madonna are a divine sign or a diabolical trick: the supernatural event could be merely paranormal, and the paranormal can easily be faked; distinguishing icon from idol, saint from charlatan, has occupied many fine minds and animated many struggles between reason and unreason, between faith and superstition.

Mary and marvels are never very far apart: she is a virgin mother, after all. Throughout the history of her cult, icons and relics (from Byzantium's miraculous portraits of her 'made without hands' to objects like the shift she was wearing at the Annunciation, which was enshrined in Chartres Cathedral) have brought about victories in battle and recoveries in health – and, for women, surprise fertility and much wanted babies. The Mother of God has given previous signs of her love, sometimes in a capricious manner: a medieval miracle tells of a young knight who, while playing a game, slips his ring off his finger and places it for safe keeping on the hand of a statue of the Virgin, joking that he will be faithful to her for ever. On his wedding night, Our Lady chooses her moment, and appears. She reproaches him for forgetting her; he leaves his bride and becomes a monk.

Images of the Virgin have exuded perfumed oils and wept tears, often; there are currently unexplained, prolonged examples – this year in the house of Mrs Mary Murray in Co. Wicklow, Ireland, and – since 1975 – in a convent in Akita in northern Japan. In *The Apparitions of the Blessed Virgin Mary Today*, the abbé René Laurentin lists every kind of manifestation – from Belgium to Zaire via Korea, Vietnam, Rwanda, with the longest entries under Ireland and Italy.[1] The most recent miracle of this kind to be officially approved took place at Syracuse in 1953, and a basilica was built to display the miraculous souvenir, a plaster of Paris plaque; crutches hang there, dedicated after miracles, and wedding dresses, too, offered to the sanctuary by brides in hopes of a happy life.

Mary's tears of blood are a twentieth-century innovation, however. Her cult often borrows features from the cult of Jesus and blood flows in the wine, during the central mystery of the eucharist. Jesus sweated blood in the Garden of Gethsemane before his death, and he exposes his bloody heart, crowned with thorns, as well as his wounds in the numerous statues and images of His Sacred Heart. The veneration of Mary's Immaculate Heart followed the success of the cult of the Sacred Heart. Blood is the vital fluid, the mystical ink of Christianity, in which the martyrs and many saints sign their professions of faith. It communicates the vitality in sacramental symbolism as well as pain and death. As Georges Bataille, whose essays and erotica are steeped in the rituals and symbolism of the Catholic faith, has written, 'Human beings are never united with each other except through tears and wounds.'[2]

Shrines are made not born; they are brought to life by a hazardous conjunction of individuals and propitious circumstances. The anthropologist William Christian, Jr, in his recent magisterial and wise study, *Visionaries*, writes, 'The Church depends on successive layers of creativity. In the constant process of renewal, grace plays a role similar to that of oxygen in the blood stream or new water in a tide pool. For many Catholics grace is an energy that reawakens interest and provides hope and direction . . . Visions, stigmatics, prophets, new devotions, new institutes and new sources of grace in trees, soil, stones, and water make up a kind of ever changing (yet never changing) world . . . Sacralization is a process . . .'[3]

Some shrines succeed after the founding wonder, the initial apparition or miracle; but others, many others, founder, and are forgotten: the process of sacralisation fails to be completed. In 1876, the villagers of Marpingen in the Saarland attempted to make a stand against Bismarck's *Kulturkampf*, after some children saw a 'woman in white' in the forest. Their parents' and other adults' impassioned belief in the visions arose from a widespread sense of collapse among the villagers in an isolated, obscure Catholic community on the outer rim of the new, centralised Germany. The authorities of the state crushed the devotion by force, using the secret police alongside the army to drive out pilgrims and discredit the child seers and the villagers. The shrine consequently failed, and the visions of Marpingen, as David Blackbourn has shown in his detailed 1994 study, are utterly forgotten today.[4] The village of Ezquioga in the Basque country, the focus of William Christian's study, was the site of numerous visions and ecstasies during the early years of the Spanish Republic, when the Church was beleaguered. Today, it does not even rate a mention in the comprehensive registers of such shrines. In Pantano, a similar drama is being fought. A holy place of Christendom must prove its authentic connection to the divine, must argue its title to truth through a series of ordeals, some more predictable than others.

The sincerity of visionaries like Bernadette Soubirous at Lourdes and the children at Fatima and Medjugorje must first be tried: their claims are tested with all available means, from harsh interrogation to mechanical processes of verification. But when there is no special medium or seer, but a sweating icon, a wobbling statue, a bleeding image, when the divine operates through inanimate matter, then the object comes under severe scrutiny, because the merit of the seer does not count for very much towards the value of the prodigy. René Laurentin admits, 'the language of exudation causes intellectuals to bristle because of its non-rational nature'.[5]

Yet Italy abounds with sacred places, and every sacred place has its roots in a relic or a miracle, every one rises from a story, local, peculiar, comic, disturbing, sometimes all at once. Near Mantua, in the popular healing pilgrimage site of S. Maria delle Grazie, where, on the Feast of the Assumption every year, *Madonnari* – lovers of the Madonna – gather to draw her portrait in coloured chalks on the broad piazza in front of the church, there is a stuffed crocodile hanging from the Gothic vault; slightly the worse for wear after a few centuries, the crocodile commemorates a miracle worked through the Virgin's intercession. When it was fished out of the canal which irrigates the fertile Lombard plain around Mantua, it was identified with that old serpent, the dragon, the devil; with its death, the plague came to an end. The conjecture is that the crocodile had escaped from the private zoo of the Lords of Mantua, the Gonzaga; but it hangs in trophy, a sign of the Virgin's mercy and divine providence – and of the irreducible ingenuity of human fantasy.

The religious attitude holds that the sacred is absolute and inherent in a miracle or a manifestation from its original moment; the process of transformation – of *Lourdizzazione*, in the Italian papers' coinage – which can turn a nowhere place into a world-class pilgrimage site, can seem to invalidate, to cheapen the claimant to original holiness. The profane and the sacred should be mutually exclusive categories, incapable of merging or exchange. But this view runs counter to the anthropological and historical understanding that sacredness accrues, like a lovely patina on ore. It effaces the history of worship, the record of grace accumulating when different desires, springing up for various reasons, converge in a single stream. Like all desires, these meet with frustrations that have to be overcome before fulfilment can be reached: the shrine only survives, becomes established when these opposing forces sink, vanquished.

Sacred places of Christendom, even after they have won official approval, have their seasons: Paray-le-Monial, where Saint Margaret Mary Alacoque received her mystical visions of the Sacred Heart in 1672–5, still attracts the faithful in surprising numbers, but its fame has ceded to the great Marian shrines – Lourdes, Fatima, and now Medjugorje. The Bishop of Tarbes, in whose diocese Bernadette saw the Virgin, first treated her harshly; the Bishop of Mostar struggled to quell the ever growing flow of pilgrims into Medjugorje, and to control – unavailingly – the Franciscan monks who were promoting the visions and the shrine. John Cornwell, the author of *Powers of Darkness, Power of Light*, a personal, perceptive account of several Catholic cult sites, comments, 'The church is uncomfortable with miracles and suchlike manifestations. Its tendency – though there is some tension over this – is to debunk, and it's not worried about how this affects the faithful. Its view would be that the faithful are much more affected when they become disenchanted.' It's revealing that throughout the events at Pantano, *L'Osservatore Romano*, the Vatican paper and an accurate gauge of the Curia's temperature, has never written a word about the Madonnina.

But this model of ecclesiastical antagonism to 'marvellism', as the Jesuit Carlos Maria Staehner has called the popular love of miracles, does not reflect the full picture in the Church today. Both Pope Paul VI and Pope John Paul II, in their personal devotion to the Mother of God, have given permission to a new era of faith in divine intervention, and especially in the Virgin Mary's saving actions. In 1970 Pope Paul VI abolished a clause in canon law which forbade publications about visions, miracles, private messages; immediately, disclosures about Mary's working presence in the contemporary world, through images, statues, and apparitions, began to flow thick and fast, and they have continued under the present Pope, John Paul II. While being an authoritarian upholder of tradition, Karol Wojtyla has made more new saints than any of his predecessors: 594 men and women beatified between 1979 and 1994. If the martyrs of the Spanish Civil War are canonised (in 1983, the Pope allowed their cause to be reopened), 6,500 more names will swell this number. He is famous for his love of the Madonna, and his advocacy of her model womanhood pervades his many teachings on the subject of sexuality and contemporary damnation. She 'takes part, as a mother, in that "monumental struggle against the powers of darkness" which continues throughout human history'.[6] He was the first pope to recognise the visions of Fatima, when he visited her shrine in 1983: the anti-Communist thrust of the visions' notorious 'Secrets' had prophetically anticipated his own struggles in his native Poland. He believes that when a Turkish terrorist shot him in 1981, the bullet was miraculously deflected by Our Lady of Fatima. The bullet is now enshrined there, another vanquished crocodile, as it were.

The Pope represents an odd hyphen between the kind of fervour that marks out the popular underclass of mystical enthusiasts and traditional values; he's the presiding genius of both Christian New Age and New Right. Don Pablo Martin, the parish priest, is a confirmed *Madonnaro*, as well as a valiant defender of the Pope, and he strikes continuous echoes, in his conversation as well as his sermons, of Karol Wojtyla's writings, as when he describes Mary making a pilgrimage in history, marking her path with 'epiphanies of maternal assistance to the church'. His slow, soft speech lapses readily into rhapsody as he relates how he left his native La Mancha for Italy when he and some friends in the seminary received a call – a spiritual message – from Padre Pio, the Capuchin friar of Monte Gargano, Puglia. Padre Pio died in 1968; he suffered from stigmata, the marks of Christ's passion, in his hands and feet and side, and he bled from the wounds.[7] When Don Pablo went to Medjugorje in September last year, he was entering a web of strong Catholic reaction which links Lourdes, Fatima and Padre Pio, and is defended by self-appointed guardians who have little time for the rationalism and prevarications of official church caution.

Through the rosary, as hypnotic a practice as Hindu mantra, and through the cult of the Miraculous Medal, a mystical talisman given to another visionary, Saint Catherine Labouré in Paris, in 1830, this international network of Marian worshippers is spreading an alternative, populist theology for the end of the millennium: the monogram on the helpers' shirts at the shrine of La Madonnina echoes the amulet of the Miraculous Medal. Their 'marvellism' is rooted in a dualistic, Gnostic model of providence, with the forces of good and evil doing eternal battle, and the Pope's dark vision of the present time as a Second Fall invigorates it. Saint Michael struggles to stab Lucifer through the heart on the tower of the church at Pantano, and Don Pablo invokes the warrior archangel warmly in his services. The events at Civitavecchia form merely another filament spun by seekers after God's touch in a time of apocalypse.

When Don Pablo and his group of friends were studying for the priesthood, they became devoted to 'a truly extraordinary mystic, who is the key to what the Lord is doing now', says Don Pablo. Luisa Piccarreta, known as 'the Little Daughter of the Divine Will', lived in the small town of Corato, near Bari, and died there in 1947.

The Italian people haven't yet realised that they possess such a treasure [continues Don Pablo]. She lived sixty-five years in her bed, and died each day. Each day, in order for her to return to life, a priest had to come – usually one of her five confessors – to give her the order to obey him, and return to life. She lived only by nourishing herself on the Eucharist. She had almost no education, yet Jesus gave her this immense treasure, in thirty-six fat exercise books of autobiographical diary. This marvellous book is not yet published because as so often happens, her writings were sequestrated, taken away and hidden. She lived the passion of Jesus without cease.

A photograph of 'Luisa Santa', a tiny, hunched old lady propped up on pillows, like granny before the wolf ate her, hangs in Don Pablo's hallway outside his combined office and residence, next to a statue of the Virgin of Fatima.

This self-mortifying female body, patterned on the ecstatics of the High Middle Ages (like Margaret Mary Alacoque), could win for its owner a very special sphere of influence – consciously or unconsciously; Caroline Walker Bynum has written in *Holy Feast and Holy Fast* (1987), about holy women who, through extreme bodily austerities, appeared to counter biological laws and so made miracles of their bodies, and thus transformed them into persuasive, respected vehicles of spiritual wisdom. The tears of the Virgin of Don Pablo's parish similarly take the body's passionate expressiveness beyond nature's normal bounds: as in stigmata, the body weeps blood, to symbolise an anguish beyond usual grief.

From the start, Don Pablo never expressed any doubt about the truth of the sign on his parishioner's statue. Indeed, he remained, according to an early observer, 'preternaturally calm' in the event, given the remarkable affray the news caused. He seemed to take it completely for granted; the call from Padre Pio, the discovery of 'Luisa Santa', and the tears of the Madonnina form part of 'a mysterious design . . . for the next millennium'.

The bishop knew well Don Pablo's character and fervour: after Don Pablo was ordained, he and his friends formed an unofficial quasi-monastic group dedicated to prayer, the Little Brothers of the Divine Will; Don Grillo accepted them in his diocese, and Don Pablo and one other worked as parish priests in the tree-lined, prosperous hillside professional middle-class suburb of San Gordiano. But the bishop and Don Pablo began to object to the approach and conduct of one or two of the brotherhood, and in 1993, it was disbanded – interestingly, the bishop then moved into their house, leaving his episcopal palace in town. The brothers left for America, but Don Pablo was secured in the parish of Pantano.

Don Pablo's weekday evening rosary vigils in Sant'Agostino, beginning at 9.30pm and lasting nearly two hours, draw a full house:

Fabio Gregori and his wife, Anna Maria Accorsi, arrive and take the front pew, just to the left of the grotto. Two coach-loads from the Umbrian city of Viterbo, miles away, are due; when the pilgrims arrive, late, they process into the church, filling the nave to overflowing; they are carrying candles glowing against baking parchment ruffs in the breeze; they are singing. The priest begins whispering of the glories and the sufferings of Mary, blazoning her beauty, her love, her power, in a tremendous ecstasy. She's the gentle breeze and the hurricane; the flowering earth and the desert; all the birds and creatures of Creation join in singing her praises.

I can count only six other men in the church, which is full, and must seat around two hundred. These women pilgrims seem a little uneasy at Don Pablo's outpouring; it feels intimate, and they want to put their feet down on the comparatively neutral terra firma of the family rosary. Many of these praying women are pickle-brown, crooked and gnarled, like cruel Renaissance allegories of Vanitas; the one next to me waves away the hymn book cheerfully: 'I can't read!' she tells me, shaking her head, her mouth opening on empty gums. At the altar, Don Pablo is in the tube, he's surfing the big wave of Mary, *mamma cara*, and until the ocean brings him into shore, he can't stop riding her praises. As he nears it, he shifts into the first person, and speaks in her voice, exhorting his listeners: 'You hurt me, because I see you are very inattentive during my prayers.' When the rosary finally begins (after three-quarters of an hour), a plaster statue of Our Lady of Fatima is passed around the congregation; each person, when her turn comes to hold it, gives out the first versicle of the Hail Mary. A younger woman, who still has teeth, whispers to me, 'It's so beautiful, to cradle the Madonna as if she was a baby in your arms! Oh, you must do it.'

It is easy to underestimate how deep the longing to touch the sacred and to be reciprocally touched by it can be. In this stifling, packed, pent-up church, one praying woman after another gazes deep into the eyes of a plaster Madonna in their hands as if hypnotising her (it?) to weep. 'The believer can add little to approved, official devotions,' writes Bill Christian. 'By praying at new places . . . Catholics make a statement about the way heaven ought to be.'

In the last decades reports of wobbling statues, stigmata, light flashes, tears and eye signals have not quite kept pace with alien abductions, but they have been increasing. Andrea Tornielli in a recent study gives account of fifty phenomena, twenty of which feature visions of the Virgin Mary in person, while twelve involve statues or other images – including supernatural photographs. Some counterfeiters have been unmasked: in Ragusa, in Sicily, two were caught squirting blood on statues of the Virgin at night. In the case of La Madonnina of Pantano, the scientists did spring a surprise: the DNA was male.

These results lifted any suspicion from the child Jessica who had first seen the tears; though many observers had commented that the tears' course was far too fine and steady for a child's work with a brush or – God forbid – a syringe; she had just lost a front tooth at the time, and so it seemed possible she might have been playing a kind of supernatural game of Casualty or Doctors and Nurses. But the male DNA created a new set of problems – and theories. Rationalists in the press suggested testing the blood for traces of vaccines. Theologians on the other hand sprang to argue that it was the logic of providence: Mary, as a perfect mediatrix, would not weep her own blood, but Christ's; pregnant with the Sacred Heart of Jesus, she conveys His sufferings.

Two days later, after almost a month had passed since the first commotion, the Procura, the legal office of the town, received a formal denunciation from one of Italy's biggest consumer protection associations, Codacons. The accusation invoked a crime formulated in the thirties, *abuso di credulità popolare* ('abuse of the people's credulity'); this charge was followed by another from the pressure group Telefono Antiplagio – contro le Truffe dei Maghi e delle Sette (the Anti-Brainwashing Helpline against the Tricks of Wizards and Sects). Its founder, Giovanni Panunzio, who teaches religious studies in Sardinia, is a devout Catholic infuriated by the superstitions that he sees turning believers away from the true faith; he is struggling to suppress clairvoyants, hypnotists, fortune-tellers, self-styled prophets of public and personal doom, and pedlars of magic and Satanism, especially on television. 'They also prey on pilgrims in holy places,' says Panunzio. 'It is against Italian law to claim to know the future and deceive the populace, and vulnerable individuals and families can be destroyed by their emotional – and financial – dependence on such mountebanks.'

In the early morning of 8 March, police descended without warning, in simultaneous raids, on six different houses of the Gregori family – including Fabio and Anna Maria's. Nothing was found, no syringes, vials, tell-tale paintbrushes. (Panunzio of the Anti-Brainwashing Helpline immediately countered that the original statue had been switched for another.) It was at this point, completely unexpectedly, that Bishop Grillo struck the greatest coup of the whole unfolding drama. On 5 April, taking a leaf from an evangelist preacher, he made a confession of faith on the television news. Three weeks before, on 15 March, when the statue was in his custody, he had lifted it out of the basket where it lay in cotton wool and then, as he was holding La Madonnina in his hands, he saw her weep again.

On 6 April, the day after the bishop's sensational outburst on prime-time news, the attorney Antonio Albano announced that the Criminalpol (the Italian FBI) would reopen the analysis of the blood samples, sealing the Madonnina in a cupboard in the bishop's living room pending the outcome.

The inquiry into the miracles of Lourdes took eight years of discussion: so far there have been no miracles at Pantano, and the wrangling will no doubt continue well into the next millennium.

If the object of the crowd's devotion – and curiosity – had been an aubergine in which the name of Allah appeared after it had been cut in half (as happened in Britain a few years ago), or a more patent fabrication – a bearded beauty, a mermaid – the state would be unlikely to move to protect the public from parting with its common sense or its money. Likewise, to take a less frivolous example, it would be unthinkable for Canadian authorities to interfere with a Crow or Blackfoot bundle ceremony on the grounds that the bundle the First Nations were unwrapping was spurious. The belief expressed by the celebrants would be enough to hallow it; the essential process of sacralisation would be irreversibly under way.

When La Madonnina was not released in time for the town's traditional Good Friday procession, the public outcry erased the differences between cardinals and peasants, between those hungry for miracles and the judicious rationalists. In the cathedral on Palm Sunday, from his wheelchair, the aged Polish Cardinal Andrzej Maria Deskur, intimate and compatriot of the Pope, appeared to pass on the Pontiff's support: he recalled that in 1967 the Communists in Czechoslovakia had confiscated the sacred icon of Our Lady of Czestochowa, which hangs in the diocese of Krakow, where Karol Wojtyla, the present Pope, was then bishop.

On 17 June, the tests completed (but inconclusive, of course), Bishop Grillo himself carried La Madonnina back to Sant'Agostino to enshrine her, and delivered a passionate homily during the open-air mass. After this, the bishop began travelling the world, far from the heated scene of the miracle.

The street talk and the newspaper theorists spinning the *giallo* (the thriller) which so enthrals observers propose varying motives: a 'macabre joke' could have been played on the fervid piety of Don Pablo and the Gregori, and gone wrong when it was taken in earnest and spiralled out of control; or – in a more sinister twist – a sect wishing to discredit the Catholic faith could have fixed the events. The prosecution isn't dismissing the paranoid theory that a nationwide organisation, bent on profiteering, is engineering a series of prodigies to gull the populace. What does seem most likely – and coincides with the narrative the Procura seems inclined to offer at this stage – is that after someone stained the face of the Madonna with blood, once, twice, maybe three times, for motives still unknown, the several people who then saw the tears flow on different occasions suffered a collectively induced hallucination. And after that, a muddle developed, a convergence of desires, the sacredness accruing, the patina growing.

Some of the most committed partisans of the story weren't religious, but seekers after wonders. As Carlo Maria Montini, the widely respected Cardinal of Milan, observed, '[There's an] itch people feel to see, to touch the supernatural, but this itch can arise from little faith.' The Turin philosopher, Gianni Vattimo, wrote 'the so-called "need for miracles". . . is perhaps a need that has been largely induced, invented and underscored by the same people who wish to satisfy it: the mass media . . . above all, the bringers of television news, who as never before, perhaps, have been the protagonists'. Calling on newspapers and television to show more responsibility, he criticised the media's tendency to level all news into sensation (murder crimes, war atrocities, miracles), and despaired that any religious message could ever be communicated on the airwaves, on camera, without losing integrity.

The whodunnit approach, the 'yellow' version, neglects however the needs and dreams behind the vision of the Virgin's bloody tears, which has placed so many more hundreds and even thousands of people under a spell. It does not even register, let alone explain, what Bill Christian calls 'the rush of grace in a time of upset'. Visions or other prodigies take root during crises of confidence when formerly stable authorities and institutions are collapsing and bitter conflicts are ensuing: the time was/is ripe. Cicero, commenting on the omens and portents so important in Roman history, wrote, 'These events, moreover, appear more frequently and more seriously in times of war, when people are frightened: in times of peace nobody pays them much attention. But there's another thing: in times of terror and danger, as these things are more easily believed, so they are also fabricated with greater impunity.'[8]

During the political convulsions of the Nineties, many familiar moorings have been cut; the fault lines in Italian society heaved and brought many old structures tumbling down. Giulio Andreotti, a once seemingly eternal figurehead of the church-going, middle-ground Christian Democrats, is facing trial for collusion with the Mafia: as if Margaret Thatcher turned out to have been supplying the IRA. Once in power, Berlusconi held one referendum after another to redefine power in the country; he even asked the Italians to vote on his right to privatise and then take possession of state television. He won, after a small turnout which reflected the disillusion of the voters with his blatant exploitation of the plebiscite. Such uncomfortable invitations to make decisions create an atmosphere hospitable to visions and miracles: in Ireland, in 1981, around the time when referenda on divorce and abortion were causing anguish among the Catholic population, a statue of the Madonna began to rock on her plinth at Ballinspittle; this 'wobbling statue' was seen by huge crowds, and there followed copycat signs and wonders in other sites.

As the Pope, ailing but obdurate, enters the eighteenth year of his reign, he's clinging to a storm-battered rock: in Austria, half a million Catholics recently rebelled against his conservatism, signing a petition for reform under the slogan 'We are the Church'; Germany, one of the most powerful communities of Catholics in the world, has followed suit as it haemorrhages lapsed lay members, spoiled clergy. They are protesting against John Paul II's silencing of debate over urgent questions – sexuality, contraception, divorce, priestly celibacy – and demanding change so that the Church may survive and grow. But the Pope will not listen, and loyal traditionalists stand firmly behind him: Don Pablo speaks bitterly about enemies within – more terrible than heathens and pagans – who refuse obedience to the Holy Father.

The novelist Susanna Tamaro observes that of all the European countries, Italy is nearest to the former Yugoslavia: 'If they wanted to bomb us from Serbia, they could – it's just across the sea.' The countries share historical connections, traditions of holidays, family links, and the experience now of many, many refugees. 'At the end of the century,' she says, 'with these terrible wars in Europe, death and devastation almost on a medieval scale, the imagination turns to archaic forms – and to the idea of a good mother, the one we would all like to have, who comes, who tells us things, who cries for us.'

Susanna Tamaro's last novel, the bestselling *Va dove ti porta il cuore* ('Follow Your Heart'), a spare, bittersweet tale based on her own harsh childhood in Trieste, has sold two million copies in Italy alone and been translated into fifteen languages; she believes that its portrait of an abused child matches the pity and the terror and powerlessness people feel:

> We have lost our respect for death, for the sacredness of the body. Every day, so many pictures of people without heads, children without legs – an obsession with damaged bodies. I've been told about photographers who tread on someone dying to get a picture of someone who is dying better – more spectacularly – something that's even worse than the war itself . . . They cannot even stay to hold the hand of someone dying. I was talking with an African friend and she told me that for them, when a people, a society, a group loses its respect for the body in death, that it's the end, because they've lost hold of the basic meaning of life.

In a Catholic context, the Madonna's message of pity for murdered children has a specific meaning, very different from protest against the war in ex-Yugoslavia. John Cornwell comments, 'The great key to this Papacy was exposed during the Lenten retreat in the Vatican Wojtyla gave the year before he became pope – he stunned the audience with his extraordinary vision of how the world is ever more a burial ground, a vast planet of tombs, a great planet of death . . . this laid the ground for his whole obsession with the culture of death through abortion and contraception.'

Don Grillo, in his sermon celebrating the Madonnina's enshrinement on 17 June, echoed the Pope's grief when he included a prayer: 'O Mary, we wish to dry your tears for the violence, for the crimes . . . for the disappearance of the sense of sin, for the millions of men swept away by the massacre of wars and abortions . . . Here . . . a great Sanctuary will rise, but a sanctuary of people who want to walk again in the way of the Gospel.' When I asked Don Pablo where the blood samples had been put after they were analysed, since in his view they are sacred relics, he replied: 'They treated them as if they were any old piece of police evidence . . . perhaps they threw them away.' And then, with bitter emphasis in a clear reference to foetuses, he added, 'Together with so many things they throw away.' Of all the prayers in front of the Madonnina, for peace, for innocence, for salvation, for the end of Sodom and Gomorrah, there came a sudden access of blatant, specifically directed anger from Don Pablo, which resonated in the crowded church: 'Let us pray for those aborted foetuses, that their hard-hearted mothers be converted.' It's significant that the legal right to abortion, which was granted in Italy after a referendum, in the face of bitter opposition from the Christian Democrats, is under challenge, and it's likely that it will again be put to the vote.

In this atmosphere, the Virgin's mercy becomes desperately necessary. But it can also turn into a flail: while the mass media adore a miracle in the same way as they love a scandal, the Pope and the resisters of humane social reform in the Church turn signs and wonders to their own ends. It is very difficult for a miracle to resonate in the interior castle of the soul, as mystics have advocated down the years, without distortion of its note, without interference, without loud, ear-crunching feedback. Bernadette's version of the Immaculate Mother was used in support of the dogma of papal infallibility, proclaimed twelve years after her visions: La Madonnina's bloody tears are adduced as proof of the wickedness of warmongers and mothers, as if these acts were equal. Even Christopher Hitchens wouldn't equate Milošović and his troops with Catherine Deneuve or any other woman who has had an abortion.

During the sermon in Pantano, I felt the congregation around me shrink, grow more hunched; the faithful dropped their heads further over their beads. They were, as I have said, mainly women, and old women, old country women who have known – and possibly handled – all the problems of a woman's life. Italy enjoys one of the lowest birth rates in Europe, and that isn't the result of widespread problems of infertility or even late marriage, but because Italian women – those famous witches and gossips – command traditional expertise in areas of bodily mysteries, including sexuality. Such wonders as the weeping Virgin are essentially ambiguous, disturbing, not simply consoling. Is the sorrowing Mother crying because of harm done to you, or harm you are doing? Do her tears offer you reprieve, or reproach? Are you guilty of making her cry?

1996

Since I wrote, the Gregori family remain under investigation for 'pious fraud', and refuse to take DNA tests; Don Pablo Martin has been replaced; the Church's commission of inquiry, presided over by Monsignor Grillo, has closed, but its conclusions remain unknown. In 1999, Grillo laid the foundation stone of a future shrine, and launched a website to raise funds.

It will be run by Mother Teresa's order of nuns. The Madonnina still attracts thousands of pilgrims every year: she has not wept again. Padre Pio has been canonised and is currently the most popular saint in Italy, and further afield.

2003

Omens of Millennium

Review of Harold Bloom, Omens of Millennium: The Gnosis of Angels, Dreams, and Resurrection

Hermes, god of messengers and of secret sharers, is one of myriad divine beings who populate this impassioned and quirky new book by Harold Bloom, but he is the author's most appropriate tutelary spirit. For Bloom here presents himself as a mystagogue and a soothsayer, a psychopomp of our times, conducting souls into unknown territories, reading the entrails of our present troubles; as Hermes does with his healing wand, he wants to clear away the shadows that lie across our path. *Omens of Millennium* is born of despair, but it focuses throughout on possibility, with a true teacher's refusal to give up the job of stimulating and informing, no matter how restless the class, or desolate the wasteland in the school yard outside.

Angelic sightings, cherub pins on lapels, daily headlines reporting alien abductions and near-death experiences, bleeding icons, signs and wonders of the new millennium, have filled Bloom with dismay at the degradation of the intellectual mystical legacy of the world's great religions. But he has not chosen to pour scorn or lament, Jeremiah-like. Instead he mounts a rescue operation: he wants to deepen our grasp of Zoroastrian dualism, of early Christian Valentinian Gnosticism, of medieval Sufi ecstatic wisdom, sixteenth-century Kabbalistic arcana, in order to create an antidote to the New Age. He wants to oppose the negative energy of apocalyptic dread with the energy of inward spiritual love and recognition of self; he confronts the fatalism of the established Churches and their doctrines of damnation and their eschatology of Doomsday with radiant intimations of immortality: 'There is always a world to come, not a world elsewhere, but one to be known here and now.'

If you want to speak with the tongues of angels, you must first go to the phrase books, the glossaries, and learn them. We are whisked through a bewildering number of theories about angels, dreams, prophecy, death, souls, signs, and apocalypse. Names of characters who sound as if they should belong in H. P. Lovecraft or Dungeons & Dragons fall thick and fast; civilisations lost and gone follow swiftly upon one another; diagrammatic analyses of consciousness from different thinkers, earlier variations on 'the astral body', are reviewed.

Angelology in particular has inspired resourceful research: one fifteenth-century bishop calculated the number who fell with Satan and came up with the figure 133,306,668. So 'our current domestication of angels' does violence to their natures and their history. Among what seem like scores of fiery, inimical predecessors, Metatron emerges as 'the authentic angel of America'. When he entered heaven (in his other persona, Enoch), 'the holy creatures, the ophanium, the seraphim [etc. etc.] smelled my odor 365,000 myriads of parasangs off, [and] they said, "What is this smell of one born of woman?"' Even more startling, Joseph Smith, founder of the Mormons, is Metatron's latest avatar, and the 'greatest and most authentic of American prophets, seers and revelators . . . charismatic and fearless'.

Harold Bloom is puzzled; he writes that 'transcendent intimations, once vouchsafed to spiritual adepts and powerful intellects, now seem available mostly to devotees of dank crankeries'. The book closes with a rallying cry, 'A Gnostic Sermon' in which Bloom blithely blasphemes: 'the God of this world . . . is only a bungler, an archangel-artisan who botched the False Creation that we know as our Fall'. His own efforts will not, I fear, do much to ease the situation, however formidable his knowledge and trenchant his expression. He dreams of releasing a new force of inward renewal: 'An America of welfare riots, an enforced contractual Gingrichian Virtual Gospel, founded upon an informational monopoly, might well provoke a large-scale Gnosticism of the insulted and injured, rising up to affirm and defend the divine spark in themselves.' This does not quite persuade (alas); for what has also changed, as Bloom is indeed aware, is that while William Blake's radicalism was mystical and political, American millenniarism has a different, more authoritarian history; even the New Age, for all its dope and wind chimes and Indian sacred chanting, is unsound in this respect as well, and 'is less a product of counterculture than it initially seems to be'.

The most persuasive argument in *Omens of Millennium* invokes the

Sufi tradition, as interpreted by Henri Corbin, and it returns Bloom to his home ground: the ideal of great world literatures. 'Between the sensory and the intellectual world, sages always have experienced an intermediate realm, one akin to what we call the imaginings of poets.' He calls this realm 'imaginal', and different adepts' degrees of access to it can explain why Blake and Emerson are readable and Emanuel Swedenborg and Joseph Smith are not (however much poets have absorbed from their thought). The 'Garment of Light' with which the indestructible astral body is clothed is ultimately woven from language and from the images that language invents and assembles; the Sufi paradise – Harqalya, the 'Earth of Light' – might turn out for Bloom, one suspects, to be a library, stocked with the Western canon, but augmented by some of these other favourites – Valentinus, Joseph Kora the Kabbalist, Corbin the Sufi exegete.

His book makes a welcome, bold stand for the value of what Isaiah Berlin has termed 'the Counter Enlightenment' – the frequently mocked and relegated esoteric and mystical tradition. Harold Bloom – at sixty-five a mere apprentice magus – has conjured up, somewhat stiffly but with evident urgency and sincerity, the imaginal realm where reason sleeps and from its dreaming head does not beget monsters only, but also gods and angels.

1998

Suffering Souls

Review of Jean-Claude Schmitt, Ghosts in the Middle Ages: The Living and the Dead in Medieval Society, *translated by Teresa Lavender Fagan*

A young priest called Walchelin, returning home one clear night in Normandy around a thousand years ago, heard a great clash and din of an army approaching; he assumed it was the soldiers who followed a local warlord, and hid himself in fear behind some medlar trees. But what he saw instead was a ghostly troop – first the lay folk on foot, weighed down by terrible burdens; then the clergy, bishops as well as monks, all black-cowled and weeping; another black-robed, fiery army of knights then rode by on black chargers. All these numbers of the dead were suffering horrible tortures, the women especially, for they were riding saddles of burning nails, and were being lifted in the air by invisible forces and dropped down again on to the points. Walchelin recognised the procession: it was the *familia Herlequini*, or Hellequin's hunt, the grim and unquiet crowd mustered by the lord of the dead, about which he had heard many stories.

The account is dated 1 January 1091 and it's the earliest extant literary telling of this phantom army, taken down by Orderic Vitalis, an Anglo-Norman monk, from the report of his colleague, the eyewitness. Walchelin related how he thought he wouldn't be believed if he didn't bring back proof: so he left his hiding place and tried to catch and mount one of the riderless black horses going by: the stirrup burned his foot and the reins froze his hand. Fifteen years after his experience, the scars remained, an authenticating brand from the other world; Walchelin showed them to the chronicler.

He watched several thousand of these dead go and recognised many he knew – murderers, wantons, renegades, but also many he was surprised to find in this tormented parade, for they had seemed to lead exemplary lives. As Eliot later paraphrased Dante, another visitor to the land of the dead, 'so many, I had not thought death had undone so many'. Several of the dead wished to talk to Walchelin, and give him messages, but he entertained only his brother, who reproached him bitterly for forgetting him, and implored him to pray for him and release him from the heavy penance he was paying for all his bloody deeds as a knight.

This early vision of the nameless, vast crowd of the damned lent support, Jean-Claude Schmitt argues, to two campaigns of the early medieval Church: to control and pacify the godless and lawless military, and to promote the liturgy of the dead. In this history of ghosts from around 500 to 1500, Schmitt searches for precise social functions for the stories he has patiently excavated from the archives, from annals, compendia of sermons, letters, treatises, anthologies of tales. That accursed rabble of Hellequin's hunt reflects the clerical grief and disapproval that would lead to the founding of the Christian orders of knights, the Templars and the Hospitallers, in an effort to discipline the crusades and their Christian militia. 'We cannot define any better the ideological function that the church assigned to Hellequin's hunt than in this moral mirror that it held up to those for whom violence was a trade.' (The Gallic accent is audible throughout this translation.)

At the same time, masses, rituals, prayers – the suffrages of the saints

– on behalf of suffering souls formed part of the clergy's bid to control secular lives and property: many a ghost who appeared to a priest confirmed the efficacy of churchmen's offices, expressed a wish that his family should bequeath more money or land to continue the monastic task of intercession in masses, chantries and dedicated prayers, or warned that the recipient of the vision was about to die and go to hell unless . . .

The French title of this book was simply *Les Revenants*, and it catches better than 'Ghosts' the author's view that the commemoration of the dead, in Christian ritual, seeks to still them so that they won't come back; 'the *memoria*,' he writes, 'as a form of collective memory, was a social technique of forgetting'. The restlessness of ghosts reveals the limits and failure of the system, for these are the dead who cannot find peace until more is done for them. In the medieval past, revenants haunted survivors if their death had been unexpected, premature, violent or otherwise untoward: suicides, victims of accidents, babies who died unbaptised were greatly feared. (The Litany still begs to be delivered from 'sudden death'.) The idea of limbo was invented in the twelfth century as a refuge for miscarried or aborted foetuses' wandering souls, that could never reach paradise.

Many of the ghosts Schmitt describes here are children, sometimes they have been seen by children, too, as in the case of a certain William, who was sent away from his home in Apt after a series of violent incidents and died in 1211 after a brawl; soon after, on several nights, he appeared, naked except for some rags, to his eleven-year-old girl cousin, who had been very fond of him. The news of the visions spread, and many local figures gathered to put questions to the ghost through the little girl – the bishop sent a questionnaire, to which William, prompted by Saint Michael who had appeared in support, gave full replies – about death, the afterlife and the structure of heaven and hell. He uses the word 'purgatory' – an early instance of the noun – and he clarified the condition of the bodies of the dead: they are but 'images' (*effigies*) but they feel acutely; the fires of purgation are corporeal, though the souls that feel them are not. Gervase of Tilbury reports these events, but does not tell us the name of the girl, an interesting predecessor of Saints Bernadette and Thérèse of Lisieux, and many more young females who have altered their status and their influence through their persuasive skills in clairvoyance.

A vision and a haunting are different, however, because medieval ghosts were sinners, petitioning the living to help them join the community of saints. The various phenomena of spectres, phantoms, apparitions, reflections and shades aren't easily distinguished, and the theology tangling with them remains knotty. Saint Augustine pondered the mobility of dream figures: he heard that he had appeared in someone's dream a long way away 'on the other side of the sea, at that very same moment I was doing something else entirely . . . in any case, I was not thinking at all of his concerns'; he dismissed such 'imagos' as mere semblances, having nothing to do with the person they invoked, and warned that the devil could assume many forms, including the appearance of dead loved ones. Souls, not bodies, should be Christians' sole concern. He was distancing Christian practice from the pagan emphasis on ancestor worship, on family tombs and mortal remains. Christians should concentrate on the hereafter, on otherworldly salvation not worldly memorials.

However, as Schmitt shows here, neither Augustine's scepticism about apparitions of the dead to the living nor his denunciation of dreams as a medium of true messages from the other world stifled the ghost story in Christian culture. Self-reflexively, many of the phantoms explore their own condition: they ponder what it means to be a ghost. One revenant explains that he can speak, though tongueless, by resonating the words in his chest; another that the penalties he suffers are real, the fires of purgation all too corporeal, and though he himself has no body, he feels them terribly; yet another that the dead continue to know their friends from the world above, but make no other acquaintance in the underworld. A dead soul could be call a 'skia' or 'umbra' – a shadow, a two-dimensional phenomenon in nature: blotting out the light guarantees the presence of a solid body, a person possessing substance. The undead – a modern form of ghost – cast no reflections or shadows. The illuminations in the sources Schmitt has drawn on are, however, undecided: sometimes the departing spirit at a deathbed takes the form of a naked child, but ghostly apparitions never choose this shape, as it's essential they should be recognised for who they are; sometimes, the artist merely paints the reactions of awe and dismay on the part of the spectators, leaving a void where the spirit stands. Jean-Claude Schmitt claims to have identified the earliest image of the conventional hallowe'en phantom – standing, arms crossed, draped in white from head to toe, eyes only peeping from his shroud, this ghost announces the death of a child to his father in a manuscript of around 1272.

In the thirteenth century, with the establishment of the mendicant friars, tales of wonders were spread far and wide through collections of moral exempla and cautionary tales: guilty ghosts returned to make amends for their crimes on earth, to return stolen property and beg forgiveness of the wronged; guilty survivors were reminded of their shortcomings and given the chance to turn over a new leaf; a bastard child who had not been acknowledged materialised, weeping and begging for release from pain, and a vengeful husband appeared to his widow at her remarriage and dropped a mortar on her head, cracking her skull and spilling her brains. Through ghosts, the Church circulated its moral precepts and its dream of social order.

Schmitt is the author of an earlier study, *Holy Greyhound: Saint Guinnefort, Healer of Children*, about the cult of a dog in a part of medieval Alsace, and this interest in the odder byways of Christian thaumaturgy leads him to deplore the uniformity that stiffened ghost lore after the thirteenth century, when the collectors gathered their material for pedagogical use, and in the interests of universality, smoothed away local peculiarities of custom, detail and narrative, as well as obscuring the names of individuals and their specific experiences.

Yet in their crude, even lurid way, the popular preachers' manuals of Jacques de Vitry and Jacopus de Voragine induce that shudder that differentiates the pious tale from the ghost story, the saint's vision from the haunting. With his concern for functional explanation, Schmitt never attempts a literary analysis, and remains uninterested in the rhetorical devices and narrative effects of the fantastic; he seems to accept the schoolmen's exclusion of *fantasia* as a diabolical instrument of hallucination and so omits the ghost-story aspects of divination, alchemy and witch lore. He quotes only briefly, and this tendency to précis and paraphrase makes for occasionally weary reading. Also, in a study of medieval ghosts, it's wayward to allude to Dante only in passing on page one and thereafter in a single footnote. It is Dante, who with his indomitable intellectual ambition, attempts to encompass the condition of ghosts, meditating on the organs and processes, sensory and cognitive faculties of the souls he meets. In *Purgatory*, Statius carefully expounds to him the character of their ethereality, using metaphors of elements in play, as in rainbows and flames:

> e come l'aere, quand'è ben pïorno,
>> per l'altrui raggio che 'n se si reflette,
>> di diversi color diventa adorno;
> così l'aere vicin quivi si mette

> in quella forma che in lui suggella
> virtüalmente l'alma che ristette;
> e simigliante poi alla fiammella
> che segue il foco là 'vunque si muta,
> segue lo spirto sua forma novella.
> Peró che quindi ha poscia sua paruta,
> è chiamata ombra . . .

(*Purgatory* XXV lines 94–101)

As translated by John D. Sinclair: 'and as the air, when it is full of rain, becomes adorned with various colours through another's beams that are reflected in it, so the neighbouring air sets itself into that form which the soul that stopped there stamps upon it by its power, and then like the flame that follows the fire wherever its shifts, it new form follows the spirit. Since it has by this its semblance henceforth, it is called a shade . . .'[1]

Ingeniously conjured from effects of light, insubstantial and incorporeal, yet endowed with presence and sense, these Turneresque wraiths move forward, it seems to me, the possibility of making the ghostly state at least thinkable, if not plausible.

Schmitt has also drawn tight borders around his topic, refusing to speculate on the antecedents of his medieval phantoms in earlier belief or on cross-pollination with cultures ancient and distant. He writes, 'What is important to the historian is not so much the age of a tradition as the currency of its uses.' But he himself allows glimpses, when he passes on Scottish tales recorded by William of Newburgh in the twelfth century or the village hauntings taken down by the monk of Byland in Yorkshire two hundred years later, of terrifying northern ghouls and vampires who do not meekly plead for prayer but wreak havoc until their corpses are disinterred, chopped up and burned by the victims of their misdeeds and their hauntings. In these stories, some of the motifs of fairy tales recur, for the border that separates the quick and the dead is not impermeable: villagers marry fairy wives, tailors change shape and enchanted hunters blow their horns to summon the living to their enchanted places of doom. Schmitt is sensitive to the fusion of clerkly and oral literature, but he doesn't see that he could have argued that the Church, in its insistence on suffrages and preparation for a good death, was simply instrumentalising a vivid corpus of existing fantastic beliefs about the dangers the dead pose for the living. Also, he doesn't introduce comparative material which could have thrown light on the distinctiveness of Christian ghosts and ways of dealing with them: on the shaman's flight, on zombies and spirit possession, on the bloodthirsty revenges exacted by wronged vassals in Japanese and Chinese literature and drama.

In Jacques Le Goff's succinct phrase, 'purgatory imprisoned the ghosts': after the official recognition, at the start of the thirteenth century, of this penitential halfway house to heaven, Hellequin's wild rout could no longer roam the night; however, the new taste for the macabre (the word enters the French language around a hundred years later) set skeletons dancing on the walls of cemeteries and their drums rolling as they marshalled mortals to join them. The macabre introduced the particular pleasures of comic horror that later infuses the Gothic and the modern ghost story. When I looked up the footnotes to one gory tale cited here, I found that M. R. James had done the only selected edition of the manuscript Schmitt quotes: the literature of ghosts is itself haunted by revenants, as in James's own antiquarian inventions or Oscar Wilde's beguiling, medievalising comic-tender tale, 'The Canterville Ghost'. In adopting such a strict historical approach, Jean-Claude Schmitt has muffled the deeper, enjoyable repercussions of his subject.

Mourning, melancholy and the macabre have tinged the pallor of spectres, but it seems that we might be entering a new phase in the history of our connections with the dead, that memory has become the crucial and necessary means to achieve peace with the past, so that we no longer wish to lay the ghosts, but rather to bring them back for prolonged acts of reconciliation. Alongside angels, they're also now invoked – even conjured – as pleasure-giving familiars uncoupled from death, reattached to life as images of inner selves, of spirits fluttering within – the *Geist*, or breath, that gives us the word 'ghost'. The uncanny has come home to take up its dwelling there with calm eeriness, as opposed to dread, in such contemporary works as 'Ghost' by the sculptor and film model-maker Ron Mueck. This Ghost is a simulacrum of a woman, perfectly rendered in latex, with real hair and a simple bathing suit and *trompe l'oeil* thread veins on her thighs. She's an illusion of life, a modern waxwork, and she disconcerts the viewer: impossibly, she has a child's lanky limbs and a matron's thick greying hair; she's also nine feet tall. But she is also, unlike phantoms of the past, rather commonplace – that is perhaps the point. At the same time, at the Hayward Gallery, Anish Kapoor's marvellous exhibition of new sculpture concludes with another 'Ghost', in this instance carved in Kilkenny limestone, which is a close-grained rock so black that it reflects like a still deep pool: in the shadowy concavity Kapoor has carved in the block, your reflection gradually gathers definition, a distorted, mutable, uncertain shade, which does not so much announce your death as offer a shaky, dreamy, partial guarantee of your continuing presence on earth.

1998

The Greatest Saint after Sainte Marie

Afterword to Charles Péguy, The Mystery of the Charity of Joan of Arc, *translated by Jeffrey Wainwright*

Charles Péguy recognised himself in Joan of Arc; or rather, through his ceaseless reworkings of her character in his poetry, he fashioned his best image of humanity, an ideal which he then tried to live up to in his own life. In 1429, Joan of Arc raised the siege of Orléans, Péguy's homeland, and the heartland to which he remained faithful always; she came from Lorraine, like the crusader Godfrey of Bouillon, who was, in Péguy's view, a pattern of saintliness in action; she was of peasant stock, like Péguy, who based his personal, ardent Socialism on trust in the community on the land, and she was a visionary who did not belong to the ecclesiastical hierarchy but trusted her inner compulsion, her voices. Péguy had abandoned the Church as a young man, but he returned in 1910, the year of his play the *Mystery*, to a private experience of faith, not to the institution itself. His independence of mind kept him an outsider, given the right-wing, ultramontanist and authoritarian temper of the late nineteenth-century and early twentieth-century French Catholicism. As an intellectual who believed in action, a convert outside the fold, a Socialist who quarrelled with the great party leader Jean Jaurès over the latter's anticlericalism and pacifism, and as a peace-lover who took up militarism to die, in 1914, at the front, Péguy found in Joan, a saint martyred by her own Church, enough mirroring contradictions of his own intense personal conflicts.

Péguy's lifelong meditations on Joan of Arc, from the 1897 *Jeanne d'Arc* to the voluminous *Mystery* of 1910, as well as many lyrics, long and less long (very little of Péguy could be termed short), develop his profound feelings for 'la sainte la plus grande après Sainte Marie'. His rockabye alexandrines, his lulling caesuras, his fondness for mantra-like repétition, the pent-up accumulation of questions, exclamations, praise and *improperia* – reproaches – give his verse a rapturous involvement with their themes and their own existence that is erotic in character: the subjects are robed in the finery of cadence and image, to be beheld with the same love that Péguy shows us he feels for them. In spite of the stasis on stage in the *Mystery*, and the sparseness of reported incident too, the play exercises a hypnotic fascination over the reader and the audience as it plies back and forth over the issues of damnation and salvation, over wickedness and goodness. Péguy's technique reproduces the cumulative mode of the liturgy and some psalmodic parts of the Bible, and this patterning is reflected in the stage direction, that Joan should be spinning all the while. With repeated movements, she draws out a single thread from the wool, as Péguy's text seeks to do from the different strands of his inquiry. When I read that Péguy's mother worked caning chairs, it struck me that as a boy Péguy must have watched her create, out of reeds, a mesh strong enough to give someone support and that with the frailty of verse he was attempting to do the same.

Hauviette was one of Joan's childhood friends, and gave evidence at the hearings vindicating her that were held twenty-five years after her death. A voice of the people who accept their lot, stalwart, hard-working, 'a little girl who has never cried', Hauviette represents one path of action in the world – but like Joan, though he feels sympathy with this child of the land, Péguy cannot bring himself to submit to the restrictions of her way. Yet we can feel his pain, in Joan's anguish that she has turned from the loved ones of her childhood in her shameful but unstoppable contempt for the choice they have made. ('Everything in your life rings as though it has a crack running through it,' Madame Gervaise tells her.) Treachery to the class of one's birth, to the blood in one's veins, that modern predicament of the educated writer, informs Joan of Arc's suffering here.

Madame Gervaise speaks for a different path of acceptance, through withdrawal from the world. Péguy pictures her converted by Saint Colette of Corbie, the reformer of the Poor Clares, whom Joan of Arc may just have known, and her meditations on Christ's incarnation and passion, with their special concentration on his human ordinariness, reflect the themes of medieval Franciscan literature, and such poetry as the *Planctus Mariae*, in which the Passion is seen as a human tragedy through the eyes of Jesus's weeping mother. Péguy's contemporary, Saint Thérèse of Lisieux, also developed a strain of quotidian metaphysics, focusing on the human Christ in her spiritual autobiography, *The Story of a Soul*, published after her death in 1899. Hauviette and Madame Gervaise interpret different aspects of the Little Flower's message of humility, retirement and patient self-sacrifice. Canonised in 1925, three years after Saint Joan, Saint Thérèse represents her polar opposite, resignation rather than challenge, silence rather than outcry.

Nothing could be more of a stranger to contemporary English sensibilities than such Roman matters, one would expect. Yet Geoffrey Hill has brought Péguy back into English consciousness again with his intricate and moving tribute, *The Mystery of the Charity of Charles Péguy*, published in 1983. In this long poem, the French poet becomes for Hill an exemplary figure of a thinker who tried to live by what he said, like others in Hill's work: Robert Southwell, the Catholic recusant martyr, Robert Desnos, the Surrealist who fought for the Resistance and died in a camp in Czechoslovakia, and Dietrich Bonhoeffer, the Protestant theologian who stood up against the Nazis. In *The Mystery of the Charity of Charles Péguy*, Hill asks, 'Must men stand by what they write?' So often the stand costs the supreme sacrifice. Hill has said about Péguy, that he is attracted to him partly out of 'a moral imperative . . . certain people do seem . . . to bear about with them some secret of life and experience that one would like to know more about'.

Jean-Paul Lucet's adaptation, from different strata of Péguy's writings about Joan of Arc, and Jeffrey Wainwright's English translation have compressed and effectively dramatised Péguy's mystery play, without losing the cyclical, musical leisureliness of Péguy's poetic manner or the ambivalent traversing and retraversing of his thinking. The play, in this shortened version, still sets before us the insoluble dilemmas Péguy contended with: the place of sin in the scheme of redemption, the fallibility of saints, the mismatch of words and deeds, the limits on the greatest of saviours' salvation. If there are souls that are eternally damned, Joan cries out that she wants to offer up her own to save them; but it is not possible. The *Mystery* also presents Péguy's thoroughgoing patriotism, to which he was entirely made over, without irony, without disingenuousness. Geoffrey Hill has called his brand of nationalism 'militant pastoral', and by concluding the *Mystery* with the successful resistance of the Mont St Michel, taken from a posthumously published fragment, Lucet's play confirms Péguy's adherence to the way of action and engagement, preferably on French soil.

Though so original in his paradoxical beliefs, Péguy was by no means an isolated devotee of Joan of Arc at the time. In the wake of the publication of her trial, historians, poets, novelists and other playwrights claimed her as a heroine – for all seasons and all causes. The Dreyfus affair in particular sharpened the struggle to make her the exclusive champion of opposing camps: Dreyfus's enemies argued she had upheld law and order and the army, Dreyfus's partisans, like Péguy and Jaurès, saw her as the forerunner of all martyrs at the hands of corrupt and malign institutions. Shaw caught the prevailing excitement, and wrote his famous play, *Saint Joan*, in 1924, a decade after Péguy's death, and two years after Joan's canonisation. Unlike the *Mystery*, *Saint Joan* moves with brio from Joan's departure from Domrémy to her death at the stake and even into her afterlife in myth; it is typical of Péguy that his Joan never leaves off spinning in her own native fields. Unlike Péguy the believer, Shaw the sceptic sets great store by Joan's miracles, prophecies and voices, as well as showing her performing traditional pieties. He shows less interest, as might be expected, in the spiritual aspects of her struggle than in the legal and social implications of her cross-dressing, her rebellion, and her heroically individual stance. Shaw's Joan of Arc also dramatises the playwright's concerns, and with her no-nonsense approach and witty repartee, provides a self-portrait, a Supergirl rather than a Superman; she can nevertheless still be very touching in performance. Péguy's Jeanne communicates her trouble to the audience with less dazzle. He was not concerned with the sexual politics of her life, but with the possibility of sainthood in a world of the damned, and manages in the *Mystery* to show us the turmoil of a soul aspiring to goodness. If any single conviction can be picked out of the web of Péguy's antitheses and unanswered questions, it is that humankind is ultimately redeemed by its impulse towards the good, by its *bonne volonté*, even if it is doomed in the attempt. Though out on the limb with the militant pastoral ethic, Péguy created a Joan agonistes, a twentieth-century heroic voice, dark in the midst of self-assertion, cracked with doubt, who unlike many of Joan's other manifestations in literature and on stage, will not be comforting, or ever satisfied.

1986

The Triumph of the Moon

Review of Ronald Hutton, The Triumph of the Moon: A History of Modern Pagan Witchcraft

Many historians fall for their subjects in the past but suspect deep down, that, if their heroes returned alive, if they could see them plain and speak to them today, they might not like them: Richard Cœur-de-Lion might turn out uncouth and Elizabeth I squalid. Ronald Hutton has reversed this common, cautious position. In his new study of 'post-Christian Britain', he shows a bracing and candid scepticism about the architects of pagan witchcraft, belief in the past, about fantasies of Mother Goddesses and cannibal Druids, about Templar shenanigans and the hocus-pocus of 'The Beast', Aleister Crowley. But when it comes to 'the now luxuriant complexity of pagan witchcraft in Britain', he has been enchanted (bewitched?). He avows himself to be a votary of Wicca, an enthusiast of covens, an admirer of present-day enchantresses, and he concludes this book with a rousing endorsement from within the redoubts of scholarly historiography.

Pagan witchcraft is an independent 'revived religion', Hutton writes, which should command as much intellectual and social attention as, for example, the Baha'i branch of Islam. It invigorates and consoles its followers, especially women, who are revered within it as living vehicles of goddesses, and take pre-eminent roles as priestesses; it has no truck with Satanism, or indeed with Christian dualism in any form. There are no ceremonies involving sacrifices – or flagellation, or group sex. He vigorously defends witches against current fears and prurience, but writes in his preface that, unlike anthropologists, he has decided to respect covens' protocols and not divulge anything more than what the witchcraft movement itself has made public. His account of the contemporary scene is consequently evasive.

Ronald Hutton is professor of history at Bristol, an exhaustive researcher whose last book *The Stations of the Sun* adventurously explored the explosion of 'traditional' festivals in Britain. In *The Triumph of the Moon*, he shows energetic rigour when exposing the fallacies and fantasies suffusing paganism's canonical texts, such as J. G. Frazer's *The Golden Bough* or Margaret Murray's *The Witch Cult in Western Europe*, and then, with his next breath, goes on to praise the innovatory genius of Doreen Valiente, who rewrote *Ye Bok of ye Art Magical*, a modern grimoire used in current pagan ritual. Of Starhawk, a leading American witchcraft activist, Hutton writes: 'it is difficult to take notes from her books without copying entire sentences, so perfectly are her thoughts expressed and so marked is her genius for aphorism'. He gives no examples, no doubt too stunned to copy them down.

This partisanship is spoiling and entirely unnecessary, for *The Triumph of the Moon* has a very interesting story to tell; the book covers a vast depth and breadth of field with eager curiosity, and, like the earlier *Stations of the Sun*, reveals how recently most ancient rituals and beliefs were invented. It puts a richly peculiar slant on Victorian values and on their Edwardian successors. Hutton tells of vicars who led processions to hail the great god Pan in rural England, and of Elspeth Thomas soaking her muslin dress in morning dew and winding her hair with daisy-chains before her wedding to Kenneth Grahame (*The Wind in the Willows*). His cast of neo-pagans includes the familiar – Swinburne, the Kipling of *Puck of Pook's Hill*, and Robert Graves – and the not-so-familiar – the American journalist C. G. Leland, for example, who was given a Vangel, or secret witch's manual, by a young Italian woman, known only as Maddelena. This became the basis of his occult novel *Aradia* (1899), about the goddess Diana and her followers' night-flying; it was to provide the structure and some of the imagery of witchcraft rites today. Leland is one of many colourful self-fashioners in this book who invoked antique ritual in order to add shine to something they'd probably made up; several witches today, whose careers Hutton reviews, still claim descent from an ancestral line of cunning folk.

Hutton's survey brings in utopian experimenters who revolted against repression, both personal and political, like D. H. Lawrence; he identifies as especially important the belief that paganism affirmed life and love and joy and freedom against all the constructions of convention. But although he finds Pan the goat-footed faun behind 'the horned god' of witchcraft gatherings, he stresses that all the gods have been eclipsed by their female counterparts, in a dramatic reversal of custom and morals. The counter-culture was in the making, though, as he interestingly points out, many early pagans were right-wing; its radical tendency has only grown since the Sixties.

How has this country come from a certain mocking indifference towards magic and sorcery beyond the fringe to its current state of high-street avidity? A schoolboy hero like Just William would have probably ducked a witch without a qualm, but here is Harry Potter, his natural successor, learning to be one – at Hogwarts, a recognisably old-fashioned ghastly public school in every other respect.

Hutton reaches for possible reasons for this major shift in *mentalité* and he finds the principal culprits, not among the working witches, but among the highest and most established Victorian and later scholarship, among respected archaeologists and classicists and literary and religious history. He attacks the widespread belief in a universal Goddess, represented in megalithic figurines from Ireland to Mongolia, which was upheld by mythographers like Jane Harrison, who posited an unbridled primordial matriarchy and a Triple Goddess, eventually deposed by sky gods and soldier-statesmen. In the chapter on American feminism, Hutton reviews the received wisdom of the Seventies about the genocide of medieval witches in the time of 'the Great Burning', and shows that all recent historians concur to reduce this massacre to around 40–50,000 people, over three hundred and fifty years – a significant number, but not the nine million alleged before.

Hutton also suggests an influence from the travels and contacts of empire: the first period, of recoil from primitive rites and savages' diabolical and horrid superstitions, gave way to admiration, and thence to imitation and plagiarism. Mme Blavatsky's Theosophy melded Hindu ideas of reincarnation and astral bodies with Victorian spiritualism. It was after her death in 1892 that Samuel Liddell Mathers founded an inner order of 'the Golden Dawn' which he called 'the Rosy Cross'. The ritual he invented for it uniquely combined elements from the Golden Dawn – initiations using symbolic instruments (pentacle, mask, swords) – with an open-door policy, idolisation of the female principle and eclectic hermetic cut-and-paste of quotations from ancient Egyptian papyri, Tantric magic and Christian symbols; the aim was individual spiritual development, not worship, self-fulfilment, not social bonding.

At times, *The Triumph of the Moon* picks at the finest threads in the present religion with excessive diligence – as with the parson coming to tea, one can have too much of a witch. One character does however stand out of the throng for eccentricity, flair, and brazen chutzpah: Gerald Gardner, a founding father of modern paganism. As a colonial officer in Malaya, he studied the local religion, espoused naturism, and collected ceremonial weapons. When he retired home to the suburbs, he started a mystical order to practise ritual magic, and claimed to have raised 'a Cone of Power' on the south coast, to prevent Hitler's invasion: a ring of witches danced naked all night, several of them dying in the process.

Hutton painstakingly combs the evidence, and, not surprisingly, finds nothing to corroborate the tale. Gerald Gardner did however purchase a 'witch's cottage', a museum replica of a sixteenth-century half-timbered house with Cabbalistic signs painted on the inside, where he and his muse, the witch Dafo, met their fellow-adepts to perform rituals: this is 'the birthplace of modern pagan witchcraft'. It was Gardner who in 1954 named the new religion 'Wicca', after a mysterious word possibly meaning 'wise people'. Wicca now has, Hutton estimates, around ten thousand witches and ten times as many followers. Some university campuses have appointed a Pagan 'chaplain'.

The title *The Triumph of the Moon* implies the crucial role women have played in the shaping of this new religion and the corresponding ascent of beneficent, poetic, female symbols within it. Writers and scholars like Jessie L. Weston, Mary Renault, Jacquetta Hawkes, Marija Gimbutas, Mary Daly, quite apart from the practising witches themselves, have put together over the last century the alternative 'Wicca' history, sometimes in the spirit of conscious myth-makers, but often as believers. Ronald Hutton shows how their desires shaped the story they told, often in the face of the evidence, how wishfully they assembled tiny tremors of information into massive quakes of female power. He scathingly demolishes this mythopoeic history, not without an underlying tinge of contempt for women's stuff. And yet, he still gives his support to thought systems that are inextricably interwoven with them: pagan witchcraft today worships the Goddess whom Marija Gimbutas found.

What empire-builders minded when officers went native was that their behaviour upset the premise of colonial superiority. Hutton wants it both ways: as a historian, he puts Wicca in its place intellectually, but he also wants to dance by the light of the moon with nothing on. He's become a player in the masque that he undertook to unmask, undermining the very edifice where he had found shelter. The historian seems to have begun with the tools of rationalist inquiry, thinking that it mattered whether the sources were authentic and correctly interpreted; then in the process, the man found himself with a pentacle and an *athame*, or witch's dagger, in his hand. *The Triumph of the Moon* tells the story of a conversion experience, with its internal and probably painful contradictions.

1999

Dom Sylvester Houédard

Obituary

A letter from Dom Sylvester Houédard was an archive (though always pithy), a poem (of an unusual kind), a meditation on arcane mysteries, and, sometimes, a personal message of touching kindness: 'i hope the coqueluche soon disappears,' he wrote on a postcard from the abbey at Prinknash when my son had whooping cough. I only met him half a dozen times, I think, though I can hardly believe it was so seldom, as through letters he was such a vivid presence.

He used to come to London in the Sixties, when the life of concrete poets was more exciting than today, and he was austere, skilled and never tricksy with his typewritten works: in one, the word *sol*, repeated over and over, traverses the word *thalamus* arranged like a rectangular bedchamber – a characteristically spare evocation of the bridal mysticism of the Song of Songs. He was a great scholar, reading industriously for the *OED* in order to find prior early usages and changing meanings, and he was a stickler. The conditions of his vow meant he was always anxious for books, but he managed to know more than many who have great resources to hand. And he was never superior with his learning, patronising or excluding, but always ready to share it, with a bob of his birdlike head and a light in his eye.

In those days, he was also helping Derek Jarman doctor the Latin dialogue of the film *Sebastiane* (1976), and for more than a decade he gave me references, comments, illuminations – though we first met in the offices of *Vogue*, where we had discussed the lost skill of goffering. (He had recently been in the Vatican and was very struck by the maintenance the lacework of the papal raiment required.)

After that, he wrote to me these incomparable letters, all the signs – the words, always in lower case, the numbers, the spaces – sprinkled on the page with controlled grace. He directed me to saints of every kind, including the many 'monachoparthenics' in the Christian pantheon (monachoparthenics being the *mot juste*, known only to DSH, for women who dressed and lived as monks); he suggested, for instance, that the origin of the popular legend of Saint Catherine of Alexandria might lie in the true story of the Neoplatonist Hypatia, who, like the legendary Catherine, was a philosopher who was stoned to death on the quay in Alexandria – with oyster shells, Dom Sylvester pointed out, the same shells that traditionally appear like knives in the felloes of the 'Catherine wheel'.

He came to London less often in recent years, but he stayed with me once. Derek Jarman had warned me not to leave out my bath essence, if I had any I particularly liked. It turned out he was a perfect guest and, on returning to the abbey, sent a sheaf of remarkable heraldic lore to help me with research I was doing then on Joan of Arc, as well as a list of the possible saints my son could choose as his patron: twelve Conrads all told, in chronological order, with curricula vitae attached.

Recently he worked hard for ecumenism, at a spiritual rather than political level, attending conferences on Buddhism; for him the love of Christ transcended distinctions of faith. His last letter to me was filled with excitement about the close connections between Saint Benedict's rule, which he followed, and the monastic tradition of the East. He seemed to have learned Chinese in the meantime, in order to deepen his searches into the peaceful communion of mystics. His life and thought should be studied, his poems and letters should be collected. They would form a remarkable anthology of a modern sage, who was wise enough to be foolish now and then.

1992

Showers of Toads

Review of Jan Bondeson, The Feejee Mermaid and Other Essays in Natural and Unnatural History

Jan Bondeson has poked about in dusty seaside museum stores for lost stuffed mermaids and moth-eaten garments made of vegetable lambs-wool; he has unearthed mummified toads that lived inside rocks before the Flood (or so claimed clergymen, rocked by Darwin); has uncovered the perils, sorrows and achievements of pet elephants and prophetic pigs, and recorded showers of toads and eels and bricks (and frying pans). To amass this truly impressive heap of detailed material about natural wonders, preternatural phenomena, amazing monsters – and, it must be said, about the measureless human appetite for fantasy – Bondeson combed the arcana of medieval encyclopaedists and Renaissance magicians, dossiers of the natural sciences in the eighteenth and nineteenth centuries, and catalogues of freak shows.

The Feejee mermaid who inspires his title was exhibited in London in 1822 to enthralled crowds; a certain mad captain, Samuel Barrett Eades, sold his ship to have her. She was a grimacing, fanged, withered and charred goblin, spliced and dried from bits of orang-utan, baboon and sea salmon, more like a witch's poppet from the storeroom of the imperial uncanny than the sinuous, wavy-locked siren of myth. Many good men and true pronounced her genuine, and plenty more mermaids were fished from the seas and stuffed for the profit of owners like P. T. Barnum; in *A Tourist in Africa* (1960), Evelyn Waugh noted seeing one advertised.

In real life, as they say, Bondeson works as a research physician specialising in rheumatology. But in writing, he abandons any sobersides approach to experiment, and takes as his acknowledged models eclectic and eccentric Victorian scientific hobbyists such as Frank Buckland or even Charles Fort, investigator of the unexpected and paranormal. *The Feejee Mermaid* follows on from Bondeson's first remarkable compendium, *A Cabinet of Medical Curiosities* (1997), and it similarly adopts a light-hearted, *Old Moore's Almanack* tone, closer to Believe It Or Not! sideshows than to the exploration of historical mentalities. Bondeson shares the impresario's glee in whipping off the handkerchief or whipcracking up another curtain on another monster, relishing the absurdity and the fun of it all.

His stories of animal trainers and ringmasters, entrepreneurs and fairground performers traverse centuries and milieux; Louis XI once expressed a whim for a pig orchestra. The abbé de Baigne zealously complied, contriving an organ of kicks and pricks: when he touched the keys, a row of pigs, staggered like pipes in order of size, were poked in the rump and squealed in sequence. In early Victorian London, something similar provoked cats to wail in counterpoint. Starlings that played cards, canaries that acted, rabbits that drummed, and pigs that told the time, spelled out words and guessed ladies' thoughts displaced tightrope dancers and acrobats from top billing, even causing a walk-out at Sadler's Wells in 1785.

Affections were lavished on performers: Jan Bondeson furnishes vivid contemporary comments on the horror of the death of Chunee, the first actor-elephant, who was gunned down in his London cage in 1826 by a barrage of 152 missiles, because it was feared he was going on the rampage. It was discovered, after his grisly end, that he was suffering from toothache (tusk ache). (His horrible crib, the Exeter Change menagerie, was pulled down three years later to make way for the National Gallery.) The popularity of costumed, articulate, clever and adaptable creatures would appear to lead directly to Walt Disney and other film-makers' staging of performing animals today. One of Bondeson's liveliest sources, fellow-teratologist and American conjuror Ricky Jay, describes in his book *Learned Pigs & Fireproof Women* (1986) how mice and rats performed tableaux of battles with cats, and flea circuses dramatised historical battles and ballroom extravaganzas. These are the forerunners of Tom and Jerry, Mickey and Minnie, Jiminy Cricket and other unlikely twentieth-century heroes, like the current singin'n'dancin' heroes of *A Bug's Life*. Dick King-Smith's *Babe: The Sheep Pig*, who (it seems only proper to use the personal relative pronoun) speaks with such fetching innocence and sense in live animation, excites something similar to the response that greeted Toby the Sapient Pig.

The Feejee Mermaid intermingles such histories of animal cuteness and gruesome early zoo-keeping with several energetic excursions into the territory of mirabilia. Among natural wonders that defy natural law and so, by implication, reveal the miraculous omnipotence of God, Saint Augustine singled out the salamander, and he warned against investigating such mysteries too closely. Bestiaries and travellers' lore described several more fantastic creatures: the basilisk, born from an egg laid by a cock, and hatched by toads, was exterminated by a Saint Patrick-like champion, who, arrayed in a coat of many mirrors, walked the length and breadth of England forcing the monsters to take a look at themselves – and die of the sight. The vegetable lamb of Tartary grew on a stem from the ground until it was old enough to fall, like a fruit, to the earth; like its cousin in oddness, the barnacle goose, hatched from barnacles attached to ships' hulks or other timbers, it broke down boundaries between genera and confounded due order. (Such creatures did, however, serve the extremely welcome purpose of providing meat-that-was-not-meat during the fasting season.) It was the encyclopaedic amateur Sir Hans Sloane, who collected an example of the vegetable lamb as well as a cap made from its fleece, who rightly surmised that this particular mirabilium was an arboreal fern.

Like other recent contributors to the history of the *Wunderkammer*, Lorraine Daston and Katharine Parks in *Wonders and the Order of Nature* and Christoph Irmscher in *The Poetics of Natural History* (1999), Bondeson accepts retrospectively the response of wonder as the organising principle of his material. This approach tends to blur important questions about the social or epistemological contexts that made such beliefs possible and such taxonomies satisfactory. Explorers in the field suffer from an unusual difficulty: their subjects continue to exercise such power to entertain that it relaxes the need to search for historical changes and patterns. But performing horses and Siamese twins don't keep company comfortably today, while mermaids, dragons, unicorns and other wonders (angels) haven't enjoyed such a revival since Mandeville first brought back news of the world's far-flung marvels.

The reader of *The Feejee Mermaid* comes away buzzing with miscellaneous and enjoyable information, but often perplexed as to what it amounts to. The most penetrating section of Bondeson's new book focuses on arguments about spontaneous generation, and here he makes a succinct and valuable contribution to the history of science for this lay reader, whose knowledge of biology began and ended with jam-jars of tadpoles (that died). In his account of experiments conducted by seventeenth-century scientists into the fertility of putrefying matter, Bondeson lays aside his top-hat and his ringmaster patter, and one begins to hear the humming excitement of early natural science and biology. Anomalies pose problems that catalyse thought, and errors in scientific proposals may be exploring the right areas of mystery, and turn out not to be so wrong after all. The presence of worms in cheese or flies in dung provoked analyses that went further than the immediate mystery. Most fascinatingly, spontaneous generation is enjoying a period of rehabilitation, it appears, in current theories about the origin of living matter that appeared 3.85 to 4 billion years or so ago – the Vital Dust, in Christian De Duve's phrase, where it all began. One generation's natural wonder may not always turn into another's folly or fable.

1999

Amber

Review of Ciaran Carson, Fishing for Amber: A Long Story

The Northern Irish poet Ciaran Carson has dedicated this exuberant, idiosyncratic and bravura performance, *Fishing for Amber*, to his father,

William Carson/Liam MacCarrain, a Belfast postman who joined the Esperanto movement. Esperanto must be the most benign of utopian, universalising endeavours, and it inspires his son Ciaran to write some of the tenderest and funniest passages in this book. But the dream of a synthetic discourse and of universal harmony underlies Ciaran Carson's achievement here in another way. *Fishing for Amber* is local, provincial, and ethnic in the strongest and best sense, but wildly cosmopolitan in its polymathic excursuses on disciplines and stores of knowledge far and wide.

Carson remembers his father's Irish storytelling, his yarns about red-herring fishing fleets and Dutch dairy farmers sailing to the moon 'in argosies of hot-air drifters, there to mine the lunar cheese deposits'. His book often echoes this kind of madcap blarney, but it lays it down in a multi-track, polyphonic babel of storytelling voices, drawn from Celtic legends of the Sidhe or fairy folk, Greek and Latin metamorphoses, natural science, optics, botany, hagiography – in short from a lifetime's reading. It's also an extended, vibrant piece of writing – a prose poem, rattled off at high speed but sharply detailed, with every word chosen for its spring, echo, texture, and the whole glowing (amber-like) from a pervasive mood of delight at the variety of the world. Meditating on the sources of argot, or thieves' cant, Ciaran Carson lists the cast in a kind of delirium: 'Picture the roads and the inns thronged with tinkers, tooth-drawers, pedlars, ostlers, carters, porters, horse-gelders and horse-leeches, idiots, apple-squires, broomsmen, bawds, chive-fencers, kinchin-coves, soothsayers and sow-gelders' and so it goes on, irrepressibly, through 'vampers', 'waste-butts' and 'bosom-buddy bugger-lugs'.

Chapter headings from 'Antipodes' to 'Zoetrope' by way of 'Ergot' and 'Foxglove' and 'Nemesis' and 'Opium', give the dictionary a flavour of Carson's browsing; the book is even ornamented with vignettes from a 1927 illustrated encyclopaedia. Amber doesn't have a chapter to itself, but studs the text throughout, a string of beads told off at intervals: we learn that 'electricity' comes from the Greek for amber, *elektrum*, because the Greeks noticed it produces static when rubbed; that one Demonstratus declared lynxes pissed amber, the males the tawny variety, the females more lemony. In one of his typical fugues, Carson whirls us from the use of amber as a prized varnish for paintings, then, via *vernis* (French) and *berniz* (Spanish) to Queen Berenice who cut off her golden hair (her amber hair) and offered it to the temple in exchange for her husband's safe return, whence it was transformed into a constellation to honour her faithfulness, the Coma Berenices. 'So, when a hair strays from the stock of an artist's brush to flaw the application of paint or varnish, it is known as a berenice.' And all this in one short paragraph.

In the wake of *Tales from Ovid*, several myths of rape and shapeshifting are quite solemnly retold here; but then by leaps of imagination, Surrealist happenstance and oblique chains of association, Carson can't sustain the earnestness, and he keys the classics into a much more arcane body of lore: his chapter on Jacinth, or the properties and associations of the bluebell, opens with Hyacinthus, the youth whom Apollo loved – and killed by mistake while playing discus together (like frisbee champions on Muscle Beach in Venice, California); it then weaves to Saint Hyacinthus, who began life as Jacko Odravag, was converted when he witnessed Saint Dominic resurrect a rider who'd been thrown from his horse, and became the most ardent of proselytising Inquisitors, ranging from Muscovy to Tibet and back again. Lithuania was one of his more successful missions, and he's the country's patron saint; the well of Saint Hyacinth is fished for amber pebbles on his feastday.

A dominant track of the book, ravelled into all the fairy-tale telling and yarning, takes up the social history of the Netherlands during the scientific revolution of the seventeenth century. Carson introduces a garrulous old character, a Dutch sea captain, to tell tales that extol the civic harmony and energy of that culture. He talks of a mermaid who paints portraits of fish as yet undiscovered, but real-life figures, like Vermeer and Jan Steen, also make vivid appearances. Carson's personal excitement really shows through when he turns to innovators in the preeminent Dutch field of optics. The consequences of seeing in a new way, through new instruments, grips him, for it clearly offers a model for his own vision of writing. In 1674, a draper in Delft, Anthony van Leeuwenhoeck, first used his invention, a microscope, to look at a glass of lake water. He wasn't appalled to find thousands of creatures swimming and wriggling in it. He found their teeming independence 'a vision of the ideal republic'.

Carson skims on, like one of his ebullient Dutchmen in a painting of a great frieze. The Dutch are also much cherished here for their love of smoking – Carson extols tobacco as a peace-maker, a sedative, a means of communication and concord: 'When you have had a quarrel with your brother, you may wish to kill him. Sit down and smoke a pipe . . . When the bowl is empty you will be ready to go to your brother and forgive him, or ask him to forgive you.' Could this be so? That peace pipes work? That what all those negotiators should do is sit down and smoke together?

Fishing for Amber is a dictionary, an encyclopaedia of natural history, a handbook of simples, a calendar of saints, an inventory of a *Wunderkammer*, a quiet riposte to the anti-smoking lobby, and an anthology of tales collected in the field. Eluding all limits of genre, neither altogether fiction nor faction, travel nor memoir, it belongs to a growing literary species: books that are simply acts of imagination. For their forerunners, we must skip back to Plutarch, and to Petrus Comestor ('the Gobbler') and thence to Montaigne and Francis Bacon and on to the Borges of *A Book of Fantastic Beasts* and Calvino; today, *Fishing for Amber* keeps company with W. G. Sebald and with Robert Calasso (though less high-toned). Most recently, Celeste Olalquiaga's beguiling study of aquatic fantasies of underwater cities and the like, in *The Artificial Kingdom: A Treasury of Kitsch Experience*, has entered this expanding category. Ciaran Carson has hatched the literary equivalent of a platypus – an unclassifiable and engaging marvel.

1999

Poison

Review of Gail Bell, Poison: A History and a Family Memoir

Like goblin fruits, poisons flourish their seductiveness under pretty, appetising colours: they lurk inside the plumpest, reddest mushrooms and the loveliest flowers, inside the trumpets of datura, in poppyheads and foxglove bells. They come dressed in beckoning words and phrases, too: mandragora, belladonna, henbane, fly agaric, 'green dream', 'green dragon'. The wicked Queen in the fairy tale offers Snow White an apple which she has tampered with; her progenitor, the stepmother in Shakespeare's *Cymbeline*, decocts 'violets, cowslips and primroses' for her deadly pharmacopoeia. Medea sends Jason's new wife a new dress: it is envenomed and burns up her hated rival on contact with her skin. Similar deep knowledge of substances and simples inspires Thetis to dip her son Achilles in the waters of the Styx so that he might become impervious to all things that harm mortal human creatures (but she holds him by his heel, and that, as we know, stays vulnerable). Gail Bell quotes the great proto-scientist Paracelsus' perception that 'All substances are poisons; there is none which is not a poison. The right dose differentiates a poison and a remedy.' From the apothecary and the herbalist to the witch and the murderer is but a little step.

Gail Bell herself is a trained pharmacist, who worked as a dispensing chemist in her native Australia, and she therefore knows intimately the dangers of the medicine cabinet. She also inherited a secret history: her father warned her against opening the box full of small glass stoppered bottles which had come to him from his father. '*Never* never do that. You could die,' he said, snatching the vial she was about to sniff. William Macbeth, the paternal grandfather whom Bell never knew, was a travelling healer, a layer-on of hands, a maker of a patent tonic and author of a treatise on preventing 'premature decay'. In 1927, his three-year-old son Patrick died from drinking strychnine; he was the second of William Macbeth's sons to die within a year: Bell was told, and on good family authority, that their father had done away with them.

Her book, *Poison*, measures out, in small loving spoonfuls, grains of information about this private, family story, as she teasingly hooks the reader into the tragic plot of the two boys' deaths. There is a riveting aside when she remembers how, 'long ago, when I was stuck in the back room of an old pharmacy compounding medicine in a trance of boredom, I put a glass to the common wall between the dispensary and the surgery next door to better hear the muffled voices that hummed off and on all day'. This secret listening-in, to which she confesses with blushes (but clearly at the same time with a kind of pride), continues in this book, in which Bell eavesdrops on the rivalries and sorrows among her own immediate kin. Fractures appear: it is surprising how very recent history, in a country keen to own a past, should so quickly fall into ruins. But Gail Bell's father was orphaned at the age of ten, and sent, as a kind of indentured child labourer, to the country to be brought up on a smallholding, when his connections to his birth family were severed.

The shame in which the aspirations of British colonial gentility can wrap an emerging national identity, even in Australia where many can trace their ancestry back to convicts, created a great silence around William Macbeth; 'family lore', Gail Bell writes, is 'the dead zone of secrets, severity and things withheld'. But, as she discovers, her poisoner grandfather was clearly a charmer, a dandy who wore a morning suit and drove expensive cars: his is also a pioneer story, for frontiers have always offered opportunities to snake-oil merchants, and long before the coming of Viagra, druggists have promised sexual vigour (unfortunately Bell could find no trace of 'Macbeth's Strengthening Tonic, tested in the Highlands of Scotland on the descendants of the great warriors of Culloden').

Her narrative method weaves in and out, sometimes frustratingly, and at times the reader longs for a more steady, ample texture. It would have been interesting, for instance, to hear more about a quack's role in and around suburban Sydney and the summer resorts of the Blue Mountains, but Gail Bell is less interested in social history than in the practice of storytelling itself. Her book gradually turns into an oblique, suggestive meditation on family memory, on false hopes and promises, and opens up into an inquiry into the intricate cheating games romancing and revenge play with the truth.

In *La Peste*, Albert Camus writes that every prisoner and every exile experience the 'profound suffering of living with a memory that has no purpose', and Bell's family story, like many others, provides an antidote to this existential emptiness. Her relatives obeyed the emotional dynamic that requires painful memories to have a rationale, that seeks to impose some kind of purposeful narrative on the unbearable, random, hopeless strokes of fate. Since Bell has constructed her story as a tease, a quasi-suspense tale of decryption, it would be a spoiling act to disclose the outcome. But it conforms to the general thrust of her book, that poisoners fascinate us far in excess of their incidence, that the fatal draught, the bitter pill, the medicine bottle labelled 'Drink me', issue above all an invitation to the fabulous imagination. Bell tells an emblematic tale of a circus elephant on tour in Australia, which died of arsenic poisoning: lurid suspicions of dark strangers from out of town were soon circulating. But eventually, an analysis of the poor beast's stomach contents revealed – weedkiller. Gail Bell's poisoners are the bogeymen we love to fear: the strangers who hide razor blades in apples, the gypsies who steal babies. But though she makes her case quietly but surely, she does not explore the complex difficulty that presents itself so urgently today, that such false texts and made-up stories have the power to drive events in the real world, that life imitates art; the distinctions she draws, between story and history, between fantasy and fact, are increasingly themselves ground up into a compound chemical that works its way with passions and ideas.

Poison is also frequently despised, for example, as a woman's instrument, the typically deceitful and cruel vengeance of the sisters of

Circe, but again, the history of female murderers who have resorted to this means reveals only sad banality – drudges rather than enchantresses. Bell does mention, however, that distillations of parsley were used as an abortifacient: one of the most common uses of all poisons, sometimes self-administered, of course. The reference to parsley gives a most interesting insight into the fairy tale of Rapunzel, in which a mother craves a herb or leaf growing in a neighbouring witch's garden. In early versions of the story, the title – 'Persinette' in French, for example – records the connection specifically with parsley. So it becomes likely that the story enfolds a buried tale of a mother who tries to abort her offspring – and the hideous penalties that ensue.

Into the quiet drip feed of her personal memoir, Bell mixes stronger flavours: she grinds and crushes together ingredients from criminology and psychology, botany and chemistry. She gives an inspired account of the original story of *Hamlet* and the poisoning of Hamlet's father from its medieval source, and adds several twists. Cleopatra's death, a conspiracy theory about Napoleon's murder by arsenic and Flaubert's sadism towards Emma Bovary find their place in her poison chest. From the Chamber of Horrors, the obsessions of thrillers and newspaper records, she analyses uses, dosages and symptoms – of cyanide, hemlock, arsenic, and her grandfather's favourite, strychnine. Her book belongs to the new fascinating corpus of substance biographies, of which Primo Levi, with *The Periodic Table*, and Sidney Mintz, with *Sweetness and Power*, his study of sugar in history, remain the two great forerunners. The genre will soon require special display sections in bookshops: Ciaran Carson, in *Fishing for Amber*, and Simon Garfield with his history of the colour *Mauve*, for example, have extended the range of this approach, into myth and poetry on the one hand and the history of manufactures and inventions on the other. Gail Bell has given this cunning and original history of poison an intimate inflection, in keeping with the current autobiographical tendency. Her ear to the glass against the partition wall has caught fascinating private exchanges, and these overheard stories confirm that even if the poisoned apple is not much more than gossip, its potent dangers should not be underestimated.

FIVE

SHAKESPEAREAN TRANSFORMATIONS

Rough Magic and Sweet Lullaby

BBC Radio lecture

Spirits haunt the plays: ghosts walk and prophesy – in a history play like *Julius Caesar*, and famously in *Hamlet* and *Macbeth*; in *Henry VI, Part One*, Joan of Arc figures as a baneful, lying, sexual witch, a 'devil or devil's dam'; *The Comedy of Errors*, another early work, takes place in the city of Ephesus, notorious for its pagan witchcraft, where the hapless protagonist Antipholus of Syracuse believes that his many misadventures have come about through local sorcery. In *A Midsummer Night's Dream*, a comedy of more musing, lyric puzzlement, a fairy king knows a secret juice with magic powers, and his messenger, Puck, is 'that shrewd/ And knavish sprite', a hobglobin 'sometimes called Robin Goodfellow', who goes about frightening maidens, curdling milk, leading wayfarers astray. Aspects of Puck are carried over into the character of that later, captive airy messenger, Ariel, who in *The Tempest* works spectacular magic at Prospero's bidding and can also fly around the earth. Like Puck, Ariel is a master of metamorphosis.

At every stage of his playwriting, and in every genre – comedy, history, tragedy and romance – Shakespeare's plays break through the barriers of the senses to convey faery, enchanted, supernatural dimensions of experience, teeming with prodigies and phenomena, with signs and wonders. As Bottom says of his dream, 'the eye of man hath not heard, the ear of man hath not seen, man's hand is not able to taste' such marvels, some sinister, some charmingly seductive, as Shakespeare stages for us.

Fairies and aerial creatures are shape-shifters; they also change others' shapes. Bottom the Weaver is 'translated' into an ass. Puck boasts he can change himself into 'a filly foal' or 'a roasted crab'; Ariel, under orders from Prospero, changes gender and turns into a harpy, a water-nymph, as well as the lightning of St Elmo's fire; both of them know how to disappear from human sight – indeed the paradoxical stage direction occurs, twice, 'enter Ariel, invisible'. The shadow of Christopher Marlowe stretches over these images of witchcraft, for Dr Faustus's devil reveals to him powers of metamorphosis as well as practical jokes.

A diverse, uncanny population flourishes, bursting from Shakespeare's teeming lexicon: lobs and pucks and sprites and phantoms and elves and even ouphes, who are a kind of elf, conjured up by name among the troop of fairies by Mistress Quickly, when, at the comic finale of *The Merry Wives of Windsor*, she stages a mock supernatural assault on Falstaff in Windsor Great Forest, pinching and buffeting and taunting the fat knight like the mock devils jabbing revellers with pitchforks at a Caribbean carnival. Oberon discriminates between the many different orders of supernatural beings: talking of ghosts, he says, '*We* are spirits of another sort.'

Imagine a visitor from the New World to Shakespeare's England, with a twentieth-century ethnographer's curiosity about other people's religions and beliefs: would such a tourist have been able to deduce much about Christianity as a faith or a moral system from Shakespeare's plays? The plays provide plenty of research material on magic as an expression of supernatural powers, but on the Christian scheme of redemption? Unearthly phenomena move the action, stir the characters to their next move: think of the opening of *Macbeth* and the creepy oracle of the three weird sisters, of Hamlet's father's eerie call for remembrance and revenge. Fiendish motives, devilish plots, the narrative heartbeat of pagan and Renaissance magic: supernatural spirit forces, not the incarnate saviour or the Holy Ghost, work at a great depth in these stories; they nourish the very bone marrow of the plays. On the one hand, Shakespeare invokes 'rough magic', the phrase Prospero uses when he breaks his staff and abjures his 'art'; on the other, he also creates his own verbal music to counteract sinister forces of harm.

The fairies in *A Midsummer Night's Dream* often used to be tots costumed in confections of gauze and tulle and glitter. But recent productions have paid more attention to their odd, eldritch, dusty or piquant names: Cobweb and Moth, Peaseblossom and Mustardseed. Still, these dingy sprites range themselves against even darker forces of night-time disturbance, against the horror of slugs and snails and puppy-dogs' tails, as it were: Titania asks them to sing 'a roundel and a fairy song' before she goes to sleep and before they go off on their 'war' against cankers in the musk rose, against bats and owls – a struggle for good in the sphere of botany. In the 'sweet lullaby' that follows, these elvish guardians of freshness, ripeness and light list the creatures that endanger even the Queen of the Fairies: newts, snakes, blind-worms – ingredients more familiar from the witches' cauldron, for they are tossed into the brew accompanied by that other, famous charm, 'Double, double, toil and trouble' in *Macbeth*. Into the pot the weird sisters stir, chanting:

> Fillet of a fenny snake,
> In the cauldron boil and bake;
> Eye of newt and toe of frog,
> Wool of bat and tongue of dog,
> Adder's fork and blind-worm's sting,
> Lizard's leg and howlet's wing,
> For a charm of pow'rful trouble,
> Like a hell-broth boil and bubble.

The fairies' lullaby in *A Midsummer Night's Dream* offers a counter charm to this grisly soup: or rather it attempts to protect Titania from such a potion. The fairies also enlist the nightingale, Philomele, to add her voice to their magic song:

> *1 Fairy*: You spotted snakes with double tongue,
>   Thorny hedgehogs, be not seen,
> Newts and blind-worms, do no wrong,
> Come not near our fairy queen.
>
> *Chorus*: Philomele, with melody,
>   Sing in our sweet lullaby,
> Lulla, lulla, lullaby, lulla, lulla, lullaby.
>   Never harm,
>   Nor spell, nor charm,
> Come our lovely lady nigh.
> So good night, with lullaby.

In his ground-breaking edition of *The Tempest*, Frank Kermode discussed Shakespeare's distinction between theurgy, good magic, and goety, or sorcery – the dark arts, and their foul deeds, called by the witch-hunters, *maleficium*. But in the plays, the two modes of supernatural manipulation are in practice confused, because the same persons perform both: Prospero, Oberon. Nor are ghosts and spectres raised only by adepts, sorcerers or witches: after Hamlet's father has appeared, Horatio recalls the public portents that warned of Julius Caesar's death. But above all, both malignant and beneficent magic phenomena inhabit analogous zones of metaphor, they speak or sing through related patterns of imagery and of prosody. Any clear difference between witchcraft and fairy lore, and between good or evil origins, true or false messages, totters and falls, though the plays tend – especially but not only the comedies – towards resisting harm and releasing, fostering, allowing blessings to flourish in order to 'restore amends', as Puck puts it in the closing line of *A Midsummer Night's Dream*. The conflict between good and evil never takes the Manichaean form of a simple combat myth; the power of Shakespeare's uncanny rises from this ambiguity, that questions around the supernatural can never be settled. The guardian fairies of Titania's rest, for example, don't themselves altogether escape the cauldron's realm of reptiles, night creatures and other 'creepy-crawlies'. They're bug-like in scale and she gives them sinister-sounding tasks: her close instructions to make candles for Bottom's siesta are practical, in the manner of a cunning woman, but also rather more surgical than one might want:

> The honey-bags steal from the humble-bees,
> And for night-tapers crop their waxen thighs,
> And light them at the fiery glow-worm's eyes,
> To have my love to bed and to arise;
> And pluck the wings from painted butterflies,
> To fan the moonbeams from his sleeping eyes . . .

The imagery of insects dominates the visual lexicon of horrors and frights today; scales, probosces, pincers, gleaming carapaces, elaborate mouthparts and bristling antennae from the hidden, subterranean territory of creepy-crawlies characterise the scary cast of current fantasy. Dislocations of size belong with the unsettling capacity to change shape, and they don't belittle the fairies' power, but increase their eeriness: Titania can stroke Bottom's large soft ears in a woman's way, even though her attendants flit about hanging dewdrops on cowslips. It's not anachronistic to respond to Titania's imagery of bees' legs and plucked insect wings with a shudder. The word 'bugs' used to mean demons: Beelzebub, after all, is 'Lord of the Flies' (2 Kings 1:2). Today, entertainment imagery is again closing the gap between bug meaning 'insect' and bug meaning 'devil'; this is the intermediate space where Shakespeare's busy elves are poised.

The ambiguous contingency of types of magic suffuses the 'insubstantial pageant' of *The Tempest*: around fourteen years after *A Midsummer Night's Dream*, this late play again draws the audience into the instability of the supernatural in Shakespeare's work. In *The Tempest*, the whole island is bewitched. It exhibits many of the special features of diabolical enchantment, according to both classical tradition and current Elizabethan and Jacobean beliefs, yet Sycorax, the dead mother of Caliban, is the only witch who is named as such in the play. Through his 'secret studies', his 'so potent art', Prospero performs the magic metamorphoses of witchcraft, but he embodies the presiding consciousness of the drama, and his perspective provides the moral viewpoint and the emotional colour. So his magic does not figure as malign – except to Caliban, of course, who rains down curses on his head. (Peter Greenaway's film script of *The Tempest*, in which he gives the entire play to John Gielgud as Prospero to intone, catches accurately this unusually condensed first-person angle on the unfolding drama.) Yet in the course of the play Prospero spellbinds the survivors of the storm which he commanded Ariel to raise, he conjures spirits to harass his victims, torments Caliban with phantom pinches and stings and beatings and pursues him with dogs; he performs these magus-like feats through Ariel his airy messenger, and Ariel creates an historical as well as emotional link between Prospero and Sycorax. More particularly, Ariel, who was once bound in a cloven pine by Sycorax, now serves Prospero against his will.

For whereas Puck performs some of his magic independently, Ariel is a bondservant, enslaved to Prospero, who promises him freedom in return for the magic this fairy being can perform on his master's behalf. He's both greater than Prospero – he can fly, for example – and his captive – a familiar, as opposed to a devil like Mephistopheles. The play does not admit in so many words that Prospero has usurped his magic powers from Sycorax, along with the island kingdom he has seized from her 'freckled whelp'. But Prospero tells us that Sycorax was a mistress of the elements:

> His mother was a witch and one so strong
> That could control the moon, make flows and ebbs . . .

And he claims powers in the same terms for himself in his fervent speech of renunciation:

> I have bedimm'd
> The noontide sun, call'd forth the mutinous winds,
> And twixt the green sea and the azur'd vault
> Set roaring war . . .

As is well known, Prospero's grandiloquent abjuration borrows heavily from the dramatic incantation of the sorceress Medea in Ovid's *Metamorphoses*, so Shakespeare put words from one of the most famous witches of antiquity on to the lips of his island magus. In classical myth, Medea is Circe's niece, and the Homeric enchantress also haunts the character of the 'foul witch Sycorax'. The name Sycorax echoes phonetically the English pronunciation of Circe: mistress of transformations, she changes Odysseus' companions into swine and alters men's minds so that they forget their duties, their homes, their own nature. Circe and Medea, these two malignant but alluring witches, seem to be standing in the wings of the play and the lights behind them cast their interlaced shadows across the stage, forming the phantom, Sycorax, whispering to Prospero how to command the insubstantial pageant of the action.

Proper indeed to an isle of mysterious music, made by spirits and voices that float, unanchored to bodies, this score gives Sycorax's former role to Prospero and accords their duet the backing support of past figures of female magic. Titania can be invoked here too: her quarrel with Oberon over the changeling boy has upset natural harmony, causing rivers to burst their banks, fogs to descend and harvests to rot. She scolds Oberon in *Midsummer Night's Dream*, that their 'brawls' have upset nature, including the rhythm of the moon:

> Therefore the moon (the governess of floods),
> Pale in her anger, washes all the air,
> That rheumatic diseases do abound.
> And thorough this distemperature, we see
> The seasons alter: hoary-headed frosts
> Fall in the fresh lap of the crimson rose . . .

Although she is Queen of the Fairies, the 'sweet lullaby' sung by her attendants doesn't work; nor does the fairy sentinel manage to ward off danger. For, with the last chord of the spell, Puck enters and drops the magic potion in Titania's eyes. He's Oberon's jester, a prankster, making mischief of one kind or another: his tricks in *A Dream* recall the peculiar buffoonery that, in Marlowe's earlier play, Mephistopheles and Dr Faustus enjoy, spiriting away dishes and cups from diners' hands at a banquet, and selling a poor sap a horse that turns into 'a bottle of hay' between his legs. In Shakespeare's comedy, the prankishness trips along merrily on the light fantastic toe: the fairies, as Oberon says, are 'frolic'. But elsewhere the same pinching and pecking can leave darker bruises. Prospero with his earnest spells raises spirits from the dead, he claims, and Caliban names, among his tormentors, hedgehogs and adders. Fairies, although distinct from witches, share their powers: that 'tricksy spirit' Ariel whistles up the wind that wrecks the boat at the opening of *The Tempest* – another splendid supernatural engine, moving the plot – in a similar way to the weird sisters on the heath, when they torment the ship's pilot whom theys cry in their magic cauldron.

Puck's a 'merry wanderer of the night,' a lord of misrule, a spirit of contrariness, and linked to the fairy activity most feared in seventeenth-century accounts of magic: their snatching human children and leaving a changeling behind. The original quarrel between Titania and Oberon arises from the fairy king's desire for the Indian boy that she has adopted after the death of his mother. Puck helps Oberon achieve his end: indeed they concoct the whole scheme of Titania's enchanted passion for Bottom in order to distract her from clinging to the boy – whom Oberon then happily acquires for himself. The Scots pastor, the Revd Robert Kirk, in his book *The Secret Commonwealth* (around 1690) relates how mothers and nurses would place a piece of iron – a horseshoe or a poker – in infants' cots, because iron had the property of turning away mischievous night visitors who intrude on human affairs, stealing babies, curdling milk. Puck's name is related etymologically to a cluster of boo-words, to 'pook' and 'bogle', and 'boobagger' and 'boggart' and 'bogey'.

Though Shakespeare's effervescent development manages to conceal this canker within the bud, *A Midsummer Night's Dream* turns on a bed-trick: a husband getting his wife into bed with someone else, and not just anyone, but some 'vile thing'. So Shakespeare in this comedy doesn't tarry on the story of the changeling, or on Oberon's nasty and contrary uxoriousness, but he does open the space in the woods as a kind of thalamus, or nuptial chamber, a site of eros and its power, where two pairs of all-too-human lovers are lost and find themselves and two pairs of heroic or divine couples in dissension are reconciled. Puck's erotic jackanapes show a certain affinity with the god Eros, in his naughty boy Cupid form: Maureen Duffy, in her study *The Erotic World of Faery*, quotes an earlier instance of a fairy's misconduct in an Elizabethan play, *The Maides Metamorphosis*, where an imp is called 'Little, little Pricke'. 'O you are dangerous little fairy!' exclaims someone, whereupon he explains, 'When I feel a girl asleepe, Underneath her frock I peep./ There to sport, and there I playe,/ Then I byte her like a flea,/ And about I skip.'

The woods where the lovers prove their love converge with the dream zones of the supernatural, as conceived elsewhere in the plays: with Queen Mab's territory, for example. Her hazelnut-shell chariot is equipped with yet more insect parts and 'her waggoner [is] a small grey-coated gnat,' Mercutio tell us. Queen Mab is another merry wanderer of the night, who excites dreams of gratification, including erotic dreams: 'she gallops night by night/ Through lovers' brains, and then they dream of love . . .' (*Romeo and Juliet*). Her royal title might arise from a mishearing: the fairies' midwife is a cotquean, or bawd – queen with an *a* rather than an *e*, a common Elizabethan word for a brothel madam or a hussy, and Mercutio's gay gallimaufry of spiders, gnats, worms, crickets, grasshopper bits and pieces again raises the spectre of bugs, those ambiguously devilish emanations.

Mercutio's bravura speech – over forty lines of fanciful fairy lore – is embedded in an exchange with Romeo on the truth status of dreams: Mercutio plays the cynic, whose verbal exuberance seeks to corral the mind's imaginings in a fantastical undergrowth, and to contain their danger by rhetorical flourishes and scornful relegation to fairyland. But Romeo remains uneasy: Mercutio speaks of 'nothing' he says, in other words, he's talking nonsense; for Romeo, it is still disturbingly possible to 'dream things true'.

This conflict over the status of dreams stirs in many of the plays: dreams can indeed be true portents, uncanny oracles (think of the dream of Caesar's wife, Calpurnia, and of Lady Macbeth's recurrent, somnambulist nightmares). They're above all a distinguishing feature of human brains, setting them aside from fairy thought, as Hamlet implies when he invokes the impossibly tiny character of Queen Mab and Ariel, 'I may be bounded in a nutshell and count myself a king of infinite space, were it not that I have bad dreams.' Here dreams appear in antinomy to fantastic features of fairy folk: Hamlet seems to be saying that he could imagine he commanded the fantastic powers of fairies, except that bad dreams – an index of truth – do not allow him such self-delusion.

Similarly, Lady Macbeth fatally underestimates the warnings that arise in fantasy when she scorns Macbeth's fears, saying, 'Tis the eye of childhood/ That fears a painted devil.' Intermediate, supernatural beings bring dreams, as Queen Mab does; they dwell in dreams, as Titania does in Bottom's fully fledged fantasy; they are the agents, objects and contents of dreams, but they themselves, Hamlet seems to be saying, do not suffer from the self-consciousness of 'bad dreams' as he does. Dreaming things true is possible, but Caliban, in his famous speech "The isle is full of noises . . .', recalls his longing for the imaginary bliss and consolation that dreams can also bring,

> And then, in dreaming,
> The clouds methought would open, and show riches
> Ready to drop upon me; that, when I wak'd,
> I cried to dream again.

The people in the plays believe in the supernatural that they conjure: Prospero doesn't doubt his art, it's so manifestly present, active and reliable to him that he has to renounce its instruments – his staff, his magic cloak, his grimoire or handbook of spells – by extreme measures of shattering and drowning. Nobody else doubts his powers, either, or Sycorax's for that matter before him. In *Hamlet*, the watch on the battlements sees Hamlet's father's ghost before he does: these are shared, unchallenged sightings of spirits. In *Macbeth*, the uncanny becomes internal, a private, agonising haunting of the criminal and his accomplice: this tragedy plumbs inner depths more deeply than even *Hamlet*, for it blurs the boundaries between inner and outer manifestations of the supernatural, depicts individual fantasy itself as possessed by devils, so that nobody else, besides guilty Macbeth, sees Banquo. Vision here becomes subjective dreaming only, the private conscience fabricating phantoms, not verifiable by shared experience.

Theatre realises illusions: setting up a perceptual paradox that can't be resolved. The dramas which seem to resolve the problem of the supernatural, by breaking the spell, ending the enchantment, relegating or at least limiting the powers of ghosts and fairies, are the selfsame plays where Shakespeare meditates most obsessively about the nature of the state of illusion itself, the power of fantasy. 'These are all actors,' Prospero tells his new son-in-law, Ferdinand, 'all spirits, and/ Are melted into air, into thin air.' The visions Ferdinand has experienced stand on a 'baseless fabric'. In this famous speech, Prospero doesn't allow his audience to rest safely in the knowledge that the dream is fled and real life, the solid ground beneath one's feet, has returned. No, this vision is the condition of 'the great globe itself': 'We are such stuff as dreams are made on,/ And our little life is rounded with a sleep'. We're not made *of* dreams, as the phrase might be expected to put it. Dreams are made *on* our stuff, as visions projected into the mind, or on to screens and flats and even smoke on stage.

Theatrical illusion offers an analogy to the spectral conjurings of enchanters as well as to the phantasms of haunted minds. In *A Dream*, Theseus talks of 'shaping fantasies' and Titania of 'fancy's images'. Reversing Prospero's metaphor, Theseus also says, actors themselves are 'shadows', something Puck repeats in the play's envoi ('If we shadows have offended . . .').

The puzzle this produces relates to the condition of language itself, oscillating between an event with consequences, and an utterance or description as airy and ephemeral as the breath taken to speak. Shakespeare explores language as event: he makes his poetry work to change experience: 'So long lives this, and this gives life to thee,' he concludes, sacramentally, at the end of one of the sonnets. In the plays, curses, blessings, spells, incantations perform crucial dramatic acts to push forward the story, transform the characters. These kinds of speech thus become the very tools of metamorphosis. But can this supernatural agency spill over the edges of the stage, diffuse its mists with the dry ice and fork its lightning into the audience's interior spaces of fear and terror? Can it get into our dreams? Or, to put it the other way around, in the phrase of Calderón de la Barca, is Life Itself a Dream? And what does this imply for the status of dreamed realities?

The answers to these questions interestingly do not appear to depend on the audience's belief at any one time: you could say, 'Oh, but people then believed in ghosts and oracles and omens, in magic and even, perhaps, metamorphosis, that a man could become a donkey. But we don't entertain such childish fancies now; it's different for us.' It is different for us: most of us no longer fear witches. But this dismissal doesn't describe the experience of being in the audience at a production of *Macbeth* now, or of *The Tempest* or *A Dream*. Sceptical, rational, sapient humans today don't suspend disbelief for a time and then return to normal; we're not tricked into colluding with something we don't believe in. The plays make us part of their world. The magical or supernatural machinery of the stories doesn't present a problem because the effects are created in the virtual realm of theatre, which we enter, accept and inhabit (Coleridge's famous 'suspension of disbelief'). But we also recognise a shared experience of cognition. This enchanted realm embodies a map of the mind, in which fantasy and dream produce impossible phenomena. The supernatural becomes an extension of imagination itself, enacted through theatrical representation. In one of the crucial speeches in Shakespeare's thinking about writing, Theseus meditates on this exact interrelationship. First, discussing the lovers' madness, he comments, 'such tricks hath strong imagination . . . how easy is a bush suppos'd a bear'. His mind is still running on this while watching the performance of Pyramus and Thisbe, when he says of the actors: 'The best in this kind are but shadows, and the worst are no worse, if imagination amend them.'

Fantasy, applied to theatrical enactments, can supply something more, as it also does for dreamers and lovers – 'the imagination bodies forth/ The forms of things unknown'. This movement of the mind makes amends, which art's reparatory power imitates through invention. For the poet's pen 'Turns them to shapes' – that is, wields the magic power of metamorphosis and 'gives to aery nothing/ A local habitation and a name'.

This activity doesn't contain the power – or the threat, however. The convergence between the dream space of magic and metamorphosis and the theatre space of performance, acting and illusion makes one leak into the other both inside the plays and outside them. Inside the plays, Hamlet stages 'The Mouse Trap' to spring Claudius from his equanimity – and succeeds: for Claudius, the events enacted on the stage prove too real to endure and he calls for lights and storms out. The play Hamlet has composed for the Players crosses the divide between insubstantial pageant and actual existence. Life and art get mixed up: this is the dangerous magic of acted words, this is the basis of casting spells, as the weird sisters demonstrate, as the fairies' lullaby attempts.

How does Shakespeare achieve the reality effect of the supernatural? Magic is a form of performative speech: its commands bring their contents into being, as when the priest officiates at a sacrament. Oberon's lovespell on Titania makes her fall in love with Bottom. The words 'chant' and 'incantation' and 'cantrip' reveal the relationship of song to spells and charms; such verbal formulae don't record or describe, they produce events, as I said, they inaugurate change.

In this respect, it's worth looking at a heated exchange in *Henry IV, Part One* between Harry Hotspur and Owen Glendower. They're disagreeing about signs and wonders, Glendower claiming portents at his birth and magic powers to summon devils. Glendower boasts, 'I can call spirits from the vasty deep . . .' At this highflown language, Harry Hotspur replies, 'Why so can I, and so can any man,/ But will they come when you do call for them?'

Their quarrel grows naturally to include language itself – and poetry, which Hotspur rejects as furiously as he rejects Glendower's 'skimble-skamble' with devils and spells. Glendower talks of his polite upbringing in the English court, where he learned to sing to the harp 'Many an English ditty lovely well'.

At which Hotspur rails:

> I had rather be a kitten and cry mew
> Than one of these same metre ballad-mongers.
> I had rather hear a brazen canstick turn'd,
> Or a dry wheel grate on the axle-tree,
> And that would set my teeth nothing an edge,
> Nothing so much as mincing poetry.

The orotund, courtly style of Glendower's boast strikes Hotspur's ears as 'mincing poetry' – he prefers grinding and screeching – or so he says.

Shakespeare, faced with the tradition that cast magic in the language of bombast – the 'vasty deep' – can also ventriloquise most eloquently Hotspur's disgust, and protest against the literary mode. Prospero does indeed wax Glendowerish when conjuring. But Shakespeare's most potent charms and spells do seem to turn to the non-literary, performative tradition of utterance. The devil's works are associated with duplicity, not simplicity, with counterfeit contrivances, not direct utterance. So the counter-magic or theurgy of Shakespeare's own verbal art sometimes rejects 'mincing poetry', the courtly style, the learned measures of classical necromancers; it pursues instead an earthy, aural, natural language that lies outside these cultured purlieus – the mew of the kitten, the grinding of a candlestick on a lathe or the screech of an ungreased wheel. Hotspur's hideous list of noises brings a touch of the grotesque to the issue, and Shakespeare does indeed like to introduce grotesque touches at moments of intense magic. For

example, Ariel's eerie, beguiling song 'Come unto these yellow sands'
ends inexplicably, 'Bow wow bow wow' – a nod to the canine
metamorphoses of spirits in the play perhaps, but also a jarring note
after the lyrical picture of the preceding lines. It's not for comic effect
alone, however, that Shakespeare puts near-doggerel to work: the
witches' uncouth rigmaroles from *Macbeth*, grotesque as they are,
don't inspire laughter.

Shakespeare's own enchantments, his rough magic, arise from his
use of such rhymes. For he characteristically casts magic charms in verse
– often in popular, vernacular metres, to the rhythms of ditties and
nursery rhymes, popular songs, nonsense, and yes, ballads (through
Hotspur includes them in his derision). This habitat – anonymous,
verbal music – coincides with the realm of the supernatural, that
supplementary dimension of fancy and dream that Shakespeare puts on
stage and especially on the lips of mere mortal fools. 'Bottom's Dream'
will be a ballad, so Bottom promises. And in *The Merry Wives of
Windsor*, during the assault on Falstaff, Mistress Quickly reveals
unexpected – indeed magical – verbal dexterity. As Anne Barton has
pointed out, she becomes quite Titania-like in her self-styled role of
Queen of the Fairies:

> Fairies, black, grey, green and white,
> You moonshine revellers, and shades of night . . .
> Attend your office and your quality.

When the masquerading elves and ouphes hit Falstaff, the witchy bounce
of the lines grows tighter, simpler in metre, more grounded:

> Pinch him, fairies, mutually!
> Pinch him for his villainy!
> Pinch him, and burn him, and turn him about,
> Till candles, and starlight, and moonlight be out.

But the best illumination of this poetic device, combining rhythm,
grotesquerie and uncouthness, occurs in the scene when Bottom begins to
sing to himself after he has been translated and his friends the rude
mechanicals have fled from his new, monstrous shape. He says, 'I will
walk up and down here, and I will sing, that they shall hear that I am not
afraid.'

His whistling in the dark, so to speak, calls upon a sequence of birds, natural musicians, in the same way as the fairies had called on the nightingale in their earlier lullaby to Titania. Birds, like fairies, occupy an intermediate zone, they're nature's airy spirits, and in this richly comic passage, Bottom, braying between verses, calls on their company to protect him:

> The ousel cock so black of hue
> With orange-tawny bill,
> The throstle with his note so true,
> The wren with little quill – . . .

Titania [*Awaking*]: What angel wakes me from my flow'ry bed?

Bottom [*Sings*]:
> The finch, the sparrow and the lark,
> The plain-song cuckoo grey,
> Whose note full many a man doth mark,
> And dares not answer nay –

'The isle is full of noises/ Sounds and sweet airs': so are the woods. Bottom's self-fortifying song falls within a sequence of dances, ditties and other music that close *A Midsummer Night's Dream*. The supernatural is summoned by spells and charms; its intrinsic affinity with goety can be countered by verbal and other music, natural not counterfeit, as in that most perfect lyric song, 'Fear no more the heat o' the sun', from *Cymbeline*. This is elegy as sweet lullaby, sung over the supposed corpse of Imogen to lay her to rest.

Sounds, sweet airs, true notes, plain song can act as a counterspell, an antidote to fancy's tricks and their ambiguous shapings, the manifestations of the supernatural. Of course there's much art in the artlessness. Within rough magic lie involutions of art upon art, spell upon spell.

2000

Shakespeare and the Goddess

Review of Ted Hughes, Shakespeare and the Goddess of Complete Being

Like Black Elk, whose visions he invokes in *Shakespeare and the Goddess of Complete Being*, Ted Hughes has received a shamanic call, and so has his Shakespeare: an adept of occult Neoplatonism, a highly conscious mythographer, Hughes's Shakespeare deploys his dramatis personae as concelebrants of a sacred ritual, fusing Celtic legend (transmitted from a Welsh schoolmaster), Gnostic philosophy and even Buddhist motifs with more current classical and folklore sources. The Elizabethan poet's works function over and above the level of literature, as 'modern England's creation story, our sacred book, closer to us than the Bible'.

Hughes himself plays hide-and-seek behind the figure of Shakespeare, unlike Robert Graves, who did not place any mask between himself and the Muse in *The White Goddess*, a study which stands as a mother to Hughes's and has much in common with its offspring. In both books, through a brilliant combination of intoxicated dreaming and deep scholarship, a male poet struggles to still the turbulence of his heterosexuality by giving as full an account of it as language can be pressed to make.

This book, however, emerges at a moment very different from Graves's in 1948, and it stirs at a deeper, more painful level. Male self-reckonings have taken on a sharper, beleaguered tone. Hughes's text keeps its fingers in its ears, as it were, against the cries of feminism, but the reader can hear them all right, still there between the lines, like the spectral voices in the several Shakespearean storms Hughes evokes so well. *Shakespeare and the Goddess of Complete Being* is an *apologia pro vita mea*, and it must rank as one of the keenest anatomies of misogyny undertaken since *The Glory of Hera* by Philip Slater (1968 – a study which should be better known).

And yet, while the poet in the present day unswervingly faces the loathing, destruction and burial of the female in Shakespeare, and celebrates the reassembly of her scattered bones and the restoration of her shattered voice, as he sees it, through the last romances till the final consummation of *The Tempest*, he reproduces the axioms of that selfsame misogyny; it is rare for a subject not to stick to a writer, so there's no special culpability in this, but it does reveal how even the keen-sighted among us cannot see behind our own heads, and that in some ineluctable way we cannot think ourselves out of ourselves. He faces honestly, in anger and in pain, the ambiguity of 'the double vision', the loving and the loathing of women by men. The Shakespeare he has made, and vehemently, is a portrait of the artist as a man.

His exegesis takes the two long poems, *Venus and Adonis* and *The Rape of Lucrece*, as a proleptic Genesis to the economy of Shakespearean salvation, worked out through the exiles, wrongs, passions and blood sacrifices of the Tragedies, in which 'the beloved Female must die', via the mediating apotheosis of mutual love in *Antony and Cleopatra* to the transcendental theophanies of the four late plays, where victims are mystically healed and restored to life (Hermione and Perdita; Thaisa and Marina; Miranda and Ferdinand united). He calls the figure that he discerns in the carpet 'The Tragic Equation' – and the words remain capitalised throughout – as he sets out in impassioned pages the workings of this Shakespearean 'algebra': Venus, the principle of 'unconditional, total love', woos the pattern of princeliness, or rational man, in the form of the beautiful Adonis; her' sweating Lust' rejected, she returns, in the form of the boar which gores the youth in the thigh and kills him; he is changed into a flower which she mourns and cherishes. Shakespeare's poem, Hughes argues, presents this pagan icon – young god sacrificed in the arms of his mother and lover – as the old, Catholic faith repudiated; the nascent puritan in Shakespeare scorns the mother goddess of love and renewal.

In *Lucrece*, by contrast, Shakespeare occupies the Catholic viewpoint through the eyes – and voice – of his paragon and heroine, and sees, in Tarquin, the rapist bent on destroying her soul as well: suffering Adonis has 'pupated', and a puritan fury has emerged, the iconoclast enemy of the goddess, hammering at cult statues of the Virgin Mary. But her soul is his, too, and he tears himself as he tears at her; his soul is England's spirit, cloven by the Reformation. Shakespeare internalised the schism, and became 'a shaman, a prophet, of the ascendant, revolutionary, Puritan will . . . just as surely as he was a visionary, redemptive shaman of the Catholic defeat'. Densely interwoven insights – historical, biographical and psychoanalytical – produce here some of the most stimulating and convincingly argued oratory in the book. Hughes then concludes his first section, announcing that Shakespeare's work – our scripture – represents 'his heroic, lifelong, patient attempt to rescue the Female – in some way or other to salvage the Goddess'.

As every retelling of a myth flows back to become the myth itself, criticising Hughes for wearing conjuror's sleeves when using his classical sources shouldn't count harshly against him. However, as 'the charge of the Boar' provides the essential tragic catalyst in his argument, sounding in Hamlet's fury against Ophelia and his mother, in Lear's turning on Cordelia, in Othello's rage and so forth, and as Hughes so closely identifies the Boar with the furious, rejected goddess, it's worth stressing that, in Greek myth, the boar is commonly sent by either Ares or Apollo, for various motives of their own, while, in Ovid, Venus warns her darling about his reckless hunting of wild beasts, explicitly dissociating herself: 'I hate their whole tribe!' For Hughes, the boar rushes from the infernal regions as Persephone's emissary, and Persephone is merely Venus under another aspect; this she-boar, this sow, becomes fiercely, incontrovertibly female, and he accords her a blazing passage:

> Her combination of gross whiskery nakedness and riotous carnality is seized by the mythic imagination, evidently, as a sort of uterus on the loose – upholstered with breasts, not so much many-breasted as a mobile tub entirely made up of female sexual parts, a woman-sized, multiple udder on trotters. Most alarming of all is that elephantine, lolling mouth under her great earflaps, like a Breughelesque nightmare vagina, baggy with overproduction, famous for gobbling her piglets . . . swamping the senses . . . As a country boy . . . Shakespeare enjoyed a familiarity with pigs that is not irrelevant to this myth.

This prose-poem, as harsh old Crow is startled into cawing again, has been relegated to a footnote; as has almost all fleshy imagery. The dominant metaphors derive from science – from the invisible operations of the new physics (Rupert Sheldrake's 'morphic resonance' is invoked), computer mathematics, atomic fission. The effects are jolting, deliberately forced, even ugly: 'Meanwhile, in the long poem he has shifted his private, subjective situation into the giant step-up transformer of this mythic narrative . . .'; 'Or, to stick to the bomb image, as it explodes here [*Troilus and Cressida*] for the first time it does so in slow motion, and Shakespeare registers – as on a computerised simulation – the composite chemical signature of each phase of the process.'

Such images, grinding at quickening new perceptions with Donne-like modernity, place Ted Hughes in line of succession to English literature's Protestant illuminati, and indeed, this volume, learned as it is, comes with no bibliography and no notes, as if it were indeed a sermon of Traherne or a *Pilgrim's Progress*. The forced, autodidact lexicon is interesting, too, because it reproduces one of the dialectical conflicts – one of the steps in Hughes's Tragic Equation, when Rival Brothers, the rational and the irrational protagonists, often literal usurpers of their own flesh and blood (Claudius; Antonio) contend murderously with each other. In these cases, the Boar charges in the form of the villain in the play; the enraged Queen of Hell takes possession of him to destroy the tragic hero. Hughes's exaltation rises to the theme of such Dioscuri, and he allots rationality and irrationality male and female gender respectively, quite according to convention; thus his text, written by himself in the male persona of Adonis, draws on a rebarbative, empirical, scientistic vocabulary to lay claim to the rational brother's legitimacy, while the footnotes explode with the force he identifies, at the very end, as Caliban's, the power of the curse, of the wound, of the darkness, of the irrational brother. (The word 'Equation' itself conceals, under its solid, balanced mien, all kinds of inchoate and turbulent forces, of course.) The new physics might have led, though, to a less dualist model, a language less riven, more 'holistic', no longer turning on this antique stand-off between reason and unreason.

Yet the readings Hughes offers again and again are dazzling; perhaps other people know Shakespeare's poetry as he does, but I've not come across them. His high-wire performance – as he cross-refers, sounds echoes of image and device, takes off with magnificent cadenzas on certain motifs – is never less than enthralling; but at the same time, it partakes of that world of masque that Prospero conjures out of the air, with Ariel's help – not quite an insubstantial pageant, but yes, such stuff as dreams are made on. Because, like those detailed maps that prove all of England has been laid out in pentacles by space visitors, the Goddess of Complete Being cannot exist except as a dream, a moving dream from a fallen world of damage and incompleteness (Hughes might acknowledge this much). More to the point, the book does not succeed in convincing us that she exists in Shakespeare as such a dream. *The Tempest*, far from healing the split and bringing her back, even as a balancing part of an equation, consecrates the masculine order: Miranda is a daughter who has never known a woman, and she is given by her father to the man he chooses for her and lures by his enchantments. In the Masque, when Juno, Iris and Ceres appear, the first and only other women to enter the stage, Venus is explicitly excluded. Meanwhile Sycorax, reviled as a foul witch, a hag, never achieves any kind of release or redemption, nor her son Caliban. Reconciliation for Prospero, yes, a return for Miranda, yes, on her father's terms; but the crowning rescue of the Goddess? Rather, Hughes reveals how Shakespeare, who spliced Hippolytus' rejection of Phaedra's love into the story of Venus and Adonis, has even more firmly banished female eros from the proper order ordained by Prospero; how Shakespeare at the end chose Protestantism, and forswore Mary and merry-making, rewards and fairies.

In the very last pages, Hughes makes the avowal that explains the collapse of the Tragic Equation's sum, as he has worked it out; the 'Goddess', he writes, 'is only a manner of speaking, or of thinking' about 'the totality of this individual's natural, biographical and instinctual life', as opposed to his 'rational ego' – 'this individual' being 'one man'. He goes on, 'The Goddess, *being his own nature*, insists with constant pressure that the fullness of her life be somehow expressed . . .' (my emphasis). Yet Shakespeare has created some of the richest female dramatic characters since Euripides; of course, they partake of his self, but they do not collapse into aspects of the male. In the same way as interpreting the plays as sacred rituals attenuates the moral subtleties of the tragedies, Hughes's psycho-sacralisation of the anima, embodied by Cleopatra, or Hermione, or Imogen, empties the plays of some of their complex, spiritual, inner life, which flows in the sensitivity of individual predicaments and responses. Perceiving overall patterns can finally blind one to the interest of the stitches; questers for Woman tend to mistake or overlook mortal women; Goddesses screen persons from view.

Hughes writes eloquently, towards the end of the book, of the long shade of Dido in the works, from the Players in *Hamlet* to the allusions in *The Tempest* which make Dido kin to Sycorax by Hecate, both of them destroyed, maddened, pagan queens of magic. He suggests that Shakespeare was constantly approaching the story of Dido and Aeneas, of the abandoned wife who kills herself when the hero leaves to fulfil his higher vocation and found Rome, and that in Miranda he resuscitated her, and her happiness with a new Aeneas. Ted Hughes gives an account of Aeneas's soul racked by the memory of the suicide Dido; maybe now, out of his own sensitivity to the boar's charge, out of his own keen experience of its tusks, he could give us his own Dido and Aeneas, in a play.

Maps of Elsewhere

Early maps of Elsewhere showing lands beyond known trade routes, or territories on either side of trodden ways, are inscribed: 'Amazons', 'Dragons', or – 'Cannibals'. Some people today believe in Amazons; and some in dragons, too; but the concept of 'cannibals' arouses much the most complicated responses of assent or dissent.

The cartographers of the Renaissance, following the accounts of wonders in Mandeville and others, imagined the dwellers of unexplored places as fantastic creatures; but fantastic because unknown, rather than the products of fantasy. Now, we know differently, or at least we think we do: Amazons, dragons, and cannibals have been sifted into different categories of reality and history, to be granted different degrees of credence. When Albert Eckhout in 1641 painted a woman of the Tapuya tribe of Brazil with a severed foot in the basket on her back and a severed arm in her hand, was he recording the evidence of his eyes? Was he looking at her in the same way as he scanned the seedpods and rinds of the novel and wondrous fruits he painted to meet the scientific curiosity of his patron, Prince Johan Maurits of Nassau, who had commissioned his work as a record of the Dutch possessions in the 'New World'? Brazilian flora and fauna were consenting subjects, which could be laid out for inspection by the documentary painter of still lifes, but his living subjects, the Indians who appear in the eight magnificent full-length studies now in Copenhagen, may not have posed for the artist – and he may have supplied features from his imagination, while all the while thinking he was faithfully recording actual circumstances. In the case of the Tapuya, their anthropophagy 'formed part of their funeral rites', according to the contemporary observer Zacharias Wagener. Eckhout's composition, showing a cluster of warriors out on a hunt or a raid, positioned on the horizon between the woman's legs, right under her cache-sexe of leaves, while her hound laps between her feet baring its teeth, suggests unmistakably barbarous appetites, a cannibalism of unprincipled assault rather than mourning.

'Cannibal', a corruption of 'Carib', is the customary etymology given for Caliban, the continually reviled native of the isle in Shakespeare's *The Tempest*: the 'salvage and deformed slave', the 'freckled whelp, hag-born', the 'mis-shapen knave', the 'abhorred slave', etc. etc., who learns language from his masters, but can use it only to curse. Caliban, in the essays and poetry of numerous Caribbean writers, has become the emblematic figure of the colonised subject: from Octave Mannoni's seminal essay on the topic ('La psychologie de la colonisation, 1950'), to George Lamming's novel *Water with Berries*, to the revision of Shakespeare's play in Aimé Césaire's *Une Tempête*, in which Caliban takes on the exact fate of a freedom fighter, something of a cross between Joan of Arc and Che Guevara.

Shakespeare does not actually impute cannibalism to his character, and indeed he follows the evidence of the shipwrecked colonists in the Bermudas in 1609 when his Caliban describes how he first helped the new arrivals on the isle to survive, gathering the unfamiliar food and fish for them. Nevertheless, interpreters who have developed Caliban as the scapegoat of white racism have responded to the bitter conflict of the play, in which Caliban is denied human characteristics. Cannibalism is still the commonplace mark of the alien (a Cornish builder, whom I was sitting next to on a plane coming back from Amsterdam, laughed in answer to my comment that I had often been to a village in the south of his county, and remarked, 'Oh, they eat their young down there'); the cannibal is someone who is not you or me, and the border between you and me and all the others is being redrawn all the time, and never more acutely than at this moment of rising migrancy and new nations.

The Dutch have stretched the word *allochtonen* – born elsewhere, the opposite of 'autochthonous', native, homegrown – to include foreigners who are born in Holland but are still perceived as foreign on account of their history, a history often announced by skin colour. In a similar way, English flounders when attempting to describe the 'ethnic minorities', often calling them 'immigrants' when they are second- or even third- or fourth-generation born-in-Britain citizens. It was while I was thinking about these knots and tensions, these gaps and blanks in the social fabric, that I came across a striking article which proposed another origin for Caliban's name.[1]

In 1610, a certain African prince arrived in England; his name was Dederi Iaquoah, and he was about twenty years old and had been put on board the merchant ship *Abigail* in the care of her master, one John Davies, to be taken to England to be christened. Or so the register declares, of the Church of Saint Mildred, Poultry, in the City of London, where the baptism took place on 1 January 1611. The prince's father, the entry says, was 'Caddi-biah, king of the river of Cetras or Cestus in the country of Guinea'. As the writer of the article points out, *The Tempest* was first performed either in the winter of 1611 or soon afterwards, and the

City, with its now vanished theatres – the Rose, the Globe – its numerous parish churches and inns, and its main artery of transport, the Thames plied by watermen, formed the London Shakespeare knew, and he might have heard about this unusual christening (the priest at Saint Mildred, Poultry, certainly thought it warranted a long, circumstantial entry). 'Caddi-biah' might be the long-lost, displaced father of Caliban; the Caliban who, with his last words, seems indeed to offer himself as a kind of catechumen: 'I'll be wise hereafter/ And seek for grace . . .'

Even if the thesis isn't altogether convincing, this account of an African's baptism in seventeenth-century London disturbs many easy notions of the past and upsets specifically received ideas about racial history. Dederi Iaquoah wasn't the only black to be christened in the city of London;[2] around that time there were also children born to Africans in Britain and baptised here. The register of Saint Olave's in Southwark records the ceremony was performed on 19 February 1586 for 'Edward, the son of Reasonable, blackman silkweaver'; and at Saint Benet Fink, 'a man Child called John born of a blackamoor woman & supposed to be the son of John Edwardes, a boarder in the house of William Conradus', was received into the Christian faith on 2 June 1606.

The Church of Saint Mildred, Poultry, where the young prince from Guinea professed his Christianity, was bombed in the last war. I went there to try and recapture the atmosphere of the merchant city in the Elizabethan and Jacobean period and found nothing but the smooth, blind glass and steel of postwar insurance blocks. The disappearance of the buildings has followed the disappearance of the population – the only inhabitants of the dozen parishes that still make up the City of London today are the Bishop and his vicar: at night security men patrol the Square Mile, and technically, they do not live there.* It's hardly surprising, and not really reprehensible, that these transformations should trail forgettings in their wake – including the forgetting of the earliest autochthonous English blacks, who at the same time as they were adopting their host country's religion, living at the hub of its activity, and no doubt adapting in other ways, were still perceived as dwellers in other places, the mapmakers' and playmakers' monsters, amazons and cannibals.

Scraping the earth from this archaeological layer in my own native town has made me realise even more strongly how deep has been the British sense of separateness from its former colonised peoples, and how

---

* The new development of the city has changed this, and there are today around six hundred residents of the square mile.

fallacious; *métissage* has always taken place, from the first contacts, but it has always been denied, and if possible, erased. Prospero turns on Caliban because he attempted to 'violate the honour of my daughter' – Miranda. The settlers did not exactly practise segregation, neither in the early colonies, nor, as it turns out, on home territory. But they strenuously maintained that they did, and in their possessions, the British built the hierarchy of master-servant relations on the fantasy that the races did not mingle. The reverse side of the cannibal fantasy must be the fiction of pure, undiluted autochthony.

Yet there are instances, in our larger Western traditions, which express a different vision. The legend of the doctor saints, Cosmas and Damian, relates how they looked after the sick for no pay, and pioneered many effective medical techniques, including dream diagnosis and transplants. Their most astonishing cure was performed on a young Christian man who was dying of an ulcerated leg; the saints amputated the limb below the knee and sewed on another leg, taken from the corpse of a dead Moor.

The artist Joseph Beuys liked this story, and included the Fra Angelico image of the operation in one of his vitrines; the patchwork patient, the white man with his black leg appealed to his sense of possibilities, his dream of universal reconciliations. The 'miracle' certainly offers an opposing example to the recent episode Rian Malan recounts, when a Boer family discovered that the heart of their father, who had died in an accident, had been transplanted into a black man's body. They complained; they grieved; the story reached the papers, and Rian Malan was sent to cover it. The door was opened by an ordinary enough young woman who was speaking for her family. They wanted the heart back. Rian Malan italicises the sentence, *'They wanted the heart back.'*[3]

The paintings which depict the operation of Saints Cosmas and Damian show them handling severed limbs as they attach the new, healthy, black leg. It's ironical how like traditional cannibals they look, flourishing cut-up bits of human bodies, how they indeed resemble the Tapuya Indian in Eckhout's painting – if you look at the imagery with other people's eyes, if you imagine for a moment that you are related to the Moor whose leg has been donated, not to the young man who is being returned to life; if you think that the saint-doctors are in fact devils from elsewhere.

1992

Shakespeare's Caliban

Review of Alden T. Vaughan and Virginia Mason Vaughan, Shakespeare's Caliban: A Cultural History

One of the many originals proposed for the character of Caliban seems to have been a Yeti of some kind, 'a Big-Foot' or 'Patagon' as Magellan is meant to have exclaimed when he first set eyes on the giant tribe of Tehuelche Indians. Bruce Chatwin's *In Patagonia* tells the story, and having checked the crew-lists and finding no one in Magellan's crew who could have exclaimed in the necessary Greek, he suggests instead that Magellan had a copy in his cabin of *Primaleon of Greece*, one of the romances Cervantes would later spoof, in which the eponymous hero does doughty battle with the Grand Patagon, a dog-headed, hooved, lascivious monster gifted with human intelligence. With the help of two pet lions, the knight brings him back as an added item in his sovereign's cabinet of curiosities. Queen Gridonia rejects the creature as 'nothing but a devil'; the princess, however, strokes him and makes much of him, and teaches him her language as Miranda once did, or so Caliban, that 'puppy-headed monster', tells us in wounded anger, during the course of *The Tempest*. There was an English translation by Anthony Munday that Shakespeare could have read.

The Patagonia of chivalric imagination figures, however, as only one of several birthplaces for Shakespeare's Caliban. The word 'cannibal' seems to have originated with the people of 'Caribia', in whom Columbus recognised the famed anthropophagi of myth. Like the gold which he was certain was always round the next headland, it was always the tribe over the next ridge who were feasting on human flesh. The invisibility of the practice did not prevent De Bry, in Holland, from illustrating barbecued banquets of limbs in painstaking and realistic detail, and rather more recently, in a part work published to accompany a BBC series on the Empire, the introductory note states, 'when the British first arrived . . . the necklace of lush tropical islands . . . was still largely the preserve of cannibals'. This was written in 1972 – it is really only in the past decade that historical study has established the crucial operations of fantasy in the story of the Caribbean conquest.

Frank Kermode, in the Arden edition of 1954, set out vigorously how Shakespeare was exploring in *The Tempest* ideas about natural man stirred by the voyages to the Caribbean and the first English colonial adventures. Like the Indians whom buccaneers treated with– Roger North in Guyana and Ralegh in Virginia – Caliban shows the new arrivals, Prospero and his daughter, 'the wonders of the isle'; later, he promises to do the same for Stephano and Trinculo. Despite the associations of Caliban's name, Shakespeare seems to have been influenced more by Montaigne's defence of the Indians than by conquistador or planter attitudes. He doesn't represent his 'monster' as a consumer of human flesh at all, but rather of 'pig-nuts' and 'filberts' on an island which, like Montaigne's Mexico and Peru, was 'all naked, simply-pure, in Natures lappe'. In the figure of the native slave, ruled and punished by Prospero, there again sounds an echo of Montaigne's appeal to civilise rather than kill: 'yet have we not whipped and submitted the same [infant world] unto our discipline, or schooled it by the advantage of our valour or naturall forces'. *The Tempest* explores the possibilities of just such 'education', and part of its contemporary fascination springs from its open-eyed understanding of the approach's limits.

The authors of *Shakespeare's Caliban* favour another origin for Caliban's now mythic name: 'cauliban', the Romany word for 'black'. They argue that in Jacobean society, gypsies were abused in much the same way as Caliban is in the play, and were associated with pagan gods (like Setebos, Caliban's deity) and with canting (the magic language, incomprehensible to Prospero and Miranda, which Caliban and his mother speak before their arrival). Kermode also covers this ground, and the Vaughans cannot add much persuasive material – oddly, given the later history of *Tempest* studies. Caliban does not figure as especially black in the play, unlike Othello (he's called 'a freckled whelp', for instance, at one point, not a description of the dark-skinned gypsy the Vaughans propose).

Alden T. Vaughan specialises in seventeenth-century history, and his studies include *American Genesis: Captain John Smith and the founding of Virginia*. This expertise brightens the pages which discuss Caliban in the context of Elizabethan England's acquaintance with Indians – Trinculo immediately thinks of taking Caliban home to put him on show as a freak. 'Kidnapped Indians' were frequent 'London Showpieces', so much so, apparently, that the Vaughans declare that 'by 1611 American natives were part of every English man and woman's common coinage'. They go on to develop the perception of the Indian by comparison with the wildman or wodewose, the pagan spirit of nature and woodland, the Robin Goodfellow, or Puckish imp who figures in pageants of the time, usually making obeisance to the monarch and acknowledging the falsehood of his creed, as Caliban seems to do in his closing lines.

The co-author, Virginia Mason Vaughan, has published an annotated bibliography on *Othello*, and her skills too are marked in this volume. Though at times the inventory feels tired, some remarkable *Tempest* lore has been unearthed. Dryden collaborated with Davenant on the botched melodrama which passed for *The Tempest* from 1667 onwards (until Macready at last returned to the First Folio in 1838), and in an essay he made much of Caliban's descent from the union of 'an incubus and a sorceress': 'He has all the malice of a witch and of a devil ... gluttony, sloth and lust are manifest; the dejectedness of a slave is likewise given him ... his language is as hobgoblin as his person.' Dryden concluded by affirming the utter singularity of the monster: 'in all things he is distinguished from other mortals'. However, in his version of the play, he did not put such a safe distance between Caliban and his fellow-humans, for he gives him Sycorax for a sister whom he tries to pander to the new arrivals. Today, it is rather Caliban's universal mirroring of humanity that dominates understanding of him; Auden, in *The Sea and the Mirror*, gives him voice as the beast inside us all whose face in the mirror we do not wish to see.

The corresponding, rich history of Latin American interpretations begins, surprisingly, with the Uruguayan José Enrique Rodó's essay, 'Ariel', of 1900, which identifies the monster Caliban with the uncouth, violent and rapacious 'Yanqui' tyrant – a most discordant view today, when the sympathy between Caliban the slave and the colonised subjects of empires, British, Spanish or American, has inspired so much polemic and poetry. Indeed, it is difficult from the vantage of the quincentennial to grasp Rodó's point of view, though, at the time, his stand against North American materialism and utilitarianism was profoundly influential. It was the essay of a French colonial doctor, Octave Mannoni, which transfigured the base and contemptible slave into a tragic symbol of the alien and the oppressed; Fernandez Retamar, in a subsequent impassioned apology, focused on Caliban's blackness. These writings mark the beginning of the contemporary Caliban, who curses and dreams through many, varied and powerful metempsychoses, in the work of Aimé Césaire, George Lamming, Derek Walcott, Kamau Brathwaite, Gloria Naylor, David Dabydeen. Caliban has passed into the common mythological lexicon; *The Tempest* offers itself as a pattern book, from which to cut new clothing, like the stories of Oedipus or Medea, or, in the past, of the crusader hero Orlando/Roland.

Shakespeare's Caliban is really a misnomer – only part of this book probes the playwright's meanings. It is more concerned with other men's Calibans (there have been fewer women interpreters), but the authors seem temperamentally ill at ease with symbolic and mythical hermeneutics. The material is organised with a cataloguer's sense of taxonomy, so that the accounts of stage design and visual representation follow separately after the sections on historical context and interpretative changes. Puzzlingly, artists do not seem to have absorbed the same influences the authors describe; Caliban often looks like a stranded manatee, or even an orang-utan (F. R. Benson's wife commented he looked 'half monkey, half coco-nut' in the part), but rarely like Puck, or the last of the Mohicans, or even the monster Patagon. The authors have also been unfortunate that so much lively argument has surrounded the subject of colonial encounters this year; they seem to have decided to retreat from the terrain staked out by Todorov's *L'Amérique, ou La Conquête de l'autre* and Stephen Greenblatt's remarkable essays on *The Tempest* as well as on Columbus, but they needed to give a much fuller account of such recent thinking. Their book tends to be diligent and a bit insipid; they have patiently carried the logs of Caliban lore into large, neat piles, but more like Ferdinand than Caliban, they haven't explored its language enough, either to pray or to curse, sing or woo.

1992

The Silence of Sycorax

Talk given at the Free University of Berlin

After reading about the conquest of the Indies, Montaigne wrote, 'So many goodly cities ransacked and razed, so many nations destroyed and made desolate, so many infinite millions of harmless people of all sexes, states and ages massacred, ravaged and put to the sword. And the richest, the fairest, and the best part of the world topsy-turvied, ruined and defaced for the traffic in pearls and pepper.' He was writing almost a hundred years before the first English and French settlements took place in the Caribbean, and he is referring principally to the dominions of the Spanish and the Dutch, before the market in sugar surpassed the trade in pearls and pepper, spices and indigo, and became intertwined with the history of slavery.

Ibsen once wrote that a writer's task was 'to sit in judgment on himself'. I have taken this as a banner, and it so happens that I was dealt a hand of issues worth examining, demanding some kind of judgment. In my novel *The Lost Father*, I looked at the political and social nexus of circumstances on my mother's side, especially her upbringing in southern Italy during the Fascist years. It was a logical move to pass on to my father's side, and his family's history in the West Indies. The power of the British empire has gone, but its effects have hardly disappeared. The exile that began with the dislocation of lives there, the diaspora which scattered British men and women overseas to the four points and has brought so many back from those countries, has become a common contemporary condition and a symbol of our times: flight, exile, asylum, and in Rushdie's phrase, imaginary homelands. History doesn't happen only in the past, contrary to what people think. It goes on being made in the present. And actions only contribute in part to its making, it seems. Words, storytelling, remembering, also play their part in history as it is made. As someone says in *The Tempest*, 'The past is prologue.'

Memory is two-faced, and the writer who works with memories, like me, is stuck in a dilemma. Memories can help, they can gild the past, they can ease the story, they can shape it as solace, as comfort. But they can also reveal what was concealed, and match experience with the tale more closely. In the long run, it seems to me, the disturbing myth or story can sometimes be of more help than the consolatory fable, the story intended to soothe and offer solace.

With *Indigo* I chose to rework *The Tempest*, a *locus classicus* in current re-visionings of imperial encounters; I felt presumptuous in doing so, but my reason – my excuse – was that it seems to me that if people who are descended from the wrong side, as it were – the colonial side – don't examine what that inheritance holds, that if speaking is left to those who are justified by oppression in the past and in memory, then in one sense one part of the story has been written out of it. It is as important to tell the ugly story as it is to tell the reparatory tale. To sit in judgment on oneself, perhaps, not only on others.

At a certain moment, in a kind of blaze, I realised that the First Folio of Shakespeare's plays, in which *The Tempest* appears first, was published in 1623, while the royal charter instituting an Englishman as the first Governor of the West Indies was granted by the King, Charles I, two years later, in 1625. A copy of the magnificent manuscript hung over the mantelpiece at home, and as a rebellious child of the Sixties, I used to be furious with my father when he boasted of this ancestry, and used to say, 'We come from a long line of pioneers.' One's childhood creates however these points of reference, and the history nagged at me and my sister Laura, and we wanted to know more. I began researching the story, and *Indigo* is the result.

Indigo is about migrations, geographical, colonial, imaginary and emotional. It's about crossing barriers, and about erecting them, about being foreign and strange in the eyes of someone else, and about undoing this strangeness in order to find what can be held in common. It's an attempt in a work of fiction to migrate itself through fantasy into lives that have been effaced and lost. I called the novel *Indigo*, with a subtitle, 'Mapping the Waters', because I wanted to introduce a pattern of many colours, and suggest their mingling. The light I was trying to shed on history was made up as light is from strands of different colours – themes and moods, not races or flesh tones. The book moves through indigo to maroon, the point being that indigo sounds related to 'indigenous' (though this isn't so) and is the original colour used in 'blueprints'. It's the colour of the ink used for the first pattern. I wanted the novel to look for the story or scheme that lay beneath the visible layers. That is not to suggest that an original truth exists which could be retrieved and re-traced. But there is always another story beyond the story, there is always as it were another deeper blueprint. I was writing about change from the beginnings, as far as they could be disclosed.

The idea of maroon, with which the books ends, again plays on words that have no etymological connection in fact. But the name of the colour echoes the word maroon, or escaped slave, which comes from French *marroner*, to run away. The maroons, in Jamaica and elsewhere, struggled bitterly against the colonial powers and established their own enclaves and economy. The image of these rebels haunts Caribbean history as the lost hope of the past, and by analogy has become the imaginative symbol of the fugitive in our time, because the maroon can also run away to an imaginary homeland; he crosses borders and breaks out of boundaries and inhabits a place of elective affinities.

I was also writing a study of fairy tales, *From the Beast to the Blonde*, and I constructed *Indigo* as a classic fairy tale. I wanted it to speak in the way fairy tales do, for hope, against despair. But at the same time, as I argued in *Beast*, I wanted not to scant the difficulties. In a fairy tale, the whole space of the narrative is taken up with ordeals. It's only the end – usually perfunctorily handled – which promises change. Most of the foreground is crammed with cruelty and horror, with sufferings and problems. Besides this, I also wanted *Indigo* to catch another theme from fairy tale, and to pay tribute to the oral culture of women, to all pre-Gutenberg female voices, including the storytellers of the Caribbean.

When I was in Trinidad I was delighted to find in a gallery there a sculpture, a wooden carving of a beautiful woman, slender and swaying with a large hat on her head, clearly dressed in her best to go to church, with a flounced skirt. She was lifting this skirt and one of her feet was a cloven hoof. This figure of Caribbean lore is called *la Diablesse*, the she-devil; she had been carved by Louise Kimmé, a German-born artist living in Tobago. *La Diablesse* is a powerful and familiar predator in local storytelling, associated with spirits from European folklore who similarly steal children, seduce men and prowl in the night. The idea of the deformed foot of such devilish enchantresses was extremely important to me in *From the Beast to the Blonde*, as the distinguishing mark of the storyteller. For the storyteller often occupies a position both inside the society to which she belongs, and outside, sequestered from it. She understands her own world, having an inside track on what is permitted and what is not permitted, and the stories she tells often illuminate for her hearers what lies ahead and the ways they can manoeuvre in order to survive. 'Cinderella' is a cautionary tale about how to cope with common difficulties – neglectful stepmother, jealous sisters, for example.

But this insider is also at the same time very often positioned as an outsider, in sympathy with characters in the fairy tales who are themselves outsiders. The classic structure presents someone who is stigmatised – a beast, a ragged girl, an orphan, the runt, the youngest child, a beggar-woman who is taken for a witch and reviled – and then offers the hope that they will somehow arrive at belonging, become included, achieve insider status too, without forfeiting their intrinsic self, their own personality. The beast is changed into a human being, but that doesn't mean he has to relinquish who he is, but rather that he becomes recognised as belonging to the human species. A transformation has taken place. This ideal of metamorphosis lies at the heart of the hope fairy tales present. So as I say, I was delighted when I found in the Caribbean the figure of this ambivalent enchantress who lives in both worlds, because she corresponds to the storyteller Serafine in *Indigo*, who is a *conteuse* in the Caribbean tradition. She has many precursors: she owes a great deal to Jean Rhys's Christophene, the nurse in *Wide Sargasso Sea*: there's even an echo of the name.

Serafine teaches my Miranda how to pass, how to survive, how not to attract attention and punishment. On the one hand, a storyteller will mould listeners to conform, but on the other hand she will try to open up possibilities by calling the rules into question. The relationship between Serafine and Miranda operates in this doubled way: Serafine is a captive of the colonial world and there is no other way she could be – in those times, at the beginning of the twentieth century – but at the same time her stories open up alternatives for Miranda. So Miranda is brought up by Serafine to resist, even though the surface messages of the stories she tells her are conformist; covertly, Miranda learns otherwise. It's also not possible to allot women a smooth slot in the division of roles. The mythical part women have played in the inauguration of societies, of new histories and new dynasties demands a fresh look at their historical role as well.

The Tempest is central to *Indigo* not only because it's a shared area of contest around the issues of empire, but precisely because it's a play in which the voices of women aren't heard. Many Shakespeare plays feature women as marginal presences only: *Henry V*, *Coriolanus*, to name two. But in *The Tempest*, Miranda is a particular and singular case: a girl who has never consciously known another person of her own sex. She says she can just remember her mother's face, and then asks Prospero, 'Did I not have some women that attended me?' Otherwise, the play features the three goddesses of the masque, and Ariel who shifts gender (and is sometimes played by an actress). So the play conjures various divine and fairy-like feminine apparitions. But – and this is of course the point – there is an overarching female presence in the play who never appears on stage: Sycorax. Sycorax, who is the original ruler of the island before Prospero's arrival. The political thrust of the plot, which meshes with concerns in several other plays, aims at reinstating a rule of order in the male line when a threat from female unruliness and heterodoxy has occurred. This tendency is reflected in other pieces of the story: the marriage in Tunis in which Claribel is given to a king; the betrothal of Ferdinand and Miranda through Prospero's enchantments so that his domain will also be established in the male line. The desired restoration of order after the storm will take place through male governance.

Ted Hughes, in his eccentric but perceptive study *Shakespeare and the Goddess of Complete Being*, argues that *The Tempest* conveys the relief felt in the whole country at the accession to the throne of a king, James I, after the long anomalous female reign of Elizabeth. The Virgin Queen has been replaced by a true Protestant heir. Elizabeth's pageantry of virginity and sovereignty was steeped in Catholic symbolism, and this rendered her rule uncomfortable, Hughes writes, for a population who had suffered the trauma of mass conversion to Protestantism. Elizabeth stirred memories of the old Church of Rome, and of the cult of the Virgin Mary, and her symbols destabilised efforts to create an image of Protestant authority. It's a thoughtful suggestion, and Hughes gives numerous examples of Shakespeare's distaste for female authority, and especially of independent, unmarried female rule. Sycorax is never spoken of as married; Caliban's alleged father, the pagan god Setebos, does not exactly summon up a picture of family stability.

One of the necessary conditions of subordinating women is to silence them. In a sense, the absence of Sycorax from the stage gives the most convincing signal that her power has passed. Silence plays an important role in Shakespeare's dramatic technique: think of Cordelia, in the first scene of *King Lear*. In their filial relationship to their fathers, Cordelia and Miranda almost form a diptych. 'Your story put a heaviness on me,' says Miranda after listening to Prospero for several dozen lines and then falls asleep. She is enchanted by his story, and drifts off into the plot that is of his devising. From then on we only see her move in obedience to his fantasy, through the enchantments that her father has conjured.

I wanted to revisit *The Tempest* from the point of view of these hidden and silenced characters. I wanted Miranda to extricate herself from her father's plot. My Miranda is very muddled, but with the help of Serafine she has glimmerings. Serafine has given her fables to use as her path through the forest, as the crumbs on the ground. I wanted also to reverse the drift of the values, and to restore the 'foul witch Sycorax' and her 'freckled whelp' to power, value and presence in my novel. I wanted Sycorax in the foreground; Ariel becomes her daughter. When Shakespeare took Medea's speech from Ovid and gave it to Prospero, he was silencing the enchantress, swallowing words celebrated in the chronicles of female magic. I took them back, and rewrote them for Sycorax.

The cultural critic Nikos Papastergiadis has written about the concept of re-visioning, that 're implies the emergence of an alternative story . . . [it] is an affirmative gesture, it holds out the promise of a new form of power, not necessarily one that will expose the failure of the past and offer itself as a model of the future, nothing as utopian as that, but as a supplement to the conventional. But *who* can claim this position?'

Who indeed? I feel that acutely. But in a sense, the business of writing demands that one should stop being self-conscious about the work of storytelling.

And so I wrote.

1996

Its Own Dark Styx: Caryl Phillips

Review of The Nature of Blood

'Memory says: Want to do right? Don't count on me.' So writes Adrienne rich in a poem from *An Atlas of the Difficult World*, opening an unpunctuated sequence of horrors: lynchings, pogroms, Auschwitz, Berlin, Palestine, Israel:

> I am accused of child death   of drinking blood
> . . .
> there is spit on my sleeve   there are phone calls in the night . . .

She concludes: 'I am standing here in your poem   unsatisfied/ lifting my smoky mirror.' Memory's smoky mirror, like the witch's crystal, or the burning glass of the Aztec god who demands human sacrifice, has become the prime instrument turned on history by several of the most powerful recent or contemporary novelists. In its shadowed and unreliable depths Toni Morrison, Kazuo Ishiguro, Leonardo Sciascia, Alejo Carpentier have searched out their material, reflections of ourselves; and from *A State of Independence*, his second novel (1986), to *The Nature of Blood*, Caryl Phillips, too, has been scrying for glimpses of troubled histories.

The Nature of Blood opens in a Displaced Persons camp in Cyprus after the Second World War, where the British are holding Jews before releasing them in quotas to travel to Palestine; a boy asks, emblematically, the name of the country to which they will be going. Israel, replies the doctor-soldier, Stephan Stern. Dr Stern threads through the story like the implied key of a sonata; for Phillips's construction is musical, and his predominant motif – of an unsparing minor starkness – is provided by Eva, Stern's niece. In her parallel story, she's liberated from another (Nazi) camp; having lost her much loved sister Margo and her parents somewhere unnamed in Germany, she goes mad in the aftermath. The novel's phrasing strikes echoes across different movements, as the several stories and characters twist through time and place, until Phillips brings the various themes together in a beautifully poised, tender and melancholy coda. The Holocaust and its victims (among whom Phillips counts the survivors: this is a novel in which no one escapes damage) occupy the foreground, but it is Israel as the dream of the Promised Land that provides the book's tragic core. For Israel, in the sense of home, cannot exist except as yearning. However clearly it appears on the atlas, it eludes the explorer and the refugee alike in the restless involutions of the mind's desires. In the closing scene, a nurse from Ethiopia, one of the Falasha invited 'home' to Israel, meets Dr Stern at a dancing club; they make love, the single act that attaches; she can't find work in racist Israel; he has become a lonely old pensioner, a stranger without moorings in the country he gave up wife, child and birthplace to create.

Both in its contemporary theme – the desolate condition of diaspora and the impossibility of a resolution – and in its diachronic approach, *The Nature of Blood* extends the methods Phillips developed in *Cambridge* and *Crossing the River*, his most recent novels. Both of those, however, explored black identity directly. *Cambridge* returned to the Caribbean, to an eighteenth-century slave plantation, where a young woman from England voyages to set her father's estate in order. Phillips tells much of the story in her words, unflinchingly voicing the plantocracy's assumptions of racial superiority, and setting up against them the figure of Cambridge, the dignified, literate, ironically named slave who unsettles her received ideas. It is as if Sir Bertram had died and Fanny Price had slipped through the gates of Mansfield Park to see for herself what the family's fortunes entailed in Antigua: Phillips drew for his portraits on the literature of abolition, including such powerful witnesses as Olaudah Equiano, who wrote one of the most eloquent and detailed accounts of life as a slave. *Crossing the River*, Phillips's last novel, and his most intense to date, took up an even less familiar corner of black history, and explored the failure of the American experiment in Liberia, the West African nation that 'enlightened' citizens sent freed slaves to settle after the Civil War.

He has distinguished himself in these three works by his refusal of pieties. There's a quiet dourness and cussedness in his handling of the material; he pits himself against any kind of received wisdom, including the prevailing feel-good tendency of some black American writing. His ironies work at everyone's expense: no one, black, white, patrician, serf, is spared. He is a sympathetic impersonator of women (Eva in *The Nature of Blood*) and white idealists (Stern the well-meaning terrorist/freedom fighter), but his pitiless irony projects their self-deceptions, too: Eva, befriended in the camp by an English soldier who gives her chocolate, follows him to London after the war, where he turns out to be married. He jilts her, abandoning her in a pub with a gin and tonic. But before we can align ourselves against this betrayal, Phillips discloses, in one of his fingertip asides, that in her dazed condition, she had forged the letter of invitation from him with which she arrived in the country.

By setting out, in *Cambridge*, the beliefs that underpinned slavery, by playing parts far beyond the borders of his own autobiography, by choosing to write about the Holocaust when he is not Jewish, Caryl Phillips is making a political statement, angled strongly at the United States, where he lives and teaches for half the year. But he's not simply flouting the parish boundaries of PC, in which only a woman may write as a woman, or only a black may address the themes of race. Phillips's contumaciousness arises from a more philosophical view of identity, which his fictions propose in their ventriloquism and polyphony, without assistance from the authorial voice. Much current writing takes up similar issues, but it is dominated by the confessional or advocacy mode, reflections of America's legal and religious culture. Hilton Als's recent essays, *The Women*, Henry Louis Gates's *Colored People*, the reportage of Keith Richburg in *Out of America: A Black Man Confronts Africa* square up to the way in which the black individual is the perceived representative of his race, and of 'being black'; the writers fight against it, plead furiously as they realign the coordinates and propose re-evaluations (for example, Ebonix, or black street slang). Phillips sets aside this direct mode of address in order to avoid group labelling and the corral of designated racial character. The regulation of difference, *The Nature of Blood* seems to tell us, has excited more hatred and bloodshed than the weaving and binding of societies according to elective affinities between persons. The blurb on the jacket – and authors are routinely asked to provide this nowadays – says: 'What emerges through these inextricably linked stories is the realisation not only of how we define ourselves but also, shockingly, that we sometimes determine who we are by destroying others.'

Questions of national place, of roots, of where one belongs, depend on psychic identifications: where hostility and contempt are projected, there fear springs. Conversely, affinities are elected where sympathy rises, where love happens. Narrative, when it throws its voice, can dissolve hatreds by deepening understanding: *The Persians*, in which Aeschylus dramatises the terrible grief of the enemy Xerxes' mother, represents an early instance of this potential.

In pursuit of this possibility, Phillips contrasts in *The Nature of Blood* two stories taken from the past and plaits them into his Holocaust theme: a blood libel occurring in the small town of Portobuffole near Venice in 1480 and the story of Othello, the African general who, according to a glancing reference in the sixteenth-century Venetian drama that inspired Shakespeare, served the Serenissima and thanks to his 'good qualities' won the love of one of the Republic's most nobly born daughters. With his love of helical structures, Phillips twists together the story of a fair-haired child beggar's disappearance and the subsequent trial, torture and execution of a group of Jews charged with his sacrifice; his Othello crosses into this world when he enters the ghetto – that stifling, overcrowded, indeed concentrated city within the city – in search of a scribe who will write a love letter to Desdemona for him. Labelling is libelling; only personal contact can efface the characteristics attributed to groups: Desdemona's father reacts with furious bigotry to his daughter's choice, but she is steadfast; Dr Stern, looking at the colour of the nurse Malka's skin as she sleeps beside him, sees her as someone who has made him a belated gift, not as a representative of her Otherness, her tribe, her race.

The choice of Othello leads to some richly worked passages on Venetian courtship rituals, on the lore of gondolas, on oligarchical banqueting, as well as on the harsh expediency of the Republic's politics. But Shakespeare's tragedy necessarily throws its long shadow over the steadfast love that grows between Desdemona and the older stranger. Phillips has decided not to trace their story to its conclusion, nor to revise it. Given the harshness of the novel's general music, the reader cannot dare hope for a happy ending, though the couple are last seen in Rhodes feasting. Two brief passages, in an external, anonymous voice, then interpellate Othello:

And so you shadow her every move, attend to her every whim, like the black Uncle Tom that you are. Fighting the white man's war for him/ . . . The republic's grinning Satchmo hoisting his sword like a trumpet/ You tuck your black skin away beneath their epauletted uniform, appropriate their words (*Rude am I in speech*), their manners, worry your nappy woollen head with anxiety about learning their ways . . . O strong man, O strong arm, O valiant soldier, O weak man. You are lost, a sad black man, first in a long line of so-called achievers who are too weak to yoke their past with their present; too naive to insist on both; too foolish to realise that to supplant one with the other can only lead to catastrophe. Go ahead, peer on her alabaster skin . . . My friend, the Yoruba have a saying: the river that does not know its own source will dry up. You will do well to remember this.

This passage, and another that comes soon after it and closes, 'Brother, jump from her bed and fly away home', are hard to interpret, and in their apparently direct and rootsy Afrocentrism, run counter to the disillusion recorded by Phillips as far back as *A State of Independence*, in which his protagonist returns to St Kitts, the island where Phillips himself was born, tries to rejoin the society of his extended family, but fails. The taunting of Othello by this unanchored late twentieth-century voice is disruptive in a book whose title implies, surely, that blood of its nature is common. Yet the discomfort it produces reintegrates itself into the novel, which refuses comfort from any source; these cries from outside the narrative express Phillips's sense of the futility of his general enterprise as he tries to locate homelands outside the formal geography of the difficult world. Novelists can't be shut out of exclusion zones, but novels, it turns out, can't be charters for newfoundlands.

There is, however, another clue to the way Phillips sees this existential and perpetual displacement: his prose. He belongs to the current school of ironists who button their lip; his sentences mimic the histories he's excavating: indecipherable fragments are picked out of the mud in which they were buried and handed over to be pieced together, making the reader work to read them. (We are only allowed to suspect that his Dr Stern is the Stern of the Stern Gang and that Anne Frank haunts Eva's sister's story.) This is also Ishiguro's unemphatic method and, to some extent, Graham Swift's, and it could not be more different from Rushdie's, or Angela Carter's: they are baroque ironists, for whom the interest swirls and flares on the mobile and sumptuous surface of the prose. Ishiguro and Phillips are elliptical encrypters: what is happening is not what you see, but what you can't see, until you adjust your perception – Wittgenstein's duck/rabbit. Both writers perform quasi-autistically as they draw the rabbit and make the duck at the same time. Phillips's storytelling manner is flat, his sentences short and bare of ornament; the rhetorical finesse exists entirely in the mimicry of voices (as it does in Graham Swift and Ishiguro). How this reflects – and indeed extends – his inquiry into history and belonging can be seen in the effect of paralysis that the flatness creates. History itself – in this book the Holocaust, in the earlier novels other great themes, slavery, emancipation, utopias – gives up its evidence grudgingly: a damaged child in a case-study whose rare and enigmatic utterances must be carefully collected and examined and pressed to yield meaning, which often enough they stubbornly refuse. The lacunae between them open, but meanings hide.

The temperature of this latest novel runs a little low. The several lost lives and loves that crowd the banks of its own dark Styx are too numerous to bind the reader emotionally in the way his three dominant protagonists did in *Crossing the River*. The effect is a little remote, the method a little schematic, and here and there the research still pokes through the extreme reticence. But in a blur that itself reflects lost history, the maimed subjects of events – Eva maddened by surviving her sister and the camps, Dr Stern desolate in Zion, the murdered Jews of Renaissance Venice, Othello travelling ineluctably towards Iago, the novel's population of exiles and immigrants, so many of the undone and unbelonging – appear in the cracks that fissure the clouded mirror Caryl Phillips is holding up as he stubbornly wills memory to articulate something we can maybe count on, in spite of everything.

1997

Castaway on the Ocean of Story

Lecture given at the Deutsche-Gesellschaft Shakespeare Conference, Weimar

Metamorphic lives, resurrected texts

Magic and metamorphosis suffuse contemporary fiction: a phenomenal translation has taken place, bearing books governed by mythological plots and psychology to thousands, perhaps millions of adult readers – some of these are written originally for children, but have crossed over, as the saying goes, to be avidly consumed by adults as well. J. K. Rowling's *Harry Potter* series and Philip Pullman's *His Dark Materials* trilogy have both been given new, sophisticated jacket designs and new prices to attract older readers. Their passage has been magnetised, I believe, by the longer-established success of magical psychology in acclaimed works of contemporary literature, such as the novels of Toni Morrison and Margaret Atwood. In works such as *Beloved* and *Paradise*, or, in Atwood's œuvre, *The Robber Bride* and *Alias Grace*, supernatural devices propel the action: the protagonists are spellbound, haunted, possessed – enchanted. Dreams of various kinds deepen the characters' sense of themselves and their destinies: from prophetic warnings to injunctions from spirits visiting from elsewhere. Such states of consciousness, which occur in classical mythology and were explored of course by Shakespeare, are returning within a new spectrum of psychological meanings. Many effects of enchantment strip agency from the heroes and heroines and substitute other powers as motive forces, and while there are some voluntary shape-shifters in classical myth, notably the Olympians in pursuit of their lusts, on the whole, metamorphosis does not take place at will. A sudden, profound, often ineluctable transformation of outer shape offers a last resort, to escape a worse fate, or to inaugurate a new era.

Shakespeare drew on the magical and metamorphic tradition in the late plays especially, where he pieced and patched many different motifs and instances, with Ovid's *Metamorphoses* and Apuleius' *The Golden Ass* threading bright strands throughout the fabric. His polychromy – at the level of language of course and of psychology and plot – offers a reassuring vindication of romance and mythological devices to someone writing fiction today, such as myself. Shakespeare's late manner in the telling of stories, depicting character, handling of time, dealing with verisimilitude and fantastical improbabilities has provided a continual resource for a heterogeneous group of writers – novelists, poets and dramatists – in many parts of the world.

Magic, being a compact between practitioner and client, requires an audience for its accomplice; it depends on the consent of the spectator, on that 'willing suspension of disbelief' Coleridge famously invoked, and does not possess inherent, stable meaning. The 'aery nothing' and 'insubstantial pageants' of Shakespearean enchanters produce different resonances with different audiences at different times and express different relations to the unknown and the unknowable.

With regard to re-visioning the metamorphic tradition, it is curious that frequently a story that is very well known has no source extant that is in any way expansive or detailed; for example, when I wanted to look at the story of Leda and the Swan, in relation to my heroine, Leto, I went straight away to Ovid's *Metamorphoses*, and checked the index. Offhand, I couldn't remember reading the story in Ovid, and then I did indeed find that there is only one line given to it: 'She [Arachne] made Leda lie down under the swan's wings.'[1] The laconic allusion occurs in the course of the extended description of Arachne's tapestry and the crimes of the heavenly gods, which she defiantly embroiders there. Her pride and insolence in this respect bring down punishment on her head, and Minerva turns her into a spider.

But the elusiveness of Leda's full story isn't uncommon in textual embroidery: Snow White, for example, can't really be pinned to a particular source, and claims of discovering such origins reveal the mythological hunger for stable genealogies – something that can never be appeased. (With regard to *Cymbeline*, Snow White resonates strongly: it's a play in which the Queen – Imogen's stepmother – is explicitly described as very beautiful, and schemes against her. In her very first speech, she alludes to 'the slander of most stepmothers' and hastens to reassure Imogen that she will not act accordingly. It also seems to me the two rustic boys, so eager and so doughty, with Imogen as Fidele keeping house for them in the cave, oddly foreshadow the singing dwarfs of Disney's famous, inaugural cartoon!)

But to return to the vanishing sources of famous stories: an indeterminate and shapeless legacy of imaginary and anonymous fictions offers us a common ocean of stories, as it is called in a very early Indian collection (one of the very first such vehicles is called 'The Ocean of Story' – a phrase Salman Rushdie adapted for his fable, *Haroun and the Sea of Stories*).[2] We swim, float or navigate this ocean of stories all the time in our daily lives, even in today's world in which people constantly criticise the mass media and television for impoverishing the culture. In fact the mass media, television, game shows, video games, and every kind of popular entertainment, navigate this same element. There are many mythological allusions, narrative references, and thematic and structural similarities between the most popular forms of storytelling and the ancient myths.

The Czech poet Miroslav Holub compared writing to the raising of Jairus's daughter: in the New Testament, Jairus comes out of his house and calls out to Jesus to help him for his twelve-year-old daughter is dying; when Jesus goes into the house, she has in fact already died. But he comes out again saying that she's merely sleeping. He has resurrected her. What Holub meant was that literature is always a resurrected body, or a body that is continuously being resurrected. Its existence, he writes, lies in its metamorphoses.

This word 'metamorphosis' is key to the practice of rewriting and re-visioning ancient and traditional story material: not only because the practice itself is of course a metamorphic practice, transforming the text or stories that it adopts. Contemporary writers are grasping the body of classical texts, like Ted Hughes in his *Tales from Ovid*, and throwing their clay into a new shape. These translations are variations, interpretations of the original Ovidian stories, but full of departures from the original, in content, tone, and versification. (In an earlier incarnation, the practice was called imitation, rather than translation; Robert Lowell, taking a similar path in the Sixties, fell back on the old term, and actually called his translations *Imitations*.)

Metamorphosis thus takes over the texts themselves. Rewritings stretch their authority into other writers' imaginations and over their work; they glimmer through the meshes of the translations; alternatively, you could put the matter the other way round, and say that new treatments abrogate the authority of the forerunner, that the new author usurps and seizes his or her textual progenitor as the metamorphic process takes hold: Seamus Heaney causes Sophocles to speak of Ireland, in his version of *Philoctetes*; Philip Pullman overturns Milton and Blake's visions of human nature's fallen state. Both embody the disruptive violence of classical metamorphosis, but in synergetic combination with the organicity that Ovid, for one, also hymns in his Pythagorean view of all things changing continually and nothing dying.

SCATTERING THE SELF

Metamorphosis also infuses the actual subject matter of stories, their theme and drama. Such myths are not only about change, but also about magical change, change that is supernatural or preternatural. There's a difference, because supernatural change is caused by some divine agency that could be Fate or the gods, but preternatural change takes place within the possibilities of Nature, according to Ovid's proclaimed philosophy, as when a young woman turns into a spring or a tree (Arethusa, Daphne, Myrrha), or some living creature turns into stone (Niobe becomes a mountain).

If the themes of the stories are metamorphic, so are their effects. Borrowings take possession of the borrower: it's a psychological as well as a material translation. Ideas of persons, and personhood, have been transformed by cross-cultural narrative exchanges, as I argue in my book *Fantastic Metamorphoses, Other Worlds: Ways of Telling the Self.* The encounter with the New World, at the very end of the fifteenth century, and thereafter through the sixteenth century and the subsequent epoch of settlement and empire-building, introduced Europeans to another corpus of narratives, besides classical myth, that was governed by belief in soul migration and spirit possession. This material was born in the early chroniclers, historians and ethnographers of the Americas, and transmitted profoundly different ideas of metamorphosis, that nevertheless resonated with earlier Greek and Ovidian precepts, that human nature was not stable; human beings could be changed by Fate, or by magical devices and spells. The instability at the heart of personality meant everyone was subject to Fate, subject to metamorphosis, to entropy.

Soul migration, or metempsychosis, challenges individual uniqueness as held in the Judaeo-Christian tradition. Broadly speaking, the idea of metamorphosis sets a huge tension around the idea of subjectivity, because to find yourself within a world that is in flux, that is metamorphic, that is constantly changing, offers two possibilities: one, that you are fragmented and dispersed, that you are scattered, that your identity is actually lost and dismembered across the whole scenery; the other is that you are capable of any form of transformation, that you could or can be anything. In several women writers' re-visionings of metamorphic stories, these two states are often present and in conflict: on the one hand, you are under threat of disappearing, because your identity is subject to outside forces, and on the other you are actually capable of entering the plot of your own life and changing it. A determined, voluntarist, utopian sense that the female being could actually find herself, shape and control her own destiny and take charge of her story was a feature of the writings of the Seventies and Eighties; the heroines in a Margaret Atwood or Angela Carter novel were often presented as the victims of circumstances, but of circumstances which they could overcome through force of personality. Sometimes, as in *The Handmaid's Tale*, the search for autonomy was fatally perverted; but nevertheless, an underlying idea drove the action: that the desideratum was to control personal identity and arrive at self-possession and self-expression.

Personal transformation would provide the happy ending of the postmodern fairy tale of the Seventies and the Eighties.

But since the Nineties, I believe we are experiencing the collapse of that heroic project, and accepting a decentring of subjectivity and a dispersal of identity; the idea of agency is weakening. Sylvia Plath prophetically cried out in her diaries in a passage singled out for comment by Jacqueline Rose in *The Haunting of Sylvia Plath*. Rose asks, 'How can women assert themselves against social oppression . . . without propelling themselves beyond the bounds of identity, without abolishing identity itself? For there is no such thing as an ego on its own, since the ego exists, comes into being only as difference from itself.' She is asking, How does Sylvia Plath find herself? Plath's great enterprise was to find herself through language, and in her own life too, but through language primarily. What provoked Rose's question was Sylvia Plath's outburst, in her diaries in 1949: 'there has always furthermore in addition and inescapably and forever got to be a Thou. Otherwise there is no i [the I in Sylvia Plath's journals is in lower case] . . . because i am what other people interpret me as being, and am nothing if there were no people.'[3]

If we take that 'i am what other people interpret me as being, and am nothing if there were no people', I think that we can apply it in a context of stories and rewriting. We can say 'i am what other texts interpret me as being, am nothing if there are no texts'. In the Seventies and Eighties, when women readers went back to the texts, we first sought out the great women of literature and the great figures in history, and we found pioneers. In the fifteenth century, Christine de Pizan, the poet and historian, was herself a rewriter of earlier material. She transformed Boccaccio's disparaging and hostile book about women, *De claris mulieribus*, and compiled a book of heroines, *The City of Ladies*, in which she recast the stories of some notorious figures to make them exemplars of virtue; they were then claimed as role models for the first wave of postwar feminists. We celebrated female texts, female-authored texts. But they are not in infinite supply, or rather, in the history of literature they dwindled in number and quality, and soon the need arose to find, scattered among the dismembered limbs of literature, fragmentary parts of women, embodied in existing texts that were perhaps written or authorised by men. One of the guiding principles of borrowing and re-visioning for women like myself moves us to find a voice through engagement with texts from the past. We struggle to find our own subjectivity in relationship with stories. I for one have always seen this as a Shakespearean process of narrative exploration.

My novel *Indigo*, published in 1992, re-scored *The Tempest* through the muffled voices of the play's female cast of characters; it attempted to restore voice to Sycorax, the vilified, offstage mother of Caliban, and to Miranda, the compliant daughter, and it closed in classic romance manner, with a union, and a baby, an echo of the happy ending of 'Cupid and Psyche' of Apuleius' fairy tale, told in *The Golden Ass*. *The Leto Bundle*, my new novel, is by contrast an anti-romance, perhaps because the tumultuous and vicious conflicts which so many of the people in the world are enduring have rather withered *Indigo*'s emancipatory wishfulness, that cunning and high spirits I tried to muster a decade ago. Foundlings, twins, tokens, shipwreck (maroonings), pirates, abductions, wanderings, misadventures, recognitions, are all found in my Bundle. My Leto is a refugee who begins as a goddess, who, raped by a god, then drifts westward with her twin babies across the Mediterranean until she ends up in Albion, an asylum seeker without papers, wearing clumsy, handed-down clothes. She borrows from many late Shakespearean heroines who are also lost and then found after long sufferings and many shifts of outward shape. They then reinstitute order by their rediscovery and restored identity. Like many heroines in the wronged maiden or slandered bride tradition, Leto is denounced, and orders issued for her death. But, as in *Cymbeline*, as in 'Snow White', the servant ordered to kill her cannot bring himself to perform the deed.

Into the figure of Leto, I also wanted to bind the stories of many persecuted nymphs and mortal women, who after being pursued and raped by the gods, inaugurate cultures and civilisations: Europa, who gives her name to the continent; Io, who after being turned into a cow, becomes the mother of the Danaïds, and hence of the Greeks themselves; and the Titan Leto, mother of the Sun and the Moon. Recently, I saw that the demonstrators against Le Pen, during the presidential elections in France this spring, were marching under the slogan, 'We are all the children of immigrants.' This is the banner my protagonist, the teacher Kim McQuy, also raises, in the name of Leto, the spectral mother whom he finds again on his computer screen. But *The Leto Bundle* ends with a deliberate flouting of the conventions of romance because, as I say, something about the harshness of the times demanded it: the foundling prince is not found, the foundling princess is not recognised.

Romance typically shares out first-person subjectivity over a wide keyboard: it plays many notes in many voices, and for this reason particularly suits dramatic development for the stage, as masque, as dream play, as frieze or tableau. In *The Golden Ass*, Apuleius' hapless Lucius, his alter ego, tells his story in the first person, retrospectively. Nevertheless, the whole book, with its interpolated stories and long excursus, in the voice of the old woman narrator who tells the tale of 'Cupid and Psyche', reads as an adventure story, a picaresque sequence of disasters, comic, tragic, tragicomic and finally, mystical. Like Ovid, who switches into the first person to intensify the immediacy and vividness of his subjects' physical transformations, Apuleius uses first-person narration to bring us close to his character, indeed inside his donkey shape and all its shame and piteous sufferings, but he doesn't use it as a search tool into the interior self or as a constitutive agent of Lucius' character, as the tragedians do. Similarly, my Leto is a character who is portrayed as almost waxen, pressed out by Fate into different shapes, moulded by hardship and accident, by social disintegration and civil wars; for the most part she remains, in romance heroine style, passively subject to Fate's twists and turns – though, like Hermione, or Marina, or Imogen, she shows throughout remarkable toughness, forbearance and an inextinguishable resourcefulness in distress.

The lack of inwardness that the frieze-like structure of romance entails, in Shakespeare's late plays, has the effect of multiplying viewpoints – of giving the story to many different characters to tell. This helps account for the choral counterpoint of texts that sometimes reverberate in romance, as for example in *Cymbeline*, in which the action moves through a flurry of letters, real and forged, reports, false and true, documents, oracles, and other written elements, including a copy of Ovid which Imogen is famously reading before Jachimo lets himself out of the chest to spy on her sleeping.[4] This series of conflicting messages spurs on the dramatic course of events, somewhat creakily, some might think, but they also deepen the play's questions about character, about consistency and inconsistency. The various messages cause confusion, in their deliberate mendacity, or their mistakenness, and in this they extend, or perhaps even embody, the romance's anxiety about instability of character: Posthumus believes, instantly, that Imogen might lightly betray him with Jachimo, while Cloten, the lout and braggart, fits Posthumus's clothes exactly and exclaims at the likeness. His resemblance does indeed lead Imogen to take his body (headless) for her husband's(!).

In *The Lost Father*, the novel I wrote in 1988, one character keeps a diary; in *The Leto Bundle*, many different textures of missive, including e-mails, track the changing time zones through their characteristic forms of communication. I like dispersing points of view through different characters, and grounding these conflicting visions in texts of different kinds. The title of *The Leto Bundle* alludes, at one level, to the heterogeneous sheaf of different objects that carry the story – from inscribed buttons to the linen bands wound around Leto's body – taken together, finally, these various documents tell Leto's story. It is a method that challenges unified character depiction, unified narrative viewpoint, and consequently – as I'll now explore – a concept of stable epistemology. Magic and metamorphosis are literary topoi that, in the current ways of reading, communicate this most powerfully.

RAPE AND TRANSFORMATION

The catalyst to several sudden, violent metamorphoses in Ovid's great poem is rape: Shakespeare, in his early *Titus Andronicus*, follows the story of Philomela's violation and mutilation closely: Lavinia's attackers actually invoke the precedent of Philomela and decide to circumvent Philomela's stratagem, by cutting off Lavinia's hands and thus prevent her weaving her story into a cloth. Here the tongueless and handless maiden communicates only through Shakespeare's play: she has become document, her mouth and lips thereafter used to carry Titus' severed hand like a dog, not to speak.

With respect to the same Ovidian metamorphosis, Shakespeare alters the focus of his attention in *Cymbeline* from the horror of Philomela's physical maiming to meditate on the extraordinary reprieve Ovid describes, when, at the moment that mayhem is about to break out again and catch up Tereus, Philomela and her sister Procne in Tereus' maddened revenge for the death of his son, Itys, they are all suddenly transformed – literally lightened and swept up into the air in the form of birds. Ovid doesn't specify that Philomela becomes a nightingale – that is made clear in other sources where, in exchange for her muteness, she becomes the sweetest singer of all, the emblem of poetic eloquence and the talisman of the lyric poet. Ted Hughes's version, in *Tales from Ovid*, is called 'Tereus', after Shakespeare's reference to the story in *Cymbeline*.

Metamorphoses deny death and fold time; they bring ancient stories into everyday scenery and populate the landscape with living characters, they overturn destruction and death through miraculous escapes, through transfigurations: to Pythagorean ears, Philomela doesn't only escape murder, she lives on in every nightingale. For Ted Hughes, time bent back against itself through poetry in the same way as Ovid's phenomena of nature were cast into new shapes by original miracles that suspended nature's laws. He commented that Ovid was interested in 'passion where it combusts, or levitates, or mutates into an experience of the supernatural', and that Tereus' tale is one in which 'mortal passion makes the breakthrough by sheer excess, without divine intervention'.

NARCOLEPSY, SACRIFICE AND SMELLS

So nearly two decades after *Titus*, around 1609, Shakespeare again alludes to the same terrifying episode in Ovid: this is the passage that Imogen has been reading, for three hours, in bed, before she goes to sleep, and she leaves the book by her bedside, with the page marked, as Jachimo finds:

> *Jachimo*:   'Tis her breathing that
> Perfumes the chamber thus. The flame o' th' taper
> Bows toward her, and would under-peep her lids,
> To see th'enclosed lights, now canopied
> Under these windows, white and azure lac'd
> With blue of heaven's own tinct. But my design!
> To note the chamber, I will write all down:
>   *[Takes out his tablets.]*
> Such and such pictures; there the windows; such
> Th'adornment of her bed; the arras, figures,
> Why, such and such; and the contents o' th' story.
> . . . She hath been reading late
> The tale of Tereus; here the leaf's turn'd down
> Where Philomele gave up. I have enough . . .[5]

Here we see dramatised one of the false texts in the making: Cloten inscribes the tablets, pressing out a true impression of the chamber but one which will bear a fallacious message. Imogen's surroundings include two stories at least, one woven into the tapestry, another in the book she's been reading. Later, Posthumus discloses that the first tells the story of Antony and Cleopatra's meeting, as described in Shakespeare's own play written around three years before, while the other tells one of the most savage stories of rape and metamorphosis in Ovid. Later, in Jachimo's treacherous report to Posthumus, it transpires that the chamber also includes a sculpted scene of Diana and Actaeon over the chimneypiece. Interestingly, Lucius, in *The Golden Ass*, enters a room with a similar sculpture, embodying the Ovidian story of Actaeon's punishment for glimpsing the goddess at her bath, in what must count as the harshest warning against peeping Toms ever conceived.

The arras, the figures: these strike resonant Ovidian notes, for *figura* is the word the Latin poet uses for changes of shape at the metaphysical conclusion of the poem:

> utque novis facilis signatur cera *figures*
> nec manet ut fuerat nec formam servant eandem,
> sed tamen ipsa eadem est, animam sic semper eandem
> esse, sed in varias doceo migrare *figuras*. [Emphasis added]
>
> (As the pliant wax
> Is stamped with new designs, and is no longer
> What once it was, but changes form, and still
> Is pliant wax, so do I teach that spirit
> Is evermore the same, though passing always
> To ever-changing bodies.)[6]

Above all, it's in Arachne's tapestry, as mentioned earlier, that the stories of the Olympians' pursuits and lusts are figured by her skilful fingers before she's turned into a spider; and Philomela communicates her sufferings to her sister in a similar embroidered cloth.

A figured arras presents the most familiar medium, in domestic and vernacular settings, of picturing mythological stories, and its presence in Imogen's chamber, where she is reading Book VI of Ovid's *Metamorphoses* (which opens with Arachne and moves on to Philomela), hints proleptically at the possibility of rape. But in bringing in Ovid in this way, the tapestry also draws attention to the difference in possible developments, and hence to Shakespeare's late manner in revising classical metamorphosis. For within his late plays, physical meta-morphosis – bodily mutilation as in *Titus* – no longer satisfies his dramatic interest; this magical or grotesque device exceeds the limits of the play's conventions, however improbable the plot might be in other respects. Bottom could be translated into an ass by the spells of Puck, Oberon's messenger, but here, as in *The Winter's Tale* and the wonderful scene of the statue Hermione coming to life, Shakespeare draws on Ovid to pull magical changes of shape on to human, even humanist ground and to turn the thrust of the story inwards: the reanimation of Hermione reunites her with Leontes and alters his nature, or so we are promised; and the transformations in *Cymbeline* affect consciousness, above all, not bodily shape.

The physical voice that Philomela has lost rises volubly in the Shakespearean tragic soliloquy, the precursor of the cinematic voice-over, as it follows the transformations of the protagonist's mind under pressure from the crises in the plays. Romance heroines, cognisant of their silenced, put-upon victim forebears, struggle to dislodge the lords of their utterance – to use Coleridge's phrase from 'Christabel' – and achieve voice after inner metamorphoses. In Plath's cry, 'Otherwise there is no i, no me, no i', we can catch echoes of this struggle with inevitable contingency.

The Holub image of Jairus's daughter is perhaps especially appropriate to recall in connection to this play, because Imogen – twice – lies in a deep sleep while events unfold around her, and is then miraculously reanimated. Again, I feel a medieval Snow White story hangs around *Cymbeline*. Shakespeare's many acts of resuscitation – fatal and melodramatic in *Romeo and Juliet*, ingenious and sentimental in *Much Ado about Nothing*, a miracle drama in the reworking of the Pygmalion story in *The Winter's Tale* – communicate his continual turning over of dream states and their effects. But these twists of plot also convey an enhanced sensitivity to scents: *Cymbeline* is his most olfactory drama – after *Hamlet*, and that tragedy's rank cabinet of poisons.

The effect of fumigations, brews, perfumes and vapours on mental states pervades Shakespeare's plays, but it's seldom as personal as in *Cymbeline*, in which Cloten, on his first entrance, is described as rank and provokes one of his attendants to say: 'Sir, I would advise you to shift a shirt; the violence of action hath made you reek as a sacrifice.' When Pisanio gives Imogen the letter in which her husband orders her death, the metaphor for its slanderous contents again moves from sensation of pain to pestilential stench:

> No, 'tis slander
> Whose edge is sharper than the sword, whose tongue
> Outvenoms all the worms of Nile, whose breath
> Rides on the posting winds and doth belie
> All corners of the world.

Here the reek of monsters' breath *posts* from place to place, like a letter, like a document, to spread confusion and distort thought and true feeling. These worms of Nile follow close upon a reference to the basilisk, and Shakespeare may have also come across, in Topsell's bestiary, the catoblepas, or shaggy-headed monster whose hot and reeking breath scorches the ground as it tries to graze.

Some kind of metaphorical cluster throughout the play associates divinity, smoke, mind-altering substances, and smells. For example, Posthumus hears his father Sicilius tell him in a vision how Jupiter had appeared to him, a portentous deus ex machina: 'He came in thunder, his celestial breath/ Was sulphurous to smell . . .' And towards the very end, Cymbeline, giving thanks for restored peace, announces: 'And let our crooked smokes climb to their nostrils/ From our blest altars . . .'

The evocation of pungent sacrifices conforms to pagan ritual; but the accompanying resonance of the imagery in *Cymbeline* of flowers and poisons deepens the peculiar olfactory connections with inner metamorphosis, erupting at moments of crisis and pressure. The transformation of the sacrificed creature, or of the 'violets, cowslips and primeroses' in the Queen's pharmacopoeia into deadly poisons, replicates the mental metamorphoses worked by the plot. Ovid's many flower girls and boys – Daphne, Hyacinthus, Myrrha, Adonis, Narcissus, to name only a famous few – reappear not physically transformed, but inwardly changed, and the appearance, on stage, of flowers marks this often tragic passage: Ophelia's mind gone as she gathers weeds and herbs, and Lear entering, in that stage direction, 'fantastically dressed with wild flowers'.[7] The Queen calls her venoms 'perfumes' and distils them from dew-soaked flowers. Imogen lies in a drugged sleep, as does Juliet, in the tomb, her slumber brought about by the herbal decoctions of the Friar.

The Queen's drugs, oddly enough, specify species of flowers which are elsewhere invoked in connection with Imogen: the mole on her breast, the tell-tale token that Jachimo later uses to deceive Posthumus, is 'cinque-spotted, like the crimson drops/ I' th' bottom of a cowslip . . .' Later, when the brothers lay Imogen out in her grave and strew it with flowers, the primrose appears in their bouquet, and yet again, they invoke the sweetness of her breath.

The elegy they sing, 'Fear no more the heat o' the sun', one of the most truly enchanting songs (a kind of elegy-cum-lullaby) in all the plays, may also draw on flower imagery: Jonathan Bate has connected these verses with Ovidian floral metamorphoses; He notes that golden lads and girls were names for the dandelion in country speech:[8] 'Golden lads and girls all must,/ As chimney-sweepers, come to dust . . .'

The whiff lingers that Imogen herself is a sacrifice, an Iphigenia ready to offer herself for distillation or sublimation in order to bring about a new harmony, a concluding peace. Later, making a chain of voluntary offerings, Posthumus suggests he should atone for his little faith through sacrificing himself.

In *Cymbeline*, the return of perfumed imagery lays an original stress on the nose, because, as in classical or biblical sacrifice, scents rising from smoking altars sublime the physical: breath manages to be both material and immaterial at once, a symbolic hyphen between worlds of body and soul or spirit. The imagery thus lends itself, with precise appropriateness, to Shakespeare's transmutation of metamorphosis itself as a device of showing character undergoing change.

Some of the earliest stories conveyed across the Atlantic reported the sniffing and snuffing of tobacco and other drugs by indigenous peoples and their powerful psychic effects. Traces of Shakespeare's reading of *Purchas's Pilgrims* and other early American documents, such as Richard Eden's translations from Spanish chroniclers, can be found in *The Tempest*.[9] But before writing that play, Shakespeare could have begun dipping into the histories by Oviedo or Peter Martyr, where accounts of trance rituals and healings, involving nasal intoxicants such as yucca seeds, receive awed, precise and vivid attention.[10]

For example, Oviedo reported, 'Among other evil practices, the Indians have one that is especially harmful: the inhaling of a certain kind of smoke which they call tobacco, in order to produce a state of stupor. . . . they would inhale the smoke until they became unconscious and lay sprawling on the ground like men in a drunken slumber.'[11] Ramón Pané, the earliest ethnographer to live among the Indians on the island of Hispaniola, also lays emphasis on their use of narcotics in making contact with their divinities, the *zemis*, as a method of medical diagnosis: 'they take a certain powder called *cohoba*, inhaling it through the nose, which inebriates them in such fashion that they do not know what they are doing; and thus they say many senseless things, affirming therein that they are speaking with the *zemis*, and that the latter tell them that the sickness has come from them.'[12] *Cohoba* has now been identified with *Anadenanthera peregrina*, a kind of bean still very much in use in New Age shamanism, (known as one of the sacred plants on the Girdle of Gaia, if you look it up on the Web!) Next to vision, scent enjoys the deepest relationship to consciousness. Shakespeare, as a member of the first generation of Europeans that smoked tobacco (I don't mean to claim him personally as a smoker), could not but be aware of this property of smells as overpowering mental stimulants; his era, one of expanding trade, provides the background to the fumes and odours that he conjures again and again in *Cymbeline*.

When Imogen wakes from her own death-like stupor, she meditates on the unreliable narration of her brain, moving from the flowers strewn on her corpse to the effect of smells on the mind:

> These flowers are like the pleasures of the world:
> This bloody man, the care on't. I hope I dream:
> For so I thought I was a cave-keeper,
> And cook to honest creatures. But 'tis not so:
> *'Twas but a bolt of nothing, shot at nothing,*
> *Which the brain makes of fumes . . .*
>
> (Emphasis added)

But we know, in the audience, that she's not dreaming at all.

MAGIC REALISM?

In the late plays, Shakespeare grasped the shape-shifting body of stories tossed up from the Mediterranean, and even perhaps, collected flotsam coming from the Atlantic, in order to psychologise magical metamorphosis, and to project inwards the prodigious natural transformations Ovid or Apuleius so vividly renders, and that he had playfully represented in *A Midsummer Night's Dream*. Jonathan Bate, in his perceptive study, *Shakespeare and Ovid*, argues that 'throughout his career Shakespeare transformed into metaphors the metamorphoses which Ovid played out at the level of mythic narrative.'[13] In the romances, Shakespeare particularly struggles with mental transformations, and these are not exactly metaphorical since minds are indeed transfigured. These plays work out the implications of Hippolyta's response to Theseus' comments on fantasy, and stage the effects of Imogen's near-death experience, Hermione's supposed petrifaction, and, above all, Ariel's spells and songs, his sea-changing powers of transmutation. Personal organic metaphors burgeon into organic social and familial structures of harmony and restored order. In a comedy such as *A Midsummer Night's Dream*, Shakespeare staged a transmogrification of Bottom into an ass, but in the romances that follow, the narcolepsy of his heroines supplies the translation from one state to another that in Ovid rape so often brings about. Their minds are changed by their fates, and then subsequently work to change the minds of others – of the two men enraged by jealousy, for example, Leontes and Posthumus.

How does all this relate to the questions with which I began, about the vitality of magic and the recurrence of soul migration and metamorphosis in contemporary fiction? It can help loosen some of the tangles around the writing mode called magic realism, I believe, in the following fashion.

First, to the obvious point that magical romance motifs, their artificiality and improbability, create an atmosphere of unfamiliarity that estranges the world and everything in it: not for nothing does Miranda say to Prospero, as she too falls asleep at the quasi-narcotic effect of his message from the past: 'The strangeness of your story put/ Heaviness in me ...' This estrangement helps open up other pathways for characterisation to take, offers a way of exploring minds and their movements: the protagonist of *Beloved* by Toni Morrison is haunted by the daughter she killed, in accordance with spirit beliefs in duppies and revenants of the Afro-Caribbean diaspora; Margaret Atwood's heroine in *Alias Grace* is possessed by the spirit of her murdered friend, and wreaks vengeance on her behalf. This form of personality – embedded in the novel most persuasively in the history of early North American psychiatry – also depends on fundamentally non-Christian, non-Judaic ideas of soul migration, of the self changing under psychic pressure from mental images and impressions. In Philip Pullman's inspired trilogy, *His Dark Materials*, one of his most original and captivating innovations materialises every character's daimon as an animal familiar, a kind of external soul, who accompanies them, and embodies their true inner self.

Exploring the nature of consciousness, questioning the status of 'fancy's images', those memories, dreams and daydreams that fiction and drama compound of their very nature, staging the paradoxical reality of fantasy: these enterprises also form a crucial part of contemporary fiction writers' uses of past stories. Metamorphic identities inside the plot, a metamorphic plot itself, represent this conflict, in its productiveness and its open-endedness. The dispersed and scattered self bobbing hither and thither on the streams of story meets and clashes with the unified authorial self who controls the parcelled body of the narrative, the polyphony of the voices in the story. In the context of current metamorphic writings, I also see my own protagonist, Leto, as a woman in flux, belonging to several times and places, a resurrected body subject to a sequence of ordeals, including at the beginning the assault of a god in a classical mythological rape scene. She finally turns herself into a cuttlefish in order to escape him, and leaves the print of her inky witness on the documents that tell her story. Later, Leto appears over the Web to my male protagonist, the political agitator Kim McQuy; she is a romance victim turned techno-communications vision of our time.

For me, the impossible journey of Leto in her various guises across time and through different media, messages, and documents operated as a way of giving voice to a woman of our time, a refugee such as we see every day, in the streets of our cities and, above all, on our TV screens, a hate figure, a scapegoat for our ills. She is for me a heroine: but I couldn't enflesh her as a realist protagonist in the tradition of the great nineteenth-century social novel; I borrowed and adapted the stratagems of mythic romance narratives, full of metamorphoses and magic.

The term 'magic realism' does not meet the character of the fantastical fictions that are now being written: it's too exotic, too ornamental, too fabulous – in short, too supernatural. Contemporary metamorphic fictions are engaging with issues of consciousness, rooted in the physical realities of psychology, not with signs and wonders, portents and prodigies. Metamorphosis offers the novelist today a language of personal description rooted in physical possibilities. Magical devices and seemingly impossible events – such as the tears in time in *The Leto Bundle* – do not obey the laws of space and time as we live in them, but they do track the movements of thought, memory and fantasy as they fill our heads.

In the wonderfully distilled exchange between Theseus and Hippolyta towards the end of *A Midsummer Night's Dream*, Theseus develops his slighting line on magic's deceptions: 'such tricks hath strong imagination,' he says. To which Hippolyta replies:

> But all the story of the night told over,
> And all their minds transfigur'd so together,
> More witnesseth than fancy's images,
> And grows to something of great constancy,
> Howsoever strange and admirable.[14]

Magic, Hippolyta is saying, works on the mind to enduring effect; she associates its enchantments with some faculty higher than fancy, and so for her, the consequences of transfigured minds aren't altogether to be deplored or, indeed, doubted.

2002

SIX

CREOLE

Between the Colonist and the Creole

My grandfather was born a Creole, but I didn't know it. The French include whites in the term Creole, and so do the Spanish, but to English ears, 'Creole' sounds foreign, French, or worse, native, but native of another place besides England. To my grandparents' generation, the word connoted an Elsewhere where foreign words were spoken as a native tongue, and various kinds of foreigners mingled and became natives in the process. And it was of course impossible, then, for an Englishman to be a foreigner at all, and perilous (though regrettably not impossible) for an Englishman to become a native. The Warners had been born in the West Indies for generations and lived there, mainly in St Kitt's, Antigua and Trinidad, in ever-increasing numbers (this grandfather was one of twenty-one children). But they had still remained English-bred in the bone.

It was startling to me to realise, when the recent nationality laws were passed, that my family's Britishness would have been abolished. For nothing could have been more English than my father and my father's family. If they could have been bottled, their voices, their walk, their dress (the ties, the hats, the sticks), their phrases, their laughter (my father's boisterous English laughter used to help me locate his whereabouts when I was a child), if they could have been pressed and fermented and drunk, they would summon up, in a single draught, an era and a world that was thoroughly and indisputably English. And yet, as I say, they weren't exactly English; how it would have shocked my grandfather to be refused a British passport, as would happen now. (Though being white, and of ancient pioneer stock, the immigration police would probably bend the rules, I know.)

The Warners, like other planter families, maintained their connections to the mother country by a series of strategies. For the lime demarcation lines in the turf that divided Englishmen from foreigners and natives could be rubbed out in the climate of the islands all too easily by passing feet. Inviolate Englishness, in a family like my father's and his father's before him, was kept up by methods both subtle and brutal, conscious and unconscious, acts of convenient memory and sins of omission; the field of memory, which is the writer's testing ground, was carefully laid out in a certain way, and returning there in imagination, as the granddaughter of Pelham Warner ('Plum'), I chose different markers, boundary lines, posts and goals from the ones that had been handed down to me in the family history.

However, because contexts and definitions are always in flux, I still cannot say that the Warners were Creoles as a simple statement of fact; the relations of the former plantocracy to the islands which they colonised and inhabited for nearly three hundred years make it fallacious, even opportunistic, for a descendant now to grasp the label and wear it with new pride. It's too easy a solution to the problems of the past, to make a few realignments – like moving the furniture to improve the look of a room. The history of denial in the past has forfeited someone like me the right to own the inheritance in the present, much as I should like to. Indeed, I sometimes felt that by writing *Indigo*, the novel I set partly in the Caribbean, I was interloping on territory from which accidents of history had morally barred me; but then I also argued to myself that it is important, too, for anyone and everyone to challenge received ideas, and that I had tried to do this before, in a book about the cult of the Virgin Mary and a novel about women in Fascist Italy, themes which sprang directly from my family history too.

My grandfather's memoirs begin: 'I was born in the Island of Trinidad, in the West Indies, where my father was, at one time, Attorney-General, and my earliest recollections of cricket are of batting on a marble gallery to the bowling of a black boy, who rejoiced in the name of Killebree.'[1] He begins the book with this memory because he went on to become the England captain of cricket, and then, for a long time, President of the MCC. When I was a little girl, Sir Pelham was still a famous figure, a slim, brittle old man with a piercing look in his pale blue eyes, the effect of the precision vision which had helped score him all those runs on the pitches of the Empire. The London flat in which he and my grandmother lived in their old age was entirely decorated with cricketing memorabilia: from the bookcases beamed the curious harsh yellow of the Wisden almanacs, the game's scrolls of the law, and the walls were hung with caricatures ('Plum brings back the Ashes') and photographs (Plum carried shoulder-high off the ground after a particular triumph; Plum with King George VI at Lord's; Plum with Queen Mary, receiving a trophy).

My memory may not be altogether accurate, because I was small during the time when both our families were living in London (1952), but in the dark, corridor-dominated, typically stuffy mansion-block flat in South Kensington, with its smells of boiling vegetables and chlorinated waterpipes, there was an atmosphere of worldly glory that had been deservedly earned and relished to the hilt. Sir Pelham was a beloved figure: he had played the civilised game of cricket all over the pink parts of the map and deepened the warmth and wisdom of that rose colour. As C. L. R. James points out in his inspired account of cricket and Empire, *Beyond a Boundary*, there existed a deep connection between the game and British power. Remembering his schooldays, James passes seamlessly from his passion for cricket to the way history was then taught:

> I would fight and resist in order to watch the big boys playing cricket, and I would do this until my grandmother came for me and dragged me home protesting . . . Later, when reading elementary English history books, I became resentful of the fact that the English always won all, or nearly all, of the battles and read every new history book I could find, searching out and noting the battles they had lost.[2]

Cricket pitches would become, for James, a place where that balance could be redressed.

The image of Killebree – Creole patois for 'Hummingbird', which the French spell *colibri* – stuck in my mind and helped inspire the reckoning I attempted in *Indigo*. Without that 'black boy' bowling to my grandfather again and again, perhaps he might not have learned to bat, so early, so well, been trained up to the game which made him a kind of national hero in the 'home' country. It seemed to me that in this exchange, as the nicknamed servant bowled to the young master in the 'marble gallery' of his father the Attorney-General's house, I could see the crucible in which my grandfather's skills were sublimed, and through this vision, by extension, the whole relation of coloniser and colonised: the whiteness of the batsman unconsciously enhanced by the marble gallery in which he stands at the ready, waiting to hit; the 'boy' infantilised by the affectionate but nonetheless patronising sobriquet of the tiniest bird in the world: the easy confidence with which the writer, my grandfather, acknowledges his debt to his childhood trainer, that 'old world courtesy' which makes up for what it takes for itself by a show of exquisite good manners ('breeding').

My father's favourite adage was 'Noblesse oblige' – he said it whenever we did anything disagreeable socially (a boring party, a tedious chore), making it clear that we had to do it, not because we needed to, or might gain thereby ourselves, or were in any sense dependent on the goodwill of others, but to confirm our superiority. He wasn't an unkind man, my father, nor an especially arrogant one, but he descended from a line of Empire servants and he had absorbed – and never re-examined, let alone repudiated – their intensely hierarchical view of social organisation, which grants importance to every stratum by teaching it to despise the orders beneath and defer to the orders above. Moving through life as his daughter became a complex dance, something like an eightsome reel, in which we were continually 'setting' to partners, ducking and twirling and curtsying as we passed along the files attempting to define their rank with respect to ourselves and make the correct steps accordingly. But above all, I found in Killebree's bowling a repeat of the pattern in the carpet, first figured three centuries before, of the hospitable helpfulness that the indigenous peoples of the Caribbean had offered the first settlers; the Indians of Guyana showed the English buccaneers who arrived in the sixteenth century how to grow tobacco and other crops that were unfamiliar to them. Some were later taken to the islands to assist there; and were promised they would return after the plantings and first harvests. But that promise went the way of all flesh. Like many others.

My father was very proud that the Warners had been significant figures in this early history. Alongside the cricketing memorabilia which we inherited after my grandfather's death, we also were left documents about the family's story in the West Indies: a copy of the charter granting Sir Thomas Warner, founding settler of the 'Mother Colony' of St Kitts, governorship of the West Indies on behalf of King Charles I; a photograph of his tomb in the churchyard of Old Road on that island. A marble slab, protected by a fretwork canopy, mourns his death in 1648 and records his 'acts of fame', 'brave exploits', and 'large narratives of military worth' in fourteen lines of rhyming couplets. I heard, recently, the poet David Dabydeen give a paper on the English language, and he said that he had seen similar glowing epitaphs to the liberality and nobility of slave-owners in the graveyards of the West Indies. They had been made by stonecutters who did not know how to read and write, who were their slaves. When I heard this, I felt prickly shame creep over me. For of course the Warners became planters, and as planters, became slave-owners.

There was one way this Creole past was acknowledged in my family: my father went to Trinidad in the Sixties to sell the last piece of land the Warners still owned on the island. There were so many heirs (the descendants of all those twenty-one siblings) that the parcelling-out of the rents from this section of Port of Spain was proving an expensive nightmare. It wasn't exactly lucrative land, anyway – I suspect the rents could not be raised as the quality of the housing was so poor. When my father returned from the sale, aglow with Carnival and other excitements, he talked a lot about our Warner cousins, and when he showed us a photograph, of one he'd taken a special shine to (cousin Lucy), I was very surprised to see that she wasn't white, but black. My sister was too, and because times have changed and we are different, we were intrigued and pleased; it was a kind of secret, something that kindled the same conspiratorial pleasure as the contents of the treasure drawer I had in my bedside table, which I only showed to very special friends.

My father explained that Warner was a very common name in the West Indies because the Warners had been enlightened owners and so the slaves were happy to take the same name. This was how we came to be related to cousin Lucy, he implied. But when I started reading to research the background of my novel, I came across another story. Not only that no evidence exists which suggests that the Warners were any different from the rest of the plantocracy, who on the whole were the sorriest crew of ugly, greedy and often vicious self-interested parties ever to lobby Parliament, as they did in strength against the abolitionists, and even against the 'ameliorists', who merely wanted to improve the conditions of the slaves. But the story was different also because the breakdown between 'foreign' and 'English' happened from the start; and was always denied, though it was plain from the law records, as well as the early chronicles of the islands, and had not been expunged entirely from the history books. My great-uncle, Aucher Warner, my grandfather's elder brother, wrote a biography of Sir Thomas, the founding father, and in it he tells the story of the colony's early years, including the episode which concerns a certain 'Indian' Warner, son of Sir Thomas.

Thomas Warner, when he arrived in St Kitt's, 'married' a local woman called Barbe, and had several children with her, including a son, also

Thomas, but known as 'Indian' Warner, who grew up to become Governor of Dominica, appointed by the colonial governor of the islands, and the active leader of the large community of Caribs on that island. Another son, Philip, was born later, by Sir Thomas's marriage to the English wife who joined him once the colony was established, and in 1672, Philip was appointed Deputy Governor of Antigua. In this capacity, he led a raid on Dominica, to punish the Indians for alleged harassment of Antiguans. The two half-brothers met in conflict, but it was agreed they should talk; there was a feast, discussion of their differences, a quarrel flared; the peace conference ended with the deaths of Indian Warner and all his followers. Philip was accused of serving rum in order to intoxicate his enemies so that he could kill them more easily, and for this treachery, he was transported to the Tower of London and tried.

The massacre and Philip Warner's subsequent imprisonment took place around 1675, and the story, with its Cain and Abel overtones of mythic violation, remains startling. It would be even more astonishing, however, if Philip had been found guilty. After many protests from his fellow-planters, and many affidavits as to his good name and character, many reports of the cruelties of the Caribs and accusations of Indian Warner's conspiracies with their raids and thefts, Philip Warner was transferred for trial to Barbados and acquitted. He was not, however, restored to the governorship of Antigua.

'This is a strange story,' concluded my great-uncle, who had found the documents to the case in the Colonial Office, and to his credit, reproduced them.[3] It was such a strange story, so uneasy-making, so full of bloodshed and strife, that my father never mentioned it: though he was a historian by inclination, an often brilliant chronicler, a *flâneur* who could bring breathing men and women from the past with all their struggles, their mess, their violence, into the streets of the different cities where we used to walk together, though he was a bookseller with a true reader's love of browsing and searching, the history of the West Indies in the pioneer years of the seventeenth century had to appear a graceful, controlled, law-abiding act of conquest in the interests of civilisation. It had to be cricket, rather than this bristling and bleeding tangled mass of loose ends, betrayals, and fratricide.

Père Labat, the Dominican missionary who lived in the Caribbean from 1693–1705, wrote in his *magnum opus* that he once met Indian Warner's mother, the first Governor's first wife, who was then a hundred years old and bald, he wrote, but had kept most of her teeth. The story of her son's life and adventures are more complex than can be related here, and a good history needs to be done of this period.[4] But the way that I was told his story, or rather not told his story, points to the edginess English empire families felt about miscegenation, interchanges between colonised and coloniser, about the translations of one culture into another that happened even while the hierarchical blueprint denied they could. Cricket, when it became the game of the colonised, and one in which they could compete as equals and defeat the colonisers, provided an allegory of the future; it also in another way encapsulated the buried facts of the past, that buccaneer and maroon could be father and son, that governor and slave could be brothers – and their wives and daughters, sisters.

As I say, this wasn't the story I was told, and indeed, as the Creole, colonial status of my father's family was never admitted as such, the Empire was something that I took for granted as belonging to us, unproblematically. But in my case, I was given a lamp which I could rub to transport me far, far from this condition of British complacency: my father, during the war, married my mother, who is Italian and Catholic. In this way, I became a foreigner. The kind of foreigner it was permitted for me to become, too, because Italian women were exotic, reputedly beautiful and voluptuous and vivacious and conscious of their femininity, their obligations towards men and children. An Italian son-in-law would not have won such approval from Sir Pelham and Lady Warner in their mansion block as they lavished on my young mother. She stood within the permitted degrees of foreignness, and Catholicism, as my father once remarked – unforgettably – was a good religion for a girl. But it wasn't the religion of the British empire, though French and Belgian and other missions carried it far and wide through their empires, and the infamous French Code Noir of 1685 declared, in the same breath, that slaves were chattels, and should be given Christian instruction and baptised immediately on purchase and that unless this were done, the owner would be subject to *une amende arbitraire* – a heavy fine.[5] Nearly three hundred years later, at my convent school in Berkshire, England, we were still 'adopting' black babies by making an offering, and following it up by regular prayers in order to earn, as sponsor, a photograph of the designated, newly baptised fosterchild.

My family's Creole past, gainsaid, erased, became the inspiration for *Indigo*. I wanted to call the novel 'A Deeper Bite' from the Spanish proverb I used as an epigraph, 'The tongue has no teeth but a deeper bite', because the book is about survival through language, in the face of military and other strengths; about the power of memory, transmuted into stories, to shape experience both fallaciously and truthfully, harmfully and helpfully. *The Tempest* gave me a structure to work with; it was first performed in 1611, twelve years before Thomas Warner arrived and settled in the West Indies, and was most probably inspired by a shipwreck of some Englishmen on Bermuda. The First Folio, in which the play appears, was published the same year that Thomas Warner landed and began the 'Mother Colony' – changing the island of Liamuiga into St Kitt's, the first of the British holdings of Empire. *The Tempest* has often been interpreted as a drama about colonialism by contemporary directors; it was recast as a cry of liberation by the Martiniquais poet Aimé Césaire in his play *Une Tempête* of 1969, and has been discussed and explored by numerous writers from the Caribbean, inspiringly by George Lamming, for instance, in *Water with Berries*. But as far as I know, nobody had attempted to discover in Caliban's mother, Sycorax, another being besides the 'foul hag' Prospero invokes. Yet, in the play, Caliban says, 'This island's mine,/ By Sycorax my mother.' It was she who ruled before Prospero came, and in my book, she becomes the embodiment of the island itself, of its inner life, as well as a woman of ordinary passions and skills who – I hope – grows to the dimensions of a full humanity.

Because our family was involved in an enterprise that so resembles Prospero's theft, that foundation act of Empire, I felt compelled to examine the case, and imagine, in fiction, the life and culture of Sycorax, and of Ariel and Caliban, whom I cast as her foundlings; I wanted to hear their voices in the noises of the isle.

1993

Noonday Devils

Review of Elaine Breslaw, Tituba, Reluctant Witch of Salem: Devilish Indians and Puritan Fantasies

The French historian Arlette Farge has described coming across a letter, written on linen in a fine strong hand, in which a prisoner, long incarcerated in the Bastille, writes to his wife, affectionately, imploringly; he adds a message, to the laundrywoman who will find it among his washing, asking her to embroider a blue cross on one of his socks to tell him she has managed to pass it on. But the document's continued melancholy presence in the Bastille archive attests to the failure of his ruse.

Then, in another bundle of letters, Arlette Farge finds a sachet pinned to a request from a country doctor to the Société de Médecine. He writes that a young girl he knows exudes handfuls of corn from her breasts every month: could the learned gentlemen in Paris please comment. She is 'sincere and virtuous', he assures them.

The historian unpins the sachet; the corn is still there, 'as golden as on the first day; it scatters in a rain on the yellowing archive,' writes Farge. 'A brief sunburst. What if it were indeed a bit of that young girl in flower whose doctor believed in her.' She notes 'the surprising power of these intact grains . . . deemed to be the fruit of a body and a scientific explanation of menstruation'. This letter was sent in 1785: a material missive from the Enlightenment about the willingness of men (and women) to be gulled by wonders, about the role of young women as suppliers to the appetite for the fantastic.

Farge's evocative book, *Le Goût de l'archive* (1989), is the only study I know that expresses the frisson of that moment of encounter with the past when the edges of the data seem to catch alight: the moment of recognition. She writes:

> The archive is a rent in the fabric of days, a tense glimpse of an unexpected happening. There, everything is focused on a few instants in the lives of ordinary people rarely visited by History . . . Archives do not write pages of History. They describe in everyday language and on the same note the trifle and the tragedy, where what matters for the administration is to know.

Tituba is one of those ordinary people who would not have visited with history, and whose trifled-with life would have passed unremarked if she had not been bought in Barbados as a slave by Samuel Parris, who then left for America and became pastor at Salem in 1692 – the man at the centre of the witch trials. Elaine Breslaw, the author of this biography, must have experienced one of those epiphanies Farge describes so well when she found, in the Barbados archives, an entry in the inventory of property from an estate being sold on the island, made in a notary's careful copperplate: in the third column of the register of slaves – a long list – under the heading 'Boys and Girls', came the name, spelt 'Tattuba'.

This was 1676–7. In 1692, on 1 March, after Tituba had been in America with Parris her master for twelve years, she was interrogated in Salem by the two Justices of the Peace appointed by the court. Betty Parris, aged nine, whom Tituba looked after, had fallen ill with mysterious pains and was also suffering from hallucinations; two other girls soon began to complain of ailments too. Samuel Parris alerted the authorities to the possibility of witchcraft. Tituba first denied that she was a witch and was hurting them. But soon, in response to the men's artlessly leading questions ('What evil spirit have you familiarity with?'), she poured out a vivid tale of hogs and cats and rats and 'upright hairy things', of a tall man in black with a yellow bird, of a woman in a hood. Animals and humans kept turning into one another; in another transcription of her testimony the details conform even more closely to European witchcraft lore: Tituba says she flies on a broomstick to Boston, for example.

Tituba was the third woman to be questioned, and the only one of the three to confess during this early phase of the witch-hunt. Of her two co-defendants at the beginning, Sarah Good denied everything, Sarah Osborne accused Sarah Good. The self-owned witch Tituba has consequently become, in the ever-swelling literature about the horrors of Salem, the catalyst for the tragedy: hers was the original, circumstantial account which proved witchcraft was at work in the afflictions of the accusers. As the evidence proliferated, other incidents emerged which supported her role as 'Dark Eve', in Bernard Rosenthal's phrase, through whom the original innocence of the New World was lost. Black magic with dolls and pins, fortune-telling with raw eggs dropped into a glass – and the witchcake. The 'witchcake' was made in the Parris household, one of several devices used to discover what Betty and the other girls' problems might be: rye meal was mixed with their pee, baked in ashes and fed to the dog. It's not known what was supposed to happen, but Breslaw suggests that according to folk remedies shared by both the Puritan and the indigenous communities of seventeenth-century New England, the animal would then reveal 'the name of the witch causing the problem'. Apart from the problem of a dog being able to do this, my understanding of magic leads me to believe that the function might have been sacrificial rather than diagnostic: the dog would absorb the poisons and the victims would then be reprieved, purified.

Tituba and her husband, John Indian, also owned by Parris, prepared the witchcake under the supervision of a neighbour, who provided the recipe. Later, under questioning, Tituba said she had learned the recipe from 'her mistress in Barbados'. In spite of their ancillary position, the two slaves have been unequivocally blamed for the introduction of magical practices in the community and for the outbreak of malign forces that brought about the death by hanging of nineteen people as witches and the imprisonment of many more, and which above all conjured a noonday devil. In the present-day climate of punitive litigiousness about child abuse and sexual harassment, he is still playing havoc with men and women's wits.

One of the oddest things about the aftermath of Salem – this is a point Bernard Rosenthal makes in his admirable study, *Salem Story: Reading the Witch Trials of 1692* (1993) – is that the accused are still called witches, and that their memory is kept by some as wronged practitioners of ancient skills, as women victimised by official repression. Elaine Breslaw – her title makes it plain – also equivocates on this point: of course, her Tituba doesn't fly to Boston on a broomstick, or pinch Betty Parris or stick pins into her at long distance. But she is skilled at magic, she is able to fall into a trance, she uses dreams to probe mysteries, she divines by witchcakes and other methods.

Breslaw thinks that Tituba was captured in a slave raid around the Orinoco, and first sold in Barbados when she was a child, but that she would have retained memories of the Taino and/or Arawak beliefs and rituals of her tribe, which continued in the barracoons of West Indian plantations. In Barbados, she might also have (the conditional perfect perforce the dominant tense of this kind of conjectural history) participated in rites imported from the lost Yoruba and Igbo home territories of some of the men and women with whom she had contact. Breslaw stresses, however, the particular character of Amerindian as opposed to African beliefs, and links Tituba's lapses into mutism under trial to shamanistic trance. She also explores some of the fantasies circulating at Salem in the light of Amerindian soothsaying: among the Arawak, the subject of a dream could be held responsible in real life for something done in another's sleep, for spirit doubles roamed everywhere, malignant, active and invisible.

The scene in the courtroom at Salem would make one laugh, as they say, if it did not make one weep: three girls, between the ages of twelve and eighteen, would become convulsed from the assault of the 'witches' sitting across the room from them – if the accused denied doing them any harm. Rosenthal asks, wisely, why it never occurred to the interrogators to wonder why the defendants should send their spirit doubles out on the attack at that very moment, when they faced trial, and so reveal their guilt in open court. If the accused confessed, the accusers calmed down. The vicious logic of the witch-hunt was under way: protestations of innocence only brought about more severe convulsions, whereas confessions inspired a kind of truce, and even, in a bizarre reversal of most inquisitorial trials, could save your life. But they also left you branded, feared, ostracised and pauperised, and failed to bring the cycle of suspicions and denunciation to any kind of respite or closure.

As the terror spread, and more and more victims were caught in the web of accusation and counter-accusation, the first male to join the group of accusers was John Indian, Tituba's husband. She had chosen confession, and had not named names, but stuck to vague figures of tall men and rats and cats: he chose the other escape route from the trap sprung by witch scare – the condition of slavery helped him to understand the rules of this macabre Wonderland, where the masters' sympathies were tending, who was determining what words meant.

As catalyst of the Salem crisis, Tituba clearly makes her mark; and Breslaw does not want to deprive her of this place in history. At the same time, she actively wants to relimn her portrait: no hoodoo, no more Dark Eve of the American Fall. She discreetly deplores Maryse Condé's 1986 novel *Moi, Tituba Sorcière . . . Noire de Salem*, in which the Guadeloupe-born novelist glories in Tituba's avenging sorcery against the community which enslaved her. For Breslaw, Tituba hyphenates the two New Worlds more cunningly; she responded to the scare – Breslaw is taking her cue from Natalie Zemon Davis's study of storytelling – with 'a carefully crafted tale that provided satisfactory answers to the questions in the seventeenth-century mind'. Borrowing a term from biology, Breslaw proposes that Tituba survived through 'creative adaptation'. Her central thesis is that when Samuel Parris had recourse to law 'to punish Tituba for her countermagic', he 'created an intellectual crisis in New England that finally forced a convergence of the two disparate traditions'. She wants to navigate clear of the Uncle Tom problem, and define Tituba's difference, between voodoo and African superstition, on the one hand, and Puritan conformism and acculturation, on the other. She does not want to lose her for the pantheon of female heroes (and of history's victims), but is clearly uneasy as well as unconvinced that she was a wholehearted subversive.

In complying with her accusers' charges, Tituba did survive: she was sent to gaol, and remained there as the witch-hunt became fullblown. After it had at last expired, Samuel Parris sold her on – to pay the expenses of her stay in prison. After that, she gets lost to view, though Breslaw, in another archival epiphany, finds her daughter, Violet, still registered as a slave in Parris's will of 1720, nearly thirty years after the events in Salem.

There's a wishfulness about the arguments in this biography; the novelty of the witch trials lay, not in their belief that spirit doubles existed, but in the officers' admission of 'spectral evidence', as the accusers twitched and writhed in the grip of the spirit doubles – Tituba cannot have introduced such thoughts to the community, or even, on the evidence presented at Salem, modified them much. Prospero curses Caliban, after all:

> For this, be sure, tonight thou shalt have cramps,
> Side-stitches that shall pen thy breath up . . .
> Thou shalt be pinch'd
> As thick as honeycomb, each pinch more stinging
> Than bees that made 'em.

Is Ariel a kind of spirit double, working Prospero's *maleficia* invisibly, from a distance? *The Tempest* was performed in 1611, a good while before the credulity of Salem. Influential manuals of witch-hunters like the *Malleus Maleficarum* and James VI's *Demonologie* warn repeatedly that the devil can remain unseen, take possession of one of his votaries and, through this instrument of his will, cause prodigies as well as mayhem.

Theories to explain the Salem witch-hunt have followed fast and furious on one another: mass hysteria, adolescent susceptibilities, Puritan sexual frustration, Parris's precarious economic situation, political unrest in the pioneer colony. Rosenthal suggests, even though he is aware that the idea is modish, looking at abuse. It's not been much remarked – and Breslaw quotes but does not seize the implications – that Tituba withdrew her confession on grounds of the treatment she received at her master's hands. 'The account she since gives of it,' wrote one contemporary witness to the whole tragedy, 'that her Master did beat her and otherways abuse her, to make her confess and accuse (such as he call'd) her Sister-Witches, and that whatsoever she said by way of confession or accusing others was the effect of such usage.'

There are hints and scraps of coercive violence throughout the Salem story: in Tituba's repeated references in her testimony that the spirits 'say more hurt to the Children'; she says she was told to hurt Betty Parris, but 'I would not hurt Betty, I loved Betty, but they call me and make me pinch Betty'. There are the scars her husband John Indian showed on his body; the statement of one of the most active accusers, Ann Putnam, that her dead sister appeared to her in a dream asking for vengeance because she had been whipped to death.

Whippings and beatings on a scale horrifying today and long illegal, scarred the pioneer communities of America, as Mary Beth Norton recounts in her big new book, *Founding Mothers and Fathers*. She has the research historian's true taste for the archive; and touches those rents in the fabric of history through which ordinary people speak. She tells of the lives of children and slaves and servants in the generation before Salem, from around 1620 to 1670. They are routinely thrashed; but what is most alarming is that obloquy rarely fell on the abusers and violators – even when the hidings ended fatally. Norton found 'one of the most tragic cases' concerned a maidservant called Elizabeth Abbott, who in 1624 turned to neighbours for help again and again against the beatings 'with smale lyne or whip corde . . . sometimes with fish hooks attached' to which she was subjected by her master and mistress and 'other servants acting at their direction'. One youth testified that he was ordered 'to fleay her or ells his Mr wold flay him'. Yet, Norton chillingly informs us, the good neighbours always returned her to her employers' household; and her case was not untypical. After Elizabeth Abbott died, and in spite of seventeen depositions of brutality, her employers were not charged with any hand in her death.

Rosenthal's surmise, that the terrors of Salem, stirred up half a century after this house servant died, may have arisen from systematic, institutionalised and accepted cruelty at a domestic level among the Puritans, at least offers a context for the terrible internecine calumnies against innocent women and men by their own family, neighbours and – in Tituba's case – households. It would help to illuminate – if only partially – the initial hysterical behaviour of the children and young women, if they can be seen as escaping from violence, however misguidedly and inarticulately. When that original, unconscious stratagem proved more effective in detaching them from everyday brutality than they can have foreseen, they were caught, dragging others with them into the ever more widely trawling nets of obsessed and credulous witch-hunters. A much less heroic, much more pathetic interpretation of Tituba's part than Breslaw's colourful forced immigrant presents itself: like Joan of Arc, her experience and her perceptions were reconfigured by someone else's powerful fantasy of the devil, always a prime pretext for the abuse of power. To adapt Hume on miracles, it's belief in the devil that makes the mischief.

1996

Siren/Hyphen; or 'The Maid Beguiled'

'This female savage,' noted the missionary Jean-Baptiste Labat, in his *Nouveau Voyage aux Iles de l'Amérique* 'was, I believe, one of the oldest creatures in the world. It is said she was very beautiful at one time.'[1] He was describing a Carib known as Madame Ouvernard, who, when he met her in Dominica in 1700, 'was more than a hundred years old'. She was held in great esteem on account of her great age rather than her past, he writes, though she was also remembered as the wife of the late Sir Thomas Warner, English governor of St Christopher's and Nevis. 'She had a lot of children by this Warner,' wrote Père Labat, 'so that her Carbet, which is very large, was peopled with a marvellous number of sons, grandsons, and great-grandsons.'* Among them, one son only has left a strong trace in the records: the former Governor of Dominica, 'Indian' Warner, who had died in 1676. Labat met Indian's mother a quarter of a century later. Other offspring or their descendants are not recorded, as far as I can tell, in official genealogies, documents or gravestones, in contrast to the issue of that branch of the family descending from Thomas Warner's first two English wives, Sarah and Rebecca.'[2]

Père Labat and his company were on their way to Guadeloupe, but they interrupted their journey for a few days' visit to Mrs Warner's carbet, though the missionary hung up his own hammock rather than lie in one of hers and risk a dusting of the red roucou powder which Caribs used to decorate their bodies. He tells us little more about his time there, but he does describe his hostess: 'This good woman was completely nude, and so naked that she had not two dozen hairs on her head; her skin was parchment, wrinkled and dried in the fire. She was so bent that I could not see her face except when she leant back to drink. However she had plenty of teeth, and still lively eyes.'[3]

---

* 'A Carbet' is the family compound of the indigenous Caribs.

Labat does not connect this Madame Ouvernard with a story a compatriot had told earlier in his history of the conflicts and massacres which led to the establishment of French and English power in the area. Jean-Baptiste du Tertre, in his *Histoire générale des Antilles* of 1667–71, shows a more full-blooded commitment to the 'picture page' and rather less discretion about the ethics of pioneering empire-builders when he describes the complex struggles that took place between indigenous peoples and the colonists. Describing the settlement of St Christopher's by the French (under Pierre Belain, Sieur D'Esnambuc) in collaboration with the English (under Thomas Warner), he relates how the settlers had been welcomed at first and helped 'libéralement', by 'les Sauvages'.[4] But relations soon changed – he does not dwell on the causes.

Du Tertre gives his account of a founding act of conquest. He writes how in 1625 or 1626, a Kalinago (Carib) woman named 'Barbe' learned that the indigenous inhabitants of several neighbouring islands were planning an ambush on the night of the full moon.[5] She passed on the information to the English, because 'she held them in affection and esteem' – she was Warner's mistress. On learning of the danger they were running into and in order to forestall a massacre, the incomers decided to commit one themselves instead, and that night they fell on the savages in their beds, and stabbed them, leaving a hundred or two hundred dead. But they kept, Du Tertre continues, 'their most beautiful women'.[6]

Through the treachery of a woman, more women are obtained, and authority over their people; or, to express it differently, the changed allegiance of one islander inaugurated the transfer of her compatriots' obedience as well; as in founding myths like the 'rape of the Sabine women', the acquisition of females and the settlement of new territories are inextricably intertwined.

Du Tertre gives her the name Barbe,[7] but this seems so punningly close to the idea of Barbarian, and the tale itself echoes another crucial legend of encounter and empire, of Pocahontas who saved John Smith out of love. As a figure of mediation between coloniser and indigenous peoples, Pocahontas or 'Barbe' has another, notorious precursor: Malinche, interpreter and consort of Cortez, about whom a great deal has been written.[8] Malinche provides the hyphen of language between Aztec and Spaniard, and that small cipher of union translates into a sexual bond, which then translates her name, too, and commutes her identity. This triple exchange – of land, of body, of name – institutes a new order of power, in the case of the Spanish conquest of Mexico, the settlement of the Algonquin territories of Virginia, and, in alignment with historical precedent, in the newly annexed islands of the British Caribbean in the early seventeenth century.

But this kind of tale is the irresistible stuff of legend, cartoon historical romance, boldly drawn and highly coloured as a Hollywood costume drama. The love of Pocahontas for Smith is an originary myth of the New World, sensitively analysed by Peter Hulme in his book *Colonial Encounters*.[9] (In spite of the alertness Disney production teams show towards current research, they chose shamelessly to ignore this sceptical, historical reading and to press romance to the service of legitimising propaganda in *Pocahontas*, the the film recycling the figures of the 'female savage', another Indian princess.)

'Barbe' may have been altogether legendary, and her warning invented to excuse an assault in cold blood, but she merges with the historical Madame Ouvernard in the folklore of Empire: her act of heroic treachery becomes attached to the Indian wife of the first governor of the West Indies for the British crown. Or so the story came down to me, and was preserved in my memory (or was it my fantasy?)[10] and found its way into one of the tales Serafine tells Miranda in my novel *Indigo*.[11]

Serafine is a *conteuse*, and she has many ancestors and precursors: like the figure in Simone Schwartz-Bart's *Pluie et Vent sur Télumée Miracle*, Christophine in Jean Rhys's *Wide Sargasso Sea*. In real life, Derek Walcott has paid tribute to his Aunt Sidone, whom he remembers telling him and his twin brother stories after school as darkness fell in St Lucia; Gisèle Pineau has described her grandmother Man Ya, passing on, in France, memories from the narrative store of her native Guadeloupe. 'For us, as children, she added coloured silks to her words and hung stars on her life in the Caribbean. In Creole – her only language – she told of vampires and spirits, of men turned into dogs and three-legged horses, of witches and enchanters, of demons and good angels.'[12]

The writers Jean Bernabé, Patrick Chamoiseau and Raphaël Confiant have reclaimed the *conteur* (male) as a spiritual forebear, and through him, have mounted a controversial attempt to reaffirm the Uncle Tom figure, who does not run away from the plantation to the forest, or *morne*, but stays at home, obedient and docile.[13] The chattering, genial servant in the big house becomes the polar opposite of the incendiary maroon, that ultimate male hero figure of the Caribbean. These French Caribbean writers offer another view of language's possibilities as an expression of resistance – from within: 'So he (the storyteller) protects himself, protects his role, protects the message of devious resistance that he propagates. The words of such a good slave, so the Boss says to himself, cannot turn out dangerous.'[14]

Quiet storytelling works as a fifth columnist, while rebel sloganeering burns itself up in its own heat.[15] A. James Arnold is right to point out how odd and how misleading it is that Bernabé, Chamoiseau and Confiant leave women and women's voices out of their discussion of the maroon and the storyteller as opposing models in history.[16] But at the same time, women cannot be smoothly allotted their place in the same division of roles; the historical – and mythical – part they play in the inauguration of new histories, new societies, new families demands a fresh taxonomy. Women, through their bodies, become the hyphen between the forest/*morne* and the *habitation*/house/plantation, either by force, or by choice. Madame Ouvernard, in her carbet in Dominica, is neither maroon nor docile house slave; she figures as the connection between the two societies, a connection that has been effaced from memory just as her own name has been lost under 'Barbe', and under her married title.

The English phrase 'natural' son, which is how Indian Warner is described in contemporary documents, catches the way the fertility of a native woman produces offspring who *naturalise* – or can be perceived to *naturalise* – the new social and historical power, who can cancel – or, again, can be seen to cancel – the denaturing character of the process by which that power is established.

But the documents of the time reveal a rather different sequence of events from the highly coloured adventure of love and betrayal in the legend – it would be surprising if they didn't. The material emerges from the confused story of Indian Warner, his political allegiances and changes of policy as a Kalinago leader, involved in the resistance the local inhabitants put up to British and French ambitions in the Windward Islands. This resistance took both military and political forms, as Hilary Beckles has shown; by playing the Europeans against one another, in a variety of divide-and-rule, the Kalinago were able to stall the settlement of St Vincent and to retain some authority over Dominica.[17] Indian Warner was deeply involved in this shifting strategy.[18]

Interpretations of his moves were complicated in the view of contemporaries by his birth. However, in the depositions at the subsequent trial of his half-brother and murderer Philip Warner, Indian Warner's mother never comes into focus in the foreground: as Hulme and Whitehead remark, Indian Warner's 'legitimacy' as the son of Sir Thomas Warner is ccaselessly disputed, but the one person who could have testified as to his birth – his mother – was never asked.[19] Some fragments in the record do however concern her, a few subordinate phrases relate to her, and they reveal how crucially women's bodies and identity mirrored the conquest of land and renaming of territory.

Hulme and Whitehead, in their annotated edition of documents from the Public Record Office, began investigating this tangled episode of collaboration, treaties, and treachery, and they give rich source material for 'The Case of 'Indian' Warner'.[20] But there is more material; it is difficult, some of it written in a particularly rebarbative script of the seventeenth century, and the remarks which follow merely attempt to scratch the surface of the story.[21]

When Philip Warner was being tried for the murder, several of his colleagues and acquaintances among the English in Barbados and other islands wrote to the court to plead in high dudgeon on his behalf; they defended the killing on two principal grounds, that Indian was not the son of Sir Thomas, but a slave, and Philip was therefore no Cain who had slain his brother; and that secondly (and consequently) Indian was just that, an undifferentiated Other, not an Englishman, who had been moreover seditious, treacherous, and predatory. These complainants did not deny, however, that the boy had been brought up in the Warner household, but to determine his exact relation – or rather insist upon his lack of relation – to Sir Thomas, they tried to distinguish between two kinds of chattel: a slave and a child. Both were family, in the seventeenth-century usage of family as household, still saturated with the Latin meaning of *famuli*, servants.

Colonel Randall Russell testified, in Nevis, in the presence of Colonel William Stapleton, then Captain-General and Governor-in-Chief of the Leeward Islands, that 'in the month of July in the year 1637' he arrived from England at St Christopher's (St Kitts) and 'was recommended unto the House of Sir Thomas Warner (then Governor-General) and there Lived in his Imploy several Years and by his Command to mind, and to keep account of his *family, both of Indian Slaves (and others)*' (my emphasis).[22] Russell then describes how 'several [of the slaves] had run away from St Xtopher's to Dominicoe [sic] and one of them was the Mother of [Warner] so named, being the first borne Slave on St Xtopher's in the aforesaid Governor-General's family, and Carried with her Son in his Infancie'.[23]

This reference to the naming of a first-born slave was remembered in more vivid detail by two more witnesses who came forward to clear Philip Warner of fratricide. Lieutenant Robert Choppin, who had worked as a servant in the household forty plus years before, described how within a short time after Sir Thomas's return to St Kitts from one of his voyages back to London, 'Thomas Warner Called All his Slaves before him, being All Indians, to the Number of About Twenty-four, and One Indian boy, or Male child, the first Born in his family of Slaves, being about Six Months old, how the Said Sir Thomas, named him Warner'.[24] This witness, like others, went on to make it clear that this public ceremony of naming, this custom of installing the child in the family or household by giving him the same surname, had not been a christening.

Whether this ceremony of inclusion was widespread in colonial households in the Americas is debatable, but certainly the first witness, Colonel Russell, thought the reason that Indian was given the surname Warner as 'the first borne Slave' might suffice to persuade his listeners (who would by the 1670s be accustomed to the slave trade's habit of naming slaves after their owner). Yet the image of the Governor, returning from the 'mother country', gathering his household around him to greet the arrival of an infant son, points to an idea of community in which relations were not as regular as the law (or the Church) might have wished. The witnesses' testimony, to modern ears, achieves the opposite of their intention, and rather confirms that Indian was publicly acknowledged as Thomas's son, and welcomed. If he was indeed the first child born in the house, it would mean that fourteen years had elapsed between Thomas Warner's first landing, in 1623, and the new arrival of the son in 1637 – a prolonged (and unlikely) period of time, but certainly a cause for rejoicing. 'Family' had not yet acquired its modern implication of blood tie, but it was about to be narrowed in order to do so, as Indian's case illustrates.

Imputations of barbarism move in two directions; and in family arrangements as well as the conduct of war, the English colonists were very quick to anticipate the savagery they ascribed to their opponents, and to make a pre-emptive strike. Everyone interprets barbarism according to their own lights (Montaigne's axiom could be reversed: not that 'Men think barbarism that which is not common to them' but 'Men think barbarism that which is common to them (but understand to be shameful)'). Empire-builders could render unto the savage what the savage of their own *imaginaire* desired. A letter from the King – Charles II – written by Sir Henry Coventry to Sir Jonathan Atkins, Governor of the

Windward Islands, offers a most notable example of imperialist projection at work – more notable than the massacre that took place in order to prevent a massacre. His Majesty has heard of the death of Indian Warner, and he expresses his very great displeasure: the murder has damaged the delicate and complex diplomacy of the English in the area and given the indigenous peoples cause to love the French more. 'Since there is reason to believe that the Windward Islands may have been much alienated from the English by this action,' writes Sir Henry, 'His Majesty leaves it to the Governor to give that people some signal and public demonstration of his justice upon the authors by *sending them some heads*' (my emphasis). The letter continues, 'and by some other proper way which he shall think fit that they may be satisfied of the detestation His Majesty and the whole nation has of this proceeding of Colonel Warner's'.[25]

A propitiatory offering of 'some heads' does not suggest policy based on Christian principles. It is difficult to know how Christian early life in the settlements would have been, and whether religion would have marked a strong difference between the Caribs and other Indians and the English; but it does not seem very likely in this atmosphere of concubinage/polygamy, piracy and pillage that the lack of a christening would matter very much when it came to owning or disowning a child.

After describing the naming and presence of the baby in the household, the testimony of Colonel Russell then went on, as we saw, to relate how several members of the household ran away, Indian's mother with them. So, 'Madame Ouvernard' was a runaway as early as the 1640s, and her son was not brought up in the household, but in Dominica, among the Kalinagos of his mother's carbet.

Russell then went on to tell another most interesting episode in the life of Indian Warner, about his reunion with his father 'many years after'. He reports that a captain of a Scottish ship, one Fletcher, calling at Dominica met Indian Warner and, 'Inveigled by the Aforesaid Slave,' says Russell, took him on board after he identified himself as the son of Sir Thomas. Then, 'It came to the knowledge of Sir Thomas Warner that he had on board the same Scotch ship one Indian slave which slave [was by] Sir Thomas Warner', who immediately asked that he be 'delivered' to him, which he was 'upon Satisfaction given to the aforesaid Fletcher'. 'And as a Slave,' concluded Russell, 'So Lived in the aforesaid Sir Thomas Warner his family [sic] until the day of his death.'[26] Recalling events of forty years before, the Colonel appears to me to be trying to impose on the story the more recently developed market structures of the slave trade, and turn a family drama into a typical transaction in the history of slavery, of a runaway restored to his owner with due payment of a fee to a middle man. But the feelings expressed, the interest implied in Indian's actions at the time, do not altogether bear out this construction.[27] The first impulse towards inclusion – Thomas Warner's ceremony of naming the native-born child – is replaced, within that child's lifetime, by the contraflowing impulse, to exclude him. The mother's part, while obscured in the background, is crucial: she moves from the plantation house ('runs away') to another island, where the Kalinagos historically sustained some degree of autonomy alongside colonial arrangements; raised for a time in this atmosphere, the child returns to reopen the relationship. The history of Indian Warner's activities as a Kalinago leader, summarised and analysed in Hulme and Whitehead, reveals the complications of his negotiations.[28]

Du Tertre gives the later part of Indian's life the colour and the cruelty of a fairy tale. After her husband's death in 1648, Lady Ann (the last of Sir Thomas's three English wives, and herself childless) tormented the love child of his illicit Kalinago wife, and, out of jealousy, 'made him work in the fields with the slaves of the household'.[29] Indian, who had been taken back into the household apparently at the mutual wish of himself and his master/father, continued to live there afterwards 'some years with this Lady Ann Warner, till he ran away again to the island of Dominicoe'. Colonel Russell in his evidence also related that after Thomas Warner's death, Indian ran away to Dominica, 'Carrying Several Other Indians with him'.[30] And rejoined his mother there, perhaps conducting from her carbet the diplomacy with contending French, English and indigenous inhabitants of the islands which eventually led to his death in 1676 at the age of thirty-eight. His mother, who survived him, might not have been quite as old as Père Labat thought: if she had been in her twenties when she was Thomas Warner's consort, she would have been in her eighties in 1700.

The figure of the native wife haunts colonial memory, as Bertha haunts Thornfield, and took possession of Jean Rhys's great novel. She lives in the shadows, or disappears altogether from view in the towers of narrative, just as Bernabé, Chamoiseau and Confiant forgot to include her case in their account of the *conteur* in the plantation household. But she does make a powerful appearance in Robert Louis Stevenson's short story, 'The Beach of Falesá', and though it may seem a big leap, from the Caribbean to the South Seas, from the seventeenth century to the late nineteenth, there are some telling points of comparison for any inquiry into the meaning of such marriages as Thomas Warner and Madame Ouvernard's.

In 1892, towards the end of his life, R. L. Stevenson sent the story to Clement Shorter, the editor of the *Illustrated London News*, whom it shocked deeply, so deeply, that to the fury of Stevenson, who did not know until after the fact, he censored it.[31] The story was not published in Britain in its complete form until 1979 in the Penguin Classics collection edited by Jenni Calder, though it had appeared unexpurgated in the USA in 1956.

Censorship can often touch those tender, distempered parts of a society, and it was the opening scene, in the chapter called 'A South Sea Island Bridal', that upset the earliest readers. Stevenson describes the arrival of a new white copra trader – Wiltshire – on the imaginary Polynesian island of Falesá; Wiltshire is met by one of the veterans, a man named Case, one of Stevenson's most brilliantly realised villains. Case offers to fix Wiltshire with a native wife, and Wiltshire chooses Uma, while his pander comments, '*That's* pretty (my emphasis). Case promises to arrange the 'marriage' and when Wiltshire demurs at this, assures him: 'Oh, there's nothing to hurt in the marriage. Black Jack's the chaplain.'

Uma arrives for the ceremony, which is to be performed in the house of the 'Captain', another of the scoundrels Stevenson records with such familiarity, and 'she was dressed and scented; her kilt was of fine tapa, looking richer in the folds than any silk; her bust, which was of the colour of dark honey, she wore bare, only for some half a dozen necklaces of seeds and flowers; and behind her ears and in her hair she had the scarlet flowers of the hibiscus.' This picture, for all its Gauguin-like accessories, is quiet, recollected, and it leads without break in tone to the narrator's first glimmer of self-knowledge: 'She showed the best bearing for a bride conceivable, serious and still; and I thought shame to stand up with her in that mean house.'

Black Jack is dressed up as a priest, and performs the service in English. Uma is given her wedding certificate: 'This is to certify that Uma, the daughter of Faavao, of Falesá, island of—, is illegally married to *Mr. John Wiltshire* for one night, and Mr. John Wiltshire is at liberty to send her to hell next morning.'[32]

The *Illustrated London News* removed this paragraph altogether. Later editions changed 'one night' to 'one week' (as if that showed willing at least). The barefaced breach of promise of 'A South Sea Island

Bridal' stuck in the craw of a London editor in the 1890s and the tenor of the 'unwholesome' story disappointed a public expectant of Stevenson's more rollicking and heroic yarns. Yet it is another of his studies in gentlemanly hypocrisy, more nuanced and more poignant than the famous *The Strange Case of Dr Jekyll and Mr Hyde*.

'The Beach of Falesá' then chronicles Wiltshire's gradual attachment to Uma, whose own sincerity and true affections and generosity of spirit contrast sharply with her husband's. Stevenson is too subtle a portraitist of human character to show Wiltshire's wholehearted redemption. He rather exposes through him the sexual exploitation that he had observed in the islands, and unravels its connections with trading and other forms of power.

Wiltshire says at a later point in the story that his name is pronounced Welsher – but he does not in this instance 'welsh' on his promise, but decides to come square and marry Uma for real. When Mr Tarleton, a missionary, opportunely arrives on the island, Wiltshire commandeers him to perform a true wedding – tearing up the bogus and insulting contract; Uma first turns pale, crying 'Aué!' She thinks herself, at that moment, what Wiltshire knows he has already made of her – 'a maid beguiled'.

Stevenson resists moral sentimentality and shows the trader hoping to profiteer to the end, and only restrained from cheating his customers by his bargain with the same preacher who married him and Uma truly in the sight of God. The pair remain married; Stevenson's impersonation of Wiltshire grows ever more the jocular Englishman abroad (he praises her as his 'A1 wife'), and ends with Wiltshire sending his 'eldest' – a boy – to Auckland to be educated, and worrying about his daughters: '. . . the girls. They're only half-castes, of course; I know that as well as you do, and there's nobody thinks less of half-castes than I do; but they're mine, and about all I've got; I can't reconcile my mind to their taking up with Kanakas, and I'd like to know where I'm to find them whites?'

'Kanaka' is the slang word in Stevenson's South Sea stories for islander: Uma is a Kanaka. 'The Beach of Falesá' would not hold the interest it does today as a clear-eyed setting forth of colonial bad behaviour if the ambivalence of traders' consciences ended with Welsher/Wiltshire's frustrated thieving and muddled prejudices. Stevenson develops Uma in the background – she speaks in pidgin throughout. This speech mimesis, at once childish and inaccessible, effectively muffles her for a reader unfamiliar with the dialect and the literary convention (which must have held true for Stevenson's contemporaries too). Since Stevenson names his characters meaningfully (Welsher/Wiltshire; Hyde hiding inside Jekyll), there may resonate in her very name the idea of Mother – You-Ma, or even, Ur-Ma – and her name gave the story its original title. Less fancifully, the genealogy Stevenson sets up polarises boys and girls in the same manner that different gateways, inscribed 'Boys' and 'Girls', gave entrance to the same Victorian schoolyard. Uma appears in the story with her mother, Faavao, who is depicted as strange, almost bewitched; it emerges that she arrived on the island with Uma, trailing after a white trader: Uma's father is not mentioned. The last paragraph of the story suggests that the boy who has gone to Auckland to be brought up an Englishman (it is implied) has escaped the condition of the half-caste, for whom Stevenson has Wiltshire so frankly declaring his distaste.

This contrast between the mothers, wives, daughters who remain of their race – or are named as mongrel – and the men who can be taught to belong, reflects the polarity of nature/culture which occupation of the newfoundland, or marriage to the native wife, attempts to ease – by hyphenation. Stevenson's story also reverberates with another, interesting comment on South Sea Island arrangements: when Wiltshire approaches the Captain's house for the mock wedding he tells us 'we had come into view of the house of these three white men: for a Negro is counted a white man, and so is a Chinese!' The narrator comments: 'A strange idea, but common in the islands.' The category 'white man' does not denote complexion, or race (as do 'Negro' and 'Chinese' in the same sentence), but a social group, a perception of alliance, founded, the story will unfold, principally in economic interests and alliances. Stevenson in passing widens the standing metaphor of 'whiteness' to describe hierarchical arrangements – what would now be called 'the construction of race', just as the deponents in Philip Warner's trial were attempting to exclude Indian Warner from the 'family' to which he had once been publicly admitted.

However, relative as Stevenson's perception of 'white' is in the story, and open as the category becomes in consequence to realignment, it implicitly excludes women. Indeed, when the villainous Case dies, his widow, to whom he has, against all expectations, left all his worldly goods, leaves to return to Samoa, to her own people: 'she was in a hurry to get home'.

The female characters in the story are sexually movable goods, commonly exchanged, lightly and callously without thought for their feelings, as the travesty of the original 'South Sea Island Bridal' shows. But their nativeness remains rooted in homeland, with all its associations with nature, and remains outside the embrace of the construction of 'white man'. The very name of the imaginary island, Falesá, means 'sacred house', and though it was used by Samoans for 'church', it may have reverberated, for Stevenson, with the idea of a newly inaugurated home itself, to which women are the magical door, the enchanted means of access.

Uma's own mother, Faavao, for example, is marked out as uncanny, potent, an irrational force of nature, and at her entrance to the story she deploys witchcraft and magic: 'a strange old native woman crawled into the house almost on her belly. She said no plain word, but smacked and mumbled her lips.' Uma herself enjoys superior intimacy with the supernatural in her husband's eyes, even though her sweetness of character dilutes its dangerousness. Immediately after the false marriage, Wiltshire opens his new store, and finds that nobody comes to trade copra in exchange for his goods. The islanders stand away from him, staring, giving him the creeps, as Uma's mother did. He finds, from Case, that he is tabooed, or as good as, and that Uma is the culprit: alliance with her has, at this stage in the story, embroiled him in the native and alien world of magic and witchcraft.

The plot pivots on Case's manipulation of the islanders' beliefs: he is exploiting local legends about hauntings and enchantresses for his own ends and Stevenson's racy yarn focuses on Wiltshire's unmasking of Case. Stevenson has been criticised for portraying South Sea Islanders as vulnerable to colonial magic, gullible when a mockery is made of their own religious system, but again, 'The Beach of Falesá' contains, in this respect, another assumption regarding the place of women, all the more interesting because it appears to be unconscious. For the villainous Case has appropriated a local legend about women's powers of enchantment. It is Uma, however, whom Stevenson chooses to pass it to Wiltshire, who protests at her credulity, and her people's.

The story tells how six youths had been shipwrecked on the coast of the island about six miles away: 'They were scarce set, when there came out of the mouth of one of the black caves six of the most beautiful ladies ever seen; and began to jest with these young gentlemen.' Only one of them refuses to join in the revels, and he alone is saved. For when the others return from the cave, 'they were all like drunken men, and sang and laughed in the boat and skylarked and the same night the five young gentlemen sickened and spoke never a reasonable word until they died.'

The enchantress who lives with her handmaidens in a lonely place, in a cave, on an island, has different names, and the South Seas is by no means the only place she is found. Demonesses with lovely faces, nymphs who turn into foxes, Circe in the *Odyssey*, Alcina in the *Gerusalemme Liberata*, the Sibyl of the Sibylline Mountains in Umbria in Italy, Venus of the Venusberg who tempts the knight Tannhäuser, all display their cloven hoof and much worse in the morning, after the first night of love, or in the aftermath of a thousand years of heedless bliss.[33]

It is as they say, an old story; a story as old as the hills. Was it a South Sea Island tale Stevenson had heard, or was he drawing on his own Scottish home lore about Tam O'Shanter and the night-roaming beauty who heartlessly consumes a mortal with her love? It does not matter, but it is significant that when Wiltshire is lying in the undergrowth waiting to ambush Case, his mind turns to the island folklore: 'Little noises they were, and nothing to hurt; a bit of a crackle, a bit of a brush: but the breath jumped right out of me. It wasn't Case I was afraid of, which would have been common-sense, I never thought of Case; what took me, as sharp as the cholic, was the old wives' tales – the devil-women and the man-pigs.' Then, he sees: 'There, coming right up out of the desert and the bad bush – there, sure enough, was a devil-woman, just the way I had figured she should look.'[34]

But it is (only) Uma, coming to find her husband and help him, whom he has mistaken for a sorceress of local legend (those overtones of 'the bad bush'!). The fear needs to be experienced by Wiltshire in the story because it is part of Uma's enchantment for him   it's part of sexual charm, part of 'nature' *ipso facto*, according to the concept of woman in such a narrative (with its associations to legendary temptresses such as the cloven-hoofed *La Diablesse*).

Carlo Ginzburg, in *Ecstasies*, his study of witchcraft, analyses the recurrent motif of the limping shaman, or the sorceress with one hoof, or even Cinderella and her single glass slipper.[35] He sees such lopsidedness as the symbol of belonging in two worlds, of being able to gain access or give entrance to another sphere. Uma, once a 'maid beguiled', is mistaken for a devil-woman with magic powers; marriage to her and children with her have indeed opened the door to a new world for Wiltshire at many levels – emotional, social, familial, national.

Barbe/Madame Ouvernard created a connection between the native inhabitants and the English which Indian Warner embodied; the conflicts around his identity, his place of belonging, reveal the way anxiety around the issues of nationality and race grew between the first encounter and the establishment of imperial power. In the struggle to define ever more tightly zones of inclusion and exclusion, women constantly disrupted the boundaries, offering different ways of belonging, of stepping across a border into another home, giving a symbolic entrance to the enchanted cave of native land, offering alternative nativity stories.

1998

Cannibals and Kings: *King Kong*

The full title of the film is *King Kong – the Eighth Wonder of the World*, and it appears immediately before a cod piece of story-setting: 'And the Prophet said: "And lo, the Beast looked upon the face of Beauty. And it stayed its hand from killing. And from that day, it was as one dead."' This is then identified as an 'Old Arabian Proverb'. Needless to say, no old Arabian dictionary of proverbs would turn up the source of this adage. The combination of mock-Koranic phrasing, biblical vocabulary, and Poe-like morbidity arose in the mind of the co-writer of the screenplay, and one of the film's two directors, Merian C. Cooper.[1]

The preamble has a clear aim, which succeeds: it frames the story as a fable with a moral; it casts the protagonists as universal antagonists in a conflict with oracular significance for all; it sets the action at a distance – an imaginary exotic space of pleasure and dread. It also, stylistically, stamps this classic early adventure-cum-horror movie as authentic kitsch: the proverb itself typifies the patchwork of wilfully fictive history found in kitsch, as well as ironising its own overt moral message. Though the Beast's hand is stayed from killing by Beauty, somehow this does not seem to be quite as welcome as it should be: Beauty is implicitly reproached for her power. Throughout *King Kong*, the titillation of the action itself undercuts the supposed edifying battle: though we are invited to take the part of the humans against the monster, it is with the monster we find ourselves in growing sympathy; though we are expected to feel manly outrage at the Beast abducting and assaulting Beauty, the audience ends up entering into his feelings about her rather than identifying with the laddish hero Jack and his old-world protectiveness. *King Kong* is one of the film children of melodrama which present the primitive as horror, but make no secret that horror ranks very high in their hierarchy of desired passions.

At the end of the film, the police chief says that the aeroplanes got the Beast. The manmade avatars of the lethal pterodactyls shown attacking Kong on his crag in the wild, they succeed in undoing his kingship – in the urban jungle, he becomes a victim. But not of the aeroplanes. Carl Denham, the leader of the expedition to capture Kong, corrects the policeman: 'No, it wasn't the aeroplanes,' he says. 'It was Beauty killed the Beast.' In the novelisation of the film, by the celebrated and prolific thriller-writer Edgar Wallace, the final sentence includes an intensive, 'As always it was Beauty killed the Beast.'[2]

The odd thing about this formula is that it is doubly untrue: the film itself gives it the lie, while the famous fairy tale, familiar since Greek romance, traditionally ends with the Beast restored, transformed into a handsome prince by the Beauty, who has been able to melt away with the power of love the evil enchantment which had held him spellbound in a false and monstrous form. When the writer added that emphatic 'As always', it is as if he was trying to persuade himself of the truth of this blatant distortion.

Nevertheless, the story of King Kong, by quoting the fairy tale throughout, offers itself as a variation on the theme; and it does supply fruitful material regarding Beasts and Beauties, especially as the famous conclusion of the movie, with Kong killed on the pinnacle of the tallest building in the world, symbolises the danger civilisation faces at the hands of nature unleashed, and then shows the beastly wrecker of civilisation overcome and Beauty saved. It also recognises, explicitly in the script, that this formula is needed to camouflage the real dynamics behind the killing of Kong. 'Play up that angle, boys,' Carl Denham urges the press: Kong as victim of love makes a good story, an acceptable, unproblematic story. Society must not be guilty of murder; but the girl can be. The conflict about possessing the creature, with all its undertones of slavery and subsequent racial oppression, will be swallowed into the fairy tale. As James Snead wrote, '*King Kong* is able to cloak and leave unresolved a potential explosive allegory of racial and sexual exploitation by manipulating the codes whereby films typically portray romantic conflict and resolution.'[3]

King Kong was made in 1933, and while it is one of the most famous early American movies, it is not always noticed that the story begins with a film project: Carl Denham is a celebrated film-maker who has already brought back wonders on celluloid to show the public at home.[4] Ann (Fay Wray), in their first encounter, has heard of him: 'You make movie pictures in jungles and places,' she says. He's also famous – and feared – for being reckless, and secretive. He has now heard of this prodigious creature, and plans another adventure movie, on the theme of Beauty and the Beast. Saying he is shooting 'tests', he poses Fay Wray in the 'beauty costume', a flimsy medievalising gown with gold ribbons that frame her pelvic triangle. When she lets down her shingled hair, she reveals that she has long blonde curls, like a heroine from a children's fairy-book illustration. He then asks her to imagine something horrible: 'Higher, still higher,' he commands as she lifts her dewy eyes. 'Now you see it. You're amazed, Ann. Your eyes open wider. It's horrible but you can't look away. Scream for your life, Ann.' Though the script never clarifies the point, it seems that Carl Denham mingles fact and fiction in his adventure movies; that he makes documentaries of distant marvels ('jungles and places') into which he mixes invented, plotted reactions. This approach has various effects, all of which are important in the audience's relation to the creature himself, after Kong appears. Psychologically, he already exists as a spectre in the mind of the screaming girl before she sees him. He matches inner fears. *King Kong* is a classic movie and its central figure a mythic creation, because it focuses on the thrill of confronting exactly this, the terrors of the imagination. Myths handle extreme areas of fear and desire, and *Kong* qualifies for a part in this process of exorcism through fantastic narrative.

Fay Wray became one of the 'screamers', the movie actresses famous for being scared till they screamed, just like the audiences watching them screamed with them. The sexual politics of the film, however, only form part of its social message. The potency of the id, invested in the form of the huge black animal, engages the spectator – becomes 'thrilling' – ambiguously, as both an image of a dreaded other, and as an image of a desirable self. The racial implications of this are as contradictorily handled as the love story, also to mythic effect.

Everything about the voyage to find Kong stresses his distance from humanity as the ship's passengers know it. The name of the 'Beast' is defined within savage (native) culture; the ship, called *The Venture*, is sailing to an island off the chart, 'west of Sumatra', known only before to one sea captain in Singapore who is now dead. The mysterious island is skull-shaped, which gives it its name, Skull Island, and its coastline consists of vertiginous precipices all round except for a single spur of accessible shore. This is the territory of turn-of-the-century adventure-cum-empire fiction, Rider Haggard, John Buchan. Cooper even directed the designer to look at Doré's engravings for *Paradise Lost*, apparently, and this signifies, because the diabolical is never far from the natural as evoked by the film. At the sound of the name, Kong, the skipper comments: 'Some native superstition, isn't it? A god, or a spirit or something . . .' The film-maker breaks in: 'Neither beast nor man. Something monstrous, all-powerful, still living, still holding that island in a grip of deadly fear.' At this stage, the script uses the neuter 'it' to refer to Kong, in spite of the sexual interpretations already circulating in the film, brought out into the open by the presence of the Beauty, Fay Wray, whom Carl Denham is preparing as a bride for the monster.

The setting characterises Kong before we see him as mythic, a monster of the imagination made real. This corresponds to the fictional film-making of Carl Denham himself, and to the enterprise of the popular cinema. He is making a film about a real monster out there who fits our deepest fears; we are watching a film in which this imagined monster has been actualised on screen with all the latest technical skills of the 1930s. The film itself demonstrates the powers of the medium to show extraordinary marvels: the trick photography's extreme contrasts have helped *King Kong* attain its kitsch cult status, and they were more awe-inspiring to the audience then, when they were unprecedented, than they are to spectators accustomed today to *Alien* and *Terminator* movies.

Photography, an invention of the nineteenth century, matched that epoch's appetite for taxonomy, for accumulating and arranging data, and *King Kong* reveals the accepted link between collecting knowledge, gathering specimens and artefacts and recording their image. Kong is a natural phenomenon to be classified and documented and shown – a kind of giant butterfly for the cabinet of curiosities. Merian C. Cooper, who had the founding idea of the film, had made what he called 'natural dramas', documentary films in Africa and South-East Asia, and he had had the idea for Kong when he became fascinated by a colony of baboons on the set of a feature movie, *The Four Feathers*, in Africa in 1929. His codirector Ernest Schoedsack had worked with him on these ersatz documentaries – *Grass* (1925, transhumance of a tribe in Persia), *Rango* (1931) and *Chang* (1927, Laos) – and it was Schoedsack's wife Ruth Rose who came in to work on the script, who made Denham and the first mate Jack into portraits of her husband and his partner. The team's motto consisted of 'the three d's: danger, distance and difficulty'. Theirs was a *Boy's Own* ethic, rip-roaring, empire-building, macho, and *King Kong* openly dramatises both Cooper and Schoedsack's fantasies about their experiences in Africa and other distant parts. They had both had buccaneering careers in the army – Cooper had returned to fly for the Poles against the Russians after the First World War. In the final scene, the two directors are seen piloting the plane that finally takes out Kong.

The frame story – about the film-maker – grounds the fantasy in a documentary process and aims successfully at suspending disbelief. Indeed, when Denham sees how utterly remarkable his quarry is, he abandons the idea of the film, and decides to bring the creature back on the boat with him, to exhibit him in reality on stage. So while the audience are shown flocking to the event which features a live giant ape, we perceive them as an expensive film-première audience, in evening dress, appropriate to the spectacle the movie is making of its own skills. There is an atmosphere of high society and bootleg prices for tickets, until the show goes wrong, and Kong breaks his shackles. The film develops the implicit idea of 'monster' from the Latin *monstrare*, to show: Kong is a showpiece, a demonstration of something people want to see. 'Carl Denham's Monster' proclaims the advertisement. But what is the image he will not let them perpetuate? What is being shown to the world in the shape of the Beast killed by Beauty? What did the directors first want to shoot to reveal, and then shoot to kill?

Carl Denham picks up Ann Darrow, the character Fay Wray so famously created, from the Depression streets where she is wandering, one of the twelve million unemployed of the period. When she steals an apple he saves her from a shopkeeper's anger by paying for it. In effect, as Judith Mayne has pointed out, he purchases the girl for himself.[5] He plans to cast her in the film, to show her too, and when they reach the island where Kong lives, to deliver her to the creature, to show her to him in turn, to lure him with the girl as bait. In this the entrepreneur-film-maker conforms to the role taken by the father in the traditional fairy tale 'Beauty and the Beast' – for it is the father who hands his daughter over to the Beast in his own interests – the Beast has threatened his life, after he has picked a rose from his garden. In the event, however, the Fay Wray character is abducted from the boat by the islanders in a canoe by moonlight – it is they who are usurping Carl Denham's ambition to present her to Kong as a bride.

The film-maker inherits the showman's work: Carl Denham is a ringmaster, a tamer of wild things, a revealer of marvels and mysteries and freaks, who breaks the boundaries of the known world to penetrate into the unknown and bring it back. The island where Kong lives is presented in the film as a compound of fancies about the unknown found in the work of showmen who preceded him, and in early as well as nineteenth-century ethnography. Drums, the cipher of the 'native' in empire literature, give the first evidence of the islanders' presence. Next, we see dancers stomping round in shamanistic costumes, and a Gauguinesque young beauty prepared for Kong with garlands of flowers. The natives are presented wearing hybrid costumes from the *Wunderkammer* of early travellers: a cross between Aztec, Zulu, New Guinea, Sioux and Hawaiian dress – any feather, bone, grass skirt, face paint and ornament that will read to the cinema audience as primitive. They are also worshippers of the deity who lives behind the huge rampart: Kong. The dancers, going round and round (rather half-heartedly and apparently wearing plimsolls, too), are covered in fur sleeves and fur rompers, in honour of Kong. When the film opened, at Grauman's Chinese Theater in Los Angeles in 1933, a fifty strong African choral ensemble accompanied the première, and an 'African troupe' performed a 'Dance of the Sacred Ape'. It's noteworthy that the press reports never specify which African country. It is all merely 'Africa' – while Kong's island, west of Sumatra, can hardly be said to be in Africa at all.

A wonder of the world, a native god, a devouring power which has to be contained behind walls and placated with sacrifices of maidens, Kong lives at several removes from human beings: not only from the society of crews of both film and boat coming from America, but also from the quintessential savages who worship him. In their elaborate fantasy primitiveness, they serve to throw into relief the even greater distance between Kong and the human present to which the savages belong. When the intrepid film-maker and his team cross the wall, they pass into the primeval – animated dinosaurs trundle past, pterodactyls' shadows fall across them, some of their number are devoured by a Loch Ness monster from the beginning of time. Thus Kong, even before he appears, has been placed as a primordial throwback in history, a chapter out of evolutionary time past, as well as a savage beast who requires human sacrifices to appease him. He combines popular Darwinism, a kind of current wisdom of the Thirties, with mythological topoi present in the legends of the heroes Theseus and Perseus: the Minotaur, you will recall, required an annual tribute of young girls and boys from Athens, and Andromeda was lashed to a rock as an offering to a sea monster before Perseus rescued her.

Kong embodies appetite, buried as deep down as his shape is supposedly lost in the prehistoric past – yet both are made present by the film.

It is highly significant that Kong is never called an ape or a gorilla until he's captured and put on show. Then one of the audience comments, 'It's a kind of gorilla.' And another wisecracks, 'Gee, haven't we got enough of them in New York already?' His appearance – the erect, tailless body, the distribution and colour of hair, his features and his gestures – chest-thumping, trumpeting – are distorted approximations of a giant male gorilla. But in other respects – his sabretooth-tiger-like fangs, his carnivorousness – he differs from the apes. His species is not defined in the film, except in one aside at the end, which seems almost inadvertent, when someone calls out that Fay Wray must be saved 'from the ape'. Above all, Kong is presented as a monster of unique character: 'We came here to make a moving picture,' cries Denham, 'and we've found something worth more than all the movies in the world.' He is somewhere in between human and animal – a racist's hybrid. That passing remark about having so many gorillas in New York gets as near as anything in the film to calling Kong a man.

Off screen, the Kong figure stood at about eighteen inches tall, and was covered in nothing more ferocious than rabbit fur. For the closer work, however, huge models of his head and hands were made, with eyeballs twelve inches in diameter. The movements were operated by compressed air and motors. In this case, forty bear hides were used to make the fur convincing in close-up. The creator of the special effects was Willis J. O'Brien, who had worked on the Conan Doyle adventure *The Lost World* in 1925 and animated there Kong's direct predecessor, a brontosaurus who wrecks London.[6]

With the abduction of Fay Wray, the plot of *King Kong* takes the shape of a rescue drama, and Kong himself acquires the third-person masculine as a pronoun: the 'it' becomes a 'he'. The proverb's promise that the beast will stay his hand from killing is about to be fulfilled. The innovative twist in the film – not present in Greek material – is that when the beast seizes the girl, he does not eat her at once or violate her, but finds her fascinating.

His followers anticipated his feelings, for they had offered the landing party six native women in return for the blonde. When Kong carries her up to a rocky height – anticipating the last sequence on another pinnacle – he examines her, and we in the audience are involved in his wonder at her. She stands or sits in the palm of his hand, a Thumbelina of tiny size, much smaller in relation to Kong in this sequence of the movie than at any other time, in order to set up clear oppositions between them: big/small, black/white. These oppositions imply deeper value ascriptions: monstrous/ beautiful, savage/civilised.

With the establishment in the USA of the Hays Committee in 1934, censorship laws came into operation and the episode was cut. The restored version, first shown in the Sixties, does indeed contain some explicitly intimate sexual gestures. Kong picks off Fay Wray's torn skirt; and goggles at its flimsiness appreciatively. She's unconscious. He then sniffs the torn sections. She comes to, and struggles, and he tickles her. His nostrils twitch, and then, again, he smells his fingers.

In the aesthetic hierarchy of the senses conveyed in Christian teaching and Renaissance allegories, smell ranks very low; sight traditionally conveys the knowledge of higher things, and touch knowledge of earthly matters; taste is associated closely with flesh, through food, of course, while smell is ranked, in the schema of the five senses, as the base, animal faculty. Thus Kong, negotiating the identity of this novelty, this blonde titbit, by using his nose, reveals his utter creatureliness, and the gestures are disturbing, even to a spectator today, in their grounded intimacy.

After Fay Wray escapes, Kong breaks out of his corral, battering down the huge gates that separate his dinosaur time from the present; his irruption into the modern signals the arrival of a major symbol of what we have left behind, come back to haunt us. The grotesque is never far away, as happens with any combination of spectacle and cruelty: when the battle against Kong breaks out, he is shown plucking warriors from the fortifications and the ground and casually stuffing them in his mouth, like so many sticks of candy: the legs of one victim go on squirming between Kong's teeth. These close-ups were also cut from the 1933 version. The spectre of cannibalism, together with the implied mating of human and animal, proved to be the sticking point for the censors. This is important: in the case of other hybrid creatures, their threat focuses on these two transgressions against the human: consuming human flesh and sexually crossing the distinction of species. In Cocteau's fairy-tale film *La Belle et la Bête*, the beast wears courtly dress and conducts himself reverently with *la belle*; he is masked by a cat-like face which his deep purring voice matches. But he reveals to her his menace when she sees him hunting, tearing creatures limb from limb with his bare paws. Eating raw flesh, he is a monster. His fur, his paws and jaws literally smoke afterwards with the bloodshed.

Once the terrifying beast Kong has been captured and tied, Carl Denham cries out, 'We'll give him more than chains . . . We'll teach him Fear. We're millionaires, boys. I'll share it all with you. Why, in a few months, it'll be up in lights on Broadway: "Kong, the 8th Wonder of the World!"'

The chains recall slavery, and the mention of fear the conditions of tyranny. The period in which Kong appeared was marked by high migration of black workers from the South to the cities of the North, the growth of the Ku Klux Klan in those same cities, like Chicago, and a wave of riots caused by different, racial problems. The figure of Kong, crucified on his gallows on stage before he breaks free, has symbolised to some viewers the eruption of the proletariat under Roosevelt's New Deal, to others the conservative fear of black men and desire to repress their perceived threatening sexuality. The film's power, as the Surrealists recognised, rises from its indeterminacy on this point: inconsistent, implausible, illogical, and unresolved, it often contradicts its own apparent purpose, and stirs up contrary allegiances in the imagination.

When the monster lies stunned by Denham's gas bombs on the beach, and Denham promises to chain him, his opportunism fills his promise with irony for the audience, whose sympathies are gradually becoming divided between mankind and the monster, in spite of his ferocity. When Kong beats off a savage assault by a pterodactyl to prevent the bird carrying off Fay Wray and is wounded in the struggle, the music turns soft and tender; when he lies trussed on the beach, the tone of the movie does not lean to exulting, but rather pity.

The film's ironical critique of civilisation, its sympathy with the Beast rather than the Beauty, grow stronger as the symbol of the primitive is freighted on board, bound for display and for profit. The primitive, epitomised by the so-called Kong monster, carries ambiguous value; he is a wonder of the world. Wonder, as Stephen Greenblatt has argued in the context of Renaissance conquest and travel, acts to define self and the identity of the beholder.[7] The 'I' of the humanist self finds a means to knowledge, by establishing ownership through knowing, and by drawing a boundary by recognising or imagining difference between self and the object of wonder. Wonder is composed of mixed feelings: 'When we wonder,' writes Stephen Greenblatt, 'we do not yet know if we love or hate the object at which we are marvelling; we do not know if we should embrace it or flee from it.' It is the response to the new and the alien: the traveller's common experience, the reaction of Miranda in *The Tempest*, creature of the old world who has been exiled from it, when she first sees men of her own kind. Her name derives from wonder, and she utters the famous line, 'O brave new world . . .'. Though she was born in the old world, she has never known the people there, and so her own kind strike her as new – a profound paradox Shakespeare creates and one which reveals that all appears new when it is not known, however like it is. It is important that Miranda exclaims with love at the first sight of Ferdinand; the response of wonder often enfolds desire; discovery and erotic susceptibility are connected, and wonder in its very ambiguity matches erotic emotions of longing and fear. But I will come back to Miranda – and to Caliban – later, after looking at the undoing of King Kong.

At one level, the monster represents nature versus humanity, but at another, he represents men versus women. The proverb announces that after seeing Beauty the Beast will be as one dead – later, Carl Denham adds a contemporary twist to this warning when he tells Jack, the first mate and the tough guy on board, that 'The Beast was a tough guy, too. He could lick the world. But when he saw Beauty, she got him. He went soft, he forgot his wisdom and the little fellas licked him. Think it over, Jack.' The men's separate manliness is bound up in Kong's singleness: he is, if you like, a bachelor on the loose.

While Kong represents primitive alterity in all its fascination, he is more and more identified, as the film develops, with human freedom, specifically male nature and its power buried within, and the unmanning of this kind of maleness by women, the carriers of civilisation's codes. The fellow-creature of dinosaurs, found to be still living, walled off from human society, bodies forth the primeval within. History and consciousness are built like houses, and both have buried layers. The adventure movie inherited from nineteenth-century ethnography imagined this stratum down deep below: the primitive, as the word conveys, comes first, and this can be understood in temporal terms – the start of time – as well as in anthropological terms – the start of civilisation – as well as psychological – the id. These first emotions include instinct, desire, horror and wonder. Those 'chains' Carl Denham heaps on Kong, that fear he wants to teach him, symbolise the end of the wilderness for him: repression, domestication. As a king in his prehistoric jungle, Kong exudes a sinister form of alienness which does not excite sympathy; but as a captive, as a crucified exhibit on a scaffold on stage, taunted by the presence of the blonde in another man's arms, he becomes the emotional core of the movie, with whom spectators – men and women – identify.

The final blow for Kong comes when the press start popping flash-bulbs, and he takes them for blazing firearms, imagines they are going to hurt Fay Wray, and bursts his bonds, freeing himself from his 'slave auction' platform and starting his rampage. Fay Wray's horrified rejection of his sudden tenderness for her inaugurates a rich tradition in the movies, of stories about monsters unrequited in love; the plot neatly carries the double pleasure that it flatters women with evidence of their remarkable powers to excite and tame the primitive and excuses men the desires of their id and their necessary failure to realise them.

No Beast in the long history of the fairy tale of 'Beauty and the Beast' had been perceived as explicitly ape or ape-like before King Kong, as far as I know. Bears, wolves, hogs tend to predominate in the illustrations and description of the fairy-tale bridegroom. The ethnographical aspects of the story and the emphasis on the primitive, in terms of inherited attitudes, contributed to shape the physical image of Kong. Structurally, in the film, King Kong inherits the part of the Beast, the embodiment of unbridled sexuality. Like the fairy tale, the film plunges long roots into the soil of Christian mystery dramas about the battle with the devil, traditionally envisaged as a hybrid species of different types. Two indices connect Kong with Christian demonology: the chthonic colouring of his skin and pelt and his overall hirsuteness. Dark and hairy, he is related to ancient representations of menace and temptation. Above all, he embodies the struggle with ideas about what is good in the natural. His overwhelming desire for Fay Wray characterises lust as his dominant motif – concupiscence was above all, in the view of Augustine and Aquinas after him, the passion of the tempter which he communicates to human beings. Taken together with his anthropophagic rampage in the movie, Kong embodies the flouting of human norms, the breaking of rules, the unruliness of nature. In itself, this marks him as outside social laws. Through the twin threat of rape and cannibalism, he must be sequestered from the human nature he so nearly shares or appears to share. In this respect, he has a precursor: the 'salvage and deformed slave' from *The Tempest*, Caliban.

When Stephano and Trinculo discover Caliban hidden under a gaberdine and smelling fishy, Trinculo's first reaction to his oddness of appearance is that he will be able to show him:

> Were I in England now, as once I was, and had but this fish painted, not a holiday fool there but would give a piece of silver;

There would this monster make a man; any strange beast there
makes a man: when they will not give a doit to relieve a lame
beggar, they will lay out ten to see a dead Indian.

Stephano picks up the idea with warmth, 'If I can recover him and
keep him tame . . . he's a present for any emperor that ever trod on neat's
leather [cow-hide].' Both are impresarios in the making – Carl Denhams
before his time. *Freaks*, the famous silent film, continued the medieval
and Renaissance entertainment of the peepshow.

Caliban's physical attributes, alluded to in scattered images
throughout Shakespeare's play, do not approximate to any species, and
productions have varied imaginatively, from portraying him as a kind
of walrus to acting him as a semi-naked islander. Favourite sources
have been the classical satyr, as in a faun-like portrait by the Victorian
fairy-painter Joseph Noel Paton, as well as the green man or
wodehouse of medieval forest legend. But *The Tempest*'s profound and
multi-faceted arguing about nature and art, its deployment of different
degrees of magic, centre on the opposition between Caliban, the
usurped heir of the island, and Prospero, the prince usurper. Caliban
represents a former time, too, a past that has been altered irrevocably
by the coming of the Duke of Milan from the city: the nature Caliban
was so expert in adapting to his needs has been changed, even renamed:
'thou wouldst . . . teach me how/ To name the bigger light, and how the
less,/ That burn by day and night.'

This aspect of Caliban inspired Browning, in his poem 'Caliban upon
Setebos', to meditate on the savage arriving at an understanding of
himself as a person and learning to speak in human language, using the
first pronoun. Caliban as missing link between the animal and the human
also influenced some stage interpretations, as for example, Robert Atkins,
in an outdoor production in the summer of 1933, the same year as *King
Kong*.

In another salient aspect, *The Tempest*'s savage prefigures King Kong,
with the attempted rape of Miranda which Prospero describes:

> I have us'd thee,
> Filth as thou art, with human care; and lodg'd thee
> In mine own cell, till thou didst seek to violate
> The honour of my child . . .

To which Caliban howls in reply:

> O ho, O ho! would't had been done!
> Thou didst prevent me; I had peopled else
> This Isle with Calibans.

The transference of fear seems patent in this speech: one rape could hardly have produced a 'population' for the island. The racial conflict concealed in *King Kong*'s allegory of slavery and revolt also lies at the root of the coloniser's maltreatment of the colonised, and beneath that lie male sexual fears about the control of women. Prospero's need to make alliances and his fear of misalliance inspire the fantasy about Caliban's progeny which Shakespeare gives to the slave to speak in the play. It is a fear continually reiterated by anti-immigration politicians to this day.

For the plot of *The Tempest* focuses on the disposal of Miranda's body – the body of the true, white daughter to her father: where it is to be bestowed by Prospero. He conjures the storm itself to bring his enemies into his power, but also to summon Ferdinand, his choice of husband, for Miranda. The drama is filled with images he makes up out of the air, with the help of Ariel: a kind of cinema of the imagination. Without wrenching the structures of play and film, it's quite possible to interpret *King Kong* as indeed progeny of *The Tempest*: with Denham the impresario in the Prospero role, cut in with a little bit of Stephano and Trinculo's robustness, Fay Wray as Miranda, the cardboard Jack as the equally insipid Ferdinand and Kong as a Caliban, king of his island before the invaders, a captive afterwards, who rages and curses his 'civilising' masters and rivals Ferdinand for her love.

The popular film has developed the traditional terrors about the savage latent – and offstage – in the play: rape, miscegenation and cannibalism. In Shakespeare, Caliban isn't portrayed even as a carnivore, let alone a man-eater – he does promise Stephano and Trinculo he will snare them 'the nimble marmoset', though this could be for a pet. But of course his punning name hints at the taboo, in the ears of Shakespeare's audience as well as later.

The Tempest concludes with the restoration of harmony, the obedient love of Miranda and Ferdinand, the penitence of Prospero and all others – except Antonio; and the promise of Caliban that he will 'seek for grace'. The order it ostensibly lays down in its happy ending turns out to bristle with question marks, and King Kong is one of the many transformations of the myth to which Caliban also belongs. Both figures flesh out fantasies of control, directed at inner drives as well as outer objects.

But the Beast's condition as a beast is not stable: the processes of art, like the fairy tale itself, are likely to find the fascinating prince beneath his hairy features and frightening, big hairy body. No metamorphosis into human shape is needed for redemption, either. Little girls watching King Kong identify with the gorilla's plight, not Fay Wray's; and at the fiftieth anniversary showing of *King Kong*, one member of the public came dressed as a gorilla, and never took off the costume at all: audience identification taken to an ultimate surrender.

1995

Bananas

The frond of the banana has straight seams, as a good pair of nylons used to have, so it's easy to tear along them and make squares of bright luminous green, nature's own shot silk. Which is what Adam and Eve probably did when they made shift with 'aprons' to hide their shame from God in the garden. In some countries where Spanish and Portuguese are spoken – which means parts of the Caribbean as well as Latin America – the word for 'fig' is used of the banana, so this may be another example of those inspired clerical slips which result in widespread conventions. That the figleaf is hard to fix to the body every child confronted with a Renaissance statue has noticed. Banana leaves, on the other hand, can be draped and threaded – like cloth.

In the seventeenth century, when savants were as keen on gardening as on the Bible, the general opinion of herbalists and botanists and connoisseurs of simples was that the banana was the strongest candidate for the original tree of the knowledge of good and evil. (The palm was preferred for the Tree of Life.) Such books aren't always reliable guides – the 'vegetable lamb', which grew on a stalk in Scythia, also makes an appearance in them as part of God's flora. Though nobody put themselves wholeheartedly behind the banana as the fruit whereof Adam did eat, Linnaeus believed in the story enough to give the tree the name *Musa paradisica*. The sister species, the plantain, he called *Musa sapientum* – on account of another legend, that those gymnosophists or Wise Men whom

Alexander the Great encountered sat in the shade of such a tree and occasionally ate a banana.

But the link to the fruit of knowledge developed from those features which make people laugh aloud at the mere mention of the banana, the same bawdy that inspired the *Sun* to put a cut-out banana on its front page ('Now they've really gone bananas'), in a fresh outcry against Euro-madness, when 'Brussels' issued specifications (at least 5.5 inches long, no more than 1.1 inches thick).

In the Caribbean, where bananas are the staple crop of several islands, the fruit isn't so funny and banana jokes are wry. In the Fifties, in the Dutch, French and British islands, the end of the imperial era was marked by a transition from large sugar plantations worked for a short season by labourers, to smallholdings growing bananas that fruited all year round and were harvested by the farmers who owned them. The harvest was then delivered to harbour and shipped by companies who paid the farmers cash on the dock: Fyffes and the formerly Dutch company of Geest, who used to sail from St Lucia to Dominica by schooner before loading the fruit on to steamships bound for Britain.

The banana is a kind crop: a perennial with no need of cross-fertilisation, it produces abundantly a food rich in nutrients, and provides a continuous income. In this sense it made a change from the punishing ordeal of sugar. It's the chief export of many Caribbean countries, and it has come under huge' pressure. In 2003, the Lomé trade convention expires, and the protective economic shield it now guarantees will be removed. Lomé has made it possible for Jamaica and the Windward Islands, which include Dominica and St Lucia, to grow bananas and export them competitively, against the might of the multinationals operating in Central America. In Honduras, the daily wage is around $1.50 to $2 for a plantation worker; in Jamaica, not exactly one of the wealthiest countries in the world, expectations are nevertheless rather higher, the standard of living is a little better, and a farmer's daily earnings are nearer $6. In Honduras, on huge estates of flat ground the yield per acre is held consistently at 22 tons; on a good smallholding in Jamaica, assiduous cultivation would be lucky to produce 14 tons per acre.

So the Caribbean fruit is much more expensive than the 'dollar banana', and its marketability is sustained only by punitive tariffs and quotas against its rivals. But, as the head of the Banana Export Company in Kingston, Jamaica, told me, 'the Americans used to get bananas tariff-free, from Colombia and so forth. Now the price is twice as high and they're screaming.' It's not only the Americans who are screaming, and fighting the EU's resolution last year to continue to subsidise the Caribbean fruit. Germany is furious, too: the Germans eat so many bananas that their consumption averages out at 19 pounds per person a year. In their view, the Lomé measures flout Gatt's free-trade principles. France is in yet another special situation since its Caribbean islands remain full *départements* of metropolitan France within the European Union. Martinique and Guadeloupe's bananas have no problems in the market; they're French, not Third World produce.

In Dominica, Dame Eugenia Charles, Prime Minister since 1980, and magnificent champion of her island's interests, is not giving in to the pressure of international free trade. She has said that if her people can't make a living from bananas they will not starve: they will turn to something else.

The banana isn't indigenous in that part of the world: the word is African and it is likely that the fruit travelled to Africa from the East, possibly in the same long-distance canoes in which Javanese sailors brought rice to Madagascar two thousand years ago. Arab traders carried it across the continent to Guinea on the west coast, where Portuguese navigators found it; they took the root stocks (known as 'bull heads' from their appearance) to the Canary Islands, where (Spanish) bananas are still grown. A Spanish monk, one Thomas de Berlanga, may have been responsible for the fruit's subsequent journey to the Americas, for he planted it in San Domingo in 1516; the English, those comparative latecomers to the New World, saw its wonderful obliging nature, and took many banana plants from the Spanish-dominated islands to the doomed colony of Roanoke. Around a hundred years later, in 1699, the buccaneer Lionel Wafer, who had decided to stay in Panama with the indigenous people there rather than continue to sail north with the explorer William Dampier, thought the cultivation methods worth reporting: 'the Indians set them' – banana plants – 'in rows or walks, without under-wood; and they make very delightful groves. They cut them down to get at the fruit; and the Bodies being green and sappy, they are cut down with a stroke of an Axe . . . The Fruit is short and thick, sweet and mealy.'

Methods of planting and cutting down the banana trees haven't changed; but a banana grove doesn't seem like Eden any more. The tree – it is in fact not a tree but a vegetable, strictly speaking, with no bark or wood – thrusts upwards from the ground in a rolled sheaf like a fat Cuban cigar, and the leaves push out from the middle in tender green quills, furled on the slant so that a small section glows transparent at the top where the leaf isn't folded on itself. A single flower grows on the tree, and after it has produced an exuberantly huge bunch of bananas, it is then cut down, to make way for the 'follower' and the 'peeper' – the suckers which will in turn grow tall and bear fruit. In the heyday of the export trade, Banana-men posed for sculptures and wall frescos and other images which showed them hauling the massive candelabra of the green fruit like fly fishermen with their prize catch: a single stem might carry ten or more round clusters of twenty or more bananas each – the weight of a woman ripened from a single flower.

The flower which produces this wonder was described by an early observer, the eighteenth-century mercenary J. G. Stedman, as 'something like a calf's heart': it is a huge bud shape, with a bluish-purple bloom on fleshy red petals and a soft whey-like scent, and it hangs down and then pokes out from the end of a bizarrely corrugated thick stem in a manner that is definitely lewd. Wallace Stevens captured the look of it in a poem called 'Floral Decoration for Bananas', and I had no idea what he was describing until I saw it for myself:

> Fibrous and dangling down
> Oozing cantankerous gum
> Out of their purple maws,
> Darting out of their purple craws
> Their musky and tingling tongues.

The future bananas hide under each petal of this monstrous protuberance, and though the light and shade are flecked under the trees' fronds, and the earth underfoot is all soft and loamy and red-rich (the banana is semi-aquatic and sucks up water like a clump of reeds), the effect of a tropical paradise is diminished these days by the blue plastic sheaths which are used to bag the developing bunch, and which lie discarded all over the ground after harvesting.

This blue sheeting has been treated with chemicals to destroy any thrips that might mar the banana's beauty with small dark scars on its skin. The requirement is purely cosmetic: the fruit's taste isn't affected. But supermarkets demand bright yellow, unmarred fruit. Jean Dixon, from the Banana Export Company in Jamaica, at first sighed, as she ran through the requirements, but then grew angry: 'I have a background in Environmental Studies, and all the marks we lose are simply for aesthetic reasons, and we're intimidated by these regulations.'

Videos are being used to teach growers ways of handling the fruit: the flowers must be pruned from the end of the developing banana, so that the latex (again not harmful) does not stain its skin; the huge bunches must be cut down at the exact stage of greenness so that they will not turn ripe on board. The banana boats still call weekly and still bring the fruit to Britain, along with the post (as a result, surface mail to and from the Caribbean is surprisingly quick – as booksellers told me).

The peasants who used to nurture their grove, deliver the week's harvest, then rest (or party – it's called 'liming' there) over the weekend, have had to become more professional, much more systematic and scientific to meet rising international standards of appearance. But if you look at some of the earliest paintings of tropical fruit – such as the National Gallery is showing in the wonderful 'Spanish Still Life' exhibition – you can see that they are never smooth and immaculate, almost laminated, the way they are gradually becoming today. When the first cargoes were landed in Liverpool, the dockers found all kinds of things still nestling in the trash – the banana leaves and stems – in which they were packed. A stowaway marmoset was then a sailor's prize pet. Now a mere spider can put you out of the market.

Although it seems too easy to blame America, this is definitely an area where American consumerism has shaped worldwide taste and led demand: only six years ago in California, when I first saw the green-grocer's section (how quaint that word is now) in my neighbourhood Safeway, I was open-mouthed at the wet-look glossiness, the high colour of the fruit on display: not the trace of a thrip, not the spoor of floral latex anywhere. Concealed rose-bulb illumination on the stands, automatic drizzle to freshen them up every now and then. But, as I soon found out, this picture-perfect fruit is soapy and wan to the palate.

In St Lucia, where the crop produces 60 per cent of national exports, and there are ten thousand farmers (with families) and twenty thousand connected workers (stevedores etc.) out of a population of 150,000, the distinctive light green shagpile of the trees hugs the slopes for mile after mile as well as coating the valley bottoms. The banana has been a bonanza crop: it has continued to bring new wealth to thousands of small farming families, it still accounts for the hundreds of private four-wheel-drive pick-up trucks and the pretty pastel-coloured houses with verandahs perched on St Lucia's volcanic hills. 'Lots of people criticise it,' said one banana trader, 'but it's one of the most efficient ways of distributing wealth that there has ever been: actual money that comes back to the islands – *weekly.*'

From the air, as I was arriving. I saw great open weals gouged in the earth of these hillsides, but it wasn't until I visited the research centre of Winban (the Windward Banana Company) that I learned what these were: landslides from the freak deluge called Debbie, which according to James Ferguson, an agricultural adviser, 'illustrated in ten hours what will happen in ten years unless something is done to stop it'. More and more unsuitable high ground is turned over to bananas to try and keep up the supply, and the terrain can be – will be – simply washed away, leaving the kind of scars in the former forest that cannot be prevented by applying a few plastic bags. The solution would be to restrict land use to high-yield farms on suitable, flat terrain: but no politician could ever formulate such a policy and be elected (unless huge compensation was offered to the dispossessed). And then, they would still have to offer something to do.

I was in the Caribbean giving talks and reading, courtesy of the British Council (yes, it's true, and yes, I did do some work). But I was interested before I went in the banana problem. I'd read that the hidden issue was the farmers' easy alternative: marijuana. Though marijuana plants are routinely grubbed up by the forces of law and order, the law enforcers I met were surprisingly ready to recognise that the problem isn't ganja, at least not in itself. It's the crop's connection to the drug baronies; to blackmail, intimidation, gangs, murder, Colombia, the whole invisible crime network. I was startled how often I heard a sobersides with a short haircut, in a suit and a tie, tell me that the solution was to decriminalise drugs. But this is another policy that no politician could ever deliver – not there, and not here. These men who certainly never inhaled, these interesting representatives of new approaches to law and order were not locals, by the way – feeling in the islands, contrary to their reputation, runs extremely high against all drugs. The 'dons' riding around in pimpmobiles, flashing their cellnet phones and gold chains, provoke anger and dismay in people who work as accountants and teachers – or banana-traders. Especially in Jamaica, where the recent television portrait of Kingston as a Bronx of the Caribbean caused bitter sorrow – and of course does little to help the country's economic problems.

The Caribbean is highly vulnerable, an area in an acute state of flux: there are thirty-two satellite stations beaming in programmes from Florida, and Jamaicans joke that the dish has become their national tree. The farming population is ageing: young men, in particular, don't want to live in the same way as their parents. They're drawn to the luxury hotels on the coast, in St Lucia, for instance, where a sailboard coach for holidaymakers might be paid an hour what a banana worker earns in a month. It is in St Kitts (where there is till some sugar cane, but no bananas) that the problems of a small Caribbean island nation are most acute. Contact with Latin American drug-dealers, using the island for transhipment of cocaine to the American mainland, has resulted in a series of murders, the head of the island's Special Branch and the Prime Minister's son among them.

Against this background, the idea of decriminalising drugs may sound preposterous; but if they were no longer illegal, they could be controlled more effectively. The trade would no longer bring in the profits it does today, or offer the same temptations to ordinary citizens. Or, more important, to politicians. As children, we used to try and smoke old banana skins, as I recall, even though we didn't know anything then about paradise lost or the fruit of the knowledge of good and evil.

1995

Zombie: The Devil Inside

The vision of transmigration that closes Plato's *Republic* describes the souls of Homeric heroes choosing the form of their next existence, which Plato calls a 'daimon'. This daimon can be a person, or an animal, or even an inanimate object. As in Ovid's *Metamorphoses*, souls live on, transmogrified, in 'all kinds of mixtures'. Legends about the Hindu gods, like the myths of the Olympians, also permutate multiplying selves, gender switches and phantom likenesses: transformations of the self depend on an idea of souls migrating from one shape or species to another.

Today, developments in biology, stemcell research and genetic engineering have repositioned the concept of metamorphosis within a practical arena: the flower of immortal life that Gilgamesh brought back from the underworld, the ointment of youth and beauty that Psyche fetched for Venus, are no longer the sheer stuff of fairy tales in an era of Michael Jackson's face, genetically modified tomatoes, middle-aged first-time mothers.

Contemporary culture revels in the potential of metamorphosis as a curse or a boon: mutants, replicants, monsters, aliens, cyborgs and a rich variety of other quasi-scientific life forms teem in comic strips, films, video games and genre fiction for adults and children. The tendency isn't confined to popular media or to sci-fi and cyberpunk: several esteemed writers of literary fiction, such as James Lasdun in *The Horned Man*, the Canadian poet Anne Carson and the French novelist Marie Darieussecq, not to mention the celebrated magic realists, Ben Okri, Gabriel Garcia Marquez, Isabel Allende, Salman Rushdie, adopt a magical model of psychology, which allows one person to take possession of another, to make huge leaps across time, to shape-shift.

In contemporary fiction, Philip Pullman has woven metamorphosis into the concept of the self in the trilogy *His Dark Materials*, re-imagining the Platonic daimon as a personal animal familiar that accompanies every character. These external doubles, which he spells 'daemons,' with a life of their own as well as a symbiotic, vital connection to their 'owners', have a shape-shifting character.

Children who are divided from their daemons in the course of Pullman's plot become zombies: he uses the word, which entered the English language in 1819, according to the *OED*. The idea of a zombie was an early nineteenth-century import from West Africa via the Caribbean, through the diaspora brought about by the traffic in human beings.

Zombies used to be primarily victims of voodoo masters. Today, it's become an existential term, about mental and physical enslavement, a deathly modern variation on the age-old theme of metamorphosis. Researching my new book on growing stories of metamorphosis, possession or soul-theft, I went to the British Library to look up the passage cited in the *OED* for zombie's English-language début: Robert Southey's *History of Brazil*. I found that the British Library's copy had actually been presented by Southey to Samuel Taylor Coleridge, his friend and brother-in-law, and that Coleridge had made notes on it.

Southey is recounting the terrible revenge taken by the Portuguese in 1694 on a group of escaped slaves who had established their own community, ruled by an elected chief, 'chosen for his justice as well as his valour . . . it is said that no conspiracies or struggles for power had ever been known among them. Perhaps a feeling for religion contributed to this obedience; for Zombi, the title whereby he was called, is the name for the Deity, in the Angolan tongue.' Southey then added a note that 'the word means Devil in their language'.

In the margin, Coleridge comments that Southey is wrong to assert that zombie means 'the Devil'. No, he writes, it means *a* devil, in the sense of a daimon, or indwelling vital principle.

Finding Coleridge's neat pencil annotation against the word 'zombie' gave me a frisson. It makes such sense with his obsessions, with the entranced and spellbound figures in his most famous poems. For with regard to the modern idea that a living person can lose all power over his or her being, that the soul or inner core can die while the body remains alive, it is Coleridge who makes the first declared link between the West Indies and a new psychology of the supernatural when he writes that he was influenced by his readings about spirit cults in the Caribbean and North America. In 'The Rime of the Ancient Mariner', the Mariner is a stricken, enthralled automaton; the doomed ship moves, bewitched, laden with its 'ghastly crew', all of them living dead whose sounds and terrible, accursed looks deepen the Mariner's own spellbound state.

William Empson linked the 'Ancient Mariner' to Coleridge's anti-slavery stand in the years he was writing the poem: the extreme, anguished guilt the Mariner feels arises from Coleridge's view of the personal effects of public wrongdoing. The 'Ancient Mariner', Empson wrote, is 'the great ballad of maritime expansion and empire'.

Zombies as we know them today arrived by another route from the Caribbean, however, through travellers' reports and the films they inspired: *White Zombie* (1932), for instance, is an early gothic nasty, in which Bela Lugosi plays the zombie master, known as 'Murder' Legendre; he hammed it up, in diabolical make-up – widow's peak wig, beetling brows – while sinister close-ups of his hypnotic eyes show him bending his victims to his desires.

The film was influenced by *The Magic Island*, a first-person account of voodoo rituals written by William B. Seabrook, an American living in Haiti. His often lurid book had first inspired a play, simply called *Zombie*; when the makers of *White Zombie* announced their film later that same year, the playwright sued, saying he owned the concept. His suit was thrown out, the law deciding that zombies by this time belonged in the public domain.

Eleven years later, another B-movie, also destined for cult status, *I Walked with a Zombie*, reworked the plot of *Jane Eyre*, with the 'madwoman in the attic' played as a beautiful, dumb, spellbound voodoo victim. The film, directed by Jacques Tourneur, sets the story on an imaginary Caribbean island, and may well lie behind Jean Rhys's ingenious reworking of *Jane Eyre* in *Wide Sargasso Sea* in 1967. But the movie that sealed the appropriation of the zombie for white conscious-ness was – is – *The Night of the Living Dead*, made in 1968 in Pittsburgh, once the great steel capital of America. By then, the mills were closing and

Pittsburgh was facing decline; the team of George Romero and John Russo recast the Caribbean living dead as a ravening, restless, super-annuated white proletariat rising up, under the effect of a radiation leak, to contaminate all with their condition.

So the zombie first appears in English culture as a terrifying new possibility at the peak of commercial and industrial power, when slavery was providing labour across the Empire. The Death-in-Life in which the zombie exists stands at the very opposite pole from individualist, self-propelled metamorphosis of upward social mobility, which promises, as the credit card advert claims, 'you can be whatever you want to be'.

2001

SEVEN

FAIRIES, MYTHS AND MAGIC

Aesop

Review of Aesop: The Complete Fables, *translated by Olivia and Robert Temple*

The biter bit. Sour grapes. Swan song. Pride comes before a fall. Borrowed plumage. Crying wolf. Once bitten twice shy. In the skin of a lion. Let sleeping dogs lie. Blowing hot and cold. One swallow does not make a summer. These proverbial phrases still stud common speech today, approximately twenty-six hundred years after they were written down as the work of one Aesop, a slave.

When I bought S. A. Handford's postwar translation of *Aesop's Fables* in the Sixties, the Penguin Classic was already in its twentieth printing. There is something fustian and schoolmasterly about its renderings, while the pen-and-ink illustrations, by Brian Robb, carefree and charming in the postwar pastoral sketchbook style of Edward Ardizzone, planted the fables firmly on juvenile territory: this was the homespun wit and wisdom of granny or Mother Goose, savvy, cynical, practical, perennial, and handed down to the younger generation to develop their 'cunning and high spirits' (Walter Benjamin's telling phrase) in dealing with life.

Olivia and Robert Temple's new version is based on French classicist E. Chambry's scholarly edition, published in Paris in 1927, but includes the mythological stories featuring Zeus and Hermes and Aphrodite that Handford omitted, thus swelling the corpus by 151 more fables. This husband and wife translation team are also intent on taking the fables out of the nursery and putting them back into history: they present the fables as the kind of crib notes that have always supplied the oral tradition in the long ongoing symbiosis between print culture and storytelling.

This practice is by no means extinct: the Arabist Robert Irwin reports that he heard a blind bazaar ballad-singer in Damascus and then, a few days later, saw the same man in a coffee house with song sheets spread out on the table in front of him, learning up another number. This was not pure charlatanry, as Irwin was quick to point out, but demonstrated that the public requires, even today, that a fabulist should appear a true bardic descendant of Homer or Aesop, an original, spontaneous conduit of a popular, unlettered art uncontaminated by high culture or scholarship.

Aesop was likewise set apart by handicap – by an arresting and unique ugliness, according to the rich body of legends that circulated about him from medieval times. He figured there as a tongue-tied brute who appeared a dolt because he could only stammer. The poet who drew on animal imagery to express the human condition was himself invoked under the aspect of a variety of beasts. 'Is he a frog, or a hedgehog, or a pot-bellied jar, or a captain of monkeys, or a moulded jug, or a cook's gear, or a dog in a basket?' the children's writer and publisher John Newbery asked in the early nineteenth century. He went on to introduce into the nursery the novel twist on the legend that Aesop, being a slave, was also black: 'his complexion was so swarthy, that he took his name from it, Aesop & Aethiop, according to their account, signifying the same thing'.

When Aesop is sold on by one master to another, called Xanthus, he offers to act as a bogeyman to frighten children into good behaviour. Illustrations from Renaissance editions of the fourteenth-century *Vita Aesopi* show him swollen and misshapen and huge, as everyone runs in alarm from the sight of him. But this outcast, this stigmatised and abject hobgoblin, has a quick and brilliant mind inside his freakish outer shape. The goddess Isis eventually takes pity on him and restores his powers of speech; he begins to entertain his master with his cunning tricks and clever ripostes. Many of these turn on puns and wordplay: the fabulist's arsenal mines the inherently ludic properties of language itself, as do much more recent exponents of the genre like Lewis Carroll and Salman Rushdie. For example, Xanthus one day orders Aesop to prepare the best banquet available. Aesop serves four courses of tongues all differently dressed, whereupon Xanthus falls into 'a most outrageous passion' and belabours Aesop. He responds, ' "Sir . . . you charged me to make the best entertainment I could . . . & if the tongue be the key of knowledge, what cou'd be so proper as a feast of tongues for a philosophical banquet?" '

Aesop's gifts in this regard make him the counterpart of such tricksters as Anansi the spider from Yoruba folklore, Coyote of the Navajo repertory, and Brer Rabbit, their US cousin; in many ways, this legendary

Aesop is the generic precursor of 'the signifying monkey', who by flyting, by repartee, by doing the dozens, reverses his low status. Aesop is the earliest figure in classical Western culture to use stories and language as defensive weapons in the struggle for survival.

The low humour of the fables and their progenitor gave them their bite: Velázquez portrayed the poet as the nemesis of great men and their pretensions. He was inspired, the art historian Nicholas Tromans has persuasively suggested, by the episode in the *Vita* when Aesop scoffs at his master for worrying that when he defecates, his brains leave him with his stools. The vessel and the rag at Aesop's feet in Velázquez's famous portrait in the Prado can be identified, in relation to this scatological anecdote, as a nightsoil bucket and toilet rag.

The Temples' new version attempts to bring out this ribald, adults-only, shameless side of *Aesop's Fables*; they are following a current trend to desanitise traditional material such as fairy tales, taking the sugariness out of Disney, dyeing darker the pastel hues of wonderland. ' "It's a jungle out there!" could be taken as the motto of Aesop,' they write in their Introduction. For them, the fables are patently cynical: this is territory where a cat may not look at a king. The messages of the stories are often highly conservative, and the appended moral tags cumbrously underline the warnings against presumption, vanity, greed, ambition, etc. It seems best to keep your place, accepting that a jackdaw will never be a peacock, that a bird in the hand is worth two in the bush, that one good deed may deserve another but is unlikely to be thus rewarded.

But can this be right? Aesop would not have acquired his fame as the adversary of tyrants' follies and of the arrogance of lions and wolves if his stories upheld the status quo in this manner. A fable is not the same as a parable, a bar-room joke not the same as an exemplum from a pious sermon: from childhood we read Aesop knowingly, against the grain of the text. Indeed, he gives us some of the most brilliant and fundamental lessons in irony, for our sympathies are aroused to run counter to the manifest lesson of the fable. Take the famous tale of the ant and the cricket, immortalised by La Fontaine's 1668 collection of fables after Aesop. The improvident cricket, who has sung all summer long instead of hoarding for the lean winter like the thrifty ant, is clearly the surface target of this cautionary tale about human folly. But the sympathy of the fable runs with the cricket nevertheless: it shows up the ant's meanness, and in so doing, offers as much of a rebuke to selfishness as it does to thoughtless hedonism. It's significant that La Fontaine placed this fable first and that in the biography of Aesop he included, Aesop refers to himself as a cricket and says, 'All my business is my song.' The story's piquancy lines us up with the cricket, against common sense, against natural selection, against the law of the jungle, just as it yokes us to donkeys, mice, rats, tortoises, frogs, and the other foolish and put-upon underlings who people the fabulous menagerie.

The Temples show a keen historical interest and scatter notes here and there to correct the circumstantial as well as the zoological record on the animals and their representations in the fables. They reckon that Aesop was a spoil of war rather than born basely into slavery, and worked as 'a personal clerk/secretary', even pleading a case before the assembly of Samos. Likewise, in point of accuracy, the famous crafty talking cats of fable turn out to be house-ferrets or polecats, apparently as common to Greek hearths as mongooses are in households of India. The editors note that the ubiquitous wild ass, protagonist of numerous warnings about knavishness and folly, is portrayed against nature as carnivorous; consequently they suggest that the fables, many of which originated outside Greece, starred hyenas rather than donkeys. Similarly, the fox may have begun as a jackal, which would link its character in fable even more closely to a Coyote's.

There are several problems, however, with this edition. The diction is often stilted, even compared to Handford's polite version (the Temples' opening line of the opening fable is almost incomprehensible: 'The things brought by ill fortune, taking advantage of the feebleness of those brought by good fortune, pursued them closely.') Adopting Chambry's arrangement, which follows the Greek titles in alphabetical order, means that the tales are clumped by character – the Fox tales all together, ditto the Monkey stories and the Lion's and the Wolf's; this decision intensifies the danger of repetitiveness and dulls the very different saltiness of each fable.

La Fontaine declared in his preamble to the Fables, 'On ne saurait trop égayer les narrations' ('One can't do too much to enliven the telling of stories'), and made an eloquent plea for 'gaieté' as the principle of fabulism. Though the Temples consider Aesop 'essentially a joke collection' for adults, gaiety and liveliness have been lost. They have decisively withdrawn Aesop's Fables from children, and present them instead as the equivalent of a journeyman artist's pattern book, supplying sallies, anecdotes, and epigrams for the party piece, the political speech, the satirist's diatribe, the cleverclogs op-ed writer. The result is almost a fable in itself, too close for comfort to the one about the kite who wanted to neigh as beautifully as a horse and by dint of croaking so hard, ended up mute.

1998

Roberto Calasso

Review of The Marriage of Cadmus and Harmony

In many religions the demiurge keeps a special treasure under his throne: not riches, powers or talents, but a box full of stories. A trickster may try to steal it, fail, and find himself turned into Anansi, the spider, protagonist of a web of stories that connects Africa with America, and North with South, in an ever-widening mesh.

Roberto Calasso's book is a box of stories, too, filled, like that of a conjuror, with an unfailing chain of coloured scarves and naked boys and girls, of blooms and wounds and plots and magic, all knotted together and displayed to the soft, cajoling sound of charms and spells. It's a more familiar box than Anansi's – here are Dionysus and Apollo paired and contrasted, here is Zeus raping yet another nymph or beauty, here are catamites and gods coupling happily – but in other ways Calasso has refashioned altogether the Greek legacy: there is no schoolmasterly fustian paraphrase here, or psychoanalytical dreamwork, but striking, mischievous tales told with enjoyment in 'the rapturous gliding' of intelligence (as Calasso himself writes of that other tale-teller supreme, Odysseus).

The book lies somewhere between fiction, diary jottings, philosophy and prose poetry, and Tim Parks's translation does it proud. The stories often feature snakes, oracular and sexual, and Calasso himself moves with a serpentine motion, sidling into thickets of related images to open up plots and characters hidden inside: the bull, the garland, the net (of Necessity), the clay mould, the phantom, the meal of sacrifice, the alphabet. Through a sequence of densely clustered chapters, he traces curves between one figure and another, between for instance Theseus, hero of the golden Fleece, Nemesis, goddess of Revenge, and Helen of Troy, all the while insinuating significance and laying eggs of a gnomic, oracular, slightly sinister sort.

When Odysseus pretends to be mad by sowing salt instead of barley in a furrow because he wants to avoid going to fight the Trojan war, Palamedes unmasks him; Odysseus does not forgive this, and callously frames him for treachery. This is the most shocking story in the book. The most edifying features the orphan girl Charila, who asked for food from a king at Delphi. He hit her in the face with his sandal, and she hanged herself. After this there was drought, until the oracle revealed her stiff body swinging still and reparation was made annually in gifts of food, etc. The most erotic story? Well, there are many, but perhaps Hippodameia, who leaves off casually sleeping with her father to marry Pelops, the stranger with the ivory shoulder, might be given the prize.

Calasso draws from many different sources little read today – his favourite is Nonnus, writing as late as the sixth century forty-eight books about Dionysus and another about Jesus Christ, apparently at the same time and with the same degree of engagement. Calasso disdains the need to believe – or to place one's faith exclusively. Nonnus enjoyed 'faith in redundancy as the way in which the cosmos makes itself visible'. This sounds like Derrida *avant la lettre*; he is there all right, in Calasso's mental underworld, but the figure who casts the longest shadow is Nietzsche.

In his syncretism, Calasso is a man of our time, even though he protests that he – and the rest of us – are still living in 'the realm of Zeus ... that of the Greek stories'. Writers of myths and about myths often find their own images reflected in them; Calasso writes that 'the enemy of the aesthetic is meaning', and his elliptical, gliding enigmas certainly elude explanation. 'Myth is the realm of risk,' he writes, 'and myth is the enchantment we generate in ourselves at such moments ... it is a spell the soul casts on itself.'

So where does it lead, this new Ovid's *Metamorphoses* or Lemprière's *Dictionary*? It isn't a genealogy of the gods (no index, even!) – any reader wanting clarity would do much better to buy the family tree of the Olympians on sale in the British Museum. Calasso doesn't want to explain the origin of things, or use myths to turn keys to mysteries. He rejects theories about their relationship to ritual, to social structures, to laws. He likes myths the way they are, muddled and multiple and mysterious. Novels are poor things by comparison, 'a narrative deprived of variants'; the visible world is insubstantial, 'a cascade of copies', desperately in need of the invisible prototype. Unlike some of the brilliant classicists at work today – Jean-Pierre Vernant, Pierre Vidal-Naquet in France and Ruth Padel here – Calasso isn't interested in intelligibility, or in throwing light on the Greeks so that we may understand our world better. He's arbitrary, guru-like, often solemn and a little tricky in the oracles he pronounces ('the heroic gesture of a woman is betrayal'). And he doesn't appreciate at all the pungent satire against gurus, against mystification, against cults, mounted by that brilliant Swift of the ancient world, Lucian. Calasso feels close to Odysseus (he's hardly the first writer to do so) but, to do him justice, he is able to recognise in Odysseus the mountebank as well as the poet.

The book begins with Europa carried off by the bull, and comes full circle at the end when her brother Cadmus marries Harmony the sister of Eros. With Cadmus, writing begins: he invents the alphabet. And with writing, historical record starts – and stories ready to be dropped into the divine box and stored, waiting for a Calasso to pull them out with such dazzling feints and passes that we in the audience know something fantastic is happening in front of our eyes but cannot be sure quite what it is.

1993

Talk at the Italian Institute on Ka: Stories of the Mind and Gods of India

Ka is a mysterious book, about the most mysterious myths we have. The Sanskrit cycle of stories about gods and goddesses, about the origins of the cosmos and human society, approach the questions that myths in every culture from Alaska to Tasmania struggle to set out, if not to answer. What do the stars mean? What is time? Where do we come from? Why the difference between the sexes? What is that difference anyway? Why pleasure? What is death? Roberto Calasso has given his reinscription of some of the sacred Indian formulations of these questions a title which is itself a question: the monosyllable 'Ka' means who?, like the Italian monosyllable 'chi?'. 'Ka' is also, as his book unfolds, a space, a gap, a presence in absence, a valency, a demon: it embodies the energy of that knowledge which is the acceptance of ignorance.

Calasso tells here, in brief, elegant, often gnomic sentences, some terrible and extraordinary tales: of the body of Indra opening with a thousand yonis, or female organs of generation, each of them like a waking eye. Of the protracted, elaborate, savage mutilation and sacrifice of a horse in a solar ritual involving several hierodules or sacred prostitutes, murder, and bestiality. Of the weaknesses and wantonness of the divinities, their quarrels and their lusts, their powerlessness in the midst of omnipotence.

But the Sanskrit myths still wear a disreputable air, for one can almost hear the thundering scorn of a Saint Jerome or a Saint Dominic denouncing these polytheistic demons and their wanton, wild excesses, fantastic orgies and massacres. Multiplicity of heads and limbs for the bodies of the gods – and goddesses – are matched by multiplicity of plotlines and subplots and incidents. As Calasso tell us, the *Mahabharata*, one of his chief sources, is the longest epic poem in the world, far far longer than Homer and a Bible in scale to the single sonnet, if you like, of the *Epic of Gilgamesh*. He writes here:

> In the beginning stories were no more than appendices to knowledge, but gradually the time given over to them grew in the gaps in that knowledge like grass between the bricks of the altar of fire, expanded and multiplied in stories that generated more stories, until they covered the whole construction of knowledge in which they had made their first furtive appearance as no more than an intermezzo.

Ka sets aside all Judaeo-Christian revulsion against pagan monsters, hybrid forms, grotesque pluralities of bodies and stories, against metamorphosis, by re-visioning the legends as a classical compendium, meditative, enigmatic and controlled. The earlier book *The Marriage of Cadmus and Harmony* purposefully imitated Greek mythography: it offered a kind of alternative reading of Hesiod's *Theogony* and Ovid's *Metamorphoses*, using lesser-known writers like Nonnus as sources. For, as Lévi-Strauss pointed out, there is no original version of a myth. Every retelling is a myth itself – every variation another story to set alongside the one that may precede it chronologically but does not therefore take precedence as truth – or as fiction. Calasso is a mythographer for today: he is passing on the myths of the mind and gods of India as his subtitle to *Ka* promises, but he is also making a new text, shaped to his own taste, his own emotional centres of pleasure, his own learning – which is vast – and his perception of his readers' desires.

Ka is a very oblique book, and so I want to end by an oblique reference or two to other stories that illuminate, I think, Calasso's concept of writing myth on the one hand and historical ideas about writers of myths themselves.

In 1921, J. G. Frazer, author of *The Golden Bough*, translated and edited '*The Library* by Apollodorus' as it is known, and as it is called in the Loeb edition. This book, composed in the first century BC, is one of the many deep reservoirs of classical stories from which later poets, dramatists and all manner of artists have drawn. But it isn't by the learned Apollodorus, a much earlier historical character who was a stickler for truths and something of a rationalist. The flamboyant anthology borrowed his name to dignify itself, in a manoeuvre that was very common in the ancient and medieval worlds: authors were as much fictions as their works. Much later, the strange figure of Nonnus of Panopolis put on another pyrotechnical display, in the *Dionysiaca*, in honour of the god of wine and excess. But he was so all-embracing in his interests – and allegiances – that he also composed a paraphrase of Saint John's Gospel in Greek. The borders between creeds in the Hellenistic world were not closed, and in many ways our times, at their best, reflect the heterogeneity, catholicity, effervescence and dynamism of those changing times when the Greek and Roman hegemonies were failing. Porousness between languages, between cultures: both Calasso and Salman Rushdie exemplify this condition.

Shakespeare draws his own portrait of a mythographer in *The Tempest* in the figure of Prospero whose magic arts arise from his books – the magician-writer as scholar, as alchemist, as wonder-worker and plotter of stories. Calasso performs, rather Prospero-like, this kind of conjuring: his so potent art is bookish, and it reinvents him, the author, as a presiding mystagogue as much as it stages the subjects of the stories he tells. *Ka* does not show, it tells; it deepens the mystery rather than dispels it. It does not decipher the myths in the manner of the work of the Sanskrit scholar Wendy Doniger, for example in her books *Women, Androgynes and Other Beasts, Splitting the Difference* and *The Bedtrick*, or comment on the circumstances of their making, as Robert Irwin does for *The Arabian Nights*. In *Ka* Calasso is retrieving the myths for literature, not for scholarship.

He is clearly fascinated with the myths' exploration of language: how 'VAC', Sanskrit for 'Voice', exists at the beginning as a generative force in herself; how metres – poetic metres – are also formative and performative – they bring phenomena into being.

As he points out, no other trace of these civilisations exists besides these documents, the Vedas and the Upanishads – only these words remain. So, in India, it's not only at the beginning but also at the end that there's only the word and the word made flesh.

1999

Louis XIV

Review of Peter Burke, The Fabrication of Louis XIV

When the future Sun King was born, after twenty-three years of childless marriage, he was already seen as the hero of a famous story: Anne of Austria identified herself with miraculous mothers in the Bible, who like her had borne a son and heir in late age, their barrenness lifted as a direct blessing from God. The Dauphin was sometimes even portrayed as the Christ Child: he was brought up from the start to see himself from a mythological angle of vision. Later, he would be cast as Alexander, Cyrus, Hercules, Roland, as Saint Louis reborn, as Charlemagne, and as the Good Shepherd.

The Christian repertory was by no means the only script on offer; as Peter Burke unfolds in this lucid study of art and power in the *ancien régime*, the personage who became Louis XIV in the eyes of posterity was polymorphously mythic, the star of a state theatre of rhetoric and spectacle which spoke only of his *éclat*, his *gloire* and his *grandeur*. In 1671, he formally called himself Louis le Grand, and the name and its handle were customarily printed in upper case whenever they appeared, making a printed page jump with the words, as if a herald was still trumpeting them today into posterity's ears.

The word 'fabrication' contains a hint at fraud, and the title echoes Biondi's book *La Fabbrica del Duce* about Mussolini, who was indeed a charlatan and an adept at the uses of propaganda. Burke develops the theme of Louis's make-believe and the increasingly necessary half-truths told by the inscriptions, medals, statues, paeans to the King's achievements. He draws a troubling picture of artists' and writers' services to the state: when Louis wanted the story of his life told in cartouches beneath the Lebrun paintings in the Grande Galerie at Versailles, he employed no less a writer than Racine.

Racine was already on the King's payroll, as were many other great names – including Charles Perrault, the writer of fairy tales. These fabricators of *l'histoire du roi* met, under the auspices of the *petite académie*, founded in 1663, to compose another kind of fairy tale. The King had told them, 'I am entrusting to you the one thing in the world that is most precious, which is my glory.' The *petits académiciens* were responsible for generating panegyrics in every medium and supervising that they contained the correct praises. More than 320 medals were struck celebrating the King's deeds; and in spite of the Revolution's destruction of statues and reliefs, the Sun King can hardly be missed in the stones of Paris today, let alone Versailles.

It was of course at the Palace of Versailles that Louis performed his *gloire* in person. At five feet three inches, he was around the same height as our present Queen; he compensated with high heels, and, after his hair fell out during an illness, was rarely without a towering periwig too – he once took so long choosing which one to wear that he caught a severe cold. The famous *levers* and *couchers du roi* were attended by courtiers who could not sit down; the King himself occupied his *chaise percée*, his commode, in their presence, to the surprise of visitors from abroad. So sacred he sallied forth to touch for the king's evil on scores of occasions in his life (in the tradition of medieval kings of England as well as France), he could make a show of his most intimate bodily functions, it seems, and not lessen the sense of majesty. Courtiers had to remove their hats in the mere presence of the place laid for him at table, and it was forbidden to turn one's back on his image in any form. When he suffered from a fistula, in 1687, the courtiers responded with an avalanche of odes and madrigals to the King's recovery. The monarchy today might have inherited many of the traditional functions of royal publicity – dressing the part, and touching of the sick, for instance – but Princess Diana, bulimia or no bulimia, exists in a rather different relation to public opinion.

Burke has written a famous book about popular culture, and he seems to have come to this story of absolute monarchy through an interest in the flourishing, anonymous pamphleteering of the time, which denounced Louis for his costly – and sometimes disastrous – military campaigns as well as his religious intolerance. Burke surveys this lively propaganda in Holland, which had suffered so much from French invasions, and in Britain and Germany, as well as France, but he does not grapple vigorously enough with internal dissent and corresponding police activity. The pamphleteers and fabulists and even some of the more acerbic fairy-tale writers were punished by exile to the provinces or captivity in the Bastille; some offenders seem to have turned spy to obtain a pardon. Burke prefers a cool, even-handed approach, refusing the pictured narrative style of a Simon Schama, and he scants the full impact of an official press, of the growing number of royal academies, the supervision of printing presses and the attempted control of their numbers, the forced recantations of poets like La Fontaine.

The closing chapter, potentially the most interesting, promises to compare the myth machines of today's leaders with absolutism's methods. With Gaddafi's costume changes on billboards on one hand, and Fergie's holiday *couchers* on the other, the theme is timely. Burke points out trenchantly the historical change in the public's identity as well as the effects of suffrage and the press; power now depends on persuasion, while for the Sun King, he was simply making a proper show of his divinely ordained role. However, Burke again skimps a full development of the argument. It's as if the hyperbole and the bombast of Louis's self-presentation, the profusion of legends and allusion in his history, have driven Burke to develop a distaste for baroque fabrication altogether, and instead deal very plainly with the glory of the King.

1992

La Fontaine

Review of Jean de La Fontaine, Œuvres complètes Vol. 1: Fables, contes et nouvelles.

The young Duke of Burgundy, grandson of Louis XIV, was overjoyed when he heard that La Fontaine had repented of his tales and even renounced the royalties due on a forthcoming Dutch edition. He immediately sent a purse of fifty golden *louis* to tide the poet over, saying that he considered 'que ce n'était pas raisonnable qu'il fût plus pauvre pour avoir fait son devoir' ('it didn't stand to reason that he should be the poorer for having done his duty'). This action was entirely spontaneous, not promoted by anyone in the prince's entourage, or so reported the Oratorian confessor who had administered extreme unction to the seventy-two-year-old fabulist and received his recantation in turn.

Several of La Fontaine's fellow-*académiciens* were called to the bedside to witness the auto-da-fé of 12 February 1693. La Fontaine confessed, 'j'ai eu le malheur de composer un livre de Contes, infâme' ('I've had the misfortune of composing an – infamous – book of Tales'). The comma indicates the intake of breath, perhaps, the cost of the admission. He continued: he had not realised the degree of the book's perniciousness, but now saw that it was 'un livre abominable'. He was angry that he had ever written it, and begged forgiveness of God, the Church and the Académie for perpetrating it; he wished that it was in his power to withdraw all copies. If he survived, he would dedicate himself to penning only 'ouvrages de piété'. This is what gladdened the heart of the Duke of Burgundy, then ten years old.

If the convergence of circumstances – clerical pressure, comic story-telling and political safety – carries proleptic echoes of Salman Rushdie's enduring predicament today, it is not in the least surprising: laughter and dogma are natural enemies.

La Fontaine lived on another two years, but his deathbed palinode can't be judged simply as a panicky response from a former seminarian, who had left an Oratorian noviciate after only eighteen months and had some written fun at clerical expense. The infamous and abominable book in question was first published in late 1664; a collection of *Contes*, or tales, after the Italian for the most part, its tone was zestful, frivolous, piquant, and ribald; the author appeared to take very little seriously, and this was of course rather serious. La Fontaine's retraction marks an important crux in literary history, a cardinal point in the establishment of official culture's authority, when the laughter of the secular, unruly medieval buffoon is silenced, stifled as licentious, and levity loses to high-mindedness its larger functions of social criticism and philosophical reflection.

The narrative poet of the risqué *Contes* is not nearly as familiar a voice as the canonical author of the *Fables*, and the new Pléïade edition brings out into the light a merry fellow, a cynic and an epicurean, a Renaissance clown who survives his melancholy knowledge by trifling. The first two tales were printed in January 1664: 'La Matrone d'Ephèse' ('The Widow of Ephesus'), after Petronius, and 'Joconde', after Ariosto. Both treat of women's frailty with classical obsessiveness; to cuckold or be cuckolded emerges as the supreme defining enterprise of man. These male anxieties threaten at first to overbalance the humour for a modern reader who happens to be female to boot; the terrors of *cocuage*, like the conventions

of duelling (which are connected, of course), have waned in our times –
one of the many benefits of sexual egalitarianism and women's
comparative financial independence. But La Fontaine's skill, his
sprightliness of line and biting concision of phrase soon overcome reader
resistance to the social conventions embedded in the material, and many
of the story poems are comic triumphs, bringing about deeply satisfying
pardons in their resolutions. Voltaire, in the entry on 'Fable' in the
Dictionnaire philosophique, considered that of all tales, the tale of 'Cupid
and Psyche' from Apuleius's *The Golden Ass* was 'la plus belle', but 'The
Widow of Ephesus' the most 'plaisant' ('amusing'): it describes how a
most virtuous widow decided to follow her husband to the grave by
starving herself to death in his mausoleum, but had a change of heart after
meeting a soldier. La Fontaine puts it in monosyllables, keeping the tone
dry, very dry:

> Il fait tant que de plaire, et se rend en effet
> Plus digne d'être aimé que le mort le mieux fait.

'He does so much, he makes himself so pleasant, that he does indeed
become more worthy of love than the most well made corpse.'
Unfortunately, this worthy soldier stands in danger of swinging in the
morning; with presence of mind, and help from her maid, the widow
substitutes her beloved spouse's corpse on the gibbet instead.

When La Fontaine published a whole volume of *Contes*, he responded
to his critics in a preface, rebutting charges of licentiousness and
misogyny with blithe confidence. He first appeals to Roman tradition,
situating himself as a mere disciple of the Ancients and their Italian
imitators, then adduces an interesting argument for the defence of levity,
and its close cousins, salaciousness and laugher: 'S'il y a quelque chose
dans nos écrits qui puisse faire impression sur les âmes, ce n'est nullement
la gaìeté de ces contes: elle passe légèrement: je craindrais plutôt une
douce mélancolie, où les romans les plus chastes et les plus modestes sont
très capables de nous plonger, et qui est une grande préparation pour
l'amour' ('If there is something in our writings which might make an
impression on certain spirits, it's not at all the gaiety of these tales, which
passes by lightly: I would rather fear a sweet melancholy into which the
most chaste and modest novels are capable of plunging us, for this is a
great preparation for love'). Comic lightness turns away sin; it creates
resistance rather than weakens it.

However, in 1666, when he came to publish a third volume of stories, including many equally robust and raunchy borrowings from Boccaccio, Ariosto and Marguerite de Navarre, the tone of the preface had become more embattled. There's a similar appeal to precedent, and a plea that fundamental unities of genre be observed: characters must not be too odious or a happy ending would no longer be seemly, readers must not find themselves crying and laughing during the same story. He calls the mixing of tones 'bigarrure' (motley) and cites Horace when he rejects grotesque works, 'moitié femme, moitié poisson'. The image of repellent mongrel literature as a kind of Mélusine, or monstrous mermaid, anticipates La Fontaine's ally and fellow-*académicien*, the stern defender of classical purity, Boileau, who in 1690 condemned Rabelais in the same metaphorical terms: 'son livre . . . c'est une chimère, c'est le visage d'une belle femme avec les pieds et une queue de serpent ou de quelque autre bête plus difforme'. ('His book . . . it's a chimera, it's the face of a beautiful woman with the feet and the tail of a serpent or of some other even more beastly deformity'). The repugnance revealed in such phrases would eventually lead La Fontaine, as one of the party of the Anciens (those who defended classical tradition against the Modernes), to protest that he was setting aside *cocuage* and merry widows and amorous priests and other *gai* and *plaisant* themes.

Yet his prefaces seek to ward off criticism by giving a false description of the book's contents: his *Contes* teem with scot-free adulterers and their mistresses, with innocent peasants beaten by tyrannical masters who get away with it. In a high-spirited variation on a *Decameron* episode, 'The Geese of Brother Philip' (also exuberantly treated by Pasolini in his film of Boccaccio), La Fontaine paints the result of keeping a boy secluded from human society: as soon as his hero sees girls, he's transported with delight, and begs his austere hermit father to tell him what they are. Geese, replies the 'bon veillard'. To which the son responds:

> Mon père, je vous prie en mille et mille fois,
> Menons-nous une en notre bois;
> J'aurai soin de la faire paître.

> Father, I beg you a thousand times over,
> Let's take one into our woods;
> I'll make sure she'll graze her fill.

Playing with ambiguities of humour, La Fontaine was adept, in these pithy and dashing verses, at having everything both ways: he promises a story that does honour to the 'beau sexe', then ends on all the mocking and even smutty innuendoes of geese and grazing.

Though *The Decameron* dominates the *Contes*, La Fontaine sometimes adapted *faits divers*; one of his genuinely funny cuckold stories was a local joke, from his home province of Champagne, in which a servant turns the tables on her master with her quick wits. When Mme de Sévigné recommended La Fontaine in a letter to her daughter, she enclosed a poem, 'Le Curé et le mort' (The parish priest and the dead man'), also based on a real-life incident: a hearse crashed and the aristocratic corpse decapitated the priest who was accompanying him to the funeral.

> Le Paroissien en plomb entraîne son Pasteur;
> Notre Curé suit son Seigneur;
> Tous deux s'en vont de compagnie.

> The Parishioner in lead leads away his Shepherd,
> Our parish priest follows his Lord;
> The two of them off on their way together.

Her daughter did not see the funny side, and was chided for her irresponsiveness. It was perhaps a symptom of the coming generation's dislike of dirty stories and gallows humour in general.

Jean-Pierre Collinet's Pléïade edition gives La Fontaine's remarkable range of sources: some of the most familiar tales are Eastern in origin, and derive from the Sanskrit *Pancha-Tantra*, the legendary Brahmin Pilpay (or Bidpai) and the sage Lokman, which La Fontaine could have come across in various ways, from meeting in the salon of Mme de la Sablière the doctor-philosopher François Bernier, who had lived and worked in India, and from fairly recent translations, by clerics and orientalists. A cautionary tale, 'The Dairymaid and the Pot of Milk' (rather like the cumulative English nursery rhyme, 'For want of a button the shirt was lost . . .'), demonstrates the extraordinary degree of communication between the Arab, Greek and Romance language worlds in early modern Europe, on the verge of *orientalisme*; the community of mythology and wisdom seems startling today, and not in the least suspect, but rather enviably humanistic and inquiring, and due for emulation.

Born and brought up in Château Thierry, La Fontaine inherited from his father a civil post as Maître des Eaux et des Forêts, but he let it lapse, and seems to have led an improvident life, increasingly dependent on patrons. His marriage to the fourteen-year-old Marie Héricart in 1647 was soon a failure, and he played *cavaliere servente* to a series of great ladies, beginning with the Dowager Duchesse d'Orléans, Henrietta of England, 'Minette'. The fall of Nicolas Foucquet in 1661 taught him the inconstancy of princes, yet he remained loyal to the disgraced minister. This volume of his works does not, however, present La Fontaine's work chronologically, so it omits the pieces he wrote during his early years, such as a sequence of letters to his wife from travels in the Limousin, and his evocations of Foucquet's glittering circle, inspired by the fabulous palace of Vaux-le-Vicomte.

As a middle-aged provincial poet seeking his fortune in times of centralised absolutism, La Fontaine dedicated the first volume of the *Fables* in 1668 to the Dauphin. It is very valuable indeed to have this Pléïade edition, with all the preambles to the famous opening fable, 'La Cigale et la fourmi' (The cricket and the ant'), because La Fontaine embedded his virtuoso variations on Aesop and Phaedrus inside a labyrinthine mass of material, guiding the reader to the fables that follow through a sequence of diversions. A preface follows the dedication, to which the anomalousness of the *railleur* courtier introduces a note of strain: he gives an illustrious genealogy for the form of the fable (Socrates, he says, 'employa . . . les derniers moments de sa vie' rendering Aesop into verse). Then, he defines his own kind of suave, civilised, Montaigne-like humour: 'Je n'appelle pas gaieté ce qui excite le rire; mais un certain charme, un air agréable, qu'on peut donner à toutes sortes de sujets, même les plus sérieux' (I don't call gaiety that which excites laughter; but a certain charm, an agreeable air, which one can give to all kinds of subjects, even the most serious'). He stresses the pedagogic value of animal stories, bringing in Plato this time as an equally imaginary witness: the philosopher is alleged to have banished Homer from the Republic, but placed Aesop there in honour. In the last paragraph, he again defends himself: 'Toute la vie de Socrate n'a pas été sérieuse' (not all of Socrates' life was serious).

The preface does not lead into the *Fables* themselves, however, but to another introductory piece, a 'Life of Aesop', one of the revelations and pleasures of this definitive edition. The portrait of the father of fables in the West follows the legendary biography by Maximus Planudes, written in the fourteenth century, which drew substantially on a life of the oriental sage Ahiqar, composed two thousand years earlier, in the sixth century BC. The Aesop that emerges from this astonishingly ancient tradition is the epitome of a trickster, a slave who saves his own hide by cunning, by riddles, by parable and story. At birth he's hideous, even malformed, 'ayant à peine figure d'homme', and as good as dumb – as beast-like as the characters in the fables ascribed to him. His goodness of heart wins him favour from the gods, who loosen his tongue. What he cannot achieve by beauty, power, wealth, however, he can by cleverness.

La Fontaine gives him gnomic utterances, and follows his misadventures and near-misses from Greece to Egypt and back again; like many other tricksters, Monkey in China and Anansi the spider from West Africa, Aesop and his exploits do not strike us now as so dazzlingly ingenious, but as improbably effective stratagems, though entertaining. Such a trickster's value today lies in his emblematic affirmation of the lowly against the exalted, the feeble against the mighty, the word against the sword. And with regard to La Fontaine, offering this first book of *Fables* to the son of Louis XIV, the ironies are many. Almost Aesop's last words he cites are 'Grand roi, je ressemble à cette Cigale; je n'ai que la voix, et ne m'en suis point servi pour vous offenser'. ('Great king, I resemble this cricket; I have only a voice, and I've never ever used it to offend you'.) But if La Fontaine identifies with Aesop, he also chooses to disparage the singing of crickets in the famous first fable – 'La cigale ayant chanté tout l'été' ('The cricket, having sung all summer long') – which then follows immediately.

As everyone knows, the *Fables* are full of cynical morals ('La raison du plus fort est toujours la meilleure') which conjure up between the lines a ghost print of the possible, opposite case. But La Fontaine proceeds here too by indirection, as if through a maze, attacking tyranny of kings in one poem, then covering himself by revising the parable of the stomach and its members as a tribute to monarchy. It is intrinsic to his skill that he does not quite let us know where he stands; like a Renaissance fool, he keeps peeping from behind a mask, with a grin and a frown and vice versa. The first books of *Les Fables* are crisper, leaner, sharper than the twelfth and last volume, dedicated to his benefactor the Duke of Burgundy and published after his recantation. But even here, he navigates between high and low with marvellous nimbleness, has his moments of rebellious laughter (he slipped in a reprint of his old poem on the Widow of

Ephesus) and shows the strength of his irregular rhymes and anti-classical prosody, what Collinet calls in a fine phrase his 'esthétique de la négligence', aesthetic of carelessness. In 'Le Chat et les deux moineaux' ('The Cat and the Two Sparrows') he brings off the Ogden Nash-style feat of rhyming 'Pénates' (household gods) with 'pattes' (cat's paws).

The heir apparent, the young Duke of Burgundy, was given the verses by his tutor Fénélon as Latin translation exercises, and when la Fontaine died, in 1695, the royal preceptor wrote the poet's eulogy, in Latin, repeating terms of praise like 'dulces nugae' ('sweet bagatelles'), and 'natura nuda et simplex' ('the unadorned and simple nature [of his language]'). La Fontaine had become a pet, a dear, sweet old pet.

The courtier could survive as a fabulist by giving up subversive bawdy and embracing world-weary social fatalism. The upshot of the *Fables*' message is deeply pessimistic about human nature; pessimism tends to leave the status quo in place, and work to stabilise topsy-turvy. It consequently suits men in power, however harshly the powerful might be portrayed. La Fontaine's career exemplifies in the seventeenth century the dilemma of the social satirist and jester who wins official approval and follows a public career; the balance between dissenting and conforming begins to tip against comedy, against jokes. He was indeed a cricket, and one who had learned that singing was no good if supper didn't follow.

The apparatus is splendidly generous, with full chronology, Notes on the Text, annotation of variants, as one expects; there is much valuable material in support – a strong survey of the *Fables*' inspired illustrators, with reproductions, showing Oudry and Cochin's elegance, Grandville's pungent fantasy and Doré's Darwinian melodramas; the volume ends with tributes and appraisals, including an abridgment of Taine's doctoral thesis, the origin of his influential *La Fontaine et ses fables* of 1860. Jean-Pierre Collinet's knowledge appears exhaustive. But it must be said that the Pléïade format makes it hard of access. Biographical, bibliographical, and critical information is scattered haphazardly through several different sections; the *Fables*, which were published after the *Contes*, precede them, no doubt by conventional order of merit (though this isn't necessarily a foregone conclusion). This first volume feels like a missal, bulky and sleek at the same time; trying to move back and forth between the texts and the apparatus also baffles in the manner of a missal, as when the priest comes on in surprising liturgical colours, and one hunts for the appropriate saint in the calendar, then for the matching epistle, collect and gospel elsewhere; but perhaps this ecclesiastical atmosphere is appropriate for reading a comic poet who learned to wipe the smile off his face when *les grands* didn't appear to be finding him funny any more.

1991

Under the Executioner's Sword

Introduction to The Arabian Nights, *for the Folio Society edition*

Like one of the djinns who appear in a pillar of cloud, *The Arabian Nights* or *The Book of the Thousand Nights and One Night* has taken many forms and has answered to many masters. Now in this version, now in that, it has no known author or named authors, no settled shape or length, no fixed table of contents, no definite birthplace or ultimate origin (India, Persia, then Syria, Egypt, Iraq have all contributed since the earliest vestiges of such tales were found in the ninth century). A kind of orphan with no established textual parents, it found fortune, and with a dazzling train of admirers and followers that include Marcel Proust, Jorge Luis Borges, Salman Rushdie, it has risen like one of its own heroes, through many vicissitudes and even a taint of illegitimacy, to take its place among the greatest classics of world literature. As a child, I found the scene in the cruel Sultan's bedroom a picture of the world, and the two sisters' conspiracy, with Dinarzade, the younger sister, obeying Scheherazade and urging her in the Sultan's presence to tell a story, seemed to me the fullest metaphor for love against death, expressed through the alliance of girls against men, and ultimately for imagination over experience. That dot dot dot which intervenes between one break of day and the next night, that ellipsis which the French rightly call *points de suspension*, packs all the excitement of an unknowable future that is nevertheless thrillingly and inevitably round the corner.

The huge narrative wheel of the *Arabian Nights* includes fairy tales and fables, proverbial anecdotes, riddles, lyric songs and love poems; it spins out erotic incidents, bawdy scenes, cross-dressed encounters, seamy pranks and jokes such as that perennial comic subterfuge, often adopted by Shakespeare, of the bed trick. Magic flights and spells and fumigations and potions bring dreams – and disaster – at the whim of capricious powers. Young women are changed into dogs, young men are turned half to stone, for the human shape is not constant, and souls can be spirited away to inhabit other forms. Crowds of demons, 'djinns' and fairies ('peris') and other magical creatures appear and determine the action; they can fly to the zenith and dive to the depths of the sea. If rewards fall at random, so do punishments. Curses work. Luck rarely holds. Lessons are hard to draw, and often dubious. Cruelty and violence erupt at every turn, heads are lopped off, the earth opens and swallows the unwary; kings practise summary justice, viziers plot and deceive, beggars become kings and dewy young princesses turn out to be deep-dyed in the arts of sorcery. There is really no rhyme or reason for the unfolding of the plots. When a motive drives the action, envy often rules. Besides envy, lust is the supreme catalyst of human behaviour.

A woman's breasts can be round like pomegranates, her sex like 'a husked sesame', her neck 'a cake for a king', her teeth 'a row of pearls set in coral'; lips are sugared and skin perfumed; fountains play and breezes lift the blossom in the inner courtyards of palaces; the local market overflows with scented oils and waters, ambergris, musk and rosemary. Young men's beauty can put the moon to shame, while the moon's beauty makes lovers ache.

Oracles decree a future that cannot be thwarted; several of the tales turn on human attempts to prevent the fulfilment of such a prophecy: three men are warned they will meet Death under a tree and indeed, when they dig up buried treasure there, they kill one another (B. Traven's *Treasure of the Sierra Madre*, filmed by John Huston, modernised this tale). However deep the beloved child is hidden from the death that has been foretold, however far the doomed victim runs, the appointment with fate will be kept. Kismet surpasses the Greek *moirai* in fatality, shows even less mercy, and never explains, unlike the Olympians who usually argue their position. The tales also break with the narrative conventions of romance and fairy tale, which one might expect they might obey. Even a blessed youngest son, for all his virtue and courage, will not be spared (as in the story of Judar and his brothers).

Pier Paolo Pasolini made a voluptuous, ripe and haunting version of the *Nights* in 1974 in the moonlit desert of the Yemen and its beautiful capital, Sana'a; he commented, 'Every tale in the *Thousand and One Nights* begins with an "appearance of destiny" which manifests itself through an anomaly, and one anomaly always generates another. So a chain of anomalies is set up . . . The protagonist of the stories is in fact destiny itself.'[1] This ineluctability, imposed by the magically summoned insubstantial pageant of the stories, delivers one of the most blissful satisfactions a reader can experience.

Borges, who took his cue from the nesting boxes and self-mirroring regression of the *Nights*, judged that 'All great literature becomes children's literature', and his apparent paradox perhaps depends on the deep universal pleasures of storytelling for young and old: stories like those in the *Arabian Nights* place the audience in the position of a child, at the mercy of the future, of life and its plots, just as the protagonists of the *Nights* are subject to unknown fates, both terrible and marvellous.

It is fantasy — fantasy and heterogeneity — that tend to mark out literature as childish. The *Nights*' tales of the fantastic exist in a heterogeneous tangle of styles and a polyphony of vocal registers: poetry and prose mingle; high-flown court lyrics from the Persian tradition will interrupt a comic tale. The *mise-en-abîme* effects, as one narrator within one story picks up from another, dizzyingly plunge the reader from one level to another, sometimes at three or four removes from the voice of Scheherazade herself. The extravagant acrobatics and vertiginous flights of language and metaphor, the ingenious plying of action and reversal, do not so much suspend disbelief as bring the impossible into embodied life, and — the tales charm us into thinking — the fantastic appears real.

Through all the twists and turns, metamorphoses and transmogrifications *The Arabian Nights* has undergone, the central theme remains and remains known to every hearer and every reader: Scheherazade has been sentenced to die in the morning by her husband King Shariyar who has vowed that he will cut off the heads of his wives every day after sleeping with them, in revenge for the infidelity of his first wife (he found her and all her handmaidens cavorting with her slaves). But Scheherazade, by telling him stories, defers the day until he relents. An Arabian Penelope, she works against death at the tapestry of her story, and through the power of storytelling, holds his curiosity, wins her reprieve and, through her heroic practice, vindicates her sex. There is a paradox here, too, because several, if not most, of the stories Scheherazade tells reiterate the frame story's message that women are not to be trusted. Within the stories-inside-stories, several also dramatise ransom obtained by storytelling (the tales told within 'The Fisherman and the Djinn', for example). Characters thrive on stories, and the stories of their woes (for woes they most often are) nourish us, the listeners and readers, who, like Shariyar, will be lifted from our misanthropic depression. For in the event none of the woes matters — in the classic happy ending, Scheherazade's sister

Dinarzade marries the Sultan's brother; Scheherazade herself presents Shariyar with the three children to whom she has given birth during her three or so years under sentence of death. This conclusion, in all its preposterous, cruel unlikelihood, accords of course with the fairy-tale conventions of the kind of stories Scheherazade herself knows and has been so busy spellbinding him with, and it still has the power to work its spell of release and contentment on the reader.

The *Arabian Nights* presents the supreme case for storytelling because Scheherazade wins her life through her art. This is why she has attracted so many writers to identify with her, from William Beckford in his orientalist confection, *Vathek*, to the eighteenth-century Polish nobleman Jan Potocki's extraordinary fairy-tale novel *The Manuscript Found in Saragossa*, to A. S. Byatt today. The Egyptian Nobel prize-winner Naguib Mahfouz has set his *Arabian Nights & Days* in the shanties and dives of present-day Cairo, while the Lebanese-born Amin Maalouf recently wrote *Balthasar's Odyssey*, a portrait of the cosmopolitan mercantile culture of the Ottomans, packed with portents, coincidences and marvels in the manner of the *Nights*.

The *Arabian Nights* was created by traffic across the frontier of Islam and Christendom, a frontier that was more porous, commercially and culturally, than dedicated ideological history will now allow. From their first appearance in print – not manuscript – the tales mirrored Arabian civilisation and *mentalité* for the West, but at the same time communicated a fantastic European dream of Araby. As Robert Irwin vividly discusses in his excellent *The Arabian Nights: A Companion* (1994), it conveys the motley, mobile, tumultuous, polyglot and polymorphous urban culture of the Near East, which ravelled up different social and linguistic groups, various religious allegiances, and conflicted value systems, all jostling in a state of perpetual, energetic becoming. But the book's history has been a fabulous muddle, and, it is fair to say, without colonialist aggression, that the book that appears here is a hybrid, formed through cross-fertilisation over time between Europe, Asia, and the Middle East.

The book first appeared in Europe in the French translations of Antoine Galland of 1704–17. Galland was a traveller, classicist, diplomat, and brilliant Arabist, who travelled to the Sublime Porte of the Ottoman empire in 1670 in the train of the Marquis de Nointel; he studied Turkish, Arabic, Persian and modern Greek, and collected antiques and manuscripts. He became a leading, scholarly orientalist, at a time when the fashion for Ottoman romancing was beginning to inspire the use of exotic settings in tales by Jean de la Fontaine and Marie-Catherine d'Aulnoy. (Among Galland's works there also appears a short eulogy to coffee, as yet unfamiliar in the salons of Paris.) Galland worked first from a three-volume manuscript written in the fourteenth century, which he found in Syria. Surprisingly, this manuscript turns out to be the earliest extant; for later volumes, he also set down stories told him by a Maronite Christian from Aleppo called Hanna Diab, who was living in Paris. Diab's repertoire, for example, included the much loved romance of 'Prince Ahmed and Peri Banou'. However, one or two of the most famous tales of all, such as 'Aladdin' and 'Ali Baba and the Forty Thieves', do not exist at all in Arabic texts before Galland: it is pretty much accepted now, by the best scholars in the field that Galland wrote them himself. Were they tongue-in-cheek parodies of the *Nights*? Sincere homages to the magical tale of the exotic?

Imitation wasn't considered in the same light then as it is now, and Galland's inventions are certainly brilliant examples of the genre, and his exuberant, learned, witty work, as translator and imitator, inaugurated the tremendous vogue for oriental settings and fantastical fables that spread throughout Enlightenment Europe and caught up Voltaire, Montesquieu, Samuel Johnson, Jeremy Bentham in the enthusiasm. The *Arabian Nights* joined the home-grown fairy-tale tradition, which in France had begun with the *Contes du temps passé* of Charles Perrault in 1697, and brought oriental sumptuousness to *Le Cabinet des fées*, an anthology of fairy tales which appeared in forty-four volumes at the end of the eighteenth century. In many ways, the Ottoman disguise gave writers a cover for ironical philosophising and satirical perspective on their own social mores and aberrant despots (the horrors in *Candide* catch some of the flavour of *Arabian Nights* misadventures).

The first English version, 'the Grub Street' translations, appeared in 1706–8, soon after Galland's first publications, and quickly sparked pantomimes on the stage and literary imitations. The subsequent story of the *Nights* becomes almost as shifting as the tales themselves: in Egypt in the eighteenth century, one of the influential and founding manuscripts was packed with all kinds of additional material, in an attempt to eke out the required thousand and one nights. 'Thus authentic came to mean complete and, ironically, spurious,' comments the most recent translator, Husain Haddawy.[2]

In the Victorian era, adventurer-explorers such as Hugh Lane and Richard Burton, both ardent lovers of Araby, produced translations based on these Arabic compilations. Their editions reflect their own attachments: Hugh Lane's edition is stuffed full of ethnographical details of Old Cairo (some of it densely researched and nostalgic, other parts rather fanciful); Burton's version is an almost Chattertonian exercise in auncient tongues, prolix and rococo, and is also truffled with lore (much of it salacious, earning Burton his nickname, Dirty Dick).

Through these translations, the *Arabian Nights* flowed to join the streams of folklore anthologies such as the Grimm Brothers' fairy tales and several volumes of *Teutonic Mythology* and Andrew Lang's series of *Fairy Books* in all colours. These compendia grew in popularity with the fashion for vernacular, ethnically identified literature/orature, but it's a mistake to receive the *Arabian Nights* as another monument to national identity in the Victorian fashion. As Robert Irwin describes, the tales reveal their historical and social roots in the seething bazaars and busy trade routes of the Mameluke empire of Egypt from the thirteenth century onwards, with their performing jugglers, conjurors, snake-charmers and professional farters, their perfumed gardens and cooling fountains, their polymorphous seductions. But the *Arabian Nights* also shares in the multiplicity, exuberance, outlandishness, multicolouredness of those tangled webs of stories woven by founding poets and fiction writers of non-Arabian literature rising from the shores of 'Our Sea', the Mediterranean: Ovid's *Metamorphoses*, Apuleius' *The Golden Ass*, Boccaccio's *Decameron*, Chaucer's *Canterbury Tales*, the Venetian Straparola's *Pleasant Nights*, the Neapolitan Giambattista Basile's *Pentameron*, and many besides. The languages differ, the settings too, but the exchanges that brought them into being were shared, and the enterprise bears a deep family likeness.

In spite of the popularity of fantastic tales, in spite of the standing of several of their composers and collectors, a critical atmosphere still hung around such freewheeling cycles of romances and fairy stories, nursery rhymes and other magic narrative forms that do not involve authors or scholars, but oral performers who aim at diverting listeners – and readers – of all classes and ages. The word *conte* (tale) was even defined by the French *académiciens*, around the time Galland was producing the *Arabian Nights*, as the nonsense foolish old people tell children to put them to sleep. This brand of literature was coded low, tinged by association with the illiterate, with women and servants and children, 'the lower orders'.

Something similar happened to the *Arabian Nights* over its history, for a certain condescension towards the amusement afforded by the tales colours some of the earliest allusions. One of the first references, from an Indian scholar in the tenth century, uses the word *khurafas* to characterise them, meaning they are tall stories, enjoyable but somehow not worth serious attention. As an American Arabist commented early in the last century, 'It is unfortunate that the Arabic world has never regarded [the *Thousand and One Nights*] as belonging to polite literature.'[3] For this reason, among others, no standard text in Arabic existed for this canonical work, until the Iraqi Arabist Muhsin Mahdi established an edition in 1984.

Throughout the plethora of recensions and variations, Galland remained a blueprint, and his edition has shaped almost every successive version. Powys Mathers (1892–1939) produced his English version in 1923 from the French of Joseph Charles Mardrus; his version had appeared in 1899–1904. Mardrus was a fin-de-siècle aesthete and a friend of André Gide, and he had been born in Cairo in 1868 and had spoken Arabic in his childhood. He claimed to be using Arabic sources, but many traces of Galland throughout reveal how much he relied on his predecessor. Mardrus also followed Galland's example by introducing new stories, and some of his contributions have a decided decadent and Symbolist character, striking the French orientalist note of Gustave Flaubert in *Salammbô*, and of Oscar Wilde in *Salome*. This languid, erotic, heady atmosphere, communicated by Mathers after Mardrus, epitomises the Western vision of a magical lost kingdom of pleasure, beyond classical and humanist rationality. For this reason, the *Arabian Nights* has excited fantasies in many forms of Western entertainment, in ballet, opera, theatre and film. Ottoman Tartary and Asia became the favoured settings for Russian composers, such as Rimsky-Korsakov and Prokofiev, while in the cinema, Georges Méliès at the turn of the century invented magical flights, changes of shape, sudden vanishings and apparitions and other visual illusions, against a background of oriental splendour. Some of the most ambitious early special effects of the Hollywood cinema were developed in films like *The Thief of Baghdad*, to approximate the magical feats described in the tales. (The fabulous 1924 silent version features Douglas Fairbanks as a bazaar pickpocket in harem trousers, energetically performing vanishing acts and rope tricks.) Even Sigmund Freud's famous couch is draped in an oriental rug, surely a salaam in the direction of the magic carpets of the *Nights*, which whisk you off to worlds of inner fantasy.

The *Arabian Nights* is both a work of literature and a genre in the process of growing. The stories are not confined by the texts they inhabit, or by the nights over which they are told. They spill out from the covers of the books in which they are translated and printed and escape from the limits of time that the narrative struggles to impose. They constitute a genre in themselves, a type of story, a whole dimension of entertainment possibility, and they therefore keep generating tales, themselves different but alike: the stories themselves are shape-shifters. Borges enters the best plea for the turbulent history of the *Nights'* transmission: 'I think that the reader should enrich what he is reading. He should misunderstand the text; he should change it into something else.' The power of stories to forge destinies has never been so memorably and sharply put as it is in this cycle, in which the blade of the executioner's sword lies on the storyteller's neck. The *Arabian Nights* proclaims the life that is language, the human reality of stories as a light in the dark and a charm against death.

2003

Laughter and Hope in the Old Wives' Tale

On Rossini's opera La Cenerentola, *and Prokofiev's ballet*, Cinderella

Cinderella has left her footprint, if not her shoe itself, on shores far and wide, and her 'once upon a time' took place a very long time ago. The earliest traces reveal her in a comic mood, for fairy tales used to offer entertainment and reassurance to adults, providing robust consolation about grown-up matters, like marriage and money and earthly justice.

In Apuleius' romance novel *The Golden Ass*, a young bride is abducted by bandits and held captive in a cave with only a donkey and a 'drunken and half-demented' old woman for company. The donkey is the book's unfortunate author-narrator, Lucius himself, a predecessor of Shakespeare's Bottom, and the whole book describes his adventures as he struggles to undo the enchantment and become a man again. In the cave meanwhile, he overhears the story the old woman tells the distraught bride to cheer her up. It is the famous tale of 'Cupid and Psyche', and it contains many of the motifs of the Cinderella story: the prince who is Love personified, Psyche who is first chosen and transformed, then discarded and lost, and at last recognised and found and married to her true love. Her two wicked sisters are jealous and plot against her; Venus, the mother of Cupid, plays the part later taken by the wicked stepmother. She beats, scolds and demeans Psyche, setting her absurd household tasks: she orders her, for instance, to separate millet and wheat and other grains into heaps. In Apuleius, ants come to Psyche's rescue and fulfil the conditions imposed by Venus, her future mother-in-law; in the Grimm Brothers' version, 'Ashpüttel', written down at the beginning of the nineteenth century, Cinderella has to perform the same impossible task before she can go to the ball, and it is birds who help her – more particularly doves, birds sacred to the goddess of love, and appropriate creatures in a fairy tale with such deep connections with Greek romance.

'Cupid and Psyche' ends with the wedding feast, and the promise that the child of their union will be called Pleasure. Apuleius' tone is never straightforward, however, but tender and bawdy, sentimental and cynical, innocent and knowing all at once. Later variants, retellings and elaborations of a fairy tale about a forlorn heroine questing for her true love remain true to this early romance's mixture of flavours.

Charles Perrault wrote the most familiar version, *Cendrillon, ou La petite pantoufle de verre* ('Cinderella, or the Little Glass Slipper'), and included it in his collection of 1697, *Contes du temps passé* ('Tales of Past Time'), where it appears alongside other nursery favourites like 'The Sleeping Beauty in the Wood', 'Red Riding Hood' and 'Puss-in-Boots'. Perrault was a member of the Académie Française, a poet and polemicist as well as a courtier who had served Colbert, Louis XIV's financier, and he published his famous fairy tales at the end of his life, when he was in his sixties. He uses throughout a tongue-in-cheek, worldly-wise manner, as if he cannot resist poking fun at the wonders and adventures he is passing on, and wants to make sure that we, the hearers or the readers, know that he is not so silly as to take such trifles seriously. He can be slyly witty: the cook, when ordered by the wicked queen to serve the Sleeping Beauty for supper, wonders if her flesh will have become a little tough, as she was 'more than twenty years old, not counting the hundred years she had slept'.

Perrault was the first storyteller to introduce the magical transformations of the pumpkin, the mice, the rat, the lizards from 'behind the watering can', and he was having some fun at footmen's expense, for they were proverbially lazy and, like lizards, would lie back and bask in the sun all day. Perrault also chose the pumpkin advisedly, making light of the fears of witchcraft that had been circulating in France with heavy consequences only thirty years before. His fairy godmother's powers of metamorphosis are identical with the practices ascribed (in dread) to witches, but Perrault, in anticipation of Enlightenment reason, shows such Hallowe'en magic to be both harmless and benign.

In Apuleius, Psyche is forbidden to look at her lover in the dark, and when she breaks the prohibition (and prohibitions are a necessary dynamic of fairy tales), everything disappears: Cupid, the enchanted castle, and all the attendants and luxuries which had surrounded her there. Perrault adapted this idea when he introduced the godmother's curfew, and again, at the stroke of midnight, all the magic comes to an end and Cinderella runs home in rags (to the melody that was Prokofiev's favourite moment in his score).

In their ballet of 1941–4, Sergei Prokofiev and his librettist Nicolai Volkov follow Perrault's story very closely, but they expand the role of the godmother to conjure many more of the gossamer creatures from fairyland who had become such defining figures of Romantic ballet, from *Giselle* to *Les Sylphides*. These scenes deepen the story's connection to the realm of enchantment, where the destinies of humans are given and directed. Frederick Ashton, however, resisted the whimsy and even mawkishness that could arise from too much faery, and, by drawing on the British pantomime tradition, held to the down-to-earth spirit of Perrault's original, in which the sisters want to show off such slim waists at the ball that they break several laces to their corsets. In a similar vein, the heroine's nickname is first given as Cucendron (Cinderbottom), but Perrault adds that the kinder of the two stepsisters softened it to Cinderella.

'Cupid and Psyche' can also be invoked as an ancestor of fairy tale as it is understood today because Apuleius presents it as a story told aloud by a narrator for a purpose – 'Let me tell you a fairy tale or two,' says the old woman in *The Golden Ass*, 'to make you feel a little better.' The Czech fantasy writer and critic Karel Čapek remarked, 'A fairy tale cannot be defined by its motif and subject matter, but by its origin and function.' 'Red Riding Hood' and Rossini's *La Cenerentola*, for example, do not stop being fairy tales because they do not feature any fairies: they remain fairy tales because they originate in popular, anonymous, familiar folk stories and aim to amuse, while at the same time drawing clear moral distinctions about the way things should be rather than the way they are. The ballet of *Cinderella* does not need a long synopsis to explain the story – novelty is hardly the point. The ancient, consolatory fable about 'The triumph of goodness' (as Iacopo Ferretti subtitled his libretto for Rossini's operatic version) delivers its pleasure without need for further narrative complications.

It is also significant that Apuleius' storyteller is a hideous crone, for Perrault, in his early editions, did not put his name on the title-page of the collection, but instead invoked in the frontispiece the traditional scene of the hearth, with an older servant gathering the children of the house at her knee, to listen to her while she spins. On the wall behind them, a placard reads, *Contes de ma mère l'oye* ('Tales of Mother Goose'), one of the earliest printed references to the proverbial teller of tales and voice of nursery rhymes. In his preface, Perrault declared that he was only passing on stories everyone knew, trifles and old wives' tales they had heard from grandmothers and nurses when they were young. Perrault the *académicien* and scholar was making a brave stand about popular literature and the culture of the illiterate by publishing fairy tales at all: many of his colleagues openly expressed their scorn of the genre. For fairy tale was considered a low branch of literature, circulating among menials and children and other vulgar, lesser mortals who would credit such foolishness as happy endings or talking animals. But like other so-called low forms – farce, riddles, fables, pasquinades, caricature and pantomime – fairy tale could also offer scope for expression and even risk-taking.

Ashton's exuberant use of drag for the two Stepsisters, the roles he and Robert Helpmann created, seized on the French idea of Mother Goose and adapted her to the vulgar native version of the *commedia dell'arte*. Mother Goose was a much loved comic character of the stage from the early nineteenth century onwards. The nursery rhyme describes her in slightly risqué terms:

> Old Mother Goose
> When she wanted to wander
> Would fly through the air
> On a very fine gander.

On stage she was traditionally played by a Dame; with her magic goose that laid golden eggs, she featured in a popular Victorian pantomime, whistling up a wind and performing other magical feats on behalf of Jack, her lucky simpleton of a son, who is a kind of boy Cinderella for whom all comes right in the end. It was this sturdy, rude, vulgar tradition that

Ashton boldly hauled on to the Royal Opera House stage and installed at the heart of one of the most lovely pieces of romantic ballet music.

Ashton's ebullient sense of the absurd strikes at many targets: at old bags titivating, of course; at human folly and vanity in general; but also, much more daringly, at the feminine conventions that ballet itself had naturalised. The Stepsisters stomping and galumphing caricature the featherweight ideals of the ballerina, pointing out good-humouredly the human impossibility of so much grace, light and airiness. In some sense their absurd cavortings satirise the romantic ballet's vision as it is going on next to them, personified by Cinderella and the fairies; yet, at the same time, they also enhance, by contrast, their counterparts' unearthly success in the ideal. Ashton's mischievous inspiration does not clash with Prokofiev's lush and passionate music, but renders the lyrical yearning in *Cinderella* the more acute.

For generations of stage-struck children who buy miniature ballet shoes, or pore over pairs worn by Markova or Fonteyn, the fairy tale of 'Cinderella' offers a related message: here is a heroine who is so small and so light that she can walk in glass shoes without breaking them. Perrault may have written down *verre* ('glass') when the oral version said *vair* ('ermine') but his mistake, if mistake it was, was inspired: Cinderella's glass slipper stirs associations with crystal purity, with virginity and hence nubility, with translucent honesty and so forth, far more than any common fur-trimmed mule ever could. Though the ballet – for obvious reasons – changes the slippers to gold, with all its connotations of value, Perrault's original choice goes on resonating, in the hint of a threat. When the Stepsisters in the ballet try and squeeze their big fat feet into the shoe, they cannot help evoking dancers themselves, whose toes are shaped into *pointe* shoes and used to give the illusion of weightlessness; Cinderella's slipper also mirrors her future as a bride, when she will have to fit in with what is required.

Perrault concluded his story with two morals: the first pointed out that charm is more important than good looks; the second reminded readers how crucial it is to have a well connected and powerful godmother. Cinderella's story, for all its magic and froth, deals with real-life problems of dowerless girls and their chances of marriage. Rossini's *La Cenerentola* shows a stepfather scheming to advance his own daughters over a third, unwanted child, and comes dangerously close to tragedy when he treacherously tells the prince's messenger, in Cinderella's presence, that she is dead.

In the Renaissance brides took their trousseau or dowry to their husband's home in a *cassone*, or 'hope chest'; these were painted with scenes from well-known stories like 'Patient Griselda' or 'Potiphar's Wife' or 'Cupid and Psyche' – cautionary tales about the torments, infidelities and dangers that a bride can face in her marriage. The tales were seen as suitable material for future wives and mothers, full of anticipatory advice of what are called today, 'worst-case scenarios'. Fairy tales offer hope against the odds, and the comfort that others have been there before, and survived – to laugh.

The anthropologist Claude Lévi-Strauss has remarked, famously, that every retelling of a myth, or story, becomes part of that myth, enters its life and its identity. There can be no Ur-version, though there may be early first-hand evidence, in texts or elsewhere. His valuable idea can be used to obscure, however, the importance of differences in the same story; the diffusion and antiquity of a tale like 'Cinderella' can lead to a false sense of its unchanging unity. For what is most fascinating is that all the retellings that make up a body of story are still different, in particulars – in tell-tale particulars. At one level 'Cinderella' offers hope to wronged children everywhere that the days of their suffering will come to an end, their inner nature will be seen for what it is, their true worth will be rewarded, their enemies will be confounded and their prince will come. These are the broadest outlines of meaning in the tale, which the psychoanalyst Bruno Bettelheim developed along symbolic lines in his important book *The Uses of Enchantment*. He argues that the figure of the wicked stepmother, for instance, helps children vent the antagonisms they feel against their real mother on a fantasy Bad Mother; this process is therapeutic for it does not damage their love for their natural mother and helps them accept her anger and her punishments.

But interpreted at other levels, paying attention to the places and other circumstances of its telling, a fairy tale like 'Cinderella' reflects the audience who heard it, takes on the colour of the circumstances in which it is told. Like the chemistry between palm-reader and client, a storyteller meets certain variable needs and responds to certain accepted values in the circle that has gathered to hear. In the days when mothers frequently died in childbirth, and stepmothers and stepsiblings were common, Cinderella stories concentrated on this loss: in the Grimm Brothers' version, Ashputtel weeps on her mother's grave, where she has planted a hazel wand. Watered by her tears, it grows into a tree, answers her prayers and shakes down the three dresses she wears to the ball, and her golden ·

slippers too. In early Scottish and English versions, which were collected in the last century but which contain memories of earlier times, the heroine's dead mother returns to help her by nursing her when she's hurt, feeding her when she's starving and clothing her when she's in rags. Hundreds of versions all over the world, from the Highlands to the west coast of Africa, invent a dead mother's saving role in her child's survival. Angela Carter has written a shivery, beautiful modern version:

> The little cat came by. The ghost of the mother went into the cat.
> 'Your hair wants doing', said the cat. 'Lie down.'
> The little cat unpicked her raggy lugs with its clever paws until the burned child's hair hung down nicely, but it had been so snagged and tangled that the claws were all pulled out before it was finished.
> 'Comb your own hair, next time', said the cat. 'You've maimed me.'

This 'Ashputtle' then picks the man she wants and leaves home, and the story ends:

> 'Now I can go to sleep', said the ghost of the mother. 'Now everything is all right.'[1]

The death of mothers and the cruelty of their successors were realities in the lives of many until recently and were brought about by powerful economic and dynastic interests as well as physical conditions. Audiences certainly identified with the Cinderella heroine at an immediate level, in fear that her plight might become theirs, if it had not already done so. The history of the tale is also a history of female cruelty, spite and ambition: it has inspired many a male interpreter, from Walt Disney to Maurice Sendak, to expand gleefully on this aspect. Perrault does not so much reproach the father in his story, but mentions that Cinderella did not complain to him of her maltreatment as he would have scolded her, being 'entirely dominated' by his new wife. Rossini and Ferretti, in *La Cenerentola*, are unusual when they lay the blame squarely on the male head of the household, the malevolent buffoon Don Magnifico. The idea that Cinderella's father is also a victim of the wicked stepmother and her offspring proved much more popular: in the Victorian pantomime, he is a figure of fun, Baron Hardup or Baron

Stoneybroke, and so henpecked he is incapable of standing up for his beloved daughter. This also gave Ashton a chance to lampoon sexual conventions, with his horrid viragos terrorising the poor little man. The music-hall joke, full of Victorian ideas about proper female conduct, has replaced an older narrative tradition in the history of the Cinderella story, in which the heroine is the victim of her father's rage, or even, in some cases, of his incestuous passion.

Shakespeare, for instance, in *King Lear*, was inspired by a medieval tale, closely related to the Cinderella cycle, about a king who had three daughters and banished the youngest when she would not tell him how much she loved him, beyond stating that she loved him as meat loves salt. Later, according to the tale in Geoffrey of Monmouth, he's beggared by his two elder daughters and wanders, in rags, into a wedding feast. He does not recognise the bride, but she recognises him, and she orders the cooks to serve the meal without salt. As soon as the guests start eating they push the food away in disgust, because it is entirely tasteless, and the old king realises what his youngest meant all those years ago. Then the bride reveals herself to him as his outcast daughter, and they are reconciled. Not in *King Lear*, of course, and the distance between the comfort of the medieval tale and the Shakespearean tragedy is very great – as it is again between Don Magnifico and Lear or between Rossini and Prokofiev. In the parentage of fairy tale there exist cousins who bear a family resemblance but are completely distinct, in mood and meaning.

At the turn of the century the folklorist Marian Cox collected over three hundred different variations of the Cinderella story; since then, dozens of others have been added to her archive, from Dahomey, New Mexico, Brazil, Japan and Russia, Iraq and Armenia, as well as Europe. Many of the best-loved and familiar fairy tales are also closely related to 'Cinderella' – like 'Beauty and the Beast'. But all these versions are rooted in the cultures that gave birth to them and can reveal to us individual facets of their societies. One of the most far-flung versions, a ninth-century Chinese one, includes the losing of the shoe. Its small size, in T'ang dynasty China where the desired 'lily' effect was achieved by breaking and binding a baby girl's foot, confers a specific, historical and gruesome meaning on what has become the glass slipper of contemporary Cinderella lore.

Most people are brought up to believe fairy tales are for children, that they should be put away with childish things. But the last decades of the century have witnessed a longing to return to childhood; as if with ageing, the times wanted to dip themselves in the legendary *fontaine de jouvence* and regain youth. Childlikeness is being re-evaluated, and the fantasy, both sweet and savage, that is attributed to the state of innocence is ever more prized; with these shifts there has come a resurgence of fairy tale. Modern authors, from Gabriel García Márquez to Angela Carter, have written in the mode; contemporary films, like *Celia* and *Edward Scissorhands*, mine fairy tales for messages. Gillian Beer, in her essay 'The Romance' (1970), commented, 'Being absorbed with the ideal, [romance] always has an element of prophecy. It remakes the world in the image of desire.' Art undertakes a realistic appraisal of the possibilities in times of wealth, confidence and certainties; it resorts to fantasy and hope and fairy stories to sketch improbable possibilities in times of fragmentation and difficulty; the laughter in Prokofiev and Ashton's ballet, the goodness of Cinderella, and the generosity of her love and mercy raise all our hopes, make us all feel a little better.

1991

Mother Russia

Review of Joanna Hubbs, Mother Russia: The Feminine Myth in Russian Culture

At the beginning of the eighteenth century, Peter the Great decreed that his country was to be called the motherland no longer; henceforward, Russia would officially be known as *otechestvo*, the fatherland. The Tsar could continue to be Little Father Tsar (*Batyushka Tsar*), but he would no longer be joined, in his coronation ceremony, to Little Mother Russia (*Matushka Rus*) in an ancient rite of sacred marriage. However, as Joanna Hubbs reveals in *Mother Russia*, the Tsar's writ did not run deep. The peasants continued to think of Holy Russia as a goddess, and repeated the proverb, 'Your fatherland is your mother.'

Such shifting sexual symbolism wasn't unusual in the West. In Tsar Peter's time, patriotic Britons were rallying to Britannia; a little later, in Republican France, *la patrie* found its reflection in the female figure of Marianne. But as Hubbs makes clear in this ambitious and packed study, the Tsar's proclamation of the fatherland perpetrated a sacrilege against a faith rather more profound than the patriotic rhetoric of Marianne or

Britannia. By fiat, he was seeking to abolish a complex of beliefs in female powers.

Caricaturists showed him as a bearded crocodile, fighting Baba Yaga, the Wise Woman and Witch of Russian folklore, opposing his dream of Christianity, centralised authority and paternal rights to her natural law, her unreason, her wildness, her claims to maternal sovereignty. Baba Yaga has a Greek Fury's fierceness and Medusa's lolling tongue and ferocious grin, and the clash between her and the Tsar echoes an age-old conflict, found in its clearest form at the conclusion of the *Oresteia*, when the female Furies are brought under Athenian rule.

Joanna Hubbs musters evidence for early matriliny in Russia, and finds in the cult of the Great Goddess among the Slavs and Scythians the foundations of early Russian beliefs. Her material here is a familiar mix: neolithic figures marked with spirals or lozenges or other cryptic fertility symbols, and a seasoning of Herodotus' enjoyable stories about barbarians and their funny ways. Though the stones speak, perhaps, it is hard to be sure of what they say. It is when the author reaches figures in Russian folk religion that her book's focus sharpens, and opens on to the richly coloured world of sirens and enchantresses, sea nymphs and dryads, crones and sprites that the brilliant early twentieth-century illustrators like I. Bilibin conjured up for Pushkin's retellings of Russian folktales.

The *rusalki*, water nymphs who comb rain – 'the milk of the clouds' – out of their hair, bring fertility to young women, but kill the male wanderer who comes upon them. They live apart from men, in bands, and are identified with springs and rivers in the Ukraine, with forests and trees, especially birches, the heralds of spring, in Byelorussia. Baba Yaga herself inspired a splendid literature of the fantastic. Her fence is made of human bones topped by skulls whose eyes gleam in the forest nights, her hut strands – and runs – on chicken's feet, while her front door has hands for bolts, legs for posts and 'a mouth with sharp teeth as a lock'. As her mode of travel, Baba Yaga favours rowing a mortar with a pestle through the sky, like a vision from a painting by Bosch. Her name might derive from a word for grudge: she is Old Mother Grudge, and as defender and enemy, heroine and villain, she appears in many Russian folktales, cautionary and magical. Hubbs, however, hardly ever quotes a text directly, but summarises instead in confusing paraphrase.

Holy Russia finds her closest counterpart in the third of Hubbs's original mythical figures, Mother Moist Earth. The relation between women and the fertility of the earth was recognised in violent fashion in early Russian history: a chronicle relates how, after a failed harvest in 1070 in the north, the priests called out the women, blamed them for the famine and then stabbed them in the back, 'drawing from them meat and fish and other produce'. In the face of such episodes, the author's enthusiasm for archaic woman-centred cults makes one worry that in *Mother Russia* she isn't always keeping both hands on the wheel.

Anthropologists like Peggy Reeves Sanday, whom Ms Hubbs cites, have found that, broadly speaking, societies where women are respected have close ties with the natural world, are often dependent on the land and familiar with animals. But the complex significance of woman's identification with nature is overlooked here. The author argues that the prominence and frequency of feminine myths accompany the high status and authority that women enjoyed in peasant society, that these beliefs continued to be held after the conversion of Russia to Christianity when the rulers and the clergy from the twelfth century onwards sought to impose a patriarchal order on the Russian people. They were only partly successful: by symbiosis, by resistance, the peasants' faith survived, a kind of preliterate samizdat.

Changes in the marriage ceremony illustrate strikingly women's official degradation after the coming of Christianity. In the Ukraine before the nineteenth century, a girl would be urged by her mother to choose her man and catch him like 'a falcon bright in the open field'. Afterwards, the bride would lament the impending loss of her freedom and of intimacy with the *rusalki*; on the day of her wedding, surrounded by her girlfriends, she would defend her house against the groom and his 'soldiers'. At the ceremony itself, the bride's braid, emblem of her virginity, would be cut by her mother, not by the groom, and then, 'anointed in butter and honey' and covered in money and bread to symbolise the bounty a wife brings to the union. In areas tamed by the Church, however, the symbolism of matrimony stressed submission: the bridegroom stamped on his bride's foot until it bled, and she was required to remove his boots for him when they reached the bedroom.

The cult of Mary had been established by the time the boot became a part of the wedding service. The Mother of God represented the ideal obedience and devotion of a Christian wife; her virginity was not emphasised in Russia as it was in the Western Church, but her docility was. Yet at the same time, her powers of intercession, her mercy, her enchantments, her miracle-working icons, made of the trees sacred to the earth goddesses and the *rusalki*, often show how she had inherited some of the powers of her predecessors.

Few other female saints entered the Orthodox heaven. But Saint Paraskeva-Pyatnitsa is a wonderful revelation and a worthy companion to Baba Yaga. Her name means 'Friday', her epithets invoke her variously as 'Dirty', 'Muddy' or 'Flaxen', and she looks after women's interests and work, especially spinning. On Fridays, women weren't supposed to wash their hair, the site of fertility – truly a maidenhead. Ivan the Terrible tried to stamp out her festivities – unavailingly. She caused terrible blights to befall those who did not observe her cult, though in the only icon reproduced here she looks very well behaved.

Mother Russia encompasses a huge territory. It badly needs a map and a chronology. Sweeping through the medieval epics of Russian history, on to the rise of tsardom and the reign of Ivan the Terrible, it catches its breath with Pushkin's claims on behalf of the peasant and his old nurse's wisdom. Hubbs's procedure – accumulating and synthesising – has something in common with pioneering works of religious anthropology, like *The Golden Bough* by James G. Frazer (written between 1890 and 1936) and *The Mothers* by Robert Briffault (1927), but the continual astral and agricultural interpretations, the trust in poorly documented archaic creeds and a Jungian tendency to see similarities rather than distinctions, make *Mother Russia* finally wearisome. Throughout, nature and the old beliefs (women) are seen struggling against history – or change – and the new ideologies (men). This model of history has its limitations. Like the *matryoshka* doll with which the book begins, the rich variety of Russian beliefs seems to nest one inside the other, enfolded and interrelated, rather than meet in the lists in a continual stand-off. But the most disappointing aspect of the book is its incuriosity about narrative, its sources, transmission, audience. In a footnote, for instance, the author mentions wandering troupes of beggars, cripples and blind storytellers known as 'God's people', who sang tales from the Apocrypha and the Bible, the 'Spiritual Verses', in return for food and shelter; but she does not tell us when, or who collected their songs or why, though she claims that with such material 'in an attempt to counter the masculinized dogma of the church, noblewomen and peasants introduced their essentially feminine vision of the cosmic order into the teachings of the church.' It may be that men like Pushkin needed the myth of the wise old nurse perhaps more than the wise old nurse needed it – or believed in it.

The French psychoanalyst Catherine Clément has written eloquently about contemporary women's need to return to myths, to 'the imaginary sorceress of whom no one has any trace; except in rediscovering the desire that this figure and her acts of violence awaken in ourselves, women'. Joanna Hubbs has found the trace of Baba Yaga and the *rusalki* and Moist Mother Earth and other fascinating feminine myths in Russian culture, and has added richly to the growing interest in popular culture. But *Mother Russia* would be more convincing if the author put her subjects to the question, like oracles, rather than offered worship at their shrine.

1989

EIGHT

REWORKING THE TALE

Combat Myths

Combat myths, which tell the story of a struggle between a hero and a diabolical enemy, have gained fresh energy from the current world crisis and the world powers' political and military response. The record-breaking figures of the Harry Potter films and the new *Lord of the Rings* series of spectacular epics convey strongly the consolatory power of such dreams of overcoming evil.

Boy heroes doing battle with mighty monsters have been the staple of 'bloods', as such tales of sword-swishing, swashbuckling, dragon-slaying adventures were called when they were first published for young people in the nineteenth century. Among the forerunners of these heroes are angels like Michael crushing the devil under foot, alongside such champions as Theseus, who threads his way through the labyrinth to kill the Minotaur, and Hercules, who grapples with giants and beasts in a long series of exploits. Saints and national patrons, including that pattern of English chivalry Saint George, also overcome cannibal dragons or other enemies ravaging their home territory.

In modern fairy tales, the dragon-killers have drawn closer to everyday experience, in size and style: they have shed wings and armour and put on spectacles, their heroic muscles have shrunk and they have turned into brave young lads, hobbits and Harry Potter. J. R. R. Tolkien and J. K. Rowling, at around fifty years' interval, are writing within an epic tradition that on the one hand appeals to young males looking for a role and so acts as a male initiation narrative, and at the same time offers the larger audience a freshly invigorated cultural identity myth bonding the community together against danger. So these stories offer thrilling, consolatory entertainment for audiences fearful of what is out there in the dark. The evil Lord Sauron, from *The Lord of the Rings*, is named after the Greek for 'dragon'; in the Harry Potter stories, the implacable

Voldemort's name means Will-to-Death in a kind of made-up medieval French; both have inherited the role of the diabolical adversaries of ancient heroic combat myth.

The strength and familiarity of this dualism can make the narratives seem archetypal, in the sense of inevitable, natural. Children's writers aren't the only ones drawn at this time to such material: the Irish poet Seamus Heaney recently made an eloquent, bleak translation of the Anglo-Saxon *Beowulf*, the epic poem that formed Tolkien's life work in his professional capacity as an Oxford professor. But combat myths are only one kind of story from the great store of myths and in the tradition, they are often superseded by tales of reconciliation, transformation, redemption in the same way as the New Testament's message of forgiveness cancels the Old Testament's thirst for vengeance.

It would be a mistake to accept unthinkingly that the dualist model of story is hard-wired in the human imagination; such a view overlooks the contemporary relevance of the model's popularity now. Fantasies of evil and dreams of victory over its agents have been increasing in voltage, needless to say, in response to the terrible events of September 11 and the threats and continuing danger. Osama Bin Laden, in fact, appears eerily to be continuing Sauron and Voldemort's legacy (as well as, one might add, the earlier ambitions of the lethal, foreign antagonists of James Bond). But we still have to be vigilant that the imaginary figures of these lords of darkness do not lead our perceptions and muddle our strategic thinking. As ever, history can offer a lesson in alternatives, and by placing the mythological struggle against evil in a historical perspective several factors emerge that qualify the apparent inevitability of a stand-off struggle between the forces of good and evil. In Sanskrit mythology, in classical Greek beliefs and in numerous African and Pacific religious systems, the powers of generation, destruction, of life and death, of boon and bane, do not act in opposition to one another, but in concert, according to the complex laws of an organic cycle.

It was in the Middle East, in the thought of the prophet Zoroaster, that the gods worshipped by the ancient Persians were declared to be devils, agents of evil. In Persia in the middle of the third century the prophet Mani, further developed this ethical interpretation of the continuing struggle between light and dark, into a strong form of religious dualism; Manichaeans envisaged the clash of forces as a personal, eternal struggle between divine powers of good and evil. Both Zoroastrianism and Manichaeism have profoundly influenced the extreme warrior visions of

Islamic and Judaeo-Christian thought – Saint Augustine, for example, was a Manichee in his youth and its philosophy coloured his deep commitment to the notion of original evil. The Christian devil, though a bright angel in his beginnings, became a vehicle of irreversible wickedness: the great philosopher Origen is neither a saint nor even a Father of the Church because he held that the devil could be converted. This was heresy. Even more significantly, Nietzsche was attracted to Zarathustra's vision and wrote *Thus Spake Zarathustra*. Wagner's *Ring* cycle, a direct progenitor of Tolkien's myth, was forged in the same crucible. In many ways, the century that has just ended and the one that has just begun have not experienced the rise of Christian or Islamic fundamentalism, so much as the triumphant revival of Zoroastrianism.

Destruction, extermination, annihilation: these are the triumphant goals of the hero combat myth. Not conversion, not metamorphosis. But there is another, different, countervailing fairy-tale tradition, which has been sidelined in the epic fantasies of *Harry Potter* and *The Lord of the Rings*: the transformation story. The model of 'Beauty and the Beast', for instance, structures thousands of fairy tales, ancient and modern. This kind of myth imagines the redemption of the monster, his (sometimes her) conversion. It focuses on the possibility of change. But even to mention this now sounds inappropriate: we have lost, it seems, this hope. Yet destruction in itself produces change by another means; and the changes it produces may be more dangerous or even monstrous than before.

Transformation stories are associated with women, for it is Beauty's courage, perseverance and fidelity that accomplish the Beast's metamorphosis. One of the striking features of the current fantasies about evil is their thoroughgoing maleness: Tolkien's work includes examples of female monstrosity (Shelob, a gigantic, malignant spider), but not of female heroism; in the film, there's a token feminised elf, played by Kate Blanchett. One of the huge questions over the Harry Potter books remains Joanne Rowling's apparent failure of imagination with regard both to girls and to grown women. The pervasive *Boy's Own* tendency of the current mythological enthusiasm also leads to that strongly male-identified zone: gadgets, weapons, boys' toys. Pottermania and the Tolkien revival dramatise magic as a means to power; both films, envisaging power in terms of world domination by an enemy, invest that power in talismanic objects which must be controlled, or, if necessary, smashed. Tolkien's ring itself, alongside the invisible cloaks, Quidditch broomsticks, and other magic weapons in the Harry Potter stories, act as instruments with an instant, direct effect. Interestingly, for such fantastical tales, they reject enigma, unpredictability and wonder: the students at Hogwarts only have to learn spells, like lessons, or acquire the right brand of weapon, to become lords of creation themselves. As many critics have pointed out, this is commodity magic, the enchanted realm of the logo.

The association of magical power with weapons of destruction, not with philosophical wisdom, with devices not with deliberation, negotiation and response, takes the stories out of the human arena of personal contact into the hegemonic and depersonalised zone of technology. The history of magic shows that interest in the subject takes a wrong turn when it ceases to be a branch of inquiry and a form of knowledge (astrology's relationship to astronomy) and becomes instead a mechanical system and means of domination (astrology as a controlling mechanism for fortune-tellers to use on individuals).

It's always difficult to tell the dancer from the dance in matters of myth and ideology: do the current mega-hits at the box office reflect anxieties and dreams, or do they shape them, encourage them, even incite them? The insistence on one kind of narrative can obliterate another, as a rampant monoculture leaches fertility from land in the long term. The fantasy of the dark lord who is to blame for all harm and hurt and evil may provide immediate comfort; the vision of conquest may uncannily appear to match current realities, and offer the alluring hope that evil will be swept away for good. But the difficulty with fairy tales is always how to distinguish the false promise from the true hope. Bin Laden is not a mythic, powerful dark lord of legend; he is a ruthless political adversary who has revealed a terrible wish to harm. Still, the two phenomena remain different. The dangers of historical amnesia on the one hand, of psychological simple-mindedness on the other, will deepen and grow from the central misconceptions of dualism and the original combat myth.

2002

Donkey Business, Donkey Work:
In the House of Crossed Desires

Lecture given at the University of Wales, Swansea

When the Spanish arrived on the west coast of the New World, they called it California; this wasn't the name of one of their number or of an explorer like Amerigo Vespucci; nor was it derived, though it sounds as if it might be, from the language of the indigenous peoples they found there. The word comes from a book, or, more specifically, from a fervid Spanish romance, the kind that Cervantes parodied so playfully and so warmly when he inaugurated the modern novel. *The Labours of the Very Brave Knight Esplandián*, by a certain García Rodriguez de Montalvo, was published in 1525; among the hero's worthy opponents, it featured an Amazon queen who ruled a golden land in the west; she was dusky with golden arms and legs, and attended by a band of female warriors, all her equal in beauty, courage and wealth – except that her equal could not exist on earth. Deeds perilous, ordeals wondrous, feats prodigious followed, pell-mell.

It's her country that's called Califia, and so is she, rather like the Queen of Sheba; and as its Queen and its embodiment, she's conquered, seduced (chastely – in love, not lust) and converted (to Christianity – this romance of empire arises in the country of the Catholic kings): and so gives her name to the future cradle of later varieties of Amazons, captives, vamps and victims. Who would have played her in *Queen Califia – The Movie*? Ava Gardner? Esther Williams? Who could have composed *Califia*, the opera?

This move from a forgotten romance into continuing history shows how experience takes colour from prior imaginings; it's a small instance of the way images and beliefs press out the wax of perception. Metaphors don't decorate the languages in which communication happens, but are the very stuff of it. The Spanish conquistadores and the monks who travelled alongside them simply could not see their new territory except through the scrim of their dreams, shaped by the same romances that had earlier led Columbus to look for similar wonders – for Amazons and cannibals and lambs that grew on stalks like fruit and rivers of liquid gold.

When the composer John Woolrich approached me to ask me to write him a libretto this was one of the ideas I proposed among many others. He specifically wanted a fairy tale, in the tradition of Bartók, Janáček, Stravinsky, and Debussy and many others of the late nineteenth and twentieth centuries who turned to folk materials and traditional romance or legend for their narratives. I had to write fast – the first librettist hadn't produced anything, and the deadline was looming – or he might lose the commission from Music Theatre Wales and the Cheltenham Festival. Though the libretto doesn't occupy the foreground, and the librettist is secondary, the words and the plot provide the necessary armature without which the building would fall down – the invisible girdings.

The debate about the relevance of opera today, especially fairy tale opera, has recently been revived: in the same way as critics call for the Great Novel of Britain in Decline, so musicians and music critics have exhorted composers – or perhaps, strictly speaking, librettists – to confront contemporary issues. *Nixon in China*, not *Orlando*; *The Plumber's Gift*, not *The Mask of Orpheus*. *The Doctor of Myddfai*, with a libretto by David Pountney for Peter Maxwell Davies, attempted to bridge the distinction and do both magic and realism.

John Woolrich sees the tradition of opera performance as conjoined with the carnival art of *serio ludere* (playing seriously) with puppet plays and street games, with conjuring and tumbling, stretching back to travelling players and the *commedia dell'arte* troupes, who were visiting England from Italy in the sixteenth and seventeenth centuries. Their art didn't feed foolish and dangerous fantasies, like the romances Cervantes mocked. Their comic repertoire of antic and magic dramatised man-eating ogres, seven-league boots, caps of invisibility and talking animals in the same breath as it boldly attacked prevailing marriage arrangements, overweening aristocrats and scheming lawyers. The first *Mother Goose Tale*, performed by travelling players in Paris at the end of the seventeenth century, features an ogre who uses a magnet to draw people to him – modern technology instantly entering the fairy tale. John Woolrich also stipulated he wanted the theatrical frame to show: the opera should revel in its own artifice and manoeuvres, making a virtue of the necessarily restricted budget, so that role-doubling and costume changes and cross-casting against natural gender became part of the spectacle. Woolrich scored it for trombone, clarinet (the clarinettist also plays the saxophone), double bass, a huge and varied batterie of percussion, from saucepans to gongs, and keyboards – a very raucous, wild, jazzy palette of sound; and he wrote all the parts for female voices, regardless of the character in the story, because he likes their resonance together.

In the House of Crossed Desires takes stock characters from the *commedia* tradition, like the wicked old miser Pantaloon, who becomes the wizard Cosmo and keeps his ward Corallina prisoner, disguised as a boy. Corallina is a Columbine romantic heroine, and follows many predecessors as a breeches role. The sly fixer Sloper is inspired by one of the Zanni figures, the supporting jesters and japesters, who have given the word 'zany' to English. He's a typical unreliable servant – who works for his master but also betrays him. Mozart was drawing on this stock when he fleshed out Leporello, Don Giovanni's servant. Greasy Joan, the sottish bawd, is a variation on the Ruffiana of the *commedia* and I gave her a name from Shakespeare's wonderful winter song from *Love's Labour's Lost*, 'When icicles hang by the wall . . .' With six characters, sung and played by only four performers, I tried to create a fairy-tale opera about crossed purposes, crossed destinies, and crossed love.

The working title of the opera was 'Then Suddenly', after a little girl asked me to tell her a story: 'Tell me one of those stories,' she said, 'where it says, "Then suddenly" lots of times.'

I set these characters within a fairy-tale plot that's a freely shaken mixture of several famous stories: aficionados will notice bits of 'Donkeyskin' and 'Tattercoats', of 'Rumpelstiltskin' and 'The Sandman', of the Grimms' 'Mother Holle', Angela Carter's *The Magic Toyshop*, and, above all, of *The Golden Ass*. The other day, long after I had finished writing the opera, I was given a lovely old copy of la comtesse de Ségur's fairy tales, and found there the terrifying morbid tale of Blondine, who is tempted and misled by an enchanted Rose and her wicked accomplice, a wizard who has been turned into a parrot: the story ends miserably when Blondine helps them both to return to human form and they abandon her alone 'in the dense forest'. Ségur was very keen on punishing her heroines with great misfortunes, as in her popular collection, *Les Malheurs de Sophie*. At the end of *In the House of Crossed Desires*, I make Cosmo fall for that old oracular or fairy-tale trap: he fails to compose the terms of his wishes carefully enough and so he does have them granted, but not in the way that he foresaw: he finds himself condemned to spend his life as Corallina's pet parrot. I thought I was making up this particular metamorphosis for the end of my opera, but perhaps not . . . I did read La comtesse de Ségur as a child, and Blondine's persecutor may have lingered in the depths of my imagination over forty years.

The author, Lucius Apuleius, was born around AD 124 in that part of North Africa which is now Algeria; he was therefore a North African of Greek culture, but he wrote in Latin; his hero Lucius' misadventures as an ass have been passed on, with divergences and accretions, in Latin manuscripts. His romance features a hero who is turned into a donkey when he rubs on the wrong ointment and has to suffer terrible ordeals before he's restored to human shape. *The Golden Ass* contains lots of interleaved stories, as well as much comic business and metaphysical speculation besides. Apuleius' romance draws its inspiration from the Greek comic genius Lucian of Samosata. The relationship between his bawdy tale and Apuleius' much longer and more elaborated romance *The Golden Ass* is complicated, and classicists are still struggling to clarify it.[1] The interest here lies, however, in the contents of *The Ass*, which closely resembles Apuleius' book; both books are of consequence in the formation of fairy tale.[2]

In Lucian's *The Ass*, Lucius the hero goes to stay in Thessaly, a province famous for the magic powers of its women, and asks the maidservants in the household to let him peep at his hostess while she casts her spells. As he watches, she smears an ointment over her body and turns into a bird, sprouting feathers and flying away. Lucius begs the maid to steal the same ointment for him, but she picks out the wrong box, and when he anoints himself, he turns into an ass. He then has to undergo terrible ordeals, until at last he is fed the roses which are the only food – a flower sacred to Venus – that can restore him to human shape.

The tone of *The Ass* is jesting, joyously lewd, and cynically unremitting in its satire of human savagery and self-interest. After heroic sexual adventures with the maid, the hero enjoys even more strenuous entertainment with a woman who loves him precisely because he is an ass for obvious, pornographic reasons, and discards him when he is turned back into a mere man. Terrible tortures are plotted by the robbers; nobody behaves well; nothing is for the best in the worst of all possible worlds. Apuleius' later, longer, richer, more baroque and deeper elaboration of this story retains some of the off-colour humour and the lubriciousness, but takes the material in a novel, metaphysical direction. Lucius in *The Golden Ass* is also turned into a donkey by a witch by mistake, caught and put to work as a pack-animal, and then witnesses all the events of the novel in that dumb, long-suffering shape, including the storytelling scene in which 'Cupid and Psyche' is related, but he is redeemed and emerges from his brute experience much chastened and wiser.

Interestingly, Apuleius in real life was charged with sorcery when he married a rich widow: his new in-laws claimed he must have bewitched her. He chose to defend himself in court in Alexandria and made a long and passionate plea which resulted in his acquittal; this eloquent speech, about knowledge, wisdom and their proper uses, was published and it frames some powerful and lasting arguments about the complex relationship between magic and philosophical curiosity. It almost seems as if his book is autobiographical, that the erotic metamorphoses and ordeals he suffers, traduced as a lustful donkey, were experiences from his own life. In his old age, Apuleius became a priest of Isis, in the same way as his protagonist does at the end of *The Golden Ass*, in which the goddess descends and offers him spiritual salvation – in my opera, she takes the form of Hope, the great goddess who stirs desires and dreams and makes life bearable:

> I am Hope, the goddess who peers
> Into the distance for glimmers of light;
> I'm that damp wood that catches at last with a spark,
> The mother's face watching over her child in the dark;
> Dimly I mirror the raddled old beauty;
> Gently I wrap loss in the tissue of dreams,
> Breathe on numb hearts to quicken their springs.
> Corallina, you've suffered enough.
> What do you want?

There isn't really a word for the narrative form the Greeks invented, to which Apuleius' wild and wonderful book belongs, but it belongs to romance, and has come down in both poetry and prose texts, such as Heliodorus' 'Aethiopica' and Longus' 'Daphnis and Chloe'. The most widely read is 'Cupid and Psyche' which inspired, for example, Giulio Romano's frescos in the Palazzo del Te in Mantua. The tale profoundly shaped the 'Beauty and the Beast' and 'Cinderella' groups of stories: Giulio shows the moment when Psyche is ordered to sift beans and peas by the wicked stepmother figure, who in this story is the goddess Venus herself, enraged that her son should have squandered himself on a mere mortal.

As you remember, Cinderella, in some versions of the story, is ordered to fulfil the same task before she can go to the ball: in Apuleius, a troop of ants come to Psyche's rescue and sort them for her; in the Grimm Brothers, followed by Disney in his cartoon, it's birds who do it on the disconsolate heroine's behalf. I gave this motif to my heroine, Corallina, when she is thrown into the dungeon by the wizard.

The motifs and devices of the Hellenistic and medieval romance – what has been called by Peter Dronke, in a helpful phrase, 'the initiatory romance' – include foundlings, parted lovers, sea voyages, kidnappings, enslavement, mistaken identity, poisonings, masquerade, spells and counterspells, magic and metamorphosis. All these have become much more familiar as the very stuff of fiction through storytellers who came long after, from Spenser and Cervantes and Shakespeare to Charlotte and Emily Brontë and, in our time, Italo Calvino, Jan Swankmajer and Angela Carter. The romance is no respecter of boundaries: it can take the form of a novel, an epic poem, a puppet film, an opera.

The title *The Golden Ass* has presented a mystery for years: it used to be suggested that it was the tales within the book that were 'golden', as the ass himself remains stubbornly grey and furry throughout. But another interpretation has been put forward, that *Asinus auratus* is a scribal error for *Asinus auritus* – 'The Ass with Long Ears';[3] this makes sharp sense as a title, for an ass's ears are the beast's defining attribute, and Lucius suffers torments throughout because he overhears everything with his unchanged and alert human faculties, but cannot speak or intervene – this muteness is the chief sign of his beast metamorphosis in my libretto. It may seem perverse, when given only four singers, to strike one of them dumb in the first act, but I then distributed the thoughts in the donkey's head to the other singers, singing in chorus the jumble of words in Luca's head.

In the House of Crossed Desires takes off from Apuleius, but I took lots of liberties – in a spirit that's true, I hope, to the tragicomic quest of his romance. But critics used to Romantic opera still find this flouting of the rules of verisimilitude hard to accept: though its playfulness has been part of the theatre for far longer than nineteenth-century naturalism.

The stand-off between fable, fairy tale, fabrication and verismo in opera goes back a very long way, to the struggles of a writer for whom John Woolrich has a high regard, and who is little known or discussed today: Carlo Gozzi, a Venetian nobleman down on his luck, who wrote *The Love for Three Oranges* in 1761. Gozzi created the piece in specific defiance of the most successful playwrights of his time and city: Carlo Goldoni who pioneered bourgeois realism on stage – and who, as I was taught at school, is one of Italian literature's great masters, and his rival but also colleague and crony, the Abbé Pietro Chiari, who peddled sentimental melodrama. Both these representational types of stage fiction, which claimed to portray contemporary life and emotional situations in a language that imitated the demotic, dismissed the ancient masked tradition of the *commedia*: as the music historian Richard Taruskin comments, 'What united them was contempt for the antiquated freakshow known as *commedia dell'arte*, which together they had almost succeeded in killing off. To Gozzi, staunch upholder of the older tradition, Goldoni and Chiari were but the two faces of a single worthless coin: 'commonplace and transparent inanities on the one hand, inanities sonorous and oracular upon the other'.

When Gozzi was nearly eighty, he wrote a blithe and boastful account of his life to which he gave the modernist title *Useless Memoirs*; there, he evokes the lively flavour of eighteenth-century Venice, where he and his partisans met regularly in a bookshop, to publish squibs and satires and broadsheets and mount a sustained, gleeful assault on their antagonists.

'This literary war', as Gozzi called it, 'raged between 1757 and 1761 . . . I opened fire [he wrote] with a dithyrambic poem . . . comparing their gay farces [of the *commedia*] favourably with the dull and heavy pieces of the reformers. Chiari and Goldoni replied to my attacks and those of my associates by challenging us to produce a comedy. Goldoni, in particular, called me a verbose wordmonger.' He defied Gozzi to fill a theatre, boasting that he at least drew a huge public, even if Gozzi did think his work inane: Gozzi countered with a challenge, that he could do better by dramatising the most improbable and fantastic old wives' fairy tale in the *commedia* style – and drive Goldoni and Chiari out of business.

Gozzi's critics 'attempted to hoot it down by clumsy abuse', but he succeeded with the public: *The Love for Three Oranges* was a triumph at the Carnival of 1761 in Venice. Gozzi continued his polemic: 'I publicly maintained,' he wrote, 'that art in the construction of a piece, well managed conduct of its action, propriety of rhetoric and harmony of diction, were sufficient to invest a puerile fantastic motive, if taken seriously, with the illusion of reality . . .' In order to defend this argument, he went on to write nine more *fiabe* – also drawn, like the *Love for Three Oranges*, from the seventeenth-century Neapolitan anthology by G. B. Basile, called *Il Pentamerone*, or 'The Tale of Tales', including the libretto of *Turandot* . . . and he even influenced *The Magic Flute*, in which Tamino and Papageno echo a recurring pair of travelling jesters in Gozzi's fables. The series of 'poetic extravaganzas' enjoyed such success with the theatre-going public that Goldoni finally withdrew in defeat, leaving for Paris in a pique.[4]

Jocular as his tone is, Gozzi makes some crucial points about stage fantasy, about the artifice of masks and magic, about the spectacle of the absurd and the excessive: he mentions the allegories discovered within his texts by the public, the critique of despotism, the satire of folly beneath the enchantments and entertainments. This is the underlying dynamic of fairy tales spoken and written, the veiled but barbed depiction of true circumstances.

A contemporary composer like Harrison Birtwistle similarly draws on myth and romance for his operas: *The Mask of Orpheus*, *Sir Gawain and the Green Knight*, and most recently, at Glyndebourne, *The Second Mrs Kong*, with a libretto by the writer Russell Hoban about the tragic love of King Kong for Vermeer's painting of *The Girl with the Pearl*. It takes place in eerie in-between worlds, for Kong and Pearl are both lost in a kind of virtual reality, the space of the imaginary, not being quite real people but only fabrications, images, and at the same time possessing universal identity and recognisability. When they first descend into the underworld, they find themselves rejected: images cannot die, phantoms cannot go to hell or heaven. The first act included an enthralling scene in which Anubis, the jackal-headed god of the underworld and conductor of souls, ferries the dead across the river to the underworld. Kong and Pearl are seeking to metamorphose into full human beings, through love, through contact – but they cannot reach each other. When Kong puts out his hand to touch Pearl, she is a prisoner of her frame, or the glass, pure image.

Russell Hoban's libretto roamed fantastic and impossible imaginary settings to probe deeply into the meaning of love and death – this is what the fairy-tale form can do, because it's liberated from representation, flies free from the requirements of naturalism.

In the House of Crossed Desires didn't enjoy the budget of a Glyndebourne production, but Richard Aylwyn did an inspired job, creating an alchemist's cell, a mirrored, sparkling, dazzling jewel box, with screens overprinted with engravings, that changed it from the barber's shop to the bedroom to the dungeon. The metamorphoses are also remarkably persuasive: when Corallina is dressed up behind closed doors by the wizard as an ideal feminine love object, a pretty little doll in ribbons and lace, the change Adey Grummit achieves with the help of lighting and costume – and atmospheric music (and words, I hope) – creates a truly sinister, erotic frisson. Then Cosmo shows her her reflection in the glass and announces the main theme of the opera: the conflict between outer appearance and interior truth.

Cosmo sings, 'Mirrors do not speak in code, they capture the image of your soul.'

He then turns himself into a bird and flies away – with the help of a shadow puppet.

But Cosmo's philosophy, his doctrine of images and their reality, will turn out not to be true – outsides are deceiving, as all fairy tales tell us. True recognition must focus on the inside. In their interest in this theme, which catches at a contemporary anxiety, I believe, *The Second Mrs Kong* and *Crossed Desires* have a great deal in common. Though it's not spelled out in the opera, of course, the figure of Corallina, coerced by the guardian who loves her into what he considers desirable girlhood or womanhood as if it were a picture which can be forged, connects to the spiralling problems of anorexia and bulimia and other disorders related to identity-as-display, as spectacle.

Cosmo's false magic then turns Luca, the hero who is trying to rescue Corallina (not for entirely altruistic motives), into an ass, the image of human folly and specifically male lust, as in Apuleius' metaphysical romance. This is the opera's most dramatic metamorphosis: I wrote 'Luca turns into a donkey'. John Woolrich encouraged me to leave it at that, and see what the production could manage.

The donkey is a key actor in the comedy of wisdom and folly: the creature is one of the most popular heroes – or sometimes heroines – of fable and fairy tale. The juxtaposition of the conjuring sorceress with the man sprouting a donkey's head condenses vividly the underlying assumption that makes witches and donkeys natural allies (bedfellows): forbidden knowledge, specifically of an erotic character. The donkey belongs firmly in the bestiary of medieval witchcraft. In that most famous of fairy plays, Shakespeare's *A Midsummer Night's Dream*, Bottom the Weaver, changed into an ass, finds himself rapturously wooed by Titania, the Queen of the Fairies, who has herself been cast under a spell by her husband after a domestic quarrel. All is topsy-turvy when Oberon, with Puck his messenger, makes mischief. All is merry, too, and will be set to rights.

Shakespeare knew *The Golden Ass* well: 'Bless thee, Bottom, bless thee! Thou art translated!' says Quince when he sees sweet bully Bottom the Weaver with his ass head on. Even though the animals most closely associated with merriment and folly are donkeys they retain an association with sorcery, and occult powers, because foolish as they're perceived to be, donkeys are also the beasts most endowed with powers of divination and prophecy in fairy and folklore. Indeed they rival geese in making fools of themselves and thus showing up the folly of others.

In the same way as the genre exalts the little man (and woman) and shows up the mighty, defeats the giants and crowns the thumblings, so the stupidest of the beasts turns out to be the wisest according to the logic of the stories. This logic organises the material of fairy tales internally, but its imagery, the costumes it assumes, are borrowed from elsewhere; and, as is the case so often, the topsy-turvy exemplar of the wise donkey can be found in the Old Testament as well as the New and thence has passed on into secular folklore in tales like that of Balaam and his she-ass, who could see the angel in his path when he could not, or of Antony of Padua. This saint's legend relates how scoffers about the real presence of Jesus in the host were taught a lesson by the saint when he presented a hungry donkey with a consecrated host and the beast knelt before it instead of wolfing it down.

The miraculous donkey who speaks the truth when her master fails to see it represents the possibility that lowly creatures may prove wiser than their learned masters, that the meek shall inherit the earth – a fundamental Christian maxim that remains to be proved. So on the one hand the beast of burden acts as a totem of the most sublime of Christian virtues, humility, and is specially precious to God in consequence,[5] but on the other hand, the creature remained a rude and comic figure, associated with priapism, stubbornness, laughter and folly – the devil's turf – this is how Cosmo sees Luca and he punishes him for presuming to lay hands on Corallina or on his magic books and arts.

Donkeys were the jester's symbolic beast. The fool can speak out when the wise man stays mute, as King Lear shows: his Fool speaks in riddles, which encode a truth the King accepts as such when he will not resign himself to any honest declaration, of love or, later, hatred from his daughters or from anyone else. Mockery, play-acting, riddling, spring uncomfortable messages from the privy mind into the public domain with a freedom denied to those who speak or write in earnest.

The fool's cap marks fools out as different from the rest, belittles and segregates and demeans them. But, at the same time it resembles the magic cap of invisibility from a fairy tale, because it frees the jester's tongue as if he were not there to be accused, or caught, or punished.

The fool fools because he makes no difference; it is not perhaps poetry that makes nothing happen, but jokes. Yet neither formula is quite right somehow: both shake out the mind, air it from a new window, lighten it, like laundry in the breeze. The revolutionary Russian philosopher Alexander Herzen commented, 'In church, in the palace, on parade, facing the department head, the police officer, the German administrator, nobody laughs. The serfs are deprived of the right to smile in the presence of the landowners.' ('Wipe that smile off your face', says the bullying teacher.) Herzen concludes, 'Only equals may laugh.'[6] So the laughter of the clown, the mockery of the fool, can be the expression of freedom, the gesture that abolishes hierarchy, that cancels authority and faces down fear. Its release can lie in the way it abolishes hierarchy and authority. Riddle books in the eighteenth century, produced for children's amusement, and filled with concealed meanings, knew this function of laughter.

The braying of the beast can also express anguish at its condition rather than brute ignorance – Luca is a figure of us all, as what we most fear might be our lives, when he is put into the treadmill and robbed of his tongue. The anonymous lady who replied in high indignation to Richard de Fournival's misogynist commentary on love, *Li Bestiaire d'amours*, wrote that he had provoked her so that she felt like the wild ass who only cries out when hunger makes him rage: 'O, by my faith, I should cry out indeed!'[7] The ass could perform this empathetic role for a woman because it was the least of the beasts.

In the House of Crossed Desires features a number of disturbing magical transformations wrought by spells and songs. But there are also serious undernotes to the playful reasons for choosing wonders and improbabilities, for refusing the replication of ordinary laws and the naturalistic representation of modern life. Metamorphoses of this sort are sure indications we've entered the territory of the wonder tale; and the principal aim of magic is transformation. If the formula Abracadabra! failed to bring about a change, to change lead into gold, or at least pull a rabbit from a hat, it would be worthless. The recent show of that title at the Wellcome Institute surveyed the interwovenness of magic and medicine, of supernatural quests and scientific inquiry; implied by the connection is the capacity to bring about a transformation: in the sphere of medicine, a cure, in the sphere of magic, reprieve, requitement, revenge (and cure, of course, as well). Spells consist of formulae that bend reality to their shape; they're commonly verbal, though they may be meaningless; and they're often musical. Art, especially music, often aspires to the condition of a spell.

Fairy tales can smuggle a disturbing theme across the borders of consciousness without pushing the receivers' faces in it. They've been told to children and youths for centuries for this reason: they're stories about family strife and sexual danger, about intellectual curiosity and impatience with social hierarchy, but they remain in disguise, in the land of far away and long ago and once upon a time. The disguise means that certain themes can be tackled, which stripped might be censored out: that donkey business in *A Midsummer Night's Dream* covers a multitude of sins without ducking the issue of sex.

But censorship, as everyone knows, has frequently struck the fairy tale just the same. 'Rapunzel', in the earliest version the Grimm Brothers wrote down, describes how the heroine pulls up the prince by her hair into her tower and enjoys his company for a while until one day, she asks the Old Witch, 'How is it that my clothes are getting so tight?' So the old woman realises that her ward has been up to no good, and cuts her hair and smashes the tower and blinds the prince and performs other such openly coded acts. But the Grimms became uneasy about the explicit character of Rapunzel's plight, and they changed her question to 'Why are you, Old Mother, so much heavier than the prince I pull up by my hair when you're not looking?' – thus making a complete ninny of Rapunzel and a nonsense of the fairy tale, draining it of its traditional warning against the appeal of passing wolves.

Fairy tales are open to transformation, and the Grimms were working in the fine storytelling mode of adapting material to suit their chosen hearers and readers: in their case ideals of middle-class urban family decorum prevailed. It's anti-historical to argue that authentic, original versions should be retained. The trick is rather to retell them in fresh ways in order to ignite the special pleasure of unconscious recognition for the audience in question – as Carol Ann Duffy triumphantly achieves with her verse version *Grimm's Tales*, staged last year at The Young Vic to the delighted thrills and squeals and laughter of school parties. *In the House of Crossed Desires* attempts to transform some of the recurring motifs of fairy tale: the vicious old woman gaoler, with her threats and her whip, takes centre stage in the part of Greasy Joan, but she is translated, too, if the desired alchemy of music, performance and words works, to become a person with her own past of lost loves, loneliness, and desperate choices. It would have been possible to write the part of this 'disreputable hag' as one of the many beaten-up homeless women who sit on the pavements of Kentish Town and the Strand in London, but the strength of the conventions, rooted in both opera and fairy tale, means that she could be established as a person with tremendous economy of means: as Helena says in *A Midsummer Night's Dream*, 'Things base and vile, holding no quantity/ Love can transpose to form and dignity.' If you start with what everyone knows, you can quickly introduce alternative readings and develop them, and then, if the atmosphere of enchantment holds, you can also sidestep the dangers of overt preachiness and moralising which so undermine all attempts to rethink dreams and desires.

Philip Larkin's gift for the acerbic epigram has memorably stigmatised 'dipping into the myth kitty'; but its contents aren't so easily put in a box and shut up and the key thrown away, as his metaphor suggests; they're parts of thought, invisible, stealthy, potent. They form a language of the imagination and, especially in a medium like opera, they make new moves possible. A composer recasts existing notes and transforms time signatures and plays with given rhythms, so a librettist can attempt to translate the old spells and figures that have proved powerfully effective in the past: the star-crossed lovers, the cross-dressed heroine, the very cross patriarch, and the crossings of destinies in any life.

1996

'Large as Life, and Twice as Natural': The Child's Play of Lewis Carroll

> Twas brillig and the slithy toves
>   Did gyre and gimble in the wabe;
> All mimsy were the borogoves,
>   And the mome raths outgrabe.

The first verse of 'Jabberwocky', the most famous nonsense poem in English and perhaps in the world, appears in mirror image back to front in *Through the Looking-Glass* when Alice finds the poem in a book that's lying on a table, near the dithering White King. He's been writing in a notebook, bewailing his inability to control his pencil, and says, 'It writes all manner of things that I don't intend.'

So there is a hint that he is the author of 'Jabberwocky', or at least that the *Looking-Glass* book in which the piece appears, shares the character of this kingdom of his, where people's intentions do not deliver the expected results, where you have to run backwards in order to proceed forwards, and everything is contrariwise. Nonsense results quite sensibly from such reversals of normality: 'Jabberwocky' itself sounds like another word for nonsense talk, a kind of combination of gobbledegook and gibberish and blabber, as in 'blabbermouth' – the nursery version of the language of Babel.

The opening quatrain of 'Jabberwocky' first appeared in *Mischmasch*, a collection of comic verses, sketches, stories, parodies, cuttings and drawings that Charles Lutwidge Dodgson compiled for his family from 1848 onwards. He had five younger sisters and two younger brothers, and he called the first of these scrapbooks *The Rectory Umbrella* after a favourite tree in the garden of their home, the Croft. As Lewis Carroll, he would return often to *Mischmasch* and rework some of its material.

The frontispiece shows a bearded old man, beaming as fairies fly under the shelter of his umbrella.[1] They are bringing cradle blessings, labelled 'Good Humour', 'Knowledge', 'Mirth', and 'Cheerfulness' – among other boons. Above them, comical grimacing goblins are hurling rocks – these are 'Woe', 'Spite', Gloom', 'Crossness', 'Ennui' and 'Alloverishness' (presumably from the woeful cry, 'It's all over'). Most tellingly of all, the umbrella that is shielding the good sprites has written between its spokes, 'Jokes', 'Riddles', 'Poetry', 'Tales', and in the centre, 'Fun'. Even as a schoolboy, Lewis Carroll interposed his inventive brand of fun between himself and unhappiness; he saw humour as somewhere above all to shelter; it was fun, but it also had a purpose, and that purpose was intertwined with children and a child's way of being.

The first verse of 'Jabberwocky' appears under the title 'Stanza of Anglo-Saxon poetry'. It is written out in runish characters, not backward writing, and it contains glosses on the meanings of the words that Humpty Dumpty picks up arrogantly later. There's no point rehearsing these meanings, really, as the exegesis is offered to poke fun at pedantry and philology and to make clear language's powers to stir feelings beyond semantics and logic, through sound, glimmerings of associations, rhyme and rhythm. Carroll, as ever, comments in 'Jabberwocky' and through Humpty Dumpty on the arbitrary relation between word and meaning, between signifier and signified, and hence the independent vitality of the sign, regardless.

'Jabberwocky' encapsulates many of Carroll's most characteristic manners, as well as summing up the dominant identifying features of nonsense poetry as a genre of English literature.

The poem is of course very funny: though, like Alice at the end, we don't know quite why. ' "It seems quite pretty," she said, ". . . but it's *rather* hard to understand!" (You see she didn't like to confess, even to herself, that she couldn't make it out at all.) 'Somehow it seems to fill my head with ideas – only I don't know what they are! However, somebody killed something: that's clear, at any rate." ' Though nonsense can express the delirium of the mad, as in Poor Tom's snatches in *King Lear*, Carroll was adopting the nursery variety of nonsense that fools in a lighter vein with violence and aggression: the English language is particularly rich in this kind of verse, such as 'Three Blind Mice', 'Hush-a-bye Baby', and 'Humpty Dumpty' itself; and the wonderful riddling song, 'There was a man of double deed' which closes, 'When my heart began to bleed,/ 'Twas death and death and death indeed.'

Children are constantly generating new examples of this comic macabre spirit, in games and skipping rhymes, often with topical allusions and certainly topical concerns. Peter and Iona Opie pioneered the collection of this verse in their great works compiled from patient eavesdropping in playgrounds, *The Singing Game: Lore and Language in Children's Games*. I was recently told some rhymes that are current today in London, by the eight-year-old daughter of some friends:

> Milkman, milkman, do your duty
> Here comes Mrs Macaroony
> She can do the pam pam
> She can do the splits
> But most of all she'll kiss kiss kiss.

The child goes down each time, stretching her legs either side until she is almost doing the sideways splits:
And another:

> Hello Hello sir, meet me at the baker.
> No sir Why sir? Cos I've got a cold, sir.
> Where did you get your cold, sir?
> In the North Pole, sir.
> What were you doing there, sir?
> Shooting polars bears, sir.
> Let me hear you sneeze, sir.
> Achoo achoo, achoo, sir.

And another, a clapping game:

> I know a little Dutch girl
> Called I shoe Shemima
> And all the boys in the football team
> Go I shoe Shemima.
> How is your mother? All Right
> Died in the fish shop last night.
> What did she die of?
> Died of raw fish.
> How did she die?
> Like this.

The child imitates, falling towards the ground; another player catches her.

And another:

> Oh my Gosh
> What colour's my mum's underwear?
> Is it black? Is it white?
> Oh my gosh it's dynamite!

This child's world of babble and rhyme relates to language as it is learned; linguisticians are increasingly affirming the importance of babies and children of hearing such patter. But they're hardly the first to notice this. Mallarmé was fascinated by English nursery rhymes and songs.

Lewis Carroll's 'Jabberwocky' also belongs in the tradition of nonsense and its ancient functions in English culture when it counterposes a form of domestic magic to profound fears: it stages a terrible monster in the Anglo-Saxon tradition of Grendel from *Beowulf* and then cancels its terrors through hyperbole, parody, excess, mockery. But the attempt of comedy to unseat fear is never wholly dependable, and Carroll himself moved Tenniel's alarming illustration from the frontispiece of *Looking Glass* to the inside of the book because he felt it was too frightening and might put off his young readers.

The Jabberwock threatens to devour its prey:

'Beware the Jabberwock,, my son!
The jaws that bite, the claws that catch . . .'

This cannibalistic menace of the monster dominates fairy tales and modern fantasies – the man-eating ogres of legend haunt contemporary figures like Hannibal Lecter, from *The Silence of the Lambs*, for example. Carroll was preoccupied with such monsters: a letter he wrote from school was illustrated with one of his cartoons – showing a monster in a cave devouring a man head first while his friends, in Tudor knightly costume, attempt to pull him out. But another, deeper and more common anxiety underlies the fear of such bogeymen: the anxiety about human carnivorousness, about the necessity to eat or die. Lewis Carroll was alert to the possibilities of animated food, both as nightmare and as farce, and the *Alice* books are stuffed with food, with its pleasures and its problems.

'What are little girls made of?' asks the kind of nursery rhyme Carroll liked to echo. 'Sugar and spice and all that's nice. That's what little girls are made of.' In this piece of proverbial wisdom, little boys, by contrast, are made of frogs and snails and puppy-dogs' tails. (The Opies comment that the rhyme has been attributed to the Poet Laureate Robert Southey, but that they cannot find it in his works.[2]) Lewis Carroll liked giving his little girlfriends tea, but unlike the Mad Hatter, he always provided jam, as he carefully explained to one mother as he issued the invitation. He himself ate very little: one meal a day, only. He was ram-rod straight to the end of his life, thin as a rail, and thought little of taking twenty-five-mile walks. But he understood the pleasures of sitting down together to eat – and indeed, in Oxford, when he volunteered his services as Curator of Christ Church's common room, he took charge of the college's catering and introduced the custom of afternoon tea there for the first time.

For a man who was so austere in his tastes, food held his interest and dominates the imagery of his jokes from his juvenilia onwards. Indeed he sounded a nostalgic note for such childhood pleasures as early as 1854, when he was already recalling lost times of 'pinafores, treacle and innocence'.[3] This closeness to children's primal appetites he retained all his life: puddings and pies, tarts, cakes, and treacle wells recur alongside more elaborate fare, oysters and lobsters and mock turtle soup.

'"I know *something* interesting is sure to happen," Alice said to herself, "whenever I eat or drink anything; so I'll just see what this little bottle does." '[4] (Not a scene that would be allowed in today's children's writing.) Carroll is at his most effervescently inventive when his fantasies are trained on eating and drinking: in one early story, the villain – an early Boojum – gets reduced to 'mashed potatoe' (sic).[5] Alice finds an – empty – pot of marmalade down the rabbit-hole, and in a letter to Mary MacDonald Carroll recommended a remedy for her kitten's toothache: 'wash it carefully in hasty-pudding, and give it 4 pin-cushions boiled[6] in sealing-wax, and just dip the end of its tail in hot coffee'. 'The proprieties of food offered the absurdist in Carroll another system to juggle with, and with the Mock Turtle's instructions to the Lobster Quadrille, he grasped 'the innate hilarity of animated food', of gourmandising and surfeit which enlivens many an earlier nonsense poem.[7] Again, he makes inspired mischief with expected categories of right things to eat and wrong things to eat, until one can almost hear children's protesting laughter bubbling up from the page. Among his other inventions, the White Knight passes on a recipe for pudding:

> 'It began with blotting-paper.'
> 'That wouldn't be very nice, I'm afraid—'
> 'Not very nice alone,' he interrupted, quite eagerly: 'but you've no idea what a difference it makes, mixing it with other things – such as gunpowder and sealing-wax.'[8]

At other times, Carroll displays his humour in its most dangerous and even perverse mood, as in the 'Pig & Pepper' episode, which he added to the original manuscript of Wonderland. He stages a ferocious culinary assault on a baby: the Nurse seems to be dressing it for the Duchess to dine on, and it then turns into a piglet in Alice's arms: 'And she began thinking over other children she knew, who might do very well as pigs . . .' (Harry Graham may be echoing the scene with one of his Ruthless Rhymes for Heartless Homes:

> Nurse, [who] peppered baby's face
>   (She mistook it for a muffin) . . .
> Mother, seeing baby blinded,
> Said, 'Oh, nurse, how absent-minded.')

Then, in Looking-Glass, the fantasies about who gets eaten take a turn into gallows humour:

'Now if you're ready, Oysters dear,
  We can begin to feed.'

'But not on us!' the Oysters cried,
  Turning a little blue.

'After such kindness, that would be
  A dismal thing to do!'

But the Oysters are 'eaten every one', as the Walrus and the Carpenter weep crocodile tears.

Towards the end of his life, in 1889, Carroll wrote from Hatfield House to the child actress Isa Bowman, one of the last and closest of his 'child-friends'. He told her that he had recently met Princess Alice, the daughter of Queen Victoria's son, Prince Leopold, who was probably named after Alice Liddell and Carroll's heroine. Carroll jokes to Isa: 'Now that I have made friends with a real live little Princess, I don't intend ever to *speak* to any more children that haven't titles. In fact I'm so proud and I hold my chin so high [doodled portrait of himself thus supplied] that I shouldn't even *see* you if we met!' But then he rushes on without a break to reassure her: 'No darling, you mustn't believe *that*. If I made friends with a *dozen* Princesses I would love you better than all of them together, even [if] I had them all rolled up into a sort of child-roly-poly.'[9] So the teatime treats return to convey just how sweet and spicy is the stuff little girls are made of. If kissing can be 'aim-inhibited eating', as Adam Phillips has suggested in his essay, 'Plotting for Kisses',[10] then Carroll's fascination with tea parties and jam tarts, and his recurrent fantasies about the jaws that bite, about babies who turn into pigs and get their faces peppered, with old men devouring little oysters, become moves in his unconscious – and in his plot.

There are scarcely any married people of any consequence in the *Alice* books, with the exception of the three royal couples – the King and Queen of Hearts in *Alice's Adventures in Wonderland* and the Red and White Kings and Queens in *Through the Looking-Glass* – and in every case, the women eclipse their vacillating spouses. The triple plot of the *Sylvie and Bruno* stories does include a romance, but it is awkwardly handled. The best of Carroll's writings do not even set up enduring friendships. Alice continues on her journey alone, and her encounter with the White Knight, which is coloured by a certain poignant nostalgia for a lost intimacy, revealingly assumes that they will never meet again. Though

The Rectory Umbrella fended off 'Alloverishness', it did not admit the possibilities of mutual attachment or tackle ideas of engagement and love in the way that George MacDonald does in his children's books, through his variations on medieval quests and the chivalrous figure of Curdie, his hero.[11] MacDonald was a friend of Lewis Carroll, after they met at a doctor's in Hastings: they were coincidentally both consulting him for a cure for their stammers. The MacDonalds enthusiastically encouraged Lewis Carroll to publish *Alice in Wonderland*, and structural and thematic coincidences abound between MacDonald's *Phantastes* (1858) and the *Alice* books.[12] Carroll also took eloquent photographs of the MacDonald daughters, some of them showing the little girls dreaming. But, while the Scottish fairy-tale writer may have profoundly influenced Carroll's metaphysics of innocence, and confirmed his investment in the child as hero, Carroll did not – perhaps could not? – absorb his commitment to love as a motive force.

It might be fruitful to speculate that as a boy, Lewis Carroll was eroticised to his particular form of singularity by the many very young girls surrounding him at home. He placed himself in charge of the fun there, just as he did later with his child-friends. When Henry Liddell arrived at the Deanery, Christ Church, with his wife and their four children (more were on the way), they offered a kind of mirror image of Carroll's own family, and of his own sisters. Alice, the second of the Liddell daughters, was three when she arrived in Oxford, but she did not emerge as his best loved child-friend immediately, not until Carroll had adopted himself into the whole family of the young Liddells – photographing them, play-acting with them, arranging no end of treats and outings and surprises.

When there are couples in the *Alice* books, they tend to be *Doppelgängers*, like the Red Queen and the White Queen and Tweedledum and Tweedledee, or they represent paired contrasts, like the Gryphon and the Mock Turtle, the Walrus and the Carpenter, the Mad Hatter and the Dormouse, and, again and again, Alice engaging her 'adventure': the Rabbit, Humpty Dumpty, the Caterpillar, the Cheshire Cat. Working in binary variations, Carroll generates a sequence of doubles for himself as well as for Alice. He writes of Alice at the beginning of *Wonderland*, 'This curious child was very fond of pretending to be two people.'[13] Inside his pseudonym, he was not merely pretending to be two people in order to dialogue with himself, like Alice. Some of the doubles function as complementary mirror selves, and some as oppositional alter egos, or

anti-selves. In one sense there can be no exploration of union or engagement in the *Alice* stories because Carroll's phantasms are not separate
enough to be Others, in the sense of other people, however dazzlingly
realised and sharply drawn they are. 'The Snark *was* a Boojum, you see' –
the words which famously floated into Lewis Carroll's head – inspired the
whole epic farrago of inventive nonsense, *The Hunting of the Snark: An
Agony in Eight Fits*. The phrase encapsulates Dodgson/Carroll's sense of
concealed and interfused riddling and contrary identities within one
entity.

Alice experiences all kinds of changes, outside and in, from the
moment she falls down the rabbit-hole and grows tall and short and tall
and short. Her later transformations even hint at the monstrous (at the
Boojum inside *her*), when she nibbles at the Caterpillar's mushroom and
shape-shifts, now shrinking till her chin hits the ground, now growing 'an
immense length of neck': 'She was delighted to find that her neck would
bend about easily in any direction, like a serpent. She had just succeeded
in curving it down into a graceful zig-zag' when a pigeon attacks her:

> 'Serpent!' screamed the Pigeon.
> 'I'm *not* a serpent!' said Alice . . .[14]

Carroll illustrated the episode with two drawings of this metamorphosed
Alice in the manuscript version; they are more awkward than his usual
illustrations, perhaps on account of the patent phallic character of his
fantasy. Tenniel did not reinterpret them.[15]

The *Alice* books are tales of strictly personal quests, through the
permutations of possibility that are – almost – infinite. The modernity
of their magic – which has meant they have far outshone George
MacDonald's books, for example, in worldwide popularity – consists of
this polyvalent and solipsistic character of the Carrollian idea of the
individual. 'I wonder if I've been changed in the night?' Alice muses. 'Let
me think: *was* I the same when I got up this morning? I almost think I can
remember feeling a little different. But if I'm not the same, the next
question is, Who in the world am I? Ah, *that's* the great puzzle!'[16] This is
indeed the great puzzle that has animated post-Victorian (and post-
Christian) philosophy since Kant, and Carroll's signal contribution was to
place, at the core of the self, the experiences of fantasy and imagination.
His conception of the inner 'wonderland' and 'looking-glass country'
enriched and stretched empiricism, but at the same time profoundly

upset its assumptions, anticipating the destabilising of unitary personality in the most adventurous philosophers of psychology today, like John Elster and Ian Hacking.[17]

The enigma of Carroll is insoluble: how does the stiff, pedantic, Tory don, High Churchman and lacklustre lecturer in mathematics, fit with the light-footed, breezy, amiable, humorous inventor of stories, games, jokes, puzzles and treats? His biographers have attempted to answer the riddle. Morton Cohen emphasises his life beyond *Alice* and the well-roundedness of his personality with such anxiety that he almost manages to make Carroll dull. Michael Bakewell, with a more sensitive ear for the English nuances of Carroll's background, education and opinions, draws his subject as a historically recognisable type, a pernickety bachelor don, a Victorian scientist-inventor and favourite uncle, sometimes naively starstruck in his pursuit of acquaintances (like Tennyson), and a doughty and innovatory thinker on a range of chosen causes, including proportional representation and the fairness of tennis tournaments.[18]

But Carroll's inner processes necessarily elude, since Lewis Carroll never revealed himself, never apologised, never explained. 'Almost none of Carroll/Dodgon's surviving writing bears the imprint of ordinary, subjective first-person experience,' writes Hugh Haughton. 'Not even his letters and diaries, where we might expect to find it.'[19] Carroll's opaque, plural identity replicates the view of character in the *Alice* books as labile and polymorphous, although Carroll himself presented in so many ways a most conventional, and indeed stuffy, face to the world. But maybe this Snark *was* a Boojum, but did not want to own it himself, or anyone else to know it either.

Though Lewis Carroll did not reflect on his role and its history, he played the jester in Victorian society just as the Fool in the medieval and Renaissance court mimicked and mocked authority, convention – and the individuals invested with their power. The anthropologist Mary Douglas has pointed out in an essay on humour, 'The joke works only when it mirrors social forms; it exists by virtue of its congruence with the social structure.'[20] She goes on to discuss the 'joker', a traditional figure among certain African tribes, who enjoys privileges of open speech that are forbidden to others, and can therefore cleanse the community.

[The joker] has a firm hold on his own position in the structure and the disruptive comments he makes upon it are in a sense the comments of the social group upon itself . . . he lightens for everyone the oppressiveness of social reality, demonstrates its arbitrariness by making light of formality in generality, and expresses the creative possibilities of the situation . . . his jokes expose the inadequacy of realist structurings of experience and so release the pent-up power of the imagination.[21]

Lewis Carroll was securely placed in two of the most established high institutions of English life, a fellow of Christ Church College, Oxford, and an ordained deacon in the Church of England, and he thereby fulfils this paradoxical criterion for the eruption of fooling. It is because the Reverend Charles Dodgson existed that he could also be Lewis Carroll: the two personae, so remarkably inconsistent, meet through the character of joking itself – that it plumbs deep into shared meanings, and those meanings depend on the institutions the joker knows well and can therefore mock percipiently. In Lewis Carroll's case, however, he could not have communicated for over a century across languages and cultures from Iceland to Japan if he had only fooled with Victorian values, with the customs of High Table or the Senior Common Room or the doctrinal disputes between Anglicans and Evangelicals. He is slyly funny about these, and also covertly critical of Darwinism, and other 'progressive' ideas of his time, as William Empson observed in his acute essay, 'Alice in Wonderland: The Child as Swain' (1935).[22] But Carroll also transmuted the material close at hand in his own experiences into blithely comic scenes with pan-cultural appeal. And he was able to do this because he was deeply rooted as well in another, far more fundamental but abstract structure: mathematics and formal logic. By playing continually with the rules of language itself, by constantly drawing attention to their breakdown, Lewis Carroll's fantasies become metaphysical fooling with the very ground of meaning itself: exhilarating, unburdening nonsense.

As Hugh Haughton comments in his perceptive introduction to *The Chatto Book of Nonsense Poetry*, the English love of infantile mimicry in the nineteenth century 'forms part of a culture with a huge investment in ideas of social and intellectual authority and a dedication to the idea of moral earnestness – a critique played out in the children's books of Lear and Carroll'.[23] Nonsense rhymes and songs and catches and refrains figure in the literature of many cultures, but they make a particularly strong showing in both oral and written English literature. Noel Malcolm, in *The Origins of English Nonsense*, actually names Sir John Hoskyns (died 1638) and the 'Water Poet' John Taylor (died 1653) as the *fons et origo* of the genre as literature; they were Royalists, writing during the Puritan hegemony, and gobbledegook and gibberish – jabberwocky – both provided a shelter for insurrectionary assaults on the Roundheads, and expressed the Royalist commitment to the ludic.[24] 'For Nonsense is Rebellion,' wrote Taylor. Though this precise dating may be arguable, the point about the political context is important and too easily overlooked: English power and wealth, intellectual and social self-confidence, as well as the start of far-reaching colonial influence, created a breeding ground for the kind of destabilising and creative explosions that constitute fantastic nonsense – Jonathan Swift, Henry Fielding, Laurence Sterne, even occasionally Dr Johnson himself, William Blake, Christopher Smart, all nourish the tradition from which Carroll sprang. The genre of the *Alice* books sidles to the attack through spoofs, pastiche, riddles, and various puckish logophilic word games. It is probably not incidental that Alice Liddell's father was the great Greek lexicographer and that she was brought up in a house of words.[25]

In *Looking-Glass*, the Red Queen remarks in typically cross fashion, 'What do you suppose is the use of a child without any meaning? Even a joke should have some meaning and a child's more important than a joke, I hope.'[26] Carroll thought highly of jokes, and they structured all his exchanges with children; he kept stores of toys and games and puzzles in his rooms and brought them out to play with his visitors; he demonstrated the magic of numbers in mathematics, such as 'mystic nines';[27] he could conjure and do card tricks, knew how to make a paper pistol pop, could make various animals with a folded handkerchief, pass a halfpenny through a sixpenny hole; he invented word games and rebuses and ways of doing sums which most children found droll and absorbing (though some were bored). And he parodied in life – as in the *Alice* books – solemn lessons and high sentiments and lyric poetry. His nonsense upskittled rules and regulations. The Red Queen wanted things to have meaning, and preferred those meanings to obey rules, however Humpty Dumptyish in their capriciousness. But Carroll does not much like the Red Queen, and he very much liked nonsense.

The figure of the child united the two target arenas of Carroll's expertise: Victorian polite society and the peculiar illogicalities of common parlance and mores. A child has not yet learned the manners, rules and prejudices that govern the adult world, and sees through them – or rather Carroll could make Alice the vehicle of his own rationality, of his amused detachment from the *convenances*, and, at other times, his distaste and indignation. His wit attacks hypocrisy: he parodies the gentlemanly codes that govern fighting, most famously in the mock-heroic ballad 'Tweedledum and Tweedledee/ Agreed to have a battle'. As she watches the duel of the White and Red Knights in *Looking-Glass*, Alice is thinking: 'I wonder what the Rules of Battle are?' She tries to make sense of them, but of course cannot. In *Looking-Glass*, Alice's encounter with Humpty Dumpty is one of the most brilliant (and bruising) skirmishes between the sound good sense (of reasonable, unspoiled minds) that passes for childish nonsense and the irrational (spoiled adult) regimen that passes for sense. Nonsense is 'a mistake on purpose', Susan Stewart writes.[28] Alice's challenge to Humpty Dumpty's distortion of this in the interests of Mastery has become rightly proverbial:

> 'But "glory" doesn't mean "a nice knock-down argument",' Alice objected.
> 'When *I* use a word,' Humpty Dumpty said in rather a scornful tone, 'it means just what I choose it to mean – neither more nor less.'

The Red Queen, as she rampages across the *Looking-Glass* chessboard, personifies even more furiously the arbitrary tyranny of custom and the petty victories scored through the code of etiquette:

> 'Speak when you're spoken to!' the Queen sharply interrupted her.
> 'But if everybody obeyed that rule!' said Alice, who was always ready for a little argument, 'and if you only spoke when you were spoken to, and the other person always waited for *you* to begin, you see nobody would ever say anything so that—'
> 'Ridiculous!' cried the Queen.

Another reason for the huge popularity of both *Wonderland* and *Looking-Glass* lies in Carroll's championing of the child against the adult world and its authority; he lampoons adult moralising through the horrid Duchess in *Alice in Wonderland*, who says, 'Tut, tut, child . . . Everything's got a moral, if only you can find it.' Unlikely as it may seem, this crabby Oxford don is a natural father to the Woodstock generation. Nevertheless, it is probably a mistake to cast him as a patron saint of hedonist subversion, for his Alice plays one set of rules against another, to show up the inherently comic contradictions that govern day-to-day life.[29]

A girl-child specially embodied the spirit of argument because Carroll knew, from his close acquaintance with so many, that Victorian social pressures and expectations tight-laced growing women into shapes that squeezed out the bright spirit of their childhood. A Victorian woman was expected to put away childish things more definitely than her brother, and had travelled far farther from the character of her youth when she grew up. Alice, his heroine, is outspoken, frank, impatient, quick-witted, adventurous, passionate in her responses, curious, petulant, frequently impertinent and cross. Empson says she is 'rather a pert child . . . the underdog speaking up for itself.'[30] Alice is 'fresh' in both senses of the term, exhibiting qualities that moralists, from Aristotle and Plutarch onwards, had singled out for condemnation in the female sex. She personifies the very antithesis of the subordinate, modest, mute and maidenly angel in the house. If Alice Liddell, on that blissful boat trip that afternoon in 1862, did indeed possess such quantities of sparky effrontery, inquisitiveness and scepticism, then Mrs Reginald Hargreaves, the married woman Alice became, no longer did; Carroll later wrote her distant letters, and his last photograph of her in 1870, when she was eighteen, shows her sunken into the chair, her arms squeezed by her sides as if, out of frame, she is twisting her hands, her eyes resentful, a whipped-bitch kind of a look, not even the faintest ghost of the pert, coquettish little mischief-making madam of her enchanting child-self. It is a sad portrait, but, like so much of Lewis Carroll's photography, it achieves an unsettling collusion with the sitter: the real-life Alice herself a perfect witness to the successful crushing of female personality by Victorian conventional aspirations.

It is striking that when Carroll throws his voice to speak for his ideal audience – to see things as the girl child Alice does – his diction and vocabulary and rhythm change. He chooses a comic register, and it entails lots of oos and uus and js and ks and bs (as in 'Jabberwock' and 'Jubjub bird' and 'Bandersnatch' and 'Boojum'). These are hard, percussive sounds found more in Anglo-Saxon attitudes than Victorian sonorities of style, and Carroll's choice indicates that the natural language of a child corresponds to an earlier stratum in the English language itself, before Gallicisms and Latinisms and Hellenisms elongated the vowels and softened and aspirated the consonants and puffed long words and stretched jaunty, bouncy prosodic forms into breathy hexameters. The longing to escape from under the burden of learning into an unintelligible and pristine (uncreated till that moment) babble that communicates directly to the senses, without cultural freighting, marks some of Carroll's greatest work, including the dotty but melancholy delights of *The Hunting of the Snark*.

Carroll's love of girl children is central to his strangeness, and his interest in expanding the circle of his 'child-friends' unusually assiduous among men of his class and occupation, not only because they were, almost invariably, little girls rather than little boys, but because his appetite for them was oceanic: in 1863 alone, he made a list of 107 he planned to photograph. He was a most dedicated wooer, indefatigable in his enshrinement of their images. Mrs Liddell, the fussocking mother of Alice, was alerted to something she found untoward, and around the time of Alice's eleventh birthday, there was a rupture. But on the whole, the extent of parental cooperation with Carroll's elaborate plans for treats and outings is remarkable; such entrustment of little girls to a young single male is not usual today.

Part of the fun was Carroll's effervescent parody of grown-up norms: he mimicked for his child visitors all the rituals of seduction. Intimate tête-à-tête meals, picnics *al fresco*, rowing on the river, flurried exchanges of billets-doux, full of delightful banter and jokes and compliments and fuss and names interlaced in acrostics. He took flattering, lively photographs of his friends for keepsakes, and even, as has become notorious, began asking for his child-friends to pose *'sans habillement'* as he put it – the slide into French surely betraying *pudeur* – in the 1870s, after several years of taking many clothed portraits. One of the nude sessions happened very quickly, very mischievously, when the children ducked under the table cloth and emerged in the buff, on all fours, laughing. Later, he scrupulously negotiated agreement from them and from their parents beforehand. Kisses were his reward for all the forms his attentions took, images, jests, mock lessons: he teases in letters about the giving of kisses, and the taking of them.

The sustained parody of adult wooing in his entertainments was part and parcel of that delighting delinquency that buoys the humour of both *Alice in Wonderland* and *Through the Looking-Glass* as well as the extended poetic fantasy, *The Hunting of the Snark*. His own innocence, of course, depends on the expression of sexuality and the form it took, but his obsession with little girls was expressed in a different context of social and sexual customs; his paedophilia belonged with cultural behaviour and attitudes that made it different from child abuse today.[31] The passionate letters, vows, embraces, tears exchanged between Bettina von Arnim and Karoline von Günderode at the beginning of the nineteenth century do not proclaim the two women were lovers, even though they are expressing and no doubt experiencing fervent pleasure in their love, their contact, their intimacy.[32] But Carroll was aware of problems about his passion: and not just from Mrs Liddell. He knew perfectly well he could not circulate his photographs of naked children, for example, and he cancelled the plates so that they could not be copied. His behaviour was quite open-eyed, and the avoidance of furtiveness a declaration of independence.

In *Through the Looking-Glass* the author meditates more deeply on the nature of a child than he had done in *Wonderland*. Haigha the Messenger explains Alice to the Unicorn: ' "This is a child! . . . We only found it to-day. It's as large as life, and twice as natural!"' At this, the Unicorn exclaims, ' "I always thought they were fabulous monsters! . . . Is it alive?" "It can talk," said Haigha, solemnly.' Alice retorts that she thought that 'Unicorns were fabulous monsters, too'. The two of them strike a 'bargain' and agree to believe in each other.

It would provoke a little girl to be called a fabulous monster and referred to as an 'it'; it would entertain future child listeners and readers to be whisked out of reality into the domain of unicorns and other wonders – or, to put it looking-glass fashion, to have such wonders conjured as real. But to be 'large as life, and twice as natural' is perhaps a more revealing casual exclamation: the naturalness of pre-gendered young girls embodied for Lewis Carroll the Romantic ideal, announced by Blake and Wordsworth and Coleridge, free spirits possessing untrammelled innocence, in a providential state of natural virtue. Nonsense verse, with its tradition of disguised protest, metaphysical anxieties, and comic self-defence provided him with a code through which he could play-act a child himself and approach little girls without turning into an ogre, without letting loose the Boojum inside him.

1998

Struwwelpeter

Review of Shockheaded Peter: A Junk Opera

Raw-Head-and-Bloody-Bones, Jenny Greenteeth, the Skriker, the Child-Snatcher and the Fleshlumpchewer: frights and bogles come under different names and in different degrees of hideousness, but none was as terrifying to me as 'the long-legged Scissor-man' who leaps into Conrad's nursery in *Struwwelpeter* and 'Snip snip', cuts off both his thumbs. I was one of those children (and thumbsuckers) who can't muster healthy gusts of mocking laughter in the face of fear, that response defined by Freud as the natural reflex of a vigorous ego. As a child, when I came across once again the copy of *Struwwelpeter* I'd tried so hard to suppress, the bogeymen inside it jumped out and frightened the living daylights out of me all over again.

At first glance, nothing could be less likely material for a brilliant performance piece, richly comic, satisfyingly mysterious – and for grown-ups. Yet the adaptation, *Shockheaded Peter: A Junk Opera*, was acclaimed when it first opened, at the West Yorkshire Playhouse in 1998, and again after it transferred to the Lyric, Hammersmith, as a highly offbeat twist to the traditional panto for the Christmas season that year. John Gross was one of the many critics who admitted scepticism at first, but was 'bowled over' by the brilliant theatricality of the production, hailing it as 'a sinister evening . . . and an utterly beguiling one'. Created by Michael Morris of Cultural Industry in collaboration with the designer-directors Julian Crouch and Phelim McDermott, the play features the cult retro band, the Tiger Lillies, with the two Adrians – Adrian Huge and Adrian Stout – on percussion and bass, and the eerie vocals of Martin Jacques, a self-styled 'castrato crooner'. Their chemistry has resulted in a macabre, comic music theatre of extremes, combining puppets and masks, penny-dreadful leers, Goth whiteface and weeping mascara, grotesquely exaggerated gestures, pasteboard props, cardboard flames and streaming red ribbons for blood.

Cramped in a cut-out toy theatre, several sizes too small for them, the humans loom like giants: Julian Bleach plays Master of Ceremonies as a scarecrow cross between the vampire Nosferatu, Dr Caligari and Baron Samedi of Voodoo ritual, linking each of the stories with exultant malevolence. The production has truly transmogrified Hoffmann's Victorian pedagogy into a most weird and wonderful experience, and it has enthralled audiences in countries as varied as Israel, the United States, China (Hong Kong), Australia, and Finland where it has been touring.

It's no longer young children's fare (if it ever was, really). When I saw *Shockheaded Peter* two years ago at the Lyric, Hammersmith, some of the children in the audience were laughing, but they looked around for a comforting hand to ensure that they really were in the situation of safety and trust that makes it possible to shrug such things off. Hoffmann dedicated it to three- to six-year-olds, but under-tens are discouraged – rightly, I think – from going to *Shockheaded Peter*.

Struwwelpeter was first published in 1845, written and illustrated by Dr Heinrich Hoffmann, a doctor in Frankfurt with a philanthropic bent, who, in early editions of his collected verses, signed himself, *'Reimerich Kinderlieb'* ('the riddle-me-ree child-lover'). Hoffmann's own father had been an inspector of sewers and had been very tough on little Heinrich's urges, so *Struwwelpeter* was intended to mock the earlier generation's harsh discipline. The story goes that Dr Hoffmann went out to buy a Christmas present for his three-year-old son, Carl, and found the moralising fare of hellfire sermons and cautionary tales on offer so utterly boring that he came back and wrote his spoof. The English version, in bouncy doggerel, appeared almost immediately, and was also instantly popular. Anne Harvey, a children's writer and anthologist, has plausibly suggested that the wonderfully named Madame Clara de Châtelain, who lived in England and published other collections of nursery rhymes by German and French writers, may have been the anonymous translator.

When I first read about *Struwwelpeter*'s background, it struck me as a good example of an author's intentions failing to control the impact of his work, for it still is, for all its happy ironies, a nasty book. But 'nasty', like 'scary', like 'wicked', has turned into a term of praise; it cocks a trigger of mysterious excitement that's highly sought after, and not only by children. *Shockheaded Peter* hasn't simply adapted Dr Heinrich Hoffmann's classic for the stage; it has ratcheted up the horror, squeezed deep macabre humour out of the mocking ditties and brilliantly, savagely turned them into the stuff of adults' bad dreams. In the original book not all the protagonists meet their deaths. Little-Suck-a-Thumb, for example, only – *only?* – undergoes amputation, while Johnny-Head-in-Air falls into the pond and merely suffers the indignity of being laughed at by the little fishes. But on the stage in this production, both these culprits die, and even the cheery, gun-toting hare kills his wife and then blows his brains out (all in dazzling dumbshow with wonderfully expressive puppets).

The play's obsessive repetitions plunge the audience into the most tabooed territory of all, the most profound terror of family and society: child death. One by one, in this production, all the little boys and girls come to grief; 'And so another young life is pointlessly snuffed out,' declares the MC, with deadpan solemnity and a lick of the lips. Martin Jacques then sings of the poor victim's demise in a screech-owl lament, accompanying himself on a wailing squeezebox. As he intones, in his queer falsetto, the dreadful refrain, 'He – or She – was dead. Dead. Dead', he truly becomes a spectre to scare the stoutest.

But the sequence of fatal accidents isn't the only place where the production has seriously 'upped the death rate', in the producer Michael Morris's phrase. The cast, improvising together during the making of the play, came up with a frame story: a perfect young married couple have a child, but that child is a fright with long nails and a shock of hair, and they reject him: this is the Struwwelpeter himself, a sad rag doll, an emblem of all rejects and changelings. They bury him under the floorboards. The murdered child lies there, haunting us, throughout the action . . . his nails break through, and the scissorman snips them; but neither his mother nor his father can get him out of their minds, until, as in the final tableau of a rake's progress, the mother goes mad, the father takes to the bottle. 'What's hidden under *our own* floorboards?' asks the sinister MC.

So the subject here is no longer children's naughtiness, or adult authority over them, as in Hoffmann's cautionary tales, but the failure to care for them adequately. For all its grotesque exaggerations and Victorian vaudeville manners, *Shockheaded Peter* grows out of current crises around children as surely as the latest headlines. The German fairy-tale scholar Jack Zipes, in his recent polemic, *Sticks and Stones*, suggests 'this social normalization of cruelty prompted the Tiger Lillies to stage *Struwwelpeter* for adults as an act of confrontation . . . an attack on complacent adults who believe that we have grown more civilized in our attitudes towards children'. It is a twist of the uncanny that the production, with its staged return of the repressed, should be brought back to the West End at this time of terrible anxiety, when the inquiry into Alder Hey has just reported, and abuse in so many children's homes is being investigated. Yet it would be entirely wrong to think that this grievous backdrop prevents the work's weird and savage wit from working its magic in the theatre; rather the opposite: gallows humour really does turn into a pill against melancholy (to use the title of an old jest book).

Something else was already going on in Victorian morality tales, besides cruel lessons in manners and survival. The inventors of children's comedy were children's allies, and an assault on adult arrogance was implied by the very introduction of the comic cautionary genre for child readers. Hoffmann was entering into the spirit of mischief perceived as instinctive in children and mocking the efforts of adults to crush them. Lewis Carroll, a generation later, continued to attack angry adults and their irrational demands, generally taking the side of children against authorities and law-makers with designs upon them. He parodied Isaac Watts's pious ditties ('How doth the little crocodile / Improve his shining tail . . . ?') and Jane Taylor's twee poems ('Twickle, twinkle, little bat'), and his Alice fantasies offer an explanation for the absurdity – and cruelty – of the grown-up world: Wonderland and Looking-glass territory aren't exactly topsy-turvy, but angled mirrors on normality, on the baffling conduct of justice and the irrational procedures of power.

But Carroll's amusement doesn't seek to make the reader shiver and start; he keeps apart from the gothic and the macabre. The peculiar humour of *Struwwelpeter* stands at the start of a different family of child entertainers, flourishing in this country as well as in Germany, even though the ghoulish expressionism of *Shockheaded Peter* seems Teutonic – as both fairy tale and theatre. (Interestingly, the first English translation of the Grimm Brothers was published in 1845, the year of *Struwwelpeter*'s publication, with illustrations by George Cruikshank: the frontispiece shows a family circle round the fireside, guffawing as one of the stories is read aloud.)

In England, Harry Graham and Hilaire Belloc excelled at the offhand, deadpan callousness in the Hoffmann tradition. Graham's *Ruthless Rhymes for Heartless Homes*, published in 1899, delights in broken-necked babies and accidentally murdered aunties; it includes the sad tale of Billy:

> Billy, in one of his nice new sashes
> Fell in the fire and was burnt to ashes;
> Now, although the room grows chilly,
> I haven't the heart to poke poor Billy.

Belloc later created Maria 'Who made Faces and a Deplorable Marriage', and 'Young Algernon, the Doctor's son, [who] Was playing with a Loaded gun', as well as unforgettable Matilda who 'told such Dreadful Lies/ It made one Gasp and Stretch one's Eyes' – she goes up in flames, like her fellow-culprit Pauline from *Struwwelpeter*. Edward Gorey, who died last year, practised a similar art ('E is for Ernest who choked on a peach'); he once remarked, 'There's so little heartless work around. So I feel I am filling a small but necessary gap.' Any number of Roald Dahl stories qualify, of course; in fact, Dahl reconditioned a special English brand of sadistic sangfroid that delights young readers. *The Naughtiest Children I Know*, a new, sparkling collection, edited by Anne Harvey, reveals the extent of the tradition: writer after writer adopts the tongue-in-cheek, finger-wagging role to parade a pantheon of little rascals and mischievous cautions.

It seems to me that, beneath the ostensible lessons in behaviour, decorum, and danger, the dark horrors purveyed by such staple children's fare function in two ways at least: they don't just pass on lessons on not playing with fire, and eating your greens, but help to shape a new way of dealing with experience, refining primal instincts of recoil and terror into protective laughter. They actually teach children what a joke is or can be; they pass on humour as a strategic refuge. They line the stomach. Laughter in the face of fear may be a natural instinct, but like many things in nature, it has to be introduced and then cultivated. And irony above all requires being in the know; it's an acquired taste and needs practice.

Besides the lessons in survival humour, this macabre fantasy mode stages a pre-moral universe where children are bad and naughtiness thrives; it projects on to children wilful, even malignant wantonness, rather than lack of experience, ignorance, and weakness; they're still carrying the primal stain, as it were, on adults' behalf. Through their antics, we can enter into an experience of trespass and daring and feel that thrill of possibility; and then through the ensuing, frightful consequences, so glowingly and horribly dramatised in *Shockheaded Peter*, we're given the pleasure of breaking the rules of decency and responsibility all over again.

Revelling in hope

Review of Karel Čapek, Nine Fairy Tales and One More Thrown in for Good Measure, *translated by Dagmar Herrmann*

The Czech playwright, novelist and fantasist Karel Čapek coined the word 'robot', and in his drama of 1920, *R.U.R.* (Rossum's Universal Robots) imagined the death of the world after robots have been manufactured to spare man labour; a few years later, in spite of international success as a dramatist, Čapek decided to concentrate on journalism: 'Now I must help educate the nation.' Čapek's methods were cunning, mischievous, full of a magician's legerdemain and a comedian's verve. Just as *R.U.R.* warns bitterly against treating people like machines, so the occasional pieces Čapek wrote – his essays, squibs and stories – plead for pleasure, tenderness, mercy and laughter against the gathering forces that would exterminate these aspects of the human.

The *Nine Fairy Tales* published here in a new English translation belong to Čapek's popularising, utopian enterprise. Through flights of exuberant fancy, improbable journeys and clever animals, Čapek delivers many gentle lessons against brutality and stupidity, in a storyteller's style that addresses the reader directly. The longest story, 'The Great Cat's Tale', embroils a princess and a pauper with a detective who has the same initials as Sherlock Homes but who behaves like Phineas Fogg, rushing about the globe in pursuit of a magician who has stolen the cat. The detective knows he has reached Japan when 'All around the trees were beautifully lacquered, each grain of sand on the shore was carefully washed and polished'. He performs many heroic acts of sacrifice and generosity *en route* and is richly rewarded; there is a clever, Borgesian twist, which would have made the ending of any ordinary shaggy dog story, but Čapek carries on with a parable about the benefits of treating prisoners well, and still does not forget to return us to the princess and the pauper with whom he began. In 'The Tramp's Tale', he shows his mastery of different structures and produces a just-so story (why crows caw) woven into a moral fable about an honest simpleton who gains a king's ransom. It's characteristic of Čapek that his hero has a hole in his pocket, and so loses the fortune as soon as he has won it.

The speed of some of the magic journeys he describes, the teasing picture of petty bureaucrats and postal clerks, pompous doctors and stuffy lawyers, comical cops and gullible robbers, and Čapek's blend of wit, pity and hope evoke the cinema of the 1930s very strongly and Chaplin in particular. But he is a writer and a supple stylist, and one of his reasons for choosing fairy tales was their origin in popular speech and the saltiness of their idiom. A passionate advocate of the Czech language, Čapek saw in fairy-tale a rich vein of national culture; he considered that his greatest literary influences were 'childhood reading, folk speech and Latin prose'. As a child he heard songs, riddles, proverbs as well as stories from his mother and grandmother, who was a miller's daughter and later a miller's wife, just like in a fairy tale. Family influences remained very strong. Čapek often collaborated with his brother Josef, the artist, and Josef illustrates these stories as well as contributing one tale about a den of thieves, who are outwitted by the brothers' great-grandfather.

Dagmar Herrmann's translation catches the deadpan descriptions of prodigious exploits essential to the genre, and English can just about stretch, it seems, to match Czech's superabundance of words for 'rascal', 'devil', and 'nincompoop'. She has difficulties, though, with the names of characters: Czech puns struggle in English. But there are many literary pleasures here, in Čapek's dryness of tone ('this is a court of law, not the geographical society,' says the judge after hearing a detailed account of a thousand leagues' voyage chasing a hat around the world), and in the affectionate observation of his naturalist's eye. (He describes a puppy: 'he only knew how to count to two, so he'd get tangled in his four legs, and in the end he'd topple over, startled, showing his pink tongue that looked like a thin slice of ham.')

These stories appeared in Czechoslovakia in 1932; the year before, Čapek published an eloquent essay on fairy tale as a branch of literature. He defended the realism of the genre, pointed out that the presence of wonders and fairies does not necessarily characterize it, whereas a popular (anonymous) origin and a moral purpose do. 'Fairy stories originate in life', he wrote, and went on to stress the struggle with evil at the heart of such tales. But Čapek's combat against evil does not proclaim evil's might, as the Grimms' tales often do, nor does he use violence against violence. He clowns to attract attention; as in *R.U.R.*, where the discovery of laughter and tears are signs that the robots are becoming human, so here, he teases us into thought. The final words of these children's stories declare the banishment of the last wicked sorcerer in the land – to the Sahara, where he remains, striving to turn the desert green for the sake of his health. Čapek concludes, 'Perhaps you children will live to see it.'

Karel Čapek died on Christmas Day, 1938, in despair about the Munich agreement; after the Nazis entered Prague, the Gestapo arrived to arrest him, thinking him still alive. His brother Josef was taken to Belsen, where he died just before the end of the war. By comparison, the Grimm Brothers led quiet lives, but in their fairy tales dealt more in fatalism; Čapek's revel in hope, against all the odds.

1990

Cunning and High Spirits

Introduction to The Second Virago Book of Fairy Tales, *edited by Angela Carter*

Italo Calvino, the Italian writer and fabulist and collector of fairy tales, believed strongly in the connection between fantasy and reality: 'I am accustomed to consider literature a search for knowledge,' he wrote. 'Faced with [the] precarious existence of tribal life, the shaman responded by ridding his body of weight and flying to another world, another level of perception, where he could find the strength to change the face of reality.'[1] Angela Carter wouldn't have made the same wish with quite such a straight face, but her combination of fantasy and revolutionary longings corresponds to the flight of Calvino's shaman. She possessed the enchanter's lightness of mind and wit – it's interesting that she explored, in her last two novels, images of winged women. Fevvers, her *aërialiste* heroine of *Nights at the Circus*, may have hatched like a bird, and in *Wise Children*, the twin Chance sisters play various fairies or feathered creatures, from their first foot on the stage as child stars to their dalliance in Hollywood for a spectacular extravaganza of *A Midsummer Night's Dream*.

Fairy tales also offered her a means of flying – of finding and telling an alternative story, of shifting something in the mind, just as so many fairy-tale characters shift something in their shape. She wrote her own – the dazzling, erotic variations on Perrault's *Mother Goose Tales* and other familiar stories in *The Bloody Chamber* – where she lifted Beauty and Red Riding Hood and Bluebeard's last wife out of the pastel nursery into the labyrinth of female desire. She had always read very widely in folklore from all over the world, and compiled her first collection, *The Virago Book of Fairy Tales*, two years ago; this second volume is being published after her death, in February 1992, from cancer.

She found the stories in sources ranging from Siberia to Suriname, and she arranged them into sections in a sequence that runs from one tale of female heroic endeavour to another about generosity rewarded. There are few fairies, in the sense of sprites, but the stories move in fairyland, not the prettified, kitschified, Victorians' elfland, but the darker, dream realm of spirits and tricks, magical, talking animals, riddles and spells. In 'The Twelve Wild Ducks', the opening tale, the heroine vows not to speak or to laugh or to cry until she has rescued her brothers from their enchanted animal forms. The issue of women's speech, of women's noise, of their/our clamour and laughter and weeping and shouting and hooting runs through all Angela Carter's writings, and informed her love of the folktale. In *The Magic Toyshop* the lovely Aunt Margaret cannot speak because she is strangled by the silver torque which the malign puppet-master her husband has made her as a bridal gift. Folklore, on the other hand, speaks volumes about women's experience, and women are often the storytellers, as in one of the dashingly comic and highly Carteresque tales in this collection ('Reason to Beat Your Wife').

Angela Carter's partisan feeling for women, which burns in all her work, never led her to any conventional form of feminism; but she continues here one of her original and effective strategies, snatching out of the jaws of misogyny itself 'useful stories' for women. Her essay *The Sadeian Woman* (1979) found in Sade a liberating teacher of the male-female status quo and made him illuminate the far reaches of women's polymorphous desires; here she turns topsy-turvy some cautionary folktales and shakes out the fear and dislike of women they once expressed to create a new set of values, about strong, outspoken, zestful, sexual women who can't be kept down (see 'The Old Woman Against the Stream'; 'The Letter Trick'). In *Wise Children* she created a heroine, Dora Chance, who's a showgirl, a soubrette, a vaudeville dancer, one of the low, the despised, the invisible poor, an old woman who's illegitimate and never married (born the wrong side of the blanket, the wrong side of the tracks), and each of these stigmas is taken up with exuberant relish and scattered in the air like so much wedding confetti.

The last story here, 'Spreading the Fingers', a tough morality tale from Suriname about sharing what one has been given with others, also discloses the high value Angela Carter placed on generosity. She gave herself – her ideas, her wit, her incisive, no-bullshit mind – with open but never sentimental prodigality. Her favourite fairy tale in the first *Virago Book* was a Russian riddle story 'The Wise Little Girl', in which the tsar asks her heroine for the impossible, and she delivers it without batting an eyelid. Angela liked it because it was as satisfying as 'The Emperor's New Clothes', but 'no one was humiliated and everybody gets the prizes'. The story comes in the section called 'Clever Women, Resourceful Girls and Desperate Stratagems', and its heroine is an essential Carter figure, never abashed, nothing daunted, sharp-eared as a vixen and possessed of dry good sense. It's entirely characteristic of Angela's spirit that she should delight in the tsar's confounding, and yet not want him to be humiliated.

She did not have the strength, before she died, to write the Introduction she had planned to this volume, but she left four cryptic notes among her papers:

> 'every real story contains something useful', says Walter Benjamin
> the *unperplexedness* of the story
> "No one dies so poor that he does not leave something behind," said Pascal.
> fairy tales – cunning and high spirits'.

Fragmentary as they are, these phrases convey the Carter philosophy. She was scathing about the contempt the 'educated' can show, when two-thirds of the literature of the world – perhaps more – has been created by the illiterate. She liked the solid common sense of folk tales, the straightforward aims of their protagonists, the simple moral distinctions, and the wily stratagems they suggest. They're tales of the underdog, about cunning and high spirits winning through in the end; they're practical, and they're not high-flown. For a fantasist with wings, Angela kept her eyes on the ground, with reality firmly in her sights. She once remarked, 'A fairy tale is a story where one king goes to another king to borrow a cup of sugar.'

Feminist critics of the genre – especially in the 1970s – jibbed at the socially conventional 'happy endings' of so many stories (for example, 'When she grew up he married her and she became the tsarina'). But Angela knew about satisfaction and pleasure; and at the same time she believed that the goal of fairy tales wasn't 'a conservative one, but a utopian one, indeed a form of heroic optimism – as if to say: One day, we might be happy, even if it won't last'. Her own heroic optimism never failed her – like the spirited heroine of one of her tales, she was resourceful and brave and even funny during the illness which brought about her death. Few writers possess the best qualities of their work; she did, in spades.

Her imagination was dazzling, and through her daring, vertiginous plots, her precise yet wild imagery, her gallery of wonderful bad-good girls, beasts, rogues and other creatures, she causes readers to hold their breath as a mood of heroic optimism forms against the odds. She had the true writer's gift of remaking the world for her readers.

She was a wise child herself, with a mobile face, a mouth which sometimes pursed with irony, and, behind the glasses, a wryness, at times a twinkle, at times a certain dreaminess; with her long, silvery hair and ethereal delivery, she had something of the Faerie Queene about her, except that she was never wispy or fey. And though the narcissism of youth was one of the great themes in her early fiction, she was herself exceptionally unnarcissistic. Her voice was soft, with a storyteller's confidingness, and lively with humour; she spoke with a certain syncopation, as she stopped to think – her thoughts made her the most exhilarating companion, a wonderful talker, who wore her learning and wide reading with lightness, who could express a mischievous insight or a tough judgment with scalpel precision and produce new ideas by the dozen without effort, weaving allusion, quotation, parody and original invention, in a way that echoed her prose style. 'I've got a theory that ...' she'd say, self-deprecatorily, and then would follow something that no one else had thought of, some sally, some rich paradox that would encapsulate a trend, a moment. She could be Wildean in her quickness and the glancing drollery of her wit. And then she would pass on, sometimes leaving her listeners astonished and stumbling.

Angela Carter was born in May 1940, the daughter of Hugh Stalker, a journalist for the Press Association, who was a Highlander by birth, had served the whole term of the First World War, and had come south to Balham to work. He used to take her to the cinema, to the Tooting Granada, where the glamour of the building (Alhambra-style) and of the movie stars (Jean Simmons in *The Blue Lagoon*) made an impression which lasted – Angela has written some of the most gaudy, stylish, sexy passages about seduction and female beauty on record; 'snappy' and 'glamorous' are key words of pleasure and praise in her vocabulary. Her mother was from South Yorkshire, on her own mother's side; this grandmother was tremendously important to her: 'every word and gesture of hers displayed a natural dominance, a native savagery, and I am very grateful for all that, now, though the core of steel was a bit inconvenient when I was looking for boyfriends in the South'. Angela's mother was a scholarship girl, and 'liked things to be nice'; she worked as a cashier in Selfridge's in the 1920s, and had passed exams and wanted the same for her daughter. Angela went to Streatham grammar school, and for a time entertained a fancy of becoming an Egyptologist, but left school to take up an apprenticeship on the *Croydon Advertiser* arranged by her father.

As a reporter on the news desk, she had trouble with her imagination (she used to like the Russian storyteller's formula, 'The story is over, I can't lie any more') and switched to writing a record column as well as features. She got married for the first time when she was twenty-one, to a chemistry teacher at Bristol technical college, and began studying English at Bristol University in the same year, choosing to concentrate on medieval literature, which was then definitely uncanonical. Its forms – from allegory to tales – as well as its heterogeneity of tone – from bawdy to romance – can be found everywhere in her own œuvre; Chaucer and Boccaccio remained among her favourite writers. She also remembered those days, in a recent interview with her great friend Susannah Clapp, for the talking in cafés 'to situationists and anarchists ... It was the Sixties ... I was very very unhappy but I was perfectly happy at the same time.'

During this period, she first began developing her interest in folklore, discovering with her husband the folk and jazz music scenes of the 1960s. (At a more recent, staid, meeting of the Folklore Society, she fondly recalled those countercultural days when a member would attend with a pet raven on one shoulder.) She began writing fiction: in her twenties she published four novels (*Shadow Dance*, 1966; *The Magic Toyshop*, 1967; *Several Perceptions*, 1968; *Heroes and Villains*, 1969; as well as a story for children, *Miss Z, the Dark Young Lady*, 1970). She was heaped with praise and prizes; one of them – the Somerset Maugham – stipulated travel, and she obeyed, using the money to run away from her husband ('I think Maugham would have approved'). She chose Japan, because she revered the films of Kurosawa.

Japan marks an important transition; she stayed for two years, from 1971. Her fiction till then, including the ferocious, taut elegy *Love* (1971; revised 1987), showed her baroque powers of invention, and her fearless confrontation of erotic violence, of female as well as male sexuality: she marked out her territory early, and men and women clash on it, often bloodily, and the humour is mostly of the gallows variety. From the beginning, her prose was magnificently rich, intoxicated with words – a vivid and sensual lexicon of bodily attributes, minerals, flora and fauna –

and she dealt in strangeness. But Japan gave her a way of looking at her own culture which intensified her capacity to conjure strangeness out of the familiar. She also deepened her contact with the Surrealist movement at this time, through French exiles from *les évènements* of 1968 who had fetched up in Japan. On her return, she examined various English sacred cows as well as the style of the times (from scarlet lipstick to stockings in D. H. Lawrence) in her wonderfully pungent articles (collected as *Nothing Sacred* in 1982).

Two novels arose from her time in Japan, though they do not deal with Japan directly: *The Infernal Desire Machines of Doctor Hoffman* (1972) and *The Passion of New Eve* (1977), in which contemporary conflicts are transmuted into bizarre, multiple, picaresque allegories. Though she never won the bestseller fortunes of some of her contemporaries (she would reflect ruefully that it was still a Boys' Club out there, and did not *really* mind much), and was never selected for one of the major prizes, she enjoyed greater international esteem: her name tells from Denmark to Australia, and she was repeatedly invited to teach – accepting invitations from Sheffield (1976–8), Brown University, Providence (1980–1), the University of Adelaide (1984), and the University of East Anglia (1984–7). She helped change the course of postwar writing in English – her influence reaches from Salman Rushdie to Jeanette Winterson to American fabulists like Robert Coover.

Distance from England helped her lay bare women's collusion with their own subjection. In the new collection of her criticism, *Expletives Deleted*, she remembers, 'I spent a good many years being told what I ought to think, and how I ought to behave . . . because I was a woman . . . but then I stopped listening to them [men] and . . . I started answering back.'[2] Angela was never someone to offer an easy answer, and in her frankness she was important to the feminist movement: she liked to quote, semi-ironically, 'Dirty work – but someone has to do it' when talking about facing hard truths, and she would say of someone, in a spirit of approval, 'S/He doesn't temper the wind to the new-shorn lamb.' Her publisher and friend Carmen Callil published her at Virago and her presence there since the start of the house helped establish a woman's voice in literature as special, as *parti pris*, as a crucial instrument in the forging of an identity for post-imperial, hypocritical, fossilised Britain. For in spite of her keen-eyed, even cynical grasp of reality, Angela Carter always believed in change: she'd refer to her 'naive leftie-ism', but she never let go of it.

The American critic Susan Suleiman has celebrated Angela Carter's fiction as truly breaking new ground for women by occupying the male voice of narrative authority and at the same time impersonating it to the point of parody, so that the rules are changed and the dreams become unruly, transformed, open to 'the multiplication of narrative possibilities', themselves a promise of a possibly different future; the novels also 'expand our notions of what it is possible to dream in the domain of sexuality, criticizing all dreams that are too narrow'.[3] Angela's favourite icon of the feminine was Lulu, in Wedekind's play, and her favourite star was Louise Brooks who played her in *Pandora's Box*; Louise/Lulu was hardly someone who rejected traditional femaleness, but rather took it to such extremes that its nature was transformed. 'Lulu's character is very attractive to me,' she would say drily, and she borrowed from it to create her wanton, rumbustious and feisty heroines of the boards in *Wise Children*. Lulu never ingratiated herself, never sought fame, or fortune, and suffered neither guilt nor remorse. According to Angela, 'her particular quality is, she makes being polymorphously perverse look like the only way to be'. If she had had a daughter, she once said, she would have called her Lulu.

She liked to refer to her opinions as 'classic GLC' but in spite of these demurrals she was an original and committed political thinker too. *Wise Children* (1989) was born out of her democratic and socialist utopianism, her affirmation of 'low' culture, of the rude health of popular language and humour as a long-lasting, effective means of survival: her Shakespeare (the novel contains almost all his characters and their plots in one form or another) isn't a poet for the elite, but an imagination springing out of folklore, with energy and know-how.

She found happiness with Mark Pearce, who was training to become a primary schoolteacher when she became ill. She often spoke of the radiance of children, their unutterable beauty and their love; their son Alexander was born in 1983.

Sometimes, in the case of a great writer, it's easy to lose sight of the pleasure they give, as critics search for meaning and value, influence and importance; Angela Carter loved cinema and vaudeville and songs and the circus, and she herself could entertain like no other. She included a story from Kenya in *The Virago Book of Fairy Tales* about a sultana who is withering away while a poor man's wife is kept happy because her husband feeds her 'meat of the tongue' – stories, jokes, ballads. These are what make women thrive, the story says; they are also what Angela Carter gave so generously to make others thrive. *Wise Children* ends with the words, 'What a joy it is to dance and sing!' That she should not have thrived herself is sad beyond words.

Since her death, tributes have filled the papers and the airwaves. She would have been astonished by the attention, and pleased. It did not come to her in her lifetime, not with such wholeheartedness. It's partly a tribute to her potency that while she was alive people felt discomfited by her, that her wit and witchiness and subversiveness made her hard to handle, like some wonderful beast of the kind she enjoyed in fairy tales. Her friends were lucky knowing her, and her readers too. We have been left a feast and she laid it out with 'spread fingers' for us to share.

1992

The Inexpressible Closeness of the Deer

On the film, Institute Benjamenta

The Quay Brothers were brought up near the city of Philadelphia in the Fifties, and they used to be taken to western Pennsylvania during the summer. Their father and his brother would go hunting in the Poconoes, the small mountain range nearby, and that's where the Quays first saw – or rather heard – the deer whose fugitive trace haunts *Institute Benjamenta*. The hunting wasn't often successful: they don't remember male rituals of bloodying or slaughter, just 'the pine needles' smell, the cones, a glimpse of a tail, the sound of the animal crashing through the undergrowth – the mysterious presence of the deer'.

In the film, the brothers' first full use of live action and their first feature, the schoolmistress, Lisa Benjamenta, carries a cane: it has a tiny delicate cloven pointed doe's hoof at the end of a violin bow. Part teacher's ruler, part dominatrix's crop, part shaman's wand, it draws attention to the heroine's vulnerability, the deer-like mystery of creatureliness that Alice Krige's enraptured performance and gentle beauty bring out superbly. But the forest and its hidden inhabitants are also made present within the walls of the enigmatic Institute in other, uncanny details: in the single hoof under the trouser cuff of Herr Benjamenta, the Institute's director and Lisa's brother, who behaves ominously as if he were rather more than kin to her. There are the gleaming birch trunks, too, which the hero, Jakob (Mark Rylance), sees when he penetrates beyond the permitted boundaries. And he also finds there a glass bell jar with a small faucet and the inscription, 'Ejaculate of deer, please sniff.' The brothers took scrapings of deer antlers to create the pile of dust under the glass: horn has an acrid, carnal smell, as hair does too when it burns. Not long after, as Jakob peeps through the keyhole into these secret 'inner chambers', he sees a pair of deer rutting.

'We wanted the building itself to be the narrator,' say the brothers, 'dreaming itself, so to speak, dreaming its own existence, in the kind of fairy-tale voice which is telling the story of its past lives. Our idea was that it had once been a perfumery, and after that a museum of fragrances', where deer musk would have been collected to bind more elusive scents. It becomes in Jakob's explorings a kind of memory palace, full of doors, mirrors, deep stairwells, and upper storeys; its layout now vertiginous, now alveolar, and made all the more off-balance and phantom-like for being modelled after a baroque church interior turned topsy-turvy, so the vaults become ledges, the windows exits and entrances.

Institute Benjamenta was inspired by *Jacob van Gunten*, the 1908 masterpiece of Robert Walser, a Swiss writer whose irony, madness and lonely pathos made a significant difference to many who followed (including Kafka, of course, Hermann Hesse and Beckett, too).[1] Walser committed himself to an asylum in 1929; there he continued to write, tiny pregnant texts in a microscopic script that was only deciphered recently. But in 1933 he fell silent, saying he was 'not here to write but to be mad' and died aged seventy-eight, on Christmas Day 1956 when out for a walk on his own in the snow.

Walser was first translated into English by Christopher Middleton in the Sixties; his reception has been very divided – into 'wild enthusiasts' (including Susan Sontag) and 'those who have never heard of him', say the twins. They add that his case reminds them of the entry in Kafka's journals when he goes to the bookseller and asks how many copies have been sold of his book. 'It's selling well, Kafka's told. Twelve copies. Kafka goes back and writes in his diary, "I bought eleven, so who was it who bought the remaining one?"'

The Quay Brothers, in their famous puppet films (*That Unnameable Little Broom*; *The Street of Crocodiles*), have ventured into the forest of fairy tale before; with *The Comb*, their first (short) to mix puppets with live action, they told a similar story of an enchanted sleep: there, it's the witch's poisoned comb that has stricken the beauty. Walser wrote 'Antifairytales': a 'Cindcrclla' in which Cinderella is in love with her degradation, and begs the sisters to persist in their cruelties towards her. His writings offered the brothers an absurdist, poignant, claustrophobic scenario of enigma and wonder that has brought out their finest, and most passionate work to date. With puppets they condensed an atmosphere of eerie remoteness; the faces of very fine actors held in absorptive close-up (as well as Rylance and Krige, there's the expressive Daniel Smith) enhance the eerie, slumbrous mood, as the camera captures the near-invisible pulsations in a cheek, an eyelid, a nostril.

Ever since the brothers were at the Royal College of Art and began travelling in Europe, they have followed an original bent in their tastes – visual, musical and literary. An early fascination for the graphics of 'Eastern Europe' took them to Poland and Czechoslovakia in the Sixties and Seventies, and in turn developed their affinity with the poets and ironists and melancholics of the landlocked, forested cities of continental Europe – with Kafka and Bruno Schultz, with composers like Janáček and fabulists like Walser. There is little Mediterranean about the Quay Brothers' sensibility: they are urban nightwalkers, drawn to shadows and the pools of light under street lamps, not to sunshine. *Institute Benjamenta* is all sooty velvets and flashes of silver – a sudden gush of water shines like crystal. Every careful frame reveals their love and knowledge of the still photography of such monochrome masters as Boiffard and Kertész as well as the films of Hans Richter and Man Ray. Not since Stieglitz's prints and Cocteau's shimmering cinema has there been such polychrome tone in black and white.

In three very short earlier films, also in black and white, the Quays began to explore the themes of *Institute Benjamenta*. Called *Stille Nacht I, II, III*, they visualise, in highly compressed symbolism, a particular trauma of the deer forest. For when the brothers were designing Tchaikovsky's opera *Mazeppa* in Bregenz in Austria, they found themselves surrounded by the mythology of the hunt; they ate venison (for the first time) in restaurants decorated with stag heads with the date of death chiselled ('very beautifully') into their skulls. The brothers became fascinated with trophies in which the animal had a crumpled horn – one antler stunted and fallen – and they found one or two mounted examples in antique shops. Handbooks they read speculated that the antlers are maimed when the animal is shot in the groin, emasculated but not killed; the release of testosterone is halted, and as a result, the antlers fail to grow symmetrically any longer.

For the brothers, Herr Benjamenta was this kind of stag; and the killing – and injuring – of deer for uses like the mounting of trophies and the making of perfumes provides an underlying metaphor, only hintingly introduced, of the role of the cadets, the self-castrating male students of the Institute.

The Institute Benjamenta itself is a school for servants: Walser was obsessed with nullity, with abjection. Jakob frequently exults in how 'very small and subordinate' he and his fellow-pupils are becoming through training: 'We are small, small, all the way down to utter worthlessness.' He is aiming to be a prize pupil and such a specimen is 'a big round zero, nothing more', full of 'the zeal to serve'. Catching the Christian humility of Walser's ideal, the brothers have enshrined a crown of thorns with the rubric, 'The Beatification of Zero', for one of the background props in the film. When Jakob enrols, voluntarily, in the dilapidated Institute, he's first inspected like horseflesh, like a slave, by the Director (for this set the brothers used the photographic and measuring equipment of the forensic pioneer, Marcel Bertillon, chief of police in Paris at the turn of the nineteenth century, who attempted to classify all criminal types from their physiognomy), and he then joins the reduced class of six others. One of the most haunting – and funny – sequences, which reaches a tragicomic pitch of mock solemnity, shows the seven students performing to a haunting jazz waltz (part of the evocative score by the Polish composer Leszek Jankowski). In a kind of t'ai chi dance, they learn to bow and scrape, twirling napkins and handling imaginary dishes. They also practise useful phrases: 'Madame la Duchesse,' they parrot, 'there is a fire in the nursery.' They learn to use a fork properly. Walser himself went to a school for servants in Berlin, and worked in a castle in Silesia as a valet, 'Monsieur Robert'. In the film, the school motto proclaims, 'The rules have thought of everything.'

Christopher Middleton, Walser's translator and editor, has written, 'In the case of Robert Walser one might think of the acrobat and his wobble, or of the bicyclist's inconspicuous, near-miraculous recoveries of balance . . . Walser was able to sustain his own exhilarating kinetic wobble through self-doubt, despair, nightmare, and spates of stubborn work.' He was like a *puer aeternus*, in Middleton's view, an enchanted child-adult who refuses to grow up and then, when he realises he is old, goes mad. In the film, we see the reverent, hopeful, innocent Jakob discovering that the central focus of the fabulous inner sanctum of the school is a goldfish bowl, which he has to clean out daily.

The Quay Brothers have been droll and wry and glum before; in the true spirit of Surrealism they have revealed the ordinary magic from everyday life, its humdrum enchantments and humdrum disenchantments. But with *Institute Benjamenta*, the brothers' work pierces through to the nerves in a new way, stirring depths of sexual curiosity and emotional unease. For in spite of the lessons in repression and self-abasement at the Institute Benjamenta, feelings flare painfully: loss, loneliness, yearning. Lisa becomes the object of the students' infatuation, and in a gaggle at her door, they sing lullabies to her (the actors remembered ones from their own, varied, polyglot childhoods); clownish, clumsy, a group of ancient and haggard boys, the students at this moment in the film come closest to capturing the character of the 'dwarfs' in the fairy tale who attend the frozen Snow White (before Disney turned them into jolly chappies). The film is subtitled, 'Or This Dream Called Life', and, like the fiction of Middle Europe, its humour conceals tragic allegories.

Lisa's end is not only lyrical (a tour de force of a fairy-tale death) but genuinely moving. As in *The Lady of Shalott*, the spell which held everything in place breaks when she begins to reciprocate Jakob's love – and she breaks too with the strain of it. With her melting, the school's order crumbles.

In the history of cinema, almost nothing divides the traditions of anglophone and continental entertainment more sharply than the handling of fantasy: even the most inventive films (e.g. *Time Bandits* or *The Fisher King*) aim primarily at kids. By contrast, a film-maker like Jan Švankmajer, a clear mentor of the Brothers Quay and a subject of one of their shorts, has directed mixed puppet and live action in his *Alice in Wonderland* and his *Faust* with an unsettling fierceness that isn't really intended to appeal to children, or certainly not exclusively to children. The literary fabulists and ironists of Prague and Sarajevo and Vienna, like Kafka, like Karel Čapek in the Thirties, and, more recently, Danilo Kiš and Milan Kundera, never treat traditional fairy-tale material as childish, and so stories like 'Snow White' and 'Sleeping Beauty' haven't suffered in their part of the forest from Disneyfication, aren't put down as juvenile – even infantile – wish-fulfilment. Walser knew how desperately serious such longings can be: one of the Institute's maxims is 'Work more, Wish less.' In a desert of British costume drama and realist comedy, the Quays have remained intransigently loyal to an aesthetic tradition of inward, spectral fantasy; they say that 'the overall feel we want evoked by this film, this fairy tale, is a kind of in-between world halfway between sleep and wakefulness, simultaneously between the two'.

When one of the servants comes back to the Institute after failing in a job in the world, he tells the others, 'There's nothing beautiful and excellent left. You must dream up beauty and goodness and justice. Tell me, do you know how to dream?' Walser's dreams, like *Institute Benjamenta*, aren't sweet, though, or consoling. He could adopt the voice of a mother who's abandoning her child in the forest, so that he will learn to survive, learn to please. The forest is a school too; and fairy tales reveal, in glimpses, the risks and the bliss of going astray there.

1995

Hoopoe: Ted Hughes

Ted Hughes's poetry is often fierce; and what is fierce in literature for children is the quality that stamps *Beowulf* and Euripides and Seneca and Dante – and the Shakespeare of *Titus Andronicus*; it erupts as a pleasure of poetry from 'human passion *in extremis*', a phrase Hughes uses in the Introduction to *Tales from Ovid* (1997). Fierceness runs through grotesque and terrible acts born from the extremes of the fantastic: Grendel and his mother the mere-wife's bloodthirsty raids, mothers' cold-blooded murders of their own babies, cannibal banquets. Ted Hughes reinhabited this mythic, epic and heroic tradition in many ways in his varied work, not only in the writing for children. But his encounter with Ovid, in his versions of the *Metamorphoses*, seems to have beaten, purified and annealed his own fierceness to a new, intense radiance. It would not be putting it too strongly to say that Hughes found in Ovid a form of psychic spiritual control, someone with whom he could expose his own terrors and passions unguardedly, through whom he could speak without sounding a note of anachronistic atavism.

To do this, like any sibling, he had to overlook some qualities of his model: his tone is less urbane than Ovid's, his comedy more ghastly, his lines are less measured (they are hacked and splintered, often to go with the stories), and the glaze on the language is more raku than slipware. But *Tales from Ovid* is thrilling poetry, with the magic capacity to strip the listener/reader of all defences and catch us up in the tale as a child is carried on the rhythm of a line of verse to stare with wide eyes, whispering 'and what then?' as the story unfolds.

The present collection of *Metamorphoses* seemed to be caught in mid-flight when it appeared. I hoped there would be more and I'd assumed there would be, soon enough, though when I look back, I realise that the poet, if he had not known he was gravely ill, would probably have created a visible, shapely conclusion to the book before publishing it. It would have alighted towards the end, come full circle from the ectoplasmic origins evoked at the beginning. Ovid's final hymn to the Pythagorean credo of cyclical transformation and renewal would surely have summoned Hughes to his most Prospero-like enchantments. As it is, however, very near the end of *Tales from Ovid*, Hughes's magnificent rendering of 'Tereus' appears. This is usually thought of as the myth of Philomela, the nightingale, who was brutally violated, tortured and muted by Tereus, her brother-in-law, and 'has infested poetry ever since', as Francis Celoria comments caustically in his valuable edition of another mythographer, Antoninus Liberalis. Indeed, Ted Hughes refers to the traditional heroine twice in the Introduction, reminding us that in *Cymbeline*, Imogen is reading the tale in bed when Iachimo steals in to rape her; he also describes *Titus Andronicus* as the most Ovidian of Shakespeare's plays, and it is of course the one in which Lavinia is raped and maimed to the pattern of Philomela. But Hughes's version rightly singles out Tereus as the protagonist, the malefactor, the prime subject of transformation therapy, and his myth seems to have become, for Ted Hughes, the most Ovidian of Ovid's *Metamorphoses*.

Ovid doesn't offer any systematic classification for his transmutations. Telling 'how bodies are changed/ Into different bodies' (as Hughes renders the first line) explains the cosmos, its origins, its relations, its purposes along Pythagorean lines, with souls surviving through time and migrating across genera: this principle, with its full freight of anti-Christian significance, can often be glimpsed in Hughes's poetry. But the changes of shape come in several kinds: benign, when the god or goddess expresses pity for a mortal and saves the victim through a transformation (Daphne turned into a laurel to save her from Apollo's pursuit); malign, when the metamorphosis punishes a culprit for presumption or folly; or, magical, as in 'Erysichthon', whose daughter possesses the gift of protean shape-shifting and can therefore escape at will in any form from the clients to whom her father panders her.

The story of Tereus and Philomela and Procne appears in Ovid towards the end of Book VI, in a group of tales containing some of the fiercest, most arbitrary and most horrifying of divine acts of vengeful rage, including Arachne's transformation into a spider by Minerva and Apollo's flaying of another unwise artist, the satyr Marsyas. But interestingly, it combines all the different effects of Ovidian metamorphosis, for when Procne is turned into a swallow 'with the blood still on her breast' and tongueless Philomela becomes a nightingale, the sisters escape from the story, from the likelihood of further bloodshed and violence: it is as if Oedipus and Jocasta had been spirited away by Sophocles and changed into doves rather than meeting their pitiless ends. And Philomela, whose tongue has been cut out, is rewarded when she discovers, outside the frame of the poem, the sweetest voice with which to mourn on behalf of human loss and folly (Keats is almost unique in hearing joy, not lamentation, in the nightingale's song). As for Tereus, the incestuous rapist, mutilator and liar, as he pursues the sisters with sword drawn for vengeance, he finds himself unmanned, changed into a hoopoe, a bird whom Ovid clearly thinks of as distinguished for its look of violence with its long hooked beak and plumed helmet crest. So Tereus, too, is saved from the further consequences of his savage nature: his metamorphosis debases him, but gives him a place where he can no longer continue to do the harm he did as a man.

How does Ted Hughes write this fairy-tale reprieve? The sisters are fleeing Tereus:

> He came after them and they
> Who had been running seemed to be flying.
>
> And suddenly they were flying. One swerved
> On wings into the forest,
> The other, with the blood still on her breast,
> Flew up under the eaves of the palace.
> Then Tereus, charging blind
> In his delirium of grief and vengeance,
>
> No longer caring what happened –
> He too was suddenly flying.
> On his head and shoulders a crest of feathers,
> Instead of a sword a long curved beak –
> Like a warrior transfigured
> With battle-frenzy dashing into a battle.

Ovid's verbs pack less action: the sisters only hang from their wings, not swerve ('pendebant pennis'); the nightingale merely seeks the woods ('petit . . . silvas'); Tereus is 'velox' – swift – from grief, but governs no verb or active voice, being passively transformed ('vertitur in volucrem'). The vivid and impassioned simile of Hughes's last two lines with their hammering of the word 'battle' expands three very simple, even dull, words of Ovid's ('facies armata videtur') into a hectic, heightened image of a man berserk. (Hughes the naturalist also corrects, silently, Ovid's apparent belief that nightingales have red breasts!)

Ted Hughes's own process of metamorphosis points up throughout the Ovidian originals with fresh colour, taut rhythms, bright percussion (was he a Stravinsky, rescoring a Handel?). His English diction syncopates the sonorities of the Latin, catches the hexameter's long breath. But not all is louder and brighter and more pent up: the final stanza of his 'Tereus' reveals the enthralling quietness of his voice when he wanted to draw out the shape of the myth and modulate the screams and bellows of its mayhem to a mood of redemptive elegy:

> He had become a hoopoe.
> Philomela
> Mourned in the forest, a nightingale.
> Procne
> Lamented round and round the palace,
> A swallow.

These lines don't appear in Ovid, except as ghosts flitting between them.

Metamorphoses deny death and fold time; they bring ancient stories into everyday scenery and populate the landscape with living characters: to Pythagorean ears, Philomela doesn't only escape murder, she lives on in every nightingale. For Ted Hughes, time bent back against itself through poetry in the same way as Ovid's phenomena of nature are cast into new shapes by original miracles that suspended nature's laws. He commented that Ovid was interested in 'passion where it combusts, or levitates, or mutates into an experience of the supernatural', and that Tereus' tale is one in which 'mortal passion makes the breakthrough by sheer excess, without divine intervention'.

These birds haunted Hughes. On the bottles of Laureate's sack for which he had commissioned a label, there appeared his watercolour of the crested hoopoe with its long curved beak: for Ted Hughes, Crow had been supplanted. When I noticed this and began thinking about what the myth of Tereus meant to him, I wrote a kind of fairy-tale short story called 'Lullaby for an Insomniac Princess', about trying to hear the song of the nightingale; on an impulse I sent it to Ted Hughes, in August 1998, because there seemed to be a connection. He wrote back.

> Not sure I've ever heard a nightingale – or seen one. I've always lived beyond the bird's pale. Thousands of hours in woods at night – never heard a note. Once in S. Yorks. rumour went through the school that there was a nightingale in some woodland near Conisborough. (Rather as you now hear the 'beast' has been sighted in some copse round here.) Groups of enthusiasts were going out there. Eventually, I sat in there for a couple [of] hours and finally heard 3 piercing notes – but I could swear they were the squeals of dry brakes in the shunting yard down below the wood. That's as close as I've been.
>
> I see there are only 4,000 nightingales left. But then. Friend of mine 20 years in Australia came back last week – visited me yesterday and almost his first words were 'where are all the birds?' Then 'I was three days in London before I saw my first sparrow.' I've sat all afternoon in the orchard near the fountain that used to be crowded all day with birds. I didn't see a single bird till about 7 pm then a magpie flew across. Strange?

When the letter came I had no idea how ill he was, so I didn't understand till later why silence was on his mind.

1999

Myth and Faerie: Rewritings and Recoveries

Talk given in French for the colloquium, 'Où en est-on avec la théorie littéraire?' ('Literary theory: where is it at?'), University of Paris VIII.

What does myth mean today? Why the renewal of mythic themes in contemporary literature? How can the return to myth be understood? These are questions that arise from the success of Ovidian and other mythic rewritings, for example, and from the current interest in stories of hauntings, possession and vampirism. The old terms, 'magic realism' and *el maravilloso latino* ('the Latin American marvellous'), do not take us far enough: they give the impression that the uses of the supernatural correspond to the classical device of deus ex machina. Or rather, they lay claim to an authenticity of Otherness stamped Indian, or Latin American, and promise a kind of living, teeming local colour, associated with the exoticism ascribed to those places and their inhabitants.

Literary theory has sketched certain responses in its attempt to grasp the character and the meaning of this contemporary resurgence of the marvellous in the fabulism of many writers today, as it springs up in a world that is disenchanted and torn between religious fundamentalisms on the one hand and neo-Darwinian turbo-charged capitalism on the other. A paradox soon emerges: it's among writers who are most alert to the dangers of religious convictions and moral certainties that contemporary myths are thriving. For example, in the work of Salman Rushdie, who has good reason to suspect anything associated with belief and faith, and, similarly, in the fiction of Toni Morrison, who has explored the nearly forgotten history and lives of black people in the United States since slavery; in her remarkable essays, *Playing in the Dark*, Morrison reveals the hypocrisy and bad faith of the great and the good, including the Churches and the creators of American liberties.[1] Two spirits working in the tradition of the Enlightenment, it might appear, two fierce critics of their societies and their times, two novelists whose writings seethe with predestined fates, destinies, fairy-tale incidents, ghostly apparitions, spellbound characters, clairvoyance, poltergeists, angelic and diabolical portents and prodigies – in Morrison's *Beloved* (1987) and *Paradise* (1998), and in Rushdie's *The Ground Beneath Her Feet* (1999).

The marvellous today no longer has anything to do with belief, nor even with the sacred, it seems. It draws on fairies, nymphs, fauns, legendary characters who populate classical literature from Homer to Mallarmé, and its construction follows traditional storytelling ideas about fatality and divine providence. André Breton's *merveilleux banal* ('marvellous banality') has been mixed into the recipe, with the result that the supernatural and the prodigious play a part that is purely literary rather than spiritual, a homage to Surrealism, not to metaphysics. These developments have inspired, as I said, diverse theoretical approaches.

First, post-colonial literary theory emphasises that this way of telling a story, disrupting the rules of verisimilitude, represents above all a political manoeuvre: lost histories are retrieved from a home-grown repertory of narrative which was once upon a time neglected and even held in contempt. This folklore tradition was relegated among marginal groups, kept apart from canonical literature, with the *desaparecidos* (disappeared ones) in the long history of Western power, and, closer to hand, down among the children, servants, old people. Traditional, popular stories were dismissed as mere *bagatelles* and *sornettes*, trifles and pieces of nonsense, Donkeyskin and Mother Goose tales, even by their very first literary exponents, the first French writers of fairy tales, Charles Perrault, Marie-Catherine d'Aulnoy, Marie-Jeanne L'Héritier, towards the end of the seventeenth century and the beginning of the eighteenth.

But nearer to ourselves and our own times, Caribbean writers in English, Spanish as well as French are evoking a tradition that precedes the colonial era, which has been able to survive on the sidelines, *métissée*, mixed and mingled, but nevertheless irreducible. Similar riches can be found in the novels of the Nigerian poet and psychopomp, Ben Okri, who speaks through his alter ego, an abuki or spirit child condemned to an eternal return to life on this earth. In the work of Maryse Condé, retrieval has meant that she inverts received values and the condemnations of colonial rulers: in *I Tituba*, she reclaims the words and spells of the slave who was accused at Salem of being the source of many of the ills attributed to the enchantment from which the small town was suffering. Yes indeed, Maryse Condé agrees, taking pride in Tituba.

Fiction has become a vehicle of recovering memories that have been effaced by the conquerors of history: where documents no longer exist, imagination provides new witnesses. Myth and faerie, perceived as survivals from ancient oral culture (orature), long despised as suspect and even ignorant atavism, and consequently identified with women, children and primitive peoples, rediscover a special affinity with the unfettered, self-generated fantasy and offer the means to reinhabit the lived experience of the Other – of exiles, slaves, the disappeared.

But stories and words rediscovered and retrieved in this way never truly are restored: in the transition to text, they become an invented language. They even imitate the forms of writing while making a show of moving beyond them. Nevertheless, the imagined oral source acts as the warranty of truth – an effect Foucault has analysed, erasing the author as master, and giving voice to anonymous phantoms drawn by the victors' historical chronicles. These stories take up habitation in gaps in time, in the large shadowy places of the past. According to Homi Bhabha's famous dictum, 'Nation is narration.' The Other of the past here puts in place the Self of the present.

Salman Rushdie suggests, in *The Ground Beneath Her Feet*, that the tripartite model of human society proposed by Georges Dumézil should be increased to include a fourth function: besides sovereignty, priestly or wisdom power, and fertility, he would add . . . 'non-belongers', people on the margins, homeless, refugees, those who have nowhere to call their own, outcasts, outlaws, freaks, tramps. Characteristically, Rushdie gives an exuberantly long list of candidates.[2] They inhabit literature, he writes, as their familiar dwelling place; literature needs to invent them, readers to hear their voices.

At this point, a political theory about the resurgence of myth intersects with a rather more aesthetic approach: the book becomes a parallel world (and *The Ground Beneath Her Feet* self-consciously reflects on its own existence) where the homeless find shelter. The return to faerie, allegory and fantasy turns fiction into the pre-eminent place of imagination and of writers' freedom. The novelist demonstrates that he – or she – can make anything at all, can play with anything and everything, can create new worlds, and master anything whatsoever through the autonomy of language. Paradoxically, the legacy of the Enlightenment, positing rational human beings who observe and order the flux of phenomena through the power of cognitive reasoning, rises again in the reconfigured form of a magician of language, imposing a despotic subjective vision on his (or her) public. As Rushdie expresses it, through the voice of his hero, the singer Ormus Cama: 'Everything must be made real, step by step, he tells himself. This is a mirage, a ghost world, which becomes real only beneath our magic touch, our loving footfall, our kiss. We have to imagine it into being, from the ground up.' Here we see in play the poetic art of the novelist: the world is a mirage or a ghost, which can only come into being from the ground up through acts of creative imagination. Is it possible to find, in this process of rewriting myths and fairy tales, the ideal that Félix Guattari invoked when he dreamed of a transformation of the planet from a living hell for more than three-quarters of its population into a universe of creative enchantments?[3]

At the same time however, these two attempts at unfolding the new relation to myth – one political, the other aesthetic – do not tackle the ontological question raised by the current return to magic, portents and enchantments, to signs and wonders, to fated outcomes and malevolent interventions which recur in the contemporary fiction of the highest literary ambitiousness as well as in popular fantasy fiction obsessed with spells and spirit possession, vampires and zombies, such as the novels of Stephen King and Anne Rice (highly rated as literature of course, in many quarters). The World Wide Web, needless to say, reveals inextinguishable famishing for the fantastic. And I should admit that I share this fascination. Along with Goya (that great painter of Reason and its enemies), I can say, 'I want you to know that I do not fear witches, spirits, ghosts, braggard giants, malignant or villainous demons etc. and that among every kind of creature, it is only the human species who make me afraid.'

But at the same time, creatures of the imagination, the trooping fairies in classical literature and in writing for children today, have always fascinated me and continue to do so. I recently published a critical study, *No Go the Bogeyman*, about ogres, night visitors, watchers and stalkers, werewolves and every kind of devil, the kind of nursery horrors who give thrills and shivers of pleasure and fear. These mixed feelings seem to me peculiarly modern in character; in the tradition of the awe and terror excited by the sublime, they no longer aim to arouse pity – *pietà*, or compassion through identification – but instead to cow and overwhelm the receiver to feel the pleasure of submission to greater powers.

I would like to draft a different analysis here, to try and pick out of this renewal of the mythic a model of human consciousness and a new placing of the individual in a historical perspective – for this charting of mental processes has been fiction's own terrain since at least the seventeenth century. The model I am going to look at is still being developed and so I can't offer an exact or clear solution, since, as I shall try to show, the significant aspect of this present rewriting of the idea of a person aims precisely at dissolving the subject, at evoking the self's fragmented and scattered condition. There's no possibility, for example, that the magical elements in a story by Rushdie or Angela Carter represent an attack on scepticism on their part, a return to belief (to credulity), that the anger of Nietzsche against the notion of another world continues to resonate, without answering echo. Neither the angel-woman Fevvers, from Carter's 1984 novel *Nights at the Circus*, nor the prophet-angel Gibreel from *The Satanic Verses*, takes on the role of an otherworldly being as established in the mystical tradition of the Bible, of Milton, or of Blake. (And we know of course that this very irony with respect of the Koran instigated the fatwa against Rushdie.) The ironical humour of both Rushdie and Carter of course puts question marks around everything they write, but it's fair to say that the marvellous beings in their fictions aren't the principal targets of their mockery.

With Toni Morrison, by contrast, it's more difficult to assess the relationship between belief and metaphysical occurrences – I don't mean her own personal point of view, but the status of the supernatural in her novels. For example, towards the end of *Paradise* – an ironical title, of course, but to what extent? – a group of women gifted with special powers form a ritual circle in order to prophesy. Their activities are described with complete seriousness:

> In the beginning the most important thing was the template. First they had to scrub the cellar floor till its stones were as clean as rocks on a shore. Then they ringed the place with candles. Consolata told each to undress and lie down . . . When each found the position she could tolerate on the cold, uncompromising floor, Consolata walked around her and painted the body's silhouette. Once the outlines were complete, each was instructed to remain there. Unspeaking. Naked in candlelight . . .
> That is how the loud dreaming began.[4]

At the end of the novel, murder victims from its beginning reappear: are they revenants who walk and talk in this world, like the ghost of Hamlet's father? Or do they resemble those spectres so widely featured at the checkout counter in American supermarkets – in papers such as the *National Inquirer* – of undead idols such as Elvis and James Dean and Princess Diana, who are continually being sighted by visionaries of the New Age? Or are they rather internal spectres who haunt the social group who destroyed them, and who consequently feel individual and collective guilt? (*Our Vampires, Ourselves*, as in the title of a perceptive study of gothic by Nina Auerbach.) Or, finally, since the apparitions in *Paradise* reassure the survivors by saying that they are doing very well in their new life, are they allegorical figures of forgetting, of bad faith in the United States where a feel-good, bland culture reiterating 'Have a nice day' spreads itself over all, covering up any painful perception of responsibility?

Toni Morrison offers few clues, except that she tends to overturn expectations and juggle terms: she likes to claim that daily realities have taken the place of metaphysics. She closes *Paradise* with an image of travellers, new arrivals landing on this earth: 'Now they will rest before shouldering the endless work they were created to do down here in Paradise.' Elsewhere she writes, 'God is not a mystery. We are.'

But it seems to me too easy an epigram and too self-flattering a formula to accept.

Myth gives legitimacy to invented memories: as Adrienne Rich reminds us, memory is an unreliable narrator ('Memory says, Don't count on me'). The revenants in the novel *Paradise*, the magical protagonists of *Midnight's Children*, the spirits and phantoms in Ben Okri's *The Famished Road* don't ask us to accept a new faith from a religious perspective – the very thought raises a smile. They accustom us rather to a new way of telling the story of the past and introduce us into a new relation between human beings, time and space. Rushdie exults in inventing tangled plots, interweaving multiple coincidences, predestination, fatal and grotesque trajectories (sometimes with rather uncomfortable gallows humour). The plot of *The Ground Beneath Her Feet* swarms with telepathic lovers and families, catastrophes foretold but ineluctable, divine, titanic characters. He isn't satisfied with a single pair of twins in the protagonist's family, one of whom dies at birth. He brings on a second pair, of whom the younger has been hit on the head by a cricket ball bowled by his own father: the improbability of this accident, which plunges the victim into perpetual silence, provokes laughter as it is no doubt intended to do. Rushdie directs his storytelling in the spirit of the *Arabian Nights*' fantasies and in the footsteps of dandyish tale-spinners such as Baron von Munchhausen, inventor of impossibly tall stories where the marvellous appears in fantastic, hyperbolic guise. (The true ultimate ancestor of this genre of the marvellous comic, blithe and learned, is Lucian and his *True History*, written in the second century AD.)

Rushdie thumbs his nose at his own methods of inspiring wonder, he makes jokes at his own expense as he tells his stories. But he also draws tirelessly on an eclectic range of mythological sources, in which gods or capricious genies conduct from above the fates of creatures down below. *Haroun and the Sea of Stories*, a story for children written in 1990, his first publication after the fatwa, and one of the most accomplished, delightful and powerful writings in Rushdie's opus, concludes with the defeat of the evil power of a tyrant. It's an optimistic allegory, written against the odds, in a spirit of hope against hope, and it stages the triumph of a male Scheherazade over a spell that would silence his voice for ever. In *The Ground Beneath Her Feet*, the Hindu pantheon jostles among Greek gods: Ormus Cama incorporates both Orpheus and Armuz, a god from Aryan mythology, along with characteristics of John Lennon. Rushdie invokes without apology the old Aryan speculations of the scholar Max Müller about the resonances between the ancient cycles of Indian and classical myth. However, Rushdie does reveal from time to time a certain unease with the expansiveness of his own mythological imagination. His characters, the hero as well as the narrator of the novel, express their withdrawal from, even repudiation of, the supposed spiritual riches of India, which are so enthusiastically cherished by Westerners. The narrator, who, as a photographer, tends to realistic narrative, announces that he himself adopts 'a sternly rationalist line': 'Every so often our deep spiritualism leads us to massacre one another like wild beasts. Excuse me, but some of us aren't falling for it, some of us are trying to break free into the real.'

The ideal quest for 'the real' possesses this character of the diaspora, one of the alter egos of the author. Later, it's Ormus Cama, the protagonist and singer, who feels rationalist disgust for mythophiles: 'This England [of the Sixties] addled by mysticism, mesmerised by the miraculous, the psychotropic, in love with alien gods, had begun to horrify him . . . A revolt against the damage, the waste . . . the swallowing of various forms of gibberish that has replaced the exercise of intelligence, the susceptibility to gurus and other phoney leaders, the flight from reason . . .' But Rushdie himself can't give up the extravagant fantasies of the gods of India, nor of the prodigy-ridden mythology of Western classicism. The myth of Orpheus and Eurydice, for example, gives the novel its dominant theme and structure.

Let's return for the moment to the question with which I began: what can it mean, since neither Rushdie nor Carter nor figures like Roberto Calasso (one of the foremost mythographers of our time) present themselves to their readers as priests of the irrational, preaching adherence to an ancient faith in enchantment and magic? (Rushdie knows too well the cost of religions reinvigorated in the crucible of ethnic nationalisms) So to throw more light on this dilemma, let's go back to literary theory. In an article which appeared in the volume, *Myth and the Making of Modernity*, Steven Connor analysed the 'vocalic uncanny', his evocative expression for the Orphic turn that modernist works have taken, giving expression to voices of disincarnate characters which then resonate directly from the page: Connor invokes James Joyce, and *The Waves* by Virginia Woolf, and above all, *Krapp's Last Tape* by Samuel Beckett. Like the severed head of

Orpheus, which goes on singing his elegy on the death of Eurydice, the media of communication which were invented during the Victorian era – the telegraph, the telephone, and the radio – give a major role to the voice as the prime indication of individual consciousness.[5] Indeed they isolate a person's voice as the sign of personal presence to a degree that recalls, perhaps surprisingly, Aristotle's assertion in the *De Anima* that the soul is conveyed through the voice above all, and that consequently animals that do not have a soul cannot give expression to their thoughts. An interior life, which is transmitted by language and by speaking, will always therefore elude them.

These invented Orphic media refashioned the map of human consciousness and created a new secular metaphysics. I would like to suggest that they provide the fundamental reason for the return of myth today.

Mechanical communication technologies, such as Morse code and telegraphic signalling or rapping, began to render possible the broadcasting of the human voice over the airwaves and its recording for the gramophone, and they brought the acoustic presence of a person, living but impalpable, into everyday experience. As a result, Victorian scholars and scientists wanted to discover the matter of spirit presences, to explain life after death through experiments in which all the new phenomena were annexed. Disembodied voices, rappings, little waves and breezes made manifest, it was argued, the special appearance of revenants during séances conducted in the most elevated scientific milieux. In France, Charles Richet, a Nobel prize-winner, and the astronomer Camille Flammarion threw themselves into the project; in England Henry Sidgwick, Professor of Moral Philosophy at Cambridge and, in the United States, William James, the psychologist and brother of Henry James, were among several of the eminent thinkers involved in trying to press the new media to serve uncanny purposes.

Steven Connor, considering key works of literature at the beginning of the twentieth century in the light of the new media of the epoch, shows their intellectual link with Victorian metaphysics and the marked interest of the times in ghosts, spectres, fairies and spirits: a whole nineteenth-century mythology which still flourishes today especially in the gothic tastes of so many young consumers, in music, fashion, cinema and reading. The self wishes to perpetuate itself, and succeeds in finding consolation by the transmutations of phenomena, accomplished through technology: the incorporeal voice of the departed which speaks from on high, the ectoplasmic trace of the dead beloved on the photographic print.

I'd like to take a cue from this reflection, and propose that the use of myths, legends, fairy tales and other fantastic materials corresponds – in so far as they are forms of narrative – to audiovisual media which now dominate contemporary communications, and have supplanted simple acoustics. The Real with the capital R, as written by Slavoj Žižek, is no longer this same territory of the real, written with a small r – in which the rational author such as Rushdie can roam freely and at will. Rushdie, and Morrison likewise, testify to the strong influence cinema has exercised. In the same way as the radio and the telegraph influenced the acoustic depiction of the soul in the early 1900s, so colour movies, television and even more recently, the virtual reality of Internet displays, have forged a new fictional narrative method, which abolishes realism and welcomes the mythical, but mythic material stripped of its metaphysical and ontological dimensions. Invented memories correspond to the fabricated images of the movies; the disappearances and reappearances of characters, the ghosts incarnate, flying characters, and beings who can teleport from one place to another, who can communicate telepathically by sheer mental power, achieve realisation on the big screen and the home monitor. They belong, as it were quite naturally, to the lexicon of cinema – you have all seen *Star Trek*, *Buffy the Vampire* and *The X Files*.[6]

I want to set the complex games, techniques and motifs borrowed by writing from film-making in a larger and richer context: that of scientific metaphors which serve to explain today the workings of human consciousness, according to the arguments of a new generation of researchers who are exploring the mind and the mystery of conscious existence. (Several among them show the keenest desire to reach the biggest public possible, and their ideas, widely and excitedly rehearsed in bestselling manuals and in newspapers, are now in general circulation.)

Two different discourses dominate the debate about consciousness: evolutionary biology, with a tendency to determinism, and, on the other hand mechanical metaphors which compare *nous*, or mind, to a computer which amasses information in order to assemble personal memory. Neither genes nor computer codes think – they act without consciousness: they carry their destiny in themselves. One can perhaps perceive in the ironically fatalistic plots of Rushdie's fiction, a certain biological and mechanistic pessimism, very much current in our time, which is figured forth in fairy tale and providential metaphor, as in the earthquake which swallows up the heroine in a protracted scene of catastrophe.

But these companion theories do not capture my allegiance as much as another, different idea about consciousness, less discussed in the press, and considered 'radical'. This theory does not accept the model of a computer for the mind, but offers instead an image of the brain as a generator, as a producer of memories and of mental images by a process of simultaneous selection and connection. An American scientist, Gerald M. Edelman, lucidly put his view in the journal *Daedalus*:

> In the radical view, the selectional system of the brain is capable of dynamic reconstruction of outputs under the constraints of value, selecting from a large number of degenerate possibilities. As such, this view rejects codes, representations, and explicit coded storage. Memory is non-representational, and is considered to reflect a dynamic capacity to recreate an act (or specifically to suppress one) under such constraints. The brain is not a computer, nor is the world an unambiguous piece of tape defining an effective procedure and constituting 'symbolic information'. Such a selectional brain system is endlessly more responsive and plastic than a coded system. In it the homunculus disappears, its role ceded to a self-organizing and necessarily complex biological system.[7]

Voice and language play a dominant role, needless to say, in the formation of a conscious being. Edelman writes with regard to the acquisition of language: 'The development of a lexicon of [such] symbols, probably initially based on the nurturing and emotive relationships between mother and child, led to the discrimination of individual consciousness and the emergence of a self.'

Here, the 'vocalic uncanny' invoked by Steven Connor meets the acoustic mirror of the psychoanalytical critic Kaja Silverman, where the child first discovers herself; such an account of early consciousness also recalls the prenatal and infantile babble invoked by Julia Kristeva in connection with the maternal body (the *chora*). In my studies of fairy tales (*From the Beast to the Blonde* and *No Go the Bogeyman*), I focus on the strong association between female voices and female themes in fables, fairy stories and wonder tales, which have indeed been rather neglected by literary theory.

In relation to the rewriting of myths, what is of concern here is that these founding and constitutive moments of language and memory, of the power of thinking and reflection, of generating mental pictures, draw on the imaginary. The ancient distinction between fantasy and memory escapes definition; the fantastic twists and turns within recollections and the irrational spreads out through them. Consciousness which produces images finds its own metaphorical mirror image in narrative cinema. It's often said that the cinema is dream-like, but the idea of dream doesn't sufficiently take into account the activity of the waking imagination as well. The exchanges between mother, grandmother, nurse and child, which are embedded in lullabies, children's songs, verses and poems for children, and in the earliest stories told by one generation to another, clearly do not issue forth from an empirical world, nor do they arise from intellectual processes which could be termed rational, in spite of the wishes of certain pedagogical experts, who used to advise against fantasy.

Orature corresponds not only to this mythological past, which finds an oracular and biblical voice in the haunted stories of Toni Morrison or its synthesised song in the fantastic epics of Rushdie; the imitation of orature, slanted through the untrammelled polyphony of these writers, also has the closest connection to linguistic apprenticeship, and to the imaginative experiences of one's earliest years. Moreover, it reflects the functions of the soul in contemporary discourse, where soul is understood as consciousness or as memory.

The ancient hierarchy between reason and its opposite, unreason, the traditional conflict between dreaming and waking, reverie and reasoning, find themselves abolished by the narrative representations of the imaginary: rewriting mythology lays a claim on motifs which are perceived to be irrational in order to seize more surely and express more fully what it means to be a conscious being now, penetrated by a cacophony of voices, irradiated by a pandemonium of images, solicited by a future torn between wilful, over-assertive individualism on the one hand and despairing determinism on the other. It's possible that the generative model of consciousness, rather than the computational model of the mind as a hard-drive, might be correct – but whether it is or not does not shed light on the relationship of fiction to consciousness. A novelist constitutes through images, stories, and language a metaphysical and poetic dimension of reality which repositions us as we confront our selves and our identities in these times. An imagination which thinks by generating images, choosing among fantasies and memories, allows expression to individual subjectivity; but this subjectivity keeps itself separate from the phantasmatic phenomena which whirl around us, from which choices have to be made. This contemporary subjectivity does not respect the distinction that used to seem so clear between lived experience and dreams, between actual and unreal events, either in the forms they take or the degree of intensity with which they impinge.

I often find these days that I cannot remember if I've seen such and such a thing in real life, if I went to a film where I saw it happen, if I've read it, if someone else told me about it, or simply, if I've made it up. And I don't think I'm the only one to be so disassociated, nor do I believe myself to be ill. Nor do I live in the disorientated modern state of exile, when the loss of home brings with it a collapse of consciousness and its subjective store of memories. A writer like the ex-Yugoslav essayist and novelist Dubravka Ugrešic lives this confusion between what she remembers and what she fears, between nightmares she saw herself and those she witnesses on the television, and of necessity, she believes, she has practised in consequence a new form of the novel, a hallucinatory fiction. In *The Museum of Unconditional Surrender* (1999), the female narrator meditates tenderly and bitterly how ' "dreamed reality" began to unravel before our eyes'. Later she puts the question: 'Did my acquaintance dream the horrors of war, which then actually happened, or had the horrors of war already occurred some time in the future, and she just dreamed them?'

This state of hallucinatory experience brings to mind the struggles of medieval thinkers with visions and states of possession, and their arguments can help, surprisingly perhaps, to illuminate our present dimensions of fantastic realities. At the beginning of his remarkable study, *Thinking with Demons*, the historian Stuart Clark questions how belief in devils can take root, often in strong, otherwise sane minds: 'To make any kind of sense of the witchcraft beliefs of the past,' he writes, 'we need to begin with language. By this I mean not only the terms in which they were expressed, and the general systems of meanings they presupposed, but the question of how language authorizes any kind of belief at all.'[8]

By language, let's designate technical languages as well: the new means of representing the world have complicated the question, for they have realised things that could not be made possible before except in fantasies – the voice of the beloved in one's ear from a mobile phone in a faraway country, the doubling of a child who can watch himself in a home video on the television as he was four years earlier. These technical processes reproduce – approximately but uncannily – the generative, image-producing faculties of the soul according to the model that some scientists propose. And I haven't even mentioned the fictive possibilities of Photoshop, virtual reality simulations and digitised processes of image-making. Some contemporary fiction aims to reproduce this experience.

With regard to the interpretation of the contemporary mythological novel, I hope I have presented some ideas that literary theory offers which might illuminate the satisfactions and the pleasure given to readers by the magical and fantastic devices of the imagination in certain writings today. They do not conform to the world as we think it to be, but to thought as we live it today.

1999

CODA: WHO'S SORRY NOW? PERSONAL STORIES, PUBLIC APOLOGIES

Amnesty Lecture in Human Rights, given at Oxford

THE WRITER'S DILEMMA

Writers, pen-pushers, ivory-tower dwellers, bookworms and clerics – we often wonder what part can we play? Where does literature intersect with life – with lives – how can we contribute to an increment of justice in the world? What are the jump-leads from a work of writing – fiction or poetry – to the statute book? This is the writer's dilemma. Can literature truly be 'strong enough to help', as in Seamus Heaney's declared hope for poetry?

In the wake of the September 11 attack, I had an email from a teacher of English literature in the island of Réunion, which is in the Indian Ocean but is still a département of France. She wrote, 'I've been worrying about why people don't seem to learn from what happens. And in spite of all the literature which is almost prophetic . . . I've been thinking about how literature works, and how it is not politics. It seems to me that literature works on the imaginary domain, on the discourses representing reality, and if mentalities are changed, on an individual level, then collective behaviour can change. But literature can only influence in the world *to come*. It doesn't work immediately.'

What Eileen Wanquet, the English teacher in Réunion, says here strikes me as important – important and perceptive, in its guarded optimism that there exists a link at all, and in its emphasis on the imaginary domain and *mentalités* as the ground of change. It is an area of *mentalité* and of sensibility that I am going to explore today, sensibility as it is embodied in writings of different kinds. I'm going to probe the apologetic state, and the feelings associated with apology, in order to throw light, if possible, on the meaning of public apology in the many distempered areas of the past and the present where human rights are violated. As we go, we shall meet beckoning figures, as if travelling on some allegorical map of a pilgrim's progress: Vindication, Confession,

Regret, Remorse, Recognition, Exculpation, Retraction, Responsibility, Repentance, and then towards the end of the journey, Expiation/Atonement, Placation, Reconciliation – flanked by two pairs of strong twins, Reform and Redress, Reparation and Restitution, with the angel of Redemption hovering overhead. The re-prefix that recurs so frequently in these words denotes that these states of mind arise in response to something that has occurred; they respond to a prior act or event and are made in relation to an object, which then bears back on the subject – an apology is in this sense an agreement, a compact between different parties, not a lone initiative. I'll be coming back later to this recursive recombining and mutual self-fashioning.

I am going to look at four scenes in literature which illuminate states that seem to me to follow upon one another in the act of apology:

First, the existence of an injustice, testified by the sufferer: for this, I am going to take the figure of Io from Aeschylus' magnificent study in suffering, *Prometheus Bound*.

Second, the apologist, the one who accepts responsibility – or takes the blame – and speaks of regret and – it is implied – pledges reform and redress. Here my principal subject will be the Saint Augustine who speaks through his *Confessions*.

Third, the response of the apologee: the person to whom the avowal of guilt is made; and here I'll look at *The Marriage of Figaro*, and play the exquisite music of forgiveness and reconciliation in the last act.

My fourth, and final scene, looking at what the future may hold, will come from Gillian Slovo's most recent novel, *Red Dust*, a popular, accessible page-turner and bestseller that vividly explores the issues raised by the Truth and Reconciliation Commission in South Africa. As you know, the TRC asked people to tell their stories. It proposed – and reached – a revolutionary form of trying to achieve some kind of peace or modus vivendi in a country that had been torn by internal strife by offering amnesty to all crimes committed in pursuit of political ends, provided they were admitted, with the significant exception of rape. Slovo's book also constitutes a challenge to J. M. Coetzee's bitter pessimism, in his allegory of post-apartheid retributive and redistributive justice, the Booker prize-winning, controversial novel *Disgrace*: by contrast, in its own ironical way, *Red Dust* explores the circuitous paths to healing, and a new future.

THE PRESENT STATE OF APOLOGY

But before I turn to these four scenes, a quick overview of the present state of apology.

The Pope has apologised on nearly a hundred different occasions, and at a special Mass for the Millennium, he bundled up two thousand years of Church injustice into one comprehensive plea for forgiveness and purification. He invoked crimes against Jews, women, minorities in general, and some historical episodes in particular, such as the crusades and the Inquisition. After invoking each category, what he actually said was, 'We forgive and ask forgiveness.' He did not mention the complicity of the Vatican with Fascism, both in Italy and in Germany, and he left out homosexuals. So while his acknowledgment of the Church's guilt and his repentance were convincing to some and warmly welcomed, they did not go far enough for others.

Bill Clinton apologised to many groups, including the ex-prisoners who were used in human experiments over syphilis; he has also done so regarding the victims of the civil conflict in Rwanda. The Queen formally apologised to the Maoris for the treaty that dispossessed them of their lands, and in India for the massacre of Amritsar. Tony Blair has followed suit, with regard to the Irish famine. I read that in Australia there's a 'National Sorry Day' when sympathisers go around wearing badges, declaring, 'I'm sorry.'

More seriously, President de Klerk apologised to the victims of apartheid; and Swiss bankers for their part in safeguarding Nazi gold. In terms of responsibility for the sufferings at issue, there is a clear difference between Swiss bankers, President de Klerk and . . . Tony Blair.

The public apologies made by leaders of world affairs cast them in priestly roles: Tony Blair is not *directly* implicated in the acts for which he has apologised, nor is Clinton. Indeed they show themselves rather more reluctant to do so when they are directly involved. Their verbal retractions are magical, sacramental acts, designed to ease and soothe and purge hatred and grudge, as religious rituals exorcise demons. These apologies differ from public statements of responsibility and regret from persons who are involved: the police in the Stephen Lawrence case, for example.

Apology is a new political enthusiasm: especially when it concerns the sins of the past; it unites two different forms of speech, both of them deeply intertwined with ideas about self-examination, and self-disclosure, with, in short, ways of remembering oneself: a theological and sacramental language of repentance and atonement, on the one hand, and on the other, the psychoanalytic practice of the 'talking cure', and the psychotherapy group meeting to help relieve bereavement, mental distress, and the victims of abuse. The French have even introduced a new word, *répentance*, to describe these contemporary acts of apology and atonement.

Neither of these discourses is, properly speaking, juridical or political: in this regard, presidential politics has become less presidential than priestly. But, as Roy L. Brooks writes in his book of essays, *When Sorry Isn't Enough*, 'what is happening [in the age of apology] is more complex than "contrition chic" or the canonization of sentimentality'. In the wake of the Second World War, the possibility of healing grief and easing social conflicts through speech acts, through rites of mourning and expiation, through an evolved, secular verbal magic, has passed into the public arena all over the world. Many tributaries, very tricky to navigate, flow from this main current of public avowals and disavowals: not least, must an apology lead to reparation to be meaningful at all? That is, without a subsequent act of reparation or restitution, can it be fully constituted as an apology? Or is it a performative speech act that changes something of itself? Is it the soft answer that turneth away wrath? Is the recognition of wrongdoing that it embodies efficacious of itself? In other words, as Wole Soyinka asked, 'Is knowledge on its own of lasting effect?'

Or again, is an apology in and of itself a plea for forgiveness, which reaches completion only if and when that pardon is granted? The sacrament of penance in Catholic rite sets out three stages: contrition, which if sincere will be granted absolution; the confessor then sets a penance to be performed in order to make the absolution take, like finishing the course of antibiotics even after you're better. In several languages, the word 'apology' does not exist independently of the word for forgiveness: 'Je vous demande pardon', the French phrase, and likewise, the Italian, 'Mi scusi', differ from English 'I'm sorry' (French was 'Je suis désolée'), so the nuanced degrees in English between the formal 'I apologise' and the personal 'Forgive me', don't operate. However, 'pardon' contains the admission of fault, while the weaker phrase for regret, 'Je m'excuse', includes a hint of a reason for the act – an excuse. As the French also say, 'Qui s'accuse s'excuse' ('To accuse oneself is to excuse oneself.'), English appears to be unusual in its range of differently inflected terms: the formula for apology in Ibo, for example, one of the languages spoken in Nigeria, also turns on pardon: 'Biko gbaghala mm', means 'Please forgive me.'

Among the many bitter issues, past and present, in which victims, survivors or their descendants are demanding apology, are some very serious, large questions of the historical past: in Australia, the government has refused to apologise to the Aborigines for their oppression during the colonial era, though it has done so to those called 'the stolen generation', who were forcibly separated in infancy from their parents to be brought up in white homes. In Japan, the 'comfort women' conscripted during the Second World War have not accepted the conditional apology so far on offer. Most burningly of all, a campaign in America calls for an apology for slavery. This last almost destroyed the UN conference in Durban last year, when Britain, alone among EU countries, refused to agree to apologise, and argued for – and eventually negotiated – a strong statement of regret and repudiation instead.

Fear of the consequences that would follow a public apology – demands for reparation, for monetary damages along the model of an insurance claim – is the most patent reason for official reluctance to apologise. But there are other reasons, which I hope will emerge from this talk.

THE GENDER OF SORRY

Hard questions are raised by the rise in official statements of responsibility framed in the language of apology, and by the growing demand that they be forthcoming for different actions in history. These questions are related to issues of sex and gender in the first place not simply because women are frequently the subjects of the wrongs – not least the victims of rape in wartime. The issue of slavery, and the calls for an apology from European nations and the United States on account of their slave-trading and slave-owning pasts, of course concern women, and the reparation that the demand entails would have to include the female descendants of slaves.

For this lecture in a series on Sex, Gender and Human Rights, I want to look at the gender of sorry, and focus on the gendered inflection of apology as a form of speech, at the utterance's relationship to female character and expected roles, and what this implies for the practice in the political arena. When I asked a friend of mine, the writer Jonathan Keates, who is also an English teacher (at a central London boys' secondary school), if he ever asked his pupils to apologise to one another, he told me that on some occasions he had done so, and it cost the boys dearly to do so, because, as he put it, 'It's a girly thing.' This is also my impression – and I think the scenes I am going to explore will help us understand why, and also other aspects of apologetic public behaviour.

At the anecdotal level, the word 'Sorry' is almost my way of saying 'Hello'. It's probably the word I habitually use most often – sometimes as a way of hailing a waiter, or, even, I'm not beyond saying it when someone treads on *my* foot. There may be a class aspect to this, of a certain upbringing and a liberal conscience, but nevertheless, saying sorry can be a way of life. Rather more seriously, I want to give my support to acts – verbal utterances – which represent revulsion against wrongdoing, to accept that to forgive and forget is the better part and to acknowledge the enchanting power of language to bring about changes in the air – aery nothings, however insubstantial, are aery somethings too; as Hippolyta says in *A Midsummer Night's Dream*, a story made up of immaterial words can make a permanent impression, can 'grow to something of great constancy'.

But, but, but. I'm still very uneasy about the currents carrying the spate of apology today. The personal is political, yes, but maybe that is the problem – the feminist slogan has won an extraordinary, moral victory, that different groups want their sorrows recognised in a language of compassion and, at the same time, the Lords of Creation want to show adherence to it, by accepting a vicarious guilt and expressing their sorrow for it. As Meursault comments wryly to himself in *The Outsider* by Albert Camus, 'In any case, you're always partly to blame.' Nevertheless, this self-inculpation for events in the past is a deep irony, for should politics be personalised to this extent? Should an existential model of subjectivity encompass the structure of human rights? I feel I'm getting in very deep here, but I wanted to find out why I laughed a hollow laugh when I arrived in San Francisco the day that the Archbishop of California was apologising to all those who had been abused as children by nuns and priests. The thought of Blair shucking off the inconvenient complications of the colonial past in Ireland by saying he was sorry also made me snort; and I want to shake the Pope, frail as he is, when he says he forgives and asks for forgiveness – from God – for two thousand years of sins of the Church against women. Yes, well, what are you doing about us now?

It's significant that the Catholic sacrament, if all the conditions are met, shrives the penitent of the sins that have been confessed and lifts guilt from the wrongdoer; Puritan or Protestant guilt, by contrast, cannot be shed by mere contrition or even subsequent acts of penance: this may underpin the difference between the Pope's acts of apology, and the consequences of apology in the USA and in Anglican Britain – also of course the birthplace of making gains through the insurance market.

Scene One: Io
So to my first scene: Aeschylus' *Prometheus Bound*. The play opens with the heroic Titan brutally tied and staked to a rock by the figures of Strength and Violence; he justifies the acts that have roused the gods' anger against him, his outrage taking the form of passionate accusation of Zeus and the new, *arriviste* gods on Olympus and an equally impassioned self-justification for his acts in stealing fire, and other exploits that defy the gods. This tragic, archetypal figure of human heroic suffering will not bend his will or retract his action. The God of the Sea, Oceanus, rising out of the chasm roaring round the rock where Prometheus struggles against his bonds, chides him, saying:

> Have you not learnt, Prometheus, anger's a disease
> Which words can heal?

But Prometheus holds to his sense of right, and doesn't offer a soft answer. He broods instead on revenge. At this point Io erupts on to the stage – Io, one of the many young women who had the misfortune to catch Zeus's roving eye, has been changed into a heifer – by his wife – and is being driven without rest, bitten continually by a gadfly: Io cries out against the stings as she rushes on; Prometheus recognises her, and, in his prophetic role as the one who sees ahead, tells her he can see her future destiny – but the Chorus interrupt and ask to hear Io's story from her own mouth. Prometheus takes up their call; he says,

> Tears and lamenting find their due reward when those
> Who listen are ready too with tears of sympathy.

Io speaks: she describes Zeus's desire, the divine decrees that she and her parents obeyed, and the terrible penalty that fell upon her as a consequence.

She is one of the many victims in Greek tragedy and myths who tell of 'the heavenly crimes' of the gods, as Ovid puts it in the *Metamorphoses*; she is only one of a host of girls or nymphs who are raped by the

Olympians and then condemned for this pollution to terrible punishments, sometimes to banishment, to pariah status, to social exclusion, to transmutation into animal or plant or watery form. Callisto becomes a bear after Zeus makes her pregnant; Leto is assaulted by peasants who refuse to let her use their water supply after she's given birth and needs to wash herself. They prefigure, it seems to me, all the women with bundles, the scattered, fleeing figures on the roads of Europe and of Asia and of Africa. But what is odd, unexpected and important, is that these female heroines of ancient mythology speak of their sufferings, and that they figure, crucially, in the imaginary past of humanity: they are the founders of culture.

Io closes her testament to her own plight with the words:

> That is my story . . .
>   do not out of pity comfort me
> With lies. I count false words the foulest plague of all.[1]

Prometheus then informs her, gleefully, what lies ahead: and he modifies Io's tale of woe into a promise of revenge: she will be the ancestor, after thirteen generations of the Greeks, including that most Dorian of heroes, Heracles himself. So Io, the fly-blown cow, becomes the foremother of civilisation. Writing about Io's wanderings, Julia Kristeva, in her essay on being a foreigner, sees her case embodying the existential contingency of women: 'The fact remains,' she writes, 'that in Greece the bride was thought of as a foreigner, a suppliant . . . The wedding ritual stipulated that the bride was to be treated neither as a prey nor as a slave but as a "suppliant, placed under the protection of the hearth, and taken by the hand to her new abode".'[2]

In Aeschylus' vision, history itself is grounded in personal trials and tribulations; his tragedy tells the story of a male inaugurator, Prometheus, bringing useful gifts to earth – fire, knowledge – while the woman, Io, acts as the biological mother of the race. In this language of sexual polarity, Prometheus defies the Chorus of women when he proclaims:

> Never persuade yourself that I, through fear of what
> Zeus may intend, will show a woman's mind, or kneel
> To my detested enemy, with womanish hands
> Outspread in supplication for release. No, never!

Io personifies this abjectness, she exercises no power, no authority, and as the gadfly bites her again, she interrupts Prometheus in terrible pain, and cries out, making her exit with the line: 'I can't govern my tongue; words rush out at random . . .' Excess of language, spilling out beyond control, beyond organisation, under pressure of a genuine state of suffering here marks the extreme agony of persecution in Io's case; this index of suffering will recur in convincing testimony from those who are wronged. Indeed, the very word 'wronged' sounds the closing note of the whole play, as the heavens fall in and the ocean rises up to engulf Prometheus, still chained, in a cataclysm.

The wronged, like Io, do not however want the consolation of 'false words' in response to their genuine cries of woe. But the call she makes – and tragic figures like her make – stirs our pity and fear, in Aristotle's famous definition; makes us sorry for her, and through her, for the plight of sufferers like her.

The move from empathetic sorrow to public apology is of course unthinkable within the order of Greek fate; its appearance today, as a response to tragic injustice, results from the growth of our ever deeper investment in concepts such as responsibility, blame, accountability, which search out individual human agents, actors, perpetrators. Apology, a secularised ritual, grows out of identity politics, and its particular, Ionic aspect of victimhood. Victim politics have a long reach into the past, but they have acquired a new salience.

History can be lost to view when it's personified in a suffering subject: and this is where the work that I do, the writing I am committed to, converges with the issue, and turns it into a bristling and jagged, intractable problem. Since the Eighties, women writers in particular have been recomposing 'the book of memory' in order to give muted subjects their voice: novelists like Louise Erdrich, Cynthia Ozick and Maxine Hong Kingston have been actively engaged in reconstituting, through empathy and imagination, lost histories and lost strands of courage and invention; they have summoned reserves of 'Negative capability' in order to engage passionately with the past. Adrienne Rich, the American poet, has been credited with coining the term, 're-visioning', with reference to the political enterprise, within feminism, of recasting the past, of reascribing value, of working against the grain of received opinion and received stories. If history is an agreed fable, as Voltaire said – 'l'histoire est une fable convenue' – then any initiative to change things must begin with stories. Adrienne Rich's vision of the writer's engagement includes a dark and mordant perspective on Memory, in *An Atlas of the Difficult World*, a fine and complex series of meditations on contemporary issues. One poem begins 'Memory says/ Want to do right?:   Don't count on me', and then as Memory speaks she remembers the twentieth century and she goes through some of the things that have happened, using the first person and the present tense: 'I am a canal in Europe where bodies are floating/ I'm a mass grave . . ., I'm a woman bargaining for a chicken . . .' She continues, taking us through more of the atrocities and horrors of the recent past and says, 'I have dreamed my children could live at last, like others . . .' Elsewhere, when Rich asks 'what does it mean to say I have survived?' With fierce irony, she is calling for a newly imagined, reactivated history, a new storehouse of stories that will reconfigure Memory, for a way of speaking that forces the silence to open up its secrets.

The embassies of campaigners for apologies belong to this same enterprise, and their popularity reflects the unexpected success, it strikes me, of the fictional revisionist mode since the Eighties. The reason that fiction and women figure in the forefront of this development is that such storytelling has been explicitly concerned with the sufferings of the silenced, invisible, oppressed and unchronicled past: with anonymous, marginal and disappeared peoples. Toni Morrison, in her novel *Jazz* (1992), writes, in the narrator's voice, about the black protagonist, 'I want to be the language that wishes him well.' In the field of apology, it can likewise work as language that wishes someone well.

Her fictions, like *Beloved*, embody voices of the voiceless: drawing on first-person accounts such as the autobiography of Mary Prince, the first woman to write about a life in slavery,[3] Morrison turned the lens of history around to look, not at the victorious – or defeated – generals of the Civil War, but its consequences for ordinary individuals. Through this act of imaginary identification, a writer like Morrison follows in the footsteps of the abolitionists who supported historical women like Mary Prince to stand witness; she is pressing literature into the service of liberty and justice. As Jacqueline Rose has succinctly summed up the relation between such acts of writing and the struggle for rights, 'All the evidence suggests that people do not kill if they can imagine themselves in the other person's shoes.'[4]

An economy of virtue flourishes around claims of injustice; like pilgrims kissing the wounds of the crucified Christ, contemporary political subjects seek to touch these springs of sympathy, and apologists – by consenting and yielding and admitting wrong – strive to reach the same condition of pathos, and consequently partake in the currency of merit.

Roy Foster has pointed to the problem and shown, with a dose of sharp scepticism and withering wit, how wishful, imaginary narratives, not historical inquiry, have impinged and shaped political allegiances and even policy in his recent book, *The Irish Story: Telling Tales and Making it Up in Ireland*: this new coin of sympathy risks turning into a black market in competitive injury, an inflationary spiral of self-pitying self-justification.

How did we reach this point? How has tragic pathos, such as Aeschylus communicates, or the polyphony of a Toni Morrison novel stirringly arouses, become instrumentalised to deepen conflict, not the intended opposite? How has grief become grievance, to echo Seamus Heaney once more?

In order to supply some light on this question, and see how strongly it bears on the issue of apology, we need to take a detour through the contradictory somersaults of the word in its long history.

Apology's first meaning is 'vindication', as in the term, *Apologia Pro Vita Sua*, used by John Henry Newman as the title for his great testimonial to his own conversion; but, slanted through the idea of vindication as an avowal, a confession, apology has acquired its present, widespread meaning as a formal statement of culpability. Plato calls Socrates' defence at his trial 'The Apology'; pleading for his life, against charges of corrupting Athenian youth, Socrates emphatically does not apologise. How did the concept – and the practice – shift from this righteous reasoning in self-defence to the abject, self-abasing petition of apologising, as we understand it today? From the Promethean stand of heroic defiance to the adoption of the Ionic suppliant?

So to the second scene in literature, which I hope will illuminate the issue:

Scene Two: Saint Augustine's *Confessions*

In the *Confessions*, the Bishop of Hippo invokes the God he loves, calling him unceasingly in the vocative: *Tu* – Thou or You. Augustine searches his heart, his conscience, his mind; he inaugurates self-portraiture in fiction.

Apologies take place in dialogue: they must be made in the presence of someone, the letter must be sent, the message delivered, the speech made to an audience, there must be an addressee. They share this character with confession, and in Augustine's accents, the effect is 'unusually intimate', a personal heart-to-heart, which '[breaks] down the boundary', the historian Peter Brown writes in his recent introduction to *The Confessions*, 'between prayer and literature'. Echoing with the pleading, praise-singing, breast-beating and lyric laments of the Psalms, Augustine analyses his self, his life and character up to the year 397 when he is speaking to God through these words (with 'his back turned to us').

Like Io, he cries out of wrongs done – *but in this case by himself*, the particular individual with an individual case history, but also Augustine, a man like any other, he writes. He doesn't start with his own memories, but with the ordinary first experiences of any baby just as he has observed in others. He addresses God with insistent, plangent intensity: '. . . my confession, O my God, in Your sight is made silently, and yet not silently, for it makes no sound, yet it cries aloud in my heart . . .'[5] Through the deep-digging psychic archaeology of the book, Augustine commands our interest – and our admiration – today because his probing is so unrelenting and often breathtaking in its penetration, because he shows us someone scrutinising feelings for their value, their honesty, their depths – their truth. In so doing, in writing this way and making this canonical text, Augustine also inaugurates the utterance of the I or ego as a major, if not *the* major point of origin for truth-telling. This is where Augustine holds up a model of the apologist: he makes a reckoning of his inner being, he begs for God's love and understanding for his faults – and for forgiveness in exchange for his sincerity. The *Confessions* admits some small, particular crimes – stealing pears when a young lad – and grieve over a general predicament of human sinfulness, evidenced in himself especially as carnal lust. The act of avowal leads to acknowledgment of wrongdoing, and thence to renunciation. This text institutes, it could be said, the high virtue of putting oneself in the wrong.

Or, to express the same thought differently, Augustine's *Confessions* enact the way an offender, seeing the offending part and plucking it out, as it were, anneals and refines and lightens his being. Augustine is too subtle, too eloquent, too persuasively anguished to be self-serving; but his example presents a warning of what supplicating self-scrutiny can profitably achieve for the confessor.

Peter Brooks's recent book *Troubling Confessions* tackles the relationship between law and literature, legal confession and autobiography, and he has shown lucidly and with great sensitivity how the urge to confess in order to feel better can propel an accused subject to admit to crimes he or she never committed: the psychological hunger to gain the approval that confessing itself confers overcomes even the instinct for survival, and innocent men and women consent to incriminate themselves.

In this personal story Augustine tells he doesn't only express his sorrow at his own transgressions: in doing so he presents himself to God stripped of all his worldly achievements and authority; he abases himself, never dwelling on his position as a powerful bishop in a city in the largest province of the Roman empire at a moment when the Church embodied authority; after all, Augustine was presiding in court dispensing justice daily. But he lets little of this show: his *cris de cœur* not only shed layer after layer of the psychic defences of self-love, but also deny the world's returning gaze and its esteem; the narcissism here takes the form of pressing himself on God, the beloved: Augustine, having parted from a long-cherished sexual companion, and renounced all sexual activity at great cost to his own nature, adopts God as his lover instead:

> It is with doubtful knowledge, Lord, but with utter certainty that I love You. You have stricken my heart with Your word and I have loved You. And indeed heaven and earth and all that is in them tell me wherever I look that I should love You . . . But what is it that I love when I love You? . . . in a sense I do love light and melody and fragrance and food and embrace when I love my God – the light and the voice and the fragrance and food and embrace in the soul . . . I breathe that fragrance which no wind scatters, I eat the food which is not lessened by eating, and I lie in the embrace which satiety never comes to sunder.[6]

The founding document of autobiography, the model for the two great Catholic Saint Theresas and their monumental works of autobiography, a forerunner of Freud's talking cure and of Proust's fiction, the *Confessions* grounds subjectivity in affect, and within that category of consciousness, in emotional, needy, supplicating lovingness. I think you will catch the drift of what I'm saying: that the subjectivity in Augustine's literary self-portrait wagers all its sincerity, its powers of persuasion in his humbling himself, by speaking as a woman to his beloved Lord God. Who else cries out in his book as he does? His mother, Monica. In the fourth-century Roman empire, his representation of himself in this abject and powerless, Ionic state was even more startling – there really was nothing to compare with Augustine's *Confessions* before he wrote them, probably because no man would have thought of showing himself in such a demeaning light – with such womanish weakness.

I'm not saying, by the way, that women *are* weak: but that womanly weakness, as exemplified by Io, could be coopted as a persuasive form of speech, and its representations confer unexpected authority on a non-female speaker.

The public apologies issued by statesmen and by the Pope on behalf of past transgressors live under the sign of Augustinian thought, it seems to me. For the Pope, humbling himself, and with him the whole Church in order to beseech God for forgiveness and purification for all the two thousand years of wrongdoing, echoes the great confessing saint's accents.

The Queen is head of a Church, and her apologies, issued in her capacity as Head of the Commonwealth, have rubbed off some of the chrism of her ecclesiastical office. As for Bill Clinton and Tony Blair, their apologies – their confessions – seek to heal and cleanse as vicars, by proxy, standing in for agents to whom they do not stand in apostolic succession. Whom are they speaking for? In politics this is a false genealogy of power, it seems to me. There are several more problems here: not least the violence done to history, to imagine it can be parcelled up and put away, that it can be *ended*. But, you might rejoinder, what if the actions do good, if they calm the trouble, ease the pain, or, in the language of conflict resolution, recognise the wrong? And in so doing manage to give right to the victims?

If these are the consequences then apology, as in Augustine's *Confessions*, can add to the sum of justice in the world. But it can do so only when it meets and merges with the response to the apology: it is by consenting to the spell, by the one who grants pardon, that the spell takes hold.

So to my third scene, and ideal, perhaps, in which an apology is given and accepted and forgiveness ensues.

Scene Three: *The Marriage of Figaro*

We skip on several centuries again: from Augustine in what is present-day Algeria to Lorenzo da Ponte and Mozart in Vienna in 1786, and *The Marriage of Figaro*. And on, to the last act: and the complex masquerade that gradually sheds its masks as the imbroglio turns from conflict to harmony, mirrored in the music.

The Countess, disguised as the servant Susanna, is going to the assignation which her husband, the Count, has been scheming to set up with Susanna all along; Susanna, disguised as the Countess, is looking on, as they meet in the dark in the garden; so is Figaro, who thinks it really is Susanna yielding to the Count's seduction. But he soon realises his mistake. Then, knowing the Count is watching, Figaro makes love to the false Countess and enrages the Count, who steps out and cries foul, calling for the guards – this is the opening of the last scene.

The Count rages at Figaro, and at the supposed Countess, until everyone, still in disguise, and of course in the know, begs 'perdono'.

But with defiant masculine pride, he refuses. This is a feudal aristocrat who has been angling for his *droit de seigneur* with Susanna and lives by a double standard as if by divine right.

The musical exchanges repeat his grandiloquent rejections of their pleas, his 'no' tolling to their entreaties.

Finally the real Countess issues from her hiding place, and sheds her disguise; she asks for 'perdono' on behalf of all. The Count, and his supporters, seeing his mistake asks her, in a lovely, slow phrase that is marked in the libretto 'in a supplicatory tone', to forgive *him*.

Then there's a pause, the action all suspended, and a silence in the music – will *she* accept *his* request for pardon, *his* apology?

Or will she, following his patrician lead, refuse?

With ineffable grace, she accepts his plea for forgiveness. (And this is, as I said before, the equivalent of an apology in Italian.)

She sings, 'Più docile sono, e dico di sì' ('I am more amenable (kinder) – and I say I will').

And the moment of horror and quarrelling, betrayal and dishonour is lifted up and away by the music of unity, serenity and pleasure, ending on the word *festeggiar* – feasting.

Here the peace-making power of the apology granted appears in all its beauty and promise of reconciliation.

It is striking that the Countess, of all the dramatis personae in the opera, reflects most intensely and inwardly on her state, her feelings and – her sufferings; she's the most poignant, and by far the least comical person in the plot. Her blessing, healing forgiveness, arising from her love for her philandering and tyrannical husband and her wronged state, unites and delivers them all from strife; the librettist da Ponte's sharing out of the emotions definitely consigns this 'docility' to the female social role – in a comedic outcome that presents an absolute test case for ideas of feminine virtue.

The original play by Beaumarchais notoriously stirred up a furore and was banned by the King, on account of the valet Figaro's insubordination, and the plot's critique of aristocratic privilege. The dénouement of the drama is therefore ironical: the Countess has in the end allowed her husband, her master, to carry on as before. Mozart's music puts a soothing patch over this bad cluster, but it may be that the rousing call to feasting with which the whole opera ends sings against that defeat. Few expect the Count to change his spots; he is clearly unregenerate: perhaps this is what Jacques Derrida means when he writes, apropos of Abraham killing Isaac, 'one only ever asks forgiveness for something unforgivable. One never has to forgive the forgivable, there's the aporia of the impossibility of pardon.'[7]

Now to my fourth scene.

Scene Four: *Red Dust* by Gillian Slovo

Gillian Slovo's *Red Dust* dramatises an emblematic case of amnesty for the murder of a prisoner, heard before the Truth and Reconciliation Commission in a small, imaginary town in the dusty wilderness of the South African interior. Clearly and cleverly plotted, *Red Dust* dramatises several characters twisting and shifting around the act of owning up.

In 1985, two policemen tortured a suspected ANC fighter, the local schoolmaster's son, Steve Sizela, and killed him; quite early in the book one of them, Dirk Hendricks, admits, 'Ja, . . . In hindsight: it was wrong. I am truly sorry for the hurt I caused.' This is the only unmistakable apology in the story; and it proves hollow. His fellow-torturer, Muller, on the other hand, is not inclined to recant or repent; he even engineers his own death in order to avoid appearing before the Commission to give evidence and admit his guilt. The novel plays with many different permutations on honesty and dishonesty, on deception and self-deception, on loyalty and disloyalty, on lies and conflict, in the public quest for truth and reconciliation. It's a cynical, ironical fiction in the spy-thriller mode, but shot through with a kind of fervour of hope that arises from its unique historical origins.

The TRC did not require apology as such; as I said at the beginning, if the crime were committed to political ends, full disclosure was deemed sufficient. Above all, it did not follow up any crime, however heinous, with penalties if the perpetrator cooperated. By implication, the witnesses combined the two opposing historical discourses of apologia and apology: by explaining what and how they had done what they did, they were somehow divested of it; by fully acknowledging their guilty participation in evils, they contributed to the purification of the nation's memory.

The philosophy of the Commission, developed under the sign of Christian penance, was also inspired by a Zulu concept of peace-making called *ubuntu*, meaning compassion, empathy, the recognition of the humanity of the other.[8] Archbishop Desmond Tutu, one of the principal architects of the Commission, calls his autobiography *No Truth without Forgiveness*, and, as so many women appeared to testify to the disappearance and sufferings of victims – they were the widows, orphans, mothers of those who had been killed – they had to do plenty of the work of forgiving: and were thereby also cast in the Countess's role. They stood to lose most by the terms of the Commission, which amnestied murderers – Gillian Slovo and her sister Sean attended the hearing of the man who killed their mother, Ruth First, and they have both written, in different ways, about this ordeal. Of the 7,128 applications for amnesty, only fifty-six came from females who had committed crimes themselves.

From the point of view of personal storytelling, the Truth and Reconciliation Commission in South Africa worked with a radical form of relativism in respect of historical narrative. It actually invoked four different types of truth as basic principles, partly conceived by the formerly imprisoned activist, now judge, Albie Sachs. The first kind of truth was 'factual and objective truth' – what actually took place. This is the equivalent of Freud's 'material truth'. The second truth was 'social or dialogue truth', which, according to the document, was established through interaction, discussion and debate. The devisers then added something we can recognise very strongly from today's world, 'narrative truth', which was victims' recitations, including 'perceptions, stories and myths': witnesses or participants talking of 'their own . . . perceptions . . . how they saw events, both subjectively and in accordance with the collective memory of the group'. This corresponds to Freudian psychoanalytic confession. These truths were seen not in synthesis but in apposition. Most interestingly of all, I think, in terms of what the work of repair or work of words can achieve, how the work of reconstituting the self through speech and storytelling can develop, was the fourth kind of truth, 'healing truth' – 'the kind . . . that places facts and what they mean within the context of human relationships'. This implies that 'healing truth' might even diverge from narrative truth, testimony and objective truth, that these things might actually be in conflict or in opposition.[9] One severe critic of the TRC's procedures was outraged by the indifference this pursuit of healing truth showed to establishing the actual sequence and character of events as they had occurred and pointed to the Commission's equal disregard of rules of evidence in a court of law. Another political commentator, Ian Buruma, more anxiously than angrily, wrote in the *New York Review of Books*, 'the steady substitutions of political argument in public life with the soothing rhetoric of healing is disturbing . . . Memory is not the same as history, and memorialising is different from writing history.'[10]

But the model followed wasn't primarily a legal tribunal, however much it may have resembled one in formalities; it was, as I said before, ritualistic and therapeutic. Jacqueline Rose uses the language of psychoanalysis to indicate the problem in relation to justice: that justice belongs in the realm of the superego, whereas apologetics – speaking bitterness, narratives of wrongdoing, personal cries of anguish – arise from the unconscious – and these utterances can be fantasies, as we know. In the Freudian perspective, they are truth to self, whether or not they took place in actuality. The two discourses are incommensurate, though the TRC attempted to hyphenate them, by eliminating the retributive character of justice, its meting-out of penalties.[11]

Gillian Slovo has written that attending the amnesty hearing for her mother's murderers first enraged her, that there was to be no justice in the form of punishment, but that eventually the experience did bring some kind of peace, as the creators of the TRC intended so ardently. But she has very conflicted feelings about 'restorative justice' and her own novel *Red Dust* explores these complications, for the healing that takes place in the book only happens deep down in the inner psyches of those who have suffered from the crimes of the past, beneath layers and layers of deception and intrigue, political bargaining and expediency, egotistical jockeying for survival and reputation that constitute the hearing in the small town at the centre of her book. *Red Dust* ironises the TRC's good intentions and undermines the sincerity of apology. It dramatises a theatre of male simulation, contest and performance, but, and it's an important but, it shows that forgiveness – the Countess's mercy – helps the victims, even while the perpetrators remain unredeemed. We are back with Derrida's perception of the impasse around pardon: that only the unforgivable asks for forgiveness.

It is one of the principal ironies of the TRC that women's voices, telling the story of violence done to themselves, rather than speaking of crimes they witnessed, were few: a special Gender Commission was convened to encourage women to come forward, with mixed results. Antjie Krog, the poet and rapporteur for the TRC, and author of the remarkable report, *Country of My Skull*, diagnoses the problem in a chapter actually called 'Truth is a Woman'. The problem is circular: rape did not fall under the amnesty provision because it wasn't considered political. So rapists could not confess with impunity. But, as the harrowing stories she reports reveal, political crimes committed against activist women almost invariably involved rape or other sexualised brutality. And the victims of these crimes did not want to speak of them: this particular atrocity escaped the bounds of language – of the talking cure, of the healing truth – and fell outside the remit of apology, in the form of it practised by the TRC.[12] Even the limited speech of the poor cow, Io, was withdrawn – with the best possible intentions – from the range of possibilities of women in the South African conflict. Cynthia Ngewu, one of the mothers who testified before the TRC, called for 'the real-real story [that] nobody knows'.[13]

So, a kind of discourse patterned on the exclusion and humility of the suffering subject, coded feminine, was not ultimately available to women themselves. Or rather, it was available, but when they adopted it, they did not command the same possibilities of release or authority or reparation as the men. Gillian Slovo has written herself out of this impasse by refusing, in *Red Dust*, emotive language, lament, confession and autobiographical modes in general, and created an alter ego who is a smart, shrewd, unattached and childless Manhattan-based human rights lawyer.

As Bob Marley says, 'No Woman No Cry'.

Conclusion

So now, as I come towards the end, today is Saint Valentine's Day; it gives couples the chance to celebrate, but those without a beloved feel the lack more acutely on this day – however much they tell themselves it's a profiteering manoeuvre at a slack time of year on the high street, that it's another tawdry example of the commodification of everything that lives that's holy. The current swell in apologies draws up into its energies many causes and griefs: since I began writing this lecture, I note offers of – and demands for – apologies everywhere: the Belgian government has apologised within the last month for the murder of Lumumba (though it was carefully phrased not to admit direct guilt) while, here, in this country, the father whose premature baby's body was found in a hospital laundry refused the hospital's apology. Every week brings fresh reports of similar statements, some attempting to put right trivial mistakes, others to redress calamities.

Like lovers on Valentine's Day, apologies are also now more conspicuous than ever by their absence. An apology has become a very powerful instrument of recognition, and retention or refusal to give one withholds that recognition with new sharpness. In Australia, the Prime Minister who has refused to apologise to the Aborigines found himself facing a hall in which the audience turned their backs to him and stood like that throughout his speech to return the deep insult he had inflicted. This fresh stimulus to anger has sharpened in turn the potentially placatory use of apology: when one is rejected, the attempt to placate is shown up as an empty gesture: it's not enough to say you're sorry. However, as Elazar Barkan, the author of *The Guilt of Nations*, says, the debate around the issue can be applied at best to finding a way forward: 'lack of apologies, demands for apologies, and the refusal to give them are pre-steps . . . a testimony to the wish and the need of both sides to reach the negotiating stage'.

Apologising has come to seem the necessary grounds in which new values can take root and grow into social and human rights for groups that identify themselves as wronged. It's a form of communication, in which the subjective self is implicated, and which, when made in public, stresses the display of humility, the loss of authority of the apologist; it adopts a language of passionate and personal sincerity identified with degraded, weak suppliants, with victims like Io, with sinners like Augustine, and so its expressions of empathy help redeem the perpetrator of the wrong by association with the object of the apology. It adapts a feminine form of self-presentation to exculpate acts undertaken with socially recognised authority – kings and bishops, prime ministers and popes love to assume its inflections.

Apologising represents a bid for virtue and can even imply an excuse not to do anything more about the injustice in question. Encurled inside it may well be the earlier meaning of 'vindication'. So it can offer hypocrites a main chance. It can also, as in the case of the priestly self-fashioning of some political leaders, make a claim on their own behalf of some sacred, legitimate authority.

Apologies consent to the story told by the wronged victim or victims in question, and contribute, today, to the re-visioning of national history and the shaping of group identities. But whereas writers struggle with the complexity of meanings, these 'agreed fables' often exacerbate grudge and grievance.

When sought by such an aggrieved community, an apology can restore dignity and spread forgiveness, by recognising, as in *ubuntu*, the dignity and presence of the oppressed. It seems that the dignity restored by the apology can make the wronged feel eased. In this way the fully compacted apology works as a spell, a verbal formula that effects change. The redemption lies not with the one who apologises but in the mercy that the one who accepts shows.

But again this fails to redress the trouble, to institute reforms. It represents retrospective avenging rather than prospective action. At its harshest, it might even maintain the parties in their disequilibrium: the Count still getting away with it, the Countess, still wronged. In South Africa, the circumstances were exceptional, and the TRC offered an exceptional remedy; but its religious and ritual confessional and expiatory processes should not be followed, in my view, in other contexts, for example the Balkans. Of course, Slobodan Milošović would be no more likely to make a clean breast of things in return for amnesty at a TRC hearing than he is going to collaborate with the court in The Hague. But is it thinkable that an apology could ever be acceptable in such a case?

Then, on another twist of this writhing problem, do restitution and reparation require apology, the admission of wrong, before they can begin? Should they? Again this surely represents a failure of the law, which should be able to institute human rights on first principles, not only in response to a personal story. Apart from the almost intractable inequities in tracing lineal descendants – of famine victims, say, or slaves – justice through economic compensation diverts resources from measures that would strengthen human rights, here and now. I am entirely with Paul Gilroy, author of *The Black Atlantic*, when he commented to the *Guardian* on the campaign in the USA for slavery compensation: 'This is what consumer culture does, makes financial transactions and commodities out of injustices. It'll be, "There's your money, now shut up." '[14]

In summary, it seems to me that the closer the two parties stand to the events at issue, the more genuine – and even effective – an apology can be, if it is followed by reform of the circumstances in which the act took place: it was entirely proper for the Chief Constable to apologise to the Lawrence family for the conduct of the police, because the police were also giving a solemn undertaking to change their ways. This of course still has a very long way to go. Concomitantly, the farther the apologist and apologee stand from the events in question, the more symbolic, religious, diversionary and obstructive and even false the exchange seems to me to be. Writers indeed have their work cut out in the quest for justice, the theme Aeschylus so intensely explored.

We must still say, with Io:

> . . . do not out of pity comfort me
> with lies. I count false words the foulest plague of all.

2002

NOTES

Prologue: Seeking the Slant
History Today, November 1998

1. EARLY ENCOUNTERS

The Bitch Route 13
Spectator, 1 July 1972.

The Crushed Butterflies of War
Guardian Extra, 4 July 1972.

My Day
Vogue, April 1973.

Jessica Mitford
Obituary, *Independent Magazine*, 28 December 1996.

Bob Treuhaft
Obituary, *Independent*, 20 November 2001.

The Female Form Defined
Vogue, October 1983.

Mrs Thatcher
Vogue, September 1975.

Making It Big in the New World
Listener, 28 August 1986.

Angela Carter
Published as a foreword to Marina Warner's short story 'Ballerina: The Belled Girl Sends a Tape to an Impresario', in *Marvels & Tales, Journal of Fairy-Tale Studies* 12:1 (1998); reprinted in *Angela Carter and the Fairy Tale*, ed. Danielle M. Roemer and Cristina Bacchilega (2001).

2. WORDS AND SYMBOLS

St Paul: Let Women Keep Silent

'The First epistle of Paul the Apostle to Timothy', in *Incarnation: Contemporary Writers on the New Testament*, ed. Alfred Corn (1990).

1. See J. N. D. Kelly's introduction to *A Commentary on the Pastoral Epistles: I Timothy, II Timothy, Titus* (1972). He believes they are by Paul himself. See Elaine Pagels, *Adam, Eve, and the Serpent* (1988), for the opposite view.

2. See the *Acts of Paul* in *The Apocryphal New Testament*, trans. M. R. James (1969); Pagels, *Adam, Eve, and the Serpent*.

3. Karen Horney, 'On the Genesis of the Castration Complex in Women' and 'The Flight from Womanhood', in *Feminine Psychology*, ed. Harold Kelman (1973).

4. Mary Ward (1586–1646) entered the Poor Clares in 1606, founded the Institute of the Blessed Virgin Mary three years later, and opened convent schools for girls in France, Belgium, Germany, and Italy until the suppression of the order. She returned to England in 1639 and continued her struggles to re-establish her ideas of an active female vocation.

5. From 'Reply to Sor Philothea', in *A Sor Juana Anthology*, trans. Alan S. Trueblood (1988), quoted by Michael Wood in 'The Genius of San Jeronimo', *New York Review of Books*, 13 Oct 1988.

6. Using the Ronald Knox translation, published in 1945, reflected the special pride of English Catholics in their heritage: Monsignor Knox was a scholar connected to the recusant families, the aristocracy of the faithful, about whom Evelyn Waugh wrote in *Brideshead Revisited*. I never liked his version as much as the King James or the Jerusalem Bible. I have used the King James in this article – its style still remains a standard for all writers of English.

7. See Ian Maclean, *The Renaissance Notion of Woman: A Study in the Fortunes of Scholasticism and Medical Science in European Intellectual Life* (1980).

8. Woodcut by Anton Woensam (1525) in Christine Megan Armstrong, *The Moralizing Prints of Corneliz Anthonisz*, 1989.

9. Antonia Fraser, *The Weaker Vessel* (1984).

10. Seen in the exhibition 'L'Enfance et l'image au XIXe siècle', Musée d'Orsay, Paris, 1988.

11. *Father Flog*, broadsheet, n.d.

12. See Pagels, *Adam, Eve, and the Serpent*.

Christine de Pizan: *The Book of the City of Ladies*

Foreword to Christine de Pizan, *The Book of the City of Ladies*, trans E. J. Richards (1982).

Watch Your Tongues

Review of Howard Bloch, *Medieval Misogyny and the Invention of Western Romantic Love*; Margaret King, *Women of the Renaissance*; Brigitte Cazelles, *The Lady as Saint: A Collection of French Hagiographical Romances of the Thirteenth Century*; Fulvio Tomizza, *Heavenly Supper: The Story of Maria Janis*, translated by Anne Jacobson Shutte; Tina Krontiris, *Oppositional Voices: Women as Writers and Translators of Literature in the English Renaissance*, London *Review of Books*, 20 August 1992.

Obscenity

Times Literary Supplements 12 February 1981.

Fighting Talk

From *The State of the Language*, ed. Leonard Michaels and Christopher Ricks (1990).

1. Nigel Swain, in 'Ex-Ulster Officer's Terrorism Drama', by David Lister, *Independent*, 24 August 1988.

2. *De La Primaudaye's French Académie*, trans. Thomas Bowes (1586–94), vol. 2 (1594).

3. From the same roots as 'ghastly', it turns out: so, literally 'terrifying' or 'alarming' flab.

4. *The Life of Saint Teresa of Avila*, trans. J. M. Cohen (1957).

5. Elaine Scarry, *The Body in Pain: The Making and Unmaking of the World* (1985).

6. Scarry, *The Body in Pain*.

7. Primo Levi, *The Drowned and the Saved*, trans. Raymond Rosenthal (1988).

8. Communicated to the author in conversation, for which much gratitude.

9. Catalogue, *GI Joe: A Real American Hero* (1987).

10. *China Daily*, 13 May 1986; *Guardian*, 19 May 1986. I am grateful to Frances Wood for this information.

11. See Marina Warner, *Monuments & Maidens: The Allegory of the Female Form* (1986).

12. Tom Disch, 'On the Use of the Masculine-Preferred', *Times Literary Supplement*, 23 January 1981.

13. See Christine Megan Armstrong, *the Moralizing Prints of Corneliz Anthonisz*, (1989).

14. Emily Dickinson, 'They shut me up in Prose', in *The Complete Poems*, ed. Thomas H. Johnson (1986).

15. Caroline Walker Bynum, *Holy Feast and Holy Fast: The Religious Significance of Food to Medieval Women* (1987).

16. Raymond of Capua, *Life of Catherine of Siena*, quoted in Bynum, *Holy Feast and Holy Fast*.

17. Dickinson, *Complete Poems*.

18. Hélène Cixous, 'The Laugh of the Medusa', trans. Keith Cohen and Paula Cohen, in *New French Feminisms*, ed. Elaine Marks and Isabelle de Courtivron (1981).

19. Angela Carter, from the jacket of Louise Erdrich, *The Beet Queen* (1986).

20. See Hélène Cixous and Catherine Clément, *The Newly Born Woman*, trans. Betsy Wing (1986).

Saint Cunera's Scarf

Talk given at the Writers' Conference, Dublin, 1991, published as 'A Few Thoughts about Europe and Its Legacy' in *PN Review*, November/December 1991

Language, Power, Fear

Talk given in Oxford on European Languages Studies Day, published in *Oxford Magazine*, Michaelmas 2001,

1. Stéphane Mallarmé, *Les Mots d'Anglais* (1877); and Mallarmé, *Recueil de 'Nursery Rhymes'*, ed. Carl Paul Barbier (1964).

The Sign of the Dollar

Lecture 'The Pillars of Hercules', given at the Palazzo Steri, Palermo, January 2003. A version was published in *Raritan*, 22:3 (2003), and a short version in *Tate Magazine*, September 2002.

My thanks to John Onians, who first drew my attention to the possible connections of the dollar sign with the Pillars of Hercules; to Piero Boitani for his study, *The Shadow of Ulysses* (1994); Philip Attwood, of the Coins and Medals Department of the British museum; Peter Hulme for his inspiring essays on the theme of 'Traffic' in the ancient Mediterranean; Valerio Lucchesi, Meg Bent, Helen Cooper, Peter Hainsworth, Richard Cooper, Gervase Rosser and other members of the Dante Society, Oxford, for their comments when I first offered these thoughts.

Translations of Dante are from Robert Pinksy, *The Inferno of Dante* (1994); of *Purgatorio* and *Paradiso*, from John D. Sinclair, *The Divine Comedy*, 3 vols (1958).

1. 'sì ch'io vedea di là da Gade il varco/ folle d'Ulisse, e di qua presso il lito/ nel qual si fece Europa dolce carco', *Paradiso* XXVII, lines 82–3.
2. 'l'ardore/ ch'i' ebbi a divenir del mondo esperto/ e delli vizi umani e del valore.' . . .
3. ma misi me per l'alto mare aperto
   sol con un legno e quella compagna
   picciola da la qual non fui deserto . . .
   Io e' compagni eravam vecchi e tardi
   quando venimmo a quella foce stretta
   dov'Ercule segnò li suoi riguardi
   acciò che l'uom più oltre non si metta:
   dalla man destra mi lasciai Sibilia,
   da l'altra già m'avea lasciata Setta.
   'O frati,' dissi, 'che per cento milia
   perigli siete giunti al l'occidente,
   a questa tanto picciola vigilia
   d'e nostri sensi ch'è del rimanente,
   non vogliate negar l'esperïenza,
   di retro al sol, del mondo sanza gente.
   Considerate la vostra semenza:
   fatti non foste a viver come bruti,
   ma per seguir virtute e canoscenza.'
4. Primo Levi, *If This Is a Man*, trans. Stuart Woolf (1979; first English translation, 1960).
5. Dante, *Inferno* XXVI, vv. 137–42
   chè della nova terra un turbo nacque,
   e percosse del legno il primo canto.
   Tre volte il fè girar con tutte l'acque:
   alla quarta levar la poppa in suso
   e la prora ire in giù, com'altrui piacque,
   infin che'l mar fu sopra noi richiuso.
6. 'Or, figliuol mio, non il gustar del legno/ fu per sè la cagion di tanto essilio,/ ma solamente il trapassar del segno,' (lines 115–18). My translation.
7. 'Ella sen va notando lenta lenta;/ rota e discende . . .'
8. Apollodorus, *The Library*, ii.v.10.

9. See Earl Rosenthal, '"*Plus Ultra, Non Plus Ultra*", and the Columnar Device of Emperor Charles V', *Journal of the Warburg and Courtauld Institutes*, vol. 34 (1971).

10. Marcel Bataillon, '*Plus Oultre*: La Cour Découvre le Nouveau Monde', in *Les Fêtes de la Renaissance*, vol. II, *Fêtes et cérémonies au temps de Charles Quint* (1960), especially Appendix.

11. Erasmus, *Correspondence: Letters 1523–4*, trans. R. A. B. Mynors and Alexander Dalzell, in *Collected Works*, vol. 10 (1992).

12. Richard Doty, *America's Money, America's Story* (1998).

13. See Minoru Yamasaki, *A Life in Architecture* (1979).

14. *Aristotelis Opera, cum Averrois Commentariis* (facs. ed. of Venice 1562–74), vol. V, quoted Rosenthal, '*Plus Ultra, Non Plus Ultra*'.

15. Peter Hulme, 'Beyond the Straits: Postcolonial Allegories of the Globe,' in *Postcolonial Studies and Beyond*, eds., Antoinette Burton et al. (forthcoming, 2004), kindly lent by the author.

3. BODIES AND MINDS

Harmoniously Arranged Livers

Review of Caroline Walker Bynum, *The Resurrection of the Body in Western Christianity 200–1336, London Review of Books*, 8 June 1995.

Magic Zones

Review of Richard Sennett, *Flesh and Stone: The Body and the City in Western Civilisation, London Review of Books*, 8 December 1994.

The Virtue of Incest

Review of Marc Shell, *Elizabeth's Glass, London Review of Books*, 7 October 1993.

The Marquise Unmasked: *Les Liaisons Dangereuses*

Published as 'Valmont – or the Marquise Unmasked', in *The Don Giovanni Book: Myths of Seduction and Betrayal*, ed. Jonathan Miller (1990).

1. Choderlos de Laclos, *Les Liaisons dangereuses*. I've used the Garnier edition of the novel, ed. Yves Le Hir (1961).

2. Albert Camus, 'Le Don Juanisme', in *Le Mythe de Sisyphe* (1942).

3. Christopher Hampton, *Dangerous Liaisons: The Film* (1989).

4. Joan Rivière, 'Womanliness as a Masquerade', and Stephen Heath, 'Joan Rivière and the Masquerade' in *Formations of Fantasy*, ed. Victor Burgin, James Donald and Cora Kaplan (1986).

5. Ovid, *The Technique of Love*, trans. Paul Turner (1968).

6. Hampton, *Dangerous Liaisons*.

'Wild at Heart': *Manon Lescaut*

Programme note for Puccini's *Manon Lescaut*, Glyndebourne, Summer 1997.

1. See *Violetta and Her Sisters; The Lady of the Camellias; Responses to the Myth*, ed. Nicholas John (1994).

2. Abbé Prévost, *Manon Lescaut*, trans. Jean Sgard (1991), Introduction.

3. 'The Subtle Princess', trans. Gilbert Adair, and 'Bearskin' trans. Terence Cave, *Wonder Tales*, ed. Marina Warner (1994).

4. See Warner, *Wonder Tales*, Introduction; and Marina Warner, *From the Beast to the Blonde: On Fairytales and their Tellers* (1994).

5. Prévost, *Manon Lescaut*.

6. John Weightman, programme note to *Manon Lescaut*; see also Robert Darnton, *The Forbidden Bestsellers of Pre-Revolutionary France* (1995).

7. See for example, Catherine Clément, *Opera, or the Undoing of Women*, trans. Betsy Wing (1988); Elisabeth Bronfen, *Over Her Dead Body* (1992).

8. See Ruth Padel, '"*Piangi, piangi, o misera*": Putting the Words into Women's Mouths: The Female Role in Opera', *London Review of Books*, 23 January 1997.

In the Mirror of Madness: Elaine Showalter

Review of *The Female Malady: Women, Madness and English Culture, 1830–1980, Times Literary Supplement*, 4 September 1987.

Fasting Girls

Review of Joan Jacobs Brumberg, *Fasting Girls: The Emergence of Anorexia Nervosa as a Modern Disease, Times Literary Supplement*, 21 April 1989.

Bloated

New York Times Magazine, 8 June 1997.

Body Politic

Review of Madonna, *Sex, Observer*, 18 October 1992.

Sites of Desire

Review of Peter Brooks, *Body Work: Objects of Desire in Modern Narrative, Times Literary Supplement*, 2 July 1993.

Love's Work: Gillian Rose
Review of *Love's Work, London Review of Books*, 17 July 1995.

Is There Another Place from which the Dickhead's Self Can Speak?
Review of Alan Hyde, *Bodies of Law, London Review of Books*, 1 October 1998.

4. FAITHS AND MARVELS

Wrestling with the Oldest Rules: The First Commandment
Self, December 1997.

Signs of the Times: Touching Tears
An edited version of this article appeared in the *New Yorker*, 8 April 1996.

1. René Laurentin, *The Apparitions of the Blessed Virgin Mary Today* (1988, revised 1991).
2. Georges Bataille, 'The College of Sociology' (1938), quoted in Denis Hollier, ed., *Against Architecture: The Writings of Georges Bataille* (1992).
3. William A. Christian, Jr., *Visionaries: The Spanish Republic and the Reign of Christ* (1996).
4. David Blackbourn, *Marpingen: Apparitions of the Virgin Mary in Bismarckian Germany* (1994). reviewed by Marina Warner, *London Review of Books*, 16:7, 1995.
5. Laurentin, *Apparitions*.
6. Pope John Paul II, *Redemptoris Mater*, Encyclical (1987).
7. Padre Pio was canonised in 2002.
8. Cicero, *De Divinatione* II, 58.

Omens of Millennium
Review of Harold Bloom, *Omens of Millennium: The Gnosis of Angels, Dreams, and Resurrection, Washington Post*, 15 September 1998.

Suffering Souls
Review of Jean-Claude Schmitt, *Ghosts in the Middle Ages: The Living and the Dead in Medieval Society*, trans. Teresa L. Fagan, *London Review of Books*, 18 June 1998.

1. Translation from John D. Sinclair, *The Divine Comedy*, 3 vols (1958).

The Greatest Saint after Sainte Marie
Afterword to Charles Péguy, *The Mystery of the Charity of Joan of Arc*, trans. Jeffrey Wainwright (1986)

The Triumph of the Moon
  Review of Ronald Hutton, *The Triumph of the Moon: A History of Modern Pagan Witchcraft*, *The Times*, 25 November 1999.

Dom Sylvester Houédard
  Obituary, *Independent*, 22 January 1992.

Showers of Toads
  Review of Jan Bondeson, *The Feejee Mermaid and Other Essays in Natural and Unnatural History*, *Times Literary Supplement*, 1 October 1999

Amber
  Review of Ciaran Carson, *Fishing for Amber: A Long Story*, *Independent on Sunday*, 28 November 1999.

Poison
  Review of Gail Bell, *Poison: A History and a Family Memoir*, *New York Times Book Review*, March 2003.

5. SHAKESPEAREAN TRANSFORMATIONS

Rough Magic and Sweet Lullaby
  BBC Radio 3 Lecture in the Purcell Room, South Bank Centre, London, 31 October 2000.

Shakespeare and the Goddess
  Review of Ted Hughes, *Shakespeare and the Goddess of Complete Being*, *Times Literary Supplement*, 17 April 1992.

Maps of Elsewhere
  First published as 'Letter from London, 4' in *Lettre Internationale*, Autumn 1992.

  1. Roslyn L. Knutson, 'A Caliban in Saint Mildred Poultry', paper given on 13 August 1991, University of Arkansas, Little Rock.
  2. James Walvin, *Black and White: The Negro and English Society 1555–1945* (1973).
  3. Rian Malan, *My Traitor's Heart* (1990).

Shakespeare's Caliban
  Review of Alden T. Vaughan and Virginia Mason Vaughan, *Shakespeare's Caliban: A Cultural History*, *Times Literary Supplement*, 1992.

The Silence of Sycorax

Edited version of the talk 'The Silence of Sycorax: Listening to the Noises of the Isle', given at the Free University of Berlin, 19 January 1996.

Its Own Dark Styx: Caryl Phillips

Review of *The Nature of Blood, London Review of Books*, 20 March 1997

Castaway on the Ocean of Story

Edited version of the lecture given at the Shakespeare Deutsche Gesellschaft Conference, Weimar, April 2002, and revised for *Jahrbuch*, 2003

1. 'Fecit olorinis Ledam recubare sub alis . . .': Ovid, *Metamorphoses* VI, line 109.

2. The *Panchatantra, or Five Books*, written in Sanskrit around the sixth century, consists of a cycle of fables, many of them made familiar through the Aesopic and fairy-tale traditions; these were included in the *Katha Sarit Sagara*, which was translated by C. H. Tawney and reprinted in ten volumes under the title *The Ocean of Story*, edited by Norman Penzer in 1928. See Robert Irwin, *The Arabian Nights: A Companion* (1996).

3. Sylvia Plath, *Notebooks*, quoted in Jacqueline Rose, *The Haunting of Sylvia Plath* (1991).

4. Kenneth Gross, *Shakespeare's Noise* (2001).

5. *Cymbeline*, ed. J. M. Nosworthy (1955).

6. Ovid, *Metamorphoses* XV, lines 165–8, trans. Rolfe Humphries ([1955], (1983).

7. *King Lear*, ed. Kenneth Muir (1972).

8. Personal communication.

9. See Barbara Mowat, ' "Knowing I Loved My Books": Reading *The Tempest* Intertextually', in Peter Hulme and William H. Shearman, eds., *The Tempest and Its Travels* (2000).

10. See Richard Eden and Richard Willes, *The History of Travayle in the West and East Indies* (1577), where they describe how a priest falls 'heavy-headed and faynte a good whyle after' the ritual, and how his disciples 'blow a certain powder in his nose to rouse him'.

11. Quoted in G. Cabrera Infante, *Holy Smoke* (1986).

12. Ramón Pané, *Account of the Antiquities of the Indians*, trans. José Arrom (1999).

13. Jonathan Bate, *Shakespeare and Ovid* (1999).

14. *A Midsummer Night's Dream*, eds. Anne Barton, Frank Kermode et al. (1974).

6. CREOLE

Between the Colonist and the Creole

Published as 'Between the Colonist and the Creole: Family Bonds, Family Boundaries', in *Unbecoming Daughters of the Empire*, ed. Shirley Chew and Anna Rutherford (1993)

1. P. F. Warner, *My Cricketing Life* (n.d. 1920?).
2. C. L. R. James, *Beyond a Boundary* (1963).
3. Aucher Warner, *Sir Thomas Warner: Pioneer of the West Indies. A Chronicle of His Family* (1933).
4. Jean-Baptiste Labat, *Nouveau Voyage aux Iles de l'Amérique*, 6 vols (1724). Peter Hulme, *Colonial Encounters – Europe and the Native Caribbean 1492–1797* (1986) and *Remnants of Conquest: The Island Caribs and their Visitors, 1877–1998* (2000).
5. Jean Meyer, *Esclaves et négriers* (1986).

Noonday Devils

Review of Elaine Breslaw, *Tituba, Reluctant Witch of Salem: Devilish Indians and Puritan Fantasies*, *London Review of Books*, 6 June 1996.

Siren/Hyphen; or, 'The Maid Beguiled'

First published in *New Left Review*, May/June 1997, and reprinted in *Caribbean Portraits: Essays on Gender Ideologies and Identities*, ed. Christine Barrow, 1998

I would like to acknowledge the help and inspiration of Barabara Mowat, who read the talk in draft and offered her most helpful insights; also Kenneth Gross, correspondent of oracular learning, generosity and incisiveness.

1. Jean-Baptiste Labat, *Nouveau Voyage aux Iles de l'Amérique*, 2 vols (1724), quoted in Peter Hulme and Neil L. Whitehead, *Wild Majesty: Encounters with Caribs from Columbus to the Present Day* (1992).
2. See Aucher Warner, *Sir Thomas Warner: Pioneer of the West Indies. A Chronicle of His Family* (1933); I am also grateful to Desmond Nicholson, of the Museum of Antigua and Barbuda's Historical and Archaeological Society, for his database of epitaphs and other documents relating to the Warner family in Antigua.

3. Labat, *Nouveau Voyage*, quoted in Hulme and Whitehead, *Wild Majesty*.

4. Jean-Baptiste du Tertre, *Histoire générale des Antilles Habitées par les François*, 4 vols (1667–71), vol 1.

5. I am adopting Hilary Beckles's usage here. See Hilary McD. Beckles, 'Kalinago (Carib) Resistance to European Colonisation of the Caribbean', *Caribbean Quarterly* 38:2–3 (1992).

6. Beckles, 'Kalinago'; Aucher Warner, *Sir Thomas Warner*.

7. Du Tertre, *Histoire générale*.

8. See for example Tzvetan Todorov, *La Conquête de l'Amérique: La Question de l'autre* (1982).

9. Peter Hulme, *Colonial Encounters: Europe and the Native Caribbean 1492–1797* (1986).

10. Aucher Warner, *Sir Thomas Warner*, tells the story of Barbe, but discreetly, without connecting her to Thomas Warner in any special way.

11. Marina Warner, *Indigo* (1993). When Serafine passes on this interpretation of Ariel/Barbe's actions, she becomes the conduit of a false narrative, her own storytelling voice taken over, overwritten, as the names of Mme Ouvernard and her son Indian Warner have also been written over by history. Serafine could not be otherwise than an unreliable narrator, because traditions change stories and individuals on their own can't shape them outside the frame of those traditions; but this moment, when she tells Miranda about Ariel's treachery, is intended to create one of the sharpest ironies in the book.

12. '*Pour nous, enfants, elle mettait des soies colorées à ses paroles et accrochait des étoiles à sa vie des Antilles. Elle racontait – en créole – sa langue unique – les soucougnans et les esprits, les hommes tournés en chien et les chevaux à trois pattes, les sorcières et les envoûteurs, les démons, les bons anges.*' Gisèle Pineau, 'Ecrire en tant que noire', in Maryse Condé and Madeleine Cottenet-Hage, eds. *Penser la Créolité* (1995).

13. Jean Bernabé, Patrick Chamoiseau and Raphaël Confiant, *L'Eloge de la créolité* (1989); discussed in A. James Arnold, in 'The Gendering of *Créolité*: the Erotics of Colonialism', in Condé and Cottenet-Hage, *Penser la créolité*.

14. '*Ainsi il [le conteur] se protège, protège sa fonction, protège le message de la résistance détournée qu'il propage. La parole d'un si bon esclave, se dit le Béké, ne peut pas se révéler dangereuse*': Bernabé et al., *L'Eloge*.

15. In *Indigo*, Serafine as nurse fulfils a similar role, because while she

unwittingly colludes with the master narrative of empire, she also passes on to her charges – especially to Miranda – the strategies and the knowledge she needs to survive.

16. Arnold, 'The Gendering of *Créolité*'.

17. See Beckles, 'Kalinago'.

18. Hulme and Whitehead, *Wild Majesty*.

19. Ibid.

20. Ibid.

21. Public Record Office, Kew, papers: CO 1/22; CO 1/31, CO 1/34, CO 324/2, CO 1/35, CO 1/37. I am very grateful indeed to Rosemary Hall for her help in locating the documents, ordering copies and helping me to decipher them.

22. Russell, 20 Dec. 1675, CO 1/35.

23. Ibid.

24. CO 1/35.

25. W. Noel Sainsbury, preface, *Calendar of State Papers*, vol. 9 (America and West Indies, 1675–6), December 1893.

26. Russell, 20 December 1675, CO 1/35.

27. Lieutenant Choppin corroborates this story, but places Capt. Fletcher's meeting with Indian in Antigua, and adds that he was 'employed, at fishing, & fowling.' Choppin, 18 Dec. 1675. CO 1/35.

28. Hulme and Whitehead, *Wild Majesty*.

29. *Robert Louis Stevenson: The Strange Case of Dr Jeckyll and Mr Hyde and Other Stories* (1979), ed. Jenni Calder, 'A Note on the Texts'; see also a richly detailed analysis of the bowdlerisation in Barry Menikoff, *Robert Louis Stevenson and 'The Beach of Falesá: A Study in Victorian Publishing* (1984).

30. Russell, CO 1/35.

31. *Stevenson*, ed. Calder, 'A Note on the Texts'.

32. Ibid., 'The Beach of Falesá'.

33. See Marina Warner, *From the Beast to the Blonde: On Fairy Tales and Their Tellers* (1994).

34. *Stevenson*. ed. Calder.

35. Carlo Ginzburg, *Ecstasies: Deciphering the Witches' Sabbath*, trans. Raymond Rosenthal, ed. Gregory Elliott (1989).

Cannibals and Kings: *King Kong*

Published as 'Cannibals and Kings: On *King Kong*, Eighth Wonder of the World', in *Ape, Man, Apeman: Changing Views since 1600*, ed. Raymond Corbey and Bert Theunissen (1995).

1. He co-directed with Ernest B. Schoedsack.

2. Edgar Wallace died in 1931, so the attribution of this book must be doubtful. He was also credited with working on the screenplay, though he had little time to do this before his death.

3. James Snead, 'Spectatorship and Capture in *King Kong*: the Guilty Look', *Critical Inquiry* 33:1 (1991).

4. Snead does address this very thoroughly.

5. Judith Mayne 'King Kong and the ideology of spectacle', *Quarterly Review of Film Studies* 1:4 (1976).

6. Ray Harryhausen, *Film Fantasy Scrapbook* (1978).

7. Stephen Greenblatt, *Marvelous Possessions: The Wonder of the New World* (1991).

Bananas
'Diary', *London Review of Books*, 25 May 1995.

Zombie: The Devil Inside
Guardian, 2 November 2001.

7. FAIRIES, MYTHS AND MAGIC

Aesop
Review of *Aesop, The Complete Fables*, trans. Olivia and Robert Temple, *Bookforum*, Summer 1998.

Roberto Calasso
Review of *The Marriage of Cadmus and Harmony*, *Independent on Sunday*, 6 June 1993.

Edited version of a talk on *Ka: Stories of the Mind and Gods of India*, given at the Italian Institute, 9 February 1999.

Louis XIV
Review of Peter Burke, *The Fabrication of Louis XIV*, *Independent on Sunday*, 14 June 1992.

La Fontaine
Review of Jean de La Fontaine, *Œuvres Complètes Vol. 1, Fables, contes, et nouvelles*, *Times Literary Supplement*, 1991.

Under the Executioner's Sword
Introduction to *The Book of the Thousand Nights and One Night*, Folio Society, 2003.

1. Paul Willemen, ed., *Pier Paolo Pasolini* (1977), quoted in Robert Irwin, *The Arabian Nights: A Companion* (1994).
2. Husain Haddawy, trans., *The Arabian Nights* (1990).
3. Duncan Black MacDonald, 'Thousand and One Nights', *Encyclopaedia Britannica* (1950), vol. 22.

Laughter and Hope in the Old Wives' Tale

Programme note for *La Cenerentola*, Royal Opera House, London, 1991; reprinted in programme of Prokofiev's *Cinderella*, 1991.

1. 'Ashputtle, or The Mother's Ghost', in Angela Carter, *American Ghosts & Old World Wonders* (1993).

Mother Russia

Review of Joanna Hubbs, *Mother Russia; The Feminine Myth in Russian Culture, New York Times Book Review,* 5 March 1989.

8. REWORKING THE TALE

Combat Myths

Published as 'Fantasy's Power and Peril', *New York Times*, 16 December 2002

Donkey Business, Donkey Work: *In the House of Crossed Desires*

Edited version of the W. D. Thomas Memorial Lecture, given at the University of Wales Swansea, 2 December 1996.

1. See *Lucius, or The Ass*, in *Lucian of Samosata*, ed. M. D. Macleod (1967), Introduction; B.E. Perry, *The Ancient Romances* (1967).
2. Perry, *The Ancient Romances*; Thomas Hägg, *The Novel in Antiquity* (1983); B. P. Reardon, *The Form of Greek Romance* (1991).
3. My thanks to David Scrase for this insight in a letter of 28 Oct. 1996. Scribal errors are a splendid source of altered meanings.
4. *Useless Memoirs of Carlo Gozzi*, trans. John Addington Symonds, ed. and revised by Philip Horne (1962).
5. See L. Charbonneau-Lassay, *La Mystérieuse emblématique de Jésus-Christ* (1940).
6. Alexander Herzen, *On Art* (1954).
7. 'Li Response du Bestiaire', in Richard de Fournival, *Li Bestiaire d'amours/ Il bestiario d'amore*, ed. Francesco Zambon (1987).

'Large as Life, and Twice as Natural': The Child's Play of Lewis Carroll

Combination of a talk given in Madrid, March 1998, and an edited version of the essay ' "Nonsense Is Rebellion": the Childsplay of Lewis Carroll', in *Lewis Carroll*, ed. Charlotte Byrne, British Council exhibition catalogue, 1998.

1. Lewis Carroll, *The Rectory Umbrella & Mischmasch* (1932).

2. Iona and Peter Opie, eds., *The Oxford Dictionary of Nursery Rhymes* (1977)

3. Carroll, 'Wilhelm von Schmitz' in *The Whitby Gazette*, 1854. I am most grateful to Michael Bakewell for this reference.

4. Lewis Carroll, *Alice's Adventures in Wonderland* (1865).

5. Carroll, *Rectory Umbrella*.

6. Lewis Carroll, *Looking-Glass Letters*, ed. Thomas Hinde (1991).

7. Noel Malcolm, *The Origins of English Nonsense* (1997), see review by Nick Groom,' *Times Higher Education Supplement*, 11 July 1997.

8. Carroll, *Through the Looking-Glass* (1872).

9. Morton N. Cohen, *Lewis Carroll: A Biography* (1996); see Marina Warner, review in *London Review of Books*, 4 January 1996.

10. Adam Phillips, *On Kissing, Tickling and Being Bored: Psychoanalytic Essays on the Unexamined Life* (1993).

11. See George MacDonald, *At the Back of the North Wind* (1871) and *The Princess and the Goblin* (1872).

12. See John Docherty, *The Literary Products of the Lewis Carroll-George MacDonald Friendship* (1995).

13. Carroll, *Alice's Adventures in Wonderland* [Miniature edition, 1907] (1940).

14. Carroll, *Wonderland*.

15. *Alice's Adventures Under Ground* (facsimile manuscript).

16. Carroll, *Wonderland*.

17. See for example, Jon Elster, ed., *The Multiple Self* (1986) and Ian Hacking, *Rewriting the Soul, Multiple Personality and the Science of Memory* (Princeton, 1995).

18. Michael Bakewell, *Lewis Carroll: A Biography* (1997).

19. Hugh Haughton, 'The Little White Knight's Cult of Little Girls', *Times Literary Supplement*, 8 August 1997.

20. Mary Douglas, 'Jokes', in *Implicit Meaning: Essays in Anthropology* (1975).

21. Ibid.

22. William Empson, '*Alice In Wonderland*: The Child as Swain', in *Some Versions of Pastoral* (1950).

23. Hugh Haughton, ed., *The Chatto Book of Nonsense Poetry* (1988).

24. Malcolm, *Origins of English Nonsense*.

25. See Jean-Jacques Lecercle, *The Philosophy of Nonsense: The Intuitions of Victorian Nonsense Literature* (1994).

26. Carroll, *Through the Looking-Glass and What Alice Found There*, [Miniature edition, 1907].

27. The property of the number nine, whose multiples always add up to nine.

28. Susan Stewart, *Nonsense: Aspects of Intertexuality in Folklore and Literature* (1989).

29. Empson, *Some Versions*.

30. Ibid.

31. See Carol Mavor, *Pleasures Taken: Performances of Sensuality and Loss in Victorian Photographs* (1995).

32. Bettina von Arnim, 'Report of Günderode's Suicide', in *Bitter Healing: German Woman Writers 1700–1830*, eds. Jeannine Blackwell and Susanne Lantop (1990).

Struwwelpeter

Review of *Shockheaded Peter: A Junk Opera, Sunday Telegraph,* 18 February 2001.

Revelling in Hope

Review of Karel Čapek, *Nine Fairy Tales and One More Thrown in for Good Measure*, translated by Dagmar Herrmann, *Times Literary Supplement*, 28 September 1990.

Cunning and High Spirits

Introduction to *The Second Virago Book of Fairy Tales*, ed. Angela Carter (1992).

1. Italo Calvino, *Six Memos for the Next Millennium*, trans. William Weaver (1992).

2. Angela Carter, *Expletives Deleted* (1992).

3. Susan Rubin Suleiman, *Subversive Intent: Gender, Politics and the Avant-Garde* (1990).

The Inexpressible Closeness of the Deer

Article on the Quay Brothers' film, *Institute Benjamenta, Independent,* 17 November 1995.

1. Reissued as *Institute Benjamenta* (1995).

Hoopoe: Ted Hughes
Published in *The Epic Poise: A Celebration of Ted Hughes*, ed. Nick Gammage (1999).

Myth and Faerie: Rewritings and Recoveries
Talk given in French as 'Le Mythe et la féerie: réécriture et récupération', for the colloquium 'Où en est-on avec la théorie littéraire?', organised for Université de Paris VII by Julia Kristeva and Evelyne Grossman, 28–29 May 1999, and published in *Textuel*, 37 (April 2000)

1. Toni Morrison, *Playing in the Dark: Whiteness and the Literary Imagination* (1992).
2. Salman Rushdie, *The Ground Beneath Her Feet* (1999).
3. Felix Guattari, 'Regimes, Pathways, Subjects' in J. Crary and S. Kwinter, eds., *Incorporations* (1992).
4. Toni Morrison, *Paradise* (1999).
5. Steven Connor, 'Echo's Bones: Myth, Modernity and the Vocalic Uncanny', in *Myth and the Making of Modernity*, ed. Michael Bell and Peter Poeliner (1998).
6. *Star Trek* interestingly resonates back from fantasy into reality through the Raelian sect, who claimed in 2003 to have brought the first cloned babies into the world. Their leader, Claude Vorilhon, had a dream of space invaders, and the cult's information, website and the founder's own appearance and costume recall strongly the styling of the programme.
7. Gerald M. Edelman, 'Building a Picture of the Brain', *Daedalus* 127: 2, 1998.
8. Stuart Clark, *Thinking with Demons: The Idea of Witchcraft in Early Modern Europe* (1997).

Coda: Who's Sorry Now? Personal Stories, Public Apologies
Amnesty Lecture in Human Rights, Oxford, 14 February 2002, published in a different version on www.opendemocracy.net, 2002

I would like to thank Gillian Slovo for her most helpful and generous comments and response; David Edgar, whose play *The Prisoner's Dilemma* helped me think about these issues; Jacqueline Rose for inspiring my interest in the first place; Hermione Lee, Kenneth Gross, Megan Vaughan, Timberlake Wertenbaker, Lisa Appignanesi, Eileen Wanquet, Jonathan Keates, Roy Foster, Susan Rubin Suleiman, Ian

Buruma, Alberto Manguel and Wes Williams for offering many helpful suggestions; Imogen Cornwall-Jones for help with research; and Anthony Barnett, Susan Mary Richards, Isobel Hilton, David Hayes and Rosemary Bechler at <u>opendemocracy.net</u> for their work on the web version.

1. Aeschylus, *Prometheus Bound*, trans. Philip Vellacott (1961).

2. Julia Kristeva, *Strangers to Ourselves*, trans. Leon. S. Roudiez (1991), quoting Detienne, *Ecriture d'Orphée*.

3. *The History of Mary Prince: A West Indian Slave related by herself* [1831], ed. Moira Ferguson (1987).

4. Jacqueline Rose, 'Apathy and Accountability', in *The Public Intellectual*, ed. Helen Small (2002).

5. Augustine, *Confessions*, X. ii., trans. F. J. Sheed, ed. Peter Brown [1942] (1993).

6. Ibid., vi.

7. Jacques Derrida, 'La Littérature du secret', in *Le Secret: motif et moteur de la littérature*, ed. Chantal Zabus (1999).

8. Jacqueline Rose, 'Aux marges du littéraire: justice, vérité, réconciliation', in *Actes du colloque: Où en est-on avec la théorie littéraire?* (1999), ed. Julia Kristeva and Evelyne Grossman, *Textuel*, 37 (April 2000).

9. R. W. Johnson, 'Why There Is No Easy Way to Dispose of Painful History', review of Anthea Jeffery, *The Truth about the Truth Commission*, *London Review of Books*, 14 Oct. 1999.

10. Ian Buruma, 'The joys and perils of victimhood', New York *Review of Books*, 8 April 1999.

11. Rose, 'Aux marges du littéraire'.

12. Antjie Krog, *Country of My Skull: Guilt, Sorrow and the Limits of Forgiveness in the New South Africa*, ed. Luke Mitchell (1999).

13. Ibid.

14. Ed Vuillamy, 'Black Leaders Divided over Reparations for Slavery', *Guardian*, 26 Aug. 2001.

INDEX